THE ENEMY
OF MY ENEMY

THE ENEMY
OF MY ENEMY
The Alarming Convergence
of Militant Islam and the Extreme Right

George Michael

 University Press of Kansas

Published by the University Press of Kansas (Lawrence, Kansas 66045), which was organized by the Kansas Board of Regents and is operated and funded by Emporia State University, Fort Hays State University, Kansas State University, Pittsburg State University, the University of Kansas, and Wichita State University

Library of Congress Cataloging-in-Publication Data
Michael, George, 1961-
The enemy of my enemy : the alarming convergence of militant Islam and the extreme right / George Michael.
p.   cm.
Includes bibliographical references and index.
isbn 0–7006–1444–3 (cloth : alk. paper)
1. Terrorism—United States. 2. Terrorism—Religious aspects—Islam. 3. Right-wing extremists—United States. 4. Islamic fundamentalism. 5. Religious militants. I. Title.
HV6432.M52 2006
363.3250973—dc22   2005036172

British Library Cataloguing-in-Publication Data is available.

Printed in the United States of America

10 9 8 7 6 5 4 3 2 1

The paper used in this publication meets the minimum requirements of the American National Standard for Permanence of Paper for Printed Library Materials Z39.48–1984.

To Chris, Frank, Mike, and
My Mother

Contents

Acknowledgments

Several persons helped me with this book in different ways. I would first like to thank all of those who granted me interviews for this study, including Steven Barry, Willis Carto, David Duke, Steven Emerson, Sam Francis, Jürgen Graf, Nick Griffin, Rohan Gunaratna, Ahmed Huber, Kevin MacDonald, Tom Metzger, David Myatt, Mike Piper, Jared Taylor, and John Tyndall.

It was a delight to work with the staff at the University Press of Kansas. I extend my special thanks to Michael Briggs for having confidence in this project, and I greatly appreciate the efforts of Susan McRory and Susan Schott.

CHAPTER ONE

Introduction

The events of September 11, 2001, have been seared in the conscious-ness of virtually all Americans. I recall vividly what happened on what began as a pleasant day. It was just before 9:00 A.M. when I turned on the television. On the financial news channel, to my surprise, I saw what appeared to be the north tower of the World Trade Center smoking profusely. There was no audio com-mentary, and for several minutes no other television channel covered this event. Finally, shortly after other news channels began covering the incident, an explosion was visible in the south tower. Moments later, word came in that another plane, which, it transpired, was United Airlines flight 175, had crashed into the south tower. All hopes that the collision of the American Airlines plane into the north tower had been an accident were dashed. Not long after, a third plane, American flight 77, struck the Pentagon, and a fourth plane, United flight 93, presumably headed for a high-profile target in Washington, D.C., crashed into a field in rural Pennsylvania. This horrific series of events was ob-viously a carefully orchestrated terrorist attack. It was all but certain to terrorist analysts that only one entity had both the capability and the intentions for such an assault—Osama bin Laden's al Qaeda network.

Americans were understandably stunned by attacks of such lethal and spec-tacular magnitude. As many Americans asked, "Why did this happen?" the deni-zens of the American extreme right believed that they already knew why. Shortly after these events, extremist Internet discussion groups issued numerous messages and essays proffering the "real reason" the United States had been attacked. Whereas mainstream commentators and public figures frequently asserted that the United States had been attacked for the values that the nation espouses (such as freedom and democracy), those on the extreme right saw this explanation as lit-tle more than facile propaganda . The true reason why the United States had been attacked, they asserted, was the U.S. government's unstinting support for the state of Israel. Not surprisingly, this sentiment was shared by many of those in what is generally referred to as militant Islam. This great cognitive disjunction between militant Islam and the extreme right on the one hand and the government offi-cials and media spokespersons in the West on the other merits further study.

It was hard not to infer a certain degree of schadenfreude and excitement in the tone of some of the extreme right's immediate reactions to 9/11.[1] Just a few days after the attacks, Dr. William L. Pierce (now deceased) of the National Alliance, which is often characterized as the leading neo-Nazi organization in the United States, announced to the audience of his American Dissident Voices radio program:

> The whole world is entering a new era now, where all their money and the hundreds of millions of mindless lemmings in their television audiences and being able to manipulate the political system and the government of what is still the world's most powerful country—at least, in a material sense—no longer are enough to guarantee the Jews' continued hegemony. What happened in New York and in Washington this week is just one small manifestation of this new era. George Bush and the other politicians under the Jews' control can order the bombing of every pharmaceutical factory in the Middle East in response to recent events here, but that will only take us further into this new era.[2]

Increasingly, militant Islam and the extreme right seem to agree on several salient issues.

Since the early 1980s, both right-wing extremism and militant Islam have gained considerable notoriety. At first glance, there would seem to be little common ground between the two movements. After all, the racialist segment of the American extreme right generally tends to be derisive toward nonwhites and would thus not consider Muslims—the majority of whom trace their ancestry to Third World countries—to be part of their desired exclusively white community. What's more, Christian fundamentalism has traditionally been an important feature in American right-wing extremism. For their part, Islamic fundamentalists tend to look askance at non-Muslims, whom they sometimes designate as "infidels" and whom they believe should be excluded from the *umma* (the single universal community in which all Muslims are brethren). Consequently, there would appear to be major ideological and theological differences between the two movements.

Yet they actually share some strikingly similar characteristics. For example, both movements evince a high degree of exclusivity as they endeavor to create their own utopian versions of homogeneous societies. Moreover, increasingly there is a meeting of the minds on several important political issues—oddly enough, one example is the cause of Palestinian independence. The two also offer similar critiques of American foreign policy in the Middle East, the American media, modernity, secularism, and globalization. Finally, both movements see the U.S. government as hopelessly under the control of Jews or Zionists, pursuing policies that are at cross-purposes with their own group interests. Thus under certain conditions, we can speculate that the potential exists for greater collaboration between the movements in the future.

Why should this topic be explored? First, to date there has been no in-depth study of the relationship between the worldviews of Arab/Islamic extremists on the one hand and the extreme right on the other. In this book I seek, among other things, to illustrate those characteristics of right-wing and Islamic extremism that overlap and that could presage greater cooperation between the two movements in the future. Such an alliance, if properly organized and coordinated, could pose a significant challenge to the status quo not only in the United States but in Europe as well. Both movements could conceivably attain a new synergy through such an alliance.

The current war on terror is, as a study published by the Center for Strategic and International Studies pointed out, the first major conflict in the age of globalization.[3] I take a broad view of the current crisis, examining the interplay of domestic and international factors in an era of globalization. Since the mid-1990s, the state system has grown extremely vulnerable in many countries around the world. Several multinational states have imploded due to ethnic rivalries. The ascendance of multiculturalism and the decreasing salience of the assimilationist paradigm could one day presage a similar situation in the United States, although at the present time this scenario appears highly unlikely. The September 11 attacks could potentially amplify these trends. Both the extreme right and militant Islam are highly cognizant of these trends, which they often refer to as the "new world order." Perhaps we can gain greater insight into these issues by examining their perspectives on 9/11 and its consequences. Dissident movements tend to be less constrained by political correctness than their mainstream counterparts, and as such, they may be able to provide alternative insights that could increase our understanding of the global war on terror in which we find ourselves.

The current war on terror has the potential to affect the domestic stability of the United States. For example, a study released in January 2002 estimated that the 9/11 terrorist attacks would cost the American economy 1.6 million jobs. The losses presumably would be most severe in the tourism and airline sectors. However, a ripple effect would spread across a wide range of industries.[4] The 9/11 attacks were the worst insurance disaster in American history, with total claims estimated at $40 billion.[5] The stock market also suffered as a result of the attacks. After reopening almost a week after 9/11, the Dow Jones industrial average plunged 1,370 points (14.3 percent)—the worst short-term decline in the history of the market. Many in extremist circles saw in these events the forebodings of an economic cataclysm that they long predicted would usher in a revolutionary era.[6]

Even in the months before the 9/11 attacks, in a survey conducted by the Council on Foreign Relations, Americans cited international terrorism more than any other issue as a "critical threat to U.S. vital interests."[7] However, few observers predicted a "war on terror" that would involve the United States and its allies in a new military campaign of global proportions. In the world prior to 9/11, terrorism was generally regarded as an isolated occurrence. The notion that the West would confront "asymmetric warfare" on a global scale did not seem credible except to the most forward-looking observers.

The Pre-9/11 World

"How did this happen?" asked James F. Hoge and Gideon Rose in their influential 2001 book on the new war on terror.[8] After all, many observers of international politics forecast that the twenty-first century would bring a period of unprecedented tranquility and economic opportunity. The 1990s were thought to have ushered in a new era of American triumphalism. Francis Fukuyama's 1989 article "The End of History?" seemed to have presaged the coming zeitgeist. According to Fukuyama's analysis, governments around the world were converging on a model of democracy and free markets. All other ideologies had been effectively exhausted and discredited. The Hegelian dialectic had run its course, and no credible ideological alternative remained. Supposedly, all that was left was mere fine-tuning.

Events in the early 1990s lent credence to Fukuyama's prognostications as the Soviet Union imploded and the Cold War ended. The old-style terrorism of various Palestinian rejectionist groups was in retreat, and a historic Middle East peace agreement was signed on the White House lawn in September 1993. However, terrorism and political extremism did not disappear. Although the largely secular rejectionist groups may have moderated, Islamist groups continued to radicalize and attract recruits. With the end of the Cold War, some observers even predicted that the West could return to a previous historical pattern in which the Occident would confront the Islamic world. But warning signs soon appeared, indicating that the march to democracy and modernity could take a radically different turn. Ethnic conflict convulsed the Balkans, and outright genocide emerged in Rwanda. More fanatical terrorists, motivated by religion rather than secular ideologies, captured attention through their attacks, not only abroad but in the United States as well.

Other voices began to express a less sanguine view of the process of globalization and saw other disturbing trends antagonistic to democratization, including the return of tribalism and the increasing attachment to affective variables such as religion. In 1993, Senator Patrick Moynihan, the long-time observer of ethnic politics, saw the specter of violent ethnic conflict afflicting nations and leading to "pandemonium" in various parts of the world. That same year, an eminent Harvard professor, Samuel Huntington, introduced his "clash of civilizations" model of international relations, in which he asserted that conflict in the twenty-first century would be most pronounced along what he termed "civilizational fault lines." In his analysis, culture and cultural identities were "shaping the patterns of cohesion, disintegration, and conflict in the post–Cold War world."[9]

According to Huntington, some of the most important characteristics of democratic systems (democratic governance and majority rule) can be exploited by populist demagogues, who often appeal to constituents on the basis of group identities such as ethnicity, culture, and religion. Thus the global spread of democracy could paradoxically destabilize world order.

Huntington took notice of the demographic and geographic dynamism of the Islamic world vis-à-vis the West. For example, at the peak of its territorial conquest in 1920, the West directly ruled approximately 25.5 million square miles, or close to half of the earth's land. However, by 1993, this territorial control had decreased to about 12.7 million square miles. By contrast, Islamic societies grew from 1.8 million square miles in 1920 to over 11 million square miles in 1993. A similar shift occurred in population. In 1993 approximately 805 million people belonged to the West, while 928 million belonged to the Islamic world.[10] The Islamic world is expected to grow faster than the West over the next several decades and comprise up to 30 percent of the world's population by 2030. Furthermore, as Huntington noted, larger populations need more resources. Hence, people from societies with dense and/or rapidly growing populations tend to push outward, thus exerting pressure on the less demographically dynamic people.[11] Massive Muslim immigration into Europe could drastically alter the politics and societies of that continent. In Western Europe there is growing concern over the growth of destitute Islamic ghettos from which native residents have been displaced as a result of high crime and periodic violence. The Muslim population also surged in the United States during the 1990s.[12] The large presence of Muslims in the West is something that cannot be ignored when thinking about the current war on terror. After all, it is that population from which Islamist groups draw much of their support.

Also worrisome to Huntington was the potential for violence emanating from the Islamic world. He observed that Muslim societies were on average more likely to be involved in intergroup violence than the peoples of other civilizations. Citing Ted Robert Gurr, he noted that Muslims were involved in three times as many intercivilizational conflicts as were the peoples of non-Muslim cultures. Furthermore, it is worth noting that of the thirty-six groups that the U.S. State Department designates as "foreign terrorist organizations," seventeen are Islamic in orientation, and six more are predominantly Muslim in membership.[13] Finally, conflicts involving Muslim populations tended to be heavy in casualties.[14]

Huntington voiced concern about a particular tendency of U.S. leaders to assiduously promote the diversity rather than the unity of the citizenry. He does not believe that the United States can endure as a coherent society by adopting a multicivilizational (read multicultural) character.[15] James Kurth has even argued that the real clash of civilizations was not principally between "the West and one or more of the rest," but rather between "the West and the Post-West within the West itself." The American intellectual and ruling class espouses values that substantially differ from those of the general population.[16] Generally speaking, the ruling class in the West—most notably in the United States—has championed multiculturalism since the late 1980s. As a result, some observers now fear that civilizational conflict with Islam could emerge in the confines of the West, with Muslims constituting a potential fifth column for groups like al Qaeda.

Since the early 1990s, Huntington posited, Islam and the West have been engaged in a "quasi-war." So far, militarily this conflict has mainly been a war of terrorism versus air power, with Islamic terrorists exploiting the open societies of the West and the U.S. military exploiting the open skies of the Islamic world to drop smart bombs and cruise missiles.[17] Ominously, Huntington warned of possible civilizational conflicts of truly apocalyptic proportions. As he observed, the forces of integration in the contemporary world were real, but he warned that they generated "counterforces of cultural assertion and civilizational consciousness."[18] As Paul Pillar said, "If bin Laden or someone of his ilk were to read Huntington's work, the reaction would not be surprise or shock but rather acknowledgement that this indeed is the conflict in which they believe themselves engaged."[19]

Some observers of international politics found merit in both Fukuyama's and Huntington's seemingly disparate theories. Not unlike Huntington, Benjamin Barber observed increasing conflict around the world driven by cultural affinities. However, he also saw a contemporaneous trend of global integration and homogenization, not unlike Fukuyama's end of history model. Barber attributed the rise of jihad (his euphemism for the new tribalism) to a reaction against an ever-encroaching Americanized global culture that threatened to efface regional, national, and tribal particularities. Barber envisioned a new dialectic in which globalization or, as he put it, the "McWorld" clashed with "jihad." The former is driven by ever-expanding global markets and the latter by parochial hatreds. In his analysis, the homogenization engendered by globalization had provoked the neo-tribal reaction. As Barber explained, "both Jihad and McWorld are at work, both visible sometimes in the same country at the very same instant."[20] As mentioned earlier, both militant Islam and the extreme right fear globalization, most notably those aspects that include American popular culture. Conceivably, both movements could share common ground in opposition to the McWorld.

The Return of History

In light of 9/11, some observers believe that history has returned and that the triumph of liberal democracy so eloquently predicted by Fukuyama was merely an interlude between the Cold War and a new era characterized by civilizational and cultural conflict. An intellectual debate began in the fall of 2001 over the "clash of theories." One side believed that Huntington's theory—long viewed with skepticism in the United States—characterized the new era. The other side held that Fukuyama's theory would endure. In any event, history does appear to have returned as politics, culture, and ideology once again appear to loom large.[21] Some even wondered if perhaps the West was not triumphant after all but merely enjoying a respite before resuming its long-predicted decline. As the prominent paleo-conservative Pat Buchanan pessimistically mused, "the end of history" may have been only a "temporary truce, a phony peace, an armistice, a time of transition from a day of Western dominance to a day when the West pays tribute."[22]

For his part, Fukuyama remained relatively optimistic about the future of the West in the post-9/11 world. In his end of history treatise, he conceded that even in the posthistorical world, terrorism and wars of liberation would continue for some time. Although Fukuyama acknowledged that militant Islam could pose a threat to the stability of world order, he saw its influence as limited, with virtually no appeal to non-Muslims. Moreover, he saw no extant ideological alternatives to liberal democracy that could pose any serious challenge. But, as Fareed Zakaria pointed out, Fukuyama did not fully appreciate the threat that the United States and the new world order posed to militant Islam—a fear that its followers feel with great intensity. Thus Zakaria posited that perhaps one side could restart history unilaterally by striking out at the West.[23]

Some analysts believe that terrorist campaigns arise from broad social and political movements. Thus, terrorism *trends* tend to follow, rather than precede, specific *acts* of terrorism. This "leading indicator" characteristic of terrorism may help us understand the nature and future direction of both international and intranational conflict. Examining various data sets of recorded terrorist events from 1968 to 1997, Leonard Weinberg and William Eubank found evidence to support Samuel Huntington's contention that there has been a substantial shift in the patterns of terrorist attacks, from those occurring within civilizations to those occurring between civilizations.[24] Their findings lend credence to the clash of civilizations theory, suggesting that terrorism may serve as a leading indicator of future political upheaval. Furthermore, they argued that the "fault line" conflicts about which Huntington warned also have the potential to manifest themselves not only between the West and other civilizations but inside Western countries as well.[25] To put it another way, in the multicultural societies of the West, there is great potential for intracivilizational struggle between various cultural groups.

In the same vein, Niall Ferguson argued that the clash of civilizations analysis is somewhat off the mark. Rather than a clash of monolithic civilizations, the contemporary world has experienced a process of disintegration, as ethnic and religious conflicts challenged the integrity of multicultural nation-states. Since 1945, civil war has become the most frequent kind of war, accounting for approximately two-thirds of all postwar conflicts.[26] From 1945 to 1990, there were approximately seventy-five important world conflicts: twenty-eight were conventional wars between armies in uniform fighting by the rules of war, and forty-six were insurrections, civil wars, or guerrilla wars. The latter category cost a total of nearly 20 million lives and was thus substantially more deadly than the conventional category.[27] As Xavier Raufer observed, the world is witnessing the end of a process that began over 300 years ago with the Treaty of Westphalia and the conclusion of the Thirty Years' War. Nation-states, the principal instigators and organizers of wars for the past few centuries, are increasingly incapable of confronting one another. Instead, armed groups at the supranational or intranational level are at the root of virtually all political violence currently being waged on the planet.[28]

Since the late 1990s, there has been a resurgence of the extreme right in Europe. Could the rightward shift, as evidenced by recent successes of extreme right parties in France, Belgium, Russia, the Netherlands, Austria, Hungary, and Romania, signify a crisis in the postwar Western world? What is more, evidence suggests that events in one part of the world affect other areas almost immediately. For example, in the weeks after the outbreak of the al-Aqsa intifada, which commenced in September 2000, over 250 violent anti-Semitic incidents were perpetrated through Europe by a variety of Islamic, left-wing, and right-wing groups.[29] Such violence has become a type of political statement about international conflict not unlike the demonstrations against the Vietnam War during the 1960s or apartheid during the 1980s.[30]

As I seek to demonstrate in this book, numerous factors, both international and domestic, have come together to form the current crisis. The war on terror ought not to be viewed as merely an overseas military conflict. The present crisis conceivably has the potential to unleash forces that could pose a serious threat to the United States. Issues such as multiculturalism, globalization, immigration, and the war on terror are all issues about which the extreme right feels strongly. Therefore, how they view this current crisis could tell us a great deal about where the United States as a nation may be heading. As Jeffrey Kaplan and Leonard Weinberg observed, for all its seeming isolation, the extreme right is relatively well informed on world events and current affairs. Thus, "in many ways the radical right serves as kind of a caged canary—the bird that miners take into the coal mines to warn of the hidden dangers long before they reach the level of consciousness. The study of this esoteric subculture can foretell national controversies yet to take place."[31]

For example, in 1994, National Alliance leader William L. Pierce wrote an article titled "Stay Out of Tall Buildings," which was published in the organization's journal *National Vanguard.* In it, he warned that the attack on a Palestinian mosque by a Jewish fundamentalist settler in Israel, Dr. Baruch Goldstein, that killed twenty-nine worshipers could one day redound against the United States as a terrorist attack on the World Trade Center: "New Yorkers who work in tall office buildings—anything close to the size of the World Trade Center—might consider wearing hardhats to work for the next few months." Not long after the 9/11 attacks, Pierce was quick to point out the prescience of his earlier remarks.[32]

Increasingly, both militant Islam and the extreme right share similar rhetoric. Their critiques of U.S. foreign policy have converged, as they both decry U.S. military intervention in the Middle East. Is it conceivable that this meeting of the minds on certain issues could one day lead to an operational alliance? Or is there too much that divides the two movements as to preclude cooperation? These are some of the questions that I seek to answer in this book.

Overview of the Book

A review of the contemporary extreme right is provided in Chapter 2, which identifies the major groups and individuals that comprise it and explains the various ideologies that motivate the movement. The primary focus is on how the extreme right has been radicalized since the mid-1990s and is now more amenable to other variants of extremism, including militant Islam.

The development of contemporary militant Islam is charted in Chapter 3 from its roots with the founding of the Muslim Brotherhood. The history of Islamic extremism in the United States is surveyed in Chapter 4, including acts of terrorism. In that chapter I also detail the connections between Islamic extremists in the United States and their coreligionists overseas.

On previous occasions, representatives of the extreme right in North America and Europe have explored the possibility of collaborating with both Arab and Islamic extremists. In Chapter 5 I examine some of these previous episodes to find common ground among these groups and the significance of these efforts for today.

Not surprisingly, the activities of both Muslim and right-wing extremists have captured the attention of authorities. In Chapter 6 I explore the U.S. government's response to domestic terrorism and political extremism, with special emphasis on the response to the extreme right and militant Islam. Several nongovernmental organizations (NGOs) have long sought to counter the activities of the American extreme right and, more recently, militant Islam. In Chapter 7 I examine the role that these NGOs play in generating public policy and shaping media coverage and public perception of both right-wing and Islamic extremists.

Many issues about which both the extreme right and militant Islam feel very strongly feature prominently in the current war on terror. In Chapters 8 and 9 I review how the extreme right and militant Islam, respectively, view this crisis. In those chapters I draw upon their statements and communiqués. I have conducted numerous interviews with extreme right activists, thus allowing voices that are usually shunned by the mainstream media a chance to be heard.

The prospects for collaboration between militant Islam and the extreme right are explored in Chapter 10. Finally, in the Conclusion, I speculate how the war on terror could unfold and its consequences for the United States.

CHAPTER TWO

The Contemporary Extreme Right

By most accounts, right-wing extremism made a comeback in the United States during the 1990s, although this trend did not manifest itself in electoral success due in large part to the nature of the U.S. electoral system. What is more, the Internet has enabled the extreme right to reach out to a potentially larger audience than it has in the past. Finally, some high-profile confrontations with law enforcement authorities and horrific acts of political violence—most notably the 1995 bombing of the Alfred P. Murrah Federal Building in Oklahoma City—have seared the issue of right-wing terrorism into the public's mind.

Although observers have sought to define the term "extremism," there is still no general consensus on what it means. Drawing upon the academic field of deviance and social control may give us a better understanding of the nature of extremism. According to the absolutist position of deviance, there is something obvious within an act, belief, or condition that makes it different from the norm. Deviance is viewed as that which is not "determined by social norms, customs, or rules, but rather is an intrinsic essence that stands apart from and exists prior to the creation of these socially created codes."[1] Thus deviance is an objective fact according to the absolutist position. In the constructionist position, in contrast, deviance is lodged in the eyes of the beholder, not the act itself. The fluid nature of extremism suggests that the constructionist position may be more useful. What constitutes extremism depends in large part on both public and elite opinions at a particular point in time; thus the concept of extremism is essentially socially constructed. In this vein, Christopher Hewitt identified three ways in which extremism can be defined. In the first case, extremism can be defined statistically, with attitudes toward particular issues arranged on a continuum. Those people who favor positions on the far left and right of the continuum would be labeled extremists, whereas those identifying with positions in the middle would be identified as moderates. Second, extremism can be defined in terms of style. Citing the research of John George and Laird Wilcox, Hewitt posited that extremism can also be defined more in stylistic terms such as "self-righteousness, fanaticism, and hatred" rather than any specific ideological substance. Finally, Hewitt took the position that extremism is most cogently understood as being socially defined:

> In any society at a given time, certain social and political views are considered normal and acceptable, while others are not. The range of acceptable views may be broad or narrow, and change over time. Nonmainstream views and beliefs may be thought of as ridiculous, dangerous, or both. To characterize someone as "extremist" is to view him as holding opinions that are beyond the pale, not to be taken seriously, to be mocked or punished. The reader can perform a mental experiment to determine which views would be considered extremist by considering what opinions could *not* [emphasis in original] be said in a social gathering, and would not be published in a major newspaper.[2]

A description of the term "extreme right" is also in order. In the context of American politics the term is difficult to define, owing to the vast geographic size, large population, and heterogeneity of the country. The contemporary extreme right is a variegated movement composed of many disparate groups and individuals. Therefore it is difficult to find a bare minimum classification into which all right-wing extremists could be placed.

With these definitional limitations in mind, I have assembled a list of characteristics that, although it does not rigidly define the extreme right, may adequately *describe* and capture the essence of the right-wing extremism:

- Particularism. Unlike other political ideologies and orientations, the extreme right usually takes a more parochial outlook, as it is more concerned with a smaller locus of identity, such as the nation, republic, race, or ethnic group. It tends not to have ambitions to proselytize the whole world to its belief system, in contrast to other ideologies such as liberal democracy, communism, and some variants of socialism, which are seen as suitable, indeed desirable, for export. The whole world is encouraged to adopt them as its model.
- Low regard for democracy. Although extreme right political organizations and individuals by and large tend to play by the democratic rules of the game, they seem to be less enthusiastic about democracy than mainstream political orientations.
- Antistatism. Right-wing extremism often evinces a severe disaffection with the government, or at least the scope of government. Although certain segments of the racialist right—most notably those that draw inspiration from National Socialism—may in principle approve of the idea of a strong state, they regard the current U.S. government as hopelessly under the control of outsiders who use their power in a way that is inimical to the national community.

- A conspiracy theory of history. Denizens of the extreme right have a tendency to look beneath the surface of American politics and find elite cabals at work subverting society.
- A racial or ethnic component, which could include racism, anti-Semitism, or xenophobia.

Although *all* the preceding characteristics may not pertain to each and every right-wing extremist group and figure examined in this study, at least *enough* of these characteristics apply to each of them so that they could reasonably be classified as "right-wing extremist."[3]

Although it is axiomatic to say that virtually all terrorists come from the ranks of extremists, most extremists are not terrorists. Furthermore, in the United States—a country in which free speech is enshrined in the First Amendment—dissident viewpoints, at least in theory, are considered essential to the maintenance of a democracy in which all voices are heard and granted at least a modicum of consideration. That said, political extremism often serves as an incubator for future terrorism.

Typology of the Extreme Right in the United States

The extreme right in the United States consists of a multitude of different groups that often disagree on a number of issues. The contemporary U.S. extreme right has several separate orientations, although there is some overlap and migration back and forth among them.

Commentators often use such terms as "extreme right," "far right," and "radical right" interchangeably. The British observer of the American right, Martin Durham, clarified the distinctions among these terms.[4] The far right consists collectively of both the radical right and the extreme right. The radical right has a long pedigree, as its ideological underpinnings can be traced in large part to the John Birch Society and the Minutemen organizations that gained notoriety in the 1960s. The militia movement is the most recent manifestation of this segment and gained much notoriety in the aftermath of the Oklahoma City bombing. The main impetus for the growth of the militias appears to be new gun control laws such as the Brady bill that threaten to weaken the Second Amendment. Repression from various federal law enforcement agencies, such as manifested in the fiascoes of Ruby Ridge and Waco, contributed to the expansion of this movement. The Ruby Ridge incident, which occurred in Idaho in 1992, involved federal law enforcement officers ambushing the home of Randy Weaver, a white separatist in Idaho. Weaver's young son and wife, as well as one agent of the U.S. Marshals Service, were killed in what many observers believed was a badly botched operation by the federal government. A Christian Identity minister, Pete Peters, held a meeting in LaPorte, Colorado, soon after this event and laid the groundwork for the contemporary militia movement by urging right wingers to organize militias at the local level. The Waco incident in 1993 further compounded resentment in the "patriot" movement.

Despite its propensity for confrontation with law enforcement agencies, the militia movement is generally considered to be less extreme than other segments of the far right, perhaps because it is seldom overtly racialist. Race creates a sharp delineation between the radical right and the more revolutionary segments of the extreme right. Generally speaking, radical right groups such as the Christian patriot movement support most features of American political culture, as evidenced by their veneration of documents such as the U.S. Constitution. Conspiracy theories associated with this movement retain considerable currency in the subterranean world of the far right, as they have been among the most strident critiques of globalization, or the "new world order." For the most part, this segment of the far right is the least relevant to this study in that it generally favors traditional patriotic themes such as individual liberty and limited government. In addition, 9/11 appears to have reduced the militia movement's volatility: some of its more prominent representatives actually voiced support for the federal government in the war against terrorism. For example, Norm Olson, the cofounder of the Michigan Militia Corps Wolverines, publicly announced that he would contact President George W. Bush and offer the services of his organization to defend the country against terrorism.[5] There would seem to be little to no potential for collaboration between the more patriotic segments of the radical right and militant Islam. By contrast, the extreme right—whose communications often feature anti-Semitic undertones—would appear to have greater prospects for such an alliance.

THE REVOLUTIONARY RACIALIST RIGHT

The extreme right differs from the radical right in that the race issue looms large in the agenda of the former, whereas the latter tends to avoid it, at least publicly. Therefore, the extreme right is sometimes referred to as the racialist right. As I show in Chapter 7, various nongovernmental organizations that monitor the far right consider this segment to pose a serious threat to the multicultural fabric of the United States. For the sake of clarity, I divide the extreme right into two major groupings, revolutionary and nonrevolutionary.

The revolutionary grouping generally holds the belief that a Jewish cabal holds sway over the U.S. government, as well as virtually all the governments of the Western world. This notion has been reified in the acronym "ZOG," which signifies Zionist occupation government. The importance of this acronym and the pervasiveness of anti-Semitism in the movement cannot be overstated. The acronym has attained great currency in the vernacular of the international "white power" movement and does much to link the disparate groups. Although much variation exists, even within the revolutionary racialist right, many individuals and groups in this segment draw inspiration from National Socialism and its attendant anti-Semitic worldview.

There are several religious sects that inspire this segment. Christian Identity posits that European-derived peoples are descendants of the ten lost tribes of Israel. Contemporary Jews are often demonized as belonging to an ancient seed line fathered by Satan or as descendants of a long-vanished Eurasian tribe, the Khazars.[6] In contrast, the World Church of the Creator rejects all metaphysical beliefs and supernatural deities. Instead it seeks to venerate the white race and protect it from miscegenation. Like Christian Identity, "Creativity," as the religion is sometimes called, posits that Jews and whites have been involved in a struggle extending back several millennia. However, unlike Christian Identity, Creativity asserts that Christianity was concocted by Jews to confuse white people and weaken their sense of tribal identity. Finally, Odinism seeks to resurrect the old Norse gods (e.g., Odin, Thor, Frey, Balder) and counter the Judeo-Christian worldview. Some people in the racialist movement sought to discover their primeval pagan roots and return to a mythical golden age unsullied by modern civilization. Thus, Odinism appears to be a white ethnic variant of multiculturalism, not unlike the black nationalist embrace of Islam.

Arguably the most significant organization of the revolutionary right is the National Alliance, which has its headquarters in Hillsboro, West Virginia. The National Alliance was founded by Dr. William L. Pierce in 1974. Pierce gained notoriety for writing *The Turner Diaries*—a fictionalized story of an underground revolutionary organization that wages a terrorist campaign and guerrilla war against the U.S. government. The book is alleged to have inspired numerous episodes of right-wing terrorism and violence. By the late 1990s, Pierce's Internet radio program, "American Dissident Voices," had gained widespread popularity on the extreme right.

Pierce was recognized as a kind of elder statesman of the extreme right and, for the most part, managed to stay above the fray in this fractious movement. When he died of kidney failure in July 2002, it was seen as a major setback, not only to his organization but to the entire racialist right as well. Eric Gliebe, a former boxer who fought under the moniker "the Aryan Barbarian," assumed leadership of the National Alliance not long after Pierce's death. Initially, Gliebe demonstrated a penchant for street activism, which included several National Alliance demonstrations at the Israeli embassy in Washington, D.C., in 2001–2002 to protest U.S. and Israeli policies in the Middle East and nationwide distribution of literature to coincide with Jewish holidays and September 11.[7] Currently the National Alliance is preoccupied with organizational survival, following numerous defections and disillusionment among members in the wake of Pierce's death. In April 2005 Kevin Alfred Strom, longtime member and Pierce's successor as host to the organization's American Dissident Voices radio program, was expelled for attempting to organize a coup against the leadership. Not long thereafter, Gliebe resigned as chairman, and Shaun Walker assumed that position. Strom created a new organization called National Vanguard, which he claimed was the legitimate successor to the National Alliance organization.

Despite some setbacks over the past few years, the revolutionary racialist right endures, perhaps because the trends that gave rise to the movement have become more pronounced. As Nicholas Goodrick-Clarke pointed out, multicultural societies in the West face a significant challenge in that they are absorbing ever-larger levels of immigration, while their political commitment to multiracialism has become an article of faith.[8] Globalization has greatly transformed Western societies, unleashing a massive flow of capital, information, skills, and personnel across national borders. Fears of economic marginalization and racial inundation have fueled the resurgence of the extreme right in North America and Western Europe. Therefore, it is no coincidence that the "Aryan cult of white identity" is now most marked in the United States, the country where the challenges of multiculturalism and Third World immigration are most pronounced. Such a development is open-ended, to say the least; Goodrick-Clarke observed that the conversion of the United States into a "colony of the world" or a "universal nation" is without precedent in the modern world.[9]

According to U.S. Census Bureau projections, by the year 2050, whites will no longer comprise a majority of the U.S. population because of huge increases in both the Hispanic and Asian segments of the population.[10] Furthermore, those in the movement generally believe that Jews will use whatever means necessary to retain power and suppress the right. Therefore, they see revolutionary resistance as their only feasible solution. The increasing nihilism of the revolutionary right could conceivably lead it to search for nontraditional allies. However, since the year 2000, the revolutionary racialist right has experienced several setbacks, as groups such as the Aryan Nations, National Alliance, and World Church of the Creator have all lost important leaders, either to death or imprisonment.

Although the revolutionary right has been hit hard in recent years, the nonrevolutionary segment has gained greater prominence in the overall extreme right constellation, for several reasons. First, representatives of the revolutionary racialist right have often acted brazenly and injudiciously, despite the formidable opposition arrayed against them, including the governmental and various nongovernmental organizations that monitor them.[11] This behavior has given authorities opportunities to effectively neutralize the more audacious among them, including Matt Hale and Alex Curtis. Furthermore, several prominent organizations on the revolutionary right have been decimated by civil suits, including Tom and John Metzger's group White Aryan Resistance (WAR), the Aryan Nations, and the United Klans of America. In contrast, the nonrevolutionary segment has remained largely intact and may actually be expanding.[12]

Second, although the nonrevolutionary right may reject the strident rhetoric of the more radical racialists, the former observes the latter and learns from its mistakes. Finally, the nonrevolutionary right has recently attracted individuals with impressive professional and educational backgrounds. Organizations such as American Renaissance, the Council of Conservative Citizens, and the Charles Martel Society attract members, writers, and supporters from among academics, lawyers, and successful businessmen. For example, Jared Taylor, the founder of American Renaissance and a prominent member of the Council of Conservative Citizens, graduated from Yale University and received a master's degree from L'Institut d'Etudes Politiques de Paris in France, speaks fluent Japanese and French, established a career as a successful business consultant, and wrote a critically acclaimed book on race relations titled *Paved with Good Intentions.*[13] His former colleague, the now-deceased Sam Francis, received a Ph.D. in history from the University of North Carolina and worked as a policy analyst for the Heritage Foundation, as well as a legislative assistant for national security affairs for the late U.S. senator John P. East (R-NC). He later worked as a columnist for the *Washington Times,* during which he received a prestigious award for editorial writing.[14] However, his open advocacy for an assertion of white racial identity and solidarity at the 1994 American Renaissance conference ultimately resulted in his dismissal from the newspaper.[15]

Unlike the revolutionary racialist right, the nonrevolutionary segment generally tends to avoid overt criticism of Jews. However, this convention may be changing. For example, David Duke, who reinvented himself as a conservative Republican in the late 1980s, has become increasingly strident in his criticism of Jews. Since the late 1990s, he has traveled throughout Western and Eastern Europe to promote various white nationalist causes and is one of the leading proponents of a global racialist movement in which Europeans and European-Americans jointly oppose globalization and Third World immigration. More recently, Duke has traveled to the Middle East in efforts to reach out to Arabs and Muslims who are critical of Israel.

The nonrevolutionary racialist right may be having some impact on the marketplace of ideas, if only on the traditional paleo-conservative movement. For example, psychology professor Kevin MacDonald, whose controversial theories on Judaism and anti-Semitism have gained, one could say, hushed attention in some intellectual circles, appears to have moved in the direction of the extreme right. Although still a relatively obscure figure, he has recently made a major impact on the intellectual currents of the extreme right. At an award ceremony in October 2004 for his trilogy on Jewish and anti-Semitic collective behavior, he discussed the applicability of the "Jewish model" as a way to ensure the "survival" of the West. The event was sponsored by the Charles Martel Society, a highly selective paleo-conservative organization that seeks to advance a platform of "white racial survival" and the preservation of Western culture.

Rejecting conventional theories, MacDonald believed that psychological research on social identity theory provides an adequate explanation of the dynamics of anti-Semitism.[16] Essentially, he argued that Jewish ethnocentrism, especially in the context of economic or other forms of competition, has produced a heightened sense of group identity in the various gentile populations among whom Jews have lived. Consequently, anti-Semitic mass movements develop in large part as a reaction to successful Jewish group evolutionary strategies.

As he argued in the first book of the trilogy, *A People That Shall Dwell Alone: An Evolutionary Theory of Judaism,* Judaism can best be explained as an evolutionary group strategy featuring such characteristics as endogamy, ethnic exclusivity, in-group altruism, and eugenics. In his second book, *Separation and Its Discontents,* he made the even more controversial argument that the various anti-Semitic mass movements that have bedeviled the history of the West have been largely reactive in the sense that they were gentile group strategies as part of a competition over resources with Jews. According to MacDonald, ethnic separatism leads to resource competition and so exacerbates intergroup tensions. Consequently, anti-Semitism is reactive and arises out of genuine conflicts of interest.

MacDonald asserted that over the years, Jews have developed and promoted numerous intellectual movements to further their group interests and combat anti-Semitism. In that vein, in the third and perhaps most popular book in his trilogy, *The Culture of Critique,* he argued that there is considerable Jewish hostility to traditional Western culture, which is manifested in various intellectual movements, such as Freudian psychology, the Frankfurt School, and Boazian anthropology, that aim to undermine the European-derived civilization in the United States and replace it with a society more congenial to Jews. According to his analysis, Jewish organizations have promoted policies and ideologies that have undermined the cultural cohesion of the West while practicing just the opposite for themselves. Specifically, he chided Jewish organizations for extolling multiculturalism in the West while insisting upon ethnic exclusivity in Israel. MacDonald argued that Jewish interest groups have sought to make American society more heterogeneous by promoting a liberal immigration policy that opens the country's borders to diverse populations from around the world. This policy diminishes the numbers of the European-derived majority, thus making the emergence of a broad-based, racially exclusivist movement less likely, as Earl Raab, an associate of the Anti-Defamation League, once colorfully explained:

> It was only after World War II that immigration law was drastically changed to eliminate such discrimination. In one of the first pieces of evidence of its political coming-of-age, the Jewish community has a leadership role in effecting those changes. . . . [17] The Census Bureau has just reported that about half of the American population will soon be non-white or non-European. And they will be American citizens. We have tipped beyond the point where a Nazi-Aryan party will be able to prevail in this country.
>
> We have been nourishing the American climate of opposition to ethnic bigotry for about half a century. That climate has not yet been perfected, but the heterogeneous nature of our population tends to make it irreversible and makes our constitutional constraints against bigotry more practical than ever.[18]

Not surprisingly MacDonald's trilogy has been well received by those in the racialist right, as it amounts to a theoretically sound justification for anti-Semitism. To his critics, MacDonald provides pseudo-intellectual support for the prejudices of anti-Semites. MacDonald's popularity could portend a major change in the orientation of the American extreme right, which since the 1980s has been characterized by radicalism and a relatively uneducated membership with little pretense to intellectual sophistication. This approach, however, was largely ineffectual; both government and various nongovernmental organizations effectively delegitimized and marginalized the movement. However, a new breed of extreme right intellectuals with tempered rhetoric and impressive academic credentials could conceivably broaden the influence of the movement as it reaches out to a more respectable audience.

Often referred to by its critics as Holocaust denial, the historical revisionist movement has pursued inquiries into many other historical topics, though admittedly, that specific historical experience still looms very large. Thus to movement members, the term "historical revisionism" is not meant to excuse or obfuscate but rather to create greater clarity.

Perhaps no other figure has been more instrumental in the development of historical revisionism than Willis Carto. The organization he founded in 1955, the Liberty Lobby, was an enduring institution that served as the nexus of the American extreme right. In 1978, Carto founded the Institute for Historical Review (IHR) and, in doing so, established an institutional basis for Holocaust revisionism that the movement hitherto did not have. However, Carto lost control of the IHR in 1993, when its board of directors terminated its relationship with him. A bitter feud ensued after IHR senior staffers accused Carto of diverting $7 million, bequeathed to the IHR, to the Liberty Lobby. Carto created a new historical revisionist organization, which publishes a journal, *The Barnes Review.* In addition, the Liberty Lobby was forced to dissolve in July 2001 as a result of a civil suit brought by IHR. Carto is not one to be easily silenced, of course, and just a few months later his defunct newspaper, the *Spotlight,* was effectively reconstituted as the *American Free Press.* Furthermore, much of the Liberty Lobby's staff has gone to work for this new project. It would appear that this segment of the extreme right is clearly waning and will probably not regain the influence it once had.

Perhaps the greatest potential for cooperation between the extreme right and militant Islam lies in the historical revisionist movement, and there are several reasons why the prospect of cooperation between this segment of the extreme right and militant Islam is strong. First, the racialism in this segment tends to be muted and much less strident. Rarely does one read claims about the racial superiority of European-derived peoples or the racial inferiority of other races. Furthermore, non-Europeans, such as the African Caribbean scholar Tony Martin, have on occasion given lectures at revisionist conferences. Finally, there is a great congruence of interests in this field of intellectual endeavor because both militant Islam and revisionists are highly critical of Zionism.

Mike Piper, a journalist for the *American Free Press* and a revisionist author who has written extensively on the John F. Kennedy assassination, described to me the contemporary revisionist movement and how it fits into the larger extreme right movement:

> Initially, I would draw a distinction between "revisionists" and "right wing extremism." While the revisionist movement and right-wing extremist

movement are very much overlapping in many respects, I think it's critical to note that the revisionist core is itself, relatively small, no more than perhaps a handful of leaders, per se, who reach, at most, ten thousand people on a regular sustained basis, at least on paper. The largest of the revisionist publications, the *Barnes Review,* has some 9,000 paid subscribers. The Institute for Historical Review, while far better known, if only because of its longevity, reportedly has fewer than 1,000 paid subscribers. So the actual core of revisionism is relatively small. The right-wing movement, as a whole, is considerably larger—although not much larger—and while it does generally subscribe to the revisionist philosophy, there are other guiding elements.[19]

Despite the opprobrium that they receive from the larger society, the revisionists persist in their efforts to alter the historiography of the Holocaust and other topics about which they feel strongly. In recent years, Swiss native Jürgen Graf gained international attention for his efforts in this area. Graf contended that the Holocaust is the Achilles' heel of Israel. As a revisionist who impugned the official version of the Holocaust, he saw great potential for an alliance with Palestinians and their supporters, especially because any effort to discredit accepted views of the Holocaust would undercut the legitimacy of the state of Israel and, by extension, the larger international community of Jews. However, it is questionable whether such an approach is really feasible, considering the scope and magnitude of the scholarship that supports the official version of the Holocaust and the acceptance it receives from the great majority of the population of Europe and the United States. In an interview, Graf offered these comments on this issue:

> By speaking of the "the scope and magnitude of the scholarship that supports the official version of the Holocaust," you are committing an error. It is hardly an exaggeration to state that there is no more "official version of the Holocaust," as the orthodox historians are making one startling concession after the other to the Revisionists, apart from the fact that they wildly contradict each other. . . . Scientifically, the gas chambers and the 6 million figure are dead. The "Holocaust" lie is but a rotten corpse, which the establishment of the so-called free world tenaciously defends for purely political reasons.
>
> It is certainly true that the overwhelming majority of the populace believes the Jewish extermination and gas chamber story, as well as the 6 million figure. This is simply due to the fact that those who profit from these myths control the education system, plus the media, of the West. As soon as the political situation changes radically—and I do not know

whether this will happen in three months or in twenty years, as I have no prophetic gifts—the truth will be made accessible to the public, and the "Holocaust" legend will collapse overnight.[20]

It is important to note that mainstream historians categorically reject the historiography of the revisionists. Yet the revisionists persist in their crusade to reveal the "truth" as they see it. In the summer of 2001, Graf, along with American revisionists, sought to organize a conference on "Revisionism and Zionism," scheduled for late March in Beirut, Lebanon. Although the event was cancelled at the last minute, it demonstrates a growing cooperation between Western revisionists and Islamic sympathizers. The IHR and the Swiss-based Verité et Justice had planned the conference, which was to include lectures in English, French, and Arabic. The IHR had interfaced with Muslims in the past; its director, Mark Weber, has been interviewed numerous times on Iranian state radio (Islamic Republic of Iran Broadcasting, or IRIB).[21] According to some accounts, Arabs were among the first financial supporters of the IHR.[22] Just prior to the founding of the IHR, it is believed that the government of Saudi Arabia funded the Holocaust denier, William N. Grimstad, author of *The Six Million Reconsidered*.[23] And on some occasions, Muslims have addressed IHR conferences, including Issah Nakleh of the World Muslim Congress, an organization that was initially led by the grand mufti of Jerusalem.[24]

Notwithstanding the efforts of the revisionists to reach out to Arabs and Muslims, the latter's interest in the Holocaust appears to be limited for a number of reasons, most prominent among them the opprobrium Holocaust revisionism receives in the West. For this reason, Holocaust revisionism is seen by some revisionists as an uphill battle that will be ultimately ineffective in combating Zionism. Thus other aspects of revisionism (e.g., lobbying against Israel in the United States, promoting Palestinian independence) are becoming increasingly popular and crowding out the Holocaust. Graf explained this development.

> Jordanian scholar Dr. Ibrahim Alloush, who organized a symposium about Revisionism in Amman in the aftermath of the failed Beirut conference and was recently arrested by Jordan's puppet regime, explained in an interview with the *Journal of Historical Review* (May–June 2001) why many Arabs are reluctant to embrace revisionism. First of all, they know that people in the West generally believe the Holocaust story and fear to alienate potential sympathizers by endorsing revisionism, even if they personally don't accept the Jewish version of World War II. For a second [reason], they often think that the Second World War is a purely Western problem, which does not concern them. As Dr. Alloush correctly stated, these arguments are utterly flawed. As

long as the average American and European believes in the gas chambers and the six million, he will always support Israel's right to exist, even if he condemns Sharon's policy as unnecessarily harsh. Israel does not really fear Western criticism of its repressive policy or of Zionism in general. The only thing it fears is revisionism.[25]

Cooperation between the extreme right and militant Islam did not arise in a vacuum. Although there was some interaction between the two movements in the past, there appears to be greater potential for collaboration today, in part because the extreme right has become radicalized.

The Radicalization of the American Extreme Right

Since the 1980s, the extreme right has evolved from a movement characterized by ultrapatriotism to one increasingly characterized by nihilism. This change can be explained in large part by various social trends that have significantly changed the racial makeup of the United States. For those in the extreme right, the United States is not the same country they once knew. Many in the movement consider the "damage" irreparable by conventional methods. Thus only radical solutions can save the nation and race. From their perspective, the increasingly desperate predicament demands that the old order be torn asunder and a new order be built upon the ruins. Out of this destruction, the remnants of Western civilization will create a new golden age characterized by creativity and racial solidarity.[26] However, this sentiment did not arise overnight. For many years, conservative patriotism tinged with nativism characterized the extreme right. Drawing upon research in the study of terrorism can give us a better theoretical understanding of how this orientation toward revolution and nihilism came about.

Breaking with the tradition of American patriotism, law, and order did not come easily for the extreme right. It took a crisis of legitimacy to spur the movement into a more revolutionary direction. Observers have noted that the notion of legitimacy looms large in the psychology of terrorists. J. Groebel suggested that terrorists go through a process of "deviant legitimation" by which they move toward the strategy of violence.[27] This process requires that two conditions must exist for a potential terrorist to decide to resort to political violence: first, the presence of a group or movement that supports his extremist worldview, and second, a set of supportive beliefs that violence is morally legitimate or at least morally justified. As explained by another observer, Jonathan Drummond, in order to socially construct violence as justified or as a moral obligation, the terrorist must perceive the threat as imminent and not preventable by lesser means. Similarly, H. H. A. Cooper theorized that terrorists cannot accept the world as it is, and after employing a type of mental cost-benefit analysis, they resort to violence when they believe that the continuance of the status quo is morally worse than the violence caused by terrorism.[28]

Terrorists must develop a sense of "self" or a community for whom they are fighting. As Drummond explained, the "self" to be defended may vary greatly.[29] Specifically, he argued that the level of terrorist retaliation is "positively related to the appraisal that an attack or affront is personal when directed not only against one's physical self, but also one's honor, family members, members of a secondary group, one's home, valued possessions, and culturally sustained beliefs and values."[30]

Likewise, terrorists must identify an enemy against whom they are fighting. Drummond described a process by which terrorists identify and construct their enemies. First the enemy is labeled. Second, there must be a validation of the label if it is to be meaningful or influential. The notion of ZOG comes to mind here. Third, construction of the enemy involves a form of mythmaking in such a way that time can be collapsed and "chosen wounds and glories" are made immediately relevant. In this sense, mythmaking is important because it is the process by which facts are framed and arranged, explanations are produced, and predictions are made. Finally, the last component of Drummond's framework involves ritual, which helps reconfirm the truth of the myth.[31]

Constructing the image of the enemy may be a necessary, though not necessarily a sufficient, condition to impel a terrorist toward violence. The immediacy of the threat posed by the enemy matters as well.[32] This sense of embattlement is amplified when the potential terrorist finds solace in a group of like-minded people. Through a process of "double-marginalization," individuals join a series of extremist groups on the way to terrorism, and through a process of "serial splintering," they arrive in a group that engages in violence. Extremists become increasingly isolated from mainstream society and find that their beliefs are reinforced by other members through a process not unlike groupthink. Violence, which was previously unthinkable, is now preferred.[33] Furthermore, as Paul Wilkinson observed, terrorist groups often reinforce group loyalty through a process of justification.[34] For example, militia members in the United States often convene so-called common law courts to render justification for their violent acts against government authorities. Likewise, Islamist terrorists issue fatwas justifying jihad against their enemies.[35]

It is not uncommon for terrorists to experience a "delegitimizing event" that propels them toward violence. For example, the U.S. military presence in Saudi Arabia was seen by Osama bin Laden as a defilement of Islam's most hallowed soil. Likewise, the 1993 raid by the FBI and the Bureau of Alcohol, Tobacco, and Firearms on the Branch Davidian sect in Waco, Texas, was one such event for Timothy McVeigh. After the tragedies at Ruby Ridge and Waco, many in the extreme right viewed the government as irrevocably lost and an implacable enemy. According to the Israeli political scientist Ehud Sprinzak, terrorist campaigns do not arise from nothing, but rather develop through a process of "delegitimization," which involves three crucial phases. The first, called the "crisis of confidence," occurs when a dissident group, movement, or counterculture articulates a critique of the regime in loaded ideological terms and begins to dissent from mainstream politics. In the second phase, the "conflict of legitimacy," the radicalization process continues, but the dissidents move from merely criticizing the government to questioning the very legitimacy of the regime or "system" as well. In this phase political action can range from angry protests to low-level violence. Finally, in the third phase, the "crisis of legitimacy," representatives of the regime are dehumanized, and the whole system is viewed as incorrigible and irredeemable. Dehumanization makes it possible for radicals to disengage morally and commit atrocities without remorse.

Sprinzak argued that the case of right-wing terrorism differs from other variants of terrorism insofar as the former goes through a dual process of delegitimization. As he explained, one of the most important differences between right-wing, or "particularistic," terrorists and "universalistic" terrorists lies in their relationship to the state. The latter are usually involved in direct confrontations with the ruling government, and thus their terror campaign is directed against its representatives. By contrast, for right-wing terrorists, the conflict with the regime is secondary. Consequently, right-wing extremists undergo an uneven radicalization as they develop animus against two separate entities. According to Sprinzak, right-wing terrorism is characterized by a process of "split-delegitimation," in which not only the "outsider" (e.g., foreigners, ethnic and religious minorities, communists, and gays) is targeted, but also the very state itself, which is seen as ineffective or, worse yet, under the actual sway of the outsiders. At first, right-wing terrorists usually avoid confrontations with authorities and direct their hostility at the "outsiders." They do not usually confront authorities and have developed no ideological critique of the regime. However, eventually they convince themselves that the government is not doing enough to protect the "original community," and the state also becomes a target.[36] On an ideological level, Sprinzak's theory holds up well, because those in the revolutionary racialist right view their governments as under the heel of ZOG.[37]

Chris Hewitt made a significant contribution to the study of political violence by collating the number of fatalities in the United States by different categories of terrorists from the period from 1955 through 1998. According to

Hewitt, since 1955, right-wing terrorism has occurred in two distinct waves. The first wave began in the early years of the civil rights era in the 1950s and ended in the early 1970s. By his calculation, there were fifty-six fatalities attributable to right-wing violence during that period. Most of the terrorist fatalities occurred in the South (forty-six deaths, or 82 percent).[38] Those targeted by right-wing terrorists fell into just a few distinct categories. Fifty percent of the victims (twenty-eight) were targeted for no other reason than some ascriptive characteristic such as race or ethnicity. This was followed closely by "enemy activists," in this case usually civil rights workers (twenty-five deaths, or 44.6 percent). Suspected informants and factional disputes accounted for two deaths and one death, respectively.

The second wave of right-wing terrorism commenced in 1978 and still continues. On an empirical level, Hewitt's data lend support to the applicability of Sprinzak's theory to right-wing terrorism in the United States: there is evidence to support the proposition that representatives of the state have been targeted with increasing frequency. Although the vast majority of victims of right-wing violence still fall into the "hate crime/random" category" (eighty-five deaths out of 120, or 70.8 percent), they include politicians and representatives of the police, none of whom were killed in the first wave. As Hewitt's data demonstrate, during the civil rights era, various Ku Klux Klan groups targeted blacks and civil rights workers almost exclusively. Government officials were not targeted. To the contrary, on some occasions local law enforcement officials were bona fide Klan members or worked hand in glove with the group.[39] However, in the second wave, right-wing terrorists have been extremely hostile to the police and have killed several of them (nine deaths, or 7.5 percent). In addition, two politicians were killed during this wave, although none was killed in the first. Several episodes during the 1990s in which members of the patriot movement targeted state facilities and government representatives also support Sprinzak's theory.[40]

In another study, Hewitt found that the timing of each major outbreak of terrorism in the United States coincides, at least approximately, with the rise of extremist sentiments and various indicators of extremist mobilization. The latter can include the formation of groups that articulate the platforms and values of extremists and the number of people who participate in such movements. Hewitt argued that when individuals holding extremist values come into contact with other like-minded people, their militancy is more likely to be reinforced. Moreover, contact between individuals becomes more likely when organizations are created to mobilize for extremism. Thus, when members of extremist organizations are likely to have their views reinforced, they are consequently more likely to come to believe that violence is legitimate and encouraged.[41]

The campaign of the Order speaks volumes for the aforementioned theories. In 1983 various extremists, who congregated at the Aryan Nations compound and were disillusioned with mere rhetoric, cohered into a bona fide terrorist organization. Led by the charismatic Robert Jay Matthews, the Order conducted a campaign of terror in the Pacific Northwest, which included several armored car heists, bank robberies, bombings, and homicides, with the ultimate goal of establishing a white separatist bastion in the Northwest. Although strategically, the Order did not accomplish much—by early 1985 virtually all known members were arrested and many would subsequently be sentenced to long prison sentences—its campaign crystallized the revolutionary orientation of the American extreme right. As former skinhead leader George Eric Hawthorne commented:

Although their precise actions mean little in the greater scheme of things, the fact that they ACTED [emphasis in original]—acted with unprecedented selflessness and sacrifice—means everything to this movement today. . . . [42] Tactically speaking, Alan Berg [an abrasive radio disc jockey whom members of the Order assassinated] was a bad choice. . . . The physical act of killing Alan Berg was about as meaningless as assassinating the White House gardener. . . . But historically speaking, in the wider context of things, it was of unfathomable significance. It marked the transition from conservatism to radicalism. It marks the beginning of the Second American Revolution, a revolution that shall strike into the heart of everything diseased that America has become.[43]

Although the Order's campaign galvanized some segments of the revolutionary right, others actually criticized the group for its lack of results. Ben Klassen, the now-deceased founder of the World Church of the Creator, believed that right-wing terrorists would be more effective in emulating their counterparts in the Middle East. Furthermore, he implicitly endorsed the leaderless resistance approach:

They [the Order] launched into a program of criminal activities such as armed robbery and even managed to assassinate a filthy Jewish talk-show host by the name of Alan Berg. The end result of all this was that these brave young racial fighters, some thirty-five of them, are now behind bars, their energetic activities neutralized and thwarted, probably for the rest of their lives. Bob Matthews is dead, having died heroically in a fiery shootout against the overwhelming odds of a massive swat team launched against him by the Jewish establishment.

I believe this is an unduly heavy price to pay in terms of our young activists for the killing of one lousy Jew. If, instead they had gone their own quiet separate ways, secretly planned and planned well a number of attacks on groups of Jews, they could, for the same price, have killed probably as many as twenty, or fifty or a hundred Jews each. The sum total price exacted for the thirty-five now behind bars could have been several hundred dead Jews, instead of one filthy talk-show host. . . .

Let's us take a look at some of the strikes the Arabs, who generally are none too bright, have successfully executed. A classic example is the bombing of the U.S. Marine compound in Lebanon on October 23, 1983. There we find one lone truck driver (presumably an Arab) who willingly went to his death with a big smile on his face. But as he did so, he took with him 240 of his enemies (dead) as well as hundreds of wounded. Now if we compare that maneuver to the effectiveness of what The Order episode accomplished, we find that the lone Arab was approximately 35 X 240, or more than 8000 times as effective as were each of the 35 some members of The Order. Now that, my fellow White Racial Comrades, is one hell of a difference. Let's give this effectiveness a name. Let's call it the Enemy Toll Effectiveness Factor (E.T.E.F.). . . . The quality of the enemy destroyed also enters in. We must remember those killed and wounded were U.S. Marines, fighting men in the prime of their manhood, a much more meaningful action than merely killing an equal number of random riff-raff.[44]

Global events shaped the orientation of the extreme right as well, most notably the demise of the Soviet Union and the decreasing salience of international communism. For many years, some in the movement saw communism as a diversion, a distraction from the "real" enemy. With the removal of communism as a major force in geopolitics, the extreme right could now focus more attention on the Jews and their putative vehicle, the U.S. government, as the prime source of evil.[45] Thus the principal object of animus crystallized. Although anti-Semitism had loomed large in the extremist subculture for many years, Jews had shared this animus with other subjects, including liberals, gays and lesbians, "insiders" (a term John Birch Society members use to refer to the shadowy plutocrats who allegedly ruled America), the Bildeberger Group, the Trilateral Commission, and the Council on Foreign Relations. What accelerated in the 1980s was the identification of Jews as the primary enemy—the puppet master of all of the enemies, in the extreme right's worldview. Indeed Jews have become an obsession, as evidenced by the popularity of the ZOG discourse. In the minds of those in the extreme right, ZOG has become a global Leviathan with tentacles reaching into the innermost recesses of government and society, a pax Judaica, if you will. This ideological development has thus led to a convergence in worldviews between the extreme right and militant Islam.

Because the revolutionary racialist right has virtually no hope of achieving power through the electoral process—at least at the present time—and because its members generally consider the broad white masses as too indifferent and even stupid to listen to their message, terrorism remains an attractive alternative. The right sees terrorism as a form of "shock therapy" that could destabilize the state and society and in so doing gain the attention of the masses.[46]

Toward this end, some extreme right activists have endeavored to create a network in which they could operate while avoiding the scrutiny of the authorities. Louis Beam, for example, advocated the strategy of "leaderless resistance" as a way of thwarting government infiltration. In essence, leaderless resistance is a type of lone-wolf operation in which an individual or a very small cohesive group engages in terrorism independent of any official movement, leader, or network of support. Despite all the theorizing by the American extreme right on this issue, however, it has seldom carried out spectacular acts of terrorism. With the exception of the 1995 Oklahoma City bombing, right-wing terrorism has not posed a serious domestic security threat to the United States in modern history. This is in sharp contrast to radical Islamists, who have demonstrated on several occasions their ability to join together for specific terrorist operations. Often with only the most tenuous affiliations to terrorist organizations, radical Islamists have demonstrated their capacity to form ad hoc amalgamations of like-minded individuals and converge to conduct serious acts of terrorism in what Bruce Hoffman referred to as the "amateurization of terrorism."[47]

Conclusion

The principal reason for the extreme right's lack of success is in large part—to use Mao Zedong's metaphor—the absence of a sea in which to swim. As the former Israeli prime minister Benjamin Netanyahu noted, the scattered movement of right-wing extremists in the United States does not constitute a sea but rather a collection of puddles. When he first made this observation in the mid-1990s, he saw no social or cultural climate for the breeding of domestic terrorist organizations in the United States. Thus the chief challenge for counterterrorist authorities, in Netanyahu's analysis, was to identify the puddles from which terrorist threats are likely to emerge.[48] However, even though potential right-wing terrorists may not at the present time have a sophisticated network of which they can avail themselves, the same cannot be said for Islamist radicals. The attacks on the World Trade Center demonstrated that they can blend in with immigrant communities and live under the radar screen of authorities. Now that they have taken up residence in the United States and established a network of supporters who can provide money, weapons, training, and housing, a serious domestic terrorist threat has emerged. They can now wage jihad within the United States.

In sharp contrast to militant Islam, the extreme right in the United States is relatively weak. However, its current marginalization could change quickly. African American scholar Carol M. Swain identified seven conditions that could fuel the growth of what she referred to as the "new white nationalism" in the near future. First, the increasing presence of nonwhite immigrants could reduce whites to minority status in certain areas. Second, structural changes in the global economy have reduced the proportion of high-wage production jobs for low-skilled workers, who must now compete with legal and illegal immigrants for low-paying employment opportunities. Third, white resentment persists over the perceived unfairness of race-based programs such as affirmative action. Fourth, the rate of black-on-white crime continues to be high.[49] Fifth, multiculturalism, with its emphasis on group rights, solidarity, and identity politics, has become more and more accepted. In this sense, white nationalism would be a logical conclusion of the multicultural paradigm. Sixth, the rising expectations of racial and ethnic minorities could lead to increased interracial competition for resources and political power. And finally, the expansion of the Internet has enabled like-minded people to share information and ideas, thus consolidating their strength and enabling them to mobilize their resources for political action.[50] The extreme right has enthusiastically taken advantage of the new medium and sees it as a powerful vehicle through which to spread its message. According to some estimates, by 1999, between 600 and 2,100 right-wing websites existed worldwide.[51]

Paradoxically, one of the chief threats that Carol Swain saw from the extreme right was its isolation in public discourse. Applying the psychological theories of Cass R. Sunstein, Swain noted that when group discussion takes place among like-minded people without the benefit of contrasting perspectives, the tendency is for members of the group to become more extreme in their views and more convinced of the rightness of their cause. Thus under such circumstances, members of an insular group tend to adopt the views of those closest to the fringe.[52] Swain believes that this finding currently applies to the extreme right. Furthermore, political correctness inhibits whites from having frank discussions about race, which she saw as the real danger for the future of race relations in the United States. In a country in which few white Americans can openly express their concerns over black-on-white crime, their impending minority status, affirmative action, and immigration, the extreme right has stepped to the forefront to offer a divisive form of identity politics that could have ominous implications for the future.[53]

One could add another item to Swain's list of trends that could bolster the strength of the extreme right: the growing salience of the Middle East conflict in American foreign policy in the future. With rapidly expanding Muslim and Arab populations in the United States, the extreme right could find potential allies on this important issue. Anecdotal evidence suggests that such a proposition has been considered.

In 1995, for example, an extreme right underground novel titled *SS Freikorps Arabien,* written by Josef Meighy, took up the fantasy of collaboration between right-wing and Arab militants, who forge a terrorist organization based on shared hostility to Israel and Jews. The short novel begins when members of the Islamic Liberation Front attack the Israeli embassy in Paris, killing several of its employees, including members of the Mossad. Galvanized by this incident, German and French neo-Nazis meet in Frankfurt to discuss plans. They decide to approach the Syrian embassy and offer their services as part of a united anti-Zionist front. The Syrians accept their offer and send twenty of the young neo-Nazis first to Syria and then to Lebanon to train with the Popular Front for the Liberation of Palestine. While in Beirut, they consort with a variety of Palestinian rejectionist groups, including Fatah of the Palestine Liberation Organization (PLO). During training they meet a former Schutzstaffel (SS) officer, Alois Brunner, who was granted asylum in Syria after World War II. They call their organization the Freikorps Arabien and even include in their ranks some Arab volunteers from the groups mentioned above. The novel concludes with the terrorist group successfully conducting a cross-border raid from Lebanon into Israel and attacking a military outpost, leaving several Israeli soldiers dead. The group then plans future terrorist attacks against Israeli and Jewish targets in Europe.[54]

More significant, if the account of Order member Richard Scutari is to be believed, before the group was quashed by the authorities, some members were working on a covert mission dubbed the "Sunshine Project" in the summer of 1984. Scutari claimed that he and Robert Jay Matthews met with two Egyptians who had belonged to the Egyptian Islamic Group—the organization responsible for the assassination of Anwar Sadat in 1981. He further claimed that he and Matthews were scheduled to travel to the Middle East with a "well-known individual." According to Scutari, Matthews's theory was that an enemy of his enemy could be useful. Finally, Scutari claimed that one of his codefendants at the 1999 Fort Smith sedition trial was a white Muslim arms dealer who supplied weapons to Afghan rebels during their war against the Soviet Union.[55] Reportedly, Order members Randy Duey and Denver Parmenter approached their leader Robert Jay Matthews about the prospect of approaching oil-rich Arab countries for funding. Matthews approved, but little is known about this effort.[56]

Was the Sunshine Project mere bluster, a boastful fabrication on the part of Scutari, a pipedream in his mind that would connect the often hapless right-wing extremists with Middle Eastern professional terrorists? Previous episodes of interaction between the extreme right and Islam will be further explored in Chapter 5, but first I turn to the development of militant Islam so that we can gain a greater understanding of this dynamic movement.

CHAPTER THREE

The Development of Militant Islam and Arab Nationalism

To some observers, militant Islam is a retrograde phenomenon, a rear-guard action against the inexorable march to modernity. Some critics even go so far as to argue that violence inheres in the religion of Islam.[1] To its followers, however, it represents an effort to return humanity to the righteous guidance of Allah as expressed in the Koran. As Bernard Lewis has pointed out, Islam is in its essence a political religion. Unlike other religious leaders such as Jesus and Buddha, the Prophet Muhammad was a sovereign leader. He promulgated laws, dispensed justice, raised armies, made war, and made peace. In short, he did all the things that a head of state does. Therefore, according to the tradition established by Muhammad, politics, government, law, war, and peace all are part of the holy law of Islam.[2] In that sense, Islam covers more areas, both spiritual and secular, than do most other religions.

But just what is militant Islam or, as it is sometimes labeled, Islamism? Not unlike the term "extreme right," it remains a nebulous concept. Surprisingly few scholars have actually sought to define militant Islam, as if they assumed the term was self-evident to readers. According to Daniel Pipes, Islamism is essentially an effort to transform the religion of Islam into a contemporary political ideology not unlike fascism and communism. Islamism offers a vanguard philosophy with a complete program to improve human beings and remake society. In short, it is an Islamic attempt to come to terms with the challenge of modernization. Pipes used the following terms to characterize militant Islam:

• Radical utopian—Islamists view all existing political systems outside their movements as deeply corrupt and mendacious. Consequently, these *jahili* (un-Islamic) entities must be discarded and replaced with authentically Islamic institutions.
• Totalitarian—Islamists seek to create an Islamic system that would touch on virtually every aspect of life. The career of the Prophet Muhammad, which included politics, statesmanship, war, peace, and civic relations, is seen as an appropriate model for contemporary Islamists.

33

- Antidemocratic—The Islamists generally do not see democracy as an end but rather a means to an end of establishing Islamic regimes. Although Islamists may seek political power via elections in the style of Adolf Hitler and Salvador Allende, it is questionable whether they would remain democrats on attaining power. As one observer once opined, the introduction of democracy could lead to "one man, one vote, one time."[3]
- Antimoderate—Islamists are aggressive and seek to export their ideology to other countries. According to the Islamist worldview, it is the historical mission of Islam to liberate man from man so that he can live in accordance with God's will.
- Anti-Semitic—Jews are identified as the arch-nemesis of contemporary Islamists.
- Anti-Western—Islamists often view the West as implacably hostile to Islam. In this respect, the history of colonialism has left an indelible imprint on the collective psyche of the Arab world.
- Unwilling to coexist—Islamists feel that they are in a struggle against the West for cultural supremacy from which only one side can emerge victorious.[4]

Islamism purports to answer all the pressing questions of the modern era. Furthermore, it seeks to revitalize the universalistic fervor of early Islam as it is repackaged as a viable model for exportation.

Militant Islam really gained momentum after the Islamic Revolution of 1979 in Iran. After many years of frustration, the elusive Islamist dream had been realized, and an Islamic republic was established. Much to the initial embarrassment of Sunni Islamists, it was the Shi'ites who had accomplished this feat. The roots of militant Islam actually go back much farther in history than the Iranian revolution, however. In this chapter I chart the development of militant Islam in order to give the reader a historical perspective to better understand other themes in this book.

Arab Nationalism and the Development of the Muslim Brotherhood

The genesis of modern nationalism in the Middle East can be traced to the second half of the nineteenth century. Napoleon Bonaparte sought to apply the humanistic ideals of the French Revolution to the other nations that his army occupied. The emancipation of the Jews and Christians during the Western occupation of Egypt, combined with new Western influences, in particular from France, led to the emergence of Arab nationalism. Western notions of freedom and political participation found currency first largely among Christian subjects and minorities and then later among the Muslim majority. Pan-Islamism emerged as a nascent movement around this time as well. One of the first proponents of pan-Islamism, Jamal al-Din al-Afghani (1838–1897), urged his coreligionists to apply the European concept of nationhood to the Muslim world so that it could develop as a major global power.[5] Afghani, along with his student Mohammed Abdu (1865–1905), led an intellectual movement to modernize Islam. To them, there was nothing inherent in Islam that was incompatible with the various progressive values proffered by the West at that time. Therefore, they sought to create a new synthesis of Islam and modernity that would revive the Muslim world. It was an early effort to transform Islam into a moderate political ideology.

However, several aspects of Islamic history militated against political moderation, prominent among them the legacy of colonialism. As the esteemed historian Bernard Lewis observed, after a series of historical setbacks vis-à-vis the West, the Muslim world asked, "What went wrong?" With the arrival of Napoleon in Egypt, the Muslim world realized that even a small European military force could penetrate with virtual impunity into the heart of their territory. By 1920, the victory of the West over Islam appeared complete. The impact of the West and Western ideas also brought new definitions of identity and consequently new aspirations and allegiances. The first, patriotism, favored by the Ottoman Empire, which lasted from the middle of the fifteenth century until the end of World War I, sought to bind heterogeneous peoples in a common loyalty to country. The second, nationalism, a more ethnic and linguistic form of identity, would have a centrifugal effect on the polyglot empire as various ethnic groups sought self-determination as expressed in national sovereignty and self-determination.[6]

The influence of the European powers had a significant effect on political developments in the Islamic world. As Yossef Bodansky pointed out, the emancipation of Christians and Jews in the Arab World eventually created complex political dynamics: Zionism for the Jews and pan-Arabism for Arab Christians. The latter sought to steer Arab Muslims away from pan-Islam to a more inclusive movement based on Arab ethnicity.

A secularizing trend swept parts of the Middle East at the start of the twentieth century, exemplified by the Turkish leader Mustafa Kemal Atatürk. He believed that Islam was a hindrance to the modernization of Turkey and blamed the religion for his nation's defeat in World War I. He spoke derisively of Islam as "the absurd theology of an immoral Bedouin." To distance Turkey from the Arab World, Atatürk adopted the Latin alphabet, abolished the koranic system of education, and declared religion to be a matter of individual concern only.[7] Today Atatürk is considered the bête noire of Islamists, and the collapse of the Ottoman Empire is generally recognized as the genesis of the crisis in the contemporary Muslim world. Secularization also engendered a backlash against Westernization and modernization and as a result intensified the fledging Islamist movement.

The Muslim Brotherhood

The collapse of the caliphate in Turkey troubled much of the Islamic world. Many Muslims were aghast as they watched how Kemal Atatürk had transformed Turkey into a secular state. They feared that such a development might take hold in their nations as well. With the collapse of Turkey, Egypt assumed the fulcrum position in the Islamic world. The most enduring institution of Islamism, the Muslim Brotherhood (Al-Ikhwan Al-Muslimun) was founded by Hassan al-Banna in Egypt in 1928. Al-Banna was born into an impoverished family in 1906. Most of the brotherhood's founders were followers of Wahhabism, a puritanical sect that seeks to return to an unadulterated, original form of Islam unsullied by centuries of history. The brotherhood movement spread rapidly throughout the Islamic world. The Egyptian branch also served as a vehicle of national liberation in that it sought to extricate Egypt from Western control and non-Islamic influences. Among other things, the brotherhood sought to counter the influence of the Wafd Party, which openly advocated the Westernization of Egypt. At that particular time, Egypt was the intellectual center of the Middle East, and the idea of an Islamic renaissance was in the air.[8] The movement also sought a moral renewal of Muslims not unlike the various Great Awakenings that have punctuated American history. Today it is estimated that the Muslim Brotherhood has branches in over seventy countries all over the world.[9] Among the major goals that the Muslim Brotherhood seeks to accomplish are the liberation of Muslim lands, the establishment of Islamic governments, intellectual and scientific progress, and the development of authentic Islamic institutions.[10]

Despite his Islamic universalism, al-Banna was not really averse to the concept of Arab nationalism. In fact, according to his version of Islamism, Arabs were seen as the guardians of the faith:

The Arabs are the core and the guardians of Islam. . . . Arab unity is an essential prerequisite for the restoration of Islam's glory, the reestablishment of the Muslim state, and the consolidation of Muslim power. This is why it is the duty of every Muslim to work for the revival and support of Arab unity.

The truth is that just as Islam is a religious faith and a system of worship, it is also patriotism and nationality. . . . As such, Islam does not recognize geographic frontiers nor the distinctions of nationality or race, but considers all Muslims as one single nation and the Islamic homeland as one single territory no matter how far-flung or remote the countries of which it is composed may be. . . . It should thus be evident that the Muslim Brothers owe respect to their own particular nationalism, Egyptian nationalism, which constitutes the primary basis of the revival that they seek.[11]

The struggle in Palestine from 1936 to 1949 transformed the brotherhood into a cadre of a broader resistance movement in the struggle against the nascent state of Israel. Al-Banna eventually ran afoul of the regime and was assassinated in 1949, reportedly on the orders of King Farouk. However, Farouk's days as Egyptian leader were numbered. Arab nationalism proved to be a dynamic force that the monarch could not squelch.

At first, relations between the Muslim Brotherhood and Gamal Abdel Nasser were amicable. The Muslim Brotherhood even supported Nasser and his Free Officers in their 1952 coup that overthrew King Farouk. By 1954, Nasser had taken over full control of the state. Early in his political career, Nasser had presented himself as a soldier of Islam, writing a pamphlet titled "Philosophy of Revolution," which was in essence a virtual rewrite of the Muslim Brotherhood's propaganda sheets.[12] However, not long into his tenure as the new Egyptian head of state, some Islamic fundamentalists began to criticize his regime. Relations broke down irrevocably between the Nasser government and the Muslim Brotherhood in 1954 when a member, Mahmoud 'Abd al-Latif, attempted to assassinate Nasser while he gave a speech in Alexandria. Soon thereafter, the regime fiercely repressed the brotherhood, many of its members were incarcerated, and the movement was driven underground. However, these measures did not silence the opposition—indeed, it became more strident. Chief among the critics of the regime was Sayid Qutb, arguably the principal theorist of the Islamist movement.

Sayid Qutb and *Milestones*

The chief ideologist of Islamism was not Hassan al-Banna but rather Sayid Qutb (1906–1966). Qutb has had a profound influence on the contemporary Islamist movement; he is believed to have inspired the most prominent Islamist leaders, including the late Ayatollah Ruhollah Khomeini, as well as

Osama bin Laden. Qutb was a prolific writer, intensely concerned about the important issues of his day. Early in his career, he gained prominence as a literary critic; in 1948 he left Egypt for an extended trip to the United States, where he pursued advanced degrees in education. At first, Qutb was a moderate who believed that Islam could be revised to meet the challenges that modernity presented to the Middle East. However, his time spent in the United States occasioned a shift in his ideological orientation. In 1951, he wrote a three-part essay based on his experiences titled *The America I Have Seen.* He told readers that he was aghast at what he had witnessed during his stay and was especially taken aback by the licentiousness of some Americans. He was particularly appalled by the convivial atmosphere that he observed in American churches, which often sponsored bake sales and dances. As a result of his experience in the United States, he became a born-again Muslim of sorts.[13]

Qutb believed that although the West in general and the United States in particular had accomplished much in the fields of science and technology, these societies had become morally and spiritually bankrupt. The hoary ideas of liberty, fraternity, and equality expressed so eloquently during the French Revolution, which had animated Western civilization for almost two centuries, had effectively been exhausted and run their course. Consequently, the West was spiritually impoverished and had no dynamic principles remaining with which to guide the world.[14]

Not unlike G. W. F. Hegel, Karl Marx, and Francis Fukuyama, Qutb recognized stages of history. But whereas these Western political theorists saw either communism or liberal democracy as the last remaining viable political ideology, Qutb believed that through Islam, man would reach his highest stage of development. As Qutb saw things in the early post–World War II era, human history was at an important crossroads:

> Mankind today is on the brink of a precipice, not because of the danger of complete annihilation which is hanging over its head—this being just a symptom and not the real disease—but because humanity is devoid of those vital values which are necessary not only for its healthy development but also for its real progress. Even the Western world realizes that Western civilization is unable to present any healthy values for the guidance of mankind. . . .
>
> The leadership of mankind by Western man is now on the decline, not because Western culture has become poor materially or because its economic and military power has become weak. The period of the Western system has come to an end primarily because it is deprived of those life-giving values, which enabled it to be the leader of mankind.[15]

Qutb argued that Islam offered a way of life regulated by God's laws and nature. All other types of government and human organizing systems—communism, capitalism, democracy, nationalism—were human constructs and thus woefully inadequate in comparison to the divine administration as revealed in the Koran. Qutb saw a limited future for both communism and capitalism. In their stead, Islam would provide a religiopolitical ideology to lead man from his current crisis. For Qutb, the Koran constituted a complete system of life; hence, no man-made additions were necessary. This belief is consistent with the Islamic notion of *tawheed,* or oneness, meaning the uniformity and unanimity of values. Furthermore, Islam is a religion of action; Muslims cannot remain aloof to the affairs of the real world. They are duty-bound to implement God's law. Although Islam, like Christianity, promises a kingdom in the hereafter, the former enjoins its followers to create the Islamic kingdom in the present world as well.

Philosophically, Qutb rejected the notion that man is the possessor of truth and the claim that all knowledge is relative.[16] In this sense, Islamism is critical of democracy insofar as it allows man to legislate his own affairs. By Qutb's literalist reading of the Koran, men are *abids* (slaves) of Allah and, as such, should follow his law as codified in sharia (Islamic law based on Koran) and sunnah (the prophet's example, along with the opinions of his immediate followers).[17]

In Qutb's analysis, the societies of the contemporary Muslim world were not authentically Islamic. Rather, they still existed in a state of *jahiliyya*—a Koranic term designating a pre-Islamic society of barbarism and ignorance. What was a *jahili* society? For Qutb, it was any society that was not Muslim. As Qutb saw it, *jahiliyya* amounted to one man's lordship over another. Therefore, it was the duty of the Muslims to implement sharia so that the sovereignty of God would rule alone. In doing so, Qutb articulated one of the most important maxims of the Islamist movement: contemporary jihadist groups are obsessed with implementing sharia. According to Qutb, Islam could not fulfill its intended role unless it took concrete form in a nation whose members lived by sharia. Only by being thus restored in its original form could Islam could once again take its role as leader of mankind.[18]

Much like the contemporary extreme right, political Islam looks to the past for inspiration.[19] The lives and examples of the first four caliphs are considered the foundation of political Islam to this day.[20] Qutb looked to the generation of the companions of the Prophet for inspiration and as a model for emulation. Like other totalitarian ideologists, Qutb believed that Islamism must endeavor to create a new Muslim man shorn of all the pernicious influences of *jahiliyya.* He exhorted Muslims to separate themselves from *jahiliyya* and then prepare themselves to liberate mankind:

Today, too, we are surrounded by *jahiliyya*. . . . in the early stages of our training and education for the Islamic movement we must remove ourselves from all influences of the *jahiliyya* in which we live and from which we derive benefits. We must return to that pure source from which the first generation derived its guidance, free from any mixing or pollution. . . . From the Koran we must also derive our concepts of life, our principles of government, politics, economics, and all other aspects of life.[21]

For Qutb, the only place on earth that could genuinely be called *Dar-al-Islam* (the abode of Islam) was those countries and territories in which an Islamic state had been established, sharia was recognized as the law, and Muslims would administer the affairs of the state with mutual consultation (*shura*). The rest of the world was *Dar-al-Harb* (home of hostility). As explained by Qutb, Muslims could have only two possible relations with *Dar-al-Harb:* peace with a contractual agreement or war.[22]

Despite the seemingly extremist undertones of Qutb's philosophy, his message was also universal. By destroying *jahiliyya,* Muslims would free mankind from the rule of men and would lead them to a utopia on earth in which God's law would prevail. For Qutb, the message of the Koran was available to all races and peoples. The Islamic society was based not on particularistic traits such as ethnicity, language, or race but rather on belief:

Islam based the Islamic society on the association of belief alone, instead of the low associations based on race and color, language and country, regional and national interests. Instead of stressing those traits, which are common to man and animal, it promoted man's human qualities, nurtured them and made them the dominant factor. Among the concrete and brilliant results of this attitude was that the Islamic society became an open and all-inclusive community in which people of various races, nations, languages and colors were members, there remaining no trace of these low animalistic traits. The rivers of higher talents and various abilities of all races of mankind flowed into this vast ocean and mixed in it. . . .

Those who deviate from this system and want some other system, whether it be based on nationalism, color and race, class struggle, or similar corrupt theories, are truly enemies of mankind![23]

Qutb believed that this universal quality of Islam and the potency of its faith had enabled its believers to prevail in the past. He used the Crusades as an example:

The unveiled crusading spirit was smashed against the rock of faith of Muslim leadership which came from various elements, including Saladin the Kurd and Turan Shah the Mamluk, who forgot the differences of nationalities and remembered their belief, and were victorious under the banner of Islam.[24]

Qutb conceded that since the nation-state is an inescapable modern-day reality, Islamist movements should first establish Islamist governments in their individual countries and then unite them into a single caliphate. By contrast, the Shi'ite position toward nationalism, which developed in the 1940s, argued that since the nation state is an un-Islamic concept, it should not be a valid consideration in the propagation of Islam.[25]

In contrast to the Shi'ite mullahs, Sunni Islamists sought to Islamicize society from the bottom up. They sought to purify Muslims at the individual level so that they would break from the manners and customs of impious society and comport themselves strictly according to the example of Muhammad and the koranic generation.[26]

Qutb followed in the tradition of Ibn Taymiyya, a thirteenth-century Islamic purist, who castigated the Mongols of his day for not (in his mind) following the koranic guidelines laid down by the prophet Muhammad. In effect, Qutb applied Taymiyya's doctrine to justify his struggle against the secular regime of Nasser.[27] Initially, Qutb actually supported Nasser's revolution in 1952 and, according to some accounts, was instrumental in its planning.[28] In fact, Anwar Sadat once conceded that Qutb was the main ideologue of the Free Officers' Revolution.[29] Reportedly, Nasser admired Qutb's writings and even offered him a cabinet position.[30] However, Qutb was unwilling to compromise when it came to applying Islamic principles. He refused to adulterate Islam by integrating it with other concepts such as nationalism, democracy, and socialism and disapproved of Nasser's attempts to apply them in Egypt.[31] His criticism and activities landed him in prison in the wake of the crackdown on the brotherhood in 1954. While in prison, he wrote *Milestones*, which became the manifesto of the Islamist movement. It was tantamount to a declaration of war on the rulers of Muslim countries, the Nasser regime in particular.

One of Qutb's most significant contributions to Islamism was his exegesis of the concept of jihad. According to Islamic law, an armed struggle can only be justified for the following reasons:

- To defend the community or nation from aggressors
- To liberate people living under oppressive regimes
- To remove any government that will not allow the free practice of Islam within its borders

There is an important distinction between defensive and offensive jihad. If infidels (non-Muslims) invade *Dar-al-Islam,* a fatwa can sanction a state of jihad, which becomes an individual obligation (*fard ayn*) for all Muslims, either directly through armed struggle or through financial contributions, charity, or prayers. By contrast, an offensive jihad to attack *Dar-al-Harb,* which can be waged to force infidels to submit to the religion of Islam, implies a collective obligation (*fard kifaya*) that can be discharged by Muslim governments, but without the personal participation of individual Muslims.[32]

In order to bring about the new Islamic order, the Islamists must wage jihad. However, doctrinal strictures in Islam militated against revolt. For example, the Islamic notion of *fitna* refers to the disunity in the Islamic community within a half century of the prophet Muhammad's death, which resulted in the Sunni-Shi'ite split. The Sunni tradition strongly condemns *fitna* within the *umma.* Even a bad Sunni leader is considered to be better than *fitna.*[33] Therefore, Qutb searched for a way to legitimize his revolt, invoking the concept of jihad to justify revolt against Arab regimes that were Muslim in name but *jahiliyya* in practice. Only through jihad could *jahiliyya* be combated. Qutb had drawn upon the previous writings of an Indian Muslim, Mawlana abu al-Ala Mawdudi (1903–1979), to formulate his theory of jihad.[34] Not unlike the Bolsheviks, Qutb argued that only a vanguard of the *umma,* or *tuliah,* could lead the masses in a revolution. And not unlike the notion of "leaderless resistance" among the radical elements of the contemporary American extreme right, Qutb asserted that it was the personal responsibility of every Muslim, both male and female, to undertake jihad against un-Islamic regimes. He exhorted Muslims to assume their individual duties to "execute the will of Allah" as they saw fit, regardless of whether they could coordinate their actions through a single organization.[35] Thus in order to create a genuine Islamic society, good Muslims must wage jihad against their own governments. To Qutb, jihad was defensive in character; it amounted to "the defense of man" against all those elements that would limit his freedom. For his part, he identified several reasons that justified jihad:

> To establish God's authority on the earth; to arrange human affairs, according to the true guidance provided by God; to abolish all the Satanic forces and Satanic system of life; to end the lordship of one man over others, since all men are creatures of God and no one has the authority to make them his servants or to make arbitrary laws for them. These reasons are sufficient for proclaiming Jihad.[36]

Qutb did not go so far as to advocate the creation of a theocracy, however, in the style of the Ayatollah Khomeini's Iran several decades later. According to

Qutb, the Islamic system (*nizam*) does not require a clergy to rule. He reasoned that in true Islam, there should be no separate class of men or religion or clergy. What was essential was that sharia be applied and Islamic principles followed. Finally, Qutb argued that the Islamic practice of *shura,* or mutual consultation, was essential in the formation of any state.[37]

Decades after his death, Qutb remains somewhat of an enigma. Through the Islamic intellectual tradition known as *ijtihad,* Qutb followed a long tradition of Islamic scholars that seek to reinterpret the religious texts of Islam and apply these teachings to contemporary times. To some observers his brand of Islamism shorn of its hoary rhetoric was mainly Leninist in inspiration in that he called for the end of "exploitation of man by man." Furthermore, he decried the "selfish individualism of liberal democracy" and sought to establish a monolithic state in which classes would be abolished.[38] However, Qutb was also intensely concerned about the legitimacy of government. His assertion that man is subordinate to God alone is an absolutist view of freedom somewhat reminiscent of John Locke, who believed that freedom is a God-given attribute and a precondition for civil society.[39] However, unlike Locke, who saw the role of government as the defender of freedom and private property, Qutb believed that the role of the state was to allow individuals to pursue moral values.[40] He also felt strongly about the concept of social justice and went so far as to write a book on the topic titled *Social Justice in Islam.*

Qutb's authorship of *Milestones* was not without great cost; it would eventually be used against him in a trial that concluded with a death sentence. Qutb was released for a short period in 1964, and he and other members sought to reconstitute the brotherhood. He would serve as the Supreme Guide of the Muslim Brotherhood until the end of his life.[41] However, the group was sharply divided on how to achieve power. One faction favored a legal approach, but the other faction favored revolutionary violence. The Nasser government cracked down on the brotherhood in 1965, and Qutb once again landed in prison. The charges against him and his colleagues were divided into two categories: (1) destructive and terrorist activities and (2) encouraging sedition.[42] Reportedly, an emissary of Nasser asked Qutb to sign a petition seeking mercy from the president. Qutb categorically rejected the offer: "If I have done something wrong in the eyes of Allah, I do not deserve mercy; but if I have not done anything wrong, I should be set free without having to plead for mercy from any mortal."[43] He was executed on August 29, 1966, and according to legend, went to the gallows with a smile on his face. Through his death, he attained the status of *shaheed* (martyr).[44] However, with his death Islamism would enter a period of dormancy.

Facing formidable state repression, Islamism soon went into retreat, having lost support among the political elite in the Middle East. However, by the early

1970s, events occurred that would redound to Islamists' favor. Qutb's influence on subsequent Islamist leaders—including Osama bin Laden—cannot be overstated. What is more, his critique of Jews and the state of Israel would provide an intellectual framework for Middle Eastern anti-Zionism.

The Development of Islamic Anti-Semitism

Jews loomed large in Qutb's worldview: he saw them as Islam's principal enemies. As one observer noted, Qutb's corpus of literature combined "a deep-rooted anti-Semitism with contempt of the West into a single ideology of Islamic superiority."[45] His chief anti-Semitic text was *Our Struggle with the Jews.* Qutb traced the conflict with the Jews back to the time of the prophet Muhammad, when some Jews opposed his rule. Turning the notion of *Ahl al-Kitab* (the people of the book) on its head, Qutb argued that Jews were actually more dangerous and loathsome than polytheists. Although the latter could not fully realize their sin in rejecting the message of the prophet Muhammad, Jews, in Qutb's view, rejected Islam intentionally and maliciously.[46] In his estimation, Zionism was only the most recent manifestation of Jewish malfeasance. He attributed all aspects of society that he considered un-Islamic to Jewish conspiracies. Furthermore, Qutb rejected the idea of Jewish "chosenness": "When the Jews claimed to be the chosen people of God on the basis of their race and nationality, God most high rejected their claim and declared that in every period, in every race and in every nation, there is only one criterion: that of faith."[47] Not unlike some observers in the extreme right, Qutb interpreted the cyclicality of Jewish history as a series of crimes against humanity followed by a series of divine punishments.[48] Qutb is significant in this regard. Historically anti-Semitism in the Islamic world never reached the same level of severity as it did in the West. It is worth examining how this development came about.

As Bernard Lewis observed, under Islam Jews were never free from discrimination but were rarely subjected to persecution. Their situation was never as bad as in Christendom at its worst and never as good as in Christendom at its best.[49] Both Jews and Christians were recognized as peoples of the book and were usually allowed to live in the Muslim world, albeit in second-class status through the institutional practice known as *Dhimmitude,* in which subject peoples would pay tribute in exchange for tolerance from their Muslim masters. That said, numerous passages in the Koran depict Jews as Islam's enemies. The early Muslim community in Mecca was often in conflict with the various Jewish tribes on the Arabian peninsula, including the Banu Nadir, Banu Qaynuqa, and Banu Quraiza. What is more, occasionally the Koran describes these

Jewish tribes as duplicitous and untrustworthy. Muhammad denounced the Jewish notion of "chosenness," proclaiming that belief, not ethnicity, was important in the eyes of God. Jews are also castigated for rejecting him. Finally, some Muslims have read the Koran to suggest that Muhammad died as a result of poisoning by a woman belonging to the Banu Nadir tribe.

Historians generally believe that anti-Semitism has been less severe in the Islamic world as compared to the West.[50] Taken literally, the term would suggest an animus not only to Jews but also to Arabs, considering their common Semitic ancestry. The term "anti-Semitism" was coined in the West in 1879 by an obscure German journalist, Wilhelm Marr, and has come to imply solely hostility to Jews.[51] During the late nineteenth century, anti-Jewish sentiment in the Middle East remained relatively low. However, the creation of the Israeli state was a catalyst in the development of contemporary Islamic anti-Semitism. In fact, in the contemporary Islamic world, it maintains substantial currency at all levels of society.

A pervasive sense of grievance suffuses Islamic intellectual currents. Over the years, various parties have been held responsible for Muslim decline. The Mongols were the first to be blamed. By the nineteenth century, Western imperialism as practiced by Great Britain and France became the chief culprit. The United States assumed this role for much of the post–World War II era. More recently, Israel—along with a putative international Zionist cabal—is looked upon as the main threat to and oppressor of Islam. The ease with which the Israeli military has defeated its Arab neighbors has come as somewhat of a shock to people who have traditionally viewed Jews contemptuously and dismissively.[52] Consequently, a variety of conspiracy theories have developed to help explain the current predicament of the Muslim world vis-à-vis the West and Israel.

Many Islamist groups seem to share the belief that their world is under attack, which necessitates a violent response for self-defense.[53] Gilles Kepel identified four principal enemies of Islamism, in the following order: Jewry, the Crusaders, communism, and secularism.[54] Inasmuch as Israel is a Jewish state, it follows that Jews control the vanguard positions on the front lines in the struggle against Islam. Slightly beneath Jewry in the hierarchy of enemies stand the Crusaders. Unlike Jews, who are all considered evil, Christians are considered contingently evil in the sense that there are both good and bad members of the Christian faith.[55] Communism is excoriated for its atheism, which hence makes it a mortal enemy of Islam. Moreover, Islamists point out the Jewish ancestry of leading communists such as Karl Marx as further proof of its insidious intentions. Finally, secularism, as exemplified by the Turkish nation builder, Mustafa Kemal Atatürk, comes under fire as well. Islamists allege that Atatürk was a Jewish agent who deposed the caliph as part of a scheme to destroy Islam and fractionalize the Islamic world. Occasionally, the Ba'ath (Renaissance) Party is cited as a more recent continuation of this plot.[56]

As Yossef Bodansky observed, all Arab regimes since World War II have constantly struggled to hold on to power despite the Islamist bent of both the elites and the masses.[57] Both pan-Arabism and pan-Islamism contain strong anti-Jewish themes in their ideologies.[58] One thing on which virtually all major parties could agree was strong opposition to Israel. In order to appeal to a larger audience, spokespeople of Arab nationalism have incorporated Islamic terms and symbols into their secular doctrines. This choice can in part explain the ease with which public discourse shifted back to Islamism when secular ideologies began their decline in the late 1960s and early 1970s.[59] As Bodansky explained, anti-Semitism became a popular instrument that Arab regimes could use to mobilize support. The Arab establishment was convinced that the presence of the "Zionist entity" constituted an existential threat to Arab security and indeed Arab sovereignty. Israel was seen as a mere spearhead of the global Zionist movement, which included the entire Jewish diaspora. Toward this end, the classic text of anti-Semitism, *The Protocols of the Learned Elders of Zion,* has gained considerable currency in the Middle East and is often promoted by Arab governments.

Bodansky also asserted that both governments and terrorist leaders in the Muslim world use anti-Semitic rhetoric as an effective instrument of populist agitation to reach the grass roots—the Arab street—to garner support. He saw anti-Semitic incitement as playing a crucial role in political Islam on two distinct levels. First, it helps to build a global conspiracy cognitive framework in which the Jewish conspiracy is used to explain the backwardness of the Muslim world. Economic stagnation, military defeats, and a host of other social problems can be blamed on an international Zionist conspiracy and, to a lesser extent, the Christian West. Second in the context of the Arab-Israeli conflict, anti-Semitism serves as a major political instrument to mobilize the entire region for the destruction of Israel.[60] The more secular, nationalist movements in the Middle East have also found anti-Semitism to be useful, as an instrument to conceptualize a common enemy and as an effective mechanism to mobilize the nation. As we shall later see, anti-Semitism—in one form or another—figured prominently in virtually all variants of Arab nationalism and Islamism.

Two schools of thought coexist in Middle Eastern grand conspiracy theories, according to Daniel Pipes. One school asserts that Israel is a puppet state run by the United States. The other school reverses the power relationship and depicts Israel and the Jews as the real puppeteers that control American policy. According to the Islamists, Jews have ingratiated themselves into the top echelons of power in the United States. Furthermore, their alleged agents are willing to employ the most unscrupulous of measures to further Zionist aims. The Monica Lewinsky scandal that rocked the Clinton administration was ascribed to Zionists as a way to discourage Clinton from pressuring Israel to make peace with the Palestinians.[61] Not unlike extreme right conspiracy theorists, some Islamists go so far as to claim that Jewish influence extends to the whole Western world.[62] The alleged control of the mass media looms large in such narratives. Zionists are thought to exert their influence through control of the world's media. This theory finds its most significant counterpart in the extreme right with the diatribes of the late Dr. William L. Pierce, who developed an elaborate theoretical model to explain how Jews control the political process through the positions that they hold in the media.[63]

Some observers argue that Israel is not the principal focus of enmity in the Middle East. For example, former Israeli prime minister Benjamin Netanyahu asserted that Middle East radicals hate Israel because it is an outpost of the Western world. In his estimation, "Israel is an island of Western democratic values in a Moslem-Arab sea of despotism."[64] However, Arab public opinion widely believes that the so-called Israeli lobby controls American foreign policy in the Middle East. As Daniel Pipes found, Zionists and to a lesser degree imperialists figure most prominently in the conspiracy discourse in the Middle East. There is little or no mention in the Middle Eastern conspiracy narratives about other entities that animate the corresponding extreme right theories in the West, such as the Council on Foreign Relations, the Trilateral Commission, the Bildeberger Group, the Rosicrucians, the Illuminati, or the Skull and Bones Society. Even communists are rarely mentioned, and even when they were, they are usually alleged to collude with Zionists and imperialists. As Pipes noted, Muslim agents in these schemes are depicted as hapless losers who are discarded by their foreign sponsors once they serve their purpose.[65]

Islamists often charge that the ultimate Zionist objective is to create a "Greater Israel" (Eretz Israel) that would extend from the Nile to the Euphrates and therefore encompass parts of Egypt, Syria, and Iraq, as well as Palestine, Jordan, and Lebanon in their entirety. As Daniel Pipes pointed out, the theory of a Greater Israel often slips into an old thesis about a Jewish conspiracy for world domination.[66] Inasmuch as the Israeli population of 5 million has repeatedly defeated an Arab population that is approximately forty to fifty times greater in size, conspiracy theories help Arabs and Muslims explain their lack of military success.[67]

In the minds of radical Islamists, Zionism is not just the archenemy of the Arab-Islamic world but also the most dangerous enemy of all humanity. A chief difference between extreme right anti-Semites and Islamist anti-Semites is that the former tends to stigmatize Jews on the bases of race and culture, whereas the latter tends to stigmatize Jews on the basis of religion. However, the fact that the Islamists' animus is based on religion in no way diminishes it virulence. As Anti-Defamation League (ADL) national director Abe Foxman indicated, that could make it all the more serious:

> The old right-wing anti-Semites exist. The skinheads exist and the right-wing fascist anti-Semites exist. They are not as significant today but they're there. . . .
>
> Today the alarming danger comes from Moslem anti-Semitism. It is more intense. It is more angry [*sic*]. It is more violent. It is tied to a political conflict. It operates in a totalitarian environment. . . . The same message can be reinforced from the mosque, to the media to government. They all play the same tune. There is no voice of dissent.[68]

These conspiracy theories are fueled in large part by the dynamics of interest group politics in the United States. It cannot be denied that certain interest groups in the United States are powerful and exert considerable influence on the public policy process. Indeed, some representatives of Jewish organizations have done little to disabuse the conspiracy theorists of their suspicions. For example, in 1992, David Steiner, then president of the American Israel Public Affairs Committee (AIPAC), boasted to a potential contributor about his organization's political clout. His interlocutor, Harry Katz, clandestinely recorded a telephone conversation between himself and the AIPAC president in which Steiner claimed that he was negotiating with then President-elect Bill Clinton over his appointments for secretary of state and national security adviser. Steiner went on to claim to have lavishly funded politicians so that they would grant billions of dollars in foreign aid and other subsidies to Israel. Soon after his remarks were released to the press, Steiner was forced to resign and explained that his statements were untrue and amounted to mere bluster designed to win over a potential donor.[69] Israeli prime minister Ariel Sharon's remarks during an argument between him and Foreign Minister Shimon Peres in October 2001 provided more grist for critics. When Peres warned Sharon that ignoring American requests for a cease-fire with the Palestinians might endanger Israel's relationship with the United States, Sharon reportedly yelled back, "Don't worry about American pressure, we the Jewish people control America."[70]

One interesting development in recent years is the worldwide cross-fertilization of anti-Semitic themes fostered by globalization and the concomitant telecommunications revolution. Just as Arab and Islamist critics of Jews used the *Protocols* for their purposes, a similar process may now again be underway, as they discover anti-Semitic propaganda originating in the West and repackage it for regional consumption. The recent comments of Osama bin Laden are instructive. Much like anti-Semitic conspiracy theorists in the extreme right, bin Laden accused Jews of economically exploiting the American people through usury:

> You build your economy and investments on usury. As a result of this, in all its different forms and guises, the Jews have taken control of your economy, through which they have taken control of your media, and now control all aspects of your life making you their servants and achieving their aims at your expense; precisely what *Benjamin Franklin* warned you against.
> . . . Your law is the law of the rich and wealthy people, who hold sway in their political parties, and fund the election campaigns with their gifts. Behind them stand the Jews, who control your policies, media, and economy[71] (emphasis added).

What is remarkable about these comments is that bin Laden alluded to the alleged anti-Semitic remarks of Benjamin Franklin—a staple in the lore of extreme right conspiracy lore. The quote, generally believed to be apocryphal and concocted by the leader of the Silver Shirts, William Dudley Pelley, was purportedly spoken by Franklin during an intermission at the Constitutional Convention of 1787 in Philadelphia:

> I fully agree with General Washington that we must protect this young nation from an insidious influence and impenetration. The menace, gentlemen, is the Jews. In whatever country Jews have settled in any great number, they have lowered its moral tone; depreciated its commercial integrity; have segregated themselves and have not been assimilated; have sneered at and tried to undermine the Christian religion upon which that nation is founded, by objecting to its restrictions; have built up a state within the state; and when opposed have tried to strangle that country to death financially as in the case of Spain and Portugal. . . . If you do not exclude them, in less than 200 years our descendants will be working in the fields to furnish them substance, while they will be in the counting houses rubbing their hands. I warn you, gentlemen, if you do not exclude Jews for all time, your children will curse you in your graves.[72]

This charge was later reiterated in an al Qaeda communiqué issued in response to an open letter signed by prominent American academics and titled "What We're Fighting For."[73]

ADL national chairman Abraham Foxman argued that the genesis of contemporary Islamic anti-Semitism has its roots in the "disillusionment and frustration over centuries of poverty and Western imperialism in the Middle East."[74] In his analysis, the Fourth Conference of the Academy of Islamic Research in 1968 (more commonly known as the al-Azhar conference) was a watershed event in this regard, in that the Koranic references to "Jewish opposition to Muhammad were removed from their historical context and transformed into symbols of an essential evil in Jewish nature."[75] Soon thereafter, Arab leaders increasingly framed their conflict with Israel in religious rather than secular terms. As Foxman noted, that was a dangerous game, but one that carried with it a number of potential benefits for Arab leaders. First, it enabled Arab leaders to tap into the power of ancient stereotypes and prejudices against Jews. Second, it served as a method to exhort all their coreligionists around the world to support the jihad against Israel. Pan-Islam could reach a potentially larger audience than pan-Arabism. Although there are roughly 300 million Arabs in the world, there are over 1 billion Muslims. Finally, scapegoating Jews could serve to distract the attention of Arabs from the failures of their leaders.[76]

Kevin MacDonald, an academic mentioned in Chapter 2, drew upon social identity theory to explain the development of Islamic anti-Semitism. (His scholarship on the topic is highly controversial and has occasioned strong criticism from his peers in the field of evolutionary theory.) Historically, anti-Semitism has been less pronounced in the Middle East than in the West, which can be explained, according to MacDonald, by the much greater emphasis on the collectivity in the Middle East. Jews as a group could not attain positions of power because impermeable Islamic groups, for whom ethnicity and religion were requirements for entry, in effect blocked them from advancing in Middle Eastern society.

Usually, Jews found the West to be a more congenial place because of its individualist tradition. According to MacDonald, Jews have had a marked advantage over their host populations in the West in competition for resources because Jews pursued a collectivist strategy, whereas Westerners were generally individualist and had a low degree of ethnocentrism. Further, MacDonald argued that Jews historically practiced endogamy and various eugenic practices enshrined in various customs and traditions in Judaism. These traits enabled Jews to attain positions of preeminence in the West that they were unable to attain in the Islamic world. However, MacDonald believed that this pattern eventually engenders a severe backlash. In order to resist this putative process of displacement and marginalization, occasionally gentile host societies develop collectivist affinities and "evolutionary group strategies" as well. Interestingly, the more "successful" strategies would tend to mimic Judaism in the sense that they encouraged endogamy, group altruism, and ethnocentrism. MacDonald asserted that the various anti-Semitic mass movements that have punctuated the history of the West, including medieval feudalism, the Spanish Inquisition, and National Socialism, are reactive evolutionary strategies that allow for gentile groups to compete with Jews.

MacDonald saw this same process at work in the emergence of militant Islam. Because Jews were not able to attain positions of power in the Middle East as they were in the West in such fields as commerce and politics, MacDonald explained, anti-Semitism never reached an extreme level in the Middle East as it had in the West. However, the creation of the state of Israel in 1948 may have redirected this trend. In a sense Israel has been a "stressor" in the region of the Middle East and has arguably contributed to the vehemence of contemporary Islamic anti-Semitism. MacDonald speculated on this development in an interview with the author.

In my opinion, social identity processes are probably always at work in the rise of intensely motivated group behavior. Individuals are more attracted to highly identified groups during times when they see themselves threatened, whether by economic insecurity or by menacing out-groups. In the case of militant Islam, Israel and the West are seen as threats. As in all cases of intense group consciousness, the threats may be real or imaginary, and scapegoating can occur. Social identity processes typically result in exaggeration of the threat.

My view is that the tribal structure of the Muslim world, with well-defined in-groups and out-groups, will work to the long-term disadvantage of Judaism. There is a great deal of historical evidence for this. Whereas Western societies typically welcomed Jews and developed anti-Jewish attitudes only after prolonged interactions with Jews, Muslim societies tended to despise Jews and keep them in a subservient, fearful position. The only exceptions were cases where Jews were brought in as the agents of alien ruling elites, in which case they were perceived by the masses as hated overseers. I do believe that the presence of Israel and its violent dispossession of the Palestinians has promoted Islamic fundamentalism throughout the region. By all accounts, the Arab—and indeed, the entire Islamic—world sides with the Palestinians in the Israeli-Palestinian conflict and sees the Palestinians as fellow-Arabs or fellow-Muslims beset by the Israelis and their Western backers. Since the West, and particularly the United States, is correctly seen as the sponsor of Israel throughout the region, Islamic fundamentalism often has a strong anti-Western, anti-American overtones. These attitudes then generalize to all aspects of Western culture—feminism, popular culture, etc., especially when they conflict with traditional Islamic values.

I do not believe that this state of affairs was inevitable. In the late 1940s, American foreign policy and military analysts unanimously opposed the U.S. recognition and support of Israel. Deprived of this in-group/out-group dynamic, the Arab world might have gradually modernized into secular regimes in a manner somewhat similar to the Far East, although I do not think that they would naturally incline to European cultural forms like democracy and relatively unfettered individualism. Beginning with the war against Iraq, the West seems set to impose its culture on the region in an effort to remake the entire region in the interests of Israeli hegemony. I suppose that this will have only temporary success and will lead to greater hatred of the West throughout the region. The Greeks conquered the area for hundreds of years but never managed to influence the indigenous culture. Neither the Crusader kingdoms nor the Mongols had any lasting influence on the region. I very much doubt that the United States will.[77]

It is worth mentioning that there is considerable convergence in the anti-Semitic narratives of both militant Islam and the contemporary extreme right. Because Jews are alleged to have been responsible for fomenting all the major wars and a host of other catastrophes, by confronting them, militant Islam sees itself as fighting a universal mission on behalf of all humanity.[78] Likewise, the extreme right has often argued that the long history of anti-Semitism in so many disparate cultures and nations confirms the universal view of Jewish duplicity and destructiveness. The fact that Jews have been despised by so many different people throughout history and in so many different societies is thought to be demonstrative of their nefarious intentions throughout history.[79]

As the Middle East conflict became more protracted, anti-Semitism began to hold much greater salience in the ranks of militant Islam. It is no longer a side issue, but rather at the front and center of the Islamist worldview.

The Resurgence of Militant Islam

The Six-Day War in June 1967 shocked the entire Muslim world and regalvanized the Islamic fundamentalist movement. Arabs discussed the defeat in apocalyptic terms, calling it "the second *Naqbah*" (holocaust).[80] The humiliating defeat at the hands of Israel bolstered the position of the Islamists at the expense of the Arab nationalists. Islamic revivalism was in large part a reaction to failed nationalist programs. As Robin Wright explained, this event was viewed as a catastrophe in the Arab world, and as a result Arabs turned inward to look for an alternative to Nasserism, and "inward they found Islam."[81] By the time of the war, Islamism had effectively established itself at the grassroots level and was thus well prepared to reach out to the Muslim masses. Islamic organizations had been deeply involved in social reform, establishing schools, hospitals, clinics, family assistance programs, legal societies, and Islamic banks and insurance companies.[82]

However, nationalist politics continued to matter in the Arab world. During the 1970s, the chief resistance movement in the region, the Palestine Liberation Organization (PLO), increasingly became leftist in orientation, although this shift arguably owed more to the zeitgeist than genuine ideological predilections.[83] Furthermore, it dovetailed well with the global movement against Western influence supported by the Soviet Union.[84]

Politics in the region were further radicalized by the introduction of terrorism. The era of modern terrorism commenced on July 22, 1968, when three armed terrorists belonging to the Popular Front for the Liberation of Palestine (PFLP) hijacked an Israeli El Al commercial flight en route from Rome to Tel Aviv. Through sensational episodes of terrorism and their attendant publicity, the Palestinians successfully internationalized their struggle with Israel. Their campaign served as a paradigm for other aggrieved ethnic and nationalist minority groups around the world.[85] Furthermore, the PLO was one of the first terrorist groups to develop a solid financial base as part of its organizational structure.[86]

During much of the 1970s, the PLO transformed Lebanon into a surrogate state that functioned as a training center for terrorist groups around the world. To the Soviet Union, these groups had great potential as seeds of future mass movements that could disrupt the U.S.-led world order. Toward this end, the Soviet Union used the PLO as a conduit to aid terrorist groups in the struggle against the West.[87]

Despite the success of the nationalist-oriented PLO, Islamists were diligently at work establishing an infrastructure as well. Events unfolding at this time favored the Islamists as they began to better organize themselves in Middle East politics. For example, Nasser died of a heart attack in September 1970, and thus one of the chief antagonists of the Islamists was removed. His successor, President Anwar Sadat, attempted to neutralize the nemeses of his predecessors by releasing most of the Islamists from prison after 1971, including the Muslim Brotherhood leaders who had been imprisoned in the 1960s. Almost immediately, they set about reorganizing, although at first, the Islamists accepted the rule of Sadat. Seeking to appease potential opposition, the new leader even went so far as to institute sharia throughout Egypt.[88]

The 1973 Yom Kippur War further bolstered the stature of Islamists. At the time, a heightened sense of Islamic identity crystallized in the Arab world, as expressed in the rallying cry "Allah Akbar" (God is great). Finally, the Organization of Petroleum Exporting Countries (OPEC) effectively employed the oil weapon, not only dramatically increasing wealth in that region of the world but also renewing a sense of political power. Increasingly, Islamism seemed a better vehicle through which to lead the Arab world out of its inferior position vis-à-vis the West.

The rapprochement between Israel and Egypt further antagonized the Islamists and increased their ranks. With the signing of the Camp David Peace Accords in March 1979, Sadat sealed his fate. His acceptance of a unilateral Egyptian-led diplomatic solution to the Arab-Israeli conflict alienated many of the Islamists and made him a marked man. On October 6, 1981, the Islamists exacted their revenge, when a group calling itself Jama At al-Jihad (Sacred Combat) staged a spectacular assassination as President Sadat reviewed a military parade. The leader of the group of assassins, Lieutenant Khalid al-Islambuli, reportedly exclaimed as the shots began to fire, "I have killed the Pharaoh."[89] Although the assassination plot succeeded, the subsequent putsch was quickly crushed.

The assassins were greatly inspired by Muhammad Faraj's book, *The Neglected Duty*. Faraj had left the Muslim Brotherhood because of its reluctance to engage in armed struggle against the government and eventually emerged as the chief ideologist for Jama At al-Jihad. According to Faraj, any means necessary was justified in order to overthrow apostate regimes, which were sometimes referred to as the "near enemy." This struggle even took precedence over the war against Jews and Israel, or the "far enemy."[90] He did, however, set some moral limits on terrorism—for example, women and innocent bystanders should be avoided in attacks. The reward for martyrdom was a place in *Jannah* (paradise). Faraj was executed in 1982 for his role in the assassination of Anwar Sadat.[91]

In the wake of the assassination, the government brutally repressed the Islamists. A large trial, which included twenty-four defendants, followed in 1982. Five of the defendants were sentenced to death. One of the conspirators, Dr. Ayman al-Zawahiri, received a three-year sentence. He was convicted only on weapons charges, though his role in the assassination was actually far more extensive.[92] Eventually, he became the mentor of Osama bin Laden.

The year 1979 was a landmark in the development of militant Islam, setting in motion many trends of great importance today. As mentioned earlier, Egypt signed a historic peace treaty with its long-time foe, Israel. The Soviet Union invaded Afghanistan. And perhaps most important, the Ayatollah Khomeini seized power in Iran and created an Islamic republic.

The Ayatollah Khomeini and the Islamic Revolution in Iran

The late 1970s through the 1980s witnessed the accelerated growth of militant Islam. No other individual had more of an impact on its revival than the late Ayatollah Khomeini. Before the Iranian Revolution, Islamism was still mainly a marginal heterodoxy.[93] The Iranian Revolution did not arise from nothing, however; the Ayatollah Khomeini had long planned to topple the government of Shah Mohammed Reza Pahlavi. At least as far back as 1972, Khomeini forged an alliance with the PLO and other Palestinian terrorist groups.[94] In November 1979, Islamic students calling themselves "the Followers of the Line of the Imam" brazenly defied the United States by seizing fifty-four hostages, whom they would not release until January 20, 1981. The re-Islamicization of Iran was imposed by clerics from above with the assistance of a large portion of the population.[95]

The success of the Iranian revolution and the imposition of an Islamic fundamentalist theocratic regime further strengthened the legitimacy of militant Islam and added to its appeal as a means by which to effect change in the Middle East. Hitherto, Sunni radicals had been in the forefront of the Islamist movement. Egypt was traditionally regarded as the citadel of Islamism because it was the homeland of the most prominent elements of the Muslim Brotherhood, and its radical Sunni clerics became the chief ideologists of the movement. However, the Islamic revolution in Iran in 1979 demonstrated that Islamism resonated with Shi'ite Muslims as well.

Historically, Shi'ites have maintained that temporal rulers have to be tolerated until the return of the Twelfth Imam, who will exercise both religious and political power. However, Khomeini was the first to claim that one man could wield both political and religious authority before the return of the Twelfth Imam.[96] The revolution demonstrated that the traditionally quietist Shi'ite population could be effectively mobilized to create an Islamic republic. At first Arab leaders scoffed at the Persian Ayatollah's boasts to export his brand of Islamism. However, his message soon reached many disaffected Muslims around the world. Shockwaves were felt in Mecca when a group of religious militants sympathetic to Iran seized control of the Grand Mosque in November 1979. In the fighting that ensued, 177 rebels and 127 government soldiers were killed and many more injured.[97]

Perhaps what it most significant about the Islamic revolution in Iran is that it truly universalized the Islamist movement. Heretofore, Islamism was in large part pan-Arabism cloaked in a religious guise. Khomeini sought to export the Islamic revolution because he saw it as a universal model for Muslims around the world. Khomeini invoked the example of the seventh-century Shi'ite martyr, Hussein, as a model to be emulated for the contemporary fedayeen (Arabic for "one who is ready to sacrifice his life for his cause").[98] According to legend, in his last stand at Karbala, Hussein and a band of fewer than 100 supporters fought to the death against thousands of troops that Umayyad Caliph had arrayed against them. Despite the knowledge that he would be overwhelmed and defeated by the numerically superior forces, Hussein chose death rather than submit to a life of injustice. To contemporary Shi'ites, his sacrifice is seen as worthy of emulation. A cult of martyrdom permeated the Ayatollah's Iran. For example, the late leader commissioned the creation of the "fountain of blood" in central Tehran, in which red water, symbolizing the blood of those martyrs who perished in the struggle against the shah and the war against Iraq, cascaded into a pool below.[99]

The rise of Khomeini-ism coincided with a gradual decline in the potency of Arab nationalism. Given the history of the Middle East, forging an Arab nation would prove to be problematic because Islam does not recognize the state in its contemporary Westernized incarnation. Rather, Islam recognizes various subnational identities such as the tribe, clan, and extended family, along with the larger universal community of Muslims, the *umma*.[100] Khomeini exhorted Muslims to identify with the latter. As he was not hesitant to point out, Arab nationalism had failed to defeat Israel in every single military confrontation. In his view, only Islam could be an effective alternative to the ineffectual ideology of nationalism.[101] Once firmly established, Khomeini believed that his Islamic republic would become a beacon of inspiration for all Muslims the world over. He cited his own country, Iran, as a government that had defied the dictates of the United States and established an Islamic republic.

In some ways the rise of Khomeini was a harbinger of the more radical strain of Islam that was incubating in the Middle East. As one observer remarked, Khomeini was the "Henry Ford of Islamic terrorism" in that his "assembly-line" model of revolutionary indoctrination, which included training manuals and videos, religious indoctrination, and paramilitary training, was copied by other Islamist movements.[102] Khomeini unequivocally identified the United States and Israel as the two principal enemies of Islam, demonizing them as the "Great Satan" and "Little Satan," respectively. Osama bin Laden would echo this theme in the 1990s.[103]

One drawback to the Ayatollah Khomeini's ecumenism was the Shi'ite nature of his variant of militant Islam. He insisted that his brand of radical Shi'ism dominate Islam. Be that as it may, Iran reportedly supported many Sunni Islamist causes despite the historical animosities between the Sunnis and Shi'ites. For example, during the mid-1980s, Iran supported Gulbadin Hekmatiyar's Hizb-I

Islami in its struggle against the Soviets in Afghanistan.[104] By 1991, Iran had also consolidated a strategic alliance with Sudan. One of Iran's principal vehicles through which to export the Islamic revolution was the militant organization Hezbollah.

Hezbollah

The conditions that led to the emergence of Hezbollah actually began in the late 1960s, with the political mobilization of the Shi'ite community in Lebanon. A decade earlier, many Shi'ites, who compose the majority of the Lebanese population, had settled in urban areas in response to the extreme deprivation they had long experienced in rural areas. In the Beirut core around which they settled, they developed a sense of communal consciousness. The civil war, which commenced in 1975, led to the mobilization of the Christian Maronite population, which in turn provoked a countermobilization by Shi'ite militants. However, the precipitating factor that contributed directly to the creation of Hezbollah was the Israeli invasion in 1982. The occupation generated a spontaneous grassroots resistance that formed the backbone of Hezbollah.[105] Hezbollah is a Shi'ite organization that grew out of the Ayatollah Khomeini's Revolutionary Guards in Iran. The organization is reportedly financed by both Iran and Syria and has an annual budget of approximately $50 to $100 million.[106]

The chief aim of Hezbollah is the establishment of an Islamic state in Lebanon. Hezbollah began as an umbrella coalition of *ulama* (Muslim clerics), under which elements from various Islamist groups and clerics united. Each cleric brought with him his own circle of disciples.[107] The new organization soon demonstrated what could be accomplished with the potent element of religious fervor. Lacking any official structure or membership list, Hezbollah is not a political party in the Western sense of the term, although it has served many of the same purposes.[108] In effect, Hezbollah can be considered the military and political outgrowth of this broad cultural movement.[109] Through the provision of social services to the needy, Hezbollah has won over the hearts and minds of many Shi'ites. What is more, Hezbollah found a strong ally in the late Syrian President Hafez al-Assad, who supported the movement as a means by which to weaken the influence of the United States, which tended to favor Maronite Christians in Lebanon.[110]

Hezbollah's ideology contains a strong critique of American foreign policy in the Middle East. A prominent Hezbollah figure, Sheikh Muhammad Hussein Fadlullah, contended that U.S. foreign policy in the Middle East is not based on genuine American interests, but rather on Israeli interests. Furthermore, Hezbollah repudiates American culture, which it views as unduly materialist. Not unlike extreme right critics such as the late Dr. William L. Pierce, Hezbollah charges that Zionists control the American media, through which they putatively wage a cultural war against Arab and Islamic culture.[111]

The eschatology of Hezbollah contains themes of millennialism and Manichaeism, as the world is divided between the forces of good and evil. The two are pitted against each other in an apocalyptic struggle from which only one will emerge victorious.[112] The notion of jihad looms very large as well, and the concept of martyrdom is integral. Hezbollah imputes great value to the life hereafter, "or the true eternal life," which renders life on earth as meaningless in comparison.[113]

Unlike other Islamist groups, however, Hezbollah does not designate those Muslims that do not subscribe to its Islamic vision as "infidels." Hezbollah has no *takfir* (i.e., identifying someone as a *kafir* or unbeliever) discourse in the sense that it does not declare the infidelity of its Islamic adversaries.[114] This approach makes it easier for Hezbollah to cooperate with, for example, secular Arab nationalists. While Sunni radicals decry the Syrian Ba'ath Party as a "Crusader party" bent on the destruction of Islam, Hezbollah tries to mitigate this apparent apostasy by claiming that the late Syrian President, Hafez al-Assad "is not an atheist." Further, this flexibility has allowed Hezbollah to sympathize with secular and even Marxist Third World leaders such as Nelson Mandela, Daniel Ortega, and Fidel Castro because of their nations' putatively oppressed status.[115]

Hezbollah considers the national borders between Lebanon and Palestine to be artificial boundaries and an artifact of colonialism. The party rejects the classification of Muslims into national, ethnic, and racial categories, as well as the notion of Arab supremacy in Islam. According to the precepts of the *Salafiyya* (venerable forefathers), nationalism and ethnic chauvinism constitute *shirk* (associating with or making others equal to God). Ultimately, the *Salafis* (those who follow a puritanical version of Islam) believe that all political boundaries should be rendered meaningless so that all Muslims will live in one polity under the sharia, devoted to God.[116] Nevertheless, some Islamists have found a way to defend nationalism as long as it does not divide the *umma.*

Despite its early doctrinal pronouncements renouncing nationalism, over time Hezbollah has developed a sense of Arab identity and nationalism. This affinity dovetailed with political objectives insofar as fostering Arab unity was seen as the requirement for defeating Israel. The significant role Christians and secular Muslims played in the intifada further demonstrated the political potency of Arab nationalism, especially when conjoined with Islam. In this context, Hezbollah does not view its efforts to foster Arab unity as an obstacle to Islamic universalism. Hence, Arab non-Muslims can be considered part of the Islamic civilization insofar as they ethnically identify with their Arab Muslim brethren. In this way, Lebanese Christians can be considered part of Arab Islamic civilization and even part of the Islamic *umma*.[117]

What is perhaps most significant about Hezbollah from the perspective of the United States is that prior to the 9/11 attacks, the organization was responsible for more terrorist fatalities against U.S. citizens than any other terrorist group, both foreign and domestic.[118] The most spectacular and lethal act of suicide terrorism by Hezbollah was the October 23, 1983, truck bombing of a U.S. Marine Corps barracks in Lebanon, which killed 241 U.S. soldiers. That same day, another truck bomb exploded at the command post of the French 1st Regiment, killing 58 soldiers. These and other attacks ultimately prompted President Ronald Reagan to withdraw U.S. forces from Lebanon. Hezbollah also takes credit for driving the Israelis out of Lebanon in 2000.

Although the Koran proscribes suicide, Islamist clerics have constructed justifications for suicide terrorism under the euphemism of martyrdom. The spiritual leader of Hezbollah, Sheikh Muhammad Hussein Fadlullah, reasoned that the Muslim world's current predicament justified suicide terrorism by fedayeen. Presently, Muslims confront the awesome power of the United States. Therefore, with such lopsided opposition, extreme measures, such as suicide attacks, were appropriate. Suicide bombings in this instance were not unlike the deaths of soldiers who enter battle knowing that there is little chance of their survival. Furthermore, since their deaths are intended for the benefit of the *umma*, they are deemed noble. Suicide in this sense is not intended as an escape from life, but rather a self-sacrificial act.[119]

Hezbollah is considered by some analysts to be the most sophisticated terrorist organization in the world. The organization retains state support from Syria and Iran and maintains a base in southern Lebanon. Furthermore, Hezbollah has established a presence in the lawless "triborder" region of South America, where Paraguay, Brazil, and Argentina meet. According to some accounts, this region has become a unique meeting ground for a disparate array of terrorists, including Hamas, Hezbollah, and even American right-wing extremists.[120]

In recent years, both Shi'ite and Sunni radicals have come to see the struggle against Israel and the United States as the chief priority. Previously, Sunni radicals considered the Islamicization of their countries to be the first order of affairs. The chief enemy for Hezbollah remains Israel. Not surprisingly, this orientation has led the movement to find common cause with Palestinian groups such as Hamas.

Hamas

The origins of Hamas can be traced to the 1960s in the Gaza Strip, when loosely affiliated members of the Muslim Brotherhood began organizing in the area. By the late 1970s, they established the Islamic Center, the predecessor of Hamas. The first intifada, which commenced in 1987, was the crucible in which the contemporary organization known as Hamas crystallized. Shortly thereafter, Hamas emerged as a significant force in Palestinian politics and is generally seen as the radical alternative to the PLO. The spiritual leader of Hamas until his death in March 2004 was Sheikh Ahmad Yassin, who was involved in the movement from its beginning.

The 1987 intifada engendered the Islamicization of the Palestinian resistance movement. Prior to the rebellion, Palestinian militants in the Occupied Territories had generally been secular and left wing in political orientation, but the new militants sought inspiration from Islam and used it as an organizing principle for resistance. Hamas has sought to establish a Palestinian state built on Islamic values. Ironically, the organization's expressed religious orientation allows it considerable civic autonomy in the Occupied Territories, which enables Hamas to maintain direct contact with the masses through mosques and charitable organizations. The social services that Hamas provides to the poor urban masses have garnered it much grassroots sympathy and support. It has been estimated that up to 90 percent of Hamas's activities and finances go to social welfare.[121] This religious orientation notwithstanding, according to its charter, Hamas still regards nationalism as "part and parcel of the religious faith," which enables the organization to appeal to Palestinian Christians as well—a population group that historically has figured prominently in the Palestine resistance movement.[122]

Despite a sincere commitment to alleviate privation among Palestinians in the Occupied Territories, Hamas has been active in terrorism and violent confrontation against Israel. Hamas sees itself as occupying the vanguard position in the jihad against Israel. Over time, two factions have emerged in Hamas with regard to the use of violence. One faction favors a politically oriented position and is willing to adjust to contemporary political realities. This faction would accept recognition as a legitimate political party that could share power. By contrast, the more militant faction favors continued armed struggle and rejection of any agreement with the Palestinian Authority that does not allow for Hamas's activities and organization.[123] This more militant faction has persuaded Hamas to ally itself with Iran and Syria in opposition to the Oslo Accords. Hamas has also been in the forefront of the more recent al-Aqsa intifada, which commenced in September 2000 after Ariel Sharon made a highly publicized visit to the third most sacred place in Islam.

From the Israeli perspective, Hamas is particularly fearsome for two reasons. The first reason is the stridency of the group's political program. This theme is reflected in the Hamas charter, into which elements of *The Protocols of the Learned Elders of Zion* have found their way: "Today it is Palestine, and tomorrow it will be another country or other countries. For the Zionist scheme has no limits, and after Palestine it will strive to expand from the Nile to the Euphrates. When it has digested the region it has consumed, it will look to further expansion, and so on. This plan is outlined in the 'Protocols of Zion,' and present conduct is the best witness to what is said there."[124] A second reason for consternation is the indiscriminate nature of the organization's terrorist attacks. A large number of Palestinian suicide bombers have carried out their attacks under the direction of Hamas.[125] As of February 2004, since the start of the second intifada, 103 suicide terrorist attacks have occurred in Israel and the Occupied Territories.[126] According to one observer, it was no accident that the terrorism campaign against Israel accelerated after the defeat of the Taliban in Afghanistan. The intifada amounted to a change of venue for the Islamist terror network, which established new foci in Lebanon and the Palestinian Authority.[127] The sheer numbers of suicide attacks in Israel in 2002 and the diversity in backgrounds of the perpetrators increased concern among American government authorities and terrorism analysts that similar terrorist attacks could occur in the United States.

Because of its theological and ideological predispositions, Hamas could move into an important strategic position in the global Islamist movement. Many Palestinian rejectionists (i.e., those Palestinians who unilaterally refuse the notion of a peace treaty with Israel) have come to support bin Laden and his Islamist worldview. One lesson that they learned was that poor planning and organization, disloyalty, and marginal dedication would undermine a revolutionary group's chances for success against a strong power like Israel.[128] Thus Islam was a way to buttress the dedication of the followers.

Since the 1980s, parochial Arab ethnic particularities have waned in favor of Islam. Saddam Hussein's invasion of Kuwait in 1990 also undercut the efficacy of Arab nationalism and solidarity. Several of his Arab neighbors—Syria and Saudi Arabia chief among them—supported the military coalition against him. Only Jordan nominally opposed the military action against Saddam. Furthermore, the humiliating defeat of one of pan-Arabism's chief proponents diminished the appeal of this ideology. Finally, advances in modern telecommunications brought both the humiliation of Arab leaders and Arabism, as well as the message of Islamist opposition, to more Arabs than ever before.[129] Increasingly, Islamism—with al Qaeda as its vanguard movement—is capturing the hearts and minds of Muslims.

Osama bin Laden and al Qaeda

The 1979 Soviet invasion of Afghanistan sounded the clarion call for jihad throughout the Islamic world. The Afghan war stimulated Islamic terrorism in three ways. First, it taught terrorist-related skills to non-Afghan volunteers (the so-called Afghan Arabs) who came to fight in the Afghan jihad. Second, the war provided the opportunity for Muslims from many different nationalities to create a truly global network. And finally, by defeating a superpower, Islamists developed an enormous sense of self-confidence that they could wage jihad successfully in other parts of the world as well.[130] After a series of humiliating defeats at the hands of Israel, the victory in Afghanistan harkened back to an earlier era in which their forebears had been a potent force in the world under the banner of Islam.[131] The war in Afghanistan also allowed radical Islamists to distance themselves from the influence of Arab nationalism, both as a doctrine and as a factor dividing Islamists seeking revolution in specific states.[132] Out of this struggle, a more ecumenical brand of Islamism emerged, which had long-term repercussions, as Afghanistan proved to be the incubator of the major jihadist organizations that would bedevil the United States in years to come.

After the war, the Afghan Arabs traveled back to their countries to wage jihad against apostate regimes.[133] Estimates of the total number of Afghan Arab fighters range from 14,000 to 22,000.[134] Chief among them was Osama bin Laden, who was born on July 30, 1957, in Riyadh, Saudi Arabia. He was the seventeenth son of fifty-two children whose father, Muhammad bin Laden, emigrated from Yemen to Saudi Arabia when he was a young man. In his adopted homeland, he established a very successful construction company, the Saudi Bin Laden Group, and became a close confidant of Saudi king Faisal and the royal family. His firm worked on several important infrastructure projects under contract for the kingdom, including renovation of the holy cities of Mecca and Medina and their mosques. Muhammad bin Laden also had the great privilege of rebuilding the al-Aqsa mosque in Jerusalem. To the young Osama, his father must have seemed a giant figure. However, he died in an accident in 1967 when Osama was just ten years old. His mother, a Syrian by birth, is still alive and is reported to stay in contact with him. By the mid-1990s, it was estimated that the bin Laden group of companies was worth $5 billion.[135]

As a young man, Osama bin Laden attended King Abdul Aziz University in Jeddah, where he studied economics and business management in preparation for the position he planned to fill in the family business. During this period, he came under the influence of his Islamic studies teachers Muhammad Qutb, brother of Sayid Qutb, and Abdullah Azzam, with whom he would create the al Qaeda organization. According to some accounts, bin Laden left college without graduating and went to work directly in the family business. His tenure at the company appears to have been unremarkable. Nevertheless, as a young man he obtained a considerable inheritance, a large portion of which—estimated between $250 and $500 million—he invested overseas.[136]

To better understand the political theology of Osama bin Laden, it is worth exploring the religious milieu in which he was raised. A small yet highly influential segment of the Saudi population, including the bin Laden family, follow the Wahhabi sect of Islam. Although it is estimated that the Wahhabis comprise no more than 15 percent of the Saudi population, they exert considerable influence on the affairs of the nation.[137] The spread of Wahhabism became a major plank of Saudi foreign policy after the oil boom of the 1970s.[138] The vast majority of mosques in the United States are funded with Saudi money and subscribe to the Wahhabi doctrine.[139]

The Wahhabi sect was founded by Muhammad bin Abdul al-Wahhab (1703–1792) as a movement to counter the influence of Sufism among Bedouin Arabs. Wahhab created a revivalist movement that sought to bring about a spiritual revolution through the purging of moral and spiritual adulterations that had accumulated in Islam since the time of Muhammad. He allied himself with a local tribal chief, Muhammad ibn Saud, to help him spread his faith throughout the region.

In the early twentieth century, an ambitious tribal leader, Abdul-Aziz Ibn Saud, used Wahhabism to legitimize his formation of the modern Saudi state. In 1902, Saud led a group of tribesmen and captured the city of Riyadh. He spent the next several years consolidating his conquests in the area and by 1926 was able to throw off the Ottoman yoke and establish a unified kingdom—the first independent state in the region of central Arabia and the Persian Gulf. The new Saudi state was formally created in 1932 and set about the task of establishing the most conservative Muslim society in the world, a position it maintained until the Taliban took over six decades later.[140] The royal family became the chief patron of Wahhabism and used the religious doctrine to obtain legitimacy and consolidate their power. The support of the Wahhabis was crucial to the military victories of the Saud family. King Ibn Saud rewarded them by making Wahhabism the official faith of the new Saudi state.[141]

The Wahhabis were greatly influenced by the *Salafiyya* movement, which sought to emulate *al-Salaf al-Salih* (venerable forefathers), that is, the generation of Muslims that lived during the life of the prophet Muhammad. The *Salafiyya* tradition spawned many other religious movements over the years, including the Muslim Brotherhood, Hamas, and a host of other voluntary religious organizations.[142] What is more, according to some sources, as many as 80 percent of the mosques in the United States are under the denomination's influence.[143] Wahhabi influence also extends to the network of madrassas in Pakistan, which have served as incubators for the global jihadist movement.[144]

Despite his Wahhabi background, bin Laden has actually parted with this denomination on several issues. Traditionally, Wahhabism has equated Islam with the Arab world. Bin Laden and his mentor, Dr. Ayman al-Zawahiri, however, have been deeply influenced by the universalist *Salafiyya* strand of Islam. This approach enables them to reach out to Muslims in various parts of the world, regardless of their race, ethnicity, culture, or Islamic denomination. Crucial to the development of social capital or a sense of trust in the al Qaeda network is religion and a shared ideology. Bin Laden's genius lies in his ability to create an overarching political ideology into which the agendas of other particular groups can be subsumed. Al Qaeda enjoys substantial prestige among the other Islamist organizations with which it interfaces. Islamists consider it the highest honor to be accepted as a full member into the organization.

Many young Muslim men find bin Laden's exhortation to jihad appealing. As with several Christian Identity sects of the American extreme right, Jean Rosenfeld sees bin Laden's concept of jihad as fitting a larger pattern of a theology of "revolutionary millennialism."[145] Members of such sects usually feel a profound sense of persecution and embattlement.

> What we see in the Al Qa'ida data is a revolutionary millennial movement that obligates its members to die and kill to achieve an ultimate reality based on a nostalgic, romanticized version of the early Caliphate. The religion of bin Laden teaches that defeat in battle will be reversed in a final victory and death is eternal bliss. Like the messianic transformative creeds, the jihadists believe that their deeds and words have an efficacious, or magical, power that exceeds the technological superiority of their enemies. They believe that they will win the final battle because they are prepared to die until they do, no matter how long it takes. The greatest fear of such a movement is that it will fail to recruit new members to carry out its violent acts.[146]

To his admirers, bin Laden is seen as a modern-day Saladin, the great Muslim warrior who expelled the Crusaders from Jerusalem. His al Qaeda network acts as an umbrella organization for a wide variety of jihadist groups. It is extremely difficult to give an accurate figure, but according to one estimate, al Qaeda consists of roughly 5,000 terrorists.[147] Bin Laden has championed Islamic causes in several non-Arab lands, including the Sudan, Chechnya, and Bosnia; has established ties with far-flung Islamist organizations outside the Middle East, such as Abu Sayyaf in the Philippines; and is reported to have even traveled to the archipelago nation in the winter of 1993.[148] Although he does not maintain central control over all of them, he has become the principal agent of what Roland Jacquard has referred to as the "Islamic Legion."[149] Furthermore, bin Laden has had considerable success in forging alliances with a cross-section of jihadist groups, some of which have been traditional rivals, such as Egypt's al-Gamaa-i Islamiya (the Islamic Group) and Islamic Jihad. And unlike other followers of Wahhabism who have historically persecuted Shi'ite Muslims, bin Laden has sought to bridge the gap between Shi'ites and Sunnis.[150] Consistent with this philosophy, bin Laden has reached out beyond Sunnis to forge links with Shi'ite groups such as Hezbollah.

However, despite these efforts, bin Laden has still not made much headway in gaining support among Shi'ites—with the exception of Hezbollah, which shares his animus towards the United States and Israel. In fact, the al Qaeda operative believed to be responsible for much of the foreign insurgent violence in Iraq, Abu Musab al-Zarqawi, went so far as to urge al Qaeda leaders to turn the Sunni and Shi'ite communities against each other to make that country less governable for American occupation forces. But other events in Iraq during the spring of 2004 may indicate the potential for common ground as traditional Sunni and Shi'ite rivals, under the influence of a young Shi'ite cleric, Moqtada Sadr, appeared to unite against U.S. occupation forces in Iraq.[151]

Perhaps bin Laden's most ostensible success in gathering a broad-based coalition of Islamists was demonstrated during the Soviet-Afghan war. During the early years of the war in Afghanistan, Osama bin Laden raised money to fight the Soviets. His fund-raising activities were carried out primarily in Saudi Arabia. Through his family's construction company, the Saudi Bin Laden Group, he was able to procure and smuggle into Afghanistan through Pakistan important equipment, trucks, and other construction tools to build roads and burrow caves. These defensive tunnels and bunkers served his al Qaeda organization in the 1990s. Accounts vary on the degree to which bin Laden was actually involved in combat operations in Afghanistan. Some claim that his role was primarily logistical and that he occupied most of his time in the rear, organizing from an office in Peshawar.[152] Others claim that he was an active fighter and commander. In both the battles of Jalalabad in 1986 and Masada in 1987 he is reported to have valiantly fought on the front lines.[153]

While working on the war effort on the Afghanistan-Pakistan border, bin Laden began working with his former professor from his alma mater, Abdullah Azzam. During the war, bin Laden's religious convictions deepened, and Azzam became his spiritual mentor. The two were instrumental in the creation of the Afghan Services Bureau (Makhtab al-Khadimat, or MAK), which raised funds for the mujahideen's jihad against the Soviets and recruited fighters. Azzam even introduced bin Laden to the blind sheikh Omar Abdel Rahman, who would go on to become the spiritual leader of the international Islamist movement after Azzam's death. However, eventually a split developed between Azzam and bin Laden, and the two competed for control of the movement. Azzam preferred to focus on supporting the mujahideen's struggle in Afghanistan and create a base of operations for the next step of his jihadist struggle. He supported Ahmed Shah Masoud, a leading Afghan warlord who was supported by the British Intelligence Service, MI6.[154] Azzam harbored no illusions of his movement overturning Arab regimes at that particular point in the struggle, as he was well aware of the government repression and brutality with which Islamists were met in places like Egypt. In that sense, his advocacy of jihad was a traditional one, albeit aggressive in that it demanded the return of formerly Muslim lands.[155] He preferred to concentrate exclusively on liberating former Muslim countries and the periphery of the Muslim world, such as the Philippines, Central Asia, Kashmir, and Palestine.[156] For his part, bin Laden wanted to export jihad to Saudi Arabia and other "apostate" Arab regimes and eventually take on their chief sponsor, the United States. As he reasoned, in order to bring down the apostate regimes, the Islamists must curtail the political and economic influence from the United States. By 1988, bin Laden had completely split from Azzam, and MAK established a separate guesthouse in Peshawar.

Ultimately, bin Laden's vision prevailed. On November 24, 1989, Azzam and his two sons were killed by a bomb explosion as they traveled a mountainous route in Afghanistan. Rumors allege that bin Laden was somehow connected to the assassination, although he has consistently denied these allegations, and no conclusive evidence has been discovered to prove that he was.[157] Interestingly, bin Laden would go on to implement Azzam's vision and create al Qaeda or "the base," which he sought to use as an underground springboard to launch jihad against corrupt Muslim regimes. Not surprisingly, such ambitions caused some consternation among the governments in the region. By 1989, bin Laden had become persona non grata with the new Pakistani government of Prime Minister Benazir Bhutto. However, with the Soviets gone from Afghanistan and his chief mentor dead, bin Laden saw little reason to stay in the country anyway.[158]

The principal lesson bin Laden learned from Azzam is that real power lay in forming a pan-Islamic rather than a pan-Arab organization. By reaching out to Muslims outside the Middle East, such as in Asia and the Far East, he could attract extensive support and build a broad-based operational infrastructure. As bin Laden has stated, his purpose is to "unite all Muslims and establish a government which follows the rule of the Caliphs."[159]

According to one of his most authoritative biographers, Rohan Gunaratna, bin Laden is not an original thinker; rather he is more of an opportunist and businessman who likes to surround himself with a solid team and manage it well while borrowing heavily from others.[160] Soon after the death of Azzam, bin Laden found a new mentor in the Egyptian surgeon, Dr. Ayman al-Zawahiri, who is credited with convincing bin Laden to transform al Qaeda from a guerrilla into a terrorist organization. He was also instrumental in forging close ties between al Qaeda and Egypt's Jama At al-Jihad Group, which was a key organization behind the assassination of Anwar Sadat.[161] During the early 1990s, he decided to shift his terrorist organization's focus away from Egypt's secular leadership to the United States. By doing so, he was able to ally his organization with al Qaeda, which also sought to target the United States. A synergy appears to have followed the forging of the alliance in that the Egyptian Islamic Jihad included many dedicated jihadists and al Qaeda had considerable financial wherewithal.[162]

After years of battle experience and organization, the event that ultimately drove bin Laden to the point of no return in his mission to reinvigorate Islam was the Gulf War. To many Muslims, the Saudi government is seen as the custodian of the two most sacred places in Islam—Mecca and Medina. Not long after Saddam Hussein's August 1991 invasion of Kuwait, tens of thousands of American armed service members began deploying in Saudi Arabia as part of a troop buildup for what would ultimately become Operation Desert Storm. The presence of foreign troops on Saudi soil appalled bin Laden, who soon returned to the country after his tour of duty in Afghanistan. The Saudi government's decision to allow U.S. troops on the holiest soil of Islam was too galling for him. Fresh from victory in Afghanistan, bin Laden approached the royal family and offered to raise an army of 5,000 veteran mujahideen volunteers to thwart any aggression by Iraq. Not wanting to risk the same fate that had befallen Kuwait, the Saudi royal family declined his offer and instead decided to accept American military assistance. This was a high-stakes decision for the Saudi royal family because their power depended in large part on the support of the radical Wahhabi clerics.

In the months leading up to the first Gulf War, the Islamist movement was undecided on what side to support. Some Islamist leaders actually voiced support for Saddam Hussein because he was confronting the United States—a chief nemesis of Islamism. In this sense, supporting Hussein's defiance of the United States was of greater importance than liberating Kuwait. Some Islamists were willing to overlook the secular aspects of Saddam's Ba'athist regime. For his part, bin Laden remained a concerned yet fiercely loyal citizen. The Saudi authorities, however, did not distinguish between bin Laden's position and that of the other Islamists. Bin Laden was extremely popular, and the Saudi government wanted to stifle any potential opposition.[163] Furthermore, bin Laden had other reasons to resent both the Saudi and American governments; he was displeased when they had ceased supporting the mujahideen after the Soviets had withdrawn from Afghanistan in 1989.

The overwhelming military superiority American armed forces demonstrated during the first Gulf War sent shockwaves throughout the Middle East. Despite its large size and relative strength vis-à-vis its neighbors, Iraq was no match for the American-led coalition. The example of Iraq was a stark lesson for the Islamists that they should not attempt to challenge the United States unilaterally. As Bruce Hoffman noted, a UN-backed international coalition under the direction of the United States was quickly arrayed against Iraq in the Gulf War. Therefore, future aggressors might prefer to use a handful of armed men with a limited amount of weaponry to accomplish what full armies, navies, and air forces have traditionally been deployed to achieve.[164] What is more, with the defeat of Saddam's Iraq, the last major bastion of pan-Arabism had dissolved. In the months before the war, the traditionally secular Hussein sought to reposition himself as a pious Muslim and even added the words "God Is Great" to the Iraqi national flag in an effort to garner support from the Muslim world.[165] Despite this effort, Hussein received little sympathy from the Islamists. Increasingly isolated, he became the chief adversary of the United States in the Middle East. Not long thereafter, Tehran began a gradual rapprochement with Washington, perhaps to avoid a similar conflict with the lone superpower.[166]

The fact that U.S. forces failed to withdraw after the war only deepened bin Laden's sense of betrayal. At this point, bin Laden dispatched al Qaeda cells into his country, and they remain to this day.[167] Furthermore, bin Laden began to openly lecture against the royal family. Cassette audiotapes of his sermons were widely distributed. Finally, he financially supported Saudi opposition groups based in London.[168] All this was too much for the Saudi government, which would brook no opposition to its rule, not even from a national hero like bin Laden. He was effectively placed under house arrest, as his travel was limited to the city of Jeddah. According to family members, he was harassed in the streets and on occasion even roughed up by groups of youths.[169] Despite government repression, bin Laden managed to leave his homeland. After his criticism of the Saudi government's reliance on U.S. troops, the Saudi government sent him to Kabul in 1992 to help stop the internecine fighting among Afghan resistance factions. However, rather than returning to Saudi Arabia, he flew to Khartoum, the capital of Sudan.[170] Seeking to further sever its ties with its defiant son, the Saudi government revoked bin Laden's citizenship on April 7, 1994.

By the early 1990s, the governments of the Middle East were able to contain the radical Islamist movement within their countries. Consequently, many Islamist organizations appeared to be in retreat because they had failed to mount a serious challenge to Arab regimes. What is more, they seemed not to offer any serious solutions to the economic and social problems of the region.[171] However, bin Laden would soon reenergize the Islamist movement. Furthermore, the marginalization of Islamist movements in various Arab nations made a large number of recruits available for al Qaeda.[172] With the connections and notoriety he established during his exploits in Afghanistan, bin Laden found a sanctuary in Sudan. He was welcomed there by Hassan al-Turabi, a charismatic Islamist cleric, who led the National Islamic Front, which ruled the country at that time. The Sudanese government and bin Laden entered into a number of business and development projects. Al-Turabi saw in bin Laden a financial benefactor who could give him the means to underwrite his broad program of pan-Islamism.[173] From this secure base, bin Laden planned attacks against the United States. In many ways, Sudan exemplifies the notion of a failed state. The jihadist movement has been able to exploit sanctuaries offered by weak regimes in such countries. Because these countries have no genuine fully functioning government and are not full members of the international community, it is difficult to exert pressure on them to expel terrorists.[174] In such a milieu, the bin Laden network was able to flourish as it prepared to launch its campaign against the United States and Israel. It was during this period that bin Laden intensified his operations and expanded his terrorist network.

Gunaratna identified several hallmarks of al Qaeda's terrorist attacks. First, al Qaeda issues a justification before attacks, usually by way of a fatwa (a religious edict). Second, al Qaeda has institutionalized the operation of suicide attacks; a cult of martyrdom pervades the organization. And third, prior to an attack, operatives meticulously plan the operation to ensure its success.[175] Al Qaeda prefers to launch a series of attacks in a short time to create a more shocking effect. Furthermore, the symbolism of the attacks is important: al Qaeda terrorists have struck icons of American power and prestige. And finally, the sheer number of suicide terrorists working together in a single operation is noteworthy.[176]

Why is suicide terrorism so prevalent among groups such as al Qaeda? In short, because it works. What virtually all suicide terrorist campaigns have in common is the specific and strategic goal to compel the adversary to withdraw military forces from the territory that the terrorists consider to be their homeland.[177]

On an individual level, arguably the most distinctive characteristic of suicide terrorism is the motive of self-sacrifice and martyrdom. Suicide terrorism can be a powerful redemptive myth as the martyr self-consciously creates a model for future emulation and inspiration. In this sense, he gains life beyond the grave when his act of martyrdom impresses his audience and is remembered. This transcendent fame can be a powerful motive for someone whose life has little significance. Furthermore, the act creates a sense of great pride in those within the organization and among future *shuhada*. The sponsoring organization identifies with the heroism and glory of the act of self-sacrifice.[178] As mentioned earlier, although the Koran proscribes suicide, Islamist theorists have defended so-called martyrdom attacks on koranic principles. According to a strict reading of the Koran, self-inflicted death for "selfish" reasons, for example, to escape an unhappy life predicament, would constitute suicide and as such is strictly prohibited. However, a selfless act in the service of jihad, which will undoubtedly result in one death, is defined as martyrdom, not suicide.[179]

The first major operation directed at U.S. interests that bin Laden is thought to have sponsored is the attack on two hotels in Aden, Yemen. On December 29, 1992, elements of al Qaeda working under the cover of the Yemeni Islamic Jihad organization detonated bombs in two hotels in that city, which killed 2 Austrian tourists and narrowly missed 100 U.S. servicemen en route to Somalia.[180] In December 1992, U.S. soldiers were deployed to the war-torn country in a humanitarian effort christened Operation Restore Hope. The Islamists feared that it was part of a campaign to extend U.S. hegemony to northern Africa, which could be used as a springboard to subjugate countries in the Middle East. Bin Laden saw Somalia as occupying a key strategic location in his struggle against the United States. In his mind, Operation Restore Hope was launched not for humanitarian reasons but to gain a secure foothold in the region, just the United States had done in the Persian Gulf. If the Americans were successful in Somalia, they could proceed next to Sudan and take over all the Islamic countries.[181]

On October 3 and 4, 1993, Somalia clans engaged in a bitter firefight with American troops in the city of Mogadishu in which eighteen U.S. servicemen were killed and seventy-five more were injured. Many more Somalis—perhaps up to 1,000—were killed, and still more were injured. (A feature-length film based on this incident, *Black Hawk Down*, was released in late 2001.) Americans were appalled as they viewed television images of a dead American soldier dragged naked through a street in Mogadishu. Although the Somalis suffered overwhelmingly greater casualties in this firefight, the incident resulted in a political victory for the Islamists when the United States abandoned the African country. It is reputed that on several occasions, bin Laden met with the Somali warlord Muhammad Farrah Aidid.[182] Bin Laden claimed that al Qaeda played a significant role in that attack. Although his operatives may not have been involved in the actual fighting, they were thought to have supplied the Somali militias with valuable logistical support.

The success of this operation emboldened bin Laden and greatly elevated the morale of the Islamists by diminishing the humiliation of the Gulf War (*al-azma,* or "the crisis," as it was often called). Commenting on the Somali campaign, bin Laden expressed a low opinion of American soldiers' martial qualities. Although much of the Arab and Islamic world was stunned by the resounding victory of the U.S.-led coalition in the Gulf War, the humiliation of the U.S. military in Somalia did much to reverse the aura of American invincibility. To bin Laden this event portended an eventual Afghan-style defeat for the United States:

> We believe that those who participated in the jihad in Afghanistan bear the greatest responsibility . . . because that with insignificant capabilities, with a small number of RPGs [rocket-propelled grenades], with a small number of antitank mines, with a small number of Kalashnikov rifles, they managed to crush the greatest empire known to mankind. They crushed the greatest military machine. The so-called superpowers vanished into thin air. We think that the United States is much weaker than Russia. Based on the reports we received from our brothers who participated in jihad in Somalia, we learned that they saw the weakness, frailty, and cowardice of U.S. troops. Only 80 U.S. troops were killed. Nonetheless, they fled in the heart of darkness, frustrated, after they had caused great commotion about the new world order.[183]
>
> . . .The youth were surprised at the low morale of the American soldiers and they realized that that the American soldiers are paper tigers. After a few blows, they ran in defeat and America forgot about all the hoopla and media propaganda after leaving the Gulf War and destroying infrastructure—and destroying baby formula factories, all civilian factories, bridges and dams that help planting food—about being the world leader of the new world order. After a few blows, they forgot about this title and left, dragging their corpses and their shameful defeat and stopped using such titles. And they learned that this name is larger than them.[184]

During 1992, bin Laden embarked on an effort to support the embattled Muslims of Bosnia. It is estimated that at the height of the conflict, roughly 5,000 Afghan Arabs fought alongside the Bosnian Muslims.[185] Bin Laden's stay in Sudan overlapped with that of many other terrorists, which enabled al Qaeda to forge more links and turn itself into a global umbrella organization.[186] Al-Turabi was instrumental in translating the theory of jihad into action. Within months of his arrival, bin Laden created the "Brotherhood Group"—a network of 134 Arab businessmen whose commercial enterprises extended worldwide. They maintained bank accounts in virtually every country and collectively shifted billions of dollars in transactions as part of their legitimate businesses, which provided an excellent cover for financing bin Laden's operations.[187]

Bin Laden's organization appears to be the paragon of the new terrorist network, which tends to be more diffuse, with less-rigid organizational structures and memberships.[188] Although bin Laden finances terrorism and directs some operations, he does not appear to have direct command and control over all operatives. Rather, he coordinates and supports many dispersed nodes in a network.[189] As one of his biographers, Peter L. Bergen, commented, bin Laden is perhaps better understood as "the Pied Piper of Jihad," in that he leads Islamists into conflict with the force of his message, which can now be easily spread in an era of twentieth-century communication.[190] As Bergen points out, Holy War, Inc., represents a privatization of terrorism that parallels a trend in many countries since the 1990s to convert state-run enterprises to privately held companies.[191] Today, terrorists are more likely to be associated with loose networks rather than established groups with state sponsors, and infiltrating them can be problematical. Moreover, state sponsors of terrorism tend to be more conservative and calibrated in their violence. Consequently, loose networks are less constrained and controllable than those groups under state sponsorship.[192] The network structure of organization offers several advantages for operating in the modern world:

Networks can often operate clandestinely and are thus not immediately visible to authorities.

1. When terrorist or other criminal networks are inherently dispersed, even when they are targeted by law enforcement, they do not provide obvious locations for authorities to attack.
2. Transnational terrorist networks can take advantage of differences in national laws and regulations in what has been termed "jurisdictional arbitrage."
3. Networks offer opportunities for redundancy and resilience. Thus, if some nodes are neutralized, others can quickly take their place.[193]

What is crucial to the smooth functioning of a network is social capital, that is, interpersonal or relational properties among individuals. Marc Sageman's research suggests that individuals tend to join terrorist organizations through acquaintances in a three-step process that involves social affiliation, a progressive intensification of beliefs and faith leading to the acceptance of the jihadist ideology, and the formal acceptance into the group.[194] The notion of trust figures very prominently in successful networks.[195] Islam, as an organizing principle, has worked effectively to cement the ties among the diverse jihadists in the al Qaeda network.

Despite its characterization as a loose network, some have cautioned about applying this construct to al Qaeda, as it does have a somewhat hierarchical structure. At the apex of the organization is believed to be bin Laden. Just beneath him on the organizational chart is his chief counsel, Dr. Ayman al-Zawahiri. Below him lies the Shura, or Consultation Council, which consists of key operatives that approve major terrorist decisions and issue fatwas. Three committees are subordinate to this council. The Military Committee oversees recruitment, training, and arms purchasing. The Islamic Study Committee makes rulings on religious matters and indoctrinates members in the Koran and jihad. The Finance Committee is responsible for corporate holdings and financing operations. According to the captured al Qaeda leader Khalid Sheikh Muhammad, there is even a "Department of Martyrs" that recruits and supports suicide terrorists.[196] These committees are connected to a vast network of cells scattered throughout the world.[197] It is estimated that al Qaeda has an annual budget of approximately $50 million.[198]

Bin Laden stepped up his terrorist campaign on November 13, 1995, when a car bomb exploded in the courtyard of a Saudi Arabia National Guard building in Riyadh. Two Indian nationals and five American servicemen were killed, and more than thirty others were injured. Four Saudis were apprehended in connection to the attacks but were executed by way of decapitation before American authorities could interrogate them. This attack put bin Laden on the Central Intelligence Agency's (CIA's) radar screen. In January 1996, the CIA Counterterrorist Center in Langley, Virginia, created a special bin Laden task force.[199] Another attack soon followed on June 25, 1996, which struck the Khobar Towers complex near Dhahran, which housed 3,000 American servicemen and women, as well as British and French troops based in the area. Nineteen U.S. airmen were killed, and hundreds more were wounded after a bomb in a fuel truck exploded just outside the military complex.

Eventually, bin Laden became too much of a liability even to the Sudanese government, which was coming under increasing pressure from the United States. As a result, bin Laden was forced to leave Sudan in 1996. In retrospect, forcing bin Laden to exit the Sudan may have been a tactical mistake on the part of the United States, as he would soon move his base of operations to a more impenetrable stronghold. Bin Laden left Sudan a wiser but reportedly a poorer man; he lost approximately $150 million in his Sudanese ventures after the Khartoum government failed to pay its debts.[200]

Bin Laden soon found safe haven in Afghanistan, where he established his headquarters in 1996. Mullah Muhammad Omar, the leader of the Taliban, welcomed him. The Taliban had recently achieved decisive victories in its battles against rival mujahideen groups and had establish control over most of Afghanistan. According to some accounts, Omar summoned approximately fifty Pashtun students from local madrassas to battle corrupt and benighted warlords, who had ravaged the country. As word of his conquests spread, more volunteers from madrassas in Pakistan made their way to Afghanistan to join the fledging movement. With the destruction of civil society resulting from over a decade of war and internecine fighting, the weary population saw the Taliban as the only viable alternative to the warlords. Omar's success captured the attention of the Pakistani Inter-Services Intelligence (ISI), which began to provide material support.[201] At first, Omar's acceptance of bin Laden was somewhat of a stressor for Afghan-Saudi relations. After all, the Taliban received significant aid from Riyadh. In order to assuage Saudi concerns, bin Laden was granted the status of a refugee and advised to remain discreet.[202] For bin Laden, the journey to Afghanistan had profound spiritual significance as he saw parallels to it in the Prophet Muhammad's emigration, or *hijrah,* from Mecca to Medina in 622.[203] According to the independent researcher Paul Williams, there were more pragmatic reasons for bin Laden's decision to relocate to Afghanistan as well. Williams asserts that working together, al Qaeda and the Taliban were able to control the opium trade in Afghanistan, which brought into their coffers $500 million to $1 billion each year.[204] To show his appreciation to his new hosts, bin Laden organized the 055 Brigade—an integrated army consisting of both al Qaeda and Taliban fighters—to battle the Northern Alliance.

According to some intelligence analysts, Iran began to sponsor conferences during this period to establish a working relationship among Middle Eastern terrorist groups.[205] At least one analyst believed that cooperation began as early as the 1980s for the purpose of turning Afghanistan into a second Lebanon.[206] Tehran resolved to transform Hezbollah into the "vanguard of the revolution." Despite its Shi'ite orientation, Iran sought to build bridges with Sunni terrorist organizations. The Iranian arm of Hezbollah had been involved in international terrorism since 1981, but this most recent initiative broadened the scope of its operations. Although Tehran had previously sponsored numerous foreign terrorist groups, it could exert only a limited amount of influence over them, mostly by financial power and ideological suasion.[207] Khomeini's successor, President Ali Akbar Hashemi Rafsanjani, established the Supreme Council for Intelligence Affairs, which was construed elsewhere as the Supreme Council for Terrorism. The council laid the foundation for a broad-based terrorist organization known as Hezbollah International.[208] In 1996 Dr. Mahdi Chamran Savehie from the Supreme Council convened a conference in Tehran, which brought many groups and leaders together, including Mustafa Al Liddawi of

Hamas, George Habbash of the Popular Front for the Liberation of Palestine, Abdullah Ocalan of the Kurdish People's Party, Ramadan Shalah of the Palestinian branch of Islamic Jihad, Ahmed Sala of the Egyptian branch of Islamic Jihad, and Osama bin Laden.[209] The summit participants agreed to the unification of their financial system as well as the standardization of training in order to establish interoperability for their terrorist operatives. Reportedly, a Committee of Three was established, which included Osama bin Laden of al Qaeda, Imad Mughniya of the Lebanese branch of Islamic Jihad, and Ahmed Sala of the Egyptian branch of Islamic Jihad. Although two of these individuals were Sunnis and one was a Shi'ite, all sides were comfortable with the arrangement, and Iran trusted them.

However, the election of the moderate Hojjatoleslam Seyed Mohammad Khatami as president in 1997 resulted in a significant shift in Iranian policy toward terrorism. Eventually, Iran relinquished control of this Islamist umbrella alliance. Khatami ended the massive financial support for the spread of Islamic fundamentalism worldwide, which sounded the death knell for Hezbollah International.[210] Bin Laden responded to this development by creating his own replacement for Hezbollah International, which he called the World Islamic Front for Jihad against Jews and the Crusaders. The group was announced to the world at a press conference in Khost, Afghanistan, in May 1998. Bin Laden used the new organization to further existing ties between groups such as Dr. Ayman al-Zawahiri's Islamic Jihad and Rifa'i Ahmad Taha's Armed Islamic Group.[211] In a more recent example of cooperation, a top operational commander of al Qaeda is alleged to have established a working relationship with an office of the Iranian government a mere four months prior to the 9/11 attacks.[212] And in November 2001, after U.S. armed forces overthrew the Taliban in Afghanistan, Iran is believed to have granted refuge to more than 250 senior al Qaeda and Taliban figures.[213] In early June 2002 the leaders of four major terrorist organizations—Hezbollah, Hamas, Islamic Jihad, and the Popular Front for the Liberation of Palestine general command—met in Tehran, Iran, presumably to work on a common strategy to oppose Israel.[214]

Although the evidence is less than conclusive, some intelligence analysts maintain that al Qaeda had also endeavored to create an operational alliance with Saddam Hussein's Iraq. The extent of Iraqi–al Qaeda cooperation is, in the estimation of Rohan Gunaratna, "purely a matter of speculation."[215] In fact, even years before the first Gulf War, bin Laden warned the Saudi government of Hussein's potentially aggressive intentions toward his neighbors.[216] Furthermore, the former Iraqi dictator's son, Qusay Hussein, once remarked that he did not have enough confidence in bin Laden to risk exposing the Iraqi regime to renewed campaigns of calumny in the international press. Finally, such adventurist cooperation with al Qaeda would have undermined Saddam Hussein's putative reconciliation with Saudi Arabia.[217]

Other analysts disagree; for example, Simon Reeve claims that by early 1999, bin Laden was in the process of forging a secret alliance with Saddam Hussein. Contact between the two sides was first allegedly made in the early 1990s when Hassan al-Turabi put bin Laden in contact with operatives from the Iraqi secret service. These contacts were supposed to have been maintained by representatives of the Iranian terrorist group Mujahedin-e Khalq Organization (MKO), which had its headquarters in Baghdad.[218] Laurie Mylroie asserted that bin Laden had known ties to Iraqi intelligence and that both parties share similar objectives, such as overthrowing the Saudi regime, ending the U.S. presence in the Persian Gulf, and having sanctions against Iraq lifted.[219] According to some intelligence sources, Osama bin Laden's right-hand man, Dr. Ayman al-Zawahiri, visited Baghdad in 1998 and received a $300,000 payment just before he merged the Egyptian branch of Islamic Jihad group with al Qaeda.[220] There is also some speculation as to an Iraqi connection to 9/11—on April 8, 2001, Muhammad Atta is reported to have met with an Iraqi intelligence officer named Ahmad Khali Ibrahim Samir al-Ani at the Iraqi embassy in Prague.[221] For his part, Saddam Hussein had voiced support for those terrorists that struck Israel. In April 2002, for example, he announced that he would pay the family of any suicide bomber who killed Israelis $25,000 in cash.[222] All of that said, recent investigations suggest that several of these Iraqi connections to anti-U.S. groups appear dubious. A commission impaneled by the U.S. government in 2004 to investigate the 9/11 attacks concluded that although bin Laden met with a top Iraqi official in 1994, there was no credible evidence of a link between Iraq and al Qaeda in the September 11 attacks. Also, the commission impugned the allegation that Mohammed Atta met with Iraqi agents in Prague.[223]

Osama bin Laden formally announced himself as an enemy of the United States with his declaration of war in August 1996.[224] Bin Laden's fatwas denouncing the United States became increasingly strident. He would go on to issue several more fatwas against the United States, including the statement of the "World Islamic Front for Jihad against Jews and the Crusaders" (now called the World Islamic Front) in 1998, in which he exhorted Islamist leaders to forge a coalition with which to confront the United States. He initially cited three major reasons why the United States should be targeted:

> First, for over seven years the United States has been occupying the lands of Islam in the holiest of places, the Arabian peninsula, plundering its riches, dictating to its rulers, humiliating its people, terrorizing its neighbors, and

turning its bases in the peninsula into a spearhead through which to fight neighboring Muslim peoples. . . .

Second, despite the great devastation inflicted on the Iraqi people by the Crusader-Zionist alliance, and despite the number of those killed, which has exceeded one million . . . despite all this, the Americans are once again trying to repeat the horrific massacres, as though they are not content with the protracted blockade imposed after the ferocious war or the fragmentation and devastation. . . .

Third, if the Americans' aims behind these wars are religious and economic, the aim is to serve the Jews' petty state and divert attention from its occupation of Jerusalem and murder of Muslims there. The best proof of this is their eagerness to destroy Iraq, the strongest neighboring Arab state, and their endeavor to fragment all the states of the region such as Iraq, Saudi Arabia, Egypt, and Sudan into paper statelets and through their disunion and weakness to guarantee Israel's survival and the continuation of the brutal Crusade occupation of the peninsula. . . .

On that basis, and in compliance with God's order, we issue the following *fatwa* to all Muslims: The ruling to kill the Americans and their allies—civilians and military—is an individual duty for every Muslim who can do it in any country in which it is possible to do it, in order to liberate the al-Aqsa mosque and the holy mosque [Mecca] from the grip, and in order for their armies to move out of all the lands of Islam, defeated and unable to threaten any Muslim.[225]

Firmly ensconced in Afghanistan, bin Laden resumed his war against the United States. According to some sources, President Bill Clinton was reluctant to apprehend Osama bin Laden before 1998 because he was unsure if a jury in Washington, D.C., could convict him at that time. Furthermore, President Clinton gave high priority to the peace process in the Middle East and did not want to offend Arab sensibilities by creating a show trial for such a high-profile figure as bin Laden. A showdown against the enemies of Israel could conceivably weaken his position as an honest broker among parties in the Middle East.[226] Instead of requesting that the Sudanese leader General Omar Bashir extradite bin Laden to the United States, the Clinton administration requested that he be merely expelled.[227] However, events would soon make such a cautious approach untenable.

August 7, 1998, the seventh anniversary of the first U.S. soldiers setting foot in Saudi Arabia, marked bin Laden's most spectacular attack. A suicide truck bombing attack on the U.S. embassy in Nairobi, Kenya, left 224 people killed and many more injured. The dead included 12 Americans. Just minutes later another truck bomb exploded 35 feet away from the U.S. embassy in Dar es Salaam, Tanzania, killing 12 people and seriously wounding 85 more. The Clinton administration responded with Operation Infinite Reach, a secret attack on August 20, 1998, which launched cruise missiles at a Sudanese factory believed to be manufacturing the deadly VX nerve gas (it later transpired to be only a pharmaceutical factory) and al Qaeda training camps in Afghanistan. Bin Laden had left the training camps not long before the attack, thus escaping injury. Furthermore, the retaliation is reported to have actually bolstered Mullah Muhammad Omar's support for bin Laden.[228]

As the attack on the Sudanese factory demonstrated, American authorities are concerned about the prospect of terrorists acquiring weapons of mass destruction (WMD). Bin Laden's first serious attempt to acquire WMD came in 1993 when he allegedly agreed to a plan to purchase a complete nuclear missile or highly enriched uranium from the former Soviet arsenal.[229] To add to this concern, the late General Alexander Lebed, former head of the Russian Security Council, once testified that over half of all atomic demolition munitions, better known as "suitcase bombs," in the former Soviet Union were unaccounted for.[230] According to researcher Paul Williams, elements of the Chechen underworld purportedly sold twenty of these nuclear suitcase bombs to representatives of Osama bin Laden.[231] Furthermore, adding to this suspicion were remarks bin Laden had made in which he claimed that his organization had acquired nuclear and chemical weapons. He threatened to use such weapons if Americans used them against his forces.[232] For his part, bin Laden has explicitly stated his ambition to acquire WMD:

Acquiring weapons for the defense of Muslims is a religious duty. If I have indeed acquired these weapons [WMD], I am carrying out a duty. It would be a sin for Muslims not to try to possess the weapons that would prevent the infidels from inflicting harm on Muslims.[233]

At a time when Israel stocks hundreds of nuclear warheads and when the Western crusaders control a large percentage of this [type of] weapon, we do not consider this an accusation but a right, and we reject anyone who accuses us of this. We congratulated the Pakistani people when they achieved this nuclear weapon, and we consider it the right of all Muslims to do so.[234]

What is all the more worrisome is that some terrorist organizations with the most violent histories, such as al Qaeda, have the requisite financial wherewithal to purchase WMD. Terrorism analyst Jessica Stern identified several indicators of a terrorist group's ability to overcome technical hurdles to the development of WMD: previous use of high-tech weapons; state sponsorship;

access to significant financial resources; a relatively large, well-educated membership; and ties with corrupt government officials, scientists, or organized crime.[235] Several of these characteristics would apply to al Qaeda. For instance, it is believed that some elements of the nuclear sector in Pakistan sympathize with Osama bin Laden and his jihadist goals. For example, Sultan Bashiruddin Mahmood, who once served as an important scientist in Pakistan's nuclear program but is now retired, has dedicated much of his time to providing social services to needy people in Afghanistan. In carrying out these laudable efforts, he has consorted with various Islamist groups and reportedly met with Osama bin Laden on at least one occasion. He is strongly suspected of having offered al Qaeda his expertise in constructing a so-called radiological "dirty bomb."[236] Clearly much is at stake in Pakistan. If the Islamists should ever manage to wrest control of the Pakistani government, they would inherit a nuclear arsenal. The prospect of Pakistani nuclear scientists selling their wares on the nuclear black market unnerves the U.S. government as well. In February 2004 concern was raised when Abdul Aadeer Khan, the founder of Pakistan's nuclear program, confessed to selling equipment related to centrifuges, which are used to enrich uranium for nuclear weapons, to several rogue nations, including Iran, Libya, and North Korea. American authorities feared that such technology might have landed in the hands of terrorists as well.[237]

As the embassy bombings in Africa demonstrated, al Qaeda has mastered the new terrorist paradigm, which researchers at the RAND Corporation have referred to as "swarming." A new operational innovation of netwar, "swarming" involves dispersed nodes of a network of forces converging on a target from multiple directions to accomplish a task. The overall aim is for members of a terrorist network to converge rapidly on a target and disperse immediately, until it is time again to recombine. This tactical flexibility allows al Qaeda to stealthily seize advantage of opportunities.[238] It was during the latter half of 1998 that al Qaeda sent reconnaissance teams to the United States to scout out potential targets for attack.[239]

Still more attacks would follow. On October 12, 2000, a small sailing ship navigated by two reputed al Qaeda members attacked the U.S.S. *Cole* as it floated in a port in Aden, Yemen, for refueling. Seventeen sailors were killed in the attack, and many more were injured. According to eyewitness accounts, the two suicide bombers stood at attention just before they detonated the charge alongside the ship's hull. The type of bomb used was a cone-shaped charge of Semtex—a destructive design that has long been a trademark of Hezbollah. The fact prompted some investigators to fear that a working relationship had been forged between Hezbollah and al Qaeda.[240]

The September 11, 2001, attacks on the World Trade Center and Pentagon were the culmination of al Qaeda's terrorist campaign against the United States. Through spectacular acts of terrorism, bin Laden has sought to polarize the Islamic world between the faithful *umma* and the regimes that ally themselves with the United States. According to some analysts, al Qaeda's strategic objective is to further the Islamist revolution, not militarily defeat the United States, which would for all intents and purposes be impossible. As Michael Scott Doran observed, bin Laden's attack on the United States was designed to overcome the weakness of political Islam in that he succeeded in striking a blow against the universal enemy, the *Hubal* (Hubal was the grandest of the gods worshiped in pagan Arabia prior to the introduction of Islam), which all *Salafiyya* movements around the world can recognize as their own. However, Doran sees the adoption of this strategy as not one of choice but desperation, born of the fact that the various *Salafiyya* movements suffered numerous setbacks in recent years all over the Islamic world.[241] Be that as it may, the attacks against the United States resonated deeply with many of the more radically inclined Muslims around the world and with some secular groups in Arab countries. With the 9/11 attacks, bin Laden has reinforced the belief that they, the *umma,* constitute one political community.

Al Qaeda has an ecumenical appeal among the various Islamist movements around the world. Bin Laden has urged these disparate groups to put aside their doctrinal differences and instead focus their efforts on striking the real enemies (the United States and Israel). Its broad-based ideology appeals to all segments of the Muslim world—the educated, the uneducated, the affluent, and the less affluent. Al Qaeda draws its membership from all strata of society. However, it remains overwhelmingly Sunni in character, despite efforts to include Shi'ites.[242] By redirecting their mostly unsuccessful efforts to cause upheaval in their own countries into a broader campaign against the West, bin Laden and al Qaeda have created a genuine strategic threat.

Conclusion

The developmental path of militant Islam has meandered over the past several decades. From its origins in the Muslim Brotherhood and Wahhabism, it has spread not only throughout the Arab world but also to the far-reaching Muslim populations in Indonesia and the Philippines and the various Muslim diaspora populations in the West. Despite its many permutations, it has demonstrated durability and a remarkable capacity to unite its followers behind some common goals. Although there are some major divisions in the Islamist movement, generally those who comprise the movement work remarkably well with one another. Their common sense of fanaticism and hatred toward their enemies "pushes all lesser animosities aside."[243]

Not surprisingly the Islamists have had a profound effect on their societies. As Samuel Huntington observed, by 1995 every country with a predominantly Muslim population, with the exception of Iran, was more Islamic, culturally, socially, and politically, than it was fifteen years earlier.[244] Furthermore, the root causes of extremism and terrorism remain endemic in much of the Islamic world. For example, current demographic trends, such as the high rate of population growth and young age structure in certain countries, coalesce with poverty to produce potentially huge reservoirs of terrorist recruits. Even a wealthy Arab country such as Saudi Arabia has experienced significant economic decline; between 1980 and 2000 that country's per capita gross domestic product shrank, after adjusting for inflation, by almost half.[245] Economic decline compounds other problems. Joblessness makes it difficult for men to marry. Furthermore, in Islamic culture sex outside of marriage is strictly forbidden, thus producing many tense, angry young men.[246] As Paul Ehrlich and Jianguo Liu point out, FBI data confirm that the vast majority of terrorists are young men between the ages of twenty-two and thirty-four. Their poor life opportunities are a source of indignation, which provides the grassroots support for wealthier and better educated leaders such as Osama bin Laden.[247]

The fanatical religious orientation of al Qaeda serves as a force multiplier and accounts for much of the organization's success. There is a tendency for contemporary terrorists to draw upon religious inspiration to justify their violence. As mentioned earlier, Christian Identity theology inspires many American right-wing terrorists. In recent years, several observers have argued that religious fanaticism is conducive to terrorism, insofar as it loosens the moral and ethical constraints that would keep more secularly inspired terrorists from committing certain acts. Although this theory may sound a bit counterintuitive, its adherents state that those terrorists who believe that God is on their side are more self-assured in their mission and hence have fewer compunctions about using violence.[248] As Bruce Hoffman has pointed out, for religious terrorists, "violence is viewed first and foremost as a sacramental act in direct response to some theological demand or imperative."[249] Furthermore, secular and religious terrorists differ in their constituencies. Whereas the former tend to see themselves appealing to a constituency of actual or potential sympathizers, the latter are at once activists and constituents involved in a total war. Unlike secular terrorists, religious terrorists are not constrained by a desire to appeal to a tacitly supported or uncommitted constituency. Religious terrorists see themselves as "outside the system" and thus have no stake in preserving it.

This profound sense of alienation and moral disengagement enables religious terrorists to contemplate far more destructive types of terrorist operations and inflict mass casualty attacks. The lethality of religiously inspired terrorism during the 1990s lends credence to this theory.[250] For example, in 1995, although religious inspired terrorists committed only 25 percent of the recorded international terrorists incidents, they were responsible for 58 percent of the total number of fatalities recorded for that year.[251] Religion is also far more enduring than political ideologies. As ADL national director Abraham Foxman stated, Islamic anti-Semitism is all the more worrisome than previous variants of anti-Semitism because religions tend to be "self-propagating, and theologies possess remarkable staying power across generations."[252]

Robert Jay Lifton has observed a common apocalyptic thread in several different extremist movements. He argues that a pervasive sense of anomie has caused many people to believe that only extreme measures can restore virtue and righteousness in society. Extremist groups often seek to decipher hermetic messages in order to understand the contemporary world and believe that society is under siege by stealthy evildoers. An ethos of martyrdom permeates these milieus. Small, and often ostracized from the larger society, they believe that they "must destroy the world to save it." A period of apocalyptic tribulation is thought to have redemptive values as it cleanses the corrupt world and ushers in a new era. Robert Jay Lifton sees a similar pattern within the idiom of Islam for bin Laden and al Qaeda. They seek to destroy a world that they see as defiled and create a new Islamic caliphate.[253]

Today, al Qaeda holds the vanguard position in the broader Islamist movement. Despite efforts to decapitate the organization's leadership, al Qaeda endures. According to some estimates, roughly two-thirds of the leadership has been killed or captured since 9/11, including many of the top leaders. Rohan Gunaratna went so far as to predict that al Qaeda would be practically extinct by the end of 2004. However, he added that numerous Islamist groups have decided to assume the role of al Qaeda and carry out its struggle as they see fit.[254]

In some ways al Qaeda has become a "state of mind" organization. Although there is a somewhat hierarchical structure for the core of the network, the periphery is much more amorphous. There is evidence to suggest that disparate individuals and groups that are inspired by the al Qaeda ideology are coordinating and conducting attacks on their own initiative—a genuine form of leaderless resistance in practice. This quality has allowed the organization to persist despite efforts to destroy it. Toward this end, the network has employed new technology to reach potential recruits and sympathizers. For example, a CD-ROM training manual released by the organization and titled *The Encyclopedia of the Afghan Jihad* has attempted "to diminish, if not eliminate, the master-pupil tutelage that forced terrorists to gather together in one spot for prolonged study." The encyclopedia functions as a "portable university for the common militant [whose] ultimate aim [is] to democratize terrorism."[255] Once al Qaeda cells are established, they may require little direction from their superiors. Rather, they can act on their own initiative when the opportunity presents itself.[256] The bombing in Bali in October 2002 was illustrative of such an operation. Indeed, al Qaeda has been transformed into a diffuse terrorist network that can still strike at U.S. targets abroad.[257] The organization has no single center of gravity, but multiple ones, enabling it to effectively prosecute asymmetric warfare.[258] By late 2002, al Qaeda appeared to have switched tactics, moving away from spectacular acts of terrorism to a campaign of attrition, as evidenced by numerous bombings in Tunisia, Bali, Kenya, Pakistan, Morocco, Saudi Arabia, and Madrid, Spain.

The agendas of other Islamic groups can be integrated into al Qaeda's grand strategy. Furthermore, the extremist ideology that bin Laden has fostered has not only helped cement ties between groups but also makes them extremely difficult for Western agents to infiltrate.[259] Finally, al Qaeda is all the more worrisome from the perspective of the United States for another reason. Although other Arab and Islamic terrorists groups have targeted American interests overseas, none had been so bold as to strike the American mainland. Al Qaeda broke with this tradition in the early 1990s. It is that topic to which we shall now turn.

CHAPTER FOUR

Militant Islam in the United States

Although various radical Islamic groups have frequently attacked U.S. interests overseas, they have generally refrained from striking domestic U.S. targets. Islamist activity in the United States has centered more on fund-raising and recruiting rather than terrorism. Their oft-expressed enmity for the United States notwithstanding, as Daniel Pipes observed, Islamists are ironically drawn to the country for a number of reasons. In their home countries they often face repression by the police and security agencies. Thus they find it attractive to flee to the United States, a wealthy country with the rule of law, separation of church and state, and an excellent communications and transportation infrastructure. Furthermore, by and large Muslims, as a demographic group, seem to fare very well in the United States.[1] However, foreign extremists have been able to penetrate the United States under the radar screen of intelligence agencies because of its liberal immigration policies and porous borders. The attacks visited upon the United States on September 11, 2001, were a tragic illustration of both an intelligence failure and an immigration policy gone awry.

Until recently, law enforcement officials have shown little concern for Islamist ideology.[2] This is all the more surprising given the fact that since the early 1990s, there has been ample reason for suspicion. The case of Sheikh Omar Abdel Rahman is instructive.

Ramzi Yousef, the Blind Sheikh, and the 1993 World Trade Center Bombing

The first significant instance of Islamic terrorism in the United States occurred on February 26, 1993, when a small circle of Islamic extremists attempted to topple one tower of the World Trade Center into the other and, in doing so, inflict horrific casualties on Americans. To better understand the import of this attack, it is worth exploring the backgrounds of the individuals who were allegedly involved in one way or the other. Several of the conspirators were followers of a charismatic blind cleric named Sheikh

Omar Abdel Rahman, whose past is enigmatic and sketchy. He reportedly was born in May 1938 into a poor family in the Nile Delta region of Egypt. Although blinded by diabetes by the age of only ten months, he demonstrated remarkable precocity as a youth; by age eleven, he had memorized the entire Koran in Braille. As he grew into an adult, he became a leading fundamentalist Muslim cleric.

An early admirer of Rahman, Dr. Ayman al-Zawahiri, forsook his medical career to become one of the founding members of Jama At al-Jihad, a highly clandestine underground movement dedicated to establishing Islamic rule in Egypt. As mentioned in the previous chapter, al-Zawahiri is regarded as Osama bin Laden's mentor and right-hand man. Eventually, two sects developed in the al-Jihad group. One faction, led by al-Zawahiri, was considered the more fanatical of the two. The other faction, led by Ahmad Husayn Agiza, came to be known as Talaa' al-Fateh (Vanguards of Conquest). Despite their differences, both factions accepted Rahman as their spiritual mentor.[3] In 1981, Rahman gave religious sanction to the assassination of Anwar Sadat.[4] Amazingly, he managed to escape justice for his role in instigating the attack.

In May 1990, while residing in Sudan, Sheikh Rahman received a multiple entry visa to the United States, valid for one year, despite the fact that he had been on a terrorist watch list since 1987 for his role in the assassination of Sadat and his involvement with al-Jihad.[5] He was also reported to have been affiliated with al-Gamaa-i Islamiya (the Islamic Group).[6] According to some accounts, the Central Intelligence Agency (CIA) is believed to have assisted Rahman in entering the country.[7] After the November 1990 assassination of Rabbi Meir Kahane (more on this later), the sheikh's visa was supposed to have been revoked by the U.S. State Department. However, miscommunication with the Immigration and Naturalization Service resulted in Rahman receiving approval for permanent residency status. To Rahman, the United States was Islam's principal enemy because it supported the creation of the state of Israel and the secular government of Egypt and stationed troops in Saudi Arabia and Kuwait.[8]

By the early 1990s, a circle of Muslim radicals began to congregate at the sheikh's Masfid al-Salaam mosque, which was located inside a dingy assortment of rooms over a Chinese restaurant in Jersey City. Malmoud Abouhalima became Rahman's part-time bodyguard and chauffer. Other followers included Ibrahim Elgabrowny, Nidal Ayyad, and Wadih el-Hage. El-Hage is believed to have served as Osama bin Laden's personal secretary in the early 1990s.[9] Another member of the circle, Emad Salem, was actually an informant for the Federal Bureau of Investigation (FBI), who supplied the agency with information on the underground group. The first member of Rahman's circle to gain notoriety was El Sayyid Nosair.

Despite numerous international terrorists attacks that targeted American interests overseas, Islamic extremists did not conduct any major attacks inside the United States until the early 1990s. The assassination of Jewish Defense League (JDL) founder and leader Rabbi Meir Kahane foreshadowed a new era of Islamic extremism in the United States. Kahane created the JDL in 1969 largely in response to a conflict in New York City involving public schools. At that time many of the schoolteachers were Jewish, and many of the pupils were African Americans; tensions developed between the Jewish and African American communities on the issue of control over public school administration. Kahane would go on to found a right-wing extremist political party in Israel called the Kach movement, which was eventually dissolved by Israeli authorities because of its extremist platform.

Kahane's assassin, El Sayyid Nosair, was a thirty-five-year-old Egyptian-born electrician who frequently attended Sheikh Rahman's mosque. On November 5, 1990, Nosair shot Kahane dead while the latter was addressing a conference of the Zionist Emergency Evacuation Rescue Operation (ZEERO) in a hotel in downtown Manhattan. Authorities generally viewed the assassination as an isolated incident and thus failed to recognize it as the start of a larger trend of militant Islamic terrorism inside the United States. In a botched escape plan, another member of Rahman's circle, Malmoud Abouhalima, was supposed to drive the getaway car for Nosair. Their signals crossed, and Nosair failed to locate the getaway car. Although Abouhalima was accused of being Nosair's accomplice, he was never convicted.

Remarkably, a jury acquitted Nosair of murder charges. He was convicted of weapons charges, however, and sentenced to the maximum seven to twenty-one years in prison. Flamboyant left-wing attorney William Kunstler served as Nosair's counsel for the trial, which became a rallying point for the followers of Sheikh Rahman. Despite his incarceration, Nosair continued to plot future terrorist operations from his prison cell. Prison notes seized by the FBI suggested plans for attacks against high-story buildings and statues, which would in effect cripple New York's tourist industry.[10]

The origins of El Sayyid Nosair's radicalism can be traced to the late Palestinian cleric Dr. Abdullah Azzam, who was Osama bin Laden's mentor during the Soviet-Afghan war. In 1979, Azzam left King Abdul Aziz University, where he was one of Osama bin Laden's teachers, to lend his services to the fledging mujahideen movement in Afghanistan. He was appointed as a lecturer at the International University in Islamabad, the capital of Pakistan. Eventually he moved to Peshawar to be closer to the Afghan border, where he could devote his time and efforts to jihad.[11] In 1984, Azzam and Osama bin Laden founded the Afghan Services Bureau (Makhtab al-Khadimat, or MAK) to recruit and train thousands of mujahideen from around the Muslim world and also to provide humanitarian aid. During this period, Azzam devoted substantial time and attention to the Islamist cause in the United States, where he sought recruits for jihad.[12]

Using the humanitarian cover of MAK, groups such as al Qaeda infiltrated many of the nongovernmental organizations (NGOs) involved in helping Muslims in conflicts around the world. All over the world MAK advertised for young men to participate in jihad in Afghanistan. Recruitment offices were opened in over fifty countries, including a half a dozen U.S. cities, London, Paris, Cairo, and many other major capitals as well.[13] Azzam had actually visited the United States frequently to raise money for MAK. An office was established in Brooklyn, New York, called the Alkhifa Center, which spun off outposts in Atlanta, Chicago, Connecticut, and New Jersey.[14] Bin Laden loyalists eventually took control of the office, and Rahman became the venue's central figure. Several of the plotters of the 1993 World Trade Center attack had strong ties to the center in Jersey City.

Islamic terrorist groups in the United States perfected the use of nonprofit organizations to establish a zone of legitimacy within which fund-raising, recruitment, and even terrorist planning can occur.[15] By delivering needed social services such as education, nutrition, and health care, these NGOs were able to win over and control local Muslim populations. The fact that Islam enjoins Muslims to help their brethren through the practice of *zakat*, or purification through charity, strengthened these NGOs. This practice creates tremendous goodwill and social capital for Islamist groups. According to a CIA study, one-fifth of all Islamic NGOs worldwide have been unwittingly infiltrated by al Qaeda and other terrorist groups.[16]

After several years of organizing and fund-raising, radical Islamists finally decided to launch a serious terrorist campaign in the United States. The bombing of the World Trade Center at 12:17 P.M. on February 26, 1993, killed six persons and wounded 1,042 others. For the attack, a 1,500-pound bomb was made from nitrate and nitroglycerine and three tanks of compressed hydrogen. According to investigators, it was the largest improvised explosive ever assembled in the United States.[17] The small band of terrorists loaded the bomb in a yellow Ford Econoline rental van, which was parked in an underground garage beneath the World Trade Center complex. The massive blast created a crater 200 by 100 feet wide and seven stories deep in the garage.[18] Reportedly, the intent was to so damage the foundation that one side of the north tower (World Trade Center One) would collapse and topple into the south tower (World Trade Center Two), thus destroying the entire World Trade Center complex and possibly inflicting up to 250,000 casualties.[19] Although few observers realized it at the time, the terrorist attack presaged a broader struggle between militant Islam and the West. As the terrorism analyst Bruce Hoffman said, "We may be talking about the opening salvo of a new conflict for a New World Order."[20]

The reputed mastermind of the attack, Ramzi Yousef, activated this cell shortly after his arrival in the United States in 1992. Little is known about his background. He is believed to have been born on April 27, 1968. In 1986 he attended the Swansea Institute in Wales, where he studied electrical engineering. Later he applied this talent to terrorism, gaining notoriety as a master bomb maker. Although American intelligence analysts are uncertain whether Yousef has ever met face to face with bin Laden, there is strong evidence to suggest that he is connected to al Qaeda. Furthermore, the two share mutual friends including Wali Khan Amin Shah and Muhammad Jamal Khalifa.[21]

Further complicating the case of the first World Trade Center attack are the putative links between the conspirators and Iraq. The chief proponent of this theory is Laurie Mylroie, a Harvard-educated political scientist. According to Mylroie, one of Yousef's accomplices, Muhammad Salameh, called his uncle in Iraq, Kadri Abu Bakr, on numerous occasions in the months leading up to the attack. Mylroie argued that Iraqi intelligence learned of the plot and decided to support it. Soon after the 1993 World Trade Center attack, Salameh foolishly returned to the Ryder office from which he rented the truck to retrieve his $400 deposit. Authorities were waiting for him, and he was arrested. Mylroie believed that the first World Trade Center bombing was essentially Iraqi-directed, with the Muslim extremists being used as dupes.[22] Adding to suspicion of a possible Iraqi connection was the fact that the attack followed on the heels of a January 17, 1993, U.S. bombing at the Al Rashid hotel in Baghdad. Saddam Hussein hosted a number of Islamic fundamentalist leaders for a conference at the hotel.[23]

Mylroie took issue with the "loose network" paradigm popular in the study of contemporary terrorism. In her estimation, this notion was greatly exaggerated. Rather, she held that state-sponsored terrorism remains the most serious variant of terrorism. She was adamant that Ramzi Yousef, the mastermind of the first World Trade Center attack, was working for Iraqi intelligence and that some of the accomplices were used as part of a "false flag operation" in order to divert attention away from the responsible party. Further, she believed that Iraqi intelligence stole an alter identity for Yousef, one Abdul Basit Karim, who was born in 1968 in Kuwait, the son of a Palestinian foreign worker. Although Mylroie believed there was such a figure, she did not believe that he and Yousef were the same person.[24] What was also significant for Mylroie was the timing of the first World Trade Center attack—February 26, 1993—the second anniversary of the liberation of Kuwait, which suggested some type of symbolic significance implicating the Iraqi government. The British investigative journalist Simon Reeve also believed that there is a strong possibility that Iraq was involved in the 1993 World Trade Center attack.[25]

Yousef was able to escape and eventually made his way to the Philippines, where he planned a new round of terrorist attacks against U.S. targets. Linking up with elements of the Islamic separatist group Abu Sayyaf,[26] he sought to broaden the influence of al Qaeda, which allegedly had sent him to serve as an emissary.[27] Bin Laden had previously financially supported the Filipino terrorists.[28] While there, Yousef made plans for "Operation Bojinka," a series of spectacular terrorist attacks that would explode several U.S. airliners as they flew in mid-air over the Pacific region. This plot was alleged to have been funded by Osama bin Laden.[29] Adding credence to this assertion is the fact that Khalid Sheikh Muhammad, a high-level al Qaeda operative, spent two months with his nephew, Yousef, in Manila in 1994.[30] However, the grandiose plot was never implemented. While preparing the explosive devices, a fire broke out in Yousef's Manila apartment, alerting authorities. They seized Yousef's laptop, which contained the plans for his various terrorist attacks. Among other things that authorities discovered were plans to detonate explosive devices aboard eleven U.S. airliners flying trans-Pacific routes to the United States, as well as the assassinations of President Clinton and Pope John Paul II when they were scheduled to visit the Philippines. Ominously, an alternate plan called for hijacking commercial airliners and crashing them into the World Trade Center in New York, the White House in Washington, D.C., the John Hancock Tower in Boston, the Sears Tower in Chicago, the Transamerica Tower in San Francisco, and CIA headquarters in Langley, Virginia.[31] U.S. authorities eventually caught up to Yousef in Karachi, Pakistan, in February 1995. On September 25, 1996, he was sentenced to 240 years in prison for his role in the Operation Bojinka plot. A year later he was convicted of the 1993 World Trade Center bombing. Yousef appears to be motivated primarily by his animus against the United States and Israel and a strong ego, rather than religious ideology.[32]

Not long after the first World Trade Center bombing, plans for another major terrorist attack soon transpired. As mentioned earlier, Emad Salem had been working on behalf of both the FBI and Egyptian intelligence. In November 1991, he began infiltrating the circle of Muslims who supported El Sayyid Nosair during his trial.[33] Through Salem, the FBI discovered a sensational plot that came to be known as "The Day of Terror," in which the circle planned to simultaneously blow up the United Nations complex, the Lincoln and Holland Tunnels, the George Washington Bridge, and the 26 Federal Plaza building, as well as assassinate New York senator Alfonse M. D'Amato, New York State assemblyman Dov Hikind, and Egyptian president Hosni

Mubarak. Laurie Mylroie believed that Iraqi intelligence also had a hand in this plot, which the U.S. government claimed began when Yousef left Baghdad and traveled to Pakistan, just before he arrived in the United States.[34] Agents from the government of Sudan were alleged to have been involved in the conspiracy as well.[35] Consequently, Sudan was placed on the State Department's list of state sponsors of terrorism.

Fortunately, the FBI's Joint Terrorism Task Force apprehended the cell in June 1993, before they could put their plan into action. Sheikh Rahman was arrested as a coconspirator in the plot. In 1995, the U.S. attorney in New York convicted Rahman on a seditious conspiracy charge for allegedly inspiring some of the individuals who participated in the first World Trade Center attack through his fiery rhetoric. The seditious conspiracy law actually dated from the post–Civil War period and was originally used to prosecute supporters of the Confederacy who continued to resist the government after the war.[36] During the Reagan administration, federal prosecutors revived the law to prosecute left-wing and right-wing radicals and Puerto Rican nationalists, but without much success. Mylroie did not believe that Rahman, despite his bombastic rhetoric and connections to various extremists, was interested in supporting terrorism inside the United States.

Throughout the 1990s, al Qaeda endeavored to establish a network in the United States. Chief among its members was Abu Muhammad ali Amriki ("Muhammad the American"), who served as bin Laden's taskmaster in California. He was eventually arrested in 1998 for plotting the terrorist attacks on two U.S. embassies in East Africa. Earlier, he had trained the guerrillas that attacked U.S. soldiers in Somalia in 1993. And a year later, he helped arrange a summit conference of anti-American terrorist organizations in Sudan. His story demonstrates that an important terrorist figure could operate freely in the United States, undetected and unmolested by authorities.

Born in 1952 in Egypt, Muhammad graduated from both the University of Alexandria and a Cairo military academy. In 1981, he joined Islamic Jihad. His organization has gained an element of elite support because it includes members of the Egyptian military. That same year, he journeyed to the United States and graduated from a special program for foreign officers at the U.S. Army Special Forces School in Fort Bragg, North Carolina. After leaving the Egyptian Army three years later, Muhammad returned to the United States and settled in the San Francisco Bay area. While in California, he raised money for Islamic Jihad. In 1986 he enlisted in the U.S. Army and was stationed at Fort Bragg's Special Warfare Center, where he trained army officers in Middle Eastern culture and geography. While serving as a U.S. soldier, Muhammad also worked on behalf of militant Islamic groups.

In 1989 Muhammad traveled to Brooklyn, where he worked at a refugee center that helped people displaced by the Soviet invasion of Afghanistan. His work with Islamic Jihad eventually drew him to Osama bin Laden, for whom he performed a variety of important services. He became a high-ranking member of al Qaeda and assisted bin Laden in relocating his base of operations from Afghanistan to Sudan in 1991. Terrorism analyst Yonah Alexander of the Potomac Institute believed that Muhammad even smuggled al Qaeda operatives into the United States via Canada. After his arrest in 1998, Muhammad was indicted along with twenty-two other alleged terrorists, including bin Laden.[37] On October 22, 2000, he pled guilty to all charges rendered against him.

According to terrorism analyst Steven Emerson, the lessons from Muhammad's story are twofold. First, it illustrates how a small number of key individuals can provide links to a sprawling terrorist network. Second, the motives of the terrorist are not simply religious fanaticism but can involve other things such as money or the desire for intrigue and adventure.[38]

Miscellaneous Islamist Groups

Al Qaeda is not the only Islamist group to establish a foothold in the United States. Hamas operated openly in the United States for several years.

HAMAS

According to Steven Emerson, Hamas has developed the most sophisticated infrastructure of all the Islamist groups operating in the United States.[39] For several years, during the early 1990s, Hamas had an office in Springfield, Virginia. The office was opened by Musa Abu Marzuq, who arrived in Louisiana around 1975 to pursue a doctoral degree. He eventually became involved with a community of Muslim extremists. In 1980, Marzuq became the founding president of the United Association for Studies and Research (USAR), which, according to some sources, was the command center for Hamas in the United States.[40] He also helped create the Islamic Association of Palestine (IAP) in 1981, which served as the primary voice for Hamas in the United States. The organization's primary activity has been its annual conferences, which host various Islamist luminaries who often give incendiary speeches. Previous speakers have included Yusuf al-Qaradawi, Sheikh Ahmed al-Qattan, Khalil al-Qawka, Abdulrahman Alamoudi, and Mohammad Abu Faris.[41]

Marzuq founded additional groups in the United States that are closely associated with Hamas. For example, in the late 1990s, USAR and IAP were joined by the Holy Land Foundation (HLF), which raises money for charitable work in Palestine. Marzuq's office in Springfield, Virginia, was shut down in 1993 after the U.S. State Department designated Hamas as a foreign terrorist organization.[42] The FBI suspects that Hamas may have established for-profit corporations in the United States. Consequently, on September 5, 2001, members of the FBI's Joint Terrorism Task Force executed a search warrant against the InfoCom Corporation, an Internet service provider based in Richardson, Texas, which was suspected of having ties to Hamas.[43] Moreover, it is suspected that the organization has even sent some of their operatives to the United States for terrorist training. Hamas member Nasser Issa Jalal Hidmi allegedly learned car-bombing techniques in the United States.

HEZBOLLAH

Hezbollah has been involved in numerous fund-raising activities in the United States, some of which include illicit schemes. For example, a Hezbollah ring based in Charlotte, North Carolina, raised money to purchase advanced military hardware and software by smuggling truckloads of contraband cigarettes into Michigan, a state with a very high cigarette tax. On July 21, 2000, FBI agents conducted a sting operation dubbed "Operation Smokescreen," which resulted in the arrest of eighteen persons on charges of smuggling contraband cigarettes and money laundering. Later, authorities charged eight men and one woman with providing assistance to Hezbollah.[44] In January 2004, two members of the ring, Elias Muhammad Akhdar and Hassan M. Makki, received nearly six- and five-year sentences, respectively.[45]

In that same month, a federal grand jury in Michigan issued an indictment against Mahmoud Youssef Kourani for allegedly raising money for Hezbollah in the United States. Kourani was arrested and pleaded guilty to entering the United States illegally through Mexico in 2001. While in custody, he was also charged with harboring an illegal immigrant. His brother, Haidar Kourani, is reportedly the chief of military affairs for Hezbollah in southern Lebanon. Finally, Dearborn residents Ali Abdul-Karim and Hassan Farhat were arrested on cocaine distribution charges. The two are also suspected of being Hezbollah supporters.

MUSLIMS OF AMERICA

The Muslims of America (MOA) is a militant Islamic group with suspected ties to al-Fuqra, a terrorist organization that has allegedly carried out fire bombings and murders in the United States. MOA claims to have offices in six U.S. cities and Toronto. Furthermore, it maintains residential communities in New York, Virginia, and California. MOA was founded in 1980 by a Pakistani cleric, El Sheikh Sayyid Mubarik Ali Jilani, who continues to lead the group to this day. Jilani—who claims to be a direct descendant of the prophet Muhammad—actively recruited American Muslims to fight against the Soviet Union in Afghanistan during the 1980s.[46] Over the years, MOA has been strident in its rhetoric against Zionism and Jews. Like Hamas, MOA has sought to establish Virginia as a stronghold for their activities.[47] Interestingly, its website features articles by right-wing extremists such as David Duke and Michael Hoffman.

MILITANT ISLAM REACHES THE ACADEMY: THE STRANGE CASE OF PROFESSOR AL-ARIAN

One of the most visible Islamic activists in the United States is Sami al-Arian, a professor at the University of South Florida. Al-Arian has been involved in the creation of several think tanks that promote Islamist causes. One of these organizations, the Islamic Concern Project, later called the Islamic Committee for Palestine (ICO), allegedly raised money for Islamic Jihad in Palestine and brought radical Islamist leaders into the United States to attend conferences.[48] Al-Arian also founded the World and Islam Studies Enterprise (WISE) in 1991. On September 26, 2002, he appeared on *The O'Reilly Factor* on the Fox network, where host Bill O'Reilly grilled him about connections between WISE and Islamic Jihad. In February 2003, federal law enforcement agents arrested al-Arian for alleged fund-raising and material support activities on behalf of terrorist organizations, including Hamas and Islamic Jihad.[49] Another professor who taught briefly at the University of South Florida in 1990, Dr. Ramadan Abdalah Shalah, served as the director of WISE. He currently resides in Syria.[50]

THE NORTHERN VIRGINIA "JIHAD NETWORK"

In the summer of 2003 the U.S. government announced the arrest of eleven men who were allegedly part of a jihad network in northern Virginia. They were charged with violating the Neutrality Act for allegedly supporting Lashkar-i-Taiba, which opposes Indian control of the Himalayan region of Kashmir. On March 4, three of the defendants—Masoud Khan, Seifullah Chapman, and Hammad Abur-Raheem—were convicted on conspiracy charges of allegedly aiding the Taliban in its fight against U.S. armed forces in the aftermath of the September 11 attacks.[51]

For the most part, foreign-born Muslims have been behind the most worrisome of Islamist activities in the United States. However, this trend could change in the future, as Islam has made headway in certain communities in the United States, most notably among African Americans.

Home-Grown American Muslims

From the outset, it is only fair to point out that the overwhelming majority of Muslim Americans are not involved in subversive activities against the United States. Nor is there any evidence to suggest that the majority of them sympathize with positions hostile to the United States. Be that as it may, anti-American and anti-Zionist sentiments have gained great currency in other parts of the Islamic world. Because of new technology such as the Internet, it is conceivable that such sentiments may one day find fertile ground in the American Islamic community. However, the Muslim population in the United States is far from homogeneous—the approximately 6 million Muslims in the United States come from more than sixty nations.[52]

In addition, it is estimated that up to 1 million Americans have converted to Islam. Of this million, the overwhelming majority are black. Whites number probably no more than 50,000.[53] One of the most important and enduring Islamic institutions in the United States is the Nation of Islam.

THE NATION OF ISLAM

Although the Nation of Islam is considered heretical by most Islamic religious authorities, it nonetheless enjoys considerable influence in the African American community. Furthermore, in a sense the organization is considered a dissident movement by both the U.S. government and Jewish monitoring groups such as the Anti-Defamation League (ADL). Be that as it may, the Nation of Islam has had a substantial impact on both the African American and Islamic American communities and therefore warrants closer examination.

Although Muslims had resided in North America almost from the start of the continent's European settlement, virtually all vestiges of Islam were gone by the end of the nineteenth century.[54] The first major effort to resurrect Islam in the United States occurred in 1913, when Noble Drew Ali (1886–1929) founded the Moorish Science Temple in Newark, New Jersey. By the late 1920s, his organization was in decline, but an obscure man believed to be one of his followers, Wallace D. Fard, founded a new sect called the "Tribe of Shabazz from the Lost Nation of Asia," which was renamed the Nation of Islam

(NOI) in Detroit in the early 1930s. The sect arose out of a black nationalist milieu, which was heavily influenced by the nineteenth-century European, primarily German, discourse on race. Race was seen as more than just a biological category; it included romantic characteristics of "a spiritual, psychological and cultural kind."[55]

For a short time, Fard led the small sect, but eventually he came under the scrutiny of law enforcement authorities in Detroit and passed control of the organization over to his most trusted disciple, Elijah Muhammad (1897–1975). Despite numerous setbacks and travails, which included imprisonment for draft evasion, Muhammad persevered and built the organization into one of the most powerful African American institutions in the United States. Furthermore, he attracted some men of considerable talent. For example, the NOI gained notoriety in the 1960s largely because of the efforts of its late firebrand speaker, Malcolm X. With the death of Muhammad in 1975, the sect split, with one faction led by Muhammad's son Wallace and the other by Louis Farrakhan. Eventually, Farrakhan would wrest control of the Nation of Islam, and he leads the organization to this day. For many blacks, the Nation of Islam has served as a gateway to Islam. Many who have sojourned in the NOI eventually leave the sect to join more mainstream Islamic denominations.

There are many tenets espoused by the NOI that differ significantly from traditional Islam.[56] According to the theology of the Nation of Islam, history moves in a cyclical fashion. The Original Man (the black man) once enjoyed supremacy over the world but suffered enslavement as a result of moral and religious backsliding. In fact, until recently the black man had all but lost his collective memory of his true religion, Islam. According to the NOI narrative, blacks are descended from the tribe of Shabazz, which traveled to the earth from the moon 66 trillion years ago. Whites, whom the NOI frequently vilifies as "devils," are the descendants of a race concocted by an evil scientist named Yakub. The NOI teaches that blacks must rediscover their true religion and their place in the cosmos. The NOI has often espoused racial separatism.

During his leadership of the NOI, Elijah Muhammad paid little attention to the Jews. However, his successor, Louis Farrakhan, has on occasion voiced criticism of the Jewish community and its relations with the African American community. The ADL has chronicled numerous anti-Semitic statements he has made over the years, which include the following: Jews largely control the American media and government, Jews control international banking, Jews have been in the forefront of the African slave trade, and Jewish doctors deliberately infected blacks with the AIDS virus.[57] However, Farrakhan's attitudes toward Jews are arguably more nuanced. On the one hand, he sees Jewish ethnic organizing as a model for African Americans to emulate. On the other hand, he criticizes Jews, not so much for existential reasons but rather "behavior." What is more, Farrakhan has on several occasions sought to reconcile his differences with Jewish leaders. However, the latter have voiced skepticism about his intentions. This reaction could be explained in part by the vitriol of his late NOI national assistant, Khalid Abdul Muhammad, whose anti-Semitic statements at a Kean College lecture drew condemnation from the entire U.S. Senate in a resolution passed 97–0.[58] According to an ADL survey, as a group, a larger proportion of African Americans evince anti-Semitic attitudes than the nation at large; over the years some 30 to 40 percent of African Americans expressed anti-Semitic attitudes, as measured by the ADL.[59] This is all the more worrisome considering that blacks have been traditional civil rights allies of Jews. There is scattered evidence to suggest that African American lawmakers, more so than other lawmakers, are more likely to express sympathy for the Palestinian side of the Middle Eastern conflict. For example, in May 2001, twelve of thirty African American members of the House of Representatives voted against resolutions in support of Israel's campaign against defiant Palestinians in the Occupied Territories. Cynthia McKinney and Earl Hillard were two of the more prominent among them.[60] The Nation of Islam's spotty record of anti-Semitism and platform of racial separation have not gone unnoticed by some elements of the extreme right.

Much of the previous interaction between the extreme right and Islam that took place in the United States involved a common desire for racial separation. This interaction occurred primarily between elements of the Nation of Islam and various white separatist groups and individuals. There had been previous efforts to work toward common goals. For example, Marcus Garvey discussed plans for black repatriation to Africa with white segregationist groups active during that period. During the civil rights era of the 1960s, two leading Klan organizations, the Invisible Empire and the Knights of the KKK, routinely informed the NOI of their rallies so that it could keep its members from participating in potential counterdemonstrations. The NOI also sought and received Klan support when it bought farmland in the South, keeping white resistance to such efforts at a minimum.[61]

In some ways, the platform of the Nation of Islam is very similar to those of so-called white nationalist Third Positionists that espouse a third way besides capitalism and communism. Both envisage the ideal nation to be a corporate community administered by a strong state. All strata of society are expected to cooperate harmoniously for the good of the collectivity. All members, regardless of class or gender, work together to create an organic new order whose membership is based on race.[62] Toward this end, during the 1980s, the NOI established contact with Tom Metzger and White Aryan Resistance (WAR), the principal proponent of this political orientation in the white separatist movement. In 1985 Metzger flew to Washington, D.C., to meet with Alim Muhammad, the minister of the NOI's mosque in the city. During that meeting, Metzger reportedly offered Muhammad and the NOI a business deal. Metzger supposedly had a friend, an oil expert, who was an ousted high-ranking Liberian public official. Through this former official, who planned on regaining his office, there was a possibility of taking control of an oil-producing company. Metzger suggested a joint WAR-NOI venture. As Metzger and Muhammad were working out the details, Minister Farrakhan was touring West Africa, when a coup attempt against the Liberian government was exposed. According to Metzger, the former Liberian official involved South Africans and four American neo-Nazis in the conspiracy. Farrakhan eventually decided to back away from the deal.[63]

During the late 1980s, elements of the British extreme right also sought to make common cause with the Nation of Islam. For example, publications of the British group the National Front (NF) contained numerous articles lauding Louis Farrakhan and his separatist agenda. The front disavowed the old "negative racism" with its claims of racial supremacy in favor of a new "positive racism" based on respect for other races and group identity. In May 1988 a senior NF official traveled to the United States and was met by American right-wing extremists Mat Malone and Robert Hoy, who had established ties with black separatist organizations. During his U.S. tour, the NF official was invited to Washington, D.C., by Minister Amin Muhammad to study the NOI's drug-busting program.[64] This black-white racialist coalition peaked in 1989, when an NF candidate, Patrick Harrington, backed by black separatists, campaigned in the immigrant-dense Vauxhall district in South London.

Louis Beam, a Vietnam veteran who popularized the leaderless resistance approach in the American extreme right, claims to have established ties with the NOI, as well as supporters in the intelligence community. He purports to have passed on information from sources such as CIA cocaine-trading operations to the NOI for its public use. The Liberty Lobby has on occasion reached out to black separatists, as both parties endeavor to establish their versions of racially homogeneous societies. In 1990, Louis Farrakhan granted an interview to its newspaper, *The Spotlight.*[65]

Mattias Gardell observed that this cooperation marks a major shift in the extreme right's perceptions of blacks and their potential capabilities. Traditionally, the extreme right has viewed blacks as intellectually inferior and as functionally incapable of leading their own struggle. The civil rights movement was considered a Jewish-orchestrated conspiracy that served Jews' nefarious ends. By the 1990s the extreme right looked with awe at the black separatist movement led by Minister Farrakhan, who could mobilize a huge gathering for the Million Man March in 1995, despite the fact that he, like the extreme right, faced fierce opposition from leading Jewish organizations. Thus many white separatists are willing to pass information to elements in the black separatist movement, which they view as more competent, better-organized, and in a better position to make use of it effectively.[66] White separatist leaders express a desire to emulate Farrakhan and the NOI, which has created its own economic infrastructure, including farmland, factories, and retail stores.

There has also been some exchange in the area of literature. For example, the Historical Research Department of the NOI published a book in 1991, *The Secret Relationship between Blacks and Jews.* According to the book's thesis, Jews, more than any other group, were the primary force behind the African slave trade. Another African American academic, Leonard Jeffries, the former head of the Black Studies Department at the City College of CUNY, has propounded a similar thesis alleging that "rich Jews" controlled the slave trade. Numerous extreme right book distributors have sold *The Secret Relationship between Blacks and Jews* because the book's thesis shifts much of the blame for slavery to Jews. The book was at the center of a controversy involving Anthony Martin, a professor of history in the African American Studies Department of Wellesley College. Martin had assigned *The Secret Relationship between Blacks and Jews* as the primary textbook for a course on African American history.[67] Critics such as the ADL argued that the book uses a highly selective reading to argue its thesis. In addition, the NOI makes use of Holocaust revisionist literature. In fact, the author of the revisionist book *The Hoax of the Twentieth Century,* Arthur Butz, was invited to be a guest lecturer at the 1985 NOI convention, and NOI members served as security for revisionist author David Irving at a public lecture in September 1996.[68]

By the 1990s, however, the links between the NOI and white separatists had withered. Farrakhan's fame, which has enabled him to become a national figure and major leader in the black community, has given him access to major national and international players. As such, he has little to gain from an alliance with the marginalized and much maligned American extreme right.

The Nation of Islam's impact on Islam in the United States cannot be overstated. Without its efforts, hundreds of thousands of African Americans who are now Muslims would presumably still be Christians. Furthermore, the NOI has had a significant influence on black popular culture: its message of black empowerment has inspired rap musicians such as Public Enemy. And as we shall see in Chapter 9, Louis Farrakhan has been highly critical of the U.S. government's policies with respect to the war on terror. The "Islamicization" of a significant segment of the African American community could foreshadow significant changes in American politics and society.

One Middle Eastern leader who has sought to use indigenous Muslims as an instrument of foreign policy is Muammar Qaddafi, who has on numerous occasions urged blacks and Native Americans to create an independent and sovereign state inside the United States and has offered to arm and train them to accomplish this goal. Qaddafi has reached out to blacks most often because he believes that they have great revolutionary potential. Furthermore, he sees African Americans as demographically dynamic. Sounding much like white racialists in their fear of black fecundity, Qaddafi wrote the following in "Black People Will Prevail in the World," a section of his revolutionary manifesto, *The Green Book:*

> Black people are now in a very backward social situation, but such backwardness works to bring about their numerical superiority because their low standard of living has shielded them from knowing methods of birth control and family planning. Also, their old social traditions place no limit to marriages, leading to their accelerated growth. The population of others races has decreased because of birth control, restrictions on marriage and continuous occupation in work, unlike the Blacks, who tend to be lethargic in a climate which is continually hot.[69]

Qaddafi has suggested that African Americans who serve in the U.S. military could form the core of such a secessionist movement.[70] Toward this end, Qaddafi has reputedly established warm ties with the NOI, extending his support on several key junctures in the organization's history, including a $5 million interest-free loan in 1985.[71] The late leader of NOI, Elijah Muhammad, along with the legendary boxer, Muhammad Ali, visited Libya in 1972 and personally met with Qaddafi.[72] Reportedly, funding from the Libyan government enabled Farrakhan to rebuild the NOI after the death of Elijah Muhammad. He expressed his appreciation for the Libyan leader: "We've come back by the grace of God and the help of Brother Muammar Khaddafi. This is why we will always love him, admire and respect him and stand up and speak on his behalf."[73]

Other Arab leaders, however, were loath to support the NOI, financially or otherwise. Some Arab leaders were put off by the Nation of Islam's overtly racialist theology, which contradicts the universalism of traditional Islam. Furthermore, some NOI representatives offended the sensibilities of Arab leaders by criticizing the role of Arabs in the African slave trade.[74]

If Muslim leaders find anything about Farrakhan endearing, perhaps it is his often-strident criticism of American foreign policy in the Middle East. He once told a bizarre story of an incident in September 1985 that took place on a mountaintop in Mexico. He claimed that he had a vision of being taken to a massive unidentified flying object, the "Mother Plane," on which he encountered the late Elijah Muhammad, who warned the minister of a putative plan by then President Ronald Reagan and the Joint Chiefs of Staff to wage war in the Middle East. Moved by the experience, Farrakhan traveled to Libya in 1986 to warn Muammar Qaddafi of Reagan's alleged plan. Farrakhan later concluded that the target of the supposed aggression was Muammar Qaddafi, whose capital was bombed by American warplanes in April 1986.[75] What is more, he saw the Gulf War as further confirmation of Elijah Muhammad's message. American authorities have taken notice of Farrakhan's rapport with the Libyan leader. The U.S. Department of Justice once sent a letter to Farrakhan warning him to register as a foreign agent for Libya if he planned to promote Qaddafi.[76]

EL RUKNS

As part of his effort to reach out to African Americans, Qaddafi is reported to have recruited members of a black Chicago street gang known as "El Rukns" to advance his terrorist agenda in the United States. The gang's leader, Jeffrey Fort, was born in Mississippi in 1947. In 1952 he and his mother moved to Chicago. Although Fort had little education—a functional illiterate, he left school after the fourth grade—gang members saw him as a charismatic leader. In 1965 he organized a coalition of gangs and named it the Black P. Stone Nation. At first he attained a certain degree of respectability in his community, as he reached out to youths and tried to channel their efforts into something constructive. His gang was even awarded a $1 million federal grant from the Office of Economic Opportunity for a grassroots education program. However, this outraged then Mayor Richard Daley, and by 1968 the grant was the subject of a U.S. Senate investigation. Fort refused to cooperate with the Senate and consequently was imprisoned for contempt of the Senate and embezzlement of federal funds in 1972.

While in prison, Fort converted to Islam and founded a Moorish religious organization. After his release from prison, Fort decided to change the name of the gang to El Rukns (Arabic for "the foundation") and assumed the more exalted moniker "Prince Malik" for himself. Not long after his release from prison, his organization began to dominate large areas of the black community in Chicago, and he became somewhat of a political force to reckon with. For example, in 1983 the Cook County Democratic organization paid El Rukns $10,000 to campaign in largely African American wards. And in 1984, Reverend Jesse Jackson publicly praised El Rukns for its voter registration drives. During the mid-1980s, El Rukns created goodwill in its community with its efforts to combat the crack cocaine epidemic in Chicago.[77] However, it was not long before Fort was in trouble with the law again; in 1982, he was convicted of participation in a cocaine conspiracy and sentenced to thirteen years in prison. Allegedly, sometime during the mid-1980s, the gang received $2.5 million from Qaddafi to commit acts of terrorism in the United States. In 1987, Fort and four other members of El Rukns were convicted of plotting terrorist acts on behalf of Muammar Qaddafi and Libya. Gang members had allegedly met with Qaddafi and agreed to blow up airplanes and U.S. government buildings in exchange for $2.5 million.[78] Fort was sentenced to eighty years in prison for this conviction.[79]

Footloose American Mujahideen

Since about 1995, it is estimated that somewhere from 1,000 to 2,000 Americans have left the United States to join the ranks of mujahideen fighters overseas. The majority appear to be Arab Americans or Muslims originally from foreign countries, but a fair number are African Americans, who make up roughly one-third of the nation's Muslims.[80] Many of these American jihadists received indoctrination and training in various camps in Pakistan and Afghanistan. In addition to tactical training, these camps also served to bind the international jihadist movement together, helping attendees develop contacts and friendships with like-minded Muslims from around the globe. Until recently, U.S. officials generally have demonstrated little concern about the presence of a fifth column in the diverse Muslim community in the United States. Furthermore, many of these American jihadists have actually fought in conflicts that the U.S. supported or took a neutral position (e.g., the Soviet-Afghan war and the Russian-Chechen wars). Some analysts are less sanguine, however, and warn that the contemporary global jihadist movement is qualitatively different in that it has become more stridently anti-American, anti-Western, and anti-Zionist.

One American jihadist who received considerable attention is Aukai Collins, a native Californian who was born on February 13, 1974. Like several of the other jihadists, he came from a broken family and evinced a high degree of alienation. By the age of fifteen, he was sent to a juvenile camp in San Diego for auto theft. Over time, his crimes escalated, and he was eventually sentenced to eight years in the California Youth Authority, the most feared institution in the California juvenile justice system. While in prison, he became a Muslim.

Upon his release, he became even more involved in Islam and eventually made his way to Chechnya to fight with the mujahideen against the Russians. While in Chechnya, he sustained a serious injury to his leg, which was eventually amputated. Collins would go on to become an informant for the FBI and gather information on the activities of radical Muslim organizations in the United States and their associates overseas.[81]

Perhaps the most notorious American jihadist is John Walker Lindh. Born on February 9, 1981, Lindh grew up in an upper-middle-class family. Like many teenagers, Lindh became an avid fan of so-called gangsta rap. Some of these rap lyrics contained references to Islam, which piqued the interest of the adolescent Lindh. By age fifteen, he exhibited a considerable degree of alienation from his peers and immersed himself in the study of Islam. By age sixteen, he had dropped out of school and started attending various Islamic centers in California. Eventually, he enrolled in an Arab-language school in Yemen. From there he made his way to Pakistan and finally Afghanistan, where he attended al Qaeda training camps and actually met Osama bin Laden, who reportedly thanked the young American for "taking part in jihad."[82] Desperate to demonstrate his commitment, Lindh volunteered to fight with the Taliban against the Northern Alliance. In December 2001, as Operation Enduring Freedom kicked into high gear, American forces apprehended him after an uprising of Taliban and al Qaeda soldiers in Kunduz in which Lindh was included. CIA special forces operative Michael Spann was killed in the fracas. On February 22, 2002, a grand jury in the Eastern District of Virginia handed down a ten-count indictment against Lindh for being an al Qaeda terrorist and conspiring with the Taliban to kill American citizens. Lindh was sentenced to twenty years in prison after pleading guilty to aiding the Taliban movement. He is currently incarcerated at a medium-security federal prison in Victorville, California. In March 2003 it was reported that a member of a white supremacist prison gang assaulted Lindh.[83]

The prospect of a radiological "dirty bomb" detonating in a metropolitan area made headlines with the arrest of Jose Padilla, a Chicago gang member who converted to Islam while in prison. He is alleged to have sought the materials to construct a dirty bomb. After his release from prison in late 1992, U.S. officials charge that Padilla traveled to Afghanistan and Pakistan, where he met senior al Qaeda officials. He was captured on May 8, 2002, as he flew from Pakistan into O'Hare International Airport in Chicago, Illinois. In June 2004, U.S. authorities announced that Padilla had also planned to simultaneously blow up several apartment buildings supplied by natural gas.[84] His arrest also brought attention to the possibility that American prisons could become recruiting grounds for radical Muslim groups such as al Qaeda.[85]

Some African American Muslims have also joined their coreligionists overseas to participate in global jihad. For example, Jibreel al-Amreekee, a young African American convert to Islam who came from a wealthy Atlanta family, took off for Kashmir to fight in jihad. While there, he joined up with Lashkar-i-Taiba (the Righteous Army), the now banned militia allegedly responsible for the attack on the Indian parliament in December 2001. Unfortunately for al-Amreekee, he was killed just two and a half months after he arrived in Kashmir, while participating in an attack on an Indian Army post.

Surprisingly, an American Jew has answered the call to jihad as well. In May 2004, the FBI announced that it wanted to question Adam Yahiye Gadahn, a twenty-five-year old American suspected of having ties to al Qaeda. Gadahn, who also goes by the names Adam Pearlman and Abu Suhayb Al-Amriki, was raised as a Christian by a Jewish father and a Catholic mother on a farm in Riverside County, California. His father, Phil Pearlman, adopted the surname Gadahn after taking up the occupation of a halal butcher. Presumably, the Arabic-sounding name would be more palatable to his customers. A seemingly alienated youth, Gadahn converted to Islam when he was seventeen years old. He eventually made his way to Pakistan and is thought to have served as a translator for al Qaeda. In October 2004, a videotape was released in which a masked man calling himself "Azzam the American" claimed to be a member of al Qaeda and threatened that "the streets of America" would "run with blood."[86]

Several Islamists and their sympathizers are suspected to have sojourned in the U.S. armed forces. The most serious and committed of the American jihadists appears to be Isa Abdullah Ali. Born on September 13, 1956, Ali grew up in Washington, D.C. In 1970, at the age of fourteen, he dropped out of high school and was able to join the army by lying about his age. By 1973, he had completed his Special Forces training and became a member of the elite Green Berets. He served four months in Vietnam, after which he was transferred to South Korea, where he concluded his three-year enlistment. Soon thereafter, he converted to Islam and eventually joined a Shi'ite sect. In December 1980, Ali decided to take action, leaving his family and departing to Lebanon, where he fought against the Israelis. An accomplished sniper, Ali reportedly killed at least five Israelis and wounded four others. During the mid-1990s, the North Atlantic Treaty Organization reportedly issued intelligence warnings that Ali was fighting alongside Islamic fundamentalists in the war in Bosnia-Herzegovina.[87]

A more recent example of a U.S. serviceman with Islamist sympathies is the case of army sergeant Hasan K. Akbar, who is alleged to have thrown a live grenade into a tent his fellow soldiers were occupying in Kuwait, just after the start of the Iraq war. Two officers were killed, and fourteen other soldiers were wounded.[88] In another case, federal authorities investigated a non-U.S. citizen and naval reservist on suspicion of his having ties to militant Islamic groups with possible connections to al Qaeda. Semi Osman was arrested on May 17, 2002, on charges of trying to illegally become a U.S. citizen and possessing a handgun whose serial number was either obliterated or altered. A federal grand jury was investigating whether Osman and other members of the now defunct Dar-us-salaan and Taqwa mosques in Seattle had aligned themselves with Sheikh Abu Hamza al-Masri, a London cleric suspected by Western authorities of recruiting for al Qaeda.[89] Although Osman was not charged as a terrorist, a search warrant issued by the U.S. District Court in Seattle noted that evidence collected from his apartment constitutes "material support for terrorists" (e.g., Islamic and anti-American literature, military instruction manuals, survival gear, and handguns). Osman had briefly served in the U.S. Army in 1998. Although no U.S. service members have been publicly linked to a terrorist group since September 11, 2001, Larry Johnson, a former deputy director at the State Department's Office of Counterterrorism, remarked that infiltrating the U.S. military would be "an intelligence bonanza" for terrorist groups.[90]

Still another soldier, Army National Guard specialist Ryan Gibson Anderson, was charged in February 2004 for allegedly attempting to pass intelligence to U.S. military personnel who posed as al Qaeda operatives. Anderson, a tank crewmember of the 81st Armor Brigade based at Fort Lewis, Washington, allegedly sought to provide information about U.S. Army troop strength, movements, equipment, tactics, and weapon systems, as well as methods by which to kill U.S. Army personnel and vulnerabilities of army weapons systems and equipment. Several years earlier, Anderson had sought out right-wing militia organizations on a Usenet newsgroup. However, he later lost interest in the militias and became highly critical of the movement. He later converted to Islam and assumed the Arabized name "Amir Abdul Rashid."[91]

The most recent former American soldier to have gained attention for answering the call to jihad is Rizvan Chitigov, who graduated from an elite U.S. subversion and reconnaissance school and once served on a contract basis in a U.S. Marine battalion. Chitigov arrived in the United States in the early 1990s from his native Chechnya. He returned to Chechnya in 1994 and fought under the famed warlord Ibn-ul-Khattab. Known by his comrades as "the American," Chitigov attained prominence in the Chechen struggle for independence. He was active in the second campaign in Grozny and managed to escape to the mountains of Georgia. Intelligence information acquired indicated that he planned to use chemical and biological weapons against Russian armed forces, thus earning him a new moniker, "the chemist." Chitigov would go on to become the third most influential warlord in Chechnya after Shamil

Basayev and Doku Umarov, but his luck ran out in March 2004, when he was killed in action in the district center in Shali.[92]

Islamic Lone Wolves in the United States

Islamist terrorists were responsible for the most lethal terrorist attacks against American interests overseas during the 1990s.[93] However, it is worth noting that there have been scattered episodes of what resembles "lone wolf" Islamic terrorism in the United States.

- In 1968 at the Democratic Party Convention, a Lebanese immigrant, Sirhan Sirhan, assassinated presidential candidate Robert Kennedy. Sirhan was angry with Kennedy for his pro-Israeli foreign policy positions.
- On March 9, 1977, Hamaas Abdul Khaalis and twelve other members of a group of Hanafi Muslims, of which he was the leader, stormed three Washington, D.C., buildings. Then D.C. councilman and future mayor Marion Barry was wounded by a shotgun blast to the chest. Another blast killed Maurice Williams, a reporter for the WHUR-FM radio station. Still another victim, Bob Pierce, was left paralyzed from a wound he received during the attack. A total of 149 people were taken hostage, most of whom were held at the office of the Jewish B'nai B'rith organization.[94]
- In Maryland on June 22, 1980, a member of a small group called the Islamic Guerrillas of America, Doud Salahuddin, assassinated Ali Akbar Tabatabai at his Bethesda home. Tabatabai was an outspoken critic of the Ayatollah Ruhollah Khomeini and the founder of an anti-Khomeini group called the Iran Freedom Foundation.[95] Salahuddin was born David Belfield in North Carolina on November 10, 1950. As a student at Howard University, he converted to Islam and changed his name.[96]
- In Colorado on October 14, 1980, Eugene Tafoya, a former Green Beret and Vietnam veteran recruited by Libya, attempted to assassinate Faisal Zagallai, a Libyan graduate student attending Colorado State University. Zagallai was severely injured but fortunately survived the attack.[97]
- Near Hawaii on August 11, 1982, a bomb placed beneath a passenger's seat exploded on a Pan Am jumbo jet en route from Tokyo's Narita Airport. The crew recovered from the blast and landed safely in Honolulu. However, a sixteen-year-old Japanese youth was killed, and fourteen others were injured. The May 15 Arab Organization is believed to have been responsible for the attack.[98]

- On January 25, 1993, Mir Aimal Kansi ambushed employees making their way to work at the stoplight in front of the CIA's main headquarters in Langley, Virginia. Two CIA employees were killed in the attack. Kansi allegedly told a roommate that he was angry over the treatment of Muslims in Bosnia and was going to get even by shooting at CIA headquarters, the White House, and the Israeli Embassy.[99]
- In Missouri on October 24, 1994, three members of the Abu Nidal organization were sentenced to twenty-one months in prison for plotting terrorism in the United States. Allegedly the three men planned to kill Jews and bomb the Israeli Embassy in Washington, D.C.[100]
- On March 1, 1994, Rashid Baz, a Lebanese cabdriver, opened fire on a van carrying fifteen Jewish students across the Brooklyn Bridge. One student was killed, and two were seriously wounded. Baz, a veteran of the Lebanese civil war, sought revenge for the shooting rampage of the American-born settler, Dr. Baruch Goldstein, who had recently killed thirty Muslims in a West Bank mosque.[101]
- On November 29, 1995, Muhammad Ali, a New York City cabdriver and an undocumented alien from Pakistan, approached Rudolph Giuliani in Manhattan and threatened to kill him because the mayor had snubbed Palestine Liberation Organization leader Yasser Arafat by ordering him removed from a concert at Lincoln Center. Ali pled guilty to charges in 1996.[102]
- In New York City on February 23, 1997, Ali Hassan Abu Kamal, a mentally disturbed sixty-nine-year old Palestinian teacher, opened fire on the deck of the Empire State Building, killing one tourist and injuring six others. He committed suicide soon thereafter. Reportedly, Kamal sought revenge for the treatment of Palestinians by the United States and Israel.[103]
- In July 1997, the New York City police arrested Ghazi Ibrahim abu Mezer for allegedly planning to bomb the subway system.[104]
- On December 14, 1999, U.S. Customs agents in Washington State apprehended Ahmed Ressam as he attempted to enter the United States from Canada. U.S. Customs Inspector Diana Dean pulled Ressam's car over and noticed that he was sweating profusely despite the fact that the weather was very cold. Agents found 103 pounds of explosives in his car. A search of his apartment in Montreal turned up a map of California with circles around the airports in Los Angeles, Long Beach, and Ontario.[105] It later transpired that Ressam was not only a former member of the Armed Islamic Group in Algeria but also a current member of al Qaeda and had allegedly plotted to attack LAX in Los Angeles. The fact that Ressam was a dark-skinned Algerian was also troubling for authorities. Director of Central Intelligence George Tenet

took this fact as a warning that the CIA had to look not just for Arab faces but also black African faces in their counterterrorism operations.[106]

- On July 4, 2002, Hesham Mohamed Hadayet, an Egyptian-born immigrant, approached the El Al airline ticket counter at Los Angeles International Airport and fired two handguns at employees. Two persons were killed, and another three were wounded before El Al guards tackled and killed him.[107] The FBI would later designate the incident as a terrorist attack.[108]
- In February 2005, Abu Ali was detained in Saudi Arabia and accused of conspiring to assassinate President George Bush and supporting al Qaeda. Ali was born in Houston, Texas, and graduated as a valedictorian of the Islamic Saudi Academy in Alexandria, Virginia.[109]

Of course, Islamic terrorism in the United States culminated in the events of September 11, 2001, when nineteen Muslim hijackers rammed planes into both towers of the World Trade Center and the Pentagon. A fourth plane, United Airlines Flight 93, crashed in a field in upstate Pennsylvania, presumably en route to an attack on the Capitol building in Washington, D.C.[110] Nearly 3,000 people lost their lives at the World Trade Center, and another 125 perished at the Pentagon. One of the principal organizers, Abu Zubaydah, recruited Muhammad Atta to be the leader of the nineteen hijackers. Zubaydah was also identified as the field commander for the October 11, 2000, attack on the USS *Cole* in the Yemeni port of Aden, which killed seventeen sailors.[111] Atta's terrorist cell originally formed in Germany nearly three years prior to the 9/11 attacks. From the start, he was in charge of the cell that would go on to gain infamy on September 11, 2001, and usher in the war on terror.

Conclusion

Since 1990, the Islamist movement in the United States has become far more active and is an invaluable source for recruitment and fund-raising. The United States remains a suitable target to strike back at perceived enemies of Islam. Islam has become one of the fastest-growing religions in the United States, partly because of immigration and partly because of conversion, most notably in the African American community. This development has not gone unnoticed by Muslims in other parts of the world. Since the 1980s, Saudi and Pakistani groups have reportedly reached out to African American Muslims, in particular by offering scholarships to study Arabic and Islam in their countries. After receiving education, they are then recruited by the more militant groups.[112]

U.S. authorities are concerned about the prospect that Islamic terrorists might strike Jewish targets in the United States. Just as the Jewish diaspora supported Israel, Muslim terrorists justified their attacks on Jewish targets outside Israel. The terrorist attacks on the synagogue in Istanbul in 1986 and the Argentine Israeli Mutual Association (AIMA) building in Argentina in 1994 come to mind as examples. In June 2002, the FBI advised local law enforcement agencies to be on the lookout for terrorists who may try to use oil tankers to attack Jewish neighborhoods and synagogues. This warning was based on information culled from interviews with captured al Qaeda and Taliban fighters who indicated that such plots had been discussed.[113]

It is also worth noting that Islamists have established a significant presence in many Western countries besides the United States. In the United Kingdom, London has become an important stronghold for the global jihadist movement, most notably in the areas of propaganda and recruitment. Some radical Islamists go so far as to refer to the English city as "Londonistan." The website Azzam.com has been in the forefront in fund-raising, selling books edited by Sheikh Rahman and another written by bin Laden's mentor, Abdullah Azzam. Most notable among the Islamists in Britain is Khalid al-Fawwaz, allegedly a trusted friend of Osama bin Laden. Bin Laden is reported to have sent al-Fawwaz to London in 1994 to manage al Qaeda's Advice and Reformation Committee (ARC) office on Beethoven Street. ARC became an important public relations vehicle for bin Laden and helped communicate his message to the rest of the world. Several other important radical Islamist clerics residing in Britain include Omar Barki Muhammad, Omar Mahmud Othman, and Moustapha Kame. Their sermons have attracted many young Muslims, including the accused twentieth 9/11 hijacker, Zacarias Moussaoui, and the failed shoe bomber, Richard Reid. Authorities estimate that Britain-based militant groups have sent from 1,000 to 2,000 Muslim men to fight for Islamic causes worldwide.[114] Mounting pressure in the wake of 9/11 has finally galvanized British authorities into action. As a result, the Islamists now appear to keep a much lower profile.[115]

The significance of Islam in the West cannot be overstated. In fact, some observers now suspect that trends in the West, such as identity politics, are actually furthering the development of militant Islam. After all, the nineteen hijackers responsible for 9/11 were not radicalized in the Middle East but rather during their time in the West. In his research sample of mujahideen who had spent time in the West, Marc Sageman noted that many of them experienced underemployment, which compounded their loneliness while away from home. Conceivably, these problems contributed to their sense of grievance and frustration, especially since many were well-educated and talented.[116] The esteemed French scholar of Islam, Olivier Roy, argues that the new breed of

Islam resembles contemporary variants of spirituality in the West, with their emphasis on finding meaning in their believers' lives. Cut off from families and acquaintances while in the West, young Muslims experience a sense of anomie and alienation and thus find solace in attaching themselves to a "virtual umma." Islam is presented as a cure for the ills of modern life and the vehicle through which to attain a larger sense of identity. Previously, the West offered numerous ideologies, such as nationalism and Marxism, that were attractive to Muslim immigrants. However, "with the old political frameworks gone, the West is unable to furnish the ideologies to go along with the process of Westernization."[117] Consequently, Islam is embraced as a worldview to help people cope in a dislocated world.

In her classic study, *The Terror Network,* Claire Sterling asserted that for much of the period from the late 1960s to the early 1980s (the time during which she wrote the book), the Soviet Union was at the center of a global terrorist apparatus. With the end of the Cold War, left-wing terrorism went into steep decline. Left-wing extremist groups lost a credible ideology and material support from communist states in the East and also their client states such as Cuba.[118] There is substantial documentary evidence to suggest that terrorism was an important instrument of Soviet statecraft. As Paul Pillar pointed out, Soviet-supported terrorism was designed to advance the influence of the communist superpower. However, there is no comparable situation today because none of the major world powers (e.g., Russia, China, the European Union, or Japan) displays any hint of supporting terrorism directed at the United States. Although state sponsors of terrorism exist, they are at least another tier lower in the global hierarchy of power. Furthermore, in an era of U.S.-dominated globalization, states presumably would have more to gain by accommodation with the West rather than confrontation.[119] However, much of the Islamic world has demonstrated an extreme reluctance toward, if not outright resistance to, assimilation into the new world order, which serves as a powerful vehicle to homogenize various regional cultures. In opposition to this development—Benjamin Barber described it as jihad versus McWorld—has emerged a loosely organized mass movement, which could be called the "Islamist international."

As one observer noted, the Islamist international terrorist network resembles the Comintern, which lasted from 1919 to 1943. However, the Comintern had a central leadership, which the Islamist international does not. Rather, the latter is bound together by a common ideology and operates on the principle of leaderless resistance, not unlike terrorist elements of the American radical right.[120] Arguably, militant Islam is the only movement in contemporary global politics that is mounting a significant challenge to the inexorability of globalization and the new world order. The spirit and determination of the jihadists have not gone unnoticed by other dissident movements around the world. Some elements of the extreme right look with envy at the strength and broad-based support of militant Islam. Furthermore, the stridency of the Islamists' anti-Zionism and their critique of American "cultural decadence" have resonated with the extreme right. Not surprisingly, the two movements have discovered that they share some common views. In the next chapter I explore the interaction between militant Islam and the extreme right.

CHAPTER FIVE

Interaction between the Extreme Right and Islamic/Arab Extremists

In the summer of 2002, *The Sum of All Fears,* a popular movie based on a Tom Clancy novel, was released. The plot centers on a global cabal of neofascists that acquires the materials and expertise to construct a nuclear weapon and ultimately detonate it in Baltimore, Maryland. Their aim was to instigate a global conflict between the United States and Russia, thus eliminating the two principal historical opponents of fascism. Early in the film, Arabs scavenging in the desert stumble upon an undetonated nuclear warhead, which was once part of a cargo of an Israeli jet that was blown out of the sky by a missile twenty-nine years earlier during the 1973 war. Originally, in Clancy's 1991 novel, Muslim extremists, not neofascists, were the villains. What is interesting is the ease with which the two villains could be switched in popular culture.

Shortly after 9/11, the United States was beset with a second round of terrorist attacks in the form of anthrax-laden letters sent to Senator Tom Daschle (D-SD) and various representatives of the media. According to one account, some top Central Intelligence Agency (CIA) and Federal Bureau of Investigation (FBI) officials suspected that domestic extremists were responsible for the anthrax attacks.[1] Perhaps the chief reason for this suspicion was that several years earlier, Larry Wayne Harris, a microbiologist by training and reputed extreme right sympathizer, had previously been arrested for possessing what authorities believed was the anthrax agent. The FBI's investigation this time focused on Dr. Steven J. Hatfill, who once worked as a research scientist at the U.S. Army Medical Research Institute of Infectious Diseases at Fort Detrick, Maryland. Hatfill had spent considerable time in South Africa and was affiliated with the Afrikaner Resistance Movement (AWB). However, after a thorough investigation, the FBI essentially cleared Hatfill of any connection to the anthrax attacks.

Some elements of the extreme right went so far as to laud the anthrax attacks. On the Aryan Update section of the White Aryan Resistance website, one post enthused: "Is there not a single person who has received these anthrax letters that isn't an avowed enemy of the white race? Tom Brokaw, Tom

Daschle, and the gossip rag offices have all been 100 percent legitimate targets. Who among us has the slightest bit of sympathy for these pukes?"[2]

Interestingly, the National Alliance later published an article in its journal alleging that the Israeli intelligence agency, Mossad, was responsible for the anthrax letters. The apparent motive was to implicate Iraq, thus justifying war against that Arab country.[3] For its part, the Anti-Defamation League (ADL) issued a report warning of the possibility of a bioterrorism attack by domestic extremist groups.[4]

Cooperation between the Third Reich and Islam

The genesis of the cooperation between militant Islam and the extreme right can be traced back to the early years of the Third Reich. During World War II, much of the Islamic world sympathized with the Axis alliance. Members of the Muslim Brotherhood would often say prayers for an Axis victory during their meetings. Moreover, some Muslims went so far as to fantasize over putative Islamic affinities of fascist leaders. For example, rumors abounded that Benito Mussolini was an Egyptian Muslim whose real name was Musa Nili (Moses of the Nile) and that Adolf Hitler too had secretly converted to Islam and bore the name Hayder, or "the brave one."[5]

The Islamic-fascist alliance was best exemplified by the cordial relationship between Hitler and the grand mufti of Jerusalem, Haj Amin al-Husseini. Perhaps no other figure did more to foster ties between right-wing extremism and militant Islam than he, as his ideology informed both pan-Arabism and militant Islam. As such, his life warrants closer examination. He was born in Jerusalem around 1895, when Palestine was a subsector of the Ottoman Empire. His family was part of a wealthy and prominent Jerusalem Arab clan. He studied Islamic law for about one year at the prestigious Al-Azhar University in Cairo. At the outbreak of World War I in 1914, al-Husseini joined the Ottoman Turkish Army, serving as an artillery officer stationed with the Forty-Seventh Brigade until November 1916, after which he returned to Jerusalem and remained on disability for the duration of the war. As a young man, he became an ardent believer in the imperial pan-Arab principle. As such, he would serve as a bridge carrying over imperialist ideas of Islam and Ottoman Turkey into modern times.[6]

Al-Husseini was a strident opponent of Jewish settlement in Palestine and used his considerable organizational and rhetorical talents to mobilize against the Zionist movement in Palestine. In April 1920, he gained notoriety when his followers went on a rampage at the festival of Nebi Musa, during which 5

Jews and 4 Arabs were killed and 211 Jews and 21 Arabs were injured. He is credited with having introduced the first modern fedayeen (Arabic for "one who is ready to sacrifice his life for his cause") suicide squads, which primarily targeted moderate Arabs who refused to support his agenda.[7] Despite this record of incitement, the British appointed him grand mufti in 1922. On August 23, 1929, he led a second massacre of Jews in Hebron, followed by a third massacre in 1936.[8] Al-Husseini's immediate aim was to halt Jewish immigration into Palestine. His anti-Jewish and anti-British activities dovetailed with Hitler's policies during this period. By 1937 al-Husseini expressed support for Nazi Germany and requested assistance in his struggle against Jews.

During the 1930s, the Third Reich had received entreaties from the Arab world. After the Nazi government promulgated the Nuremberg Laws in 1936, which greatly diminished the legal citizenship status of Jews, telegrams of support were sent to Hitler from all over the Arab and Islamic world.[9] These entreaties notwithstanding, the German government initially demonstrated a surprising lack of interest in the Arab world and its affairs. However, this attitude changed in 1937 with the publication of a report by the British Royal Commission, which explicitly recommended for the first time the partition of Palestine into separate Jewish and Arab states. The German minister of foreign affairs at that time, Konstantin von Neurath, issued instructions to German legations that explained new directives of the German government, which feared that the formation of a Jewish state under a British mandate would not be in Germany's interest insofar as it would create an additional position of power under international law for international Jewry, somewhat like the Vatican state for political Catholicism or Moscow for the Comintern. Germany therefore had an interest in strengthening the Arab world as a counterweight against such a possible increase in power for world Jewry.[10]

The Nazi regime also made overtures to Afghanistan during the 1930s and initially established good diplomatic relations with the Afghan government. The Germans even attempted to establish a political alliance with Mullah Mirza Ali Khan of Ipi, who, along with his Waziri mujahideen, resisted British rule of the Northwestern Province of Afghanistan from 1936 to 1947. In 1941 German envoys were sent to Gurwekht, which was a stronghold of Patani Islamic guerrilla action inside the British zone of occupied Sarhad. They brought with them money and a letter of support from Adolf Hitler. However, when the emissaries were en route to Kabul, they were ambushed by British soldiers, who killed one. The Afghan border police captured the others. The Afghan monarch was well aware of what happened to pro-German Iran, which was invaded by British forces. Seeking to avert a similar fate, he expelled German and Italian diplomats from his country.[11]

Nazi Germany's war against the British Empire electrified much of the Islamic world, whose people viewed it as a noble struggle against imperialism. Furthermore, Germany and the Arab world shared the same enemies (England, Zionism, and communism). The early victories of Field Marshal Erwin Rommel's Afrika Korps raised the hopes of Arabs seeking to establish independence. Some Arabs from North Africa volunteered to aid the German war effort, as evidenced by the creation of various Arab auxiliary units, including Freikorps Arabien (Arab Free Corps), the Kommando Deutsch-Arabischer Truppen (German-Arab Commando Troops), and the Deutsche-Arabisches Infanterie Battalion 845 (German-Arab Infantry Battalion 845). After the war, remnants of these units would go on to join the anticolonial struggle in Algeria.[12]

After the Wehrmacht invaded Poland in 1939, France and England declared war on Germany, thus commencing World War II in the European theater. Al-Husseini realized that his pro-Nazi activities could land him in a British jail. He therefore decided to seek refuge in Iraq, where he found an ally in Rashid Ali al-Gilani, who became prime minister of that country in March 1940. Al-Husseini had previously been involved in Iraq; in October 1939 he went to Baghdad and met with the Committee of Free Arabs, which was led by the so-called colonels of the Golden Square, to discuss plans for a revolution against the British. The Free Arabs demanded an immediate cessation of Jewish immigration to Palestine and a crackdown on violence perpetrated by Zionist organizations such as Betar, led by Vladimir Jabotinski.[13] In October 1940, representatives of the Free Arabs signed an Axis-Arab Manifesto of Liberation in Berlin. Both Hitler and Mussolini expressed strong support for an independent, united Arab nation. Al-Husseini would go on to become the spiritual leader of the Mutamar al-Alam al-Isami (the Islamic World League), a group that sought to establish Arab independence from Britain. Grand Mufti al-Husseini worked hard to win a pledge of Arab support for the Axis powers. While in Iraq, he helped organize the new government led by Rashid Ali al-Gilani and the current minister of justice, Nadif Shaukat. Al-Gilani appointed Nur Said as his new foreign minister, a choice that would later doom his short-lived regime, when the latter conspired with the British embassy. Previously, in June, Said had helped to negotiate the German-Arab Peace and Cooperation Treaty in Ankara, Turkey. On January 31, 1941, British prime minister Winston Churchill ordered the removal of al-Gilani, and a power struggle ensued over the control of the new Iraqi government. Nur Said and Abdullah bin Ali briefly seized power with British support. However, a coup d'état on April 1, 1941, restored al-Gilani to the position of prime minister. Abdullah and Nur Said escaped to Amman, Jordan. Soon thereafter, Germany recognized the new Iraqi government led by al-Gilani. On May 12, 1941, al-Gilani declared independence from Great Britain. In doing so, he sparked a greater anticolonial uprising of nationalist Muslims in Palestine, Syria, and Egypt. One of the coup plotters was an Iraqi officer named Khairallah Tulfah—the future father-in-law of Saddam Hussein.[14]

Al-Gilani's second regime was also short-lived, however, as British forces quickly deposed it, but not before troops and policeman loyal to al-Gilani carried out a pogrom in which roughly 200 Jews were killed. By May 29, the British Army had seized Baghdad and reinstalled Nur Said as the Iraqi leader. To show his gratitude, Nur declared war against Germany in January 1943.

Seeking to find a more hospitable location, the mufti sought refuge in Persia. The nationalist general Shah Reza Pahlavi, who seized power in 1925, was an admirer of Adolf Hitler's racial policies and even went so far as to rename his county Iran, which translates into Aryan in Persian. However, with the arrival of British and American troops in October 1941, the mufti was forced once again to relocate. He finally made his way to Nazi Germany, where he lived for the remainder of the war.

In November 1941, al-Husseini traveled to Berlin, where he met Hitler and offered his full support. Reichsfürher Heinrich Himmler and Foreign Minister Joachim von Ribbentrop helped prepare the meeting. In doing so, he forged an alliance between Nazi Germany and the Palestine Arab High Command, which al-Husseini led. According to some accounts, this meeting was the genesis of Nazi-style anti-Semitism as a mass movement in the Arab world.[15] Hitler recognized al-Husseini as the leader of the Arab world and pledged to install him as the Arab führer when the time was feasible. Al-Husseini remained in Berlin during the course of the war and was treated as a foreign dignitary. According to Ahmed Huber, a Swiss national depicted as a liaison between the contemporary extreme right and militant Islam, the grand mufti had many conversations with Hitler, including the one below, which Huber related to me:

The Grand Mufti of Jerusalem, Haj Amin el-Husseini, whom I met in 1965 in Beirut, we had a long talk. He told me many, many interesting things, because he had an almost friendship relationship with Adolf Hitler. He told me a fantastic story. On one night in December 1941, after the big victories of Germany over the Soviet Union, he had a long talk with Hitler about architecture, culture, the music of Richard Wagner, and so on. Hitler started talking about race theory and anti-Semitism and the Grand Mufti asked Hitler, "Did you ever think, Mr. Chancellor, that your race theory comes out of Judaism? It comes out of the Old Testament." And Hitler was very astonished by that. The Grand Mufti knew the Bible very well. He said, "All of your ideas, the doctrine of the Nazi Party are in the Old Testament. The chosen people of God are not the chosen people, but the chosen race and that blood carries the soul. And this chosen race must keep its blood pure. It must not mix its blood with non-Jews; the foreigners, the subhuman beasts called the goyim, are inferior to the Jewish master race. The genocide order of God in the fifth book of Moses and in the book of Joshua. The race laws of Ezra and Ishmael. All of these things are in the Old Testament." Hitler was absolutely astonished, and the Mufti told him [further], "You have not high esteem for the Africans, for Black people. And also this comes from the Old Testament in the first book of Moses, the Black race is doomed, considered by God to eternal slavery. It's the famous curse by God on Ham, one of the three sons of the prophet Noah. . . ."

So when the Mufti told Hitler another story, he said, "You, Mr. Chancellor, hate the Roman Catholic Church," [to which] Hitler responded, "Really?" [The Mufti replied], "Yes it's true, but you, Mr. Hitler, you never left the church. You are still formally a member of the Roman Catholic Church." Then the Mufti added, "Mr. Chancellor, you have organized your party like the Roman Catholic Church. You are the pope. Your *Gauleiters* and *Reichsleiters* are the cardinals and the archbishops. And your party congresses . . . are [like] high masses— religious ceremonies—which you celebrate as the high priest." Hitler became furious and walked out. And for three weeks the Mufti could not come back in. After three weeks the Mufti had to go to the Reichschancellary in Berlin, and he told me, "There I thought he [Hitler] would arrest me and shout at me." Hitler came and smiled at the Mufti, put his hands around his arms, and said, "Your eminence, I want to apologize to you. I behaved like an uneducated little boy." He said, "I have read the Bible and thought about what you said and now that final victory is close, Moscow will fall in a few weeks, and the Soviet Union will be gone, and then final victory will come. We must talk about all these things and try to make some changes in our ideology." And, of course, final victory never came, but Hitler dedicated a text to Christoph Schroeder and Frau Junge, his secretary, which is called the Hitler-Bormann Documents, or the Testament of Adolf Hitler. In this text, Hitler makes a criticism of his policies.[16]

For his part, Hitler was very proud of his stature among Muslims and, near the war's end, regretted that he had not done more to take advantage of this alliance.[17] Hitler even went so far as to accept the grand mufti as an "honorary Aryan" because of the red beard and blue eyes that he presumably inherited from his Circassian mother.[18] To support Hitler's war efforts, al-Husseini traveled to Bosnia in 1943 and helped organize the Waffen-SS Handschar Division in Yugoslavia, which was composed of Bosnian Muslim volunteers.[19] According to one estimate, approximately 100,000 European Muslims fought for the Third Reich during the course of World War II.[20] To further recruitment, al-Husseini wrote a book titled *Islam and the Jews,* which was distributed to Bosnian Muslim SS units during the war as motivational literature to incite the slaughter not only of Jews but also of Serbs.[21] Balkan Muslims were encouraged to identify themselves spiritually as Muslim and Arab but racially as German.[22] Al-Husseini also made a number of radio broadcasts to the Arab world, urging his fellow Arabs to support the Nazi cause. In appreciation for his services, al-Husseini was elected as the supreme sheikh-ul Islam (supreme religious leader) of the Muslim troops of the Axis.[23]

The German military also found Muslim supporters in territory that it had conquered in the Soviet Union. Once again, al-Husseini was instrumental in this effort. The German occupation government garnered some goodwill from the local Muslim populations by reconstructing mosques that had been destroyed by the Soviets. Furthermore, German authorities actually restored the institution of the mufti, which had been abolished by the Bolsheviks not long after the Russian Revolution. According to one estimate, over 500,000 Muslim Turkomans, Tadjiks, and Uzbeks from the Central Asian Soviet republics volunteered to fight on the side of the Third Reich. More than 180,000 Muslims were recruited to fight from the Caucasus, Crimea, and Itil-Ural Tataristan. Many of these Muslim soldiers came from Lithuania and Latvia and became known as "Askaris."[24] Reportedly, the Islamic Waffen-SS fought in the battle of Stalingrad.

In 1945, the German military founded the Nordkaukasischer Waffengruppe (North Caucus Armed Group) for Muslim volunteers from Chechnya, Ingushetia, and Ossetia. They were organized into nineteen independent Islamic combat battalions and twenty-four infantry companies in the Wehrmacht. Furthermore, Muslim Turks and Tartars formed a Waffen-SS division known as the Ostturkisches Waffenverband (East Turkish Armed League) and SS-Waffengruppe "Turkestan" (SS Armed Turkestan Group). Many Muslim soldiers had been recruited from Soviet labor camps by SS-Sturmbannführer Andreas Mayer. Mayer died from a Soviet sniper's bullet in 1944 while conducting antipartisan operations in Belarus. He was replaced by Haupsturnführer Billig, who ordered an execution of seventy-eight Muslim mutineers. This reprisal angered many Muslim soldiers and caused the immediate desertion of hundreds of soldiers. In April 1944, Billig was replaced by SS-Standartenführer Haruan al-Rashid (William Hintersatz), an Austrian convert to Islam. He led several Muslim units in battle against partisans in the Warsaw uprising in April 1943.[25]

During the war, Germany's Muslim allies and the pro-Muslim lobby in Berlin, led by al-Husseini, adamantly opposed any plan to expel Jews from Eastern Europe to Palestine.[26] Some researchers believe that al-Husseini may have played a major role in the Holocaust because he discouraged authorities in Germany as well as pro-Nazi governments in Romania, Hungary, and Bulgaria from allowing Jews to immigrate to Palestine.[27] In 1937, the head of the Sicherheitsdienst (Security Service), Reinhard Heydrich, sent a special envoy, which included Adolf Eichmann, to Jerusalem to meet with al-Husseini to discuss Jewish immigration into Palestine. The Nazi government was ambivalent toward Jewish immigration into Palestine. Hitler believed that it was an expedient measure that would allow him to more easily expel Jews from Germany, but he was hostile to the notion of Zionism and the creation of a Jewish state, which he believed would become a base for Jewish power in the world. Furthermore, support for Jewish immigration would alienate his Muslim supporters in the Middle East. Be that as it may, there is evidence that there was limited cooperation between the Nazis and Zionists on this issue.[28]

Despite some mutual admiration, the interests of the Axis powers and the Islamic world were not always symmetrical. For example, the grand mufti's demands for Arab self-determination conflicted with the colonial interests of fascist Italy and Vichy France, both of which were Germany's wartime allies. Al-Husseini urged Hitler to make a public declaration in support of Arab independence. He believed such a gesture would galvanize the Arab world and prepare them for a revolt against British forces. However, as Hitler explained to al-Husseini in a meeting, at that time Germany was enmeshed in a life-and-death struggle with Great Britain and the Soviet Union and could not spare manpower for deployment in the Middle East. Therefore, for strategic reasons, Hitler refrained from making a formal declaration supporting Arab independence.[29] Hitler believed that pressing too hard for Arab independence would bolster the influence of Charles De Gaulle, the commander of the Free French Forces. The declaration, Hitler feared, might have impelled the French to make common cause with England to save their colonial empire. Such an uprising would have required Hitler to divert a portion of his armed forces to the west that were desperately needed in the east at that time.[30] However, after victory over the Soviet Union, Hitler promised the grand mufti that one of Germany's principal objectives would be to destroy the Jewish element residing in the Arab sphere under the protection of the British and French colonial administrations. With his eastern front secure, Hitler would be indifferent to French reaction to such measures and would thus voice unbridled support for Arab self-determination.[31] Hitler gave al-Husseini his word that he would make such a declaration and provide material support to the Arabs once German forces crossed over the Caucasus Mountains and extended their reach into the Middle East.[32] Furthermore, he would recognize the grand mufti as the leader of the Arab world.

The grand mufti stayed in Berlin until nearly the end of the war and, while there, played a significant role in the formation of the Arab League in 1944.[33] Just three days before Hitler's suicide, the SS offered to provide him with a plane with which to escape to Switzerland, in the hope that he would eventually make his way to North Africa, where he had established spy networks that were still extant.[34] Instead, he purchased a car and drove to the Swiss border, where he was denied entrance and arrested by the occupying French forces. He remained under house arrest until 1946, when despite demands from the Yugoslav government that he be extradited to face charges of war crimes, he was allowed to escape to Egypt, where he received a warm welcome.[35] Although the grand mufti died in 1974, he had an enduring influence on subsequent Arab and Muslim leaders, most notably his distant cousin Yasser Arafat, who would go on to become the leader of the Palestine Liberation Organization (PLO). According to one researcher, al-Husseini was the true founder of Fatah, the militant arm of the PLO.[36] Notwithstanding the defeat of the Axis powers, National Socialism would continue to inspire Arab nationalists after the war.

NATIONAL SOCIALISM AS A MODEL FOR ARAB NATIONALISM

Many Arab nationalists looked to Germany for inspiration during the 1930s and 1940s and saw National Socialism as a viable model for state building. Hitler's *Mein Kampf* found a receptive readership in parts of the Arabic world. Many aspiring Arab leaders sought to emulate the German führer and his National Socialist movement. As far back as 1933, Arab nationalists in Syria and Iraq embraced National Socialism. In Egypt, a protofascist organization, Young Egypt, also known as the Green Shirts, attracted many army officers.[37] The grand mufti is believed to have been instrumental in the group's formation.[38] Members, including young lieutenant colonel and future Egyptian president Anwar Sadat, along with Wing Commander Hassan Ibrahim and General Aziz al-Masri, attempted to execute a scheme in World War II in which they would link up with Rommel's Afrika Korps and supply them with secret information on British strategy and troop movements.[39] Although hopes of a pan-German and pan-Arab alliance would be dashed with the defeat of Rommel, his early military successes gained admiration from the Arab population that endured even after the war.

In 1953 rumors spread in the Middle East that Hitler might still be alive and living in Brazil. This prompted *Al-Musawaar*, an Egyptian weekly journal, to ask public figures what they would say to the führer if they could write to him at that time. Future Egyptian president Sadat expressed admiration for Hitler in the Egyptian weekly.

> Dear Hitler, I welcome you back with all my heart. You have been defeated, but in fact one should regard you as the real victor. There will be no peace in the world until Germany again takes first place.
>
> Your principal mistake was in opening too many fronts, but everything is forgiven, for you are a shining example of belief in one's fatherland and people. You are eternal, and we shall not be surprised if we see you again, or a second Hitler, back in Germany.[40]

Although Sadat would go on to sign a historic peace treaty with his arch-nemesis, Israel, according to some sources, he never really had a change of heart.[41]

The German model of centralized government and corporatist nationalism remained attractive to many of the early pan-Arab nationalists in Egypt, some of whom sought the creation of an "Arab Reich" that would unite all Arabs into one nation.[42] The early pan-Arab leaders searched for methods to mobilize their populations and build independent nations. They were influenced in large part by European fascists who viewed the state as an organic outgrowth of the nation. As they saw it, only a strong, authoritarian state could protect the nation. Hence, the German model of bureaucratic centralization and authoritarianism looked attractive to many Arabs who sought an alternative way to modernize their countries. Moreover, the fact that Germany was opposed to the Western powers, such as England and France, made it all the more appealing to Middle Easterners, who deeply resented colonialism. Perhaps no other Arab country was more deeply influenced by National Socialism than Egypt.

King Farouk, who ruled Egypt during World War II, was initially seen as pro-Nazi, although his country was occupied by Britain. By the early 1950s, a wave of anti-British and anti-American sentiment had swept Egypt. Eventually both the U.S. and British governments decided that Farouk had to be replaced. The CIA, under the influence of John Foster Dulles, selected Egyptian army general Muhammad Naguib to lead a new Egyptian government. On July 22, 1952, with the help of the CIA, Naguib sent the army into the streets of Cairo and Alexandria and established himself as the commander in chief of military forces. Although Naguib was the titular head of state, unbeknown to the CIA, the real power ultimately rested with Lieutenant Colonel Gamal Abdel Nasser, who soon assumed the position of president. This coup was also significant because it opened the door for numerous Nazis to take prominent positions in the Egyptian government.

Not long after the war, many German military officers and Nazi party officials were granted sanctuary in Middle Eastern countries, most notably Egypt and Syria, where they helped develop the militaries and intelligences agencies of those countries.[43] Unrepentant former Nazis formed clandestine networks that occasionally included contacts in the Middle East. In the early postwar years, Egypt hosted many leading Nazi refugees. For example, Major General Otto Ernst Remer, the officer that squelched the anti-Hitler coup in July 1944, found refuge in Egypt, where he offered his services to the Nasser regime. With the help of Remer and other German military and technical advisers, Egypt developed a support base for Algerian, Moroccan, and Tunisian guerrillas fighting against France, as well as anti-British movements in Aden and the Mau Mau insurgency in Kenya.[44] Cairo became the nerve center for the Front de libération nationale (FLN, or National Liberation Front) insurgency and the seat of the provisional government for Algerian rebels. Remer also served as the front man for German arms traffickers who supplied the FLN and other Algerian guerrillas. Also, Homanned Said, a former SS volunteer who fought in the grand mufti's Handschar Division, assisted the Algerian insurrection as well, commanding FLN guerrilla operations near the Tunisian border.[45] The Algerian war, however, proved to be a divisive issue among the international extreme right in the early postwar years. As the investigative journalist, Martin Lee, noted, this conflict split the extreme right in Europe into two camps. Among the leaders of the Secret Army Organization (OAS) were several French fascists, Vichy collaborators, and French Waffen SS volunteers who did not take kindly to the support that many of the German neo-Nazis provided to the FLN.[46]

Arguably, the most important former Nazi in Nasser's employ was Hitler's commando extraordinaire, Otto Skorzeny, who arrived in Egypt in the early 1950s. According to Martin Lee, Colonel Nasser, Otto Skorzeny, and Haj Amin al-Husseini (the grand mufti) formed a triumvirate to further both their personal and common goals. Nasser is reported to have had great respect for Skorzeny. Coincidentally, a young Yasser Arafat—a distant cousin of the grand mufti—participated in unconventional warfare training under the Egyptian soldiers, during which time he developed a rapport with Skorzeny that would reportedly last for many years.[47]

Skorzeny's principal responsibility was to train thousands of Egyptian commandos in guerrilla and desert warfare. Furthermore, he organized and planned the initial forays of the early Palestinian terrorists into Israel and the Gaza Strip around 1953–1954.[48] An Arab Foreign Legion was created, whose nucleus consisted of 400 former Nazi veterans who were recruited by Arab League agents in Germany.[49] Finally, Skorzeny sought to protect German scientists, technicians, and engineers who were recruited to work on Egypt's special military program.

Not surprisingly, the Mossad—the newly created Israeli espionage agency—considered these personnel to be a serious threat to the security of Israel. Consequently, the Mossad launched numerous missions to assassinate them—usually through the use of letter bombs—some of which found their intended targets.

During this period, renascent Nazis saw the rise of Arab and Third World nationalism as an excellent opportunity to create a German-Islamic neutralist alliance that would extend from the heart of Europe to the South China Sea.[50] This idea was consistent with the late Karl Hausofer's policy of an alliance with the "Colored World."[51] Hausofer is generally regarded as the person responsible for popularizing "geopolitics." One vision of this new extreme right foreign policy was to create—with the assistance of the grand mufti and the Arab League—a German-Egyptian-dominated power bloc that could resist both the United States and the Soviet Union.[52]

Several other unrepentant German Nazis made their way to the Middle East and played important roles as well. For example, Skorzeny's uncle-in-law, Hjalmar Schacht, brokered the "Jeddah agreement" between German industrial firms and Saudi Arabia in 1954. Under the agreement, the Saudi government agreed to establish a fleet of supertankers—to be built in German shipyards—that would transport Saudi oil around the world. The Greek magnate, Aristotle Onassis, was chosen to manage the shipping side of the arrangement. The Jeddah agreement occasioned considerable consternation among various Western oil companies; not only would the agreement have been extremely lucrative for the Ruhr shipbuilders, but it would also have threatened the market dominance of the "Seven Sisters" oil companies' distribution of Middle East oil. Ultimately, with the help of the CIA, the Western oil cartel was able to block the Jeddah agreement.[53]

Former Nazis also served the new Nasser government in the realm of propaganda. For example, German expatriate Louis al-Hadj translated Hitler's *Mein Kampf* into Arabic. Johann von Leers, a former high-ranking assistant to Nazi Propaganda Minister Joseph Goebbels who worked in the Berlin Foreign Ministry, eventually settled in Cairo, where he churned out anti-Western and anti-Israeli propaganda for Nasser's government.[54] He eventually converted to Islam, assumed the Arabized name of Oman Amin von Leers, and went so far as to predict that the German people would turn their backs on Christianity and embrace Islam. He confided his thoughts to his friend H. Keith Thompson in conversations and correspondence:[55]

> The Islamic bloc is today the only spiritual power in the world fighting for a real religion and human values and freedom. . . . I think sometimes if my nation had got Islam instead of Christianity we should not have had all the

traitors we had in World War II, two million women would not have been burnt as "witches" by the Christian churches, there would have been no Thirty Years War which destroyed Germany and killed more that half of our nation.[56]

One thing is clear—more and more patriot[ic] Germans join the great Arab revolution against beastly imperialism. . . . To hell with Christianity, for in Christianity's name Germany has been sold to our oppressors! Our place as an oppressed nation under the execrable Western colonialist Bonn government must be on the side of the Arab nationalist revolt against the West. . . . *I hamd ul Allah!* . . . Indeed, for our nation there is only one hope—to get rid of Western imperialism by joining the Arab-led anti-imperialist group.[57]

Still other former Nazis who worked for Nasser included SS lieutenant general Wilhelm Farmbacher, who was the head of the original military adviser group in Egypt, and his assistant, Major General Oskar Munzel, who organized the Egyptian Parachute Corps.[58] In the realm of economic development, Dr. Wilhelm Voss, the former director of the Skoda arms factory in Czechoslovakia and the Hermann Goering Steel Mills, was the architect of the Egyptian economy in the early postwar years.[59] Working with Reinhard Gehlen, Skorzeny, and Hjalmar Schacht, he increased West Germany's trade with Egypt.[60]

During the Cold War, former Nazi officials would occasionally play off both sides of the East-West divide. The case of Dr. Fritz Grobba, a German Orientalist who converted to Islam, is instructive. Grobba was Berlin's minister to Baghdad and also to the court of King Ibn Saud at Riyadh. In the years leading up to World War II, with his colleagues and agents in the Middle East, Grobba conspired with the grand mufti to sabotage Anglo-French military and economic influence in the region. In 1941, they helped spark Rashid Ali al-Gilani's revolt in Iraq, which was quickly suppressed by the British government. Driven out of the Middle East by the Allies, Grobba, the grand mufti, al-Gilani, and their assistants took refuge in Berlin, where Hitler installed them in a special Bureau of Arab Affairs that was designed to disseminate propaganda to the Muslim world. Grobba survived the war and eventually served as the director of Arab affairs at the Soviet Foreign Ministry in Moscow. Serving as a Soviet diplomatic intermediary, Grobba brokered an arms deal between Nasser's Egypt and the Soviet Union.[61] His former compatriot, Otto Skorzeny, is thought to have helped engineer Nasser's alliance with the Soviet Union. Bolstered by the new alliance and relying on Nazi-trained military forces at his disposal, Nasser felt confident enough to seize the Suez Canal in 1956. His confidence backfired three months later, when Great Britain, France, and Israel attacked Egypt in order to regain control of the canal. Ultimately, the Egyptian-Soviet alliance undercut Skorzeny's influence with Nasser. Under pressure from the Soviets to establish relations with East Germany, Nasser alienated the German Federal Republic, which broke off diplomatic relations with Egypt and cut off all economic aid. That effectively put an end to Skorzeny's work in Egypt, including a rocket program in Helwan.[62]

Not to be left out of the action, some American right-wing extremists also sojourned in the Middle East in the early postwar years as well. For example, in 1953 Francis Parker Yockey, the author of the 600-page tome *Imperium*,[63] and H. Keith Thompson were reported to have visited Cairo in an effort to forge an alliance with the Nasser regime. Yockey was an early postwar exponent of pan-Europeanism. In his geo-political framework, the United States was a more serious enemy to the European-derived peoples than the Soviet Union.[64] He praised Hitler as the "hero of the Second World War" and the Nazi seizure of power as the "European Revolution of 1933." Yockey and an associate, Fred Weiss, reportedly sought to persuade Nasser to underwrite the development of a "cobalt bomb" on which exiled Nazi scientists were working.[65]

Other American extremists reached out to Arabs in the Middle East as well. In 1959, the founder of the American Nazi Party, George Lincoln Rockwell, was reported to have made overtures to then President Gamal Abdel Nasser of the United Arab Republic.[66] And James H. Madole, the leader of the extreme right National Renaissance Party, openly supported Arab regimes and may have received financial backing from Arab nationalists, including diplomats in the United States. There is some indication that these overtures were taken at least somewhat seriously. For example, Abdul Mawgoud Hassan, the press attaché of the Egyptian United Nations delegation, once spoke at an NRP meeting.[67] The NRP also corresponded with the grand mufti.[68] However, by all known accounts, not much ever came of these efforts.

Black September and the Black International

The rise of Palestinian terrorism in the early 1970s caused some elements of the European extreme right to once again take interest in the Middle Eastern affairs. After King Hussein of Jordan expelled the PLO from Jordan in 1970, PLO chairman Yasser Arafat created a new terrorist organization called Black September. The organization established strong ties with German left-wing radicals. Working together, they carried out one of the most infamous acts in the annals of European terrorism—the kidnapping and subsequent killing of several Israeli athletes at the 1972 Summer Olympic games in Munich, Germany.

Actually, representatives of the extreme right had collaborated with Palestinian rejectionist groups long before the representatives of the radical left had. A few neofascists even fought alongside Arab guerrillas in Middle Eastern conflicts. For example, Robert Courdroy, a veteran of the Belgian SS, died in combat while fighting for the Palestinians in 1968.[69] And, on some occasions, the extreme right actually worked side by side with the radical left in support of Palestinian terrorists.

Both the extreme right and Palestinian rejectionists shared hostility toward Zionism. Early efforts on the part of the European extreme right to assist Palestinian rejectionists consisted primarily of financial support. The case of François Genoud is illustrative. Genoud founded a Swiss extreme right organization and worked as a trusted banker for German neo-Nazis. Reportedly well connected to Arab circles in the Middle East, Genoud founded the Arab Commercial Bank in Geneva and became a formidable financial power as tens of millions of dollars were funneled through his hands for the use of Palestinians in Europe. Through his various connections, Genoud was an important nexus between groups like Fatah and Black September on the one hand, and extremist groups in Europe on the other.[70]

In his capacity as a shadowy financier, Genoud paid the legal costs for three members of the Popular Front for the Liberation of Palestine (PFLP) who stood trial for blowing up an Israeli jet in Zurich. Genoud's Nazi roots went quite deep. While studying in Bonn as a teenager in 1932, Genoud actually met Hitler. The young Genoud shook hands with his mentor and expressed his admiration for National Socialism. When he returned to Switzerland in 1934, he joined the pro-Nazi Swiss National Front. Shortly thereafter in 1936, he traveled to Palestine, where he became a confidant of Grand Mufti al-Husseini.[71]

After the war, Genoud acquired all the posthumous rights to the writings of Hitler, Martin Bormann, and Joseph Goebbels, increasing his fortune in the process. Using his Swiss banking connections, he helped many Nazis escape from Germany, an effort to which Grand Mufti al-Husseini also allegedly lent assistance.[72] Genoud also helped underwrite the costs for the legal defense of Adolf Eichmann. According to some European press accounts, Genoud sold defeated Nazis' gold and deposited the proceeds into Swiss bank accounts to finance these projects.[73]

Genoud was particularly close to the grand mufti, serving as his financial adviser. In 1958, he founded the Arab Commercial Bank in Geneva to manage the assets of the Algerian National Liberation Front. As mentioned earlier, several former Nazis, including Major General Otto Ernst Remer, assisted the rebels in their struggle against French colonial rule. Genoud was reportedly involved in financing terrorist groups, disseminating anti-Israeli propaganda throughout the Middle East, and assisting the Palestinian hijackers of a Lufthansa plane in 1972. He was particularly close to Dr. Waddi Haddad, the cofounder of the PFLP, and Ali Hassan Salameh of the Black September group. However, his activities did not go unnoticed by his enemies. In 1993 a bomb exploded in front of his house, and he barely escaped alive. Feeling trapped, Genoud committed suicide by drinking poison in May 1996.[74]

Another important financial benefactor of Palestinian causes was the wealthy Italian publisher, Giangiacomo Feltrinelli. Ironically, Feltrinelli was a financial supporter of communist groups; however, he once met secretly with the Italian neofascist Prince Valerio Borghese to discuss ways in which both the left and right could work together to battle imperialism.[75] The Black International, which operated under the name of the European New Order, held a summit in Barcelona on behalf of the Palestinians. The organization was composed of various Nazis and fascists from Nazi Germany, Vichy France, Franco's Spain, Salazar's Portugal, Mussolini's Italy, and the Greek colonels' military junta. The Spanish leader, General Francesco Franco, is believed to have endorsed the meeting. Two representatives from Fatah, the military arm of the PLO, attended the event. Reportedly, the delegates discussed raising money, organizing arms traffic, and providing ex-Nazi military instructors to help train guerrillas. A major endeavor was to recruit Caucasians to augment Fatah's forces in the Middle East and also collaborate in acts of sabotage and terrorism in Europe.[76] Several summits followed this event, including one held on September 16, 1972, barely ten days after Palestinian Black September terrorists killed eleven Israeli athletes at the Munich Olympics. Six hundred delegates to this gathering reportedly cheered Black September to the rafters.[77] In May 1979, another summit was held in Paris, where a former SS officer and Rexist Party (a pro-fascist Belgian political party that was active during the interwar years) member, Jean Roberts Debbaudt, pledged support to the Palestinian resistance.

Still another right-wing extremist who established contacts in the Middle East was Jean Thiriart from Belgium, who served as a secretary for a neo-Nazi group called La Natión Européene. He shared many of the ideas of Francis Parker Yockey, including creating a European–Third World bloc that could resist the United States. In 1968, he traveled to several Arab countries to gain support for his idea of a "European brigade," which he envisaged as a guerrilla army that would engage in armed struggle against American soldiers stationed in Europe. Reportedly, Thiriart actually served as an adviser to Fatah in 1969. He sought to convince his Arab interlocutors that it would be in their interest if the United States became enmeshed in a "silent war" against neofascist terrorists in Europe.[78] He traveled to Iraq and conferred with Colonel Saddam Hussein, the future dictator of the country. According to Thiriart, the Iraqis were enthusiastic about the plan but were persuaded by their then sponsor, the Soviet Union, to abandon the plan. Thiriart was also believed to have been close to PFLP leader George Habash.[79]

Other efforts to collaborate in the field of terrorism followed. For example, there were several instances of cooperation between German right-wing extremists and terrorist groups in the Middle East. Following the example of European left-wing terrorists, members of a small German neo-Nazi group, Wehrsportgruppe-Hoffmann, sought to develop an alliance with the PLO and other Middle Eastern terrorist groups during the 1970s and early 1980s. Karl Heinz Hoffman, the leader of the group, traveled to Damascus in July 1980 to develop links between the PLO and East German intelligence agents. Hoffman also worked out a deal that provided used trucks to the PLO in exchange for training.[80] Members of this group reportedly received paramilitary training in PLO camps in Jordan and fought alongside Palestinians in that country during the "Black September" of 1970.[81] One German neo-Nazi mercenary, Karl von Kyna, even died in combat during a Palestinian commando raid in September 1967.[82] However, Hoffman was unable to sustain the tenuous alliance, and it faltered because of the prosecution of members of Wehrsportgruppe-Hoffmann by German authorities.

One of the most notorious terrorist groups of this period was the Popular Front for the Liberation of Palestine, which gained widespread notoriety in 1968 by hijacking several commercial airplanes. The leader of the PFLP, George Habash, received support from neofascists in Europe known as the Black International. The PFLP reportedly carried out terrorist attacks against Jewish targets in Europe with the assistance of Odfried Hepp and his neo-Nazi group, which unleashed a wave of bombings at four U.S. Army bases in Germany that damaged property and injured military personnel.[83] In early 1970, a neo-Nazi group calling itself the Freikorps Adolf Hitler, founded by Udo Albrecht, was identified as having participated in the Black September war against King Hussein's government in Jordan. In 1978 German police arrested members of the Freikorps Adolf Hitler and another organization, the Hilfskorps Arabien, on suspicion of smuggling arms from the Middle East into West Germany for Palestinian operatives that were living there. In that same year, Albrecht was arrested in Germany and was found to be carrying a card that connected him to the Fatah organization. This arrest was the first direct proof German authorities had linking German radicals with Middle Eastern terrorist organizations.[84] Still another neo-Nazi with whom the PLO had contact was Manfred Roeder. Following advice from Albrecht, he traveled to Lebanon to make contact with Yasser Arafat. He never met with the PLO chairman, however, instead speaking with his deputy, Abu Jihad. Disappointingly for Roeder, Jihad refused to cooperate with him, which was a setback for relations between neo-Nazis and Palestinians.[85]

Undaunted, Roeder continued to look for supporters in the Middle East. In 1980 he traveled to Syria and Iraq to build a relationship of mutual support and trust, but these efforts appear to have failed. Other German extremists, however, were able to establish significant ties. There were also sporadic reports that surfaced during the 1980s of cooperation between German neo-Nazis and a Turkish fascist organization known as the "Gray Wolves." Mehmet Kengerle, who served with the SS in World War II, was the figure that allegedly sought to arrange this alliance.[86] The organization's most infamous member, Mehmet Ali Agca, attempted to assassinate Pope John Paul II in May 1981.[87] This alliance, like the others that preceded it, was also short-lived and of limited significance.

There is anecdotal evidence to suggest that Nazism still bedazzles some elements in the Palestinian movement. For example, Fawsi Salim el-Mahdi, the leader of Yasser Arafat's Praetorian Guard, "Tanzim 17," reportedly included the Nazi salute in a graduation ceremony for Palestinian Authority police cadets. Known to his colleagues as "Abu Hitler," his affection for the Third Reich is reflected in his choice of names for his two sons, Eichmann and Hitler.[88]

Despite efforts by members of the European extreme right to reach out to the Palestinians, an enduring operational alliance was not established. At best, the ties were sparse, shallow, sporadic, and ephemeral. However, by the 1980s it appeared that a new ecumenical ideology heralded as "the Third Position" might unite disparate anticolonialist dissidents around the world.

Muammar Qaddafi and the Third Position

During the 1970s and 1980s, Libya was perceived by the West to be one of the foremost state sponsors of international terrorism.[89] The Libyan government, under the leadership of Muammar Qaddafi, made numerous attempts to forge international terrorist alliances. Qaddafi sought to appeal to a broad coalition of anti-imperialists and popularized a syncretic ideology known as the "Third Position." In essence, Third Positionism combines numerous themes, including nationalism, anticapitalism, anticommunism, and anti-imperialism, into a populist ideology. Qaddafi codified his message in a manifesto known as *The Green Book,* which gained popularity in some neofascist circles, primarily in Europe but also in North America. Qaddafi's defiance of the U.S. government impressed anti-imperialists from both the far left and far right of the political spectrum. As the Cold War lost much of its urgency and as American popular culture became more pervasive around the world, the United States increasingly became the bête noire of the international extreme right.[90]

In order to foster a broad-based anti-imperialist alliance, the Libyan government supported numerous conferences that brought together disparate extremists from around the world. In 1986, for example, a meeting in large part financed by Libya was held in Frankfurt, Germany, and attended by no fewer than 500 persons, most of whom were Marxist-Leninist in orientation.[91] Qaddafi showed some interest in extreme right activists as well and invited several to Libya.[92] In his early years, Qaddafi generally reached out to the far right, not the far left. Several European neofascists were ready to reciprocate.

Shortly after Qaddafi seized power, Claudio Mutte, an Italian neofascist, formed the Italian-Libyan Friendship Society. Mutte even published an Italian version of Qaddafi's *Green Book*.[93] Qaddafi sought to include the extreme right in his big tent when he convened an international anti-imperialist meeting on April 15, 1987, that was attended by dissidents from across the political spectrum. One common denominator was opposition to Israel. Numerous representatives from the extreme right included Ian Verner Macdonald, Wolfgang Droege, and Don Andrews from Canada. Reportedly, approximately 2,000 Libyan, Palestinian, European, American, and Canadian delegates attended the event.[94] A young Canadian journalist covering the gathering, Christoph Halens, died after falling from his room in a three-story hotel in Tripoli. Some observers suspected foul play.[95] The American leader of White Aryan Resistance (WAR), Tom Metzger, was invited but declined.[96] Although Metzger has long been a leading exponent of his own version of the Third Position, he expressed dismay over the influence of Qaddafi on the movement. In his mind, some white nationalist groups were losing their focus as they were losing their racial consciousness by adopting a "race-mixing attitude."[97]

One year later, in September 1988, three leaders of the British group the National Front, Patrick Harrington, Nick Griffin, and Derek Holland, traveled to Libya as guests of that country's foreign office. The National Front was founded in February 1967 when a number of right-wing organizations coalesced to form a political party.[98] John Tyndall eventually emerged as the chairman, a position he would hold until 1980. As a political party, the National Front won no major elections, yet it did draw enough votes away from the Tory Party to cause some concern among conservatives. Margaret Thatcher stole much of the party's thunder in 1979, when she echoed its concern over immigration. As a result, the party became marginalized and drifted in a more radical direction. In 1980, Tyndall left the party because he was dismayed that the party had been taken over by radicals, including skinheads. In 1982, the

New National Front was renamed the British National Party, which John Tyndall led until 1999, when he was replaced by Nick Griffin in a party election. During the 1980s, younger National Front members, led by Nick Griffin, sought to build alliances with nontraditional allies, including radical Muslims.[99] They were introduced to the Libyans and other Arabs through Italian extreme right fugitives who sought refuge in Britain.[100] For the leadership of the National Front, the Libyan trip produced no demonstrable results other than a supply of 5,000 copies of *The Green Book.* Overtures were made to the PLO but were rebuffed.[101] What is more, Griffin's overtures to Arabs and the Nation of Islam alienated many of the National Front's traditional supporters. Consequently, Griffin soon formed the International Position with the Italian fascist fugitive Roberto Fiore. Not long after the 1988 trip to Libya, it appeared that both the extreme right and Muammar Qaddafi had lost interest in each other. Like earlier attempts to forge alliances, these efforts accomplished little. Moreover, Qaddafi's aggressive support for international terrorism abroad and in the Middle East ultimately isolated him, as even his Arab neighbors ostracized him. He suffered a series of foreign policy setbacks, and no fewer than thirteen countries in Africa and the Middle East, as well as the United States, broke diplomatic relations with Libya or expelled Libyan diplomatic personnel.[102] In early 2004, Qaddafi renounced the use of terrorism and went so far as to apologize for Libya's role in the 1988 bombing of Pan Am flight 103 over Lockerbie, Scotland. The Libyan government acknowledged its culpability and agreed to pay a huge $2.7 billion settlement for its role in the terrorist attack.[103] Perhaps the example of Iraq contributed to the Libyan government's reversal in policy, as it now pursues a rapprochement with the United States, its former nemesis.

The 1990s and Beyond

By the late 1980s, there was very little cooperation between militant Islam and the extreme right. Arab nationalism had waned considerably, and most of the leading Nazi fugitives were dead or in permanent retirement. The Palestinian rejectionists had begun to moderate. What is more, the new Palestinian groups, such as Hamas, had no history of cooperation with the extreme right.

However, the end of the Cold War significantly changed international politics. Furthermore, the revolution in telecommunications greatly facilitated the exchange of ideas between dissident groups around the world. As one observer noted, the Internet has been key to the development of the nascent alliance between Islam and the right. By one estimate, more than 2,000 extremist sites dot the World Wide Web.[104] Another important factor is the demise of communism. The extreme right abandoned the communist threat as its chief enemy; in its place emerged the nemesis of the new world order, which, as one observer noted, is often perceived as "a juggernaut of international corporate finance, Jewish media, and American military power."[105] The right's conceptualization of this new enemy parallels closely the principal adversaries of militant Islam. Finally, both the extreme right and Islam share a similar eschatology, in which the old order is viewed as incorrigibly corrupt, something that must be totally effaced in order to build a new order. For these reasons, new opportunities for cooperation began to emerge by the late 1990s.

THE OKLAHOMA CITY BOMBING AND THE PUTATIVE
MIDDLE EASTERN CONNECTION

Before I consider these new opportunities for cooperation, it is worth examining details of the 1995 Oklahoma City bombing because rumors persist of an Islamic connection to the incident. Despite one of the most thoroughgoing investigation in the FBI's history, some observers believe that important questions about the 1995 Oklahoma City bombing have been left unanswered. Notwithstanding Timothy McVeigh's own denials, published not long before his execution, rumors have persisted that the 1995 Oklahoma City bombing had an Islamic connection.

Stephen Jones, McVeigh's defense attorney, is one of the main proponents of this theory.[106] The connection between the various parties in this theory is McVeigh's accomplice, Terry Nichols. There is also speculation that Nichols may have met with Ramzi Yousef, the mastermind of the 1993 World Trade Center bombing, while in the Philippines.[107] Jones spent months investigating a possible Filipino link to the Oklahoma City bombing and concluded that Ramzi Yousef's close friend and conspirator, Wali Khan Amin Shah, knew Nichols's wife Marife and her sister through a mutual friend.[108] British journalist Simon Reeve noted that Nichols visited the Philippines in 1994— around the same time that Ramzi Yousef had visited that country as well.[109] In mid-November 1994, Nichols left for the Philippines to spend time with his Filipino mail-order bride, Marife, who lived in a boarding house in Cebu in which a large number of Muslim students also resided. After returning to the United States in January 1995, Nichols is reported to have made seventy-eight phone calls to the boarding house, where his wife still resided, between January 31 and March 14, 1995.[110] Shortly before he left for the Philippines, Nichols is supposed to have left his ex-wife, Lana, a package with instructions that it was not to be opened for at least sixty days, in the event that he did not return safely in that period of time. Fearing Nichols might be in trouble, Lana opened the package and discovered instructions addressed to her and Timothy McVeigh, treasury bonds, Nichols's car keys, and details of the location of a secret compartment Nichols had built into her kitchen cabinet, which contained a plastic bag into which cash and more than $20,000 in gold and silver bars had been stuffed. The instructions read, "Your [sic] on your own. Go for it." Where did the money come from? Months prior to the attack on April 19, 1995, Nichols is believed to have participated in the armed robbery of a gun collector, Roger Moore, in his Arkansas home. Reeve conjectures that Nichols may have realized that he might be consorting with highly dangerous individuals in the Philippines and thus was unsure if he would return.[111]

According to a motion filed by McVeigh's defense team, an American fitting Nichol's description met with Yousef in the Philippines in 1992 or 1993.[112] Furthermore, a senior member of Abu Sayyaf, Edwin Angeles, claimed under interrogation by Filipino authorities that he had met Yousef together with Nichols, the latter whom he had known only as "the Farmer." Allegedly, Angeles claimed that Nichols and Yousef met to discuss bomb-making techniques and the procurement of firearms and ammunitions. Some reports suggest that Nichols may have first established contact with Yousef through Muslim students in Southwest College in Weatherford, Oklahoma. While in Cebu, Yousef may have spent time in a safehouse with militant student friends from Southwest College. Some observers conjecture that Yousef may have provided Nichols with the training necessary to build the bomb used in Oklahoma City.[113] Yousef is thought to have received funding from Osama bin Laden.

Laurie Mylroie, a terrorism analyst who received a Ph.D. from Harvard, has added an Iraqi connection to the Oklahoma City bombing case. She asserted that Saddam Hussein's fingerprints were all over the 1993 World Trade Center bombing.[114] Furthermore, Mylroie was adamant that Yousef was an Iraqi intelligence agent, and believed that he probably met Terry Nichols, thus further suggesting that Yousef may have had a role in the Oklahoma City bombing. According to Mylroie, a lack of communication and coordination between the Justice Department and the national security bureaucracies contributed to the failure of the FBI to pick up on an Iraqi connection to the first World Trade Center bombing. In her estimation, there was never an adequate intelligence investigation into the incident.[115]

Similarly, Jayna Davis, a former Oklahoma City television reporter for KFOR-TV in Oklahoma City, has also researched the case and came to the conclusion that the Iraqi government was involved in the 1995 attack. Her investigative journalism on the story has been given exposure in several major media outlets, including the Fox News Channel's *O'Reilly Factor, On the Road with Greta Van Susteren, The Big Story with John Gibson,* and *Fox News Live;* · CNN's *Moneyline with Lou Dobbs;* and the *Wall Street Journal.* Furthermore, some high-ranking representatives of the U.S. intelligence community have given her theory credence as well, including former director of Central Intelligence James Woolsey and the executive director of the Congressional Task Force on Terrorism and Unconventional Warfare, Yossef Bodansky.

After a sedulous investigation to which she devoted several years, Davis averred that a Middle Eastern terrorist cell was in operation only blocks from the federal building. Allegedly, an Iraqi national, Hussain Hashem al-Hussaini, who served in Saddam Hussein's Republican Guard, was in contact with McVeigh on April 19, 1995, and also on the days leading up to the bombing.[116] Shortly after the attack, the FBI released sketches of "John Doe 2," who may have had Middle Eastern features. To buttress her assertions, Davis interviewed numerous witnesses that have identified al-Hussaini as McVeigh's consort and possible accomplice. Davis's investigation uncovered that al-Hussaini entered the United States in 1994 as an Iraqi defector from Saddam Hussein's Ba'athist regime. Al-Hussaini claims to have been persecuted by the Iraqi government for distributing antigovernment leaflets.[117] After 9/11, Davis went so far as to speculate that the hijackers might have had some connection to the perpetrators of the Oklahoma City bombing. Allegedly, the ringleader of the hijackers, Muhammad Atta, one of his accomplices, Marwan al-Shehi, and the so-called twentieth hijacker, Zacarias Moussaoui, attempted to rent a room at the Cactus motel just outside Oklahoma City in early August 2001—the same motel where the perpetrators of the attack on the Murrah Federal Building allegedly met the night before April 19, 1995.[118]

Also suspicious to Davis was the fact that Oklahoma City was reportedly a hotbed for Islamist activities, including meetings and conventions for groups connected to Hamas and Hezbollah.[119] According to intelligence reports supplied to her by Bodansky, Davis claimed that Iraqi intelligence sought "lily whites" (potential operatives whose backgrounds would not tie them to terrorism) for training.[120] However, most government intelligence officials remain unconvinced; former CIA chief of counterterrorism Vince Cannistraro referred to Davis's dossier as "total bullshit."[121] Adding to the intrigue is the fact that Cannistraro is reported to have received a telephone call from a Saudi counterterrorism official (whose name Cannistraro did not disclose) who warned of an impending terrorist plot by a group of foreign terrorists aimed specifically at the Alfred P. Murrah Federal Building. Cannistraro duly notified the FBI's Washington Metropolitan Field Office of the information that he had received. Interestingly, Cannistraro would later downplay the significance of the call from his Saudi source. Surprisingly, federal prosecutors evinced little interest in Cannistraro's story.[122]

It is interesting to note how the radical right responded to the Oklahoma City bombing. Although McVeigh was usually depicted as a fellow traveler of the militia movement, I know of not one instance in which a militia leader has publicly condoned the attack. Just the opposite is true. Quite often militia leaders blamed the attack on a government conspiracy. By contrast, the racialist right seemed much less likely to ascribe the attack to some larger conspiracy involving the government or others unknown. *The American Free Press,* possibly the most circulated organ of the extreme right, suggested that Davis had been duped into believing that Arabs were behind the attack, when a more convincing case could be made for Israeli complicity. Further, the article accused several neoconservatives and Jews in the media of hyping her theory in order to foster a public perception that Saddam Hussein was behind the attack, thus justifying the most recent war on Iraq.[123]

For his part, McVeigh dismissed the theory as "nonsense" and a "red herring."[124] According to the statements McVeigh made near the end of his life, there was no larger conspiracy, and the government's version was correct after all. Still there remains the chance that he may be covering for accomplices and thus might not be entirely truthful about what happened. Furthermore, the 1995 federal grand jury indictment proclaimed that McVeigh and Nichols had acted with "others unknown."[125] Perhaps the main reason that the Oklahoma City bombing has become a question mark for terrorism analysts is the sheer magnitude of the attack. Previous episodes of right-wing violence and terrorism are often marked by extreme ineptitude. Furthermore, the modus operandi of the April 19 attack is consistent with the type of terrorism conducted by Middle Eastern groups, most notably Hezbollah.

Perhaps the most direct connection between McVeigh and Iraq was his experience in the Gulf War, which made a significant impression on the young soldier. He seemed to harbor feelings of guilt for Iraqi soldiers that he killed during the short military campaign. As a gunnery sergeant, McVeigh destroyed an Iraqi machine-gun emplacement, killing two Iraqi soldiers and forcing the surrender of thirty others.[126] McVeigh has occasionally condemned U.S. military actions in the Middle East, including the 1998 missile strikes aimed at Afghanistan and the Sudan in the wake of the embassy bombings carried out by al Qaeda in Kenya and Tanzania. Furthermore, in an April 21, 2001, letter to Fox News, McVeigh gave tacit approval to Ramzi Yousef's 1993 attack on the World Trade Center.[127] Interestingly, McVeigh has on occasion drawn parallels between the Oklahoma City bombing and the U.S. government's policy toward Iraq. He saw the two as morally equivalent:

Hypocrisy when it comes to children? In Oklahoma City, it was family convenience that explained the presence of a day-care center placed between street level and the law enforcement agencies, which occupied the upper floors on the building. Yet when discussion shifts to Iraq, any day-care center in a government building instantly becomes "a shield." Think about it.

(Actually, there is a difference here. The administration has admitted to knowledge of the presence of children in or near Iraqi government buildings, yet they still proceed with their plans to bomb—saying that they cannot be held responsible if children die. There is no proof, however, that knowledge of the presence of children existed in relation to the Oklahoma City bombing.) [Parentheses in original.]

Yet another example of this nation's blatant hypocrisy is revealed by the polls, which suggest that this nation is greatly in favor of bombing Iraq.

In this instance, the people of the nation approve of bombing government employees because they are "guilty by association"—they are Iraqi government employees. In regard to the bombing of Oklahoma City, however, such logic is condemned.

What motivates these seemingly contradictory positions? Do people think that government workers in Iraq are any less human than those in Oklahoma City? . . .

I find it ironic, to say the least, that one of the aircraft that could be used to drop such a bomb on Iraq is dubbed "The Spirit of Oklahoma."[128]

Perhaps the full story of the Oklahoma City bombing, with its possible Islamic connection, has yet to be written. In any case, after an extremely exhaustive investigation, the U.S. government seemed unimpressed with such a theory. The theory did find renewed currency in October 2001 when some high-ranking Defense Department officials leaked a story to the national press that an Iraqi agent may have been involved in the attack on the Murrah Federal Building.[129] However, as the Bush administration sought to build support for the war against Iraq, no one in the administration except Paul Wolfowitz gave the slightest countenance to the theory.[130] This is all the more noteworthy considering the alleged intelligence failure that indicated that Iraq had been harboring weapons of mass destruction, which served as the justification for the war. Still, detractors to the official version of the April 19 attack, such as Stephen Jones and Jayna Davis, point out that the government's case against McVeigh rested on the premise that he had "single-handedly designed, delivered, and detonated the bomb."[131] To add in foreign conspirators would conceivably greatly complicate the case and possibly make it all the more difficult to secure a conviction. Relevant to this book, it is worth noting that Saddam Hussein had on some occasions sought to build alliances with extremists in Europe and the United States.

SADDAM HUSSEIN

As discussed in Chapter 3, many of the early Arab nationalists—including some of Saddam Hussein's relatives—drew inspiration from the European fascist movements of the 1930s and 1940s. Saddam Hussein's uncle and future father-in law, Khairallah Tulfah, along with General Rashid Ali al-Gilani and the so-called colonels of the Golden Square, participated in a coup against the pro-British government of Iraq in 1941. The pro-Nazi regime was ejected by a British military intervention soon thereafter, but not before the regime instigated an anti-Jewish pogrom in which 200 people were killed.[132] Tulfah had a strong influence on his son-in-law, regaling him with his vision of a pan-Islamic Nazi alliance. Not unlike Hitler, Saddam Hussein sought to implement a new order based on the principles of nationalism and socialism under the dictatorial control of the Führerprinzip.[133] His Ba'ath (Renaissance) Party had the characteristics of a European fascist party of the interwar years, seeking to mold the masses into a single organic collectivity through a program of corporatism and national regeneration. Saddam Hussein's defiant position toward the United States and Israel throughout the 1990s bolstered his image in some quarters. As a result, several representatives of the extreme right have reached out to him on numerous occasions.

In the weeks leading up to the Gulf War, some European right-wing extremists sought to provide token assistance and moral support. For example, the late German neo-Nazi leader Michael Kühnen reportedly negotiated with Iraqi diplomats in an effort to build an "Anti-Zionist Legion" to fight for Saddam Hussein and repel the U.S.-led coalition. Another German neo-Nazi leader, Heinz Reisz, appeared on Hessian state television on January 25, 1991, and proclaimed "Long live the fight for Saddam Hussein; long live his people; long live their leader; God save the Arab people."[134] A French neo-Nazi, Michel Faci, traveled to Baghdad where he and twenty or so assorted activists and historical revisionists were guests of Saddam Hussein at a government-sponsored event titled "Friendship, Solidarity and Peace with Iraq."[135] Not much is thought to have come from these efforts, as no neofascist foreign legion is known to have served in combat in Iraq.

In January 1991, the intellectual leader of the French Nouvelle Droite, Alain de Benoist, joined with a coalition that included various leftists, trade unionists, and anti-American rightists to protest the U.S.-led aggression against Iraq. Just a few years before, in 1986, Benoist released a publication, *Europe, Tiers monde, même combat* (Europe, the Third World, the Same Fight), in which he called for an alliance between Europe and the Third World, primarily the Arab Middle East, to weaken both the U.S. and Soviet blocs and their hold on Europe. This rightist variant of "Third Worldism" was not informed by the more liberal-oriented admiration of the "noble savage" or white racial guilt, but rather by geopolitical hostility to the bloc system and its hold over Europe.[136]

After the war, Saddam found himself a pariah in the international community. However, some of his policies found supporters in Jean Marie Le Pen's Front National. Christian fundamentalists in the party favored Saddam because Iraq had been a major arms supplier to the Falange in its battle against Muslims in Lebanon during the civil war. Anti-Americanism and anti-British sentiment played a role as well. In October 1990, Le Pen traveled to Baghdad as part of a delegation of right-wing parties from Europe to meet with Saddam Hussein. They returned with fifty-three European hostages that were held by Iraq in the months prior to the war. For his part, supporting Iraq was a clever way in which Le Pen could defuse criticism that he was anti-Arab and anti-Muslim.[137]

Reportedly, some elements of Jörg Haider's Austrian Freedom Party (FPÖ) have also sympathized with Saddam Hussein's regime. For example, there is the case of Abdul Moneim Jebra, a sixty-year-old Iraqi arms dealer, who has reportedly sought to strengthen ties between the radical right and militant Islam. Jebra now lives in Austria, where members of Jörg Haider's FPÖ recently established an Iraqi-Austrian Association to promote ties with Baghdad. In 1998 a plot to smuggle helicopters to Iraq that involved Jebra was uncovered during a Swiss bribery case.[138]

Perhaps Saddam's firmest supporter from the extreme right is Vladimir Zhirinovsky, leader of the Russian ultranationalist Liberal Democratic Party. Zhirinovsky accused the Kremlin of "betraying" its long-term Arab partners and clients. The Soviet Union had strong diplomatic ties with many countries in the Middle East, and until its collapse, Moscow played a key role in the region, supporting Arab leaders such as Muammar Qaddafi in Libya, PLO chairman Yasser Arafat, Syrian president Hafez al-Assad, and Iraqi president Saddam Hussein. However, Mikhail Gorbachev's government consented to the U.S.-led military action in the Gulf War, an operation that it could have vetoed in the Security Council. Furthermore, by that time, and even more so during Boris Yeltsin's tenure, relations with the United States became the top Russian priority.

Zhirinovsky has sought to reestablish an alliance with Iraq. Toward this end, he reportedly developed a warm relationship with Saddam Hussein. The Iraqi ambassador to Russia appreciated Zhirinovsky's gestures of support and has frequently been in attendance at Zhirinovsky's birthday parties.[139] Zhirinovsky visited Baghdad on numerous occasions during the 1990s and was a guest of Saddam Hussein. In one instance, he lectured the Iraq leader for four hours on the need to unite against the "American-Israeli plot" to dominate the world.[140] In 1993, Zhirinvosky went so far as to send a contingent of his paramilitary "falcons" to Iraq to fight against "American imperialism." Hussein is rumored to have contributed considerable financial support to Zhirinovsky. After his trip to Baghdad, Zhirinovsky increased the frequency and the stridency of his anti-American rhetoric.[141]

Other Russian right-wing extremists have also reached out to Muslims in recent years. For example, Heidar Jamal has sojourned in several extremist organizations. He worked briefly for the ultranationalist Pamyat (Memory) organization in 1989 and the late Ahmed Khomeini, the son of Ayatollah Ruhollah Khomeini, in 1990. In 1993, he joined the Russian branch of the Islamic Committee. He ran unsuccessfully for the Duma in 1995. Finally, in 1999, his Islamic Committee joined forces with hard-line communists Victor Ilyukhin and Albert Marashov. One constant theme that links all his projects is a virulent disdain for the West in general and the United States in particular.[142]

Hussein's defiant posture has not gone unnoticed among the American extreme right either. Some individuals have offered the Iraqi leader moral support. For example, in 1990, Gary Schroeder, a leader of the Posse Comitatus, accompanied a group of farmers for a visit to the Iraqi embassy in Washington, D.C., to voice their opposition to the impending war. Also during the Gulf War, Dennis Mahon, at the time a leader of a Tulsa, Oklahoma, Klan group, organized a small demonstration in that city in support of Saddam Hussein. Mahon claimed to have later received a couple of hundred dollars in an unmarked envelope from the Iraqi government.[143]

Like so many previous attempts to build alliances in the Middle East, the extreme right's support for Saddam Hussein appears to have produced few tangible results. For his part, Hussein appears to have actually appreciated the support he received from some elements of the extreme right. Generally speaking, although the extreme right and militant Islam on occasion share rhetoric, what admiration does exist tends to move in one direction: selected extreme right activists voice support for militant Islam, but the latter rarely voices support for the former. However, some Muslims have reached out to those in the extreme right in an effort to build a broad-based anti-Zionist coalition.

Ahmed Rami, who operates the Swedish-based Radio Islam, also has ties to Western Holocaust revisionists.[144] Born in 1946 in Tafrout, Morocco, Rami became an officer in the Moroccan Army. Angered by the arrest of Moroccan opposition leader Ben Barka, in 1965 Rami enrolled in the Royal Military Academy in Meknès with the expressed purpose "to enter the system in order to destroy it." Convinced that the Moroccan monarch, King Hassan, was a puppet of Jews and the CIA, Rami participated in a plot to overthrow the leader in 1972. He fled his country after the failed coup attempt and received political asylum in Sweden.

Rami has occasionally interfaced with some extreme right luminaries, such as the late Otto Ernst Remer, the German Wehrmacht officer who squelched the attempted coup to depose Hitler in July 1944. On his Radio Islam website, Rami offers many classic staples of anti-Semitic propaganda, including *The Protocols of the Learned Elders of Zion*. Rami advocates what might be called a "universalistic anti-Semitism," in that he exhorts all peoples, regardless of race, ethnicity, nationality, or religion, to combat Jewish influence around the world. This sentiment is encapsulated in a phrase on his website: "No hate. No violence. Races? Only one Human race, divided we fall. Only one enemy." In addition, his website carries stridently anti-American messages and essays. Rami accuses Jews of controlling the mass media and international finance, through which, he believes, they maintain a stranglehold on the world. In his estimation, Jews work to prevent the true self-determination of various peoples around the world, most notably in the Middle East and in the West.

Rami's activities have occasionally brought him into conflict with Swedish authorities. In 1990, for example, Swedish courts ruled that he was guilty of incitement against Jews. He received a six-month prison sentence, and Radio Islam was shut down. Not to be deterred, Rami reestablished Radio Islam as an Internet site carried by an Internet service provider outside Sweden. However, in October 2000, he was convicted in a Swedish court for incitement and fined.[145]

In 1992 Rami was a featured speaker at the annual conference of the Institute for Historical Review, the leading Holocaust revisionist organization in the United States. There is anecdotal evidence to suggest that other Islamic extremists are beginning to take greater notice of propaganda produced by right-wing extremists. For example, the fiercely anti-Semitic writings of Dr. William L. Pierce have found their way onto the website of Hezbollah, the Lebanese Shi'ite Muslim group linked to Iran. Furthermore, Radio Iran has on occasion interviewed Pierce by telephone from his office in West Virginia.[146] As Pierce stated, the extreme right and Islam have a common goal in that they both seek to get "the U.S. government off the back of the world and [get] the Jews off the back of the U.S. government." He stated further that there is "ground for joint action" but ruled out violence on the grounds that the extreme right was so "outgunned by the government."[147] Not long before his death, Pierce pointed out that he received support from nontraditional audiences: "I've gotten a few letters from Palestinians who have said how pleased they are that somebody in the United States is picking a reasonable position. They knew not everyone agreed with the government policies, but no one had the courage to speak out against it."[148]

THE ARYAN NATIONS' MINISTRY OF ISLAMIC LIAISON

Some of the more radical organizations have gone so far as to establish outreach programs with members of the Muslim faith. One sign of growing tolerance for militant Islam among the extreme right is the Aryan Nations' Ministry of Islamic Liaison that is featured on the Aryan Nations' website. The stated purpose of the ministry is to reach out in "solidarity, to the bona-fide adherents of Islam in the Arabic world and abroad."[149] The site points out to viewers that the Muslims' God "is our father." One story on the site, "A Turning Tide Is a Violent Tide," tells the fictional tale of a selfless Palestinian suicide bomber who stalks his target: an Israeli white slave trafficker who is thinking about his most recent import of hapless young women from Eastern Europe.[150]

Think of a throng of men and women, thousands strong. In the center of the teeming mass stand young men, warriors of God, masked and clothed in brilliant white.

Some have belts strapped with explosives encircling their waists. A wire runs from the suicide belt to a detonation device which they hold in their hands, their thumbs poised above a button that, if pushed, will swiftly and surely dispatch them from their mortal coil (along with countless others who might be in the vicinity).

Several days later, a young man in a faded green jacket, stone-washed jeans and a pair of dilapidated Nikes strolls along a crowded street. . . . if you look into his eyes, there is seen, if one would look ever so carefully, a gaze that contains much. A window to a mind that is purified, content and single in its purpose. A purpose that is obedient to the law which was written on his heart since he put out his call to heaven many years ago, as he bowed in awed reverence at the mosque, crying tears of joy, when he realized that heaven had responded.

He takes a left at the city's main thoroughfare, lighting a cigarette as he walks to a bustling street corner. On the same street corner stands a man, much different than he. This other man is tired today. . . . He received a midnight phone call a few days ago from Russia, then another one just last night from the Czech Republic. His "friend" in Russia had informed him that the business was "going sour" for him and that the Russian law enforcement had been on his tail, thus he required a "grace period" until the goods could be delivered. If they were ever delivered! Young Russian girls, anything under twenty, brought good profits on the streets of Jerusalem these days. A rich government official, a rabbi or a successful businessman would pay a very satisfactory sum for a Russian bitch. Especially one that has been "house trained" with near endless bouts of "non-consensual sado-masochism" and a long ride to Israel in a metal shipping container followed by bouncing along in the back of a van with duct tape. . . .

The man in the green jacket [suicide bomber] checked his watch, and then put his hand into his pocket as he began walking towards the entrance to the food mart. As he passes by, the businessman [white slave trafficker] notices something a bit odd. There seem to be several square bulges beneath the man's jacket.

The man in the green jacket turns to face him. And then he sees it. He sees it in the man's eyes. The look. The same look that he saw in the eyes of the masked, militant Muslim protestors as they screamed out against his people and the Jenin affair on the television network several nights ago. The square bulges beneath the man's jacket. The look. He was one of them! PLEASE NO!

The man in the green jacket ends his silent prayer and looks at the businessman and smiles, "Bismilah!"

The man in the green jacket triggers the mechanism hidden deep within his coat pocket that sets off the belt.

The last thing that the businessman sees in Jerusalem is a smiling Muslim in a green coat, before the world around him and all his anxieties, worries, and curses all become naught in the blinding glow of a C-4 explosion. . . .

The sound of a prayer being made. A clear, heartfelt prayer that is sung out of a loudspeaker mounted to the side of the mosque. . . . "Allah is great. . . ."

A young woman cries, the sister of a man who she cheered four days ago at the Hamas rally. Although he was masked like the others, she knew which one was her brother, and she was proud but mostly scared. More than any other nation that she knew, her people were under the severest persecution from the Infidels, from the children of the devil, the wretched Zionists. And the Israelis got so much money from the United States, the richest nation.[151]

The fictional story is interesting insofar as it blends the racialist right's contempt for and outrage over the illicit sex slave industry in Israel with Islamic suicide terrorism. As such, it suggests a meeting of the minds between the two parties. According to the ADL, the website openly recruited sympathizers to become "Phineas Priests." The term "Phineas Priesthood" was popularized by Richard Kelly Hoskins, a Christian Identity minister from Lynchburg, in his book, *Vigilantes of Christendom*. Essentially, Phineas Priests are lone-wolf terrorists who act on their own volition without any direction from an organization.[152]

DAVID MYATT: THE ISLAMIC–NATIONAL SOCIALIST SYNTHESIS

The Aryan Nations' Islamic Liaison website features writings from sympathetic activists, including David Wulstan Myatt, an intriguing theorist whose exploits merit further examination. Myatt has been among the most outspoken activists in support of fostering ties with militant Islam. Although he is little known outside Britain, he has arguably done more than any other theorist to develop a synthesis of the extreme right and Islam. Born in 1950, Myatt spent much of his childhood abroad, first in Tanzania, where his father worked for the British government, and later in the Far East. The young Myatt evinced considerable intellectual curiosity; he reportedly has an IQ of 187.[153] Over the years, Myatt has ventured on a series of Faustian quests. While in the Far East with his father, he began an extensive study of the martial arts. Returning to England in the late 1960s, he went on to study physics at Hull University but did not graduate because he devoted most of his energies to politics.[154] He is reputed to have been a member of the underground paramilitary groups Column 88 and Combat 18 and was twice imprisoned for violent political activism.[155] Combat 18 gained notoriety in the early 1990s when members attacked left-wing bookshops, gay pubs, and antiapartheid activists.[156] Myatt took over the leadership of the organization in 1998 after its previous leader, Charlie Sargent, received a life sentence that year for murder. However, by the late 1990s, the organization appeared to have disintegrated due to internecine conflicts and government repression.

After several years of radical politics, Myatt became disillusioned and traveled throughout England and other parts of the world. The consummate "seeker," Myatt has gone down many avenues of enlightenment. He explored the esoteric aspects of Taoism and spent time in a Buddhist monastery. Later he entered the novitiate of a Christian monastery. Still searching, Myatt is alleged to have explored the occult and dabbled in pagan and quasi-Satanic secret societies. Throughout these varied spiritual and intellectual and quests, Myatt has always remained a committed National Socialist.[157]

Myatt has been the chief proponent of the "leaderless resistance" in England and established the National Socialist movement as a vehicle through which to promote this approach. A prolific writer, Myatt pens not only political and revolutionary strategy but poetry and spirituality as well. Following his resignation from the National Socialist movement, he joined the small Reichsfolk organization, which had the twofold aim of propagating the philosophy of National Socialism and forming rural communities where the like-minded could live in accord with the "ethos of their Aryan culture."[158]

At least publicly, Myatt has adopted a form of racial-ethno-nationalism sometimes described as "neoracism," in which racial and ethnic particularism is framed not as invidious racial supremacism but rather cultural identity and self-determination. He rejects the claims of racial superiority of older variants of racism and instead respects and seeks to preserve racial and ethnic differences. In Myatt's view, the various races of the world have different destinies, different abilities, and different ways of living that should be respected.[159] Despite the pronouncements of leading Nazis, such as Hitler on the superiority of the Aryan race, Myatt sees National Socialism as an evolving, organic process of change and development and speaks affectionately of the hospitality that was accorded to him by members of other races. One incident in particular that stands out in his memory is an episode in a remote part of Africa, where he was cared for by a woman "as dark as the ace of spades."[160]

In light of his earlier adventures, it is not surprising that Myatt eventually discovered Islam. Like so many other converts to Islam, Myatt adopted an Arabic name, "Abdul Aziz." According to Myatt's account, his conversion began when he started a new job on a farm in England, which required him to work for long hours in the fields. As Myatt explained, he felt a close connection to nature in which he reflected on the cosmos and came to the conclusion that this "order had not arisen by chance." Humbled by the experience, he eventually converted to Islam.[161] As Myatt has explained in numerous essays, he became fascinated with the life of the prophet Muhammad, coming to see him as both divinely inspired and an accomplished human being of unparalleled character.[162]

Myatt conceded that he had some ulterior motives that led him to adopt the Islamic faith. He was much taken by the militancy with which various Islamist movements confronted the new world order. As he saw it, both he and militant

Islam shared common enemies, the capitalist-consumer West and international finance.[163] Perhaps more important, he came to believe that something was terribly missing in the hearts of right-wing extremists. Islamists were animated with fanatical religious conviction. Myatt was much impressed with the power of religion so evident in the ranks of Muslim militants.

> I came to understand that what motivated the fighters I and others had discussed previously was an intense faith: a real belief in an after-life; a belief that it was their duty to act in such a way, and that by doing their duty in the way they did, they would be assured of entering Paradise. And this faith was not a political belief they had acquired or accepted in adult life: it was part of their very culture. Indeed, it was their culture, their tradition, and their way of life, from birth through death.
>
> It was this type of faith, this immersion in one's own culture, which our own people so sadly lacked. We were trying to motivate people in a political way, whereas Muslim fighters did what they did because it was accepted as their duty, as their own people understood this duty and gladly accepted their martyrdom.[164]

Myatt had little difficulty reconciling his newfound faith with National Socialism. At first he found little that was contradictory between the two:

> how could a National Socialist—an admirer of Adolf Hitler and his SS—come to sit happily in the homes of a Pakistani, an Arab, an African from Chad, share a meal, talk affably about God, our dreams for the future, the need for a spiritual renaissance, and of course, the common enemy?
>
> Because the truth about National Socialism has been obscured for over fifty years, thanks to the intensive, hateful, worldwide, well-financed and unending propaganda campaign directed against it.
>
> I never lived up to the stereotyped Marxist-capitalist image of a National Socialist—that is, some sort of rabid so-called "racist" who hated other races, saw them as inferior, and who would want to create "another holocaust." Rather, and in common with all true National Socialists, I loved my own people, valued my own heritage and wished to see creation of independent homelands where the different races and cultures could live in freedom according to their own customs.[165]

Myatt explained to me his endeavor to syncretize National Socialism and Islam:

> There is some common ground, since both ways—when correctly understood—produce civilized, honorable individuals who use reason as a

guide. The differences are, first, that Islam concentrates on the next life, on *Jannah,* and there is therefore what I have called an individualistic and Earth-based ethic: individuals do what they do in anticipation of the reward of *Jannah;* and, second, that the individual is understood in relation to such things as *taqwa* [the conscious awareness that God is watching you] and *imaan* [faith or belief], for these define them. For Islam, the folk—and the diversity and difference of human culture—is basically irrelevant. For National Socialism, this diversity and difference should be treasured and developed in an honorable, rational way.

In addition, National Socialism concentrates on our connection to our folk and thus to Nature and the Cosmos, with Nature and the Cosmos being understood as living beings. That is, we, as part of our folk, are Nature made manifest, and that our purpose is to aid Nature, and thus the Cosmos, through our folk: to evolve ourselves, our folk, our culture, and thus our human species. Hence, the perspective of National Socialism— and the basis for its ethics—is a cosmic, evolutionary one, of ourselves as a nexus, a connection between our human past and our human future. National Socialism believes we can and should evolve further: that this is our unique human destiny.

In National Socialism (and folk culture, I should add) the individual is defined by honor, loyalty, and duty, just as a National-Socialist society is.

Islam depends upon interpretation of texts, and thus there are areas of difference and dispute. In National Socialism, a person is either honorable, or they are not, honor being defined by a code of honor.

As for myself, I am committed to folk culture, which I understand to be the esoteric aspect of National Socialism: what National Socialism is evolving to become.

I spent many months, last year, living alone in a tent in the high hills of Cumbria thinking about Islam, National Socialism, and folk culture, and as I wrote in the third part of my autobiographical essays, I learnt a great deal from Islam but finally concluded—as I had years ago in relation to first, Buddhism, and then Christianity—that only the natural, honorable, reasoned, way which underlies what I have called folk culture fully answered all the questions about the meaning and purpose of our lives. I just could not reconcile my belief in the importance of personal honor and the overriding importance of Nature and ethnic identity with the principles of Islam.

Essentially, I accept that my foremost duty is to Nature and that we, as a species, have evolved from primitive beginnings and not been created, almost as we are now, by God. Furthermore, I accept that Nature and the cosmos work in a reasoned way and that there are no such things as God-given "miracles" which contradict this natural order, just as there is no such thing as a God-given book, or teachings, which we must follow in order to achieve salvation or eternal life.

In the end I had to accept that Islam and the way of Nature—the numinous way of folk culture—were different ways of living.

So, in one sense Islam was part of my lifelong quest to discover the meaning, the purpose, of our lives. As a result, I do believe I understand Islam, which is why I know an alliance between Muslims and National Socialists is possible, and indeed necessary.[166]

As Myatt explained, there were several aspects of Islam that he had difficulty reconciling with National Socialism. For instance, National Socialism is inherently tribalistic in that it exalts the "folk" as the primary focus of dedication and loyalty. From the National Socialist perspective, the individual is seen as a living link in a chain of ancestors and descendants to come. Furthermore, there is an emphasis on evolutionary development in which each folk or race follows its own unique trajectory. By contrast, Islam does not recognize the concept of race and sees all humanity as potential brethren once they acknowledge Allah and Muhammad as his messenger. National Socialism sees God as intrinsic to nature. Islam views God as detached from yet concerned about human beings. However, Myatt admires what he sees as an inherent quest in Islam to build a just society, the realm of the caliph. To Myatt, the Western man must rediscover his sense of destiny and follow a similar quest to build a "numinous order" based on Aryan ethics and honor.

Myatt's initial euphoria after his conversion to Islam did not last long. At the outset, Myatt thought that he might be able to create some sort of "Aryan Islam" in which Aryan culture and identity could be expressed in the confines of Islam. He eventually concluded that this endeavor was not feasible, as National Socialism was the best worldview in which to "fully and rationally answer all the questions about life, existence, and our identity, as human beings."[167] Despite this recommitment to National Socialism, Myatt retains great admiration for Islam and still on occasions uses the moniker Abdul Aziz.

According to Myatt, the great potential for cooperation between the extreme right and militant Islam stems from both movement's shared opposition to the so-called new world order, which he defines as a collection of Western capitalist nations whose way of life is dominated by materialism. According to Myatt, the plan of the new world order is to subjugate the planet through an oppressive world police force so that no dissidents can escape its reach—in short, a one-world government, with its own police force, courts, and army that have jurisdiction anywhere in the world. In that sense, the new world order regime amounts to "bully-made law." By contrast, Myatt sees Islamic sharia as far superior in that it was putatively derived from God, thus making it superior to fallible human-derived laws. Myatt has publicly expressed admiration for the Taliban movement in Afghanistan because it sought to establish "a true Islamic society" and defended Mullah Muhammad Omar's decision to continue to grant Osama bin Laden sanctuary in the wake of 9/11.[168] Despite obvious setbacks for the Taliban and al Qaeda since 9/11, Myatt remains confident that the Islamist movement will prevail. Part of the reason, as he sees it, is that the United States will decline from within. He sees American society as totally corrupt and decadent and thus ultimately outmatched by a morally superior Islam.[169]

In Myatt's analysis, the only real significant opposition to the new world order comes from militant Islam. On previous occasions, he has expressed open admiration for Osama bin Laden and views him as an exemplary warrior who has forsaken a life of luxury to pursue his Islamic duty.[170] According to Myatt, the primary battle against the Zionist occupation government (ZOG) has shifted from the West to the Islamic world in areas such as Afghanistan, Palestine, and Chechnya. This war between Islam and the new world order, in Myatt's estimation, makes the extreme right's goals more easily obtainable. He believes that the extreme right has several choices:

1) We can, for tactical or strategic reasons, now or in the future, ally ourselves with those, such as Muslims, who are fighting the same opponents as ourselves.

However, we must understand that our own Aryan way is not the same as the way of Islam, even though we share some of the same civilized values and ideals, such as that of personal honor, reason and using our will to restrain ourselves. Our Aryan way is unique, and we must not compromise it, or our values, in any way.

Thus, if we do seek, for whatever reason, some alliance with the forces of Islam then it can and must be on the basis of mutual respect for each other's way of life and ideals. That is, we must be open and honest about our pagan way and aims . . .

2) We can eschew such an alliance with Islam, and forge ahead on our own, in our own nations, through social, political, religious, educational and revolutionary means, effectively seeking to ignore the machinations of the New World Order, and instead—if required or it is advantageous—forging alliances with our Aryan comrades in other lands. That is, we concentrate on gaining some kind of local and national influence and power, and only then turn our attention to the forces at work in the wider world.[171]

To Myatt, the principal advantage of an open alliance with Islam is its ability to strike at the nerve center of the new world order. Myatt pointed out that another advantage stemming from such an alliance is that persecuted activists in the West could conceivably find sanctuary in those countries that are hostile to the new world order. Furthermore, these friendly governments could even allow—perhaps even support—so-called extreme right liberation movements on their soil.[172]

Although no other extremist activist has done more to theorize on the feasibility of an alliance with militant Islam, it is difficult to determine just how much Myatt has accomplished in his endeavors to bring the two sides together. When I asked if he had reached out to Arabs and Muslims in an effort to forge a coalition of common interests, he responded that he had but could not "elaborate for obvious reasons."[173] One right-wing extremist who appears to have had more documentable success in this regard is the Swiss national, Ahmed Huber.

AHMED HUBER AND AL-TAQWA

Just a few months after 9/11, some observers feared that an unholy alliance between militant Islam and the extreme right might eventually take hold. Adding credence to these suspicions was the strange case of al-Taqwa (fear of God), a now defunct financial firm that allegedly funded al Qaeda. Among the other organizations to which al-Taqwa is alleged to have provided assistance is Hamas, a radical Palestinian-Muslim group active in Israeli-occupied territories, and the Muslim Brotherhood.[174] Not long after September 11, 2001, al-Taqwa's name was changed to Nada Management, and the firm announced that it was liquidating its assets. The last known board chairman of al-Taqwa is reported to have been Yousef Nada, whose connections to the extreme right extend back several decades. As a young man, Nada joined the armed branch of the Muslim Brotherhood during World War II, during which time he established ties with German intelligence agents as they sought to undermine British colonial control in Egypt. Currently, he is believed to reside in Campione d'Italia, a small tax haven near the southern Swiss city of Lugano.

According to one researcher, on July 21, 1988, several individuals involved in financing various Muslim causes and projects gathered in Lugano to create al-Taqwa. Those at the meeting included Yousef Nada, Mohammed Mansour and his wife Zeinab Mansour Fattouh, Ali Ghaleb Himmat, and Ahmed Huber. The new entity was ostensibly created as an import-export company. Reportedly, 1,000 shares were initially issued, with 333 going to Mohammed Mansour and his wife, 332 going to Huber, and the rest split between Nada and Himmat.[175] Swiss authorities believe that the late François Genoud might have been involved in the original founding of al-Taqwa and used its resources to support international terrorists such as Ilich Ramirez (a.k.a. Carlos the Jackal) and Osama bin Laden. Genoud also helped pay for the defense of convicted Nazi war criminal Klaus Barbie when he stood trial in a French court, as well as that of Adolf Eichmann during his trial in Israel.[176]

Despite accusations from the Bush administration, the extent of al-Taqwa's ties to the al Qaeda network is still unclear. On September 23, 2001, President Bush issued an executive order designating twenty-five entities as supporting terrorism, fourteen of which were owned or controlled by either Ahmed Idris Nasreddin or Yousef Nada.[177] Furthermore, on November 7, 2001, President Bush announced that "al-Taqwa is an association of offshore banks and financial management firms that have helped al Qaeda shift money around the world."[178] Finally, in April 2002, President Bush issued a list of firms and individuals with suspected links to al Qaeda. In December 2001, Swiss authorities raided al-Taqwa's local office and seized records and documents.[179]

Al-Taqwa was included on the list, and the firm's assets were frozen. The investigation into al-Taqwa soon centered on Ahmed Huber, a Swiss national, who was reputed to be the liaison between European right-wing extremists and Islamic militants. He also maintains ties with American extremists.[180] Huber reportedly first met Yousef Nada at a conference held in Iran in 1988.[181] Until late 2001, Huber sat on the board of al-Taqwa. Huber, a convert to Islam, was also accused of being an important cog in al Qaeda's global financial network. Previously, he admitted to meeting followers of bin Laden in Beirut, whom he described as "very intelligent and nice guys."[182] There is little information available about him in the secondary literature. Therefore, much of this section is based on an interview that I conducted with Huber in April 2003.

Ahmed Huber was born to Protestant parents in the city of Freiburg, Switzerland, in 1927. As Huber explained, he converted to Islam around 1960. He recounted his conversion for me in an interview and explained how it came to influence his political worldview:

Well, it was a very simple thing. I was then a member of the Social Democratic Party of Switzerland. I had been a member of the party for forty-two years, but I was kicked out in 1994 because of Khomeinism, right-wing extremist contacts, revisionism, and so on. That's another story. In 1959, the Social Democratic Party of Switzerland had asked me—I was a young socialist journalist—to hide a few Algerians. At that time, there was a war between Algeria and France—the liberation war. Some Algerians had brought weapons and arms into Switzerland. They were being arrested by the police, and so they had to hide. The party asked me if I could hide a few of them in my apartment. I lived alone. I wasn't married then. So I took in these young people, and they were brilliant people. We had long discussions. It was, for me, the first real [encounter with] Islam. I asked them precise questions and I got precise answers.

I was myself a Protestant Christian, very tolerant, liberal, and not practicing. I didn't go to church. I was religious, but not too much. And here I found something very interesting especially two things. I found a concept of God which was fascinating because it was antitheology. The notion of Allah is a declaration of war against all theology. *Allah Akbar* means Allah, not god, Allah is always greater and greatest and completely different. It is beyond all human reason. . . . And the second thing they taught me was the unity of faith and reason. . . . And then the idea that there was no church; the only authority of the message and of the messenger. In Islam, the religious, the political, the social are [all] one, are together, which does not include the separation of the state and the mosque or the church or the synagogue. . . .

This always fascinated me. And it took me two years to slowly come to Islam. Then I became a Muslim by saying the *Shahadah* [declaration of faith] in 1962 in an Islamic center in Switzerland. The Egyptian embassy knew about it, though it had to be kept secret in a certain way. I said, "I don't want it to become public"; only my superiors in the Socialist Party knew about it at the time. They said, "Religion is a private matter. We don't care, as long as you don't make Islamic propaganda as a journalist." I said, "Of course. I will not then." Then the Egyptians invited me to the embassy, and they told me, "Listen the Islamic center where you said your *Shahadah,* your profession of faith, is a group of enemies of our president, Abdel Nasser and of Egypt, and of Islam. You should go to Cairo to al-Azhar and repeat the *Shahadah.* We will invite you and do everything." And then I went to Egypt and I went to Sheikh Mahmud Shaltut, the supreme leader of Egyptian Islam, who accepted my *Shahadah.* Then I was received by Gamal Abdel Nasser. For me it was a tremendous thing, and thus I entered into Islam.

Nasser explained to me some things about the Third Reich and about the Second World War, and about Adolf Hitler and some things that I have never known. It was for me a complete cultural shock. And then I went back to Switzerland. I was invited to the embassy and there I met a young girl. She was a secretary, and we later married in the private officers' club of Abdel Nasser. There we got married in August 1963 and from then on I've been a Muslim.

The late Haj Amin al-Husseini, the grand mufti of Jerusalem, was instrumental in shaping Huber's views, not only on Islam but also on the Third Reich. By the early 1980s, Huber found a new mentor in the Ayatollah Khomeini of Iran. In fact, he is reportedly the only European Muslim to have given a speech before the tomb of the late Iranian cleric.[183] Huber spoke to me about the late mullah in glowing terms:

I was, [for some] time, an Arab nationalist. It was the Islamic Revolution in Iran which made something new out of me. I became more deeply involved with Islam. I met Iman [Ayatollah] Khomeini, the leader of the Islamic revolution. I spoke before the Iranian Parliament. The first time I went to Iran was in 1983, and since then, every year I've been in Iran. Even though I am a Sunni Muslim, I became very much touched by Shi'ite Islam and felt [sympathy] for the legality of the Shi'a Muslim and especially for the Islamic republic.

When I came back to Europe in the last ten to fifteen years, the Iranians told me that it would be good if I could make contact with right-wing movements in order to stop them from attacking Muslims and to speak of common values [that] we have and also of common enemies. . . .

In 1985 I was invited to his house with some journalists, who had converted to Islam. I met him [Ayatollah Khomeini] several times. I was in a little mosque in the north of Tehran, where he was sitting on the balcony and speaking to the people. We were sitting down at his feet and listening to him. He was an absolutely remarkable man. He was one of the greatest, maybe the greatest leader of Islam in the twentieth century. Prophet Muhammad had said centuries ago that Allah will send in every century a man to wake up the *umma* and show the way to the *umma*. Many of us think that Imam Khomeini was that man for Islam, who came in the twentieth century.[184]

Not unlike David Myatt, Huber found no contradiction in terms of his Islamic faith and his admiration for German National Socialism, as he explained:

I judge as a Muslim, I judge Adolf Hitler and the Third Reich and his movement in a different way than the Zionists, or the Marxists, or the Anglo-Americans do because I know very, very much. I have been studying the sources of what was the Third Reich. And I met a lot of people who knew Hitler personally. I have met his secretary, Frau [Gertrud] Junge, who recently died, and Christa Schroeder. I have met Anton Axman, the last Hitler Youth leader, who brought the corpses of Hitler and Eva Braun to the Reich Chancellery and burnt them. I met a lot of Waffen-SS generals from the *Leibstandarte,* who personally knew Hitler. . . .

[W]e Muslims were fascinated by the Third Reich in the 1930s because Hitler had some ideas at the political level and the economic level, and the cultural field, which were very close to the political, economic, and cultural sharia. For instance, the economic concept of an interest-free noncapitalist economy is very close to the Islamic concept of the economy. His [Hitler's] idea that art should represent God and not be degenerate and make a cult of ugliness, of lies, and of evil, this corresponds to the cultural sharia, and so on.

So this man and his movement were fascinating to many Muslim intellectuals all during the 1930s. And since 1945, Muslims have been studying all of these things. And we judge him in a different way. Even if now, of course, when the Muslims protest against America, they say Bush equals Hitler, or Sharon equals Hitler, they say that not for themselves, but [because] they know that it has an impact on Western public opinion.

You see Hitler himself had a quite positive attitude towards Islam. He said several times, "The only religion I respect is Islam. The only prophet I admire is the Prophet Muhammad." He said several times in his table talks that "After the final war the swastika will rule over Europe and will represent a new Europe. We will help the Muslims in North Africa and the Middle East to reestablish the Caliphate." That means there would be an Islamic civilization. [And Hitler said] "In the Far East, there will be the rising sun"—Japan of course. He didn't see China [laughs]. He had no thought for China. He only saw Japan with whom he had an alliance. He spoke of a new stability in the world. The swastika, the crescent, and the rising sun would be a new stability. He said in America, people will wake up [as well as] in Latin America and Black Africa. He was against colonialism, you know. After the beginning, in *Mein Kampf*, there are still some colonialist ideas he had, like all people of his time. But later in the 1930, especially during the war, he changed.[185]

Huber explained some of his efforts to build bridges between militant Islam and the extreme right:

You see, in the past ten years I have been in Switzerland, Austria, France, and Germany. I have been around with groups of young people, both Muslims and non-Muslims, and especially what we call the new right. Sometimes we hold meetings together, Muslims and people from the new right, to speak about these things and to show what we have in common. I also spoke about this at the University of Tehran. I spoke at a seminar and workshops about these problems. Explaining what was the Third Reich, what it was all about. In London, we had conferences. We had Islamic conferences in the United States between 1988 and 1998, the last time in 1998 in the United States. And, of course, I was in Beirut also.

I always tell them, the young Germans, apart from all of the stupid ideological blah, blah, blah, [that the Third Reich] had three aspects. It was a revolution, a reconsideration of the divine of God. Hitler was a man, who until the last minute of his life, believed in God. . . . And he spoke about it quite frankly. . . . He wanted a reconsideration of the creation of life, of nature—to live in accordance with nature. The Nazis were the first ecologists in Europe. They made the first ecologist Green laws in Germany. And then the third aspect was [a return] to reason, back to the normal sound reason of the individual. . . . Three aspects—the return to God, the return to the creation of life and nature, and the return to reason and common sense. This appealed to a growing number of German people. . . .

Of course, when you say this to young Muslims, they say, well this is Islam. We also have this belief in God, the belief in his creation. One should not change His creation. Allah says in the Koran very clearly there is no change in Allah's creation. And if you change the creation of Allah, the earth will turn against you. And then also, the importance of reason and of science, and knowledge, it's very central in Islam. The Prophet said, "Before you can become a real Muslim, you must first acquire knowledge. Look for knowledge from science, even if you have to go to China!"

When you talk about this to young Muslims and young right-wing Germans, they say there is common ground. The link is a criticism of the so-called modernity of the modern world, which in many ways has gone far away from God. It is against creation. It is against nature. Look for instance, at the cult of homosexuality. This is incredible. This is against common sense, against reason, against nature. It is ridiculous. If you look at modern art, it is an insult to reason and an insult to the sense of beauty, which is in every human being.[186]

Just how successful Huber's efforts to build an alliance between militant Islam and the extreme right have been is still unclear. Besides Huber, other German right-wing extremists are believed to have connections to radical Islamic groups as well. For example, in January 2003 German authorities banned Hizb ut-Tahir (the Party of Liberation), an Islamist group suspected of having ties to the German National Democratic Party (NPD), according to German Interior Minister Otto Schily. Hizb ut-Tahir called for the destruction of Israel and Jews. In Germany, radical Islamic and rightist groups have reportedly had frequent contacts to discuss their shared hatred for the United States and Israel.[187] In January 2004, it was reported that the former head of the

NPD for the Saxony-Anhalt region, Frank Kerkhoff, and another activist, Harald Bornschain, opened a business in Kosovo that sold weapons, among other things.[188] In addition, according to a report in the Milan-based newspaper *Corriere della Serra,* German intelligence services claimed that Osama bin Laden had financed extreme right organizations in Europe in the hope that they would assist him in carrying out terrorist attacks during a G-8 summit meeting held in Genoa in the summer of 2001.[189]

An organization that may have connections to al-Taqwa is the Saar Foundation, created by Suleiman Abdul al-Aziz al-Rahji, a scion of one of the richest Saudi families. According to some reports, soon after al-Taqwa was forced to shut down, elements of the Wahhabi lobby shifted operations to its backup institutions in the United States. Saar is also allegedly linked to Khalid bin Mahfouz, the former lead financial adviser to the Saudi royal family and former head of the National Commercial Bank of Saudi Arabia. French intelligence named Mahfouz as a financial supporter of Osama bin Laden. Moreover, U.S. authorities have confirmed that the Muwafaq Foundation, an entity that Mahfouz has endowed, is an arm of al Qaeda. Muwafaq's former chief, Yassin al-Qadi, assisted the financial penetration of Bosnia-Herzegovina by Islamic mujahideen in the late 1990s.

The paths of Saar, al-Rahji, al-Qadi, and Mahfouz frequently led back to northern Virginia. The U.S. government sought to dry up the sources of terrorist funding by launching "Operation Green Quest." As part of this effort, on March 20, 2002, a U.S. Treasury task force raided businesses connected to these individuals. As of April 2002, the assets of 192 individuals and organizations connected with al-Taqwa, al Baraka (a financial and telecommunications conglomerate alleged to have channeled millions of dollars to al Qaeda), and Hamas have been frozen.[190] Reportedly, their financing was significant. For example, Saar received $1.7 billion in donations in 1998 alone. Another major target of the raid was one Jamal Barzinji. His northern Virginia–based World Assembly of Muslim Youth was alleged to have been deeply involved in providing cover for Wahhabi terrorism.[191] Another former al-Taqwa shareholder, Alessandro Ghe, an Italian, has been questioned by Italian authorities for possible ties to bin Laden. Ghe belonged to the Ordine Nuovo (New Order) organization, which began to reach out to Muslim radicals in the 1970s.[192]

Despite these major setbacks, al Qaeda continues to strike out against the United States and its allies; its financial network in the West has proven to be durable, despite great efforts on the part of authorities to disrupt it.[193] The practice of *hawala,* an ancient system of banking based largely on trust and connections, facilitates financial transactions for sub-rosa organizations such as al Qaeda. *Hawala* transfers take place with little, if any paper trail, thus making them very difficult for authorities to monitor. When financial records are kept, they are usually kept in code.[194]

For his part, Huber categorically denied that al-Taqwa was involved in any way in abetting al Qaeda and insisted that the financial firm only undertook charitable work that benefited needy Muslims.[195] He expounded on this issue for me:

> After the eleventh of September, President Bush and the American
> government said it on CNN. They put several individuals and Islamic
> organizations on a blacklist of sixty-seven people and organizations. And
> among others [was] al-Taqwa Management, which was situated in
> Switzerland, in Lugano in the south of Switzerland. I was a member of the
> administrative counsel of al-Taqwa Management and the al-Taqwa Bank,
> which was in the Bahamas for tax reasons. . . . And Bush and the American
> government accused us of financing terrorism and maybe participating in
> the financing of the 11 September [attacks]. I mean these were very, very
> grave accusations. Then the American government asked the Swiss
> government to make an investigation, and the federal police and the
> federal prosecutor came to my house. They were very kind, very, very
> correct, and looked up everything. They interrogated me for three and a
> half hours. Nothing more happened. They did the same thing in Lugano
> to my friend, the other members of the council of the administration.
>
> Al-Taqwa was very small. We liquidated it in the beginning of 2002.
> The bank was also liquidated. It was founded in 1983. I joined in 1988. I
> became a member of the administration council. Our job was to finance
> very small development projects in Muslim countries and for Muslims in
> the Third World in Africa, Asia, and so on. We had a total circulation of
> about $1.5 to $2 million every year. I mean it was very, very small. We got
> our money from sponsors. These sponsors were rich Muslims and Arabs
> from the Saudi royal family. Allies of the Unites States sponsored our
> projects. And out come Mr. Bush and Mr. Ashcroft, and they say that we
> are financing terrorists. It was rubbish. The Swiss authorities made their
> investigation. They did not find anything and especially the American
> government has not given any evidence for [its] accusations. The federal
> prosecutor told me, "So far the American government has not given us any
> evidence." It's all rubbish. And now the Swiss prosecutor will publish his
> report about the al-Taqwa case and close it. I was interrogated on
> November 7, 2001, by the federal authorities and on the tenth September

2002. I was again interrogated for one hour. Nothing new. They were very polite, very correct. And they told me, "Well we will now try to establish our report, and it will come out."[196]

A spokesman for the Swiss attorney general, Hansjuerg Mark Wiedemer, remarked that he believed that al-Taqwa "could have been financing al Qaeda." However, he believed that his office did not have enough evidence to open criminal proceedings against Huber and other members of al-Taqwa.[197] The principal concern of American authorities with respect to Huber is probably his role in and the financial services that firm could potentially offer to radical Islamist groups. Despite his denial of any wrongdoing, Ahmed Huber waxed enthusiastic over the 9/11 attacks and saw them as a catalyst that would bring together elements of the extreme right and militant Islam:

> The new alliance has come. The eleventh of September has brought together [the two sides] because the new right has reacted positively. . . . They say, and I agree with them 100 percent, what happened on the eleventh of September, if it is the Muslims who did it, it is not an act of terrorism but an act of counterterrorism.[198]

HISTORICAL/HOLOCAUST REVISIONISM

The most notable instance of propaganda sharing between the extreme right and militant Islam has been in the area of Holocaust revisionism. For the most part, revisionist historians associated with the extreme right have developed a much larger corpus of literature in this area than their Islamic and Arab counterparts. Of all the various elements of the extreme right that have reached out to the Islamic world, arguably the revisionist historians have been the best received. So-called Holocaust revisionism is becoming increasingly popular in the popular newspapers and magazines in the Arab world.[199]

One notable episode of cooperation between the two parties occurred in the summer of 2001, when American revisionists sought to organize a conference on "Revisionism and Zionism," scheduled for late March in Beirut, Lebanon. Although the event was canceled at the last minute, it demonstrates a common ground between the Western revisionists and Islamic sympathizers. The Institute for Historical Review and the Swiss-based group Verité et Justice had planned the conference, which was to include lectures in English, French, and Arabic. Long-time Holocaust revisionists Roger Garaudy and Robert Faurisson were slated to appear as guest speakers. The event occasioned fierce opposition from Jewish defense organizations. The Simon Wiesenthal Center, as well as the Anti-Defamation League and the World Jewish Congress, put pressure on the Lebanese government to cancel the event. The U.S. State Department also sought to dissuade the Lebanese government. After a cabinet meeting on the subject, Lebanese prime minister Rafik Hariri announced that the conference would be cancelled. Despite the protests of the ADL, a smaller conference was eventually held on May 13, 2001, in the city of Amman, Jordan, sponsored by Jordanian Writers' Association.[200] The Swiss organizer of the event, Jürgen Graf, recounted the controversy surrounding the conferences for me in an interview:

> Vérite et Justice was founded in 1999. Its main goal is the restoration of freedom of speech in Switzerland. It has published two booklets in German and French documenting anti-Revisionist repression in our country. . . . Recently, Vérite et Justice published an abridged French language version of Henry Ford's *The International Jew.*
>
> Our organization has some hundred members and sympathizers. While I am officially still its president, although I left Switzerland in August 2000, the current leaders of Vérite et Justice are my friends Rene-Louis Berclaz and Philippe Brennenstuhl. In April 2002, Berclaz was sentenced to eight months and Brennenstuhl to three months in prison, but they both appealed the verdict, and the sentences have not been confirmed yet. A third defendant, Gaston-Armand Amaudruz, who is currently serving a three months prison term for disbelieving in the Nazi gas chambers and the 6 million figure, got another three months for criticizing his first sentence. He is eighty-two years old.
>
> As you know, Vérite et Justice tried to organize a conference about Revisionism and Zionism in Lebanon in spring 2001. As a result of strong American pressure on the Lebanese government, the conference was forbidden (although it would have been quite legal in the United States). This proves that the Washington regime is fully aware of the political impact of revisionism.[201]

Several Western Holocaust revisionists who have faced prosecution in their own countries have turned to the Islamic world for help. Jürgen Graf reportedly once fled to Iran—a country where other revisionists are said to have received a warm welcome—after his appeals of a 1998 Swiss conviction for hate speech violations had been denied. Fearing arrest by Austrian authorities, Wolfgang Fröhlick, an Austrian engineer who testified on behalf of Graf in his 1998 trial about the putative impossibility that Zyklon-B could not be used to kill humans, also found refuge in Iran in 2000. Reportedly, he still resides there.[202] Iran has become somewhat of a sanctuary for Holocaust revisionists fleeing legal entanglements in their own countries.

The prominent Iranian cleric, Ayatollah Ali Khamenei, once even suggested that the Holocaust had been greatly exaggerated in part to undermine Islam:

> There is evidence which shows that Zionists had close relations with German Nazis and exaggerated statistics on Jewish killings. There is evidence on hand that a large number of non-Jewish hooligans and thugs of Eastern Europe were forced to migrate to Palestine as Jews. The purpose was to install in the heart of the Islamic world an anti-Islamic state under the guise of supporting the victims of racism and to create a rift between the East and the West of the Islamic world.[203]

The former president of Iran, Ali Akbar Hashemi Rafsanjani has voiced moral support for revisionists in the West as well. In a sermon delivered on Radio Tehran, he once defended the French revisionist and convert to Islam, Roger Garaudy, the author of the book *The Founding Myths of Modern Israel* and one of the scheduled speakers at the Beirut conference. Rafsanjani exclaimed that he was convinced that "Hitler had only killed twenty thousand Jews and not six million" and added that Garaudy, who in 1998 was convicted in a French court for inciting racial hatred, was being persecuted because of "the doubt he cast on Zionist propaganda."[204] In some ways it is not difficult to fathom Rafsanjani's support of revisionism. After all, he is arguably one of the most rabidly anti-Zionist figures in the Middle East. He once went so far as to raise the prospect of national suicide as part of an effort to destroy Israel, musing that the nuclear annihilation of Iran as a result of a retaliatory attack by Israel would be an acceptable price to pay to destroy half of the world's Jewish population. In such a conflagration, only a small portion of the world's Muslims would perish.[205] More recently, the Iranian government invited the Australian revisionist historian Fredrick Töben to speak before the International Conference on the Palestinian Intifada, held in Tehran on August 19–21, 2003, at which he not only impugned the Holocaust but also decried American and Israeli aggression in the Middle East.[206]

The Palestinian resistance movement, Hamas, has on occasion dabbled in Holocaust denial as well. After an international conference involving several heads of state and officials from many countries was held in Stockholm in 2000 that emphasized the need to counter Holocaust denial, Hamas issued a press release that took issue with this effort:

> This conference bears a clear Zionist goal, aimed at forging history by hiding the truth about the so-called Holocaust, which is an alleged and invented story with no basis. . . . The invention of these grand illusions of an alleged crime that never occurred, ignoring the millions of dead

European victims of Nazism during the war, clearly reveals the racist Zionist face, which believes in the superiority of the Jewish race over the rest of nations.[207]

Another institution that has fostered cooperation between revisionists and the Muslim world is the Zayed Center for Coordination and Follow-up, which was founded in 1999 as the official think tank of the Arab League. The current chairman is Sultan Bin Zayed al-Nahayan, who also serves as the deputy prime minister of the United Arab Emirates. Located in Abu Dhabi, United Arab Emirates, the Zayed Center has hosted numerous Western heads of state and diplomats, including former president Jimmy Carter, former vice president Al Gore, and former secretary of state James Baker.[208] However, recently the Zayed Center has hosted some controversial figures as well, including the journalist Mike Piper from the extremist newspaper, the *American Free Press*. Increasingly, the center has become a forum for Holocaust revisionism and has released several anti-Zionist publications.[209] In March 2003, Piper presented a lecture at the center during which he accused the Israeli lobby in the United States—in alliance with Christian fundamentalists who sympathize with the aims of Zionism—of pushing for a U.S.-led war against Iraq.[210] Furthermore, Piper accused Israel of not only developing weapons of mass destruction, including nuclear weapons, but also a sinister form of biowarfare known as an "ethnic bomb" that could be targeted at specific ethnic groups (such as Arabs) while leaving Jews unharmed.[211] Piper recounted for me his experiences at the Zayed Center:

I was invited to the Zayed Center to speak on the basis of two primary factors: (1) the fact that my book, *Final Judgment,* was translated into Arabic and published by one of the leading Arab world publishing houses, the firm of Dar El Ilm Lilmalayin, based in Beirut; and (2) the fact that I have a proven, twenty-two-year track record of advocacy for the Arab cause through the venue of writing and speaking.

At the Zayed Center I spoke not only on the topic of my book—which alleges Israeli involvement in the assassination of John F. Kennedy—but on the more broad-based topic of U.S. media bias in favor of Israel and the corresponding hostility to the Arab world.

My position has always been clear and unambiguous, and for myself, I have always felt that the U.S. has never had any business allying itself with Israel, a nation that is of no benefit, in any way, to the United States, the claims of pro-Israel propagandists notwithstanding.

Although my longtime employer, Liberty Lobby, adopted a strict "hands off" policy toward the Arab-Israeli conflict, counseling against bias in favor of either side, saying that America's best interests were served by strict neutrality—certainly an admirable and respectable position shared by many people who would prefer that America stay out of the troubles of the world—for my own part, I frankly differed with that position, advocating instead U.S. alliance with the Arab world, even if it meant the exclusion of Israel.

Building friendship and alliance with the Arab world has far more potential benefits for the American people and for American national security than does a relationship with the state of Israel of the type that now exists, founded on sentimental ideals that have been betrayed by the very actions of Israel against the subjugated Christian and Muslim Palestinian Arabs.

The reception at the Zayed Center was tremendous. I was impressed with the caliber of those in attendance, diplomats, intellectuals, and media figures from the Arab world and from elsewhere, including the ambassador from one Western European state who took the time to greet me following my presentation.[212]

In August 2004, Piper conducted a ten-day speaking tour in the largely Muslim nation of Malaysia, where he lectured about "Israeli lobby influence" on American foreign policy.[213]

Piper is best known in revisionist circles for a JFK assassination theory that he advanced in *Final Judgment*. In it, he argued that the Israeli Mossad was the principal force behind a conspiracy to murder the late president, John F. Kennedy. According to his analysis, Israeli prime minister David Ben-Gurion was determined to develop a nuclear warfare program in Israel. When Kennedy resisted the project, he paid the ultimate price.[214] The theory has gained currency among conspiracy theorists in the Middle East.[215] In an interesting twist to the story, Israeli whistleblower Mordechai Vanunu, who spent eighteen years in prison for revealing details of Israel's top secret nuclear program, suggested that President Kennedy was assassinated because of his strong opposition to then Israeli prime minister Ben-Gurion.[216] It is worth mentioning that no mainstream JFK assassination research has reached a similar conclusion. Despite his efforts to build bridges with Arabs and Muslims, Piper saw only limited potential for Holocaust revisionism in the Middle East:

Although I have always been interested in Holocaust revisionism and very familiar with its emphasis and certainly associated with many of its pivotal figures, I have always felt that Holocaust Revisionism is indeed an uphill battle, precisely because it is so emotional in nature and because so many people have been exposed to the Jewish point of view vis-à-vis the

Holocaust. I think, probably, that my own views reflect those of many in the Arab world. The Holocaust revisionists are doing important work, needless to say, and I admire them for their tenacity, but I don't see Holocaust Revisionism emerging as a major force in the Arab world.[217]

Other observers tend to disagree. For example, Abraham Foxman, the national chairman of the ADL, believes that many Arabs are embracing Holocaust revisionism. As he explained, this endeavor is used to delegitimate the state of Israel. According to the reasoning of Holocaust revisionism, the tragedy was deliberately exaggerated in order to generate global sympathy for Jews and support for the creation of the Jewish state. Furthermore, it has been used to "extort" billions of dollars from the West and demoralize Aryans and the West "so that Jews could more easily control the world."[218]

DAVID DUKE

In recent years, David Duke has been in the forefront of an effort to reach out to the Islamic world. One such effort took place in the fall of 2002, when he presented two lectures in Bahrain titled "The Global Struggle against Zionism" and "Israeli Involvement in September 11." Duke claims to have found a receptive audience in that country. A group called Discover Islam Center invited Duke to Bahrain, after members were impressed by some postings on Israel that appeared on his website. Over the past several years, Duke has journeyed throughout Europe in an effort to shore up support for white nationalist movements. More recently, he has reached out to critics of Zionism in the Middle East. For example, an article Duke wrote titled "The World's Most Dangerous Terrorist" was published in the *Arab News,* a Saudi Arabian English daily newspaper. In the article he repeated his assertion that Israel had assisted the terrorists in the 9/11 attack.[219] Duke has also appeared on a talk show, "Without Borders," which airs on the al-Jazeera satellite network in Qatar. The U.S. Department of State protested to the Qatari government over the broadcast. Duke recounted his experiences for me in an interview:

I was received very well. We had packed, overflowed meetings in one hotel in Bahrain, and we actually had a huge hall there, and we had two meetings in a row on succeeding nights. Both audiences were packed. Two different lectures as to what's going on in terms of Israeli supremacism and Jewish supremacism. So the reception was fantastic. . . .
     In Qatar, of course, al-Jazeera said about 70 million people watched my program, and the response was overwhelmingly positive. . . . The U.S.

State Department, even before I went on the program in Qatar, tried to prevent the program from being aired, which is very much against the Constitution of the United States of America. What right does the federal government have to prevent an American citizen from voicing his opinion on a talk show? And when the government of this country tries to keep somebody off a talk show to talk about issues and ideas, I mean that's a very, very dangerous sign, and they literally tried to suppress the talk show and they all tried to blackmail the al-Jazeera network, that if they would have people like me on the air then they won't have journalistic rights in Washington. . . .

The ADL issued a protest to Bahrain for having me in the country. One of the things they said [was], "How can they have a white supremacist in Bahrain?" But the people in Bahrain understand very well that I'm not a white supremacist and that I am a European American who wants to preserve my heritage like all people in the world want to, but the real danger to all heritages is Jewish supremacism, which seeks to destroy every heritage but the Jewish heritage.[220]

In the months leading up to the Iraq War, Duke sought to dispel the theory that had gained currency in some left-wing circles that the principal reason for prosecuting the war against Iraq was to control that country's oil. Conspiracy theorists, most notably from the political left, often invoke oil as an ulterior motive for the current war on terror. Of course, there is scattered evidence with which to build a mosaic to support such a theory. After all, the American, Russian, and Chinese governments have indeed given serious consideration to Afghanistan as a prospective site for constructing pipelines. The journalist Ahmed Rashid has christened this endeavor as the "Great Game II." As he reported, the Clinton administration sought to assist a U.S. firm, Unocal, in its effort to build an oil pipeline to pump gas from Turkmenistan through Afghanistan to Pakistan. Pakistan's Inter-Services Intelligence (ISI) urged the United States to support the Taliban insofar as it would make Unocal's project less cumbersome.[221] However, U.S. domestic politics soon interfered as the plight of Afghani women became a cause célèbre among feminists and prominent liberals in Hollywood. Vice President Al Gore was eager to retain the support of these constituent groups in his upcoming presidential election. Furthermore, the continuing moderation of the government in Iran made that country a more attractive partner in the region. As a result, U.S. policy began to toughen against the Taliban.[222]

Seeking to debunk the "war for oil" theories, Duke argued that American petroleum companies would have little to gain from the war in Iraq. In fact, as

Duke saw it, a normalization of U.S.-Iraqi relations would lead to more oil on the world market, thus increasing supply and potential long-term profits. Duke finds preposterous the notion that somehow the United States would seize the oil fields and profit from the oil. In his analysis, the "war for oil canard" has been deliberately propounded by Jews in left-wing circles as a way to divert attention from the efforts of Jewish organizations and neoconservatives pressing for war. Furthermore, Duke contends that the notion that the war is being fought for oil leads the American people to believe that they are fighting for a resource vital to the functioning of the American economy.[223]

One obvious difference that separates militant Islam and the extreme right is religion. Interestingly, Duke has also sought to bridge the religious differences between Christians and Muslims. Not unlike the spokespeople from the Aryan Nations' Ministry of Islamic Liaison, Duke went so far as to point out the similarities between Christianity and Islam. Sounding much like an ecumenical multiculturalist, he expounded on the commonalities of the two faiths while at the same time distancing them from Judaism:

The truth is there is no such thing as Judeo-Christianity. That would be saying Satanic-Christianity. The religion now called Judaism did not even come formally into existence until six hundred years after Jesus Christ. It began with the codification of the Babylon Talmud. . . .

Interestingly enough, Islam is much closer to Christianity than Judaism. For instance, Judaism condemns the Virgin Mary as a prostitute and viciously condemns Jesus as an evil sorcerer and a bastard. . . . In stark contrast, although Islam certainly does not share all the Christian views of Jesus Christ, it views Christ as the true prophet of God, virgin-born, and that God resurrected Jesus from the dead. Ironically, the chief religious book of Islam, the Qur'an, actually defends Jesus Christ from the obscene slanders made against Him in the Jewish Talmud.[224]

Furthermore, Duke is quick to point out that many Arabs residing in the holy land are actually Christians. He castigates Christian right evangelicals such as Pat Robertson and Jerry Falwell for championing Israel while ignoring the plight of Palestinian Christians.[225]

Duke is not the only right-winger to draw parallels between Christianity and Islam. For example, Bill Baker, the head of Christians and Muslims for Peace (CAMP) and former chairman of the Populist Party, was invited by an Islamic student group at the University of Pennsylvania to speak at the institution's Islam Awareness Week. He also appeared at an Islamist conference held in Toronto called "Reviving the Islamic Spirit." In 1998 Baker published a book titled *More in Common Than You Think: The Bridge between Islam and*

Christianity, which amounts to an attempt, according to his detractors, to forge an alliance between fringe Christians and extremist Muslims.[226]

By late 2002, Duke's international campaign was drawing to an end. For much of the previous three years, he had stayed in self-imposed exile. Rather than face possible extradition, Duke returned to the United States in late 2002 to face charges of mail fraud and tax violations involving the $100,000 sale of a list of donors to Mike Foster in 1995, a year before the latter became governor of Louisiana. Duke plea-bargained with federal prosecutors to avoid trial and received a fifteen-month sentence.[227] Given the allegations that he misused donations from such a cash-strapped movement (see chapter 6) it first appeared that Duke might have difficulty regaining credibility among his supporters. However, since his release from prison in 2004, Duke has regained much of his momentum. In September 2005, he received a doctorate in history from the Interregional Academy of Personnel Management—a major private university system in the Ukraine. And in November 2005, he traveled to Syria, where he held a news conference and expressed his support for the Syrian people. He pledged to do his best to convey the "real peace-loving Syrian" positions across the world. Attendees at the event included several members of the Syrian Parliament and Arab and foreign correspondents. Reportedly, officials in the Syrian Public Relations Association announced that Duke had dramatically improved the view of the Syrian people and the entire Arab world toward Americans.

THE NATIONAL ALLIANCE

At first, 9/11 and its immediate aftermath appeared to galvanize the National Alliance. Its chairman, Dr. William L. Pierce, became even more strident in his rhetoric in his American Dissident Voices radio broadcasts. Although he stopped short of outright praise for bin Laden, al Qaeda, and the Taliban, at times it was hard not to infer a degree of admiration for these parties. His deputy membership coordinator, Billy Roper, was less inhibited, overtly praising the 9/11 hijackers. In the immediate months following September 11, 2001, members of the National Alliance boldly took to the streets to bring attention to their critique of American foreign policy. The National Alliance launched several demonstrations at the Israeli embassy in Washington, D.C., to protest American and Israeli policies in the Middle East and distributed literature nationwide to coincide with Jewish holidays and the anniversary of 9/11.

At its first demonstration in November 2001, the National Alliance released a list of eighteen demands to the Israeli government that resembled the standard anti-imperialist pronouncements of traditional left-wing groups. The demands included: (1) "stop using American military aid to commit unlawful acts of terrorism, murder, and genocide against Palestinians"; (2) "obey UN Resolution 242"; (3) "obey UN Resolution 194"; (4) "allow true freedom of speech and assembly for all people in Israel"; and (5) "turn Ariel Sharon, the 'Butcher of Beirut,' over to the World Court."[228] These efforts may indicate a desire to reach out to a larger audience than the segments to which the organization has traditionally appealed. How successful this effort has been in currying favor with other groups is questionable. Not long after the protests, several Arab Americans expressed dismay over the National Alliance's arrogation of the Palestinian cause.[229] The ADL has also voiced alarm over this development, observing that extremists often draw parallels between the Palestinian struggle against Israeli occupiers and their own struggle against what they perceive as a Zionist occupation government. Furthermore, some have lauded the selflessness of Palestinian suicide bombers. Some of the more radical elements of the extreme right have gone so far as to express the proposition that Palestinians ought to replicate their struggle against Jews inside the United States.[230]

Not long before his death, National Alliance chairman Pierce claimed that interest in his American Dissident Voices program increased significantly after the 9/11 attacks.[231] Conceivably, one factor that contributed to the success of the National Alliance was its lack of inhibition in addressing politically sensitive issues. For example, various Jewish organizations and Jewish neoconservatives in the Bush administration have been among the most steadfast proponents of the war against Iraq, but the mainstream media have been reluctant to frankly discuss this connection. The National Alliance, unconstrained by political correctness, is one of the few voices in the American political landscape willing both to protest current American foreign policy in the Middle East, as well as new measures, such as the USA PATRIOT Act, that abridge civil liberties, and to go further to connect them with Jewish organizations that support these policies. If the National Alliance's statements are to be believed, just prior to 9/11, American Dissident Voices broadcasts received approximately 170,000 downloads per week. Not long thereafter, this figure jumped to 340,000. Furthermore, membership applications have reportedly trebled since 2001. As one observer noted, these developments could propel the National Alliance out of its extremist right ghetto.[232]

Despite occasional rhetorical overtures, for the most part Pierce remained skeptical of an actual operational alliance with Muslims:

> We must not foolishly imagine that we can achieve some quick and easy
> victory by building alliances with people whose goals or interests are
> essentially different from ours—Middle Easterners or other non-Whites for

example—or even with people who believe that their goals and interests are different from ours, as is the case with any of our people who still are under the influence of Jewish ideology.[233]

It is worth mentioning that although Pierce usually expressed little fondness for Arabs and Muslims, he did not see them as implacable and inevitable enemies, as he did Jews:

> I have no real fondness for anyone in the Middle East. I do not believe that Middle Easterners, Arabs, and Jews—especially Jews—should be permitted to live in America or Europe. I have no sympathy for Islam or any other Semitic religion from the Middle East. But I do not believe that we need to go to war against Iraq or Iran or even Afghanistan in order to protect Americans from terrorism or to protect any other American interests. And I strenuously object to going to war against anyone to protect Israel's interest.[234]

In the months before his death, Pierce seemed to reevaluate his derisive views toward Muslims. For example, a story in his *Resistance* magazine featured articles on the Middle East, including photos of light-haired Palestinians with European features. The implication was that some elements of the Muslim and Middle Eastern population were descended from Europeans, as he remarked in a broadcast:

> It is interesting to note, by the way that not all of the people in Afghanistan are black-haired, swarthy, greasy, hook-nosed, Middle Eastern types. Some of the tribes are White, with reddish-brown hair, white skin, and European features. Aryan people conquered and colonized that part of the world 35 centuries ago, and there are pockets of us remaining in some of the mountainous, isolated areas.[235]

In a similar vein, in 2004 the *National Vanguard,* the recently resurrected flagship publication of the National Alliance, carried a sympathetic article on the Islamic Republic of Iran.[236] In March 2005, the al-Jazeera English-language website carried a transcript of a broadcast of one of Kevin Alfred Strom's American Dissident Voices radio programs.[237] Just two months later, Strom granted an interview to Iran's Mehr News Agency in which he criticized Jewish lobbying groups, such as the American Israel Public Affairs Committee, and their influence over American foreign policy in the Middle East.[238]

In the final years of his life, Pierce occasionally offered veiled praise for Islamic terrorists such as Osama bin Laden and increasingly spoke admirably of Palestinian suicide bombers who were "paying a terrible price" to liberate their land. Presciently, just two years before 9/11, Pierce compared bin Laden with the fifteenth-century Flemish surrealist painter, Hieronymus Bosch, whose art reflected his concern for the moral condition of Dutch society:

> Well let me tell you, it doesn't take a Hieronymus Bosch to look at this [American] society and notice that it is profoundly ill. Ordinary men and women all around the world can see that. And while Hieronymus Bosch isn't here today to chastise us for our lack of morality, other men who care about morality are: men like Osama bin Laden, for example. And the fact that men like bin Laden can look at America and see that it no longer has a soul, makes them infinitely more dangerous as our moral instructors. Bin Laden knows that the next time he blows something up a great many people will applaud him, both around the world and in America.[239]

Conclusion

As the preceding discussion demonstrates, there have been numerous phases of cooperation between elements of the extreme right and militant Islam. The potential of such an alliance lies in the fact that both share the same enemies.[240] What do these previous episodes of collaboration portend for the future? As of yet, there is no clear answer, but some recent developments are worth mentioning. According to some accounts, a convoluted web of terrorists that includes elements of al Qaeda, Iraqi intelligence, and German neo-Nazis have established a working relationship. In the fall of 2002, investigators with the German government's Office for the Protection of the Constitution reported that right-wing extremists and radical Muslims were increasingly using similar rhetoric. They both decry the new world order, which they see as controlled by Jews and enforced by U.S. military power. Both movements are also wary of democracy. Recently, German neo-Nazis have been seen sporting Palestinian headscarves at rallies and calling for worldwide intifada. Udo Voigt, the chairman of the National Democratic Party, has reportedly reached out to some Muslim extremists.[241]

Some investigators believe that Hezbollah and Argentinean right-wing extremists may have been responsible for the bombings of the Israeli embassy and Jewish Community Center in Buenos Aires in 1993 and 1994. Jewish institutions outside Israel are generally less protected, and local anti-Semitic extremists can provide logistical help for attacks.[242] In 1993, Imad Mughniya of Hezbollah masterminded the truck bombing of the Israeli embassy in Buenos Aires, Argentina, which killed 29 people and wounded over 200 others. This attack was followed by a second bombing on July 18, 1994, which destroyed the Argentine Israeli Mutual Association (AIMA) building in Buenos Aires, which housed several Argentine Jewish organizations. The attack killed 86 people and wounded several hundred more.[243] Some speculate that the Arab and Nazi expatriate communities may have assisted in the attack.[244]

Although several factors would seem to militate against such an alliance, militant Islamic groups, including al Qaeda, have previously sought to cooperate with non-Islamic militant groups. For example, in Ireland, army intelligence investigated the possibility that funds raised by the Mercy International Relief Agency (MIRA) may have found their way into the coffers of the Irish Republican Army. In Spain, authorities discovered an alleged plan hatched by al Qaeda and Euskadi Ta Askatasuna (ETA, or Basque Nation and Liberty) to car-bomb a meeting of leaders of the European Union. In Sierra Leone, the Revolutionary United Front was charged with selling millions of dollars worth of illegally mined diamonds to al Qaeda. Finally, in Sri Lanka, the media reported that Liberation Tigers of Tamil had established ties with al Qaeda.[245]

One of the chief obstacles to cooperation would seem to be a disagreement over religion. However, there may be ways in which to hurdle this obstacle. For example, inasmuch as the Koran teaches that Allah sent prophets to all major civilizations, it is conceivable that the extreme right could reconcile some of its beliefs with Islam.[246] Furthermore, the entry requirements for Islam are relatively few in number. Technically, all one need do to become a Muslim is to recite the *Shahadah:* "I declare there is no god except God, and I declare that Muhammad is the messenger of God." As we saw earlier, such a requirement was not too cumbersome for David Myatt and Ahmed Huber.

One significant difference between right-wing terrorists and the more prominent variants of terrorists (e.g., left-wing during the 1970s, contemporary Islamic) is that the former have had no significant state sponsors. This material and logistical disadvantage could conceivably make the more radical elements of the extreme right more amenable to an alliance with outside groups. Without governments to offer intelligence, funds, sanctuaries, training facilities, and other kinds of support, their effectiveness has been very limited.[247] One of the principal reasons terrorism spread from the Middle East and Latin America to Western Europe in the 1970s was that a shared ideology of anti-Americanism and anti-imperialism cemented ties among radical groups.[248] The chief difference today is that the nascent anti-American global movement lacks a powerful state sponsor. However, it is worth noting that most lethal acts of terrorism over the past decade have been perpetrated by groups and individuals unaffiliated with state sponsors.

Another very significant difference between right-wing and Islamic terrorists is the latter's propensity for martyrdom. Islamic extremists have demonstrated time and again their commitment to carry out suicide attacks, whereas such methods are virtually nonexistent among right-wing terrorists, for both logistical and ideological reasons.[249] Sophisticated suicide operations require an extensive network capable of support and planning.[250] Islamic terrorists have such a network, but right-wing terrorists do not. Perhaps more important, for Islamic terrorists, dying in a suicide operation is considered an act of martyrdom that will immediately be rewarded with splendid afterlife bliss.[251] By contrast, right-wing terrorists by and large do not evince the same degree of certainty about afterlife rewards for their terrorist acts.

Although right-wing extremists have traditionally not practiced suicide terrorism, the theme occasionally appears in their literature, most notably in William Pierce's novel *The Turner Diaries*. The conclusion is strikingly similar to the 9/11 attack on the Pentagon. The story's protagonist, Earl Turner, writes in his diary just hours before his scheduled attack:

> It's still three hours until first flight, and all systems are "go." I'll use the time to write a few pages—my last diary entry. Then it's a one-way trip to the Pentagon for me. The warhead is strapped into the front seat of the old Stearman and rigged to detonate either on impact or when I flip a switch in the back seat. Hopefully, I'll be able to manage a low-level air burst directly over the center of the Pentagon. Failing that, I'll at least try to fly as close as I can before I'm shot down.[252]

Not unlike Muhammad Atta, Turner expressed a sense of calm before his mission.

> It is a comforting thought in these last hours of my physical existence that, of all the billions of men and women of my race who have ever lived, I will have been able to play a more vital role than all but a handful of them in determining the ultimate destiny of mankind. What I will do today will be of more weight in the annals of the race than all the conquests of Caesar and Napoleon—if I succeed![253]

Finally, like Atta, Turner shares a sense of religious fellowship with his comrades. The night before his suicide mission, Turner is inducted into "the Order," the quasi-religious inner circle of the organization:

> Knowing what was demanded in character and commitment of each man who stood before me, my chest swelled with pride. These were no soft-bellied, conservative businessmen assembled for some Masonic

mumbo-jumbo; no loudmouthed, beery red necks letting off a little ritualized steam about "the goddam niggers"; no pious, frightened churchgoers whining for the guidance or protection of an anthropomorphic deity. These were *real men, White* men who were now *one* with me in spirit and consciousness as well as in blood.[254]

At the present time the cooperation between the two movements is primarily on a rhetorical level, as there does seem to be a potential for synergy in the area of propaganda. As mentioned earlier, this collaboration tends to move only in one direction, with right-wing extremists occasionally voicing support for Islamic extremists and the latter being much less reciprocal. This situation could be changing, however, as propaganda by right-wing extremists is being acquired and recycled by Islamic extremists. Furthermore, several Arab newspapers have reprinted articles written by extreme right activists.[255] Internet technology has done much to cement such alliances among seemingly disparate groups across national borders and different cultures. Abraham Foxman, the national director of the ADL, commented on how the Internet can facilitate this "globalization of hate": "Today a sermon in Cairo travels across the globe within minutes, through the network, the Internet, e-mail, and Al Jazeera. This globalization facilitates the incitement and hate that makes the message of anti-Semitism more potent and very real. It is now out there everywhere. . . . this technology has given anti-Semitism, hate and incitement a strength and a power of seduction that it has never had in history before."[256]

There is some anecdotal evidence to suggest that anti-Semitism has spread to some parts of the non-Arab Muslim World. For example, in the midst of the Asian financial crisis in 1997, Malaysian prime minister Muhammad Mahathir went so far as to blame this predicament on Jews. The high-powered currency speculator, George Soros, was seen as the chief culprit in adversely affecting the Malaysian economy. More recently, in a speech presented at an Organization of the Islamic Conference summit in October 2003, Mahathir accused Jews of trying to "rule [the] world by proxy [and] get others to fight and die for them." Further, he asserted that Jews promoted socialism, communism, human rights, and democracy so that persecuting them would appear to be wrong, and by doing so they have "gained control of the most powerful countries." Mahathir exhorted the Islamic *umma* "to face the enemy" and opined that 1.3 billion Muslims could not be "defeated by a few million Jews."[257] Mahathir's remarks were met with scorn by President George Bush and other representatives of the United States, as well as various European governments and Jewish defense organizations, such as the Anti-Defamation League. However, numerous extreme right groups and Muslims commended him for speaking out on this issue.[258] Still defiant, Mahathir reiterated his criticism of Jews and Israel in an interview in May 2005, in which he accused American politicians of being "scared stiff of the Jews because anybody who votes against the Jews will lose elections."[259]

Just as Islamists and the extreme right are beginning to find common ground, the gap between the far left and the far right may be narrowing as well. Both movements often decry globalization. Increasingly, they both share a criticism of Israeli policy toward Palestinians. A case in point is the case of Rachel Corrie, an attractive twenty-three-year-old American student at Evergreen State College in Olympia, Washington, and a member of the International Solidarity Movement, who took a semester off to work as a peace activist in Gaza. While there, she took part in a protest in which an Israel driver using a bulldozer was preparing to knock down a Palestinian's house. Corrie stood between the bulldozer and the house and refused to move. However, the Israel driver ran over her, and she sustained injuries from which she ultimately died. Despite Corrie's presumably left-leaning political orientation, various right-wing publications and websites eulogized her as an Aryan martyr. What is more, the antiglobalization rhetoric of the contemporary extreme right could conceivably make its agenda more palatable to the far left, which also champions a similar platform, including radical environmentalism and animal rights. In fact, in 2002, the National Alliance created a front group, the Anti-Globalism Action Network (AGAN), to capitalize on the left's opposition to globalist organizations such as the World Bank, G8, and the International Monetary Fund and sent it to Kananaskis, Canada, to protest a G8 meeting. AGAN added an anti-Semitic twist to the traditional left-wing conspiracy narrative.[260] And extreme right stalwarts, such as Louis Beam, the chief proponent of the leaderless resistance approach in the United States, expressed solidarity with anti–World Trade Organization protestors in Seattle.[261]

Some left-wing radicals now extol revolutionary strategies that sound very similar to the leaderless resistance approach advocated by extreme right revolutionaries. Although there have been no significant displays of overt anti-Semitism on the part of so-called eco-extremists, some elements have become increasingly strident in their opposition to the war on terror, especially once it expanded to encompass Iraq. A former spokesman for the Earth Liberation Front, Craig Rosebraugh, exhorted antiwar activists to escalate their opposition to the war. Among his suggestions to foment revolution were attacking the financial centers of the country; provoking large-scale urban rioting; attacking the media centers of power; spreading the battle to the individuals responsible for the war (the heads of government and U.S. corporations); publicly announcing that the antiwar movement does not support U.S. troops; targeting U.S.

military establishments within the United States; and when engaging in the aforementioned activities, striking hard and fast and retreating in anonymity.[262]

It was not uncommon to find a strain of anti-Semitism in the guise of anti-Zionism in the various left-wing revolutionary movements in Europe during their heyday in the 1970s. Thus neofascists could conceivably promote their ideology as a revolutionary movement of the left.[263] Currently, the far left is in a state of flux, while some of its activists question traditional tenets of their platform, such as unrestricted immigration.[264]

By aligning itself to militant Islam, the extreme right could conceivably ride on the coattails of a dynamic movement. As Daniel Pipes observed, the extreme right's emphasis on the prominent role of American Jews in business, the media, and politics makes it natural for that movement to link up with like-minded parties in the Middle East.[265] Although traditional anti-Semitism in the West is relatively weak and marginalized, anti-Semitism in the Middle East is robust and growing. Pipes lamented the fact that Jewish self-defense organizations remain preoccupied with potential anti-Semitism that could emerge from the Christian right, while they ignore what he sees as the much greater threat of anti-Semitism from militant Islam.[266]

One major drawback of an alliance with militant Islam is that the extreme right would almost inevitably draw increased attention from the government and private monitoring groups. On that note, the next two chapters examine the response to the extreme right and militant Islam by both the government and nongovernment organizations.

CHAPTER SIX

The U.S. Government's Response to Political Extremism and Terrorism

The September 11 attacks on the World Trade Center and Pentagon brought home the issue of terrorism like no previous attack in American history. The government was strongly criticized in many quarters for its failure to anticipate and prepare for such a horrific eventuality.

Yet the Clinton administration had given high priority to the issue of domestic terrorism. For example, President Clinton issued Presidential Decision Directive (PDD) 39 in 1995, the first directive to make terrorism a national top priority; he also concluded that the United States was threatened from within. This policy further articulated and defined the roles of members of the U.S. counterterrorism community. The Federal Bureau of Investigation (FBI) was designated as the chief government agency responsible for investigating and preventing domestic terrorism.[1] New legislation was also passed during Clinton's tenure, including the Anti-Terrorism and Effective Death Penalty Act of 1996, which contained the most thoroughgoing measures to that point to combat terrorism. Funding for counterterrorism was substantially increased during this period.[2]

Several factors contributed to the push for new counterterrorist measures during the 1990s. Much of the impetus for these efforts actually came from the perceived threat of domestic right-wing extremists and self-styled citizen militias. The April 19, 1995, bombing of the Alfred P. Murrah Federal Building in Oklahoma City was seen as a harbinger of further domestic terrorism. Although experts generally saw international terrorists as posing the most serious terrorist threat, it was perhaps domestic right-wing extremists, more than any others, who made counterterrorism a salient issue and put it on the public policy agenda. During the two decades before 9/11, right-wing terrorists had preoccupied personnel working in the area of domestic counterterrorism. Both government authorities and private monitoring organization took them very seriously.

The FBI continues to identify so-called right-wing hate groups, such as the National Alliance, World Church of the Creator, and Aryan Nations, as the first category of domestic terrorist threats. The most serious international terrorist threat

Table 6.1. Number of Terrorist Incidents by Type of Group

International	163	(35.67%)	Individual	13	(2.84%)
Left-wing	130	(28.45%)	Unknown	7	(1.53%)
Right-wing	83	(18.16%)	**Total**	**457**	**(100.00%)**
Special interest	61	(13.35%)			

facing the United States today emanates from Sunni Islamic extremists, such as those affiliated with Osama bin Laden and his al Qaeda network. Formal terrorist organizations such as Hamas and state sponsors of terrorism were identified as the second- and third-level international threats, respectively, to the United States.[3]

According to FBI tallies, 457 terrorist incidents occurred in the United States between 1980 and 1999 (see Table 6.1). The majority of these incidents were attributable to international and left-wing terrorists. Left-wing terrorism remained a significant threat until the mid-1980s, when a shift occurred, and right-wing terrorism became more prevalent. Furthermore, by the early 1990s, so-called single-issue extremist groups had become more active in terrorism as well. Actually, FBI statistics indicate that there were fewer acts of domestic terrorism in the United States in the 1990s than in the 1980s. However, there were more fatalities during the 1990s (176) than during the 1980s (26) due to the lethality of the Oklahoma City bombing.[4]

In this chapter I examine the U.S. government's response to right-wing extremism and militant Islam. Prior to 9/11, the government's antiterror measures, although occasionally serious, were implemented incrementally rather than sweepingly. Domestic right-wing extremists were once at the top of the list of potential threats, but Islamic extremists now occupy that position.

Historical Background

Episodes of right-wing extremism and violence have punctuated American history almost from the founding of the republic. Consequently, this issue has frequently impelled the federal government to respond. Although several agencies and branches of the government—including Congress, the Supreme Court, and the Department of Defense—have dealt with extremism, in this section I focus primarily on the FBI, which has been the chief agency responsible for investigating political extremism and domestic terrorism.[5]

Essentially, the U.S. response to domestic right-wing extremism is a joint effort by the government and various nongovernmental organizations (NGOs), which have persuaded the government to respond vigilantly to manifestations of right-wing extremism. The close working relationship between the federal government and NGOs in the effort to counter right-wing extremism can be traced back to the 1930s. A variety of measures were used during that period. By 1936, President Franklin D. Roosevelt was concerned that potentially hostile fascist and communist governments might have a subversive influence on some Americans. To meet this potential challenge, Roosevelt instructed FBI director J. Edgar Hoover to develop an intelligence apparatus to gather information on extremist groups.[6] The bureau was authorized to gather domestic intelligence by presidential directive rather than by statute.

The Anti-Defamation League (ADL) and the American Jewish Committee augmented the intelligence efforts of the government, working closely together and providing information to government authorities, including congressional committees, army and navy intelligence, and the FBI.[7] According to a claim by Arnold Forster, an important member of the ADL's fact-finding division during that period, most of the data on pro-Nazi propaganda that federal agencies possessed came from the ADL field investigators and other private organizations.[8]

By the end of World War II, the American extreme right was demoralized and imploding. However, events in the 1950s allowed it to rebound. A renascent Ku Klux Klan emerged in the aftermath of the *Brown v. Board of Education of Topeka* Supreme Court decision in 1954. In 1956 the FBI commenced a campaign of surveillance and disruption against left-wing groups in an initiative called the Counter Intelligence Program (COINTELPRO), and in 1964 this effort was expanded to include the Klan and various "white hate groups." According to the 1964 FBI memorandum that authorized this initiative, "The purpose of this program is to expose, disrupt and otherwise neutralize the activities of the various Klans and hate organizations, their leadership and adherents."[9] In total, 289 different programs of action were approved and used against various Klan and extreme right organizations.[10] These COINTELPRO measures had a devastating effect on the morale of these extremist groups, creating so much suspicion among members that they were extremely loath to initiate violence in any kind of organizational setting. By 1971, membership in the Klan had plummeted from its high of 14,000 in 1964 to 4,300.[11]

From the perspective of the government, these efforts were generally successful because the targeted extremist groups were effectively neutralized by the program. However, when details of COINTELPRO transpired, it provoked both a legislative and public backlash against the government. The negative publicity surrounding the program pressured the Justice Department to make changes to the law enforcement and investigative policies of the FBI. The Levi Guidelines were adopted on April 5, 1976, in an attempt to depoliticize the FBI. The guidelines marked a significant departure from traditional policy in that they moved federal law enforcement away from its preventive functions. Furthermore, these changes came on the heels of the Privacy Act of 1974, which attempted to stop the FBI from spying on people because of their political beliefs. The results of these changes were dramatic. The number of domestic intelligence cases dropped from 1,454 in 1975 to only 95 in 1977.[12] When determining whether to investigate a potential terrorist group, the FBI was instructed to consider the magnitude of the threat, the likelihood that it would occur, the immediacy of the threat, and the danger to privacy and free expression posed by an investigation.[13] As a result, the FBI devoted less attention to terrorism and focused more effort on traditional law enforcement.[14] Significantly, however, nothing in the guidelines precluded the FBI from opening an investigation based on information received from private groups such as the Southern Poverty Law Center (SPLC) and the ADL.

FROM OPERATION CLEAN-SWEEP TO WACO, 1980–1993

By the early 1980s, terrorism had become a salient issue in the public mind. Several high-profile acts of international terrorism against U.S. personnel overseas compelled the government to take measures to protect American territory from such eventualities. To meet such potential challenges, Oliver Buck Revell, then the head of the FBI's Criminal Investigative Division, persuaded FBI director William Webster in 1983 to authorize the creation of an elite antiterrorist division in the FBI. Webster agreed, and Special Agent Danny O. Coulson was made the first commander of the Hostage Rescue Team (HRT), an elite squad of fifty agents who could be deployed at a moment's notice.[15]

The first major deployment of the new unit occurred in 1985, when it was called upon to arrest members of the Covenant, Sword, and the Arm of the Lord (CSA) at the group's compound in Arkansas. Fortunately for the FBI, the operation was a surprising success: the violence-prone CSA and fugitive members of the Order that had sought sanctuary there surrendered without incident after two days of negotiations with HRT commander Coulson.[16] Increasingly, the activities of the radical right caught the attention of federal authorities, and a concerted effort was made to stymie them.

From mid-1983 through the end of 1985, the underground revolutionary group the Order electrified the radical right and alarmed the government with a series of spectacular crimes that included bank robberies and armored car heists. To counter the threat of renascent right-wing terrorism, in 1985 the FBI, the Internal Revenue Service (IRS) Security Division, the Justice Department, the Department of the Treasury, and the Bureau of Alcohol, Tobacco, and Firearms (ATF) joined forces in one of the largest joint efforts in law enforcement history, known as Operation Clean-Sweep, to investigate the most radical representatives of the movement.[17] It was, however, primarily a Department of the Treasury initiative and was allegedly the brainchild of an assistant U.S. attorney, Steven Snyder.[18]

Operation Clean-Sweep culminated in the Fort Smith sedition trial of 1988, in which a who's who of some of the most radical elements of the extreme right were prosecuted for conspiring to overthrow the U.S. government. James Ellison, the former leader of the CSA, turned state's evidence and was the government's star witness at the trial. Despite great effort on the part of federal prosecutors and the ADL, an Arkansas jury acquitted all the defendants, and the extreme right enjoyed a rare upset victory.

This legal victory notwithstanding, by the mid-1980s the radical right was in disarray, and the domestic terrorist threat from both the left and the right had largely evaporated. However, this lull in activity proved to be short-lived. The 1990s would witness several high-profile confrontations between political and religious extremists and law enforcement authorities.

The 1992 siege at Ruby Ridge was one of the first such incidents to gain widespread notoriety. The raid, which began as an ATF operation to arrest Randy Weaver on minor firearms violations, escalated into a firefight in which Weaver's son Sammy and a deputy U.S. marshal were killed. Once a federal agent had been slain, the FBI assumed responsibility for the incident, and the HRT was deployed. A series of bad policy decisions compounded the crisis, which tragically resulted in the fatal shooting of Weaver's wife, Vicki. Eventually, Weaver and codefendant Kevin Harris surrendered to authorities but were ultimately acquitted of the most serious charges. Moreover, the jury fined the federal government for withholding evidence and for lying and concluded that the federal government had acted with a "callous disregard for the rights of the defendants and the interests of justice."[19] The government eventually settled a civil suit with Weaver and paid $3.1 million to him and his surviving children. In sum, the incident had a devastating effect on the morale of the FBI, as several agents with stellar service records effectively had their careers ruined.

Although the Ruby Ridge fiasco captured only a limited amount of public attention when it occurred, other incidents soon followed on its heels that would later magnify its significance. Just a few months later, the siege near Waco, Texas, at the Branch Davidian compound in Mount Carmel, laid bare the consequences of faulty planning in responding to dissident groups as well as the pitfalls that can occur when authorities rely on intelligence from NGOs without adequate corroboration.[20]

The siege and subsequent conflagration at Waco galvanized the extreme right as the militia movement spread throughout many states. What is more, it provoked Timothy McVeigh to strike out against the government in revenge.

The April 19, 1995, bombing of the Alfred P. Murrah Federal Building in Oklahoma City, which killed 169 people, was the most lethal act of terrorism committed on American soil at that time. It did not take the authorities long to find the suspects. The mastermind of the bombing, Timothy McVeigh, was apprehended the same day of the attack and ultimately sentenced to death for the crime. His accomplice, Terry Nichols, was sentenced to life in prison. A third defendant, Michael Fortier, plea-bargained with authorities and received a sentence of twelve years in exchange for cooperating with the prosecution.[21]

Prior to the bombing, the FBI had not paid much attention to the militia movement. Furthermore, one of its most extensive investigations failed to turn up a significant militia connection to the bombing. However, after this attack, the association between the two stuck in the public mind, and the FBI began to monitor the militias and other extreme right organizations much more closely. In the aftermath, there were many calls to alter and expand counterterrorism policy. This event, more than any other factor, was the impetus behind the expansion of counterterrorism programs.

For starters, FBI director Louis Freeh loosened the attorney general's guidelines for investigating extremist groups.[22] He also formed the Executive Working Group on Domestic Terrorism, which meets every two weeks to cull intelligence and plan strategy. Not even a year after its founding, FBI investigations into militias increased fourfold.[23] As a result of these policy changes, the number of politically oriented domestic surveillance operations increased substantially. Just prior to the Oklahoma City bombing, the FBI was working on roughly 100 terrorist investigations. This figure jumped to about 900 two years after the bombing.[24]

After the fiascoes of Ruby Ridge and Waco, the federal government began responding to right-wing extremists more gingerly, but still resolutely. The 1996 siege of the Montana Freemen at their Justus Township estate in Jordan, Montana, was a success. Members of the Freemen were accused of committing a variety of acts of "paper terrorism" in the Midwest, such as issuing billions of dollars in phony checks and filing illegal property liens against their enemies. The FBI enlisted the support of high-profile figures in the patriot movement to help negotiate an end to the standoff. It ended peacefully, and the ensuing fallout in the patriot community led to the diminution of a movement that the FBI had identified as a serious threat to domestic security. However, both the FBI and NGOs continued to monitor extreme right groups and warn of their potential danger.

For example, in the fall of 1999, the FBI released a report titled *Project Megiddo,* which alerted various chiefs of police around the country to the potential violence that groups holding millenarian beliefs could perpetrate. The report focused almost exclusively on the political right. Surprisingly, the subject of Islamic extremism was completely ignored. Some observers suspected that both the ADL and the Southern Poverty Law Center (SPLC) had a hand in the preparation of the report. For its part, the FBI denied any such collusion. Fueling this suspicion was the coincidence that the ADL issued a report entitled "Y2K Paranoia: Extremists Confront the Millennium" at the same conference—the International Association of Chiefs of Police in Charlotte, North Carolina—at which the FBI released its report. As it turned out, no significant right-wing violence occurred at the turn of the new millennium.

Still another example that illustrates the vigilance with which the government and NGOs have responded to the extreme right is the case of Alex Curtis.[25] Until his arrest in 2000, Curtis, a young man from San Diego, California, was the most vociferous advocate of the leaderless resistance approach to right-wing terrorism. In audio programs on his Nationalist Observer website, he reviewed and critiqued recent episodes of right-wing violence. He pointed out mistakes and offered suggestions on how they could be avoided. Not surprisingly, Curtis's violent rhetoric caught the attention of authorities and watchdog organizations. In November 2000, the ADL issued a critical report on Curtis titled "Alex Curtis: Lone Wolf of Hate Prowls the Internet." About a week later, he was arrested along with two other individuals for various alleged civil rights violations. The arrests were the culmination of an extensive two-year joint investigation by the FBI and the San Diego Police Department dubbed "Operation Lone Wolf." Failing to follow his own advice, Curtis allegedly acted with others to harass several prominent figures in the San Diego area. Despite the amateurish characteristics of the alleged offenses, the authorities took Curtis and his accomplices seriously. In March 2001, Curtis pleaded guilty to all charges in exchange for a reduced sentence. He received a three-year sentence in June 2001. The case of Alex Curtis marks a return to a more proactive approach by the government to right-wing extremism, a trend that accelerated after September 11, 2001.

The Post-9/11 Response to the Extreme Right

In the aftermath of 9/11, many in the extreme right feared that the American government's war on terror could spill over into a witch hunt against domestic extremists and dissidents as well. Several arrests in the months following 9/11 gave credence to such concerns.

Since 9/11, federal authorities have adopted a more aggressive position toward domestic extremist groups, as the remarks of Department of Justice spokesman Bryan Sierra indicated: "The Department of Justice is also making every effort to shut down hate groups and homegrown terrorists before they, too, can act violently on their hatred."[26] Toward this end, the FBI stepped up monitoring of the National Alliance, which it has long considered the most dangerous extreme right organization in the United States. Presumably near the end of Pierce's career, the National Alliance developed more of the characteristics of a fully functioning organization, and its opponents began to take it more seriously.[27]

The federal government's opening salvo against the National Alliance occurred on January 23, 2003, when armed FBI and Secret Service agents, working as part of a new Counter-Terror Task Force, raided the Leesburg, Virginia, home of Byron Calvert Cecchini, a former key staff member of the National Alliance. Cecchini had been convicted in 1989 for stabbing two people, an offense for which he spent nearly four years in prison. Reportedly, he served for a short time as a mercenary in Bosnia in the early 1990s. The stated reason on the affidavit for the predawn raid was the fact that Cecchini had a violent criminal history and likely owned weapons. Agents found no weapons in his home, but they did discover T-shirts that featured a Nike swoosh logo that substituted the word "Nazi" for "Nike." Cecchini had sold the T-shirts on his website, and presumably authorities were aware of the possible copyright infringement that they constituted. Capitalizing on the situation, agents seized computers and other items from Cecchini's home. For his part, Cecchini believed that the raid was no more than a fishing expedition to gather intelligence on his extremist associations. Currently Cecchini is believed to be working as the manager of Panzerfaust Records, a CD distributor that specializes in white power music, located in Minnesota.[28]

Less than two months later, the FBI struck again. On March 7, 2003, a seventy-person FBI team arrested Chester James Doles, a leader of a Georgia chapter of the National Alliance, on weapons charges.[29] Doles was charged with six felony offenses of firearms possession. Authorities discovered a total of thirteen firearms, including rifles, shotguns, and pistols.[30] Although the firearms had been legally purchased by Doles's wife, Teresa, he was prohibited from having firearms in his residence due to a previous felony conviction. In 1993 he was sent to prison and served nearly four years for the assault of a black man. After his release, Doles had attracted attention for organizing anti-immigration rallies in Gainesville, Georgia. Furthermore, the deceased leader of the National Alliance, Dr. William L. Pierce, is reputed to have trusted Doles highly: the latter was one of only six persons permitted to speak on behalf of the organization.[31] Not surprisingly, authorities took notice, and the FBI commenced an investigation into his activities in July 2001. The FBI sent an undercover informer, whom Doles befriended, to gather information on him. After the arrest, Doles was held without bond. U.S. Magistrate Linda Walker mentioned Doles's alleged connections to local law enforcement officers as a reason for doing so.[32]

For a short while, Doles's case looked like it might catalyze a disparate coalition of civil libertarians, who feared that the government was becoming increasingly overzealous in the aftermath of 9/11. A website—freechester-doles.com—was launched to raise money for his legal defense. In an impressive display of Internet activism, approximately $75,000 was raised by members of the traditionally cash-strapped extreme right. What is more, his defense scored a major coup when former U.S. representative Bob Barr (R-GA) decided to join the defense team. Not surprisingly, watchdog groups, such as the ADL and the Southern Poverty Law Center, evinced no sympathy for Doles and supported his prosecution.

Although some observers believed that the charges against Doles amounted to a technical infraction of the law and were politically driven due to his affiliation with the National Alliance, Doles decided to plead guilty in January 2004. Judge Richard Story imposed the lightest sentence in his power to give—seventy months in federal prison, minus time served and time allowed for good behavior—which will amount to about four more years in prison. To some in the movement, the guilty plea was a letdown. They had hoped that the money raised would be used to mount a vigorous defense.

As the aforementioned cases illustrate, potential violations of firearms statutes are frequently invoked to justify raids on the residences of right-wing extremists. Once again, on July 1, 2003, authorities raided the home of a National Alliance member on suspected firearms violations. Artie Wheeler, who works out of his home as a gunsmith, is alleged to have made statements about "race war" that originally led to the search and seizure warrant, according to a Maryland assistant state's attorney, Doug Ludwig.[33] Approximately sixty members of the Baltimore Police Department's elite special weapons and tactics (SWAT) team arrested the sixty-one-year-old Wheeler for possessing roughly 62 pounds of gunpowder. Maryland state law prohibits the possession of more than 5 pounds of smokeless powder. Furthermore, Wheeler did not store the powder in its original container, which was also a violation of state law. Finally, authorities charged Wheeler with reckless endangerment, alleging that he might have had plans to blow up his neighborhood. During the raid, the police also discovered numerous firearms, a significant amount of ammunition, and National Alliance literature, which Wheeler handed out to the officers, warning them that a race war was imminent. Authorities used these comments as further justification to incarcerate Wheeler.

The police were alleged to have used excessive force during the raid, hacking through the front door with axes, ransacking the hours for seven hours, and even going so far as to handcuff Wheeler's seventy-one-year-old wife, Elizabeth, to a bed. Although Wheeler was charged with only misdemeanor offenses, his bail was set at the astronomical sum of $2 million. Moreover, a judge later revoked bail on the grounds that prosecutors believed that he posed a threat to the community.

The National Alliance sought to mobilize support for Wheeler. The organization sponsored a link to a website, www.freeartwheeler.com, devoted to raising money for his legal defense. Furthermore, Kevin Alfred Strom devoted two broadcasts of American Dissident Voices to Artie Wheeler's case in which Wheeler's wife spoke of their ordeal.[34] Mrs. Wheeler endeared herself to some people in the movement through an Internet radio program that she hosted, called "Grandmother Elizabeth's Reading Hour for White Children."

After spending nearly four months in jail, Wheeler eventually pleabargained with authorities. He pled guilty to three misdemeanor offenses pertaining to reckless endangerment, possession of gunpowder in excess of 5 pounds, and improper storage thereof. The story took an odd twist when Wheeler proclaimed during his sentencing hearing that he was "not white." Rather, he claimed that he was a "half-bred Indian" and therefore not capable of being a white supremacist.[35] His racial renunciation caused considerable embarrassment among supporters in the extreme right.[36]

The aforementioned raids suggest that the National Alliance is under very close scrutiny by the government. Ironically, the organization that is responsible for such tracts as *The Turner Diaries* and *Hunter*—considered by some to be "blueprints for terrorism"—now adopts a strict zero-tolerance policy for violence and illegality for fear that such activities would be used by the government to repress the organization.[37] The organization currently faces still more problems. Rumors have circulated that a former chairman, Eric Gliebe, might be under federal investigation for allegedly embezzling funds from Resistance Records, a subsidiary of the National Alliance that he manages. Furthermore, it is believed that the organizational turmoil following the death of Dr. Pierce in July 2002 has taken a toll, causing many members to leave and funds to substantially decrease.[38] Despite these setbacks, the National Alliance still remains the most important organization of the revolutionary racialist right.

Despite its tumultuous history, the Aryan Nations has been one of the more enduring institutions of the revolutionary racialist right. From the late 1970s to 2000, the organization maintained a "compound" in a relatively remote area of Idaho called Hayden Lake. Over the years, many right-wing extremists have attended numerous "congresses," usually held on an annual basis at the compound. It was this milieu out of which the underground terrorist group the Order emerged in 1983. By the 1990s, however, many extremists considered the compound to be infested with informants, thus rendering any serious revolutionary planning unrealistic. To make matters worse, in September 2000 the Aryan Nations suffered a major defeat in a civil trial in which the plaintiffs, represented by Morris Dees and the Southern Poverty Law Center, were awarded a $6.3 million judgment against the organization and its leader and founder, Pastor Richard Butler. The jury found the Aryan Nations responsible for the 1998 assault on a Native American woman and her son by two of the compound's security guards.[39] As a result, the Aryan Nations was forced to relinquish its compound in Hayden Lake.

A power struggle ensued over control of Aryan Nations after the group was evicted from its compound. Two members, Ray Redfeairn and August Kreis, attempted to wrest control of the organization from its founder, Richard Butler, and relocate the headquarters to Kreis's rural property in Ulysses, Pennsylvania. The two complained that undercover informants had repeatedly attempted to gain access to the top leaders in various branches of the Aryan Nations.

The government and monitoring groups still pay close attention to the remnants of the organization. In November 2002, a multiagency investigation, which included the Orange County District Attorney's office, the Orange County Sheriff's Department, the Orange County Probation Department, the Joint Terrorism Task Force, the FBI, the Los Angeles Police Department, and the Anti-Defamation League, resulted in the arrest of two persons, Christine Greenwood and her boyfriend, Patrick McCabe, on charges of stockpiling bomb-making materials, and a third person, John Frederick Steele, on charges of falsifying documents, committing perjury, and possessing a firearm with a previous conviction.[40] McCabe was already in prison at the time of the arrest. Steele was a leader of a California branch of the Aryan Nations known as the Brandenburg Division. Greenwood was a member of Women for Aryan Unity, which seeks to get women more involved in the white separatist movement. Both Greenwood and McCabe faced an additional charge of promoting gang membership through white supremacist groups in California. Previously, Greenwood had gained attention from her seemingly innocuous Aryan Baby Drive program, which distributed food and clothing to poor white families. She and her boyfriend were also believed to be members of the group Blood and Honor. Authorities were particularly concerned about McCabe because he worked as a security guard for the Port of Los Angeles and could thus be a potential security breach, considering the sensitive nature of his job duties.[41]

The charges appeared to be somewhat dubious in that the materials confiscated had uses other than bomb making. It is highly questionable whether the materials were intended for that purpose. However, during the search of Steele's house, authorities allegedly found a letter addressed to a white separatist organization, which advocated that the Aryan Nations align itself with Islamic extremists to target Jews and the U.S. government.[42] Steele pled guilty to one felony count of perjury and one count of possessing a firearm with a prior conviction, for which he received a 120-day jail sentence and three years of formal probation, on the condition that he refrain from consorting with extremists.[43] The charges against Greenwood and McCabe were eventually dropped.

For at least the past few years, the FBI has sent undercover investigators to gather information on the Aryan Nations, branches of the Ku Klux Klan, and the Christian Identity movement. This probe resulted in two arrests at opposite ends of Pennsylvania. One of Kreis's followers, Joshua Caleb Sutter, was arrested on February 12, 2003, in Philadelphia for allegedly attempting to buy a handgun from undercover agents whose identification had been illegally removed. He was also charged with possession of an illegal silencer. Sutter was a member of an Aryan Nation's spin-off organization, the Church of the Sons of Yahweh, and previously had served as the Aryan Nation's "minister for Islamic liaison." The FBI began to pay particularly close attention to him after he expressed the desire to form alliances with Islamist groups in the wake of 9/11. Reportedly, he spent much time scanning the Internet for secret messages from al Qaeda and Taliban operatives.[44] As part of the same probe, in Washington County, Pennsylvania, federal agents arrested David Wayne Hull, the imperial wizard of the White Knights of the Ku Klux Klan, who also maintained a longtime association with the Aryan Nations and various Christian Identity groups. Hull was arrested for allegedly manufacturing a pipe bomb, which he traded to an undercover informant for a cell phone. Federal authorities were alarmed when Hull allegedly attempted to purchase ten hand grenades from an informant, telling him that he needed them for attacks on abortion clinics.[45] Other members of the Aryan Nations had trouble with the law as well.

The organization's most recent run-in with the law occurred in late May 2004, when police in Longview, Washington, arrested Aryan Nations member Zachary Loren Beck after a shootout with officers and a subsequent standoff at his home. Beck was wanted by authorities for an alleged assault against a Hispanic man that occurred while he was running for local office in Hayden Lake, Idaho.[46]

Aryan Nations founder Butler died of natural causes in 2004 at the age of eighty-six, thus depriving the organization of a sense of direction. These setbacks notwithstanding, the Aryan Nations continues to soldier on. In March 2005, CNN carried a story in which Kreis expressed support for al Qaeda and publicly announced that sleeper cells of non-Muslims were ready to fight alongside the organization.[47] The fact that the Aryan Nations could manage to survive, even in reduced form, after the loss of its Hayden Lake compound and the arrest of many of its leaders, is testimony to the group's durability and stature in the racialist right.

MATT HALE AND THE WORLD CHURCH OF THE CREATOR

Although the World Church of the Creator (WCOTC) is a relatively obscure organization, it has garnered occasional publicity due to a few episodes of violence linked to some of its members. The most notable instance was the July 1999 shooting spree of former member Benjamin Smith, which left two persons dead and several more injured. Shortly thereafter, the Department of Justice commenced an investigation into the group. Matt Hale, who has led the WCOTC since 1996, refused to condemn the attacks and went so far as to eulogize Smith. Arguably, it is this uncompromising approach on the part of the young leader that has ensnared him in significant legal problems.

The theology of the World Church of the Creator syncretizes several disparate themes in history, including Roman classicism, German National Socialism, and the settlement of the American Western frontier. The church is not only stridently anti-Semitic but anti-Christian as well, which is somewhat surprising, insofar as Christian fundamentalism has been an enduring theme in the history of right-wing extremism in the United States. Arguably the organization has had an influence beyond what its membership would suggest. In recent years, one can discern a growing criticism of Christianity in the extreme right, as alternative religions, most notably Odinism, have gained popularity.[48]

In the fall of 2001, the WCOTC began an aggressive leafleting campaign in scattered cities throughout the United States. The flyers—which included quotes from a 1998 ABC News interview with Osama bin Laden—charged that the 9/11 attacks resulted from the U.S. government's unstinting support for Israel.[49] On that note, in July 2002, Hale released a booklet titled *The Truth About 9–11: How Jewish Manipulation Killed Thousands,* which examined the influence of Jewish lobbying groups, such as the American Israel Public Affairs Committee (AIPAC), over the U.S. government.[50]

In January 2003, Matt Hale, the "Pontifus Maximus" of the church, was arrested on charges that he solicited a church member to kill a federal judge. During much of 2002, the church had been embroiled in a civil suit with the Te-Ta-Ma Truth Foundation over the latter's trademarked "Church of the Creator" name. Hale argued that his church had existed prior to the Te-Ta-Ma Truth Foundation's trademark and further that the "Church of the Creator" name was too generic to be exclusively held by only one organization. Originally, U.S. district judge Joan Humphrey Lefkow ruled in his favor. However, her decision was overturned on appeal. Judge Lefkow was left to enforce the appellate court's decision and ordered that Hale's organization desist using the Church of the Creator name. Further, to add insult to injury, all the organization's books, which members consider to be holy texts, were ordered to be destroyed. Outraged by this decision, Hale allegedly solicited a church member to kill Judge Lefkow and was arrested by an FBI counterterrorism team in January 2003.[51] An informant working for the federal government, Anthony Evola, wore a concealed wire during a visit to Hale's residence in East Peoria, Illinois. According to the informant, Hale allegedly requested the address of Judge Lefkow. The informant implied that she should be killed, and although Hale did not directly endorse the plan, neither did he ever instruct the informant not to carry it out. The recorded conversation suggests that Evola sought to suborn Hale:

> AE: Are you going to exterminate that rat [Judge Lefkow]?
> MH: Well, whatever you want to do, basically. . . . My position has always been that, you know, I'm going to fight within the law and, but, ah [Judge Lefkow's home address has] been provided if you wish to ah, do anything yourself, you can. . . . So that makes it clear.
> AE: Consider it done.
> MH: Good.[52]

When Evola later requested money and an alibi to help him carry out the would-be assassination, Hale responded, "I can't be a party to such a thing."[53]

Commenting on Hale's arrest, Mark Potok of the Southern Poverty Law Center did not think the World Church of the Creator would survive its current crisis. Rabbi Abraham Cooper of the Simon Wiesenthal Center stated that if the charges against Hale stick, it would result in "the removal of the most dangerous American racist of [Hale's] generation."[54] Likewise, the ADL applauded Hale's arrest.[55]

The WCOTC launched a website titled "Free Matt Hale Legal Defense Fund," which alleged that the government's prosecution was instigated by Michael Chertoff, then chief of the Department of Justice's Criminal Division and recently appointed secretary of the Department of Homeland Security. Reportedly, he is an official of the New Jersey branch of the Anti-Defamation League; in 1992 the ADL bestowed its Distinguished Public Service Award on him.[56] Furthermore, Chertoff's wife sits on the executive board of the New Jersey office of the ADL. Interestingly, it was the Latham and Watkins law firm, of which Chertoff is a partner, that brought the suit against the WCOTC over the Benjamin Smith shooting rampage of 1999.[57]

On April 27, 2004, Hale was found guilty of soliciting the murder of a federal judge as well as three charges of obstruction of justice. His organization appeared to unravel when a leader in the church, Jon Fox, turned state's evidence and testified against Hale.[58] The story took an odd twist in March 2005, when Judge Lefkow's husband and mother were found murdered execution-style in her home. At first, authorities suspected a WCOTC connection to the crime. However, it later transpired that the perpetrator was Bart A. Ross, a fifty-seven-year-old Polish immigrant, whose lawsuit Lefkow had previously dismissed as "delusional."[59] On April 6, 2005, U.S. district judge James Moody sentenced Hale to forty years in prison for his offense.[60]

ERNST ZÜNDEL

Ernst Zündel has become a cause célèbre among his supporters in the extreme right, who have depicted him as a champion of free speech and a victim of an overzealous government beholden to Jewish interests. In February 2003, agents of the Immigration and Naturalization Service (INS) arrested Zündel in Sevierville, Tennessee, where he resided with his wife, Dr. Ingrid Rimland, also a promoter of Holocaust revisionism. Zündel moved to the United States from Canada in 2000. According to the INS, Zündel had overstayed his visa and consequently faced a deportation hearing. Nearly two weeks after his arrest, U.S. authorities deported Zündel to Canada, not his native land of Germany.

Since the mid-1970s, Ernst Zündel has gained notoriety as Canada's largest purveyor of anti-Semitic and neo-Nazi literature. As a young German expatriate, Zündel emigrated to Canada in 1958 and established himself as a successful commercial artist. Intellectually curious, he came under the influence of long-time Canadian fascist Adrien Arcand. By the mid-1970s, Zündel began publishing literature advocating clemency for Rudolf Hess and rehabilitation of the Third Reich. In addition, he authored a bizarre set of books, including

UFOs: Nazi Secret Weapons, in which he claimed that secret Nazi UFO bases operated in Antarctica.[61]

Zündel's legal problems first began in 1983, when Mrs. Sabrina Citron of the Canadian Holocaust Remembrance Association, acting on her own behalf, brought charges against Zündel for violation of section 181 of the Canadian Criminal Code, which proscribes the spreading of false news that the purveyor knows to be false. The Crown eventually took over the prosecution. The charges stemmed from two pamphlets Zündel had distributed, "The West, War, and Islam," which argued that a conspiracy existed between Zionists and international bankers, and "Did Six Million Really Die?" which claimed that the Holocaust was a hoax fabricated by Jews to extort reparations payments from Germany and elicit world sympathy for Jews. Zündel was represented by Doug Christie, whose clients have earned him the appellation the "lawyer of the damned." The defense's strategy was to attack the testimony of various Holocaust experts and survivors. The case received international attention. The first trial dragged on for eight weeks, after which Zündel was found guilty for the "Did Six Million Really Die?" tract and acquitted for charges stemming from "The West, War, and Islam." Zündel filed numerous appeals, and in 1992 the Canadian Supreme Court overturned his conviction, saying that the spreading of false news law under which he was convicted was unconstitutional, in that it posed "an unjustifiable limit on the right and freedom of expression contained in the Charter of Rights and Freedoms." After the court announced its decision, the Canadian Jewish Congress urged Ontario attorney general Howard Hampton to charge Zündel under section 281 of the Criminal Code, which prohibits spreading hate against identifiable groups. However, "Did Six Million Really Die?" was written in a dispassionate, academic style, allowing Zündel to argue that he was only presenting facts he believed to be true and did not intend to promote hate.[62]

After moving to the United States and then being returned to Canada, Zündel once again found himself in legal trouble. Canadian authorities held him in solitary confinement for much of his incarceration since he was deported to Canada in early 2003. In a controversial decision, the Canadian Security Intelligence Service designated Zündel as a national security risk. This decision was made under the provisions of a new law passed in the aftermath of 9/11—the Canadian Immigration and Refugee Protection Act—which includes tougher immigration procedures when deemed necessary by authorities. Authorities based their decision on Zündel's associations with various extreme right groups, referring to him as a "lightning rod" for white supremacists. Although Zündel has twice applied for Canadian citizenship, he has been denied both times. He positions himself as a human rights activist and went so far as to refer to himself as the Gandhi of the right for his nonviolent approach to activism. Zündel feared deportation back to his native Germany because there he could face prosecution under various hate speech provisions codified in German law. Seeking to avoid such a predicament, Zündel applied for refugee status. However, a Canadian federal court justice, Pierre Blais, ruled that Zündel constituted a threat to national security, and on March 1, 2005, Canadian authorities deported Zündel to Germany. There German authorities quickly charged him with inciting racial hatred and defaming the memory of the dead. In his decision, Judge Blais had accused Zündel of hypocrisy, in that he patterned himself as a pacifist yet "propagated[d] violent messages of hate" and worked to accomplish "the destruction of governments and multicultural societies."[63] Jewish organizations in both the United States and Canada had encouraged the deportation of Zündel.[64]

DAVID DUKE

Arguably the most prominent figure in the American extreme right, David Duke was also caught in the ongoing federal dragnet. Duke first gained notoriety in the early 1970s as a new style of Klan leader who favored business suits instead of white robes. By 1980, he had left the Knights of the Ku Klux Klan and founded the National Association for the Advancement of White People, which he sought to position as a white civil rights organization. In 2000 he founded his most recent organization, the European American Unity and Rights Organization (EURO). Duke gained national attention in 1989 when he won a seat in the Louisiana state legislature. He went on to lose senatorial and gubernatorial bids in 1990 and 1991, respectively. For a while he sought to shed his extremist image and instead patterned himself as a mainstream Republican conservative who was concerned about hot-button issues such as welfare, crime, and affirmative action. He was even elected chairman of the Republican Executive Committee in St. Tammany Parish in 1997. However, with the publication of his autobiography, *My Awakening*, in 1998, Duke appeared to have returned to his roots. In it, he warned that whites faced racial oblivion from various trends, including nonwhite immigration into the Western world, differential birth rates between whites and nonwhites, and miscegenation. He followed this book with another titled *Jewish Supremacism*, which argued that Jews are locked in an implacable struggle with white gentiles all over the world, as well as with Israel's Arab neighbors, most notably the Palestinians.

The Department of Justice spent three and a half years probing Duke's finances. Finally, in November 2000, his home, which also served as EURO headquarters, was raided by federal authorities on the suspicion that he may have misused funds that he solicited for his organization. Duke was accused of misleading donors by claiming that he urgently needed funds in order to fend off political persecution and avoid destitution. However, authorities claimed that Duke had used much of the money he received at casinos in Mississippi, Las Vegas, and the Bahamas. Furthermore, he was also charged with filing false statements with the Internal Revenue Service. Allegedly, he significantly under-reported his income on his 1998 tax return. Finally, there was an investigation into his sale of mailing lists of supporters to prominent Louisiana politicians, including then gubernatorial candidate Mike Foster and former state representative and U.S. Senate candidate Woody Jenkins. However, the Department of Justice concluded that the transaction did not violate any federal law.

During much of the investigation, Duke spent several years in self-imposed exile. He appeared to have found somewhat receptive audiences to his message overseas during extensive tours in Europe and, to a lesser degree, in the Middle East. Frequently, he spoke to Russian audiences on the topic of "Jewish supremacism" and sought to build alliances between extreme right and nationalist organizations in various nations. He achieved some moderate success in this endeavor, establishing contacts with French National Front leader Jean Marie Le Pen, British National Party leader Nick Griffin, the Russian ultranationalist Vladimir Zhirinovsky, and retired Soviet general Albert Makashov. A prominent university in the Ukraine, the Interregional Academy of Personnel Management, even awarded Duke an honorary doctorate.[65] As explained in Chapter 5, Duke also lectured in the small Arab country of Bahrain. His appearance on al-Jazeera, in which he strongly criticized American foreign policy in the Middle East, occasioned sharp criticism from the U.S. Department of State. According to Duke, that was the last straw for the federal government, which he believed was determined to prosecute him.

Finally, in late 2002, Duke returned to the United States to answer criminal charges. Facing a potentially long prison sentence if convicted in a criminal trial, Duke decided to plea-bargain. Duke feared that as a former Klan leader, he would have a slim chance of acquittal in a trial held in Louisiana, which presumably would have included a large black jury pool. Consequently, Duke pled guilty to various charges and was sentenced to fifteen months in a federal prison in Big Spring, Texas. He was also ordered to pay $10,000 fine.[66]

Duke asserted that his criticism of the United States and its relationship with Israel is the real reason why authorities have targeted him. To buttress his case, he pointed out the role of Michael Chertoff, the chief of the Department of Justice's Criminal Division, in initiating Duke's prosecution.[67] Duke claimed that the Louisiana-based U.S. Attorney's office launched a protracted campaign against him that continued after his departure under the direction of

Michael Chertoff. Duke did not stop there, however; he maintained that Chertoff was responsible for the release of members of an Israeli spy ring shortly before and after 9/11. The implication was that Chertoff sought to protect Jewish interests from fallout for alleged Israeli complicity in 9/11, a theory discussed in greater detail in Chapter 8.

In accordance with his plea agreement, Duke is allowed to pursue political office.[68] In April 2004, he was released from prison to spend the remainder of his sentence in a halfway house in Louisiana. As he has demonstrated so often in the past, Duke was quick to rebound. Over the Memorial Day weekend, he hosted a conference attended by over 250 supporters.[69] The event appeared to be a success.

WILLIAM KRAR: AMERICAN TERRORIST?

The most serious threat from the extreme right since 9/11 have come from an obscure figure, William Krar, and his girlfriend, Judith Bruey. The sixty-three-year-old Krar kept a low profile and is believed to have associated with numerous extremist groups. He claims to be the chief executive officer of International Development Corp., or as it is sometimes called, IDC America, a firm that manufactures gun parts. Krar first caught the attention of authorities in 1995 around the time of the Oklahoma City bombing, when the ATF investigated him and another unidentified man on weapons charges. The other suspect told authorities that Krar had an abiding hatred for the federal government and planned to bomb government facilities. However, the suspect later recanted the story. For his part, Krar denied the allegations and was not arrested.

In January 2002 Krar once again raised suspicion: a package that he intended to send to a militiaman in New Jersey containing five false identification documents, including a Defense Intelligence Identification card, was inadvertently sent to a wrong address in Staten Island, New York. The recipient promptly notified authorities of the package. Not long thereafter, the federal government began to investigate Krar. A U.S. attorney's statement claimed that Krar had accumulated dangerous chemical weapons, a reference to a January 2002 Tennessee Highway Patrol stop in which state police officers discovered dangerous chemicals and a note that appeared to represent instructions for carrying out a covert operation. Soon authorities began to connect the dots. Finally, in April 2003 federal agents raided Krar's home and rented storage units in East Texas. They discovered a large quantity of sodium cyanide and other substances such as hydrochloric, nitric, and acetic acids, as well as a large cache of guns and ammunition and a copy of *The Turner Diaries*. After putting together all the pieces of evidence, authorities conjectured that Krar and Bruey might have had malevolent intentions. Consequently, Krar was charged with possessing sodium cyanide and other chemicals for the purpose of creating a dangerous weapon, to which he pleaded guilty and received a 135-month prison sentence in November 2003. His codefendant, Bruey, pleaded guilty to conspiring to possess illegal weapons—an offense for which she received a 57-month prison sentence. The Krar case was one of the most extensive domestic terrorism investigations since the 1995 Oklahoma City bombing.[70]

Most of the arrests described in this chapter seem to suggest a high degree of political motivation on the part of the government. What is more, private monitoring groups, such as the ADL and the Southern Poverty Law Center, have exerted considerable pressure on law enforcement agencies to take a strong position toward the extreme right.[71] In the aftermath of 9/11, law enforcement authorities are increasingly prosecuting any illegal activity by known extremists while at the same time infiltrating the potentially more dangerous groups to guard against future attacks. As one law enforcement source commented, "You prosecute what you can prosecute."[72] In addition to its civil liberties implications, such a strategy could potentially misdirect scarce law enforcement resources away from more serious threats, most notably militant Islam.

The U.S. Response to Militant Islam

For most of the 1990s, right-wing terrorists have preoccupied government counterterrorism analysts. Perhaps more focus ought to have been placed on the better organized, more disciplined, and highly financed radical Islamic terrorists that compose the al Qaeda network. Clearly, the first World Trade Center attack of 1993, the bombings of U.S. targets in Saudi Arabia in the mid-1990s, the bombings of the U.S. embassies in Kenya and Tanzania, and the attack on the USS *Cole* should have demonstrated the formidable capabilities and intentions of this terrorist network. Despite these red flags, the FBI continued to focus the agency's counterterrorism efforts on combating right-wing extremist groups. According to a retired FBI official, this pattern held all the way up to September 11, 2001.[73] A number of factors may have contributed to this development. For example, President Clinton exploited the Oklahoma City bombing by drawing parallels between antigovernment militias and a resurgent Republican Party that advocated small government. Political correctness probably had a part in this omission as well. The FBI's much heralded report on possible Y2K terrorism, *Project Megiddo,* made no mention of Islamic terrorists. In fact, the only serious terrorist threat surrounding the landmark event involved an al Qaeda operative, Ahmed Ressam. Similarly, a Commerce Department official in charge of security went so far as to expurgate all references to Islamic extremists in a Y2K report on potential terrorist threats.[74]

For those cases involving international terrorism—defined by the FBI as terrorism inside or outside the United States involving a group with ties outside the United States—the FBI uses classified guidelines. The intelligence guidelines in international cases allow the investigation of Americans and others in the United States who are not suspected of breaking the law but are engaged in political activities.[75] In short, in the international context, the FBI does not need evidence of a criminal predicate[76] to investigate the activities of a foreign power, even if those activities are purely political and peaceful in nature.[77] Furthermore, the Anti-Terrorism and Effective Death Penalty Act of 1996 makes it a crime for both citizens and noncitizens alike to provide material support to even lawful and humanitarian activities of any group designated by the State Department as a foreign terrorist organization. To some civil libertarians, this provision is worrisome, insofar as it resurrects the notion of "guilt by association" and criminalizes humanitarian support to any group blacklisted as terrorist.[78] What make this provision all the more problematic is that many groups designated as terrorist devote most of their resources and efforts to humanitarian activities. For example, the Israeli government estimates that Hamas, a group that the State Department designates as terrorist, devotes 95 percent of its resources to legal social service activity and only 5 percent to violent or military activity.[79]

THE U.S. RESPONSE BEFORE 9/11

Throughout most of the 1970s and 1980s, it was principally the secular Palestinian rejectionist terror groups that posed a serious challenge to Western interests abroad. For example, the 1985 hijacking of the *Achille Lauro* cruise ship left an American, Leon Klinghoffer, dead. Some analysts, most notably Claire Sterling, believed that the Soviet Union was the principal sponsor of these groups. In her book *The Terror Network,* she advanced the theory that the Soviet Union was ultimately responsible for sustaining various terrorist groups around the world. During the Cold War, terrorism was considered to be just another aspect of the struggle between the superpowers and could be used to further a country's foreign policy agenda. Although some critics called her view alarmist and dismissed it as red-baiting, the book found some supporters inside the Reagan administration. For her part, Sterling never really asserted that the Soviet Union was controlling all these terrorist groups around the world.[80] Rather, she argued that the Soviet Union provided a significant amount of support, including weapons, training, and asylum, all of which was well documented. Furthermore, after the fall of the Soviet Union, the new Russian government opened some of its archives, and those documents confirmed much of what Sterling had written. Finally, it would appear to be more than just a coincidence that there was a precipitous drop in left-wing terrorism since the demise of the Soviet Union in December 1991.

But before the Cold War was even over, the United States faced a new challenge from Iran, which for years had been an integral part of the Washington-led anticommunist alliance. At first the Carter administration took a rather benevolent view of the movement to overthrow the shah, hoping that it would move the country in a democratic direction consistent with American foreign policy interests. That attitude changed when the Islamists overthrew the shah and held fifty-two Americans hostage for more than a year. Furthermore, even after the new regime showed its true colors, the Reagan administration was preoccupied with the Soviet Union and consequently gave relatively short shrift to the potential threat emanating from Iran and a renascent radical Islam, which the new theocracy fomented.[81] The Soviet invasion of Afghanistan in 1979 served as a further catalyst as well.

Afghanistan served as an incubator for militant Islam during the 1980s. Even before the Soviet-Afghan war, the political situation in Afghanistan was unstable. In the mid-1960s, revolutionary elements in Afghanistan coalesced to form the People's Democratic Party (PDP). The monarch was deposed in 1973, but an autocratic government that lacked broad support replaced him. That government was forced out in 1978 after a massive demonstration in the front of the presidential palace, in which the army intervened on the side of the protestors. The military officers invited the PDP to form a new government under the leadership of Noor Mohammed Taraki. The left-leaning government was seen as a threat by the Central Intelligence Agency (CIA), however, and the agency is reported to have recruited Hafizulla Amin, a top official in the Taraki government. In September 1979, Amin seized control of the government in an armed coup and immediately sought to establish a fundamentalist Islamic state, but within two months he was overthrown, as remnants of the PDP regained control of the government. The besieged PDP government requested that the Soviet Union send a contingent of troops to ward off the incipient mujahideen and foreign mercenaries, both of whom were recruited and funded by the CIA.[82] According to some accounts, then National Security Adviser Zbigniew Brzezinski instigated the crisis so that the Soviets would fall into the "Afghan trap." Months before the Soviet invasion, he publicly admitted that the Carter administration was assisting the mujahideen to subvert the Taraki government.[83]

It is estimated that the U.S. government sent approximately $3.1 billion to the foreign volunteers in Afghanistan during their struggle against the Soviets. Saudi Arabia is reported to have matched the United States dollar for dollar.[84] Prince Turki bin Faisal, the head of Saudi intelligence, coordinated the training and support of the mujahideen with the CIA and Pakistan's Inter-Services Intelligence (ISI).[85] Furthermore, to counter military advances that the Soviets made in the mid-1980s, the United States provided Stinger antiaircraft missiles to the mujahideen. These weapons were quite successful in neutralizing the Soviet fleet of heavily armored MI-24D helicopters, which were inflicting heavy casualties on the Afghan rebels. They are estimated to have downed more than 270 Soviet aircraft.[86]

Some observers have used the term "blowback" to describe the turn-around in the erstwhile alliance between the United States and the mujahideen in Afghanistan. For his part, bin Laden has consistently maintained that the United States had not helped him in his effort to organize the Afghan mujahideen.

The Americans are lying when they say that they cooperated with us in the past, and we challenge them to show any evidence of this. The truth of the matter is that they were a burden on us and on the mujahideen in Afghanistan. . . . We were doing our duty in support of Islam in Afghanistan, although this duty used to serve, against our desire, the U.S. interests. This situation was similar to the Muslims' fight against the Romans. We know that fighting between the Romans and the Persians has always been strong. So no wise man can say that when Muslims fought the Romans first at the Mu'tah battle they were agents to the Persians, but interests met at this point. In other words, your killing of the Romans, which is a duty for you, used to please the Persians. However, after they finished with the Romans, they began to fight the Persians. So, the conversion of interests without agreement does not necessarily mean relations of agentry. In fact, we have been hostile to them since then. Praise be to God, we gave lectures during those days in Hejaz and Najd on the need to boycott the U.S. goods and to attack the U.S. forces and the U.S. economy.[87]

Terrorism analyst Marc Sageman impugns the assertion of blowback with respect to the CIA's involvement in Afghanistan. Sageman, who served as a foreign service officer in Pakistan during the Soviet-Afghan war, asserted that U.S. support was confined to Afghan resistance fighters. He found no evidence of any direct U.S. support to foreign mujahideen. What Sageman found most striking is the virtual absence of Afghans in the contemporary global jihadist network. Finally, he maintained that very few foreign volunteers were involved in actual combat against the Soviets; they concentrated their activities on supporting functions.[88]

Eventually, the relationship between the United States and the Islamists soured, and Osama bin Laden turned on his erstwhile allies of convenience. By 1993 bin Laden was ready to attack. Ramzi Yousef, the mastermind of the first World Trade Center attack, is believed to have been affiliated with the al Qaeda network. Later that year, elements of his network provided support for Somali fighters who attacked and killed American soldiers in Mogadishu. For President Clinton, the spectacle of body bags and dead American soldiers figured prominently in his decision to withdraw troops from Somalia and hand over stewardship of the humanitarian relief effort to the United Nations.[89]

Until the 1998 U.S. embassy bombings in Kenya and Tanzania, the Clinton administration was loath to take strong action. However, shortly after those attacks, on August 20, 1998, President Clinton initiated Operation Infinite Reach, which launched cruise missiles at a Sudanese factory believed to be manufacturing the deadly VX nerve gas and al Qaeda training camps in Afghanistan. Bin Laden left the training camps not long before the attack, thus escaping injury. As a result of the embassy attacks, the State Department expanded its Diplomatic Security Service from 900 to nearly 1,200 agents.[90] CIA director George Tenet provided new guidelines for his deputies, effectively declaring war on bin Laden.[91] On July 6, 1999, President Clinton issued an executive order that placed sanctions on Afghanistan for allowing bin Laden and al Qaeda to maintain a base of operations in that country.[92] This was followed by UN Resolution 1267 on October 15, 1999, which condemned the Taliban for providing sanctuary to al Qaeda. The resolution demanded that the Taliban turn over bin Laden to a country in which he had been indicted.[93]

In hindsight, these measures appear to have been woefully inadequate. It was not until after 9/11 that the U.S. government unleashed its full fury on global terrorism.

THE IMMEDIATE RESPONSE AFTER 9/11

In the aftermath of the attack on September 11, 2001, the federal government, with support from the American public and U.S. Congress, called for more vigilant measures to root out potential terrorists at home and abroad.[94] President Bush issued several executive orders that sought to block terrorist financing, establish an Office of Homeland Security, and allow for the detention and trial of some noncitizens in military tribunals.[95] With regard to funding, the government has demonstrated that it is prepared to underwrite the cost of the war on terror. Funding to combat terrorism nearly quadrupled, as the $13 billion originally budgeted for this effort in fiscal year 2002 was increased to $50 billion.[96] Although the FBI's budget doubled after the 1993 World Trade Center bombing, still less than one-sixth of its budget was devoted to counterterrorism and counterintelligence.[97] After the 9/11 attacks, Attorney General John Ashcroft and FBI Director John Mueller refocused the bureau's efforts on detecting and thwarting future terrorist attacks rather than pursuing culprits after crimes had been committed.[98]

THE FEDERAL BUREAU OF INVESTIGATION

The FBI responded to the 9/11 attacks with the largest criminal investigation in its history, codenamed PENTBOM. Seven thousand agents and support personnel were assigned to the case.[99] The Department of Justice shifted away from its emphasis on due process to preventive investigations. Toward this end, Ashcroft instructed federal prosecutors in November 2001 to arrange "voluntary" interviews with approximately 4,800 men between the ages of eighteen and thirty-three who were of Middle Eastern descent. The purpose of the interviews was to cull information that might alert authorities to potential terrorist attacks.[100] The Justice Department is also believed to have detained over 1,200 people as part of its investigation into terrorism. Most of those detained were held on immigration charges; fewer than 100 were held on other criminal charges. Still others were detained as material witnesses who might have information related to ongoing grand jury investigations. These massive arrests alarmed civil libertarians and raised understandable fears of scapegoating in the Muslim and Arab communities in the United States.

The fact that all nineteen perpetrators were Muslims of Arab descent was not lost on the public. Some people feared that the presence of a large number of immigrants constituted a potential fifth column threat to the United States, whereas others took it upon themselves to strike out in "revenge" against the Arab and Muslim communities. In the aftermath of the September 11 terrorist attacks, there was a marked increase in the number of bias crimes, including assaults and vandalism against Muslim Americans, Arab Americans, and even those who are mistakenly identified as such because of their physical appearance. To counter this trend, many political leaders, including President Bush and New York mayor Rudy Giuliani, urged Americans not to succumb to bigotry and blame Muslim Americans for the tragedy. The Department of Justice directed its Civil Rights Division's National Origin Working Group to help counter violations of civil rights laws against individuals "perceived to be Arab American, Muslim American, Sikh American, or South-Asian American"; and its Community Relations

Service sponsored a meeting with Arab and Muslim leaders to brief them on the Uniting and Strengthening America by Providing Appropriate Tools Required to Intercept and Obstruct Terrorism (USA PATRIOT) Act.[101] The meeting was an effort to respond to the concerns of the Arab and Muslim communities related to issues surrounding 9/11 and the response thereto.[102] Moreover, some NGOs also decried the bias crime "revenge" attacks against Muslim Americans and made efforts to reach out to this community.[103]

The government was sharply criticized for the intelligence failure that had left the country vulnerable to the 9/11 attacks. Despite the earlier wake-up calls—the first World Trade Center attack in 1993 and the Oklahoma City bombing in 1995—serious defects remained in the area of intelligence. Moreover, senior FBI officials were officially informed of a 9/11 terrorist scenario in the summer of 2001. For example, the so-called Phoenix memo, written by Arizona FBI agent Ken Williams, expressed concern over the sudden rise in the number of Arabs enrolled in flight training. What is more, a CIA report received by President Bush on August 6, 2001, warned that a likely terrorist attack might involve an airliner.[104] One operational deficiency has been the shortage of analysts fluent in Arabic, Farsi, and a range of Central and South Asian languages in the intelligence agencies.[105] This lack of language and cultural skills undermined previous terrorism investigations, including the 1993 World Trade Center bombing.[106]

One persistent problem was the lack of coordination between counterterrorism and criminal investigation sections at the FBI. As one former FBI assistant director, James Kallstrom, pointed out: "We built the Chinese wall between counterterrorism agents and criminal agents higher and higher every year. We did less intelligence sharing, not more."[107] Turf battles have frequently bedeviled relations between intelligence and law enforcement agencies. Moreover, grand jury secrecy laws limit the amount of information that national security bureaucracies can receive.

As mentioned earlier, since 1976, the FBI has officially conducted surveillance of extremist and potentially violent groups under the attorney general's guidelines, which were established after misconduct and abuses arising from the defunct COINTELPRO initiative. The extremely well-coordinated attacks of September 11 underscored the gaping hole in the area of human intelligence and impelled the government to reexamine and recalibrate this policy. As a result, the FBI has loosened its guidelines pertaining to the investigation of extremist groups.[108] Under the new guidelines, field offices directors are allowed to initiate terrorism investigations without approval from headquarters. Also, the new guidelines allow the FBI to enter public places and forums, including publicly accessible Internet sites, to observe and gather information. These new measures caused consternation in some quarters, most notably from civil libertarians, who feared that the FBI would resume domestic spying against politically unpopular dissident groups.[109] Other interest groups applauded the new measures. For example, the ADL's Abraham Foxman has long advocated a recalibration of these guidelines.[110]

THE USA PATRIOT ACT

To meet the exigencies of the new terrorist threat, Congress passed the USA PATRIOT Act, which was signed into law by President Bush on October 26, 2001. The new law gave authorities more options for surveillance with less judicial supervision.[111] First, it authorizes the use of "roving wiretaps" to tap any phone line that a suspected terrorist may be using. Second, it permits surveillance of a suspect's Internet activity and gives the FBI greater latitude in conducting secret searches of suspect's homes. Third, it allows for greater sharing of information among grand juries, prosecutors, and intelligence agencies. Fourth, it expands the powers of the INS to detain immigrants suspected of terrorist activities. Fifth, it gives the government greater power to penetrate banks suspected of being involved in the financing of terrorist groups and activities. And finally, the new law statutorily creates new crimes, enhances penalties, and increases the length of statutes of limitation for certain crimes.[112]

THE DEPARTMENT OF HOMELAND SECURITY

The magnitude of the 9/11 tragedy demonstrated that the United States had not adequately prepared for such an eventuality. Consequently, the federal government undertook a massive effort to restructure and expand both its counterterrorism and homeland security policies. On October 8, 2001, President Bush issued Executive Order 13228, which established the Office of Homeland Security. In essence, homeland security is a comprehensive effort to safeguard the nation's population, property, government, and critical infrastructure. It seeks to accomplish this task by preparing for, protecting against, and managing the consequences of terrorist attacks and related crises.[113]

President Bush appointed Pennsylvania governor Tom Ridge as director of the new agency, which identified four initial priorities. First, U.S. borders must be secured. To strengthen border security, the U.S. Customs Service was granted more personnel, new technology, and a substantially increased budget.

Second, support for "first responders" needed to be increased. To support this effort, President Bush proposed $3.5 billion to enhance the homeland security response capabilities of first responders. Third, the federal government introduced several initiatives to defend the country against bioterrorism. Finally, the government has sought to improve technology systems and protect critical infrastructure systems.[114]

On June 6, 2002, President Bush announced in a national address his desire to consolidate several federal agencies—including the Coast Guard, the Immigration and Naturalization Service, the Transportation Security Administration, the Customs Service, the Federal Emergency Management Agency, and the Secret Service—into a cabinet-level Department of Homeland Security, to coordinate the efforts in protecting the nation against terrorism. And on March 1, 2003, the majority of the 180,000 personnel from these various agencies were merged to become the fifteenth U.S. cabinet-level department. This initiative constituted the most ambitious governmental reorganization since the creation of the Department of Defense in 1947. Indicative of the new department's significance, $36.2 billion was allocated for its fiscal year 2004 budget.[115]

OPERATION ENDURING FREEDOM

Immediately after 9/11, the American public cried out for retaliation. However, there was no immediate consensus in the Bush administration on the appropriate initial course of action. During the early part of the crisis, Defense Secretary Donald Rumsfeld worried that building a coalition around the goal of defeating al Qaeda would fall apart once that mission had been accomplished. Bush, however, worried about making the initial target too diffuse. Both he and Secretary of State Colin Powell believed that it would be far easier to build an international coalition focused on the specific target of al Qaeda. Deputy Secretary of Defense Paul Wolfowitz wanted to make Iraq the principal target in the first round in the war on terrorism. To him, there was no greater menace in the world than Saddam Hussein, and he argued that if the president was serious about going after those who harbor terrorists, then Saddam had to be put on the top of the list of targets.[116] In his analysis, an American military campaign in Afghanistan was wrought with uncertainty, given the history of conflict in that nation. By contrast, Wolfowitz saw Saddam's Iraq as a fragile regime that could easily be broken.[117] President Bush ultimately decided to target Afghanistan first, under the operational name "Enduring Freedom," which commenced on October 8, 2001.[118]

The planning for Operation Enduring Freedom was hasty to appease U.S. domestic opinion, which demanded swift retaliation for the 9/11 attacks. The initial U.S. strategy was directed primarily at splitting the less fanatical elements of the Taliban from the hardliners. The U.S. military relied primarily on air power and special forces on the ground to gather intelligence, provide targeting information for U.S. aircraft, and coordinate operations with the Northern Alliance. Very few American troops—no more than 4,000—were used for the original campaign.[119] However, one consequence of this low number of troops deployed was that many Taliban and al Qaeda fighters were able to escape from Afghanistan because there were not enough personnel on the ground to apprehend them. Operation Anaconda, which sought to round up and capture Taliban and al Qaeda leadership, was largely unsuccessful; many escaped to neighboring Pakistan to regroup and fight another day.[120]

The speed with which the U.S. achieved victory surprised many skeptics, who bemoaned the U.S. military's poor track record in fighting unconventional wars. However, as one observer noted, victory in unconventional war in the long term depends more on political and psychological action than on the application of military power. For the most part, the United States has focused primarily on the military dimension of the campaign rather than on winning hearts and minds and building enduring institutions.[121] Despite a thoroughgoing campaign to destroy the Taliban, there is evidence that the organization has reconstituted itself and even dominates some rural areas, primarily in the south of the country.[122] Some elements of the Taliban are working with local landlords to reassert some of their lost authority. At present, however, U.S. armed forces appear to generally have the military situation under control in the most important areas of the country.

The United States scored on other fronts as well. Shortly after 9/11, President Bush announced to the world, "you are either with us or with the terrorists." In this vein, the United States has sought the cooperation of foreign governments to help track down suspected terrorists and their supporters. Since 2001, the United States has experienced many successes, as many al Qaeda operatives, including several high-ranking leaders, were captured in foreign countries. International cooperation in the war on terror has been crucial, most importantly with Pakistan. Among the most notable captives was Abu Zubaydah. Arrested in March 2002, he is believed to have been the chief of external operations for al Qaeda. Coincidentally, exactly one year after the 9/11 attacks, Pakistani authorities arrested Ramzi Binalshibh, who disclosed that he was the principal organizer of the 9/11 attacks and the only person outside the group of hijackers who knew the exact details of zero hour.[123] For the first time, a member of al Qaeda had taken direct responsibility for those atrocities. His colleague and coconspirator, Khalid Sheikh Muhammad, was arrested in March 2003.[124] In light of these victories, Bush felt confident enough to expand the war on terrorism.

OPERATION IRAQI FREEDOM

Fresh from quick victory in Afghanistan, by April 2002, Bush began to publicly call for a policy of regime change in Iraq. This has arguably been the most controversial aspect of his war on terrorism. In order to understand just how the United States came to this position, it is worth looking into the recent history of U.S.-Iraqi relations.

During the 1980s, Iraq received support not only from other Arab regimes and the United States but the Soviet Union as well. All parties feared that an Iranian victory in the Iran-Iraq War (1980–1988) would destabilize the region and, by doing so, metastasize Ayatollah Ruhollah Khomeini's radical Islamist revolution. The Reagan administration overlooked Iraq's previous involvement in terrorism and even went so far as to remove that country from the State Department's list of state supporters of terrorism, which was all the more remarkable considering that the notorious terrorist leader Abu Nidal was living in Baghdad at that time. Some officials in Washington believed that Iraq could serve as a bulwark against Islamic fundamentalism emanating from Iran.

Although Iraq did not achieve all its war aims and suffered substantial losses, it came out of the Iran-Iraq War militarily stronger than it had entered and demonstrated the durability of Saddam Hussein's regime.[125] Saddam Hussein was affronted by what he believed was a lack of appreciation from his neighboring countries. As he saw it, Iraq had defended the Gulf states from the menace of Islamic fundamentalism. The long conflict with Iran put enormous fiscal strain on Iraq, which accumulated billions of dollars in debt from the war effort. The sacrifices of Iraq notwithstanding, the Gulf creditors still insisted upon the prompt payment of the loans. Their lack of gratitude left Hussein with a sense of betrayal. In a reckless gamble to rectify what Hussein perceived as an injustice, he invaded Kuwait in August 1990 and shortly thereafter announced an *Anschluss* with the tiny but extremely oil-rich country, under the tutelage of Iraq.

Of course, the subsequent Gulf War proved to be ruinous for Iraq. However, Saddam Hussein demonstrated remarkable durability, squelching a Kurdish uprising in the north and a Shi'ite uprising in the south. The CIA worried that

Iranian-style Shi'ite radicalism might take hold in the South and thus backed away from the proposition of toppling Saddam. Moreover, a Shi'ite victory in Iraq could have conceivably inspired the long-oppressed Shi'ites to entertain revolutionary aspirations similar to those of Iranians.[126]

The resultant sanctions regime imposed by the victors in Operation Desert Storm caused tremendous privation for the Iraqi people. Furthermore, the callous remarks of then U.S. ambassador to the UN and future secretary of state Madeline Albright in 1996, when she appeared on *60 Minutes* and commented on the morality of economic sanctions, did little to endear the United States to Islamists: she remarked that the estimated deaths of over a half a million Iraqi children due to lack of medical supplies imposed by the sanctions was a "very hard choice," but "we think the price is worth it."[127] Osama bin Laden has explicitly cited the UN sanctions regime against Iraq as one of his grievances against the United States in his various fatwas. Iraq also faced a very intrusive inspections program under the direction of the United Nations Special Commission (UNSCOM). Frustrated by seeming dissimulation on the part of the Iraqi government, the weapons inspectors left Iraq in 1998. However, this "departure" was soon followed by Operation Desert Fox, a U.S. military operation that included occasional air strikes against Iraqi targets.

By June 2002 President Bush announced that he would launch preemptive strikes against those countries believed to pose a serious threat to the United States.[128] Furthermore, he added that the United States would be willing to take unilateral action if support from the UN and traditional allies was not forthcoming. This approach, which would later be dubbed the "Bush Doctrine," caused considerable consternation in some quarters in Bush's cabinet, most notably with Colin Powell, who worried that a military operation against Iraq could destabilize the whole Middle East.[129] However, the hawks in the administration ultimately carried the day. Vice President Dick Cheney, who had previously voiced concern about a military operation against Iraq, had become one of the chief advocates for a war to remove Saddam. In the words of Bob Woodward, Cheney "was beyond hell-bent for action against Saddam. It was as if nothing else existed."[130]

Ultimately, Bush became convinced that a strategy of preemption was necessary. Two factors featured prominently in his decision: (1) another massive, surprise attack similar to 9/11 could happen again, and (2) the proliferation of weapons of mass destruction added to the potential lethality of future terrorism. If these two factors should converge in the hands of terrorists or a rogue state, then the United States could suffer terrorism of unprecedented magnitude.[131] Public perceptions also helped the Bush administration in the days leading up to the Iraq War. A poll conducted by the *Washington Post* found that approximately 70 percent of those Americans surveyed believed that Saddam Hussein had a role in the 9/11 attacks.[132]

In March 2003 the Bush administration finally launched its military campaign against Saddam Hussein, dubbed "Operation Iraqi Freedom." After just a few weeks of battle, the U.S.-led coalition won a decisive victory despite pockets of fierce Iraqi resistance. However, the elation would prove to be short-lived, as a loose collection of former Ba'athists, foreign fighters, elements of al Qaeda, and some regular Iraqi citizens bent on revenge and restoring national honor coalesced to wage a guerrilla war against U.S. forces and their allies. Some supporters of the Bush administration went so far as to advance the "flypaper theory" that it was better to fight the terrorists in Iraq than in New York City.[133] There is evidence that Muslims from many different countries have converged on Iraq to wage jihad against U.S. armed forces and coalesced around groups such as Ansar al-Islam.[134] In fact, according to U.S. intelligence, the vast majority of suicide attacks in Iraq are believed to be carried out by foreigners.[135]

The initial military victory in Iraq came at significant cost to the United States. Currently, the federal government is registering a record-high budget deficit with no real sign of improvement on the horizon. A protracted occupation and guerrilla war will only exacerbate this problem. Moreover, diplomatic relations between the United States and some of its traditional allies were severely strained in the months leading up to the war. France led the opposition against American military intervention and was followed by important nations, including Germany and Russia. Indeed, there is evidence to suggest that the United States has become increasingly isolated in the war on terrorism: a Pew Foundation Global Attitudes Project poll found a sharp disconnect on this issue between the views of Americans and Europeans. For example, most Europeans surveyed did not believe that the war on Iraq had helped the overall war on terror.[136] But by the summer of 2005, American support for the war had fallen considerably, as most Americans agreed that the war had made the United States more vulnerable to terrorism.[137] Even Turkey—a long-time stalwart ally—declined to militarily assist the United States in the war. Furthermore, there are some indications that key countries involved in the coalition may be experiencing serious domestic pressure as a result of the war. For example, in the November 2002 Pakistani election, Islamist parties won 20 percent of the vote on a platform that included calls for the establishment of sharia and the removal of American military and law enforcement personnel.[138] The Musharraf regime is not really in a position to take on the Islamic militants. From the perspective of the United States, this situation is worrisome, considering that without Pakistan's support, it will be extremely difficult to root out terrorists along the Pakistani-Afghani border.

Conclusion

By the summer of 2003, Iraq appeared to have emerged as the pivotal theater in the war on terrorism. One might even go so far to call it the potential Stalingrad of the conflict. Indeed, much is at stake in Iraq. If the U.S. government can install a new Iraqi government that establishes democracy and revives a viable economy, then this model would, as the theory goes, prove to be a great threat to antidemocratic and extremist forces in the region. If the Iraqi experiment fails, however, then American credibility and reliability would seriously wane, with great consequences for American interests and allies in that region of the world. What is more, the loss of Iraq could disrupt the American-Israeli alliance. As Abraham Foxman conjectured, if Israel were to become directly involved in the current Middle Eastern war, for example, in response to an Arab attack, it is conceivable that the conflict could metamorphose into a war between Islam and the West over the survival of Israel. In a world of rapid change and turmoil, Foxman assumes that no alliance—even one as enduring as that between the United States and Israel—can be assumed to be permanent.[139] Still further emboldened by victory in Iraq, the jihadists may decide to launch an all-out jihad against Israel.

As Michael Ledeen observed, the Islamists believe that they have found the key to getting on the right side of history. Their mass appeal depends heavily on continuous success. In his analysis, what is crucial for American victory in the war on terror is to undercut the momentum and morale of militant Islam. If the dynamism of the movement is curtailed, then he believes that it will soon collapse, not unlike the implosion of the Soviet empire.[140] However, one major problem with the idea that Iraqi democracy can spawn more democracy in the Middle East is that Iraq's democracy did not develop organically from the will of the people, like those in Latin America or Eastern Europe. Rather, the Iraqi model consists first of a foreign invasion, followed by a period of violence and chaos and finally a long period of foreign occupation.[141] There are successful examples of democracy being imposed by foreign victors, such as Germany and Japan after World War II, but both those countries had ethnically homogeneous populations, parliamentary traditions, and experience with the rule of law. Iraq has virtually none of the aforementioned characteristics in its national traditions.[142]

American foreign policy has always been pulled in two general directions, a realist national security defined in narrow terms versus an expansive sense of American idealism that rests directly on the exceptionalism of American institutions and the messianic belief in their universal applicability. Essentially, the Bush administration has favored the latter orientation. A variety of Bush administration spokespeople and advisers have suggested that a regime change in Iraq will put pressure on other governments in the region to adapt democratic reforms. In doing so, the United States is embarking on an immensely ambitious exercise in the political reengineering of a hostile part of the world— a project to which Francis Fukuyama referred as "a big roll of the dice."[143]

Besides the government, various nongovernmental organizations are working to counter extremism at home and abroad. It is that topic to which we now turn.

CHAPTER SEVEN

The Role of Nongovernmental Organizations in the Aftermath of 9/11

U.S. policy toward political extremism differs from that in other Western democracies. For instance, in Germany, an agency called the Office of the Protection of the Constitution (Verfassungsschutz) can recommend to the judiciary the dissolution of extremist groups that it deems a threat to constitutional democracy. Similarly, on occasion the British government has invoked the 1965 Race Relations Act to justify raids of homes and offices of right-wing extremists, including the National Front and the British National Party. Even in Israel, where the extreme right enjoys significant grassroots support, the government outlawed the late Meir Kahane's Kach movement because of its extremist platform.

By contrast, in the United States, with its strong civil liberties tradition and First Amendment protections, the government does not have the authority to disband extremist groups or proscribe extremist speech just because they may espouse unpopular ideas. From a comparative legal perspective, the U.S. government appears to be more constrained in responding to political extremism. However, what is often ignored is that nongovernmental organizations (NGOs) have inserted themselves into this area of public policy and have done much to fill the void. They have persuaded the government to take a strong position vis-à-vis the extreme right, and on numerous occasions they have augmented the government's efforts.

The Watchdog Community

The number of NGOs, or so-called watchdog groups, that monitor the activities of the extreme right has grown considerably since the late 1970s. A University of Florida study estimates that there are now approximately 300 such groups nationwide.[1] Like its extreme right adversaries, the watchdog community comprises a variety of groups.[2]

The first major category of watchdog groups consists of the so-called Jewish defense organizations, which seek to safeguard the interests of Jews both in the United States and overseas. The chief organization in this category, and indeed for all NGOs in this area of policy, is the Anti-Defamation League (ADL), which was founded in 1913 in Chicago. The ADL is well financed and maintains thirty-three regional offices in various American cities as well as in foreign countries, including Austria, Canada, and Israel. This NGO sets the pace for the others; it has taken the lead in countering the extreme right through such measures as the promotion of legislation (antiparamilitary training statutes and hate crime legislation, for example), cooperation with law enforcement agencies, training programs, and the promotion of software that blocks access to extremist websites. Through its nationwide intelligence apparatus, the ADL has been able to closely monitor developments in the extreme right. In 2001, the ADL announced that it would join efforts with the Israeli-based International Policy Institute for Counter-Terrorism (ICT) to coordinate and provide information to policymakers, law enforcement agencies, and the public.[3]

The American Jewish Committee (AJC) is another important organization in this category. It was founded in the early years of the twentieth century in response to the pogroms that terrorized Jewish populations in Russia and parts of Eastern Europe at that time. The AJC sought to help their coreligionists overseas. During the 1930s, the AJC, along with the ADL, worked to expose native fascists active in the United States (see Chapter 6). After World War II, the AJC focused most of its efforts once again on overseas affairs affecting Jews. In recent years the AJC has demonstrated renewed interest in combating domestic right-wing extremism, primarily by issuing reports on the topic. Its primary researcher on the topic, Kenneth Stern, published a best-selling book on the militias in 1996 titled *A Force upon the Plain*.[4] The AJC has also produced numerous reports on Islamic extremism and terrorism and has testified on the subject before the U.S. Congress.

The Simon Wiesenthal Center (SWC), which has its headquarters in Los Angeles, California, has recently gained prominence. For most of its history, the SWC concentrated on educational efforts, promoting awareness of the Holocaust, and bringing Nazi war criminals to justice. However, the number of Nazi fugitives is rapidly dwindling, and in recent years the SWC has expanded the scope of its domestic agenda to include monitoring right-wing extremist groups in the United States and abroad.

The Jewish defense groups have been the most formidable NGOs in countering right-wing extremism. Despite their relative affluence and security, American Jews, according to survey data, believe that anti-Semitism remains a dormant threat. The percentage of Jews who told pollsters that anti-Semitism is a "serious problem" in the United States nearly doubled during the 1980s, from 45 percent in 1983 to almost 85 percent in 1990.[5]

The only organization in the second category, the civil litigation watchdog group, is the Southern Poverty Law Center (SPLC) in Montgomery, Alabama. It is arguably second only to the ADL in influence and stature among these advocacy groups. The SPLC's major innovation is the use of civil suits to hold extremist groups responsible for the actions of their individual members. Some of these civil suits have resulted in very large judgments and have bankrupted several extremist organizations. Thus, the SPLC is among the NGOs most feared by the extreme right.

Progressive NGOs constitute the third category of watchdog groups. These groups tend to be critical of a broad segment of the right wing, not just the extreme right. They are generally concerned with a much broader range of so-called progressive issues such as environmentalism, women's rights, and affirmative action. Prominent among them is the Center for Democratic Renewal (CDR) of Atlanta, Georgia. The CDR has favored a grassroots approach, seeking to form coalitions with like-minded activists. Another prominent group is Political Research Associates (PRA) in Somerville, Massachusetts. Primarily a research center, it acts as a clearinghouse of information for people who want either to study the American political right wing or to organize against some of its public policy positions.[6] Much like the CDR, several members of its staff have progressive and left-wing political backgrounds.[7] Progressive watchdog groups are much less likely than their better-established counterparts to get involved in intelligence sharing with law enforcement agencies.

Understandably, the increasing stridency of militant Islam has alarmed some people. A fairly recent watchdog group is the Investigative Project on Terrorism, which monitors radical Islamic groups in the United States. It was founded in late 1995 by Steven Emerson, who currently serves as the organization's executive director. He began his career as an analyst on the staff of the U.S. Senate Foreign Relations Committee in 1977. By 1982, he had gone to work as a freelance writer, primarily for the *New Republic*. While there, he developed an intense interest in Middle Eastern affairs and wrote several books on the topic, including *The American House of Saud: The Secret Petrodollar Connection*, which was published in 1985. In 1986 he joined *U.S. News and World Report* and worked as a national security correspondent while writing two more books: *Secret Warriors* and *The Fall of Pan Am 103: Inside the Lockerbie Investigation*. He joined CNN in 1990 as a special investigation correspondent, a position for which he gained stature in the media. In 1994, his PBS video "Jihad in America" won the George Polk award for best television documentary. Soon thereafter, he left CNN to devote his efforts to the Investigative

Project. His organization has compiled a database of thousands of individuals who are known or suspected terrorists, as well as dossiers on militant groups.[8] Emerson recounted the origin of his organization in an interview:

> The Investigative Project on Terrorism is an organization I founded in 1995 following a documentary I produced for public television called *Jihad in America*. The Investigative Project on Terrorism's mission is to investigate, analyze, and combat the threat of militant Islamic extremist groups and their activities in the U.S., as well as overseas. It investigates the covert as well as overt activities, in addition to tracking the financial wherewithal by which they get their funding. . . .
>
> . . . the film *Jihad in America* that aired in 1994 came out of a series of events the previous two years when I had been working for CNN and was asked to do a special following the 1993 World Trade Center bombing. And that sparked a lot of my interest, having seen a lot of the evidence put into the record by the government showing what I thought was a far more massive conspiracy and also showing a greater degree of radicalization among various Islamic institutions than was previously thought to have existed. So, in response to the CNN request to do a one-hour special on the 1993 bombing, I prepared a proposal. CNN didn't buy it, so I took the proposal to public television and they gave me the green light and actually I did the documentary. Having done the documentary, I realized that there was no other repository of information in any domain—government or nongovernment—on this issue of Islamic militant groups and what their real agenda or activities were. So I created the organization to fill that void.[9]

Emerson's reputation suffered in the wake of the 1995 Oklahoma City bombing. When asked by reporters for his thoughts on the attack, Emerson speculated that Islamic terrorists might have been responsible, noting the physical similarities between the bombing of the Murrah Federal Building and the 1983 attack on the U.S. embassy in Beirut—an incident for which Hezbollah is believed to have been responsible. At the time this assessment was understandable in that the attack resembled the modus operandi of Hezbollah and not domestic right-wing extremists, who had theretofore never carried out such a lethal attack, at least in the United States.[10] His credibility was diminished shortly thereafter when homegrown radical rightists were arrested for the attack. Interestingly, Emerson has categorically rejected subsequent theories that implicate Middle Eastern operatives in the bombing.[11] However, the 9/11 attacks seemed to vindicate Emerson's earlier warnings, and he is once again a sought-after commentator on the topic of terrorism. Not long after 9/11, he published a book *American Jihad,* based largely on his television documentary.

He is often a guest terrorist analyst on television news programs. Furthermore, he provides advice on militant Islamic groups to law enforcement and intelligence agencies. Finally, he occasionally testifies before congressional committees on the topic of terrorism. Still, Emerson has his detractors and has come under some criticism for his supposed "Islamaphobia."[12]

Methods Used to Counteract Extremist Groups

The various NGOs in the United States take a multifaceted approach to countering terrorism and extremism. One obvious concern to both the watchdogs and the government alike is paramilitary training by armed groups. When the contemporary militia movement surfaced in 1994, more attention was brought to bear on this issue. To meet this challenge, the ADL crafted legislation proscribing paramilitary training by unauthorized groups. The thrust of the legislation was to make it illegal to operate paramilitary camps.[13] The SPLC followed suit and introduced its own legislation as well. The ADL also conducted a media campaign to heighten public awareness on this issue. The campaign has proven to be very successful: twenty-four states have enacted such statutes, thirteen of which are based on the ADL's model.[14]

Hate crime laws are occasionally used to prosecute perpetrators of right-wing violence. Right-wing terrorists very often choose targets they perceive as "outsiders" for no other reason than some ascriptive characteristic such as race or ethnicity. Moreover, because of the organizational fragmentation of the American extreme right, the distinction between terrorism and hate crimes is often blurred. And although very few right-wing groups regularly commit terrorism, some advocate violence and can presumably influence the lone wolves that do. Thus, hate crime laws can be used to counter right-wing violence. Most offenders arrested for hate crimes do not formally belong to organized extreme right groups, and even those that do belong to such groups usually act independently, without any directive from their organizations. Nevertheless, watchdog groups have done much to link organized extremist groups with the issue. The ADL has been the most important advocate of hate crime legislation by far, having begun lobbying for it in the 1970s. Its model statute, or a close facsimile, had been adopted in all but nine states by 1998.[15]

Although the perpetrators of hate crimes are usually juveniles or young adults without much wealth, the SPLC has on occasion used civil suits to hold extreme right organizations responsible for the actions of their law-breaking members. This novel and controversial use of the civil suit has effectively put some right-wing organizations out of business. In essence, this approach seeks to hold leaders of extremist groups vicariously liable for the actions of their members, even in some instances where there is no evidence of any directive to commit an illegal act. The SPLC effectively used this tactic on numerous occasions and won judgments against several extremist organizations, including Louis Beam's Knights of the Ku Klux Klan, Robert Shelton's United Klans of America, Tom Metzger's White Aryan Resistance, and most recently Richard Butler's Aryan Nations. The SPLC contends that the principal aim of these civil suits is to bankrupt the organizations and individuals responsible for crimes and effectively put them out of business.[16]

Training and educational programs are important instruments by which NGOs can influence public policy toward extremism. For quite some time, the ADL has been active in this area. For example, it periodically presents lectures on extremism at the FBI academy in Quantico, Virginia.[17] Other watchdog groups have joined in this effort as well and offer similar programs of their own, which they conduct for both government agencies and private organizations. In October 2001, the Library of Congress announced that the ADL online response to September 11 would be included in an electronics archive of the 9/11 attacks. The ADL publishes many online reports on terrorism and extremism, including background information on Osama bin Laden and al Qaeda.[18]

By far the most effective effort in countering the extreme right has taken place in the area of intelligence sharing. Once again, the ADL has taken the lead. FBI documents obtained under the Freedom of Information Act (FOIA) indicate that the ADL has made considerable efforts to cultivate a close working relationship with the FBI.[19] The SPLC has moved into this area as well, and as its founder, Morris Dees, put it, the organization "has long shared intelligence with law enforcement agencies."[20] As mentioned earlier, Investigative Project on Terrorism founder Steven Emerson often provides intelligence on militant Islamic organizations to authorities. However, this seemingly backdoor relationship with law enforcement is not without its critics; some believe that it raises serious civil liberties issues.[21] Further, some critics charge that the intelligence sharing between the FBI and the watchdog groups constitutes a circumvention of the attorney general's guidelines, in that law enforcement authorities can view the files of private monitoring organizations when they see fit. Moreover, watchdog groups do not have to concern themselves with the stringent civil liberties restrictions to which the FBI must adhere when gathering information on its subjects of investigation.

The watchdog groups have tended to confront right-wing extremism more gingerly in the area of free speech and the First Amendment. Traditionally, efforts to legally exclude extremist views from the marketplace of ideas have not been very effective in the United States. Consequently, some watchdog groups have sought to use other means to effect the same result. On numerous occasions watchdog groups have filed formal complaints with the Federal Communications Commission (FCC) against radio stations that air extremist programs. One method employed by the ADL and the SPLC that has proved effective is applying pressure directly on media outlets and dissuading them from disseminating extremist views.[22]

The cumulative effect of the various efforts by these NGOs has done much to neutralize the extreme right in the United States. However, the events of 9/11 and more recently the war in Iraq seem to have catalyzed extremist segments from across the political spectrum. Some representatives of the various Jewish defense organizations expressed concern that a new synthesis is taking place, in which numerous variants of anti-Semitism are coalescing into a new ideology that could conceivably unite disparate extremists around the world.

The Watchdog Community in the Aftermath of 9/11

The NGOs opposed to right-wing extremism—most notably the Jewish defense organizations—have responded to the 9/11 challenge with special vigor. Although the Jewish defense NGOs have historically been preoccupied with right-wing extremists in the United States, recent events have caused these organizations to take greater notice of the potential threat posed by militant Islam. Consequently, Islamic extremism is an increasing cause of concern. Daniel Pipes has even chided the Jewish defense organizations for their fixation on seemingly innocuous Christian fundamentalists such as Jerry Falwell and Pat Robertson while virtually ignoring the threat of radical Islam right now in their midst.[23] The religious aspect of Islamic anti-Semitism makes it particularly worrisome, as ADL director Abraham Foxman argued:

We saw the rise of anti-Semitism in an anti-religious, anti-Christian paganism. Now we have the religion element, and that is a dangerous element. My father used to say one should always be careful of God's Cossacks. Those who act in the name of God and believe that they have the truth, the only truth. That is very dangerous. It makes this virulent epidemic of anti-Semitism that much more dangerous, that much more virulent and that much more threatening.[24]

The perceived threat to Jewish security and interests in the United States has caused some in the American Jewish community to create new protection organizations. For example, shortly after the September 11 attacks, a group of mostly Jewish New Yorkers founded the organization Americans to Counter Terrorism. Among their aims is to rally public support for the government in its war on terrorism.[25]

A major objective of the Jewish defense NGOs in the aftermath of 9/11 has been to convince the public that the terrorists targeted the United States not because of the country's policies but because of its values—democracy, freedom, secularism, and modernism. Support for Israel, they argue, is only incidental to the grievances of the terrorists. A frequent refrain was that the attacks of 9/11 were visited upon the United States for primarily existential reasons (i.e., what the United States is, not what it does overseas), rather than its policies toward Israel. Abraham Foxman's comments are illustrative of these sentiments:

> The American presence in Saudi Arabia and willingness to protect other states in the region from extremists, whether Saddam Hussein or Osama bin Laden, make America the prime enemy. In addition, it is American culture, so predominant everywhere in the world that stands in direct opposition to the medieval, anti-democratic ideology of the Islamic extremists. If Israel did not exist, Osama bin Laden and his cohorts would still see America as their prime enemy.[26]

The Jewish defense organizations have worked hard to counteract the perception that the terrorist attacks were related to U.S. support for Israel. For example, the ADL sought to counter a *Newsweek* poll that found that 58 percent of the American public believed that U.S. support for Israel was a factor in bin Laden's decision to attack the United States. It is worth noting, however, that the same poll found that 60 percent of Americans did not believe that the United States should change its policies in the Middle East.[27] The ADL conducted surveys to determine whether the American public blamed the attack on the close relationship between the United States and Israel. According to the study, 63 percent of those surveyed rejected the notion. Furthermore, the basic sympathies of the American people were closer to the Israeli position (48 percent) than the Palestinian position (11 percent) in the current crisis. Finally, a much larger portion of the American public blamed the violence in the Israeli-Palestinian conflict on the Palestinians rather than the Israelis (42 percent versus 13 percent).[28]

Other Jewish defense NGOs responded to the 9/11 crisis as well. For example, the American Jewish Committee issued briefings pointing out that Islamic extremism predated the establishment of the state of Israel. According to this line of reason, Israel is merely a side issue in the current terrorist campaign.[29] The Simon Wiesenthal Center announced a two-pronged strategy consisting of an expansion of its worldwide monitoring coupled with increased sharing of this information with government officials, the media, and other important international figures.[30]

The ADL has also been monitoring the response to this crisis from Arab, Muslim, right-wing, and left-wing extremists. Its Internet website features a section titled "What They Are Saying," in which the comments of extremists on the 9/11 attacks are posted. The ADL has also sought to debunk various rumors circulating on the Internet, most notably the allegation that the Israeli government, specifically Mossad, was complicit in the September 11 attacks. Toward this end, the ADL issued a report titled *Unraveling Anti-Semitic 9/11 Conspiracy Theories* in late 2003.[31] Similarly, the Simon Wiesenthal Center released a study titled *9/11 Digital Lies: A Survey of Online Apologists for Global Terrorism.*[32]

Just days after the September 11 attacks, rumors circulated on the Internet that Israeli intelligence operatives in the United States had shadowed the al Qaeda terrorist hijackers yet deliberately failed to warn American authorities. (This conspiracy theory will be explained in greater detail in Chapter 8.) According to the rumor, Israeli nationals working in the World Trade Center were warned approximately two hours before the first plane struck the tower and evacuated the building. David Duke asserted in his newsletter that the *Jerusalem Post* had reported that 4,000 Jews were missing from the World Trade Center and furthermore that only one Jew was killed in the attack, which suggested Israeli foreknowledge of the terrorist plot. The rationale for failing to warn the Americans was supposed to be that the attack would so enrage the American public that it would support a broad war against those countries that sponsor terrorism in the Middle East, some of which are hostile to Israel (e.g., Iraq, Iran, and Syria).[33]

The ADL went so far as to send letters to foreign ministers of European nations urging them to make educational initiatives to counter the spread of rumors that Israel was somehow complicit in the 9/11 tragedy. These rumors have gained considerable currency in the Arab/Muslim world; the Saudi minister of the interior, Prince Nayef Ibn Abd al-Aziz, blamed Israel for the attack. According to al-Aziz, the "Zionist-controlled media" used this tragedy to turn U.S. public opinion against Arabs and Muslims.[34] Apparently, these conspiracy theories resonate in the Arab world. A Gallup poll released in March 2002 found that approximately 60 percent of the population in nine Arab and Muslim countries believe that Israel or Jews, not bin Laden, were responsible for the 9/11 attacks.[35]

Since the end of World War II, anti-Semitism has generally been con-fined to the ghettos of political extremism. Admittedly, it attained some stature in the Middle East, not only with the general public but in the leadership and media of that region as well. However, events in recent years seem to have loos-ened the inhibitions that developed in the wake of the Holocaust. ADL Direc-tor Foxman commented on how the 9/11 attacks had "created a new dynamic where the rhetoric of anti-Semites in this country is being picked up and recy-cled in some segments of the Muslim and Arab world to advance hateful myths and conspiracy theories about Israel and Jews."[36] Moreover, the ADL has ex-pressed concern that pro-Palestinian rallies have frequently turned into forums for anti-Semitism that often include classic canards such as equating Zionism with Nazism, asserting that Jews control the U.S. government, and blaming Jews for killing Jesus Christ.[37]

This renewed sense of Jewish angst was expressed most urgently in Foxman's 2003 book, *Never Again? The Threat of the New Anti-Semitism.* According to Foxman, Jews around the world face their most serious threat since the 1930s. As he sees it, a new synergy of anti-Semitism is developing around the world, as disparate extremists coalesce around a shared animus against Israel and the United States. For Foxman, the "new anti-Semitism" is all the more worrisome in that it appears more mainstream and acceptable. Thus it has the potential to reach more social and political groups that would otherwise not be receptive to such a message. Moreover, the new anti-Semitism draws upon multiple sources of financial and logistical support, including not only sympathizers in Europe and the United States but prominent individuals, businesses, and governments in the Arab and Muslim worlds.[38] To buttress his claims, Foxman cites recent ADL surveys that indicate an increase in anti-Semitic attitudes even among Americans, thus reversing a decades-old trend. According to the survey, 17 per-cent of Americans hold "unquestionably anti-Semitic" attitudes. The results of surveys in Europe were even more troubling; overall, 21 percent of European respondents were characterized as "most anti-Semitic."[39]

The fact that 40 percent of the world's Jewish population is concentrated in a small geographic location—the state of Israel—makes the situation of Jews today all the more perilous. Israel is a country surrounded by hostile neighbors, some of which may gain access to weapons of mass destruction, which could effectively wipe out the region's Jewish population.[40] What is more, Israel faces serious internal problems as well. The Palestinian segment of the population is increas-ing much faster than the Israeli portion. If this trend continues unchallenged, Foxman sees only two likely possibilities: Israel will disenfranchise Palestinians in order to maintain Jewish control, or Israel will cease to be a Jewish state.[41] In either scenario, Israel would not resemble the country it is today. Increasingly, Jewish defense organizations are recognizing the commonalities of anti-Semitic movements around the world and the threat that they pose to Israel and Jewish interests.

THE CONFLATION OF MILITANT ISLAM AND RIGHT-WING EXTREMISM

The watchdog organizations were quick to point out the ideological similarities between the extreme right and Islamists. Some even feared that an operational alliance might develop between the two movements. Mark Potok of the Southern Poverty Law Center believed that both the extreme right and militant Islam share common enemies in globalism and multiculturalism. As Potok commented, the extreme right has "come to see the United States as the global spearhead of multiculturalism and multiracialism." Interestingly, far from wrapping themselves in the American flag as patriots did in the past, today's right-wing extremists are, in Potok's words, "burning it."[42] However, Potok conceded that he saw no "big organizational bridge" between militant Islam and the extreme right.[43]

Chip Berlet of Political Research Associates noted three ideological affinities shared by the extreme right and militant Islam. First, both movements generally view Jews with disdain and see them as controlling the world through secret conspiracies. Second, both see the U.S. government as hopelessly under the sway of a powerful Jewish elite, or what in extremist circles is called the Zionist occupation government (ZOG). Finally, both movements seek to overthrow the existing governments in the countries in which they reside and replace them with monocultural states built around racial or religious exclusivity. Berlet points out that this ethnonationalist ideology is sometimes referred to as the "Third Position," that is, a third way besides capitalism and communism (see Chapter 5).[44]

This prospect of seemingly disparate movements coalescing into a larger anti-Semitic alliance has not gone unnoticed by Jewish defense organizations. One ominous development from the perspective of the Jewish groups is the increasing criticism of Jews and Israel from other parts of the political spectrum. For example, Representative Cynthia McKinney (D-GA) drew criticism from Jewish groups for remarks she made suggesting that pro-Israeli lawmakers had dual loyalties. In response, Jewish groups expended considerable resources in an effort to defeat her reelection bid. Although she was defeated, the episode strained black-Jewish relations and put a drain on the resources of Jewish defense organizations. The self-styled populist Democratic congressman, James

Traficant, went so far as to blame Congress and its support for Israel for the 9/11 terrorist attacks.[45]

In January 2002, Roger Cukierman, the president of Conseil représentatif des institutions juives de France (CRIF), an umbrella organization for secular Jewish institutions in France, warned that Jews faced the threat of an antiglobalization, anticapitalist, anti-American, and anti-Zionist alliance comprising neo-Nazis, environmentalists, and left-wing groups.[46] Similarly, Todd Endelman, a professor of modern Jewish history at the University of Michigan, announced at a conference on the topic of anti-Semitism in Toronto that a greater threat of the new anti-Semitism now comes from the political left and antiglobalization activists. He sees anti-Semitism as dovetailing very well with a renascent anti-Americanism and "Third Worldism." Criticism of Israeli policies has fueled much of this sentiment and has led to campus campaigns to divest financial holdings in Israel, which is reminiscent of the antiapartheid activism of the 1980s.[47] Much like Marxism-Leninism inspired numerous nationalist-separatist and revolutionary groups decades ago, the success and audacity of militant Islam are inspiring contemporary extremists. For example, Ilich Ramirez Sánchez, a.k.a. "Carlos the Jackal," recently converted to Islam while in prison in France.[48]

This potential for collaboration has not gone unnoticed by the government. U.S. authorities, including former Homeland Security secretary Tom Ridge, announced through a spokesman that the FBI had stepped up its efforts to monitor groups for such an eventuality.[49] There are now more mechanisms in place to deal more effectively with such threats.

SUPPORT FOR NEW COUNTERTERRORISM MEASURES

In the aftermath of the September 11 attacks, the federal government, with support from the American public and U.S. Congress, called for more vigilant measures to root out potential terrorists at home and abroad.[50] Although Jewish organizations have traditionally been among the most consistent defenders of civil liberties, they have generally been very supportive of President Bush's counterterrorism initiatives, many of which carry serious civil liberties implications.[51] Surveys conducted for the American Jewish Committee by Market Facts found that clear majorities favored expanding the investigative scope of law enforcement agencies, 92 percent supported infiltrating suspicious groups, 70 percent favored a national identity card system for American citizens, 66 percent favored expanded camera surveillance on streets and public places, and 55 percent favored monitoring Internet chat rooms.[52] The government has sought to build support for these new measures by presenting them to groups such as the ADL.

For example, former attorney general John Ashcroft defended the USA PA-TRIOT Act in a speech to the Anti-Defamation League in November 2003 in which he conveyed the Bush administration's strong condemnation of anti-Semitism.[53] Civil libertarians and political dissidents feared that the new law could be used to selectively target dissident groups that are critical of U.S. policies. The new act allows the CIA to spy on American citizens, which departs from previous policy that forbade the agency from conducting domestic operations.[54]

The ADL also supported President Bush's decision to use military tribunals to streamline the trials of suspected foreign terrorists because they allow for greater secrecy and faster trials than ordinary criminal courts. The ADL endorsed this new measure and issued a press release praising the new guidelines as "a significant step forward in efforts to balance national security interests with traditional rights accorded criminal suspects in American courts."[55]

Increasingly, the ADL sees right-wing extremism and militant Islam as two of the most serious threats confronting the Jewish community. Its annual list of top issues affecting Jews included the propagation of the claim that Israel was somehow complicit in the 9/11 attacks, the siege of Israel by Palestinian terrorist attacks, anti-Israeli protests on U.S. college campuses, the prospect of al Qaeda attacking Jewish targets in the United States, and the future of the National Alliance.[56] As I discuss in Chapter 8, these fears are not without merit. Several trends appear to be converging that could make for some odd political alignments, some of which could be potentially worrisome for Jews.

CHAPTER EIGHT

How the Extreme Right Views the Current Crisis

The extreme right's reaction to the September 11 attacks has been mixed, which is not surprising, considering the variegated character of the movement. By exploring their reactions in this chapter, I hope to clarify for readers the ideologies that animate it. To do so, however, requires the reader to develop a phenomenological understanding (i.e., get into the minds of the subjects being studied) of the worldviews of this movement. I seek clarity and comprehension, not endorsement or excusal. Greater attendance to grievance interpretation enables us to better understand the minds of the subjects we study.[1] As one observer noted: "Enemies do not just arise from the ether; they are socially and phenomenologically constructed from facts, be they actual or apparent, selectively or incompletely assembled, current or obsolete. Both accurate and inaccurate negative stereotypes are vital to understanding the construction of the enemy from 'inside the narrative'; while the latter have been prominently addressed, the former have been largely neglected."[2]

The Extreme Right's Initial Reactions to 9/11

In some quarters, most notably in Europe, the extreme right expressed a palpable degree of schadenfreude over the terrorist attack. There is scattered anecdotal evidence that suggests elements of the extreme right, most notably in Europe, were delighted by the attacks. For example, supporters of the Nationalist Front in France drank champagne on the evening of September 11. The Czech activist Jan Kopul proclaimed bin Laden to be "an example for our children." Fascist youth leaders in Switzerland wore bin Laden badges.[3] Horst Mahler, the erstwhile left-wing radical turned right-wing extremist, went so far as to proclaim that the attack marked the beginning of the end of the "Judeo-American" empire. To Mahler, the events of 9/11 were part of a larger global struggle that commenced with the promulgation of the Balfour Declaration in

1917.[4] The real significance of the attacks, in his estimation, was that they demonstrated that the United States is vulnerable and cannot control all events in the world.[5] Despite his extreme leftist past, Mahler sees no contradiction in his conversion to right-wing extremist. As he sees it, his chief enemies have not changed—he has retained his critique of global capitalism, Zionism, and American foreign policy.

Some elements of the American extreme right also expressed admiration for the valor and audacity of Islamic militants. National Alliance organizer Billy Roper exulted shortly after the 9/11 attacks:

> The enemy of our enemy is, for now at least, our friends. We may not want them marrying our daughter, just as they would not want us marrying theirs. We may not want them in our societies, just as they would not want us in theirs. But anyone willing to drive a plane into a building to kill Jews is all right by me. I wish our members had half as much testicular fortitude.[6]

Likewise, Tom Metzger of White Aryan Resistance (WAR) expressed admiration for the hijackers and believed that they served as role models for right-wing terrorists as well:

> This operation took some long-term planning, and, throughout the entire time, these soldiers were aware that their lives would be sacrificed for their cause. If an Aryan warrior wants an example of "Victory or Valhalla" look no further.[7]

A tone of envy could also be discerned in Alex Hassinger's *Aryan Loyalist* magazine:

> Where did they found [sic] the cowards [9/11 hijackers] from I will never know, but something tells me that these hijackers had balls the size of watermelons! I wish our movement had such courageous and dedicated men, as they were.[8]

R. J. Frank, the secretary of the American Nazi Party, expressed mixed feelings over the 9/11 attack. He lamented that the United States was attacked on its own soil by foreign terrorists, but he admired the hijackers' commitment to their cause:

> While I do not care for sand niggers, you can't help but admire the military precision, planning and most of all dedication. If we had a handful of our people willing to give it their all as they did any of the issues confronting white America would be non-issues today.[9]

Frank would later lament that it was sad to see how a "bunch of towel head/sand niggers put our great White Movement to SHAME" (emphasis in original).[10] Not to be outdone in rhetoric, Victor Gerhard of the National Alliance exhorted whites that they "should be blowing up NYC and DC, not waiting for a bunch of camel jockeys to do it for us."[11] However, not long after the initial exhilaration, the extreme right's mood became increasingly fearful that they might be targeted in a crackdown on political dissidents as part of a larger war on terror.

Pessimism and Fear of Government Repression in the Wake of 9/11

The U.S. government demonstrated steadfast determination to root out terrorism in the initial weeks after 9/11. Not even two months after the tragedy, President George W. Bush signed the USA PATRIOT Act into law. David Duke expressed the fear of those in the extreme right that the government would use the war on terror as a pretext to quash domestic dissidents:

> My fellow Americans, please open your eyes! Bush's first action after September 11 was to fund the creation of the biggest Secret Police apparatus in the history of the world. . . . When the billions of appropriated monies work its way, the size of our "secret police" will make the former KGB look like a kite next to a Jumbo Jet. Americans will have about as much privacy as one would have in a glass outhouse.[12]

Similarly, Sam Francis, a leading paleo-conservative associated with American Renaissance and the Council of Conservative Citizens, referred to the present American system as "anarcho-tyranny," that is, a combination of anarchy in which legitimate government functions such as spying on and punishing real criminals are not performed, and tyranny in which government performs illegitimate functions such as spying on lawful citizens or criminalizing innocent conduct like gun ownership and political dissent.[13]

According to Dr. William L. Pierce, the deceased chairman of the National Alliance, the real purpose behind the new anti-terrorist measures, such as the USA PATRIOT Act, was not to protect the public from terrorism. Rather, the unstated objective was to protect a government he saw as run by "traitors" from the patriotic segment of the American population that "can be awakened and informed and organized and inspired to act."[14]

Virtually all those leaders of the Christian patriot movement who publicly commented on 9/11 condemned the attacks. Several activists even offered to defend the government in the face of potential foreign terrorist threats. However, many in the movement also expressed consternation that the U.S. government would use the attacks as a pretext to construct a huge police state apparatus in the guise of the Department of Homeland Security. Moreover, they feared that new laws, such as the USA PATRIOT Act, could diminish civil liberties. In sum, 9/11 appears to have had a deradicalizing and demobilizing effect on the Christian patriot movement.[15]

Representatives of the British extreme right also expressed concern about government repression in their country. When I queried John Tyndall, the former leader of the British National Party, on this topic, he responded:

Witch-hunt against domestic "extremists" (the latter your word, not mine)? Yes, corrupt governments fearful of genuine opposition will undoubtedly exploit things like 9/11 as pretexts for draconian, and by all normal standards illegal, action to suppress such opposition groups—even when those groups cannot by the remotest stretch of imagination be coupled with the terrorist acts. This has started to happen in the U.S. We anticipate that it could happen here.[16]

Mike Piper, a senior journalist for the *American Free Press,* feared that extreme right dissidents would be conflated with international terrorists and thus be similarly targeted:

The American elite and the major broadcast media, in particular, have been stoking the fires of distrust against the American right "dissidents" (particularly critics of Zionism and Jewish power) for years. Now, since America is essentially in line with Israel in the "war against terrorism," American critics of Israel are being equated with being apologists for terrorism and, effectively, advocates of what happened on 9–11. In addition, because the Justice Department is (at least under George W. Bush) under the domination of a Christian fundamentalist, John Ashcroft, who is a fanatic supporter of Zionism, I do believe that many on the right have good reason to be concerned. The Bush-Ashcroft regime, with a tendency toward a police-state mentality, evidenced in the so-called [USA] PATRIOT Act and its would-be sequel, is a very real threat to liberty in America.[17]

Kevin MacDonald, a professor of psychology at the University of California at Long Beach whose research I examined in Chapter 2, stated that the new war on terror could lead to an abridgment of civil liberties, especially for unpopular dissident movements such as white racial nationalists:

I worry that the U.S. will become like much of the nations of Western Europe, where speech or writing that raises critical issues on racial or ethnic conflict—no matter how scholarly or well-reasoned—is criminalized. We are moving toward a multi-cultural police state, as I predicted in *The Culture of Critique*. The dispossession of Europeans both in Europe and the U.S. will in the end require police state controls on expression of opinions and on behavior, and we are seeing the beginnings of this already. I predict that Europeans will become increasingly aware of their reduced status and ultimately there will be movements that attempt to re-assert their interests—movements that can only be controlled by increased and more direct coercion. . . . Racial polarization is increasingly noticeable in election returns, and I expect that pattern to increase. At some point, the Republican Party will become the party of white ethnic interests or it will collapse like the old Whig Party and some new mainstream party that will assert white interests will take its place. Of course, by the time this happens such a party may be simply one more ingredient in the ethnic cauldron.[18]

Despite fears of repression, the extreme right seemed to believe that it had truth on its side and knew the real reasons why the United States was attacked. Many in the movement felt a sense of urgency to explain to their fellow Americans how they had arrived at such a juncture.

Why Was the United States Attacked?

Representatives expressed feelings of vindication, pointing out that many of the issues about which they feel strongly featured prominently in the attack. The fact that all the nineteen hijackers were immigrants underscored the potential problems of liberal U.S. immigration policy. The most pointed critic in this respect was perhaps Jared Taylor of *American Renaissance*, who warned of the possibility of more terrorist attacks in his article "Will America Learn Its Lessons?"[19] In a similar vein, Sam Francis, an occasional contributor to *American Renaissance*, responded:

While the logical response to 9/11 would have been to re-examine our Middle East foreign policy and especially to close the borders and severely restrict immigration, neither was done. There were some token restrictions on visas for foreigners. Thus an event that corroborated much of the white nationalist critique of our foreign policy and our immigration policy was interpreted by the media and the administration to mean just the opposite.

Therefore I think the net effect of the 9/11 attacks has been to make the prospects for white nationalism somewhat dimmer than they were before.[20]

Several Bush administration spokespersons have repeatedly asserted that the attacks visited upon the United States on September 11, 2001, were because of the democratic values that the country espouses. Addressing the nation the evening of September 11, 2001, President Bush explained: "America was targeted for attack because we're the brightest beacon for freedom and opportunity in the world. And no one will keep that light from shining."[21] Soon after the attack, many Americans asked, "Why do they hate us?" President Bush replied to the nation in an address to a joint session of Congress:

> They hate what they see right here in this chamber: a democratically elected government. Their leaders are self-appointed. They hate our freedom: our freedom of religion, our freedom of speech, our freedom to vote and assemble and disagree with each other.[22]

This sentiment was echoed in many American newspapers, magazines, and television talk shows. Most notable in this regard were the pronouncements of various neoconservatives, who argued that the American model posed a great threat to extremists and despots around the world. The words of Michael Ledeen, a leading neoconservative intellectual, are illustrative of this theme:

> Our enemies have always hated this whirlwind of energy and creativity, which menaces their traditions . . . and shames them for their inability to keep pace. They cannot feel secure so long as we are there, for our very existence—our existence, not our policies—threatens their legitimacy. They must attack us in order to survive, just as we must destroy them to advance our historic mission.[23]

As Ledeen's comments seem to imply, 9/11 was conceivably the opening salvo in a clash of civilizations between Islamic fundamentalism and the West. Mainstream commentators maintained that this division resulted from "what America is," but extremist commentators argued that American policy was the crux of the problem. Hence, Islamic rage toward the West was understandable.

Many in the extreme right derided President Bush's explanation that the terrorists had attacked the United States because of its freedom and democracy. The most frequent refrain from the extreme right was that the terrorist attack was visited upon the United States because of the government's unstinting support for Israel. For example, in response to my query, John Tyndall remarked, "Attacks on America because of the 'democratic' values the country espouses? Those who believe that kind of thing probably believe in Santa Claus and the

Tooth Fairy!"[24] Likewise, his successor, Nick Griffin, the current leader of the British National Party, opined:

No, it's obvious propaganda nonsense. The hatred is about Palestine and having U.S. troops in Saudi Arabia. Fundamentalist Muslims certainly are hostile to democracy and other Western values, but they are concerned with keeping them out of their own countries, and wouldn't mind at all if the USA sank into a sea of democratic alcoholic homosexuals if the USA was an isolationist state rather than an aggressive superpower with a powerful Zionist lobby at its heart.[25]

Fellow Briton David Myatt rebuked the Bush administration's official explanation as well:

The attacks were in response to American policy in the Middle East and elsewhere: a consequence of their support for the Zionist entity, which has killed and tortured Muslims and which has stolen Muslim land; a consequence of their support for sanctions against Iraq, which have resulted in the deaths of nearly one million children; a consequence of their arrogant, bullying, ways in Muslim lands and their support of the ignoble, un-Islamic leaders of Muslim countries; a consequence of them defiling— in Muslim eyes—the Land of Two Holy Places. And so on.[26]

The Swiss revisionist Jürgen Graf also rejected the line of argument that the mainstream media and President Bush had offered:

One must be very silly indeed to swallow such a preposterous argument. Why does nobody attack Iceland, the oldest democracy on earth? The radical Muslims don't care a bit about America's political system. They hate the USA because it supports the colonialist state of Israel and the enslavement of the Palestinians, backs reactionary and unpopular regimes in the Muslim world and commits genocide, by starvation and by bombing, against the people of Iraq.[27]

Jared Taylor weighed in sarcastically on this issue as well:

Does President Bush really imagine Osama bin Laden saying to his men: "Those Americans are just too damn free; they've got too much opportunity. Let's kill as many as we can?" The idea is absurd. Islamic militants have a grudge against us because of our attacks on Afghanistan, Libya, Iraq, and Sudan. But the main reason they hate us and want to kill us is that we support Israel.[28]

Steven Barry, the former leader of the now defunct Special Forces Underground,[29] expressed the belief that the terrorists had targeted the United States as a way to take revenge for that country's support of Israel:

The Bush administration's stated reasons for the 11 September attacks, that "they hate our freedoms" and "democratic values," are blatant lies. Officials in the Bush administration know perfectly well the reason behind the attacks. That reason, the sole reason, is Israel. For obvious reasons the nomenklatura must lie about it. . . . The Party Line "justifying" the "war on terror" is merely another segment in the historical toilet tissue roll of United States government propaganda.

Further, it is a lie that the United States was attacked. What was explicitly attacked was a, if not the, nerve center (not the ideological center) of international banking. What was implicitly attacked was the source of Israel's weaponry. The United States was not under attack on 11 September. "Terrorism" on the order and magnitude of 11 September is symbolism—propaganda by the deed. Indeed, Osama bin Laden expressly—and as is usual with enemies of the United States, truthfully—stated the reason for the attack: In this case United States support of Israel. The sheer emotionalism of Bush administration propaganda to the contrary is its own indictment as utter lies. That "the People" swallowed whole the Bush administration's shameless propaganda speaks volumes about the inherent stupidity of the mob.[30]

By far the most vitriolic response came from Dr. William Pierce of the National Alliance. Repeatedly since the September 11 attacks, Pierce had used his weekly radio broadcast, American Dissident Voices, to propagandize against American foreign policy in the Middle East. Other extremist organizations and figures, including the World Church of the Creator, the Institute for Historical Review, Bo Gritz, Aryan Nations, Posse Comitatus, and various neo-Nazi groups, have expressed virtually identical sentiments.

Kevin MacDonald also derided the premise that the United States was targeted on 9/11 for its democratic values. He finds this proposition absurd, especially because it contradicts the policy statements of important U.S. officials. For example, he noted that not long after the attacks, President Bush and Secretary of State Colin Powell sought to pressure Israel to restart peace negotiations with the Palestinians. This would make it easier for the Bush administration to forge a coalition, including moderate Arab states as well as Europe and Russia, in the war against terrorism. But MacDonald took this argument even further, rejecting the notion that Israel is an outpost of Western culture. In his view, just the opposite is true: he sees Israel as an ethnostate with an apartheid-style legal system that distinguishes Jews and non-Jews in many important areas of public policy. Furthermore, a significant portion of the Jewish population that forms the core of the state consists of religious fundamentalists, for whom Western culture with its emphasis on democracy and individualism is anathema.[31]

Still, some respectable scholars have conceded that American policies do figure prominently in the list of grievances of the Islamists. For example, Rohan Gunaratna, a professor at the Institute of Defense and Strategic Studies at Nanyang Technological University in Singapore, who interviewed numerous members of al Qaeda, conceded that the organization targets the United States because it is an obstacle to the establishment of Islamic states.[32]

Although many government officials have claimed that the Islamists target the United States for existential reasons, considerable evidence suggests that U.S. policy features prominently in their motives. As I demonstrate in Chapter 9, policies such as the stationing of troops in Saudi Arabia, U.S.-supported sanctions against Iraq, and U.S. support for Israel are mentioned frequently by bin Laden as his grievances against the United States. To the best of my knowledge, bin Laden has never made a public pronouncement in which he cited democracy, freedom, or diversity as grievances against the United States. Government officials who are privy to intelligence on al Qaeda and bin Laden would certainly know that. Thus the reasons they give for the attacks suggest a certain amount of deception on the part of the government and media.[33]

Not only did the extreme right scoff at the government's explanation of the underlying causes of the 9/11 attack, some in the movement go so far as to impugn the official version of the events surrounding 9/11. The extreme right has produced several conspiracy narratives that take issue with the official explanation of the events surrounding that tragedy.

Extremist Conspiracy Theories about 9/11

Various conspiracy theories that question the official version of events were proffered in the aftermath of 9/11. The *American Free Press* published several stories on this issue. Some self-styled investigators claimed that explosives were positioned in the World Trade Center towers prior to the attacks and detonated at just the precise moment at which the hijacked planes struck. Other theories posited that the planes were actually remote-controlled by way of radios to strike the towers. Perhaps the most popular variation of this theme was propounded by a French author, Thierry Meyssan, in his book *L'Effroyable*

Imposture (The Horrifying Fraud), which postulates that conservative Republicans in the Bush administration orchestrated the attacks. Meyssan advances the theory that no plane actually struck the Pentagon; rather, it was a truck bomb. Amazingly, his book has gained considerable popularity in France.

The theory that seems to have gained the most currency in extreme right circles, not surprisingly, is that the Israeli intelligence agency, Mossad, allegedly had foreknowledge of the attacks and deliberately failed to warn Americans. Furthermore, some versions assert that the Mossad may have actually supported the hijackers. Mike Piper explained to me in an interview why he believed that Israel was complicit in the 9/11 attacks:

I have written extensively on the topic in the pages of *American Free Press*, and I do share the view that, in fact, the Mossad ultimately orchestrated the 9–11 terrorist attacks in order to spark U.S. outrage against the Arab world. I am inclined to think that there were Mossad assets in place in the United States government who may have lent their influence and expertise to helping the event occur, but I am not one of those who go so far as to suggest that President Bush himself had personal foreknowledge of the attack.

I have been one of the few persons writing on the topic who has actually gone so far as to say that the alleged "Arab" terrorists on the 9–11 planes were not actually the Arabs said to have been aboard; that perhaps Jewish operatives posing as Arabs actually carried out the crime.

This is not so extraordinary a thesis to those who are aware of the finely tuned nature of Israeli intelligence operations, to the point that even a formerly secret CIA assessment on the Mossad stated flat out that the Israelis had a history of deploying Arabic-speaking Jews into Arab countries and into Arab terrorist units for the purpose of manipulation.

That same report emphasized Israeli skill at forging passports, evidently a skill that the Israelis have utilized quite successfully. So I do believe there is reason to doubt that those who are said to have been aboard the 9–11 planes were Arabs, official U.S. government claims notwithstanding.

As a final point for skeptics to digest, I would add that Israeli and Jewish history is rife with tales of suicide for the greater good and that, indeed, as Pulitzer Prize–winner Seymour Hersh noted in *The Samson Option*, Israel has a long-standing national geopolitical plan for national suicide—utilizing the "Samson Option" (setting off a nuclear bomb)—if Israel ever appears to be on the verge of destruction by outsiders.

In fact, on September 11, Israel was faced with world opprobrium for its treatment of the Palestinian uprising, and popular opinion was turning against Israel. A small-scale "suicide" operation (that is, crashing planes into the World Trade Center and pinning the blame on Arabs) would have been a small cost to Israel, in terms of losing only a handful of dedicated fanatics willing to give their lives for the greater good.

In addition, I should note that *Arab News,* the English-language daily published by the government of Saudi Arabia, picked up the story that I wrote on that topic and published it verbatim, with the result that there was a major frenzy accompanied by demands that the Saudis admit, once and for all, that there were Arabs on the 9–11 planes.

Aside from that, there is no question, based on a variety of "mainstream" sources that Israel does indeed have a history of infiltrating, financing, and manipulating Arab terrorist organizations. At the very least, I have no doubt, Israel did have advance knowledge of the 9–11 tragedy and manipulated it from behind the scenes in some fashion. It's quite their style.[34]

By far the most adamant proponent of a Mossad connection to 9/11 has been David Duke. According to Duke, the Mossad had foreknowledge of the 9/11 attack yet deliberately withheld such information so that the United States would respond ferociously against hostile nations and parties opposed to Israel in the Middle East. He cited a number of curious facts to make his case. For example, President Bush had originally claimed before a joint session of Congress that more than 130 Israeli citizens had perished in the 9/11 attack.[35] However, according to Duke's research, not a single Israeli perished in the 9/11 World Trade Center attack. (The Israeli newspaper *Haaretz* identified five Israeli victims in the 9/11 attacks.)[36] Duke found that to be a statistical impossibility, thus indicating that those Israelis who worked in the building received warning prior to the attack. Further, he cited the fact that Michael Macover, the chief executive officer (CEO) of an Israeli firm, Odigo, confirmed that two of its employees received text messages warning of an attack on the World Trade Center a full two hours before the terrorists crashed their planes into the towers.[37] The Odigo story was soon picked up by the *Washington Post*'s online "Newsbytes" column, written by Brian McWilliams.[38] It provided more grist for the rumor mill and spread around the world. Duke elaborated on his theory in an interview with me:

> I don't think that the American government had forewarning. As jaded as I think that our elected officials and bureaucrats in Washington are, I would find it hard to believe that any American, true American anyway, could have had clear knowledge of the impending attack on the World Trade Center without moving to stop the attacks. Without moving to get to the airport and arresting these hijackers as they attempted to board these planes.

But there's no question in my mind that there was Israeli foreknowledge and I think there's ample evidence that deals with Israeli foreknowledge. The Mossad is a covert operation. It's hard to get documentary proof, but if you look at the facts that we do know about 9/11, they lead inescapably to Israeli foreknowledge. And we can categorize them very quickly. There are so many things we could talk about, [for example], the death toll at the Trade Center being impossibly low for Israeli citizens. There were varying accounts, but most accounts now say zero Israeli citizens dead in the Trade Center. One Israeli was on one of the airplanes that were hijacked, but the Trade Center has been a sight of tremendous amounts of Israeli business, firms, and interests. There are many people who worked at the World Trade Center, who practically commuted from Israel. The World Trade Center was the sight of international trade, banking, and heavily represented, even a co-owner of the World Trade Center itself was an Israeli citizen, by the name of Frank Lowy. The day after the World Trade Center went down, the *Jerusalem Post* headline said that 4,000 Israelis were presumed missing, who were believed to be in the area of the World Trade Center. Part of that was because Israelis couldn't contact their relatives who worked at the World Trade Center. But even if that figure was vastly overinflated, and there were only say 400 Israelis there at the World Trade Center, they still should have had a death toll of around 1 percent of that, which would have been 40. So mathematically, it's very unlikely. Then we have physical evidence. *Haaretz* and the *Jerusalem Post*, as well as the *Washington Post* news services, had articles showing that the FBI was investigating the Israeli firm Odigo. And the fact that instant messages were sent to the offices in the World Trade Center hours before the attack, specifically warning of the attack on the World Trade Center. So we know that there were prior warnings.

We know that five Israeli Mossad agents were caught filming the attacks and were cheering and jumping up and down celebrating the attacks. They were actually caught with box cutters and large sums of cash and so forth. Why would these Israeli Mossad agents be celebrating unless they knew exactly what was going down and who was behind it? We also know that at least five Mossad agents were living on the same street as Muhammad Atta, closely monitoring the hijacker leader and about half of the hijackers were being closely monitored by the Israeli Mossad agents. These agents had the capacity for wire-tapping. The largest wire-tapping is done by an Israeli firm. In fact our federal government farms out its wire-tapping for criminal matters to an Israeli firm, believe it or not. . . . So these people certainly had the means, the knowledge, the ability, and certainly the opportunity to know the details of the attack and the specific evidence that proves that fact that they did have foreknowledge of the attack. And they treacherously did not warn the United States.

GM: How has your theory of the event surrounding 9/11 been received? Why did the government dismiss your theory?

DD: Why did the government ignore the repeated Israeli terrorism against the United States? In 1956 Israeli terrorist Mossad agents from the Israeli government actually attacked American installations in Egypt and tried to blame the Egyptians for the attacks. And even after these horrendous actions against the United States, an ally who gave Israel the money it needed to get its weapons of war. Even after this attack was revealed and exposed and the Israeli defense minister had to resign, American aid continued. I mean it's like the same thing as aiding the Japanese after the surprise attack on Pearl Harbor. It's insane but true. That's how much power they have. They even commit treason against us through these agents in our government, but they can cover up that treason.

For example, the attack on the USS *Liberty*.[39] The secretary of state at that time, Dean Rusk, as well as the chairman of the Joint Chiefs of Staff, Admiral Thomas Moorer, have both stated that there was clear evidence that the Israeli attack was premeditated and deliberate against the United States. Again, they were trying to blame Egypt. They killed 34 Americans and wounded 170 other Americans. After this was revealed, they were able to quash a congressional investigation into it, and aid and money went on to Israel.

Then, of course, in the 1980s, we had the Jonathan Pollard affair, an Israeli spy who stole critical intelligence and information from the United States, which ultimately devastated our intelligence network in Eastern Europe and in the Soviet Union. In fact, many people think that it was the very worst intelligence disaster for the United States in our history. . . . There was no cessation of aid or arms or anything to Israel. Israel stole atomic weapons secrets from us. They stole atomic technology from us. And we could just go on and on.[40]

It is important to keep in mind that Duke's theory has not gained acceptance by mainstream political researchers.

Some conspiracy theorists believed that "Jewish ownership" of the World Trade Center created a financial motive for the attacks. In July 2001, a real estate developer, Larry Silverstein, signed a ninety-nine-year lease on the World

Trade Center complex. It was the first time that control over the World Trade Center had changed hands since the Port Authority of New York and New Jersey created the complex in the early 1970s. According to some theories, Silverstein wanted the building destroyed so that he could collect insurance money. Toward this end, the theory goes, he prevailed upon an Israeli businessman who lived in Australia, Frank Lowy, to get his company, Westfield America, to insure the complex. Some theorists implied that the attacks resulted in a huge windfall for Lowy and Silverstein. Furthermore, the former chairman of the Port Authority, Lewis Eisenberg, arranged the ninety-nine-year lease for Lowy and Silverstein, both of whom were supposed to have held high positions in an Israeli fund-raising institution.[41]

Theories of Israeli complicity in 9/11 are not confined to the political fringe. For example, the first reports on the alleged Israeli spy ring actually originated from Fox News Network, which carried a story that speculated on a similar theory. The Fox News channel originally planned to carry a four-part story on a large Israeli espionage ring that had come under official scrutiny shortly before the September 11 attacks. Carl Cameron, the Fox News journalist assigned to the story, discovered that approximately 140 Israeli citizens had been arrested or detained on suspicion of belonging to an "organized intelligence-gathering operation" prior to 9/11. Shortly thereafter, 60 more suspected spies were detained. The story suggested that there might have been a connection between the Israeli spies and the 9/11 attacks.

The investigative segment of the news program reported that a private Israeli telecommunications company, Amdocs, handles most directory calls and virtually all call records and billing done in the United States. Amdocs generates the computerized records and billing data for nearly every telephone call made in the United States. This reportedly worried some officials in the National Security Agency, and as a result, a top secret information report was issued, warning that records of calls in the United States were possibly getting into foreign hands, most notably Israel. Although the FBI and other investigative agencies did not believe that the calls were being listened to, they still believed that the data about who was calling whom were still potentially valuable. U.S. government officials worried that this information could conceivably get into the wrong hands—for example, organized crime.[42] The segment alleged that U.S. investigators probing into the 9/11 terrorist attacks feared that the 9/11 conspirators might have been tipped off as to what they were doing by information leaked from Amdocs.

Another part of this tangled web is the Israeli firm Comverse, which provides wiretapping equipment for law enforcement agencies. Some investigators feared that the wiretapping system that the firm used contained a back door through which unauthorized parties could intercept correspondence. Complicating matters further is that fact that Comverse works closely with the Israeli government. Investigators within the Drug Enforcement Agency, the Immigration and Naturalization Service, and the FBI told Fox News that to pursue or even suggest Israeli spying through Comverse would amount to "career suicide."[43]

Interestingly, Fox cancelled that fourth and final segment of the investigative report, reportedly at the behest of Jewish defense groups, which feared it could provoke anti-Semitism. This fact only raised suspicions among conspiracy theorists and added verisimilitude to the story. What is more, Fox quickly pulled the text transcripts of the story from its website archives.[44]

Still more evidence was cited by conspiracy theorists to implicate Israel in the 9/11 attacks. Adding further to the suspicion that there may have been foreknowledge of the attacks were reports that the American Securities and Exchange Commission was investigating Israeli citizens who allegedly sold "short" various stocks that would have reasonably been expected to fall in value as a result of the 9/11 attacks. Essentially, selling short involves the opportunity to pass shares to a third party and then buy them back after their price falls. Reportedly, there had been a great deal of talk about insider trading involving certain Israeli groups based in Germany and Canada between August 26 and September 11. Allegedly, millions of dollars were made on various "put options" involving firms involved in tourism, airlines, and insurance—all industries that would obviously suffer in the wake of 9/11. In addition, al Qaeda is alleged to have made some stock market transactions in anticipation of 9/11, as the financial operatives in the network were suspected of having sold short on insurance companies that covered the World Trade Center.[45] In order to detect financial red flags, the Central Intelligence Agency (CIA) uses software known as *Promis* to routinely monitor stock trades as a possible warning sign of terrorism or suspicious economic behavior.[46]

Still another bizarre incident surrounding 9/11 was the case of the five Israeli citizens who were caught filming the 9/11 tragedy in New York City while they celebrated raucously. Authorities arrested the men and discovered several interesting items in their van: box cutters, $4,700 in cash stuffed in a sock, and foreign passports.[47]

Finally, revelations of official Israeli intelligence policy in the United States unnerved some people as well. According to some accounts, the Israeli government had given its espionage agency, Mossad, nearly free reign in the United States. Mossad allegedly had altered its policy to allow "targeted killings" (i.e., assassinations) inside the United States and other allied nations. Bush administration representatives treated this issue like a hot potato. When asked about the Israeli spies, White House spokesman Ari Fleischer demurred, "I would just refer you to the Department of Justice with that. I'm not familiar with the report." Secretary of State Colin Powell was evasive as well: "I'm aware that some Israeli citizens have been detained. With respect to why they're being detained and other aspects of your question—whether it's because they're in intelligence services, or what they were doing—I will defer to the Department of Justice and the FBI to answer that."[48]

Still other theories popular with the extreme right speculated that the CIA was involved in 9/11. The Swiss revisionist Jürgen Graf did not accept the official version of 9/11 and suspected a conspiracy possibly involving the CIA and Mossad:

I do not buy the official version of 9/11. If the CIA knew nothing in advance of the planned hijacking of four planes and the planned attack on the World Trade Center, it is led by idiots. If the "Arab terrorists" performed their mission at nine o'clock in the morning, when the World Trade Center was still largely empty, instead of some hours later, when they could easily have killed five times as many people, they were idiots too. I suppose that the planes were either remote-controlled, or that the hijackers, if there were any, were manipulated by an intelligence agency, most likely the CIA or the Mossad. The Bush regime desperately needed a "Pearl Harbor" to unleash a series of aggressive wars in the Middle East. Maybe there will shortly be a second eleventh of September, which will provide Bush and his gang with a pretext for further criminal adventures.[49]

Others in the extreme right were more skeptical of the conspiracy theories yet still impugned the official version of events. For example, John Tyndall explained:

I have followed some Internet discussions on this subject, and I have to say that there are a number of questions raised in them which have not been adequately answered. We are entering here into an area in which the listing of examples would take this discussion to enormous length, and so I will have to leave it there. But yes, I certainly impugn the official version of the events of 9/11. If Bush and Blair lied to the people about the grounds for the attack on Iraq (as they quite clearly did), it follows that they have probably lied about much else.[50]

David Myatt, however, discounted conspiracy theories implicating the U.S. government and Israel and was generally willing to give credit where he thought it was due:

I have considered such theories, and reviewed what evidence has been put forward to support them, such as the way the Twin Towers collapsed which may seem to some to indicate it was destroyed as a result of a covert operation by the CIA. This is an interesting theory, but my view is that the attacks were martyrdom operations by Muslims who wanted to show that America, for all its military and economic power, is not invincible. As Sheikh Usama bin Laden said in a recent statement: "We stress the importance of martyrdom operations against the enemy— operations that have inflicted damage both on the United States and on Israel: damage that has been unprecedented in their history, all thanks to Almighty Allah."

As for the US government having forewarning of the attacks and just letting it happen, they might do this as another Pearl Harbor, but it is more likely that they did not know since they have very little intelligence about the base of jihad operations, and certainly less then than the little they might have now.[51]

For his part, Ahmed Huber proffered a bizarre conspiracy theory of his own that actually implicated the extreme right:

I have my own idea about 11 September. Among Muslims it's a very controversial debate. Many Muslims still believe that the 11th of September was organized by the CIA and the Mossad to bring closer together the relationship between Israel and the United States, and to help make war in the Middle East, and to put under Western-Jewish control the most important geo-political zone on earth, which is the Middle East. I believe, that 11 September, but I have no proof, was organized by American patriots, Muslims and non-Muslims together with the help of foreign Muslims residing in the United States.

From 1988 to 1998, I was in America every year, at Islamic conferences. I made big lecture tours through the United States and I always met three groups of people at these conferences. There were American right-wing people, not American Nazis or Ku Klux Klan, not these kind of people, [but] people who were rather close to the extreme right of the Republican Party, or other independent right-wing groups. Then [the second group was] Muslims, young American Muslim patriots, who came from Muslim countries. And then [the third group was] the Nation of Islam people. And these three groups . . . always told me two things. They said, "We must free America from Jewish-Zionist rule." And two, "Then we must change the foreign policy of the United States toward the national interests of the American people. . . . We must end this Jewish-Zionist rule over America."

And when I asked them, "How will you do it?" they said, "Well, we have friends in very high places and there will be a big bang. It will happen here to wake up the American people, you know, like Pearl Harbor." Pearl Harbor was organized by Roosevelt and his Jewish [advisers] to provoke Japan to attack America. Then Hitler would immediately declare war on America. It was not Japan—they really wanted America to go to war against Germany. . . . Then the way was open to make war against Germany. And this is what these people told me. Something similar will happen here. They said, "You will hear a big bang."

And then came the 11th of September, and my Egyptian wife said, "You see the Mossad and the CIA." And I believed it also. But then I got telephone calls from American friends, and they said, "See now they have done it." I said, "What?" and then they said to me, they have done it, and then the coin was dropped. I said, "This is counterproductive. This 11 September will provoke a huge alliance of American and Israeli Zionism against Islam, against the Muslim world." And they told me, "Yes, it will be at the beginning, but then America will get into difficult days and after some time, the American people will wake up. When it is up to the nose in difficult days—political, economic, war, and so on—they will ask who is responsible for this. And they will say it's the Jews and the Zionists." One told me that around the beginning of September 2001, a telephone call, a very good friend of mine, told me, "You know Ahmed, then we will have 1933." And then of course, I knew. He said that the American people will wake up [as did] the German people [woke] up in 1933. For me, I still didn't believe it. Now the more and more things go on, I see how Bush and all his experts, I mean Mr. Wolfowitz, Mr. Perle, Mr. Kissinger, Mr. Feingold, I say maybe there is something to what my friends in America told me. It is possible now that things will go in that direction. You know, in the 1990s, when I was in America, we were talking about how to change Jewish rule in America. For me, a Swiss, it was fascinating. One of these young persons said, "You know, we may have many sympathizers in the American Army, and if necessary the American Army will make a coup d'état against the Zionist-American regime in Washington."[52]

Often, various pieces of evidence can be selectively assembled to construct an interesting conspiracy theory. The ideological predispositions of those in the extreme right, with their traditional animus toward Israel and Jews, explains in large part the popularity of the conspiracy narratives on 9/11. In addition, former Israeli prime minister Benjamin Netanyahu's offhand remark just moments after the 9/11 tragedy did little to disabuse Duke and other conspiracy theorists of Israeli complicity. When asked about the terrorist strikes, Netanyahu remarked, "It's very good." Then he quickly qualified that remark by saying, "Well it's not good, but it will generate immediate sympathy [for Israel from Americans]."[53] As the U.S. war with Iraq approached, many in the extreme right voiced alarm and put the blame squarely on their "traditional enemies."

The War against Iraq and the Critique of Neoconservatism

In the days leading up to the U.S. war against Iraq in March 2003, the extreme right tended to focus on Jewish neoconservatives as the chief party responsible for mobilizing the country into a conflict that would have far-reaching repercussions. Virtually all representatives of the extreme right believed that the war was misguided and would in the long run redound against the United States. It is not surprising that the extreme right and so-called paleo-conservatives would look upon neoconservatives with great suspicion. After all, many prominent neoconservatives began their political activism as Trotskyites. The neoconservatives have their origins in the early 1970s, when some Democratic political intellectuals became increasingly concerned that the Democratic Party was not taking the Soviet threat seriously enough. Further, these intellectuals were among the most ardent defenders of Israel. Neoconservatives found a home in the Reagan administration, where they were instrumental in planning and organizing a foreign policy that contributed in part to the collapse of the Soviet Union. Bolstered by this victory, neoconservatives believed that such sweeping change was possible in the Middle East as well. Unlike traditional conservative isolationists, the neoconservatives have a messianic desire to export democracy around the globe.

Arguably, David Duke has been the most vociferous extremist critic to speak out against the war. Duke charged influential Jews in the Bush administration and the media with dragging the United States into war in the Middle East for the benefit of Israel and was quick to point out that many of the high-profile advocates for a war against Iraq are Jews: *Commentary* publisher Norman Podhoretz, David Horowitz, Ari Fleischer, David Frum, Richard Perle, Elliott Abrams, David Wurmser, and Douglas J. Feith.[54] As Duke saw it, this war is against American interests: it will cost not only the lives of American soldiers but also an enormous amount of money, and it will destroy goodwill toward the United States around the world. Furthermore, the present conflict in Iraq could destabilize an already struggling American economy. Constitutional freedoms and other civil liberties would also be diminished under the guise of fighting terror through new laws such as the USA PATRIOT Act. Finally, the aftermath of such a conflict would embitter Arabs and Muslims, many of whom will join the ranks of future terrorists and strike out against the United States someday. Not unlike Dr. William L. Pierce, Duke saw the influence of the media as determinative in shaping the perceptions and attitudes of Americans toward the war. As he sarcastically remarked, "Right up until September 11, the media daily characterized George Bush as the village idiot who stumbled into the Presidency. Now that Bush may embrace Israel's holy war against the Palestinians and their allies, he has suddenly become a great leader who will give us a wonderful victory in the glorious war ahead."[55] He elaborated on this position in an interview with me:

The war on Iraq is an insane Jewish war. It's insane from any standpoint of benefiting the United States of America. It will cost us hundreds of billions of dollars before it's all done. It's already costing tens of billions of dollars in higher oil prices and gas prices. It's alienating our friends around the world. It's causing tremendous hatred against this country. It's spawning terrorism. It's Osama bin Laden's wet dream. I mean it's exactly what he would want. It will spur violence against people of the United States, both at home in America and the millions of Americans that are overseas. On every true point of interest of our country, it hurts America, not helps America.[56]

Duke's sentiments were echoed by virtually everyone in the extreme right. Mike Piper of the *American Free Press* also voiced opposition to the war on Iraq:

It's wrong. It's needless. It's a bloodbath that will have grievous consequences for years to come. It's a war that need not and should not be fought. America's military leaders didn't want to fight the war but, good soldiers that they are, allowed themselves to be directed into the war and now they and the young men and women in the field (not to mention the Iraqis) are paying the price.

The war is founded on the age-old Zionist dream of "Greater Israel" adapted to the modern-day realities of global geopolitics, in alliance with the Western oil interests.

The so-called neoconservative Jewish elements that dictate the Bush administration's foreign policy are, if anything, not "right-wing" at all, but instead a late-twentieth-century formulation of the old anti-Stalinist Jewish Trotskyites who reworked themselves in a mystical fashion and emerged to be the "leaders" of the conservative movement in America—a total repudiation of the traditional America First philosophy that held sway in the minds of millions of Americans for more than a century, ranging from conservatives in the mold of Robert Taft to liberals and progressives such as Burton Wheeler and others.

The "conservative-liberal" concept is thoroughly outdated and hardly useful at all: the big debate, especially that revolving around the Iraq war, is imperialist vs. anti-imperialist. The Jewish elite and their neoconservative henchmen are firmly in the imperialist crowd. Count me out.

I believe that the current war is the latest manifestation in a traditional "Jewish War of Survival" that has been waged, in one form or another, since almost the dawn of mankind.[57]

Tom Metzger of White Aryan Resistance voiced opposition to the war as well. From his perspective, the U.S. war on terror does not further the ideological interests of racial separatists like himself. He therefore believes that no effort should be wasted in supporting it.[58] He clarified his position in an interview with me:

I think that the targets were extremely symbolic of the transnational corporate economic power and that was the World Trade Center. [The attack on] the Pentagon was obviously symbolic of going to the heart of the beast of the military might that sustains the corporate structure around the world. Beyond that, I didn't see it as an attack on America itself at all. . . .

I'm just sick about it. It's like Vietnam all over again. . . . It really wrenches my stomach to see another bunch of guys going over there, "We're saving America," and all of that kind of stuff, and they're going to come back in body bags and everything else. I just despise Bush for getting us into this.

I think Bush is a very easy guy to goad, because I don't think he's too bright. I think he probably does have some of those fundamentalist Christian ideas and they scare the hell out of me, because these people believe there's got to be a nuclear war in the Middle East before Jesus can come back. I mean these people are frightening. . . . I believe there is almost insanity going on in Washington.[59]

Willis Carto, arguably the central figure of the postwar American extreme right, expressed dismay over the war in Iraq and believed that it would ultimately undercut American prestige around the world. His views also reflect a noninterventionist streak prevalent in the extreme right:

I've come to the conclusion that the American public loves war. But now there is television. It saves Hollywood lots of money, because people can really see war. They can see buildings getting blown up. They can see people getting killed and dismembered. They can see blood. . . . It's wonderful. And people love it. These dirty Iraqis. What the hell have they ever done to us? I don't know. But it doesn't make any difference. The president says we go to war. We wave the flag and we march off to war. People love war. . . . People's lives are essentially pretty boring. But war puts a great patriotic fervor in your heart. All your personal things are sublimated to this . . . atavistic desire . . . But wars have gotten out of hand. Totally out of hand. . . . And now these crazy people like Bush, he knows nothing about war. He's going to get everybody killed. He has destroyed the American image all over the world. America is most hated after the war. After the Second World War, America was the most admired and beloved country in the war. Today, it is certainly undoubtedly the most hated. I think Bush is crazy. But he loves war because of course it gives him power. . . . America is literally going around the world looking for trouble, looking for wars, looking to blow people up. Wolfowitz and the neoconservatives, of course, are totally Jewish. They want to get Syria next. And then they want to get Iran. They want to get Saudi Arabia. . . . I don't think Bush has any real historical knowledge whatsoever. He is a victim of government propaganda. America is good, everybody else is bad. And if you don't believe that, why we'll shoot you up. We're heading towards a terrible situation where American power can literally destroy the world. It looks like he [Bush] is trying to do it. It's frightening. . . . No country can control the world. It never has been able to. . . . Our foreign policy is to clear out the Middle East for Israeli hegemony. That's what it amounts to. Using our money, our weapons, and our man and woman power in the Army to do it for the Israelis. That's what it is all about. . . . Israel is the elephant in the living room that you don't want to talk about. . . . Everybody knows it subconsciously. They all know it. There's no doubt about it. . . . They all know about it. They're all afraid of it.[60]

Several paleo-conservatives spoke out against the war as well. According to Justin Raimondo, 9/11 was a godsend for the neoconservative movement. Two pillars of their ideological edifice—the projection of American military might and the sanctity of the U.S.-Israeli alliance—suddenly came back in vogue.[61] He noted a statement released by William Kristol's think tank, Project for a New American Century, that advocated regime change not only for the three countries that compose the "axis of evil" (i.e., Iraq, Iran, and North Korea) but also Syria, Lebanon, and Saudi Arabia. Raimondo cautioned that such an over-arching imperial project would have a corrupting effect on the United States, thus turning Americans into "a cruel race of conquerors blinded by hubris and a danger to one and all—including ourselves."[62] In his analysis, the costs of empire would be prohibitively expensive. Furthermore, creating an empire would lead to further strengthening and centralization of the federal government—a development that is anathema to many traditional conservatives. Raimondo asked, "Who would benefit from this war?" He answers that the Bush administration's expressed reason of finding weapons of mass destruction in Iraq is not the true motive for war. Whatever missiles Saddam still had in his arsenal on the eve of the war had a functioning range of about 400 miles—barely enough to reach Tel Aviv. Thus their intended target was surely "not Hoboken, New Jersey," but possibly Israel. To further clarify his position, Raimondo counseled, "When the first body bags come home, let the following be carved on their tombstones: He died for Israel."[63] Raimondo later wrote a book, *The Terror Enigma: 9/11 and the Israeli Connection,* in which he argued that Mossad had been complicit in the September 11 attacks.[64]

The late Sam Francis, who was a leading paleo-conservative intellectual and journalist, was also critical of the war on Iraq and thought that it was inimical to American interests:

> My thoughts on the war with Iraq are that it is at best an unwise and foolish war against a country that has never harmed the United States and which has no imminent plans to harm us. It will certainly alienate the vast majority of Arabs from us even more and probably cause a generation of terrorist warfare against us, and it may lead us into further and far bloodier wars in the Middle East in the near future. I believe it was concocted by a small group of pro-Israeli officials and media people for the protection of Israel. I think that has been documented by many journalists, right and left, beyond debate. I think also that those who concocted the war are essentially treasonable—it is an act of treason to entangle the United States in a war. They should be prosecuted for treason and sent to prison or executed if convicted.[65]

Likewise, Kevin MacDonald has also been highly critical of neoconservatives and their influence on the Bush administration. He implicated Jewish neoconservatives as the driving force in the war on Iraq:

> I believe that the war with Iraq is primarily the product of a push by Jewish neoconservative activists to advance the interests of Israel by transforming the politics of the Middle East. There is a long list of such activists, both within the Bush administration and in powerful lobbying groups and in the media. They have close ties to Israel and the Likud Party and a long

history of supporting Israel and other Jewish causes. Jews must never be represented as monolithic, but we must have ways of discussing Jewish influence—talking about specific groups of Jews, their Jewish identity, and their actual influence on public affairs, as we do with other ethnic groups. The neoconservative influence is increased because virtually the entire organized Jewish community (but certainly not all American Jews) has become pro-Likud. The Likud Party, led by Ariel Sharon, is strongly in favor of a U.S.-led war against Iraq. I suspect that the war with Iraq will achieve the short-term aims of Israel and its U.S. backers. However, the long-term effects are less clear because I do not think the United States can be an occupying power over the entire region and I do think that there will be an Islamic reaction to the invasion. The United States must prepare itself for a very long and costly campaign in order to secure Israeli interests in the Middle East. I doubt that even the powerful U.S. Jewish community can pull that off in the teeth of hatred throughout the region. I agree with the many analysts who are predicting a further rise of militant Islam and the appearance of tactics like suicide bombing, which has been common in the Israeli-Palestinian conflict. Once the initial fighting is over and the first American occupying troops are killed by Islamic martyrs, there may well be second thoughts about the wisdom of this preemptive U.S. policy.[66]

Not surprisingly, opposition to the war carried over to the extreme right in Europe. Nick Griffin of the British National Party believes that the war on Iraq is just another step in a larger campaign in the Middle East:

It's just the start. After Iraq, those who have conned us into this war will go for Syria and Iran and then occupy destabilized Saudi Arabia. The Coalition of the Stupid will presumably win the conventional war quite quickly, but the "terror" will go on until it ends either in nuclear war or with the peoples of the West ridding themselves of their self-serving rulers and secretive lobbies, and doing a deal with Islam—"you get out of our homelands, and we'll get out of yours."[67]

The Swiss revisionist Jürgen Graf was also highly critical of the U.S.-led war against Iraq:

The war against Iraq is undoubtedly the most impudent and cynical aggression of modern history. It is fought on behalf of two lobbies: the oil lobby, which wants to grab Iraq's oil, and the Jewish lobby, which wants to make the Middle East safe for Israel. It goes without saying that I admire and support the courageous resistance of the Iraqi people, but in view of overwhelming Anglo-American technical superiority, the conflict will almost inevitably end with a military victory of the aggressors. But they will have to pay a high price. Anti-American and Anti-British sentiments will run even higher in the Muslim world, and Russia will eventually be forced to oppose the United States. A positive result of Bush's and Blair's stupidity is the split of NATO. I was pleasantly surprised that both Paris and Berlin opposed the aggression, and I hope that the development in the Middle East will give birth to an alliance between Russia, Germany, and France (ideally, China could become a member of such an alliance too).[68]

David Myatt, the British convert to Islam, expressed disgust over American military intervention in the Islamic world and saw it as part of a larger effort to repress Islam:

America is acting like an arrogant, ignoble bully. It will not be a war: it will be a big, powerful bully picking on someone much smaller. A one-sided conflict, rather like that between the American-equipped Zionist army and the activists of Hamas: helicopter gunships and tanks against rifles; rockets and missiles against stones. It makes me angry to watch the television pictures of American and British troops swaggering around, showing off their hardware while experts talk about powerful American weaponry: it so dishonorable; so against the ethos of the true warrior. There will be no honor in such a conflict, at least not on the part of American and allied troops. You want true warriors in the modern world? Muslims defending Jenin. Mujahideen defending Tora Bora.

America is acting in the interests of the Zionist entity.

It is not a war for oil, and neither is the war in Afghanistan about oil. It is war to tame Islam; to extend the dictat of the NWO to Muslim lands. A war to ensure that Muslim countries do not develop weapons which can challenge the Zionist entity. In addition, it is war to ensure that the NWO can control and stifle the growth of holocaust revisionism in Muslim lands, for the truth has begun to be freely told in such lands, and were the myth of the holocaust to be destroyed, the NWO, with its Western ZOGs [Zionist occupation governments], would crumble from within. . . .

In brief, it is part of the plan to extend the dictat of the NWO to the whole world. The next target will be places like Iran and possibly Syria.[69]

It is important to point out that some of the more respectable representatives of the conservative right wing have also criticized the neoconservative war hawks who have gained influence in the Bush administration. For example, Pat Buchanan wrote a blistering article in his magazine, *American Conservative,* which sounded very similar, although less strident in tone, to the sentiments expressed by those in the extreme right. In fact, Buchanan has long been one of the most vociferous critics of the so-called dual-loyalists. In January 1991, just prior to the start of the Gulf War, Buchanan colorfully opined that men named Rosenthal, Kissinger, Perle, and Krauthammer—a group he called Israel's "amen corner"— were beating the drums for a war in which people with names like "McAllister, Murphy, Gonzales, and LeRoy Brown" would die.[70] Moreover, he referred to the U.S. Congress as "Israeli occupied territory," a charge reminiscent of the acronym ZOG used by the more radical elements of the extreme right.

In the months leading up to the most recent war in Iraq, Buchanan accused defensive neoconservatives of playing the "anti-Semitic card" by attempting to smear those who criticize them for allegedly subordinating American interests to Israel. In his estimation, the foreign policy interests of the two countries are not symmetrical. He cited an open letter sent to President Bush on September 20, 2001, just nine days after the 9/11 attacks, and signed by prominent neoconservatives—including William Bennett, Norman Podhoretz, Jeane Kirkpatrick, Richard Perle, William Kristol, and Charles Krauthammer—which amounted, in Buchanan's analysis, to an ultimatum. In order to retain the signatories' support, the president was in effect told that he must depose Saddam Hussein in Iraq and retaliate against Syria and Iran if they refused to stop supporting terrorism in the region. As such, according to some observers, the letter amounted to a warning to President Bush that he must launch a series of wars on Arab regimes—none of which had attacked the United States or were proved to be connected to the 9/11 attacks.

Buchanan has occasionally criticized Israel Prime Minister Ariel Sharon. In the spring of 2002, when President Bush urged Ariel Sharon to pull out of the West Bank, the Israeli prime minister fired back that he would not let anyone do to Israel what Neville Chamberlain had done to Czechoslovakia. According to Buchanan, this retort, along with the September 20 open letter signed by neoconservatives, amounted to a clear warning that if Bush should attempt to pressure Israel to trade land for peace, he would be denounced as an anti-Semite and a Munich-style appeaser inside his own Republican Party.[71]

There have been indications that relations between the United States and Israel have frayed during the war on terror. For example, the deterioration of the Israeli-Palestinian conflict in the spring of 2002 put pressure on the U.S.-Israeli alliance. After several suicide bombing attacks, Israeli prime minister Ariel Sharon launched an invasion into the Palestinian-controlled areas and cities of the West Bank in a campaign called Operation Defense Shield. In a press conference in Crawford, Texas, with British prime minister Tony Blair, Bush admonished Israel to "withdraw without delay." He later backtracked from these comments and softened his tone toward Israel.

How prominently have Jewish neoconservatives figured in the prowar faction? Jewish defense organizations have been very sensitive to charges of dual loyalty, citing it as a classic anti-Semitic canard. Yet there is evidence to suggest that many of these well-placed officials and advisers have played an important role in the prowar faction. For example, Deputy Secretary of Defense Paul Wolfowitz has been in the forefront of the Bush administration's push for war against Iraq. Wolfowitz obviously feels a strong bond with Israel. As a youth, he spent time in that country on numerous vacations with his family. His sister is married to an Israeli citizen. For his part, Wolfowitz has done little to disabuse the public of the association between Jewish interests and neoconservatives. When asked in an interview for *Esquire* magazine about the assertion that the war in Iraq was a brainchild of the neoconservatives, Wolfowitz sardonically replied, "No . . . Cheney can't be a neocon. He isn't Jewish."[72] Other prominent Jewish neoconservatives include Douglas Feith, who is the current undersecretary of defense for policy. Richard Perle is considered the doyen of Jewish neoconservative war hawks. Until recently, he was the chairman of the Defense Policy Board, an influential think tank on national defense issues. Peter Rodman and Dov Zachkeim serve at the subcabinet level in the Defense Department. At lower levels, the desk officers for Israel and Syria/Lebanon are held by imports from the Washington Institute for Near East Policy, a think tank spun off from the American Israel Public Affairs Committee (AIPAC).[73]

On the National Security Council, Elliott Abrams, who is viewed as very pro-Israel, has been appointed director of Middle Eastern affairs. He is the son-in-law of Norman Podhoretz, the editor of the American Jewish Committee's magazine *Commentary.* Over the years, Abrams has written extensively on the Israeli-Palestinian conflict and has opposed U.S. mediation and efforts to press for Israeli concessions.[74]

Although neoconservatives have yet to make considerable inroads at the State Department, a few have risen to prominence. For example, John Bolton, an American Enterprise Institute analyst, a former undersecretary for arms control, and an Israeli proponent, was appointed U.S. ambassador to the United Nations in August 2005. His special assistant, David Wurmser, coauthored (with Perle and Feith) at least two strategy papers for Israeli prime minister Benjamin Netanyahu in 1996.[75] One paper in particular is occasionally cited by critics as a blueprint for Israeli hegemony in the Middle East.

In 1996, Feith, Perle, and both David and Meyrav Wurmser were among the authors of a policy paper titled "A Clean Break: A New Strategy for Securing the Realm," prepared by an Israeli-sponsored think tank and written for the newly elected Prime Minister Netanyahu. The paper urged a "clean break" from the peace process, in particular the land for peace aspect, which the authors felt was a prescription for Israel's annihilation. They recommended that Israel foster a close alliance with Turkey and Jordan and work to destabilize and roll back dangerous threats to Israeli security in the region, such as Syria. They rejected the premise of making peace unilaterally with the Palestinians as a way in which to enhance Israeli security. Instead, they advocated a "peace for peace" formula that would recognize unconditional acceptance of Israel's right to exist, including territorial rights in the occupied areas.[76] The authors saw the principal threat to Israel not from Saddam Hussein's Iraq but from Syria. The paper recommended deposing Saddam Hussein and replacing him with a more compliant monarchy led by the Hashemites, who claim direct descent from the prophet Muhammad. The royal family of Jordan is the most prominent contemporary branch of the Hashemite family tree. If members of the Hashemite family were to rule Iraq, they conjecture, it would weaken Iran's influence over Shi'ites in Lebanon, including the Hezbollah organization, insofar as the Shi'ites for centuries have been tied to the leadership of their coreligionists in Najf, Iraq. Iraq was seen as a steppingstone to Syria.[77] Wursmer, a resident scholar at the American Enterprise Institute, urged both Israel and the United States to be on the lookout for a crisis that could be used as an opportunity to apply their policy strategy. Conspiracy theorists would later latch on to Wursmer's comments to buttress their conspiracy claims surrounding 9/11.

Indeed, those in the extreme right believe that neoconservatives have hijacked the Bush administration and plan to use the Defense Department to remake the entire Middle East so that it is more congenial to Israel. They find evidence of such a grand scheme in the pronouncements of the neoconservatives. For example, the term "World War IV," coined by Eliot Cohen and popularized by the neoconservative Norman Podhoretz, has come to mean a crusade against recalcitrant regimes in the Middle East (the Cold War, in Cohen's analysis, was World War III). In a speech at the University of California at Los Angeles, former CIA director R. James Woolsey added credence to the charge that neoconservatives had broad designs that went well beyond Iraq and Afghanistan in the Middle East:

As we move toward a new Middle East, we will make a lot of people very nervous. We want you nervous. We want you to realize that now, for the fourth time in 100 years, this country and its allies are on the march and that we are on the side of those whom you—the Mubaraks, the Saudi Royal family—most fear. We're on the side of your own people.[78]

Former Pentagon official Michael Ledeen has propounded what has become known as the Ledeen doctrine: "Every ten years or so, the United States needs to pick up some small, crappy little country and throw it against the wall, just to show we mean business."[79] Specifically, Ledeen calls for regime change in Iraq, Iran, and Syria. He believes that supporting prodemocratic forces in Iran can best effect regime change in that country. However, he believes that military intervention would be appropriate to bring down these governments. Also, the United States must "come to grips with the Saudis."[80] Ledeen outlined his strategy in a book called *The War Against the Terror Masters.* His book was the first significant contribution to a genre that pushed for an expanded global war on terrorism.

In early 2003, Richard Perle and David Frum released their manifesto, *An End to Evil: How to Win the Terror War,* which defended the neoconservative position and warned that the momentum of the early victories in the conflict had flagged. The authors dismissed the idea that there is a neoconservative "cabal" and argued instead that they and their like-minded brethren represent a tiny minority of visionaries. Furthermore, they assert that the "neoconservative myth" is a useful euphemism that allows leftists and Europeans to express their hostility toward Israel more comfortably.

To Frum and Perle, the war in Iraq was justified irrespective of the issue of weapons of mass destruction because it eliminated a traditional state sponsor of terrorism, taught the U.S. how to fight wars in the region and subsequently rebuild countries, demonstrated American military potency to enemies, aided the forces of democracy in the Middle East, and eliminated the "Arab world's most tyrannical ruler."[81] But Frum and Perle believe that the war on terror should be expanded far beyond Iraq and Afghanistan. For instance, North Korea must be brought to heel for its nuclear weapons program and its status as a rogue nation. The prospect of the North Korean government conveying a nuclear warhead to al Qaeda or some other terrorist group makes the small Asian nation a serious threat. Frum and Perle recommended that the U.S. government apply pressure on the Chinese government to encourage North Korean compliance on nuclear nonproliferation. Likewise, Iran, also a country with nuclear ambitions and a history of state sponsorship of terrorism, poses a challenge that must be dealt with as well. As they pointed out, defanging these two regimes is all the more urgent because weapons of mass destruction can serve as the great equalizer and thus "deter retaliation by even the most powerful and outraged governments."[82]

Nor does Syria escape their plans for preemptive aggression. Frum and Perle demanded that the Syrian government cease all support for terrorism, close its border to Iraqi guerrillas, cease its campaign of incitement against Israel, withdraw its forces from Lebanon, and open up its controlled economy and its authoritarian political system. They cautioned that recent Libyan overtures for rapprochement with Washington should be met with great skepticism and not delude "the accommodationists in the foreign policy establishment." Finally, the United States should demand total cooperation from Saudi Arabia on the war on terrorism or else tell that country to expect "the severest of consequences."[83] As they explained, state sponsorship is the prerequisite for the successful terrorist network in the sense that effective terrorists either are supported by governments (e.g., Iraq and Iran) "or else they create territorial bases for themselves in which they practically become the government."[84]

Frum and Perle also took Europe to task for its intransigence in the days leading to the war on Iraq. They even went so far as to question the desirability of a closely integrated Europe from the perspective of the United States. Specifically, French resistance to American military intervention should be punished and discouraged. They also recommended that the U.S. government reevaluate its position toward Russia in light of that country's dealings with Iran and Iraq.[85]

Some critics of the neoconservatives believed that the war against Iraq is only a first step in a broader mission to reorder the power structure of the entire Middle East. Furthermore, the critics asserted that the neoconservatives have used a considerable amount of deception in pursuit of this project—in effect, taking a page out of their mentor Leo Strauss's book, who believed that such subterfuge was necessary in politics. For their part, the neoconservatives counter that a democratic Iraq would undercut the legitimacy of various autocracies in the Middle East and, in doing so, hasten their demise.

Some critics believed that the scenario of a Middle East of prosperous democracies is illusory because many countries in the region have heterogeneous populations with many major ethnic cleavages. The absence of national unity militates against the development of viable democracies. What is more, all this could not be effected without massive intervention on the part of the United States, which would of course entail a massive fiscal undertaking—a project that would not be an easy sell to the American public.[86]

Buchanan asked rhetorically, who stands to benefit from a clash of civilizations between the West and Islam? His answer: "one nation, one leader, one party, Israel, Sharon, Likud."[87] Furthermore, Buchanan is fearful that a broad war, which would include Iraq, could destabilize friendly Arab governments. He charges that neoconservatives actually would welcome such a development. Buchanan sees the Bush administration as virtually hijacked by the Ariel Sharon's Likud Party. He does not shy from accusing them of dual loyalties: "What these neo-conservatives seek is to conscript American blood to make the world safe for Israel. They want the peace of the sword imposed on Islam and American soldiers to die if necessary to impose it."[88] In the years prior to 9/11, Buchanan had frequently warned that the United States would eventually face "cataclysmic terrorism" on its soil if it continued to embark on an interventionist foreign policy.[89] As he later remarked, "The terrorists were over here because we were over there. Terrorism is the price of empire."[90] Buchanan later expanded his critique of neoconservatism in a book titled *Where the Right Went Wrong: How Neoconservatives Subverted the Reagan Revolution and Hijacked the Bush Presidency.*

The influence of neoconservatives on the Bush administration's Middle East policy has not gone unnoticed in the mainstream media. For example, *Nightline* carried a story titled "The Plan," which examined the efforts of the neoconservative think tank, the Project for the New Century, which was founded in 1997 to pressure the U.S. government to take a hard-line position toward recalcitrant regimes in the Middle East.[91]

Criticism of the Israeli lobby comes not only from the extreme right of the political spectrum. For over two decades, former Democratic congressman Paul Findley has spoken out against what he sees as the undue influence of the Israeli lobby. Like many in the extreme right, he believed that 9/11 had its principal origins in a much broader Middle East conflict, to which the United States has been either directly or indirectly a party for over half a century. Findley saw the lack of debate on the relationship between the United States and Israel as perilous. Intimidation silences criticism, which in his analysis stifled the debate necessary on such an important foreign policy issue with potentially far-reaching repercussion for the United States. Not unlike Buchanan, he averred that the U.S. Congress behaves as if it were a subcommittee of the Israeli Knesset.[92] Other, more mainstream critics of Israel have included former congressman Paul McCloskey, George W. Ball, and Douglas B. Ball. What these critics share in common is an underlying assumption that U.S. support for Israel is misguided and incongruent with American interests. It follows that a powerful Jewish lobby is responsible for subverting U.S. foreign policy according to its own will.[93]

Still other Democrats have criticized the Israeli partiality in American foreign policy. In March 2003, Congressman James Moran (D-VA) accused Jewish organizations as being the principal advocates for the war against Iraq: "If it were not for the strong support of the Jewish community for this war with Iraq, we would not be doing this."[94] Moran is generally considered a political liberal, but his relationship with pro-Israel groups and American Jewish leaders has soured in recent years because of his perceived pro-Palestinian stance in the Middle East conflict. Six Democratic members of the House of Representatives—Henry Waxman (CA), Martin Frost (TX), Tom Lantos (CA), Sander Levin (MI), Benjamin Cardin (MD), and Nita Lowey (NY)—signed and sent a letter to House Minority Leader Nancy Pelosi (D-CA) sharply criticizing

Moran's comments. Furthermore, they recommended that he should not seek reelection in light of his remarks.[95] Moran was quick to apologize for his remarks, which drew ire from the extreme right. Sam Francis saw Moran's apology as disingenuous and noted that many other observers wrote articles suggesting the same thing, including Robert Kaiser in the *Washington Post,* Jason Vest in the *Nation,* Chalmers Johnson in the *Los Angeles Times,* and Pat Buchanan in the *American Conservative.*[96]

Several Jewish organizations quickly condemned Moran's remarks and accused him of unfairly scapegoating Jews.[97] ADL director Abraham Foxman conceded in an editorial that removing Saddam Hussein would be in Israel's best interest but added that it was unfair to ascribe an organized Jewish conspiracy as the causative factor behind the U.S. government's decision to go to war against Iraq.[98]

More recently, U.S. senator Ernest F. Hollings (D-SC) criticized the Bush administration for the Iraq War, which he argued was launched at the behest of a handful of Jewish public officials and opinion makers, including Paul Wolfowitz, Richard Perle, and Charles Krauthammer.[99] He accused Bush of cynically planning for an invasion of Iraq prior to 9/11 in order to curry favor with Jewish voters. However, as Hollings stated, the war came at great cost, because it fueled more terrorism in the Middle East region. Hollings's remarks originally appeared in an editorial in the *Charleston Post and Courier* and were later entered into the Congressional Record. Abe Foxman was quick to condemn Hollings's editorial, averring that it veered "into anti-Jewish stereotyping."[100] Likewise, Hollings's colleague, Senator George Allen (R-VA), wrote an article in which he accused Hollings of anti-Semitism.[101] For his part, Hollings refused to make a retraction. In fact, on May 20, 2004, he spoke on the floor of the U.S. Senate and expounded on the topic in a tone that was uncharacteristic by the standards of the U.S. Senate, as the following remarks make clear:

> I can tell you no President takes office—I don't care whether it is a
> Republican or a Democrat—that all of a sudden AIPAC will tell him
> exactly what the policy is, and Senators and members of Congress ought to
> sign letters. I read these carefully and I have joined in most of them. On
> some I have held back. . . .
>
> [The Israeli Defense Forces] are coming in there with U.S. equipment,
> U.S. gun helicopters, U.S. tanks that are bulldozing. That is our policy.
> That is the reason for 9/11, when Osama said, I do not like American
> troops in Saudi Arabia, get the infidel out. . . .Where do you think we get
> all this talk about hate America? I do not buy that stuff. I have traveled the
> world. They love Americans.[102]

Perhaps more telling is a series of memoirs by several former high-ranking members of the Bush administration that tell of the influence of the neoconservatives and their push for war on Iraq. Former Treasury secretary Paul O'Neill revealed that a mere ten days after the presidential inauguration, elements of the Bush administration expressed their determination to topple Saddam Hussein.[103] In March 2004, former counterterrorism czar Richard Clarke caused quite a stir when he asserted in his book *Against All Enemies* that top Bush advisers, most notably Defense Secretary Donald Rumsfeld and his deputy Paul Wolfowitz, were more focused on Saddam Hussein and Iraq than Osama bin Laden and al Qaeda, even in the wake of the 9/11 attacks.[104] Retired general Anthony Zinni, who served the Bush administration as a special envoy to the Middle East, accused various neoconservatives— Paul Wolfowitz, Douglas Feith, Richard Perle, Elliott Abrams, and Lewis "Scooter" Libby—of leading the effort to involve the United States in the war against Iraq. Furthermore, Zinni maintained that their principal objective for doing so was to strengthen the position of Israel.[105] Finally, the respected Washington insider and journalist, Bob Woodward, conducted numerous interviews with Bush administration officials for his book, *Plan of Attack*. His research also suggested that the neoconservatives figured very prominently in the push for war.[106]

Despite the protestations of the ADL, there is strong evidence to support the notion that not only have Jewish organizations been in the forefront in advocating a war against Iraq, but also that they are very influential in this regard as well. Government officials do indeed take these organizations very seriously. For example, ADL chairman Glen A. Tobias and ADL director Foxman commended President Bush for "clearly and forcefully" calling on the international community to take a strong stand against Saddam Hussein.[107] On March 30, 2003, a meeting convened by the American Israel Public Affairs Committee drew very high-profile guests, including Secretary of State Colin Powell, who spoke at the event, National Security Adviser Condoleezza Rice, White House Political Director Kenneth Mehlman, Undersecretary of State John R. Bolton, Assistant Secretary of State William Burns, one-half of the U.S. Senate, and one-third of the U.S. House of Representatives. The conference was billed as "off the record," which would certainly cause concern for those opposed to a broader war in the Middle East, especially after Secretary of State Powell made the following remarks at the event: "Syria can continue direct support for terrorist groups and the dying regime of Saddam Hussein, or it can embark on a different and more hopeful course. Either way, Syria bears the responsibility for its choices—and for the consequences."[108] More recently, in May 2004, President George Bush spoke at an

AIPAC gathering in which he pledged American support for Israel and decried the resurgence of anti-Semitism around the world, a development that he vowed to combat.[109]

The so-called Israeli lobby has indeed been very effective in the realm of foreign policy. The effort of Jewish Americans on behalf of Israel is one of the biggest success stories in the history of constituency pressure groups. At the center of this effort is AIPAC, which has become well known on Capitol Hill for its ability to mobilize support for the state of Israel. AIPAC has been able to exert considerable influence not only in Congress but also in the executive branch, including presidents, the Department of Defense, the media, academia, and evangelical Christian churches and groups.[110] In a survey of current members of Congress and lobbyists, the American Israeli Public Affairs Committee ranked second out of the 120 most powerful lobbies, with no other ethnic lobby in the top twenty-five.[111]

It goes without saying that the state of Israel is a focal point of Jewish organizing efforts in the United States. The basic idea of Zionism was to create a nation to which Jews could emigrate to escape the vagaries of the diaspora. The Jewish state would thus "give voice to a voiceless people and return Jews to the stage of history after centuries of helplessness."[112] However, as some observers have noted, Israel has in many ways strengthened the diaspora in the United States and has mobilized it on a number of issues. In doing so, American Jews discovered that they had developed enormous political clout.[113] As J. J. Goldberg pointed out, Jewish pressure groups have to a certain extent fostered the image of a powerful Jewish cabal that can punish those who oppose its public policy agenda. ADL director Foxman conceded: "The non-Jewish world to a large extent believes in the myth of *The Protocols of the Elders of Zion,* and to some extent we in the Jewish community have not disabused them."[114]

But as the war on Iraq approached in March 2003, Foxman was quick to point out that as a group, Jews were less likely to support the war than other Americans. A poll conducted by the Pew Research Center for the People and the Press "found that while 62 percent of all Americans supported Bush's plan for a war in Iraq, only 52 percent of Jews supported it."[115] It is worth mentioning that the pro-Israeli neoconservatives have found common cause with evangelical Christians. For example, that same Pew poll found that among evangelical Christians, support for the war was 72 percent. In their worldview, Israel's dominion over the area of Palestine is considered a necessary prelude to fulfillment of biblical prophecy. For many evangelical Christian conservatives, support for Israel is seen as a religious imperative. Furthermore, some believe that a Jewish conquest of the Temple Mount in Jerusalem would precipitate Armageddon and hence the return of Jesus Christ. Similarly, messianic Orthodox

Jews believe that their messiah will not arrive until the al-Quds mosque is destroyed and the Temple Mount is constructed in its stead.[116]

Just how slanted U.S. policy in the Middle East has been is open to debate. Examining U.S. foreign policy in the region, Barry Rubin found that in twelve major issues on which Muslims had a conflict with non-Muslims or Arabs had a conflict with non-Arabs, the U.S. sided with the former groups in eleven out of the twelve cases. For example, the United States backed Muslims in six out of seven cases: it supported Turkey over Greece, Bosnia and later Kosovo against Yugoslavia, Pakistan against India, the Afghani mujahideen against the Soviets, and Azerbaijan against Armenia. The only exception to this pattern was U.S. support for Israel in the Arab-Israeli conflict.[117]

As the Iraq War finally commenced in March 2003, many in the extreme right criticized the U.S. government's prosecution thereof and urged that U.S. troops be quickly returned home, lest they become targets in a protracted guerrilla war. Many defense analysts were surprised by the tenacity of Iraqi resistance in the early part of the campaign. Jared Taylor of American Renaissance remarked, however, that President Bush and the rest of his administration had managed to overlook one of the strongest collective and affective forces in the world: "the call for blood and soil." He chided the optimists who, as he explained, believe that race, religion, and ethnicity are not important and that the "combination of democracy and Coca-Cola would dissolve all parochial loyalties." In his analysis, the rest of the world does not desire to be as "rootless and raceless as Americans have become."[118] Despite the great pessimism the extreme right felt over many aspects of the war on terror, many in the movement ultimately believed that the events of 9/11 would undermine what they often refer to as the new world order and redound to their favor. Of course, the subsequent guerrilla war in Iraq added credence to this position. As reported on the extreme right Nationalist Movement website, some skinheads expressed a desire to join the insurgency but were dissuaded by an Arab, who encouraged them instead to concentrate their efforts in the United States to push for the removal of American troops from Iraq.[119]

Conclusion

Some representatives of the extreme right expressed the view that 9/11 and the war on terror would have a catalyzing effect on politics and increase the salience of the issues about which they feel strongly. As mentioned earlier, the extreme right's reaction to the September 11 attack seems to have been mixed. Many in the movement expressed feelings of vindication, insofar as many of the issues about which they feel strongly (e.g., immigration and American foreign policy in the Middle East) featured prominently in the attack. Others were less sanguine about the current state of affairs and feared that the government's war on terror could spill over into a witch hunt against domestic extremists as well. I sought feedback from various representatives of the extreme right to determine if they thought that 9/11 and its consequences would hinder or improve conditions for the extreme right in the future.

John Tyndall, a longtime extreme right activist in the United Kingdom and former leader of the British National Party, explained:

I regard the question of whether 9/11 would hinder or improve conditions for white racial nationalism as one of those "do-you-still-beat-your-wife?" questions. It is loaded in such a way as to place the person being questioned in a position in which he/she is expected to consider tragic events in terms of political profit/loss ratios. I do not intend to fall into that trap. 9/11 was a tragedy and should be welcomed by no one, whatever their politics.

Of course, it is a rule of political life—and particularly political life in the "democracies"—that some tragic events are bound to lead to consequences and provoke reactions out of which one faction will be perceived as "losing" and another faction as "winning." In the crudest example, the murders of small children could be perceived as "benefiting" those in politics who seek the restoration of the death penalty for the culprits, but no one with any fairness would accuse such a faction of welcoming such murders. Politics are a matter of reacting to tragic events in such a way as to reduce to the minimum the possibility of their occurring again. Fire brigades are organized to put out fires, but no fireman likes the consequences of a fire.

To other parts of this question, yes—9/11 has confirmed our basic case, which is that (1) the power of the Jewish lobby in the United States, and the perversions of American foreign policy that are engaged in to accommodate it, provoke outrages like 9/11 because such things are perceived in the Islamic world to be the only available response; (2) western countries should not interfere in the politics of the Islamic world or any other part of the world except where their own vital national interests are at stake and/or under threat; (3) globalism, as adhered to by the governments of the United States, UK and others, leads to this very interference; and (4) nationalism and (relative) isolationism are therefore the preferred policy. In short, were the USA to adhere to the principles of foreign policy prevailing before World War I, 9/11 would almost certainly not have happened.[120]

Nick Griffin, Tyndall's successor and current leader of the British National Party, gave his thoughts on 9/11 as it pertains to the extreme right as well:

In direct terms, it won't have any effect on conditions for us in Britain; it was simply too far away. But by giving the Zionist/Christian fundamentalist pressure groups around Bush the added influence needed to push the U.S. and Britain into invading Iraq, it will end up being a major factor in the creation of the "clash of civilizations." While it is clear that the neoconservatives want that clash, the irony is that nationalists in countries with large and growing Muslim populations will benefit from it too.[121]

The Swiss revisionist Jürgen Graf was undecided on what effect 9/11 would have on revisionism and the extreme right:

9/11 and its consequences could work either way for revisionism and the far right. The Bush regime will doubtless try to use the "war on terror" as a smokescreen to transform the USA into a police state, and it goes without saying that revisionists and anti-Zionists would be among the first victims, as they would automatically be associated with "Muslim extremists." On the other hand, more and more Americans are becoming aware that the war against Islam is primarily being fought on behalf of Israel (even some mainstream politicians, such as Patrick Buchanan, now openly say so). If this adventure ends with a failure, and if America suffers a drastic loss of prestige and influence, it would become exceedingly difficult to conceal the reasons of this development. People would become very angry at Israel and the Jewish lobby, and this would work in favor of Revisionism. Similar developments could take place in Europe, too.[122]

David Myatt predicted that initially the war on terror would be used as a pretext to suppress elements of the extreme right. However, ultimately he believed that the present crisis will redound against the present governments of the West:

The attacks have certainly been used, by ZOG [the Zionist occupation government], to increase their tyranny, as witness the surveillance, the new laws, the many arrests and detentions. They have also been used to appeal to a vacuous "patriotism" based upon the abstract, nonfolkish, concept of "the State."

In the long term, this can be to our advantage, since such things reveal the real nature and intent of those who wield power, as it reveals the insolent, dishonorable, un-Aryan nature of such governments. In the short term, it will probably lead to some government suppression of Aryan dissent, but given good leadership and the correct understanding of our own Aryan aims, goals and culture, this will not be much of a problem.[123]

Jared Taylor of American Renaissance stated that although the 9/11 attacks were a tragedy, they might have the unintended effect of forcing Americans to come to grips with the country's immigration policies:

What happened on September 11 was a terrible thing, but it has already had several positive effects. The most immediate was to stop the conversations George Bush had begun with Vicente Fox about amnesty for illegal immigrants from Mexico. Early in 2004, George Bush tried to revive the idea, but even within his own party got a very cool reception. During the more than two years during which the conversations were stalled, yet more Americans became disillusioned with the changes Third-World immigration brings to our country, and the resistance to amnesty is undoubtedly now greater than it would have been in late 2001. Amnesty is therefore less likely to be enacted, thanks in part to the terrorists.

The more important positive consequence of the attacks was that it has forced Americans to rethink the idea of "diversity." Until September 11, we were supposed to think of Muslims as yet another part of the gorgeous American mosaic. It is now clear that there is a certain group of people— young Muslim men—some of whom hate the United States enough to launch suicide attacks against us. Investigations into the mentality of radical Islamists has brought to light men who are American citizens but Muslims first. Consequently, most Americans are not shocked by the idea of ethnic profiling as part of the fight against terrorism, nor by the greater visa and travel restrictions the State Department has set on citizens of certain Muslim countries.

This recognition that at least some population groups can legitimately be evaluated in terms of whether they are good for the country is an exceedingly important intellectual breakthrough, even if it remains barely conscious for most Americans. The principle has been established: If Muslims are a threat, what about other people? What do Nigerians or Haitians add to the country? Why do we need more Hispanics when 20 percent of the population of Mexico already lives here? If young Muslim men are a legitimate category for evaluation, every group is fair game. We are slowly shifting towards the idea of "Do we really need these people?" rather than the mindless repetition of "We are a nation of immigrants."[124]

Dr. William L. Pierce, the late leader of the National Alliance, predicted that 9/11 would ultimately have a galvanizing effect on the American public. He has long derided what he saw as the torpidity of the white population in the United States, which is more preoccupied with consumerism and self-indulgence than with broader issues that affect them and their posterity:

> The psychological shock has been profound. The attitude used to be that our government could do whatever it wanted to do against the people of other countries, and Americans could enjoy the spectacle on TV from the comfort of their living rooms, watching the bombs falling and buildings burning while sipping their beer and munching potato chips. Americans felt invulnerable, and the feeling of invulnerability led to a diminished sense of responsibility. We could kick other people in the teeth all day long, kill other people's wives and children, burn other people's homes, and they couldn't do a thing about it. We didn't have to worry about the consequences of our behavior.
>
> . . .What happened in New York and Washington this month seemed very real indeed. What people saw on their television screens—and still are seeing as the wreckage continues to be cleared and the corpses hauled away in body bags—was a stark reminder of the truth in the ancient adage: as ye sow, so shall ye reap.[125]

Now that we have reviewed how the extreme right views the current crisis, it is instructive to see the response from militant Islam.

CHAPTER NINE

How Militant Islam Views the Current Crisis

In the immediate aftermath of 9/11, most of the Muslim and Arab leaders around the world sought to distance themselves from bin Laden and the tragedy for which he was subsequently determined to be responsible. Likewise, several Arab and Muslim organizations in the United States issued official statements against extremism and terrorism. For example, the American-Arab Anti-Discrimination Committee, Muslim Council, Council of American-Islamic Relations (CAIR), American Muslims for Jerusalem, Arab-American Institute, and Al-Hewar Center all spoke out against the 9/11 attacks and have voiced support for the war on terror.[1]

Some Arabs and Muslims, however, expressed satisfaction over the terrorist attacks on the United States. For example, Iraqi president Saddam Hussein announced in a broadcast on September 12, 2001, that "the United States [had reaped] the thorns that its rulers have planted in the world."[2] In that same vein, Atallah Abu al-Subh, a columnist for the Hamas weekly *Al-Risala,* rhapsodized over the anthrax attacks that occurred in the fall of 2001, "Oh Anthrax, despite your wretchedness, you have sown horror in the heart of the lady of arrogance, of tyranny, of boastfulness! Your gentle touch has made the U.S.'s life rough and pointless."[3]

Why do Islamic terrorists target American interests? Some observer have argued that "root causes" such as poverty, inequality, and large numbers of young men with restricted life opportunities contribute to terrorism. However, similar conditions exist in other parts of the developing world, yet they have not manifested themselves in terrorism.[4]

A frequent explanation offered by observers, especially those on the political left, is that the American government's desire to control the supply of oil is one factor that has engendered enmity against the United States in the Islamic world. However, bin Laden decries not so much U.S. petroleum consumption and petroleum policies as what he perceives to be its blasphemous occupation of Saudi Arabia—the custodian of Islam's most sacred sites. Therefore, oil, one could argue, is more of an indirect cause and not a direct cause of Islamic terrorism. Oil—whether it comes from Texas or Saudi Arabia—is part of a unified market, and thus the seller receives roughly the same price, no matter where and to whom it is sold. Thus, the notion that oil is major source of Islamic grievance would appear to be greatly exaggerated.

Still another explanation is that Islamists target the United States for existential reasons, including seemingly laudatory qualities such as liberty, freedom, and democracy, as well as some less than noble qualities such as cultural decadence, greed, and licentiousness. Islamists have on occasion expressed dismay over what they see as the corrosive effects of American pop culture on their societies. For instance, on previous occasions Iranian mullahs have denounced American entertainers such as Michael Jackson and Madonna as "cultural terrorists."[5] Much of this enmity against American culture hegemony stems from the fact that the United States dominates many of the media in the world. And in fact, bin Laden has on occasion decried American cultural decadence, once referring to the United States as "the Hubal of the age."[6]

The View from Osama bin Laden

Why does al Qaeda target America? Several observers and analysts have weighed in on this issue in the aftermath of 9/11. Despite the various claims that bin Laden targets the United States for cultural and existential reasons, he has actually been quite explicit in his objectives and his grievances, which include the following:

- Expel the United States from the Arabian peninsula
- Drive the West from the traditional lands of Islam
- End the repression and suffering of Muslims around the world, supposedly at the hands of the United States
- End the rule of most regimes in the Muslim world and replace them with Islamic governments that will implement the sharia and, in doing so, usher in a new Muslim golden age
- End the UN sanctions regime (led by the United States) imposed on Iraq, which has resulted in privation for many Iraqis, most notably Iraqi children
- End U.S. support for the state of Israel and punish Israel for its treatment of the Palestinians[7]

More recently, bin Laden has championed the Palestinian cause with greater emphasis and has spoken out about the suffering of Iraqis as a result of

UN sanctions. In a message released in November 2002, bin Laden clarified his positions and demands on the West. In that statement, he focused considerable attention on the Palestinian issue, which has now reached the top of his list of grievances. He excoriated the United States for supporting Israel and blamed not only the U.S. government but the people as well:

> The American people are the ones who pay the taxes which fund the planes that bomb us in Afghanistan, the tanks that strike and destroy our homes in Palestine, the armies that occupy our lands in the Arabian Gulf, and the fleets which ensure the blockade of Iraq. These tax dollars are given to Israel for it to continue to attack us and penetrate our lands. So the American people are the ones who fund the attacks against us, and they are the ones who oversee the expenditure of these monies in the way they wish, through their elected candidates.[8]

Some observers believe that bin Laden has broadened the scope of his grievances to appeal to more Muslims and thus expand his base of support.[9] That would be consistent with bin Laden's broader aim of polarizing the world into two camps, those that support the United States and its allies and those that resist them. Bin Laden has given notice that he is battling not only the government of the United States but its citizens as well:

> Our enemy, the target—if God gives Muslims the opportunity to do so—is every American male, whether he is directly fighting us or paying taxes.
> You may have heard these days that almost three-quarters of the U.S. people support Clinton's strikes on Iraq. They are a people whose president becomes more popular when he kills innocent people. They are a people who increase their support for their president when he commits some of the seven cardinal sins. They are a lowly people who do not understand the meaning of principles.[10]

Bin Laden has frequently invoked the imagery of a U.S.-Zionist–led crusader war against the Islamic *umma* (community). He saw the current war on terror not as an isolated incident but rather just one more episode in a series of events of a larger conspiracy to subjugate the Islamic world.

> Let us investigate whether this war against Afghanistan that broke out a few days ago is a single and unique one [event] or if it is a link to a long series of crusader wars against the Islamic world.
> Following World War I, which ended more than 83 years ago, the whole Islamic world fell under the crusader banner—under British, French, and Italian governments. They divided the whole world, and Palestine was

occupied by the British. Since then, and for more than 83 years, our brothers, sons, and sisters in Palestine have been badly tortured.

Let us examine the recent developments. Take for example the Chechens. They are a Muslim people who have been attacked by the Russian bear, which embraces the Christian Orthodox faith. Russians have annihilated the Chechen people in their entirety and forced them to flee to mountains where they were assaulted by snow, poverty, and diseases.

This was followed by a war of genocide in Bosnia in sight and hearing of the entire world in the heart of Europe.

Our brothers in Kashmir have been subjected to the worst forms of torture for over 50 years. Still, the United Nations continues to sit idly by.

Let us examine the stand of the West and the United Nations in the developments in Indonesia when they moved to divide the largest country in the Islamic world in terms of population. This criminal, Kofi Annan, was speaking publicly and putting pressure on the Indonesian government, telling it: You have 24 hours to divide and separate East Timor from Indonesia.

Therefore, we should view events not as separate links, but as links in a long series of conspiracies, a war of annihilation in the true sense of the word. . . . These battles cannot be viewed in any case whatsoever as isolated battles, but rather, as part of a chain of the long, fierce, and ugly crusader war.[11]

Much like those in the extreme right, bin Laden asserts that Jews and Israel control the U.S. government.[12] Bin Laden's comments in a 1998 interview excerpted below sound strikingly similar to those of members of the extreme right quoted elsewhere in this book:

I say that the American people gave leadership to a traitorous leadership. . . . The American government is an agent that represents Israel in America. If we look at sensitive departments in the present government like the defense department or the state department, or sensitive security departments like the CIA and others, we find that Jews have the first word in the American government, which is how they use America to carry out their plans in the world and especially the Muslim world.

The presence of Americans in the Holy Land supports the Jews and gives them a safe back. . . .

So, we tell the Americans as a people, and we tell the mothers of soldiers, and American mothers in general, if they value their lives and those of their children, find a nationalistic government that will look after their interests and not the interests of the Jews.[13]

Osama bin Laden had no sympathy for Clinton's successor, President George W. Bush. In fact, he found Bush to be the greater evil because early in his first term, his administration announced its intention to move the American embassy in Israel from Tel Aviv to Jerusalem. Furthermore, the fact that the U.S. Congress approved of such a political move was all the more galling for bin Laden.[14]

Despite the bombast of bin Laden's rhetoric, his organization has on occasion established a dialogue with opinion makers in the West. A case in point is the communiqué correspondence between some influential American academics and representatives of al Qaeda. In February 2002, a group of American academics released a paper titled "What We're Fighting For: A Letter from America." Signatories included Francis Fukuyama, William Galtson, Daniel Patrick Moynihan, Robert Putnam, and about sixty others, including professors of law, history, theology, public policy, and political science. The signatories conceded that there were many aspects of contemporary American culture with which they were dissatisfied. However, they condemned the 9/11 attacks and the ideology that inspired them. The signatories enunciated five tenets that centered on the themes of liberty, equality, human rights, and religious freedom. This open letter was first met with a response from a large group of Saudi clerics and academics titled "How We Can Coexist," published on October 23, 2002. Although they found much on which to agree with the Americans—including the denunciation of terrorism—the Saudis strongly condemned Israeli treatment of the Palestinians.

Amazingly, shortly thereafter, representatives of al Qaeda joined the dialogue. In their response they explained "what they were fighting for," which included opposition to American support for Israel and Israeli treatment of the Palestinians; U.S. support for various Arab and Middle East governments that suppress the Islamists; the sanction regime imposed on Iraq and its resultant privation for the population; and the transference of the U.S. embassy in Israel from Tel Aviv to Jerusalem. The document noted that insofar as the American people had democratically chosen their leaders, it followed that the former bore responsibility for the policy decisions of the latter. In addition, the response attacked the current morality in the United States citing un-Islamic practices and vices such as usury, alcohol, adultery, gambling, and American pop culture. The document announced various demands, which included a cession of support for both Israel and "corrupt" regimes in the Middle East. In a more conciliatory tone, the document enjoined Americans to come to Islam and face up to the responsibility for what it called "the worst nation in the history of mankind."[15]

Al Qaeda has proven adept in exploiting the media. Of course, the rise of new media outlets such as al-Jazeera, from which al Qaeda has on occasion received a sympathetic ear, has facilitated the organization's efforts in this regard. Not unlike Dr. William L. Pierce, Osama bin Laden has remarked on the significance of the media, "The United States has an advantage media-wise and great media power that varies its standards according to its needs."[16] Other Arabs and Muslims have echoed this sentiment as well. For example, the Palestinian Information Center announced: "The Jews can and do control the American media from *The Washington Post* to CNN, but they can't control the flow of the Internet."[17] Not surprisingly, the major American media outlets, including Hollywood movie studios, have come under threats from terrorists.[18] Despite this perception of Jewish domination, the Islamists believe that the media can still be manipulated to further their goals. Osama bin Laden saw great propaganda value in the 9/11 attacks. As Jessica Stern noted, the real audience for suicide terrorist attacks is not necessarily the victims, but rather the perpetrators and the sympathizers.[19] In that sense, bin Laden's comments are illustrative of terrorism as a form of "propaganda by the deed."

> These young men . . . said in deeds, in New York and Washington, speeches that overshadowed all other speeches made everywhere else in the world. The speeches are understood by both Arabs and non-Arabs—even by Chinese. It is above all the media said. Some of them said that in Holland, at one of the centers, the number of people who accepted Islam during the days that followed the operations were more than the people who accepted Islam in the last eleven years. I heard someone on Islamic radio who owns a school in America say: "We don't have time to keep up with demands of those who are asking about Islamic books to learn about Islam." This event made people think [about true Islam], which benefited Islam greatly.[20]

These comments were culled from a videotape of very poor quality discovered by American armed forces in Afghanistan in the opening weeks of Operation Enduring Freedom. Despite bin Laden's laudatory comments of the nineteen *shaheed,* survey data indicate that a substantial number of Muslims question whether bin Laden really was responsible for the 9/11 attacks.

Conspiracy Theories about 9/11 in the Muslim World

Despite bin Laden's words of praise for the suicide pilots of 9/11, many in the Islamic world expressed doubt about his culpability in the attacks. According to those surveyed in six Islamic countries in 2002, only 18 percent said they believed that Arabs carried out the 9/11 attacks.[21] What is more, another public opinion poll conducted in nine Middle Eastern countries found that one-third of the respondents (and even more in Kuwait and Saudi Arabia) refused to condemn the attacks.[22] A frequent refrain heard from Muslims, much like the extreme right, was that somehow the Israeli intelligence agency, the Mossad, had orchestrated the tragedy as a political windfall for Israel. It was a classic case of cui bono logic. The narrative usually went something like this: The horrific terrorist attacks of 9/11 would provoke a ferocious response by the U.S. government. Moreover, this war on terror would not be limited to al Qaeda, the Taliban, and Afghanistan. Eventually it would encompass Iraq (which it did), along with other Muslim nations, including Syria and Iran. Meanwhile, Ariel Sharon could take care of Israel's Palestinian problem while the world's attention was focused elsewhere. Thus the great beneficiary would be Israel, in that its chief geopolitical rivals in the region would be defanged and its restive Palestinian population would be subdued. A sampling of some of the statements made by Arab and Muslim observers is illustrative:

Israel is the main beneficiary of this terrible tragedy.[23]

You see these people [Jews] all the time, everywhere, disseminating corruption, heresy, homosexuality, alcoholism, and drugs. [Because of them] there are strip clubs, homosexuals, and lesbians everywhere. They do this to impose their hegemony and colonialism on the world. . . . If we take these things into account and look closely at the incident [9/11], we will find that only the Jews are capable of planning such an incident, because it was planned with great precision of which Osama bin Laden or any other Islamic organization or intelligence apparatus is incapable. . . . If it became known to the American people, they would have done to the Jews what Hitler did![24]

According to the journalist Kenneth Timmerman, Dr. Anwar Ul Haque, a self-styled koranic scholar, was the first person in the Islamic world to popularize an alleged Jewish conspiracy behind the events of 9/11.[25] Not long thereafter, the allegation that 4,000 Jews had been absent for work that day spread over the Internet and the mainstream media in the Arab world. Not unlike David Duke, Dr. Gamal 'Ali Zahran, the head of the political science faculty at Suez Canal University in Egypt, wrote in the Egyptian government daily *Al-Ahram* that despite the fact that thousands of Jews worked in the financial markets, "none were there on the day of the incident. Out of 6,000 killed [*sic*], of 65 nationalities from 60 countries, not one was a Jew."[26]

Several American Muslim clerics, along with members of the New Black Panther Party (NBPP), discussed the charges of alleged Israeli complicity in 9/11 on a three-hour-long news conference broadcast on C-SPAN2. Malik

Zulu Shabazz, the national chairman of the NBPP, asserted on the air that "European Jews have America under control, lock stock, and barrel, the media, foreign policy." His national assistant, Amir Muhammad, repeated the claim that 3,000–5,000 Jews did not go to work at the World Trade Center on the day of the attack and that "we need to take a serious look at that." Muslim cleric Muhammad al-Asi added: "The twin evils in this world are the decision makers in Washington and the decision makers in Tel Aviv."[27] Al-Asi had previously served as the imam of both the Muslim Community School in Potomac, Maryland, and the Islamic Center in Washington, D.C. On January 30, 1990, Ayatollah Ali Khamenei hosted him during a visit to Iran.[28] The Anti-Defamation League (ADL) responded to this broadcast with a letter of protest to C-SPAN, saying that it was inappropriate to allow a three-hour "open mike" news conference.[29]

Writing in *New Trend* magazine, Kaukab Siddique stated that the conspiracy theories that some Arabs have bandied about are symptomatic of an inferiority complex that they feel vis-à-vis their Israeli neighbors.

Jews are so powerful that nothing is beyond them. It is true on a realistic level that Jews are powerful, rich and well-organized. However to believe that nothing is beyond them . . . indicates a serious inferiority complex, which is prevalent among Muslim elites. [This creates] a huge gap between the jihadist impulse, which after having defeated the USSR now wants to take on the U.S., and the middle class Muslim elites who are mentally unable to even consider jihad.[30]

Although certainly not sympathetic to the Islamists, Daniel Pipes conceded that on occasion, conspiracies do indeed occur and impinge on the politics of the Middle East. He cites numerous examples. For instance, the European powers did conspire to divide up the Middle East during World War I as part of the secretive Sykes-Picot agreement. In 1954, the Israeli government bombed American targets in Egypt and blamed it on Egypt in an operation that became known as the "Lavon affair." Pipes referred to these examples as petty conspiracies in that they are a normal part of the real world of politics, which is not always virtuous. They operate within the existing order of world politics and do not evince any overarching plan to control the world. By contrast, grand conspiracies have to do with world domination. In his analysis, a grand conspiracy theory is a nonexistent version of a conspiracy.[31] Conspiracy theorists part company with mainstream historians in that the former see conspiracy as the driving force of history and ignore the context in which events occur.

The War against Iraq from the Perspective of Militant Islam

Many observers in the Islamic world have come to conclusions about the current war on terror that are strikingly similar to those held by the extreme right. For example, Saleh Abdel-Jawwad, a professor at Beir Zeit University in Egypt, argued that Israel sought to pressure the United States into a war against Iraq in order to advance its own foreign policy objectives. In his analysis, Iraq is the sole remaining Arab nation that has a powerful mix of resources unavailable to other Arab countries, mainly petroleum; financial assets; fertile soil; plentiful water supplies; a sufficiently large population; a clear national political agenda; and a military, industrial, and scientific infrastructure. He charged Israel with seeking to balkanize the Middle East into an ineffectual mosaic composed of many different ethnic and religious groups. Such a mosaic, he argues, will be no match for an Israeli hegemon with a clear national purpose. Toward this end, he reasoned that successive Israeli governments have supported non-Arab ethnic minorities such as the Kurds in Iraq or the Maronites in Lebanon. Using a logic reminiscent of the Cold War, Abdel-Jawwad argues that Israel has labored hard and long to encircle and contain the Arab world through such measures as creating alliances with peripheral nations that have been traditionally hostile to Arabs (e.g., Iran, Turkey, and Ethiopia). Further, Israel has encouraged secessionist movements in Sudan, Iraq, Egypt, Lebanon, and other Arab countries that Israel considers to be enemies. The most recent international campaign to isolate and defang Saddam's Iraq is seen as a continuation of this policy. Iraq has historically been too independent in that it has resisted pressure from the United States and Israel to conform to their dictates.[32]

Not unlike extreme right commentators, Osama bin Laden accused the "Zionist lobby" of orchestrating the war against Iraq:

> Bush has sent your sons into the lion's den, to slaughter and be slaughtered, claiming that the act was in defense of international peace and America's security, thus concealing the facts. On one hand he [Bush] is carrying out the demands of the Zionist lobby that helped him enter the White House. These demands are to destroy the military strength of Iraq because it is too close to the Jews in occupied Palestine, regardless of the harm that will happen to your people and your economy. On the other hand, he [Bush] is concealing his own ambitions and the ambitions of the Zionist lobby and their own desire for oil. He is still following the mentality of his ancestors who killed the Native Americans to take their land and wealth.[33]

On April 15, 2004, an audiotape purporting to be from Osama bin Laden was broadcast across Arab satellite channels and also translated and published in the European press. It offered a truce to European nations if they would withdraw their military forces from Iraq. In the taped message, bin Laden implicated several parties as his principal enemies, including the United Nations, George Bush, and the Zionist lobby. He referred to opinion polls measuring the war's unpopularity among Europeans and implored them to put pressure on their respective governments to change their current policies in Iraq. The March attacks on the Madrid train stations had been in that sense a warning to the people of Europe to extricate themselves from the affairs of the Islamic world. No such olive branch, however, was extended to the United States and Israel:

> We should like to inform you that labeling us and our acts as terrorism is also a description of you and of your acts. Reaction comes at the same level as the original action. Our acts are reaction to your own acts, which are represented by the destruction and killing our kinfolk in Afghanistan, Iraq, and Pakistan. . . .
>
> . . . it is both sides' interest to curb the plans of those who shed the blood of peoples for their narrow personal interest and subservience to the White House gang.
>
> The Zionist lobby is one of the most dangerous and most difficult figures of this group. God willing, we are determined to fight them.
>
> We must take into consideration that this war brings billions of dollars in profit to the major companies, whether it be those that produce weapons or those that contribute to reconstruction, such as Halliburton Company, its sisters and daughters.
>
> As for President Bush, the leaders who are revolving this orbit, the leading media companies and the United Nations, which makes laws for relations between the masters of veto and the slaves of the General Assembly, these are only some of the tools used to deceive and exploit peoples.
>
> All these pose a fatal threat to the whole world. . . .
>
> Based on the above, and in order to deny war merchants a chance and in response to the positive interaction shown by recent events and opinion polls, which indicate that most European peoples want peace, I ask honest people, especially ulema, preachers, and merchants, to form a permanent committee to enlighten European peoples of the justice of our causes, above all Palestine. They can make use of the huge potential of the media.
>
> The door of reconciliation is open for three months of the date of announcing this statement.

I also offer a reconciliation initiative to them, whose essence is our commitment to stopping operations against every country that commits itself to not attacking Muslims or interfering in their affairs—including the U.S. conspiracy on the greater Muslim world. . . .

For those who reject reconciliation and want war, we are ready.

As for those who want reconciliation, we have given them a chance. Stop shedding our blood so as to preserve your blood. It is in your hands to apply this easy, yet difficult, formula. You know that the situation will expand and increase if you delay things.

A rational person does not relinquish his security, money and children to please the liar of the White House.[34]

Perhaps suggesting a meeting of the minds, at least on certain issues, the extreme right newspaper *American Free Press* published an unredacted transcript of the broadcast soon thereafter, with an introduction that referred to Osama bin Laden as "one of the most influential men on the planet."[35]

Muslims in the United States have also been outspoken in opposition to the war. Louis Farrakhan has becoming increasingly strident in his criticism of President Bush's foreign policy, especially after the invasion of Iraq. In the past, he has frequently condemned U.S. military intervention in the Middle East. Farrakhan called Bush "spiritually blind" and charged that the president planned a wider war that would include not only Afghanistan but Iraq, Libya, and Sudan as well. Although a war with Iraq might be militarily easy, Farrakhan warned that it would be only a trigger that would ultimately lead to the United States "rolling down the hill to total destruction."[36] Further, he contended that the president would like to link him to terrorism because of his uncompromising message against American foreign policy in the Middle East.[37]

In July 2002, Iraq's state-run media quoted Farrakhan as saying during a visit to Baghdad that American Muslims were praying for an Iraqi victory in the event of war with the United States. Farrakhan held several meetings with Iraqi officials on a "solidarity trip" in which he sought to avoid a U.S. military campaign against Saddam Hussein.[38] It appeared that Farrakhan conceivably had a receptive audience for his antiwar message within the African American community. According to a Gallup poll, 78 percent of whites supported the war on Iraq, whereas only 29 percent of blacks did likewise.[39]

Farrakhan's Nation of Islam suffered a public relations setback in the fall of 2002 after it transpired that one of the D.C. area snipers, John Muhammad, was once a member and security officer for the organization. Furthermore, Muhammad is reported to have expressed sympathy for the 9/11 hijackers.[40]

Time appears not to have mellowed Farrakhan's rhetoric. In a series of speeches in 2004, he lambasted Israeli policy and the neoconservatives in the Bush administration, to whom he referred as the "synagogue of Satan." Further, he reiterated his contention that Jews were prominently involved in the transatlantic slave trade. Finally, he accused Jews in Hollywood of depicting African Americans in denigrating ways.[41]

Others believed that the current crisis had a silver lining. Ahmed Huber, the extreme right convert to Islam, speculated that the war on Iraq could help bridge the gap between traditional Arab nationalists and Islamists:

> The so-called nationalists and the so-called Islamists, who came closer together, and the war of America against Islam, because this is what the war against terrorism means, it's a war against Islam and war against the people of Iraq, because it is not a war against Saddam Hussein. It's a war against the people of Iraq. This war is now strengthening Islam and patriotism. In Iraq it's very interesting. So in the whole, I'm quite optimistic for the future. I think we will witness now the beginning of the end of Zionist-American power and the beginning of the end of Zionist-American world domination. Why, they say, "We want to liberate Iraq from a bloody regime." They should go to war first against the rogue and terrorist regime in occupied Palestine. They are the worst ones. They have made three wars of aggression against their neighbors. The Zionists have 200 atomic bombs. They have chemical and bacteriological arms. They have everything and nobody speaks about that.
>
> . . . Well, of course, now this whole development, now what happens in Iraq, it will strengthen in Europe, it will strengthen the new right, and also in the Muslim world, it will strengthen the so-called nationalists, who rediscover Islam. For me, it's quite clear, the result will be absolutely counterproductive for the Zionist-American regime in Washington.[42]

The ensuing guerrilla war in Iraq after the cessation of major combat operations supports Huber's predictions. Iraq was considered to be one of the most secular countries in the Middle East. Although it appears that most of the guerrilla fighters are Iraqis, there is some evidence that foreign fighters have been involved as well. The war in Iraq could conceivably work to bridge the gap between secular Arab/Iraqi nationalists and the Islamists and, in doing so, foster greater cooperation between the two camps. For example, after he became the bête noire of the U.S. government, Saddam Hussein displayed tendencies of abandoning pan-Arabism and increasingly appropriated the rhetoric of pan-Islam. While a fugitive in Iraq after the collapse of the Iraqi armed forces, Hussein released audiotapes in which he exhorted Iraqi "mujahideen" to wage jihad against American forces.[43] This development seemed to underlie statements from the Bush administration in December 2002, when representatives announced that the U.S. government had received credible information that Islamic extremists affiliated with al Qaeda had acquired the lethal VX nerve gas from Iraq.[44]

Instructive of the rapprochement between Arab nationalists and Islamists was a June 2004 meeting whose participants included Izzat Ibrahim al-Douri (the Iraqi vice president and deputy chairman of the Revolutionary Council before the war), his two sons, and Abu Musab al-Zarqawi, an al Qaeda affiliate believed to be responsible for many of the attacks on American forces in Iraq.[45] At the meeting, al-Douri and his sons pledged their support for al-Zarqawi. The atmosphere of the meeting was full of enthusiasm as al-Douri announced to al-Zarqawi, "You are the commander, and we are your soldiers." Afterward, hundreds of automatic weapons and large quantities of ammunition were distributed to the insurgents. Al-Douri has evaded coalition forces despite being designated as the king of clubs in the United States' "most wanted" deck of cards.[46] Many former regime loyalists have made common cause with the Islamists to oust the foreign invaders from Iraq.[47]

There are indications that the military situation in both Iraq and Afghanistan has developed in the direction of so-called fourth-generation war—that is, an evolved form of insurgency in which all available networks, including political, economic, social, and military, are employed to convince the enemy's decisionmakers that their strategic goals are unattainable and/or too costly. Characteristically, fourth-generation wars are protracted, as they are often measured in decades, rather than months or years. What is more, historically the United States has not fared well in such conflicts, as evidenced by its experiences in Vietnam, Lebanon, and Somalia.[48]

Despite the meeting of the minds on the issue of the Iraq war, is there an adequate basis for cooperation between militant Islam and the extreme right? The next chapter examines that issue in greater detail.

Prospects for Cooperation between Militant Islam and the Extreme Right

The extreme right is far from reaching a consensus on the issue of cooperation with militant Islam. Indeed, many in the movement are indifferent to this issue and have not even seriously pondered it. Still others are adamantly opposed to such a proposition for a variety of reasons, including tactical, ideological, religious, cultural, and racial/ethnic ones. However, one segment of the right has mulled over this issue and considers it worth exploring. Just as Osama bin Laden encourages Islamists around the world to view their regional conflicts not as isolated, parochial struggles, but rather as theaters of a larger war in defense of Islam against the West and Zionism, some elements of the extreme right view their individual nationalist movements as part of a larger struggle for white racial survival against a rising tide of nonwhite demographic expansion orchestrated by the forces of globalization and international Judaism. As Jeffrey Kaplan and Leonard Weinberg observed, faced with a similarity of conditions in both North America and Western Europe—for example, declining white birth rates, massive immigration from the Third World, diminishing life opportunities for working-class youth, and perceived cultural decadence—scattered elements of the extreme right around the globe found solace in a universalistic slogan of "white power."[1] Moreover, Internet technology enables disparate dissident groups to exchange ideas. Therefore, it is conceivable that increasingly some elements of the extreme right may come to identify with the anti-Zionist orientation of Islamism.

Thoughts on Cooperation

Although many in the extreme right were wary and skeptical of such an alliance, some still approached the proposition with an open mind. Although he decries nonwhite immigration into the United States and Europe, David

Duke has sought to build bridges with the Islamic world, as evidenced by his tour of the Middle East in 2002. He expounded on this issue for me.

There are some fundamental differences, obviously, between the Muslims and the Christian West and between their culture and our culture. But there's no question that globalism is an enemy of all cultures. In that way, I think there can be a friendship between many different nationalities and many different people of the world. People often say that America wants to rule the world, and it's just not true. It's not American interests that are doing this, it's Jewish interests that dominate the United States. This whole Iraq war is not about furthering the interests of the United States of America; it's about furthering the interests of Israel at the sacrifice of the true interests of the United States. We lost the twin towers because of our blind obedience to these Jewish supremacists and their political domination of this country, and the domination of our media and our support of Israel's criminal policies. That's why we lost our security in the country because we've pursued a policy which has not been in the interest of the United States of America. In fact it's been exactly the opposite of the interests of our people. . . .

. . . in the final analysis, to avoid the genocide of our people, we may have to enter into all sorts of strange alliances and combinations in the future, because at some point, our people have to survive. We have to have a homeland at some point. We have to have a land where our people can survive and thrive free and unfettered. I certainly wouldn't be in favor of this at this point, but at some point if something happened, and there were certain temporary alliances that would [have to] be formed. I could see how that could happen at some point in history. I see it a lot right now. White nationalists are very strong in Europe, and they have quite a strong support for the Palestinian cause. I think that is because there is a common problem there. And that problem is Jewish supremacism.

. . . The Jewish supremacists not only want supremacy on the West Bank of Palestine, they also want supremacy on the West Bank of the Potomac. They also want supremacy along the Thames. They want political, social, economic, and cultural supremacy in the Western World. I don't think that we can tolerate that supremacy and survive.[2]

Interestingly, Duke occasionally used the example of Islam to illustrate the way in which a seemingly obscure idea can rapidly catch on:

I think in the next decade we are going to see a tremendous shift in the ideas across the world. This whole world can change very quickly. Islam was the right philosophy at the right time for the Arabic people and it swept the Arab world in a single generation. Today with modern communication, the Internet, and all the rest, a new idea can sweep the Western world in literally a fortnight. I think we're moving closer and closer to a seminal shift in ideas and thoughts and even government in the world. I think we're seeing the beginning of it now with some of the movements in Europe standing up to the Jewish supremacists who are dominating the United States.[3]

Ahmed Huber, arguably the leading figure in the effort to bring about such an alliance, conceded that such an endeavor would be difficult, given the endemic racism among those in the extreme right. However, he still believed the differences between the two movements could be surmounted because of their mutual enemies, Zionism and American hegemony.

Well, it is not easy because on both sides there are difficulties coming from the past. You see on the so-called right wing extremist movement there has always been a certain amount of racism toward Muslim Arabs, or Turks like, for instance, in Europe. On the Islamic side there was a certain distrust toward right wing extremist movements, also because of that racism. Then there is a very important aspect, the racist doctrine, which was kept by some right-wing movements, is considered by Muslims to come out of the Jewish Old Testament, the Hebraic Bible. This is a very important aspect. Nobody ever talks about it, but now both sides meet. I have been in America meeting such groups from the so-called extreme right and I'm doing that for several reasons in Germany. I also meet such groups, and we are talking very frankly. I can explain the Muslim point of view, and they can explain their positions, and we find some common ground, which is quite interesting, both in the religious field, and of course, in the political field.

You see there are two great menaces, the power of Zionism in the United States over the United States and, as a consequence of this, the utterly hostile policies of the United States government, not only Mr. Bush, but Clinton before him, and lots of presidents before him against the Muslim world, which is of course especially the creation of the so-called state of Israel in the Palestinian part of Dar-al-Islam. This is the first thing I have to say.[4]

Huber's Swiss compatriot, Jürgen Graf, believed that there is much common ground between the two movements and thus the potential for collaboration. He was especially sanguine about the potential of Holocaust revisionism as a vehicle through which to foster cooperation:

While revisionists greatly differ in their political and religious beliefs, they are, of course, all anti-Zionist, because the "Holocaust" lie is essentially a Zionist lie, and because the Zionist organizations are the driving force behind antirevisionist repression. . . . Therefore, the revisionists and militant Islam have good reasons to cooperate, as they are facing the same adversary.

The far right, to which many revisionists belong, certainly has a lot in common with radical Islam. Both movements cherish spiritual values; they reject materialism and globalism, and as the United States is the vanguard of materialism and globalism (plus the stronghold of Zionism and the protector of Israel), both the far right and radical Islam have good reasons to regard it as their enemy.

. . . If America becomes a police state, the far right will be persecuted anyway, whether it cooperates with militant Islam or not. A pretext for repression can always be found. As for the revisionists, we hope to cooperate with Islamic movements, or indeed Islamic governments, as this would serve our mutual interest. The Achilles' heel of revisionism is its financial weakness. With a few million dollars, which we unfortunately do not have, we could massively spread our message by means of booklets, leaflets, radio broadcasts, etc. On the other hand, we can give the Arabs and Muslims a terrible weapon in their struggle against Israel and Zionism. This weapon is historical truth. It is regrettable that those Arab states which sincerely oppose Zionism have spent huge amounts of money on weapons, while 1 percent of these sums would have been sufficient to spread revisionism and thus inflict irreparable damage on the Zionist state. I trust that it is not yet too late to correct this error.[5]

Steven Emerson, the director of the Investigative Project on Terrorism, offered his assessment of the potential for an alliance between the two movements:

Well, I think rhetorically and ideologically you're definitely seeing an overlap and a cross-fertilization. . . . I think in Europe you see even more cross-fertilization between neo-Nazi groups sometimes and the Islamic militant groups. We've seen now a number of neo-Nazis convert to Islam.

Now operationally, I don't know how extensive there will be an alliance, because at least from the Islamic militant community, to really have access to the high-level operators, you have to have pedigree that these guys [right-wing extremists] would not have. On the other hand, I could envisage scenarios where there is [cooperation] when it comes to sharing resources, particularly in terms of Islamic militants perhaps needing weapons or explosives, or technical expertise without having to rely on operators themselves.[6]

A frequent refrain was that cooperation with Islam was possible, at least in theory, as long as Muslims stayed out of Western nations: "we are separate and both of us would like to stay that way; we need have no conflict," Dr. William Pierce commented.[7] In a similar vein, John Tyndall, the former leader of the British National Party (BNP), thought collaboration was possible, but only under the strictest conditions that would recognize separation and self-determination on both sides:

> In the long-term perspective I believe that we should establish strict lines of demarcation between the white and Islamic Worlds: we stay out of their lands and they stay out of ours. In the short term, certain collaboration could be possible—though there would be no justification whatever in such white organizations collaborating with Islamic groups carrying out acts of terror against this country or any other. Inasmuch as the Islamic World opposes U.S.-led globalism and Zionism, and we do also, there could be areas in which collaboration could be of mutual benefit (with the proviso that I have given) but all this would only be as short-term means towards the desired end of separation of the two worlds. That said, the whole subject of collaboration should be approached with very great care.
>
> I personally do not see Islam as any threat to Britain as long as the ethnic groups bringing it here are excluded from this country. In other words, the threat is racial, not religious. If nonwhite ethnic groups are removed from this country (or remove themselves), the tiny few white Muslims left here would present no problem, and Islam would probably evaporate in the course of time. The same would apply to the United States and other white countries.
>
> So, in summary, Islam need not be a threat, but neither should it be considered an ally, except in the short-term sense that I have mentioned—and that would depend on a number of strict conditions.[8]

Likewise, Nick Griffin, the present leader of the BNP, indicated that an alliance might be acceptable if it were based on an alliance of nations rather than an intranational coalition within Britain:

> On a global scale, I think the long-term prospects are good. Nationalist governments in Europe will need trading partners and oil suppliers; Muslim states need high technology. Both we and they share a number of ideological/moral fundamentals, such as opposition to usury. And, of course, we will also be pariahs as far as the likes of Bush or his successors are concerned. Locally, here in Britain, though, not a hope in hell. They want

to Islamify our country; their young thugs continually launch low-level ethnic cleansing attacks on our people. We'll gain power by opposing such things, not by cuddling up to them. "My enemy's enemy is my friend" cannot apply when one is looking at Islam; it's a dangerous and insatiably aggressive imperialism in its own right.[9]

Just after 9/11, Nick Griffin supported a crackdown on Islamic extremists in Europe and publicly called for British military action against Osama bin Laden and his terrorist network. However, he tempered this support by demanding that efforts be made to eradicate what he believed are the root causes of terrorism: support for the Israeli oppression of Palestinians and the blockade of Iraq, which has resulted in substantial human suffering in that country.[10] Furthermore, he derided British prime minister Tony Blair as a "poodle" who slavishly obeyed President George W. Bush.

In a strange twist to this story, the BNP launched a joint anti-Islam campaign with Sikhs and Hindus residing in Britain. Griffin reportedly reached out to Ammo Singh, a Sikh activist in West London. The two even went so far as to pose together for a public handshake. Among the aims of this campaign was to counter the "politically correct lie that Islam is a religion of peace."[11] According to the British antifascist journal, *Searchlight,* Griffin has met with Hindu extremist organizations, including Shere-e-Pubjab (the Lions of Pubjab) and the Arya Samaj Movement.[12] Griffin commented on his recent efforts to reach out to Hindus in Britain:

> Very simply, after I said on a major national TV show that the riots and attacks on non-Islamics were "not an Asian problem, but a Muslim problem," we were contacted by a number of Sikhs delighted that a British politician had bothered to make the distinction. Since then, we have worked with two in particular to produce a pamphlet and audiocassette aimed at educating people as to the "nature of the beast." A new law imposing up to seven years in prison for telling the truth on this matter has, however, somewhat curtailed such initiatives. Rhajinder Singh, however, continues to write a regular column in our newspaper.[13]

Griffin's campaign against Islam was something of a political turnaround for him. In the late 1980s he and Derek Holland split from the National Front to form the International Third Position, which sought to find common ground with the radical Muslim regimes of Muammar Qaddafi and the Ayatollah Ruhollah Khomeini.[14]

Several other representatives of the extreme right expressed the view that they were not amenable to the notion of an alliance with Islam. Norman

Olson, a militia leader in Michigan, even offered the services of the militia to President Bush in fighting Islamist terrorism on the home front.

Jared Taylor of American Renaissance saw little commonality between the two movements and hence little basis for cooperation:

> [The chances of cooperation] are slim to none. Nonmilitant Muslims come to the West because Europe and the United States are successful countries and theirs are failures. Anyone who wishes to preserve the racial and cultural heritage of the West must prefer that these immigrants stay home. Militant Muslims come to the West with the unconcealed desire to spread Islam. Especially in Europe, clerics openly preach the establishment of theocracies that would be the death knell of the West.
>
> It would be possible to debate the points you suggest on which Western nationalists and Islamic radicals agree—American foreign policy, the media, Zionism, globalization—but whatever convergence of views there might be are not the basis for an alliance. First, even if there were fundamental agreement with radical Muslims on any question of importance, cooperation with a movement that has shown itself capable of large-scale civilian killings is out of the question. Second, even with the most highly developed sense of realpolitik, it is nearly impossible to work fruitfully with people whose ultimate objectives are radically different from one's own.[15]

The most thoroughgoing critique I received on the prospect of an alliance between militant Islam and the extreme right came from Steven Barry, the former leader of the now-defunct Special Forces Underground. His analysis suggests that he has given considerable thought to the issue:

> The notion of cooperation between the "extreme right" and militant Islam falls flat on its face the instant it is examined in the light of reality rather than fantasy. The theory contends that, given a laundry list of supposed "issues" common between the "extreme right" and militant Islam, the two might cooperate on the "terror" side in the "war on terror." But nobody asks the simple question, "What does the 'extreme right' have to offer militant Islam?"
>
> Militant Islam (as "movement" writ large) possesses every quality absent in the "extreme right." Militant Islam, on the whole, has (i) organization (ii) hierarchy (iii) authority (iv) money and logistics, (v) media (vi) liaison, if not integration, between various national factions (vii) popular support, and (vii) the covert support—if not clandestine cooperation—of at least critical elements within indigenous governments.

In contrast, the "extreme right" (in the United States) is (i) disorganized and chaotic (ii) leaderless, fractionalized and defiant of subordination (iii) anti-authoritarian, more often than not to the point of anarchic (iv) bankrupt and lacking anything remotely resembling logistics, (v) voiceless (vi) uncooperative and more often than not hostile in their mutual relations (vii) utterly bereft of popular support—indeed "the People" are hostile toward them, and (viii) without the least sympathy in any government at any level.

Yet the theory ignores those obvious respective realities and instead concentrates upon another, more elaborate fantasy, *id est,* that members of the "extreme right," in return for financial support for their "cause," would serve as tradecraft surrogates in the targeting process for Arab terrorists who are incapable of performing those functions without attracting suspicion. Nobody who has done such things as targeting and mission planning (including all their associated subsidiary tasks and support requirements), and who knows the "extreme right" from the inside, would entertain such a notion for one instant.

But one issue is missing (or deliberately ignored) from the scenario's incredibleness. That issue is religion. I understand that, these days, talking about religion is unpopular. Nevertheless it cannot be avoided for the simple reason that militant Islam is engaged in jihad—holy war—against both Western secularism and Jewish Zionism. . . .

Militant Islam again possesses everything the "extreme right" utterly lacks. Militant Islam, writ large, is (i) religious (ii) militant Islam as we witness it today IS classical, traditional Islam resurrected (iii) its adherents have faith [albeit in a lie] (vi) its adherents are willing to die, even "martyr" themselves, for their faith (vii) the catalyst of militant Islam is not Jews *qua* Jews, rather Jews qua Zionism, and (viii) militant Islam is contemptuous of Western civilization because the West is indifferent to religion altogether— with the inevitable democracy, moral squalidness, ideological hypocrisy and societal anarchy that follow. . . .

So, between militant Islam and the "extreme right," where is the common cause? Jews? Not really. Jews have always flitted and floated about in any traditional Islamic society without harassment; indeed, as honored guests. It is doubtful that historical Islamism, during its rise, would have ever made any headway at all without Jews to grease the skids and open city gates to their armies—or, it is rumored, write the Koran for them. . . . Nor do I see Zionism as a common cause between militant Islam and the "extreme right." The "extreme right" had no direct experience with Zionism; their objections to it are purely academic. They have no more empathy for the plight of Palestinians than they do about the persecution of Sudanese or Indonesian Christians by militant Islam. For the "extreme right," Zionism and Palestine are foils for their hatred of Jews *qua* Jews (by way of illustration, we do not witness members of the "extreme right" rushing to Palestine to actually "fight" the Jews to stop Zionism in its tracks—that would be too real). On the other hand, Islam deals with Zionism close and personal on a daily basis.

When we strip away the surface glitter of the matter, the only common ground between militant Islam and the "extreme right" (in the United States) is their common hatred of American-invented religious indifferentism [i.e., the belief that all religions are of equal validity]—for entirely different reasons. The former because they rightfully object to the United States smearing the face of Islam with our secularism; the latter because the official secularism of the United States refuses to deify their genes and raise their race to a state religion. There is no basis there for cooperation.[16]

Several far-right leaders in Europe spoke out against Islam as well. For example, Italian prime minister Silvio Berlusconi remarked that Western civilization was superior to Islamic culture: "We must be aware of the superiority of our civilization, a system that has guaranteed well-being, respect for human rights and—in contrast to Islamic countries—respect for religious and political rights. . . . The West will continue to conquer peoples, like it conquered communism."[17] Most European leaders sought to distance themselves from Berlusconi's remarks, so as not to offend the sensibilities of Islamic countries with which they would have to work as part of an antiterror coalition. His remarks drew quick condemnation from the Arab League. Bruno Megret, formerly of the French National Front, warned of an "Islamic fifth column" inside France. He claimed that the large number of North African immigrants in French cities and suburbs could pose a threat to France like that the 9/11 hijackers posed to the United States.[18]

Immigration

Large Muslim immigrant populations could profoundly affect European politics and society in upcoming years. The two issues that would obviously divide militant Islam and the extreme right are specifically, immigration and religion. In fact, the immigration issue would appear to be the chief catalyst for the success of far-right parties in elections in recent years. Both North America and

Western Europe are experiencing substantial immigration from Muslim countries. A major fear that inhibits cooperation between the extreme right and Islam in Europe is that the former fears demographic inundation by the latter. By the year 2000, roughly 4 million Muslims resided in France, 2.5 to 3 million in Germany, and nearly 2 million in Great Britain.[19] Furthermore, Muslims have some of the highest birthrates in the world.[20] Muslims now total roughly 2–3 million in the United States and 15 million in the European Union; they now outnumber Jews and have become the second-largest religious community in the latter.[21] Ultimately, these demographic trends could significantly alter both the racial/ethnic and religious textures of these two geographic regions.

There is evidence to suggest that Muslim migration to Europe has made governments there increasingly skittish about responding to Islamic extremism, both at home and abroad. For example, France's opposition to U.S. foreign policy toward Iraq was arguably motivated in large part to appease its Muslim population.[22] What is more, European governments often ignore U.S. sanctions on countries such as Iran, Iraq, and Libya. There are historical analogs for this occurrence. For example, Pat Buchanan draws a parallel to the United States during the period from the 1850 until World War I, when the Irish, whose votes were decisive in states such as New York, effectively held U.S. foreign policy toward Great Britain hostage.[23]

Of course, immigration is a salient issue among the extreme right in the United States as well. Among the most publicly outspoken critics of the U.S. "open borders" immigration policy has been Pat Buchanan, who hails from the more respectable wing of the paleo-conservative right. He warned that uncontrolled immigration threatens to deconstruct the traditional American nation. As a result, the United States is becoming a conglomeration of people with almost nothing in common—"not history, heroes, language, culture, faith, or ancestors"—a "country nothing more than an economy." He predicted that balkanization will follow. According to Buchanan, the West faces its gravest challenge since the Black Death, which ravaged Europe in the fourteenth century.[24] Not unlike Dr. William L. Pierce, he imputes the countercultural revolution to opinion-making elites in the media and the fields of arts and entertainment. Moreover, he also accuses the "revolution" of seeking to morally disarm and paralyze the people of the West. However, he does not refer to any overarching Jewish conspiracy, as did Pierce.

Buchanan sees the demographic issue as an important factor in future politics in the Middle East as well. As he pointed out, demographic disparities between the Jews in Israel and its Arab neighbors make the future existence of the state of Israel increasingly tenuous. In the year 2000, there were roughly 6.2 million people in Israel, but there were 116.2 million people in the Arab nations of Jordan, Egypt, Syria, Lebanon, and Saudi Arabia. Demographic projections for the year 2025 are 8.3 million and 178.4 million, respectively. Furthermore, demographic projections inside Israel proper could threaten the Jewish character of the Israeli state. According to current trends, by roughly 2025, there will be approximately 6 million Jews and 16 million Palestinians living in the West Bank, Gaza, Jordan, and Israel. By 2050, the figures will be 7 million and 25 million, respectively. Thus Buchanan argues that Israel faces an existential threat in the future from demographics.[25]

As Samuel Huntington observed, in some ways the extreme right in Europe and the Islamist parties in Muslim countries are mirror images of each other. Both attacked the foreign influences in their lands and exploited economic grievances, particularly unemployment. In most instances, both the Islamist and extreme right parties tended to do better in local than in national elections. Furthermore, the Muslim and European political establishments responded similarly to this development. In Muslim countries, the governments tended to become more Islamic. In European countries, the parties adopted the rhetoric and some of the anti-immigration positions of the extreme right parties.[26]

Despite this seeming antagonism between European nativists and Muslims, the relationship between the two is ambivalent. Take, for example, Jörg Haider, whose relationship with Islam has been mixed. On the one hand, he and his Austrian Freedom Party (FPO) have called for severely restricting asylum rights for immigrants as a means of preventing terrorism.[27] On the other hand, Haider has occasionally exchanged acts of goodwill with Muslims. For example, Libyan leader Muammar Qaddafi ordered the deposit of $25 million into a bank in Carinthia in an effort to alleviate the sting of economic sanctions imposed on Austria by the European Union after the FPO joined a governing coalition in 2000. Haider described Qaddafi's deposit as "Christmas for Austria." And on two occasions, Haider visited Tripoli and met with Qaddafi. Previously, he arranged a deal with Libya to sell gas to Carinthia at a discount.[28]

David Myatt, however, took issue with the various far-right politicians who seek to gain political capital by making an issue of Muslim immigrants:

The people who make political capital out of such things and who thus strike an anti-Muslim pose—such as the BNP and Le Pen—are, in my opinion, acting contrary to honor and reason. They fail to understand their own Aryan values, as they fail to comprehend the true global situation, which is of an increasing world-tyranny, the new world order. In addition, the nationalism they propagate is outdated, [and] anachronistic . . .

Such political groups, and the people who lead them, are of the past, whereas folk culture and National Socialism are of the future: an expression of what is needed to create civilized, human, numinous societies where honor is the criteria for personal behavior and social conduct.

Seen in this way, Islam is an ally. We need an Aryan homeland: this does not mean we need the old nation-states. We need to begin again, with a new way of life, a new society, an entirely new nation. In brief, we must be the founders of a new nation. Once this principle is accepted, the movement will shed an enormous amount of excessive and unnecessary baggage. In respect of America, for instance, that would mean creating a homeland in one or more States, or even in a part of one state. It is not size which matters; it is creating a pure Aryan society, which means one where we can live among our own kind according to our own laws and customs, and where our Aryan culture, our Aryan way of life, can flourish. . . .

The reality is that we both have the same enemies: the materialistic capitalist system, and the cabal who run the NWO [new world order]. It is in both our interests to fight and destroy the NWO. If there were a nationalist or National Socialist revolution in America this would be to the great advantage of the Muslims. . . . Both the authentic Islam of the Jihadi movements, as exemplified by groups such as the Base of Jihad, and genuine National Socialism—as exemplified in my own NS [National Socialist] writings—are numinous alternatives to the insolent, materialistic, dishonorable tyranny of the NWO.[29]

Ahmed Huber weighed in on the immigration issue. In his mind, there is a great deal of misunderstanding between both parties that could be rectified:

Yes, there is a big misunderstanding here on both sides. For instance in Europe, in the last thirty to forty years, there was an artificial immigration by Muslims into Europe, which was organized by the West itself. They needed manpower. They needed foreign workers. For instance, millions of Turks and people from the Balkans, Muslims, came to Western Europe. It was in large part artificial. It was not an economic necessity. Europe could have organized its labor market in a different way. . . . And, of course, many Muslims left their countries because their countries were under the control of regimes which had been established by the West. . . .

Many Muslims who come, their grandparents, or their parents, they did not really successfully integrate in Western society for a simple reason. They did not know, or they did not respond, to a very important advice from the prophet Muhammad, *sallallahu aalayhi wa sallam*, peace be upon him.

The prophet Mohamed, the last messenger of Allah, has given to the Muslims fourteen centuries ago, Mohamed said, if you go to stay with the Romi—and the Romi is the collective notion of the West, it was the

Romans, the Greeks, the people, from the West—if you go to the West, live in a Romi culture, in a Romi civilization, behave like the Romis in all things except those which Allah has specifically and clearly forbidden to you. That means dress like the Romi. Learn their languages. Behave like them always, except don't eat pork. Don't drink alcohol. Don't run after their women. Don't do these things, which Allah has forbidden you [to do] clearly.

. . . Now we have a new generation of young Muslims, which are called the third generation, who grew up, who have become secularized, and in a certain way, Europeanized. But at the same time now, they rediscover Islam, but they have a different approach to Islam, not the one of their grandparents or their parents. They have an approach of young Europeans, who look for religion, who look for moral values, for social values. They find them in Islam, but with a new, very open-minded reading of the Koran and the Sunnah, that means the social practices of prophet Mohamed. This is a new phenomenon and we have something that we now call European Islam, which is developing among the young people.[30]

Likewise, the Swiss revisionist Jürgen Graf saw immigration as a potential wedge issue between the two movements:

Islam is a religion worthy of respect but fundamentally alien to European culture and thought. For this reason, and partly also for racial reasons, the far right resolutely opposes mass immigration from Muslim countries and demands that most Muslim immigrants be repatriated. Incidentally, one of the driving forces behind the suicidal immigration policy of the Western world have always been the Zionist organizations. . . . The Zionists want to use the immigrants as a tool to weaken and ultimately destroy white European society and culture. But this strategy might backfire as the Muslims are almost all anti-Zionist and despise the Jewish-inspired "values" of our materialistic society.

Intelligent and honest Arabs and Muslims will understand that we Europeans have the right to defend our identity and heritage. I remind you that Jean-Marie Le Pen, the well-known French nationalist and critic of immigration, was one of the very few European politicians who staunchly opposed the first Gulf War and the murderous embargo against Iraq.

The far right and Islam can (and should) become tactical allies in their struggle against a common foe. However, it would be senseless to deny that they could become bitter enemies if immigration from Muslim countries continues, as the repatriation of the Muslim (and other Non-European) immigrants will be one of the main tasks facing future nationalist European governments who will defend the interests of the indigenous

European population. But for Muslim mass immigration, there would be no reason whatsoever for hostility between European nationalists and Muslim countries. As you know, Adolf Hitler greatly admired Islam, and the grand mufti of Jerusalem spent the war in Berlin.[31]

Kevin MacDonald believed that there are too many differences between the two movements to permit any enduring collaboration:

They do share views on [some] issues, but I doubt that they will see eye to eye on other issues. Especially problematic is the desire by racial nationalists to attain an ethnically homogeneous society for themselves in America. They might cooperate with Muslims against Jewish interests and the other issues you mention, but ultimately their political aims (such as restricting non-European immigration to the U.S.) differ too much to result in a long-term alliance.[32]

Sam Francis also believed that an alliance with militant Islam was infeasible. Once again, the immigration issue loomed large in his analysis:

There may be some white nationalists who would try to make common cause with radical Islam. I would not. Ultimately, Islam and especially radical Islam is as much the enemy of the white West as any other nonwhite group or force, part of "the rising tide of color" that Lothrop Stoddard[33] foresaw nearly a century ago and part of the clash of civilizations that Samuel Huntington has recently discussed. The conflict is due not so much to any sinister motivations on the part of whites or nonwhites but rather is just part of their racial and cultural constitutions. It is in my view an irrepressible conflict, and as Stoddard made clear, whites have the disadvantage of harboring a fifth column among them that is on the side of the racial enemy. Having said that, it is also true that Muslims/Arabs cannot do the West much harm unless they come here as immigrants. I therefore have no quarrel with Islamic peoples, countries, and cultures, but I do think they should not be permitted to immigrate into white, Western countries. If it were not for immigration, the conflict between Islam and the West would remain dormant, as it did for centuries before they started coming here.

As far as the prospects for such an alliance, apart from my own views, I think it is unlikely. Some white nationalists tried to gain support from Arab states over the years and always failed. If you look at most of the people who call themselves white nationalists, you can understand why the Arabs refused to support them.

. . . I believe Islam is a greater threat than potential ally. The problem from immigration is much more serious in Europe and Britain than it is here. Islam has been an enemy of the West since its beginnings; insofar as it is taken seriously as a religion, its anti-Westernism is plain and ineradicable. Moreover, it is also, much like Christianity but even more so, antiracial. It celebrates the mixture of peoples and races under Allah; apart from Arabism itself, there seems to be no racial identity in any Muslim country I know of. American "Black Islam" is an aberration and an exception.[34]

In contrast, Mike Piper supported the notion of cooperation between the two movements, at least in principle, despite the various obstacles to cooperation:

The immigration/religion/cultural conflict is there and will be there for as long as mankind exists, and this will certainly play a part in preventing any kind of tactical alliance, really, between the Arab/Muslim world and the revisionist/right-wing elements.

This is not to say that I oppose a tactical alliance. Far from it. I have always maintained that all opponents of Zionism and heavy-handed aspects of Jewish political dominance should, each for their own reasons, form an alliance. In that respect, I've come, for example, to admire the thinking of the late François Genoud, who worked assiduously—to the dismay of the Zionist elite—to bring about such an alliance.

Personally, I believe that Islam and the Arab peoples should be potential allies, but I do not believe, based on my experience with the activities of people such as Jared Taylor, for example, that there can ever be a genuine alliance on a broad scale.[35]

Despite the potential wedge issue of immigration, there are still areas on which common ground can be found, some of which are explored in the next section.

The Palestinian Issue

Despite the overriding concern with nonwhite immigrants, the extreme right still sees Jews as the principal enemy of white Aryan peoples. Although militant Islam generally eschews racialist themes, its version of anti-Zionism parallels in many ways the anti-Semitism of the extreme right. The narratives of both movements often charge that a Jewish conspiracy is undermining their societies, not with the sword but through "cultural poisoning." Alien values are inserted in a deliberate attempt to defile the host societies. According to the standard extreme right narrative, the chief aim of the Jewish conspiracy is to defile the white race through miscegenation, thus ultimately leading to its extinction as a distinct racial group.[36] In doing so, the Jews will remove their most dangerous rivals, because nonwhites are generally viewed as posing a less serious threat than white racialists to the welfare of Jews.[37] Using a similar narrative, but in the framework of religion, Islamists argue that Jews seek first and foremost to destroy Islam because it constitutes the strongest moral challenge to perceived Jewish perfidy. Both right-wing extremists and Islamists often invoke the status of the Palestinians as a paradigm of what awaits them on the horizon if their people do not act swiftly.

The Palestinian issue is increasingly a topic of shared interest between the extreme right and militant Islam. Various commentators have remarked that Osama bin Laden has "hijacked" the Palestinian issue to legitimate his movement and gain support from Muslim and Arab sympathizers.[38] Some quarters of the extreme right have championed the Palestinian cause as well. For example, the German expatriate and revisionist Ernst Zündel once lamented the condition of Palestinians and linked it to the historical primacy of the Holocaust in the West:

> The poor Palestinians are the most abused victims of this "Holocaust" propaganda tool. What is being done to them behind the shield of "Holocaust victim" status is barbaric and unforgivable and makes me want to hang my head in shame as a white man in the year 2000. It is a reflection of how emasculated the West has become, how utterly morally bankrupt—and we should be ashamed that we don't rain paratroopers down on that place and end the carnage caused by that miserable statelet once and for all. I ask God to forgive me for my own impotence in that Palestinian question.[39]

As mentioned in Chapter 6, in an effort to solicit financial support from Arabs and Muslims for his Holocaust revisionist efforts, Zündel wrote a small pamphlet titled "The West, War, and Islam." He argued that Muslims could get a better return on investment from funding Holocaust revisionism than military weapons. As he explained, "Take the Holocaust away, and you will have severed the financial water well that feeds an evil oligarchy and repressive system!"[40]

At times it is difficult to determine if this concern for the Palestinians is sincere when their Semitic racial category would qualify them as "mud people" in the eyes of many extremists. Be that as it may, quite a few extreme right commentators have expressed admiration for the dedication and selflessness of Palestinian militants. Some of the more extremist figures in the movement have toned down their racialist rhetoric in the aftermath of 9/11 and paradoxically sound very similar to left-wing critics as they decry American imperialism, Israeli aggression, and discriminatory policies against Palestinians in Israel. The most strident in this regard was the late Dr. William L. Pierce. In February 2002 he eulogized Wafa Idris, the first female Palestinian suicide bomber. His comments illustrate several attitudes common in the extreme right milieu: a growing contempt for the American government and indeed "average Americans" (whom Pierce frequently derided as "couch potatoes" and "lemmings"), intense anti-Semitism, and an increasing tendency to identify with Arab and Islamic militants:

> Two weeks ago, on January 27, another of these Palestinian "terrorists" carried out a suicide bombing in Jerusalem, killing one Israeli and wounding 100 others. The bomber was Wafa Idris, a 27-year-old Palestinian woman who lived in Ramallah and worked as a volunteer nurse, riding in ambulances and providing emergency care in field hospitals for Palestinians wounded by Israeli soldiers. Wafa was no wild-eyed Muslim fundamentalist or fanatical Palestinian nationalist. She was not involved in politics and was not even considered to be a Muslim by her friends and family. She didn't even wear the traditional head covering for Palestinian women. She was described by everyone who knew her as a friendly, open, caring, and fun-loving young woman. She used her spare time to give free lessons in language and mathematics to children in the Ramallah refugee camp. She simply had had enough of seeing her people humiliated and brutalized and murdered by Jews. She had had enough Palestinian children die in her arms after they were shot by Israeli soldiers. She had taken care of enough Palestinian children who had lost an eye or a leg at the hands of the Israelis. She herself had been shot at repeatedly by Israeli soldiers while she was on ambulance duty and was wearing her Red Crescent uniform, and on three occasions she had been wounded by rubber bullets. Israelis consider shooting at Palestinian medical personnel to be a sport. On January 27 Wafa had had enough and decided to hit back. The spokesmen for America's controlled media consider her a "terrorist." So do George Bush and Donald Rumsfeld and John Ashcroft and Dick Cheney, and all of them vow to continue their war against terrorism and against terrorists such as Wafa Idris. And the mindless, TV-watching yahoos with little American flags on their cars cheer the Bush team on. To them also, Wafa was a terrorist.
>
> Well, maybe so. But let me tell you, when America fights against idealistic young women like Wafa Idris and for murderous thugs like Ariel Sharon, it should be clear to everyone but the most clueless, flag-waving

yahoos that we are fighting on the wrong side. And let me tell you something else: people everywhere in the world are beginning to understand this: not just Palestinians; not just Muslims; not just people who don't like Jews, but ordinary people everywhere who have any sort of clue about what's actually happening in the world, people everywhere who pay attention to the news and care about more than the latest ball-game scores.[41]

At least rhetorically, Kevin Alfred Strom of the National Alliance, Pierce's successor as host of the American Dissident Voices program, has been in the forefront of building bridges with extremists from across the political spectrum. He occasionally makes veiled entreaties to the Palestinians and other Arabs, as evidenced by an excerpt from one of his American Dissident Voices broadcasts:

It is not white separatists who are the violent threat to the nonwhite races. It is the Jewish establishment, which ordered the burning alive of 100,000 nonwhites who were peacefully retreating from Kuwait after their surrender in 1991. It is the Jewish power structure, not white separatists, which routinely pumps Palestinian children full of bullets, tortures them, and keeps them behind barbed wire in what ought to be called concentration camps. It isn't white people who commit the drive-by shootings and drug murders on our streets, but the Jewish establishment which has supported the browning of America has a lot to answer for in that regard. . . . It's the Jewish establishment that insists that no white nation on Earth can keep itself white. That's genocide. Palestinians and whites are in the same boat; it's just that many whites don't know it yet.[42]

With respect to the Palestinian issue, David Duke was ahead of the curve. He has written sympathetically on the Palestinians for many years now. Duke cited in his book *My Awakening* what he believed was the hypocrisy in the disparate treatment of Jews and Arabs by the U.S. government on the issue of terrorism. He was quick to point out that the nation of Israel was created after a long struggle, which included acts that would be defined today as terrorism. Moreover, many of the Israelis who participated in these acts—for example, Menachem Begin and Yitzhak Shamir—went on to become Israeli heads of state. For effect, Duke recounted in gory detail previous Israeli atrocities, including the massacres at Deir Yassin in 1948 and the Israeli-supported massacres in the Chatila and Sabra refugee camps in Lebanon in 1982. Further, he mentioned previous acts of duplicity, including the Lavon affair, the attack on the USS *Liberty*, and the Jonathan Pollard spy scandal. Finally, Duke decried the Israeli government's discriminatory policies against Palestinians residing in

Israel and its effort to preserve the Jewish character of the nation, while at the same time, Jewish organizations in the United States are in the forefront of multiculturalism and immigration liberalization.[43] He offered his thoughts on the Palestinian issue to me in an interview:

> I think that the Palestinian issue goes right to the core of what my philosophy has always been. That all people have a right to control their own affairs, the right to their own independence, the right to freedom, and the right to preserve their way of life, their culture, their heritage, their traditions, everything that makes them individual peoples. And that's certainly the very essence of what I believe, so it's no departure for me. Now, yes, my first concern is obviously European Americans. But the principle is there for all people. I think that the Palestinian issue is tremendously illustrative of what Jewish supremacism is around the world. It's amazing to see the same Jewish media moguls promote open borders for Americans, pushing for support for Israel, which has immigration limited to only people of Jewish descent. And these same Jewish media moguls in America that are opposed to the right of citizens to carry guns and advocating gun control for Americans, the same Jewish moguls will support Israel where every Jewish citizen carries a submachine gun if he wants. These same Jewish moguls push against European Americans preserving their communities, their schools. These same Jewish moguls support Israel, which has strict segregation for Jews and non-Jews in housing, in school, and even whole villages. I mean it's amazing, the level of segregation that exists in the nation of Israel. And there is no outcry.[44]

For his part, Tom Metzger of White Aryan Resistance voiced skepticism about the extreme right's sincerity with respect to the Palestinian issue. In his opinion, the words of support are often feigned and disingenuous. Furthermore, he was wary of such an alliance with militant Islam:

> I still feel that this is something that has to be handled very carefully because, first of all, we must demand the exclusion of the Muslim nonwhite people from North America. But we also realize that it is because of our own government and transnational corporate meddling that causes people to flee their countries and so forth because we supported and financed the dictators that caused the problems in the first place. But it's a very sticky situation. As far as the Palestinians are concerned, one can have sympathies with them now and then, but on the other hand, we feel too

that the Arabs could get together and solve that problem fairly simply. Arabs are the types that are very difficult to deal with. It's very difficult for them to deal even with each other. They have a very tough time even coming to any serious accommodation with themselves.

I believe that the white races must push the Muslims back and keep them out of Europe. . . . We want nothing to do with the Muslim religion. And since the Muslim religion, like some other religions, promotes miscegenation and race mixing, then it is an enemy. But even though something may be an enemy, we can have certain sympathies for some of its problems. Now some of the right-wing [people] have gone a little overboard with this, and there's a lot of disingenuous propaganda floating around by people who really don't like Jews, but they use the Palestinians as simply an excuse. "Oh look at the poor Palestinians." What they really would like to say is, "We hate the Jews," but they don't have the guts to say it. I don't think that they are serious at all about aiding the Palestinian people.[45]

After an initial flurry of activism on the part of the extreme right in the immediate months following 9/11, the movement went into retreat. As explained in Chapter 6, many activists were arrested and even sent to prison, which has had a chilling effect on others in the movement. However, by May 2004, the extreme right had demonstrated that it could still rebound, even under adversity. In a rare display of unity, many of its most prominent representatives gathered in New Orleans, Louisiana, for a homecoming for David Duke, who had recently been released from a federal prison. At the conference, Duke announced the "New Orleans Protocol," by which the participants would endeavor to work together to achieve common objectives.[46]

During a panel discussion near the end of the conference, members considered the prospect of an alliance with Islam. Duke averred that the Muslim world was the most steadfast opponent of "Jewish supremacism." As such, he believed that an alliance was appropriate. He called for greater understanding between Christianity and Islam, but he added the proviso that the nations of the Western world should not open their borders to Muslims from foreign lands. Further, Duke speculated that the extreme right could draw upon the resources and influence of Muslim nations that are hostile to Israel. Therefore, creating a common front could be mutually beneficial under certain conditions.

Kevin Alfred Strom of the National Alliance agreed with much of Duke's analysis but added that Islam was an expansionist religion that currently threatened much of the Western world. Support, however, would be appropriate for those Muslims that remained in their own countries and opposed Israel. With these Muslims, he found room for common ground and went so far as to say, "We are all Palestinians now." Don Black of Stormfront also saw merit in such an alliance but added that it was a delicate issue that must be approached with extreme caution.

Sam Dickson, an attorney from Atlanta who has long been involved with groups such as American Renaissance and the Council of Conservative Citizens, was averse to an alliance with Islam. He countered that the notion of receiving substantial support from the Islamic world was a pipe dream of which the extreme right should disabuse itself. Dickson reminded the panelists of the history of some of Islam's encounters with the West, most notably in the Balkans, which resulted in the oppression of Christian Slavs and Greeks. He urged the other panelists and the audience to strive for self-reliance in their efforts and not entertain alliances with outsiders. Even more troubling for Dickson were the legal and public relations consequences that could result from such an alliance. As he noted, it would be a ticket to public relations oblivion and would probably lead to an indictment for violation of a foreign agent registration law. Yet Dickson acknowledged that "white nationalists" could learn from the example of Muslims. Furthermore, they could use the plight of the Palestinians as a weapon with which to delegitimize Israel and the Jews.[47]

Conclusion: Anti-Americanism Conjoined with Anti-Semitism

In many parts of the world, the United States is both envied and feared. Thus anti-Americanism can be explained in large part by American power. As Walter Laqueur observed, great powers are rarely loved. Thus hatred is a consequence of being great and powerful.[48] What is more, the present American empire has no analog in modern history. By comparison, both the Spanish Empire of the sixteenth to eighteenth centuries and the British Empire of the nineteenth century had to contend with challenges from other empires or great powers. By contrast, the United States does not confront a great power today. One would have to go back to the era of the Roman Empire to find such a dominant empire on a global scale.[49] As James Kurth noted, the threat of Islamic terrorism has added a sense of urgency to the new growth of American empire. The specter of terrorism haunts the American empire; therefore the United States must project its power over an increasingly larger domain so that all threats may be stymied. In this sense, empire is not for convenience but rather necessity. Representatives of the American elite believe that the American values are universal and that the United States should remake the world in its image.[50] Interestingly, militant Islam and the Bush administration both pursue their own visionary quests to rid the world of evil, albeit with each party coming to different normative conclusions. Both sides are energized by their own version of intense idealism. This sense of moral clarity was most succinctly expressed by President Bush when he announced to the world, "You're either with us or you're against us."[51]

The conflation of anti-Americanism and anti-Zionism arises in large part from the relationship between the United States and Israel. The paradox of modern Israel, as Christopher Hitchens argued, is that the state was created to provide a safe, stable, and proudly independent nation to which Jews from around the world could come to escape from fluctuations in gentile goodwill. However, today Israel is largely reliant on foreign aid, most notably the annual subsidy of $3 billion from the United States. Furthermore, the tiny nation appears to be hopelessly involved in endless battles that have the effect of catalyzing anti-Zionist sentiment around the world.[52] Anti-Semitism generated in the lands of the diaspora is weak, but anti-Zionism generated from the Middle East conflict grows strong. Therefore, paradoxically, the "new anti-Semitism" appears to be engendered in large part by the existence of Israel.

In recent years, some observers have also noted the parallels between traditional anti-Semitism and the current incarnation of anti-Americanism.[53] As Walter Laqueur observed, since the 1960s the American extreme right has been transformed from an ultrapatriotic movement to one that is increasingly anti-patriotic and nihilistic.[54] This shift explains how the extreme right could find common cause with anti-American movements such as militant Islam. Both movements see the United States as being under the control of the Jews. It thus follows that with the global rise of American prominence, the Jewish threat extends to the entire world. A new synthesis has been created, centered on the narrative of a U.S.-Israeli alliance. The Israeli-Jewish hand is seen as pulling the strings of the American leviathan. Just as bin Laden has conflated the United States and Israel under the rubric of the "Zionist-crusader" alliance, so has the international extreme right reified the notion of the U.S. government hopelessly under the control of a Jewish cabal in the phrase "Zionist occupation government," or "ZOG."

For many years, the European extreme right has identified the United States and its pervasive popular culture as an existential threat to the racial, cultural, and spiritual integrity of European civilization. Ahmed Huber wrote an essay in this vein in 1982, titled "The Unknown Islam." In it he identified three principal threats to Islam: Zionism, Marxism, and finally "the American way of life," which was largely a code phrase for "Judaism."[55] Huber commented on a trend in which anti-Semitism coincided with anti-Americanism:

The Jewish organizations are very alarmed about this. They say this is a new form of anti-Semitism. There are now Jewish intellectuals who say openly that the anti-Americanism which is spread all over Europe is a new, disguised form of anti-Semitism. Anti-Americanism is strongest in Switzerland. . . . Of course, we Swiss have been attacked by the World Jewish Congress, by [Edgar M.] Bronfman, by [Under-Secretary of the U.S. Department of Commerce Stuart E.] Eizenstat and [former chairman of the Federal Reserve Paul] Volcker, because of our attitude in the Second World War [Huber is alluding to the controversy involving Swiss bank accounts held by Jews during the Holocaust].

. . . Now the anti-Americanism all over the world, which should be directed at the American government, against Zionist power in America, becomes now a general anti-Americanism.[56]

Similarly, in an audiotape released in October 2003, Osama bin Laden voiced his contempt for the United States, replete with anti-Semitic themes:

Some have the impression that you [Americans] are a reasonable people. But the majority of you are vulgar and without sound ethics or good manners. You elect the evil from among you, the greatest liars and the least decent and you are enslaved by your richest and the most influential among you, especially the Jews, who lead you using the lie of democracy to support the Israelis and their schemes and in complete antagonism towards our religion [Islam].[57]

Laqueur noted an interesting pattern to the anti-Americanism in Europe in the wake of 9/11. Although anti-Americanism in the media came overwhelmingly from the political left, protests in the streets were almost all sponsored by the extreme right and radical Muslims.[58]

Kenneth Timmerman argued that indeed the United States is a manifestation of the Judaic worldview. However, his normative conclusion in this respect is one of pride and affinity rather than hostility:

The same cultural, religious, and national identity that has maintained the Jews as a separate people for thousands of years is now being championed by America as the world moves hesitantly toward global values and global rules. We use different terms—the rule of law, not Torah; freedom, not God; republic, not nation—but the absolute and transcendent nature of the concepts underpinning the American way of life are obvious and present a constant challenge to other peoples with competing (and less significant) ideologies. If you hate the Jews, you must also hate America.[59]

Further, Timmerman posited that there is indeed a special historical relationship between "America and the Jews," of which he is quite proud:

> Is there a conspiracy between America and the Jews? Indeed there is. It's called shared values, a common heritage, a dedication to improving the human condition through compassion, and tolerance of differences: a conspiracy of freedom.[60]

Currently it is still very speculative to predict how the strange relationship between militant Islam and the extreme right will unfold and develop. Chapter 11 explores trends that could influence this development.

CHAPTER ELEVEN

Conclusion

The current war on terror should not be viewed as just a regional war in the Middle East between the United States and its allies on the one hand and militant Islam on the other. It behooves us to view the present crisis not as a localized conflict, but rather a global struggle in which many factors, both foreign and domestic, come into play. The home front could prove to be very important in a protracted war on terror, especially with regard to immigration and its modern corollary, multiculturalism.

Immigration and Multiculturalism

The openness of American society has made the country extremely vulnerable to foreign terrorists who can take advantage of the country's porous borders. In fact, the United States is the most open society in the world, as some 3.5 million people and 380,000 cars cross its borders each day.[1] Foreign terrorist organizations such as al Qaeda have demonstrated that they can flourish in the climate of the West, with its freedom of association, rule of law, and liberal immigration policies. These characteristics, long touted as among the greatest strengths of the United States, could now prove to be the country's Achilles' heel, presenting an opportunity for asymmetric warfare, the goal of which is to find and exploit an adversary's weaknesses and vulnerabilities.[2]

The increasing heterogeneity of the American population makes it easier for terrorists to blend into society. What is qualitatively different in this era is that the distinction between traditional international terrorism, which was conducted against U.S. interests overseas, and domestic extremism has been blurred. Massive immigration to the United States since the 1960s has created a huge expatriate population, some of whose members may sympathize with causes that originate overseas. One important trend over the past few decades is the rapid increase in Muslim populations in traditionally non-Muslim regions of the world. According to the U.S. Census Bureau, the Arab population in the United States nearly doubled from 1980 to 2000. It is estimated that over 1.2 million Arabs reside in the United States. Whereas earlier Arab immigrants came from countries with large Christian populations, the more recent wave of Arab immigrants come more heavily Muslim countries.[3] In addition, many non-Arab Muslims have immigrated to the United States as well. It is estimated that roughly 2–3 million Muslims now reside in the United States.[4] Furthermore, over 15 million Muslims now reside in the countries of the European Union. Significantly, Islam is the fastest-growing religion in Europe. If current trends continue, by 2020, Muslims will represent 10 percent of the total population of Europe. Presumably, the vast majority of Muslims in the West reject the extremism of al Qaeda. That said, the large number of pockets of diasporic Muslims does provide a kind of sea in which terrorists can swim. This has not gone unnoticed by U.S. intelligence services, which estimated that Islamist sleeper cells operated in at least forty states.[5]

As a group in their host nations in the West, Muslims will more than likely exert greater influence in politics in the future. As Muslims in these countries politically organize, they could conceivably have a great impact on Western governments and influence such issues as foreign policy in the Middle East. This development has not gone unnoticed by Jewish special interest groups that fear it could attenuate the special relationship between the United States and Israel. As Anti-Defamation League (ADL) director Abraham Foxman observed, "in a historic shift, the attitudes of the Islamic world are beginning to have an important presence in traditionally non-Muslim regions of the world."[6] If the U.S.-Israeli alliance ever broke down, then Israel would be forced to defend itself alone—an untenable position in the long term.[7]

American political leaders have demonstrated little resolve in facing up to the nation's immigration crisis. Rather than working for a feasible solution, the political leadership class opts for capitulation. For example, in September 2003 New York City mayor Michael Bloomberg issued an executive order forbidding the New York City police or any other city government agency from cooperating with federal immigration law, except for cases involving violent crime or terrorism.[8] In that same month in California, Governor Gray Davis signed a law allowing illegal aliens to obtain driver's licenses—an official identity document that would enable potential terrorists to live and move about the country with much greater ease.[9] Since the mid-1990s, high-profile figures associated with international terrorism have demonstrated that they can enter the United States and conduct business. As a result, terrorists who sympathize with foreign ideologies find it easier to operate within the West. Take, for example, a firm called Sakina Security Services, which allegedly offered an "Ultimate Jihad Challenge" course that consisted of two weeks of weapons and advanced combat training at rented shooting ranges in Michigan, Missouri, and

Virginia. The company said that it operated its program in the United States because of the less restrictive firearms laws.[10] More ominously, in 1995, Dr. Ayman al-Zawahiri—Osama bin Laden's right-hand man—entered the United States for a cross-country fund-raising tour.[11] And Abdullah Azzam—bin Laden's mentor during the Soviet-Afghan war—had made several trips during the 1980s to raise funds for the incipient terrorist network.

In 2004, the esteemed political scientist Samuel Huntington released a new book, *Who Are We? The Challenges to America's National Identity*, in which he argued that the massive Hispanic, primarily Mexican, migration to the United States constituted the greatest challenge to the country's national unity. As he saw it, the rise of multiculturalism and the demise of the assimilationist ethic have contributed to a predicament that could conceivably divide the United States "into two peoples, two cultures, and two languages."[12] The rise of various group identities based on race and ethnicity threatens to diminish the larger American national identity, which Huntington believed is essential for the long-run survival of the country as a unified political entity. Paradoxically, as Huntington pointed out, leaders among the elite in American politics, business, media, and academia have been in the forefront of deconstructing the nation, a situation that he noted is "quite possibly, without precedent in human history."[13] Massive immigration could compound this problem. As Huntington argued, the current Mexican immigration is qualitatively and quantitatively different from previous waves of immigration.[14] What is all the more worrisome for Huntington is the fact that American leaders actually encourage subnational group affinities, as evidenced by then President Bill Clinton's remarks in June 2000: "I hope very much that I'm the last president in American history who can't speak Spanish." A more recent example is a September 2003 debate among the Democratic Party's presidential candidates, which was conducted in both English and Spanish.[15] Huntington believed that a serious cultural division could develop between Hispanics and Anglos that could even supplant the historical cleavage between blacks and whites. He cited anecdotal evidence, such as a 1998 soccer match in Los Angeles between the United States and Mexico, during which Mexican Americans booed the American team. Eventually, these trends, Huntington predicted, will engender a backlash in the form of a new white nativism:

> It would, indeed, be extraordinary and possibly unprecedented in human history if the profound demographic changes occurring in America did not generate reactions of various sorts. . . .
> The actual and prospective continuing loss in power, status, and numbers by any social, ethnic, racial, or economic group almost always

leads to efforts by that group to stop or reverse those losses. In Bosnia-Herzegovina, the population was 43 percent Serb and 26 percent Muslim. In 1991 it was 31 percent Serb and 44 percent Muslim. In 1990 the population of California was 57 percent white and 26 percent Hispanic. In 2040 it is predicted to be 31 percent white and 48 percent Hispanic. The probability that, in this comparable situation, California whites will react like Bosnian Serbs is about zero. The probability that they will not act at all is about zero.[16]

Political correctness has had a chilling effect on frank discussion of the immigration crisis in the United States. In doing so, it has made the country highly vulnerable to terrorism. These characteristics have made the West an attractive soft underbelly for attacks by foreign terrorists.[17]

Al Qaeda's Grand Strategy against the United States

Osama bin Laden was greatly influenced by his experiences in the Soviet-Afghan war of the 1980s. In fact, he even goes so far as to take credit for the dissolution of the Soviet Union. By that, of course, he does not mean that the mujahideen rode their horses into the Red Square in Moscow. Rather he believes that the war in Afghanistan set in motion various trends and developments that ultimately contributed to the collapse of the Soviet Union. The Soviet-Afghan war and the current war on terrorism to which the United States is committed share some interesting parallels. The Soviet Union was a multinational state, with military commitments that reached far beyond its borders and eventually strained the capacity of the state to maintain them. Similarly, the United States is arguably on its way to becoming a multicultural state, as the population becomes more diverse and the trend of identity politics encourages people to increasingly identify with subnational groups, based on race, ethnicity, or lifestyle. What is more, Paul Kennedy's notion of "imperial overstretch" may be applicable to the contemporary United States, as its military is committed to numerous hot spots around the world.[18]

There are two schools of thought on how the September 11 attacks fit into al Qaeda's grand strategy. One theory posits that al Qaeda and the Taliban were caught unawares by the massive military response of the United States to the terrorist attacks. According to this view, the leadership of al Qaeda believed that the U.S. response would be limited, just as it had been in the past to previous incidents of terrorism.[19]

The other theory, which I find more interesting, asserts that the attacks on 9/11 were intended to provoke a ferocious response from the United States. For nearly a decade prior to 9/11, al Qaeda had struck American targets overseas on numerous occasions. The American response to these incidents had been limited. However, 9/11 could not be ignored. With this event in mind, one is reminded of Walter Laqueur's observation that the chief danger of international terrorism is usually not the terrorist act per se but rather the incident's potential to trigger a wider and more dangerous conflict. He once referred to this prospect as the "Sarajevo effect."[20] Likewise, 9/11 has had the same effect, as the initial response to the atrocities committed by al Qaeda has been expanded to a global war on terror and an effort to remake the Middle East.

Just two months after the September 11 attacks, an intriguing policy position paper prepared by Decision Support Systems (DSS) and titled "Al-Qaida's Endgame?" was released, which argued that bin Laden had in effect laid a trap for the United States with the 9/11 attacks. According to this analysis, al Qaeda knew full well that the attacks would force the United States to unleash a ferocious response and eventually draw the country into a protracted Middle Eastern war. Al Qaeda had determined that it could not destroy U.S. forces inside the United States. Nor could it discourage the United States from engaging in the politics of the Middle East by merely conducting terrorist tactics in that region of the world. Therefore, according to this reasoning, the most viable strategy was to draw the United States into a larger conflict in which it would be forced to deploy a large number of forces.

Bin Laden is under no illusions that his al Qaeda network can single-handedly defeat the United States and Israel. Rather, he sees al Qaeda as a vanguard movement that exhorts the Islamic *umma* to join his global jihad. According to this reasoning, once the United States is drawn into a major regional conflict in the Middle East, it could be worn down by attrition in a guerrilla war. Its growing weakness could engender a civilizational struggle and ultimately make the Middle East ungovernable. Furthermore, application of the oil weapon, or disruption and destruction of the petroleum production system, would leave the United States with greatly diminished interests in the region. Such a scenario could precipitate a severe, global economic downturn and thus dramatically alter the geopolitical balance of the world. In light of this scenario, DSS recommended that the United States make a very measured and focused response, preferably with the use of special forces because of their small size and flexibility. Large forces would be vulnerable to the guerrilla warfare strategy about which DSS warned.[21]

It is worth mentioning, however, that it could prove to be very difficult for the Islamists to sustain a guerrilla war against the United States without outside support. In his classic study, *Guerrilla Warfare,* Walter Laqueur noted that there have been only two cases in recent history in which major guerrilla armies survived without an outside supply of arms and matériel—Mao Zedong's campaign in China and Josip Broz Tito's partisan campaign in Yugoslavia during World War II. What is more, both of these cases were exceptional in that they occurred within the context of a general war that offered many opportunities for acquiring arms.[22] However, the proliferation of arms during the end of the twentieth century may enable Islamists to obtain arms for their campaign against the United States and Israel. The basic strategy of a guerrilla campaign is to raise the cost of occupation in terms of both lives and money, until the enemy leaves the land. The most obvious targets are enemy soldiers who occupy the land and enemy civilians in their own homeland. Al Qaeda has carried out both types of attacks.[23] Arguably, al Qaeda and its sympathizers have already succeeded in pressuring the Saudi government to have American military personnel withdrawn from Saudi Arabia.[24]

There is evidence to suggest that al Qaeda's strategy to wear down the United States has had some success. By the spring of 2004, opinion polls indicated some weariness among the American public with respect to the war on terrorism.[25] The initial relief over a quick military victory in the conventional war in Iraq was tempered by the ensuing guerrilla conflict. Some skeptics began to question the scope of the U.S. war on terrorism. For example, in January 2004, a report published by the U.S. Army War College, which criticized the war in Iraq, caused a stir. In the report, titled *Bounding the Global War on Terrorism,* the author, Jeffrey Record, argued that the campaign in Iraq amounted to a diversion in the global war on terrorism. The defense analyst warned that the overly ambitious and open-ended fashion in which the war was being prosecuted threatened to stretch U.S. armed forces to the limit and, by doing so, posed a serious threat to the future security of the nation. As of 2004, the United States had deployed 135,000 troops in Iraq and an additional 17,500 in Afghanistan. Although the U.S. military has an active-duty force of 1.4 million soldiers, sailors, and airmen, the great majority of them are not combat-ready. Still other peacekeeping missions in war-torn lands such as the Balkans further strain the force strength of the U.S. military.[26] All the more worrisome is the growing number of casualities in the war in Iraq. When major combat operations ceased on May 1, 2003, 138 U.S. soldiers had been killed. However, by January 2006, the death toll had reached 2,100.[27]

In Record's analysis, the war in Iraq has not made the United States any safer; rather it has created a new theater in the war on terrorism. Furthermore, by rushing to conflate Saddam Hussein with al Qaeda, the Bush administration has undercut U.S. credibility around the world, which could seriously hamper cooperative efforts such as intelligence sharing and law enforcement against terrorists. As Record saw it, the Bush administration's goal of democratization for the Middle East region is not only overly ambitious but also unlikely. He also questions U.S. willingness to sustain such a protracted effort: it is sure to cost untold billions of dollars as well as seriously challenge the public's resolve, which has historically been averse to imperial-style projects.

Al Qaeda's strategy of wearing down the United States could impinge on the home front in a variety of ways. For example, the war on terror—especially now that it includes an occupation of Iraq—will amount to an enormous fiscal undertaking. The federal and some state governments are experiencing severe budget crises. The financial cost of the war on terrorism must be taken into account. After September 11, annual defense spending exceeded $400 billion, but that figure does not even include special spending for Iraq and Afghanistan, which is averaging over $80 billion per year. Still more money is needed for the newly created Department of Homeland Security, whose annual budget reached $40.7 billion in fiscal year 2005.[28] In addition to these outlays, the United States will face still other serious fiscal challenges in the years ahead. On the horizon is a looming crisis in the Social Security trust fund that will require, according to projections, either a significant increase in payroll taxes or decrease in benefits for the fund to remain solvent somewhere after 2030–2042.[29] Related to this is the growing cost of Medicare, which is fueled by a general aging of the American population, an increase in life expectancy, and an increase in the cost of health care. Finally, the cost of immigration is worth mentioning. Estimates on the net cost vary considerably, from a low of $11 billion to a high of roughly $61 billion per year.[30] The total costs of all these programs could amount to such an enormous undertaking that they could engender a fiscal crisis never before experienced in American history.

As immigration into the United States grows, would it be unreasonable to envision a scenario in which the U.S. government could be winning the war overseas yet lose control of its border with Mexico and, by doing so, face an existential threat to its national unity? In the mid-1990s, Robert Kaplan prognosticated in his influential article, "The Coming Anarchy," that it is not entirely clear that the United States will be able to survive exactly in its present form because it is a multiethnic society, where the concept of the nation-state has always been more fragile than it is in homogeneous nations.[31] What is more, conflicts such as civil war, guerrilla warfare, and terrorism are more likely to occur in countries with heterogeneous rather than homogeneous populations.[32]

Traditionally, external threats, à la 9/11, tend to strengthen national cohesion. And immediately after September 11, polls indicated an upsurge in patriotism in the United States.[33] Historically, Americans have tended to put partisan differences at the ocean's edge. However, on rare occasions, when serious domestic conflicts exist, new external threats can have the opposite effect and diminish national unity.[34] Looking at the historical experiences of both the United States and Great Britain, Arthur Stein found that the degree of unity or disunity war produced depended largely on two factors: first, the greater the perceived threat from the enemy, the greater national unity; and second, the greater the mobilization of resources necessary to prosecute the war, the greater the likelihood that disunity would result because different degrees of sacrifice had to be made by different segments of the population.[35] As Samuel Huntington observed, by 2004, the current war on terror still involved a relatively low mobilization of resources. In fact, soon after the conflict commenced, President George W. Bush exhorted Americans to live their lives as they normally did so as to not give terrorists the impression that they had succeeded in alarming the country. As long as the perceived threat of terrorism remains high, and the mobilization of resources remains low, Huntington believed that the war on terrorism will tend to engender national unity.[36] However, the costs of the war will not be borne in isolation, because the United States will face the other fiscal challenges mentioned earlier.

One worrisome development is a seeming polarization in the United States over matters such as national identity and cultural issues. Following the 2000 and 2004 presidential elections, observers noted a rift in the electoral map of the country. Generally speaking, "red" states favored a more conservative course for the nation, whereas "blue" states preferred a more liberal orientation. If the United States were to fragment due to trends such as multiculturalism, then it may someday reach a critical stage where support for the war on terror may be more difficult to sustain. Intense competition among groups could conceivably undercut national resolve. As Huntington pointed out, the concept of American national identity has evolved during the country's history. British settlers in America initially defined themselves in terms of race, ethnicity, culture, and religion (sectarian Protestantism). A political or creedal component consisting of the principles of liberty, equality democracy, and civil rights was included in the eighteenth century to justify independence from England. By the end of World War II, the ethnic component had dissipated, as large numbers of southern and Eastern European immigrants had assimilated in American society. The civil rights movement and the Immigration Act of 1965 would eventually efface the racial component as well. Currently, the cultural component is under heavy attack by a generalized movement known as multiculturalism. Consequently, the creedal component may soon be all that remains of the American national identity.[37] For Huntington this development has very serious implications. He believed that it is highly improbable that a nation can be defined by an ideology or creed alone and long survive. As he observed, creedal societies tend to be coercive insofar as repression is necessary to bind together disparate peoples who would otherwise have little in common. To make his case, he cited numerous communist regimes, including the Soviet Union, Yugoslavia, Czechoslovakia, East Germany, and North Korea. When communism lost its appeal, all but one of these states, North Korea, disappeared and were replaced by countries defined by nationality, culture, and ethnicity. Likewise, the diminution of the communist ideology in China has posed little threat to national unity because that country has "a core Han culture going back thousands of years."[38] Huntington predicted that the American creed will unlikely retain its permanence if the United States abandons the Anglo-Protestant culture in which the country has been historically rooted. As he sees it, a "multicultural America will, in time, become a multicreedal America, with groups with different cultures espousing distinctive political values and principles rooted in particular cultures."[39]

There is some evidence to suggest that al Qaeda's leaders may have already considered this scenario. For example, al Qaeda's response to the document, "What We're Fighting For" (discussed in Chapter 9), concluded with the following statement:

> If the Americans do not respond, then they will face the same fate as the Soviets who ran away from Afghanistan to face military defeat, political fragmentation, ideological collapse and economic bankruptcy.
>
> This is our message to the Americans in response to theirs. Have they now realized why we resist and why, with the permission of Allah, we will prevail?[40]

For his part, David Myatt, the English convert to Islam, gave me his thoughts on the prospects of such a scenario:

> We can but hope! In truth, this is the real weakness of America, and one which I am sure Sheikh Usama bin Laden knows, which is why he is using the tactics he is. America has been drawn into a global conflict, and to keep this going, for many years—as it must—will be an enormous drain on its resources. What is needed to tilt the balance toward bringing the New World Order to its knees is for there to be increased social and political unrest in America. In this, the [extreme right] movement must play a part.
>
> All modern Western societies are vulnerable; their infrastructure is fragile. The movement should target this infrastructure, in an honorable

way, which means avoiding civilian casualties in the covert, revolutionary, war, which is necessary. The reality of the present is that National Socialists seem to be doing very little in a practical sense to undermine and destroy the New World Order, while Muslims are actively waging a war against it. If National Socialists are committed, they should be inciting and inspiring revolution in their own lands and doing practical things to undermine and destroy their ZOG.[41]

As riots ravaged areas of France in November 2005, some observers speculated that a similar scenario could occur in the United States as well. Ernesto Cienfuegos, a representative of La Voz de Aztlan—an irredentist group that advocates a Mexican "reconquista" of the American Southwest—opined that similar social, political, and economic conditions exist in the United States, which will eventually lead to civil unrest among disaffected minorities not unlike what happened with North African immigrants in France.[42]

Although al Qaeda's terrorist attacks may appear reckless, a closer examination reveals that their planners may have a very informed and nuanced understanding of the politics in the areas in which they occur. The case of the bombings of the Madrid train stations on March 11, 2004, is instructive. After these attacks, a document titled "Jihadi Iraqi Hopes and Dangers," which had appeared on several Islamist websites, received much attention. A draft of the document was prepared in September 2003, but it was not published until December of that year. The document was prepared by the "Media Committee for the Victory of the Iraqi People," which is believed to be an arm of al Qaeda. The main thesis of the document was that the United States could not be forced to leave Iraq by military and political means alone. Rather, the document argued that the Islamic resistance could only succeed if the American occupation was made as economically costly as possible. Toward this end, the document recommended that resistance fighters target coalition countries such as England, Spain, and Poland, so that the United States will be forced to bear almost the entire cost of the occupation. The author evinced a sophisticated knowledge of the domestic politics of these countries, most notably with regard to Spain. Presciently, he predicted that painful blows inflicted on that country near its general election could force the Spanish government to withdraw forces from Iraq.[43]

Conclusion

As the preceding discussion sought to illustrate, several current trends have occasioned some strange alliances. Although it should not be overstated, there would appear to be some potential for cooperation between the extreme right and militant Islam in that they both share a strikingly similar critique on several issues. This development has not gone unnoticed by authorities. Dale Watson, the Federal Bureau of Investigation's (FBI's) assistant director for counterterrorism, saw evidence of communication between extremists in the United States and Muslim extremists overseas, mostly through the medium of the Internet.[44] Concerned at the prospect of such an alliance, the U.S. government has begun monitoring these contacts to make sure that the two movements do not begin collaborating on terrorist attacks. Authorities are particularly concerned about overtures by American extremists to radical groups such as Hezbollah in Lebanon, al Qaeda in the Middle East, and Abu Sayyaf in the Philippines.[45] In recent years, domestic right-wing extremists appear to be more internationally inclined than they traditionally have been in the past.[46]

In the realm of terrorism, such cooperation would make for a very formidable challenge, if carried out deftly. Islamic terrorists have traditionally been foreign young men of Middle Eastern origin. Despite the pronouncements on the part of authorities that they abhor racial profiling and would not condone its use, the fact remains that young men of Middle Eastern ancestry will tend to make people more suspicious than other population groups, for no other reason than that previous Islamic terrorists shared the same ethnic and religious characteristics. If well-funded Middle Eastern terrorists could enlist the support of terrorists with white, Anglo-Saxon ethnic features, it could present an intelligence nightmare to authorities. Reportedly, al Qaeda has already entertained this scheme. According to a statement by then U.S. attorney general John Ashcroft in May 2004, al Qaeda was seeking to recruit operatives "who can portray themselves as Europeans."[47] In order to avoid the intense scrutiny received by travelers from certain Middle Eastern countries, it is believed that al Qaeda is using operatives from Chechnya, Bosnia, and even Western Europe. Furthermore, some Muslim operatives are believed to have converted to Christianity in order to obscure their backgrounds and allay suspicion.[48] Currently, would-be right-wing terrorists would not appear to have the capability of carrying out massive attacks. However, this situation could change if they were able to join forces with a group such as al Qaeda.[49] As yet, there appears to be no real evidence of such a development. Such a scenario is purely speculative. That said, the potential threat that others besides right-wing extremists might draw inspiration from the example of the September 11 attacks and act on their own initiative remains a strong possibility as well. This was tragically illustrated in February 2002, when a seemingly normal fifteen-year-old Florida youth deliberately slammed a single-engine plane into a Florida office building.[50] In another example, a former representative of the Earth Liberation

Front, Craig Rosebraugh, exhorted antiwar activists to escalate their opposition to the war in Iraq to the point of sabotage and rioting.[51] The U.S. government has warned law enforcement agencies that Islamic extremists, without any formal affiliation with al Qaeda, might carry out terrorist attacks in the United States and overseas. The FBI fears that individuals on the fringes of extremist groups may carry out attacks on their own initiative. Certain events, such as the war on Iraq and increasing tensions in the Israeli-Palestinian conflict, could act as catalysts for such attacks.[52]

One major obstacle to any kind of serious collaboration is the fact that in the United States, there is no real right-wing terrorist infrastructure to speak of; leaderless resistance—actually a sign of desperation—predominates. Thus, even if Middle Eastern terrorists were willing to collaborate with native right-wing terrorists, they would be hard pressed to find a viable terrorist network already in place. From the perspective of the extreme right, an overt alliance with militant Islam would entail many perils. The extreme right is monitored very closely by both the government and nongovernmental organizations in the United States. Thus, tactically, the extreme right would not appear to be in a good position to cooperate with militant Islam, even if it had the desire to do so. Other observers have expressed doubt about the success of such an alliance, insofar as many extremists are traditional racists and would prefer not to work with Muslims.[53] Furthermore, as Walter Laqueur argued, given the very specific and exclusive religious doctrine of al Qaeda, it would be most difficult to forge an alliance with Western infidels sympathetic to their cause—at least one of any enduring quality.[54] However, the history of terrorism has demonstrated that on some occasions, disparate groups scattered around the globe can cooperate when they share common goals and similar worldviews. For example, from the 1960s to the late 1980s, a wide assortment of both ethnonationalist and Marxist-Leninist terrorist organizations often cooperated with one another, based on a shared opposition to imperialism and sympathy for the Palestinian cause.

It is in the area of propaganda where the greatest potential for cooperation would seem to lie. There appears to be increasing cooperation on a rhetorical level between the two movements. For the most part, admiration tended to move only in one direction, with right-wing extremists occasionally voicing support for Islamic extremists. There is anecdotal evidence to suggest that this situation could be changing, as propaganda by right-wing extremists is being acquired and recycled by Islamic extremists.[55] Internet technology facilitated the networking of dispersed people across national borders and different cultures.[56] Through the Internet, various cliques can weave a grand narrative to explain their grievances and build a sense of collective identity, thus creating a "virtual community."

The significance of potential collaboration in the area of propaganda should not be blithely dismissed, as conflicts in the future will increasingly revolve around information and communication matters. So-called soft power is important in an era of globalization. Joseph Nye was the first to distinguish between "hard power" and "soft power." The former consists of traditional measures such as military and economic strength, and the latter includes culture and ideology.[57] Adversaries will emphasize media operations and "perception management" in order to get their side of the story out.[58] As David Ronfeldt and John Arquilla argued, what happens at the "narrative level" is very important to the success of a network:

> Networks, like other organizations, are held together by the narratives, or stories that people tell. . . . these narratives provide a grounded expression of people's experiences, interests, and values. First of all, stories express a sense of identity and belonging—who "we" are, why we have come together, and what makes us different from "them." Second, stories communicate a sense of cause, purpose, and mission. The express aims and methods as well as cultural dispositions—what "we" believe in, and what we mean to do, and how.[59]

Crucial to success in the area of propaganda is momentum. There are some indications that the United States is losing the war of ideas, most notably in the Islamic world. A survey conducted by the Pew Global Attitudes Project in forty-four countries and released in June 2003 found that a significant number of people in the Muslim world would trust Osama bin Laden to "do the right thing regarding world affairs." Reportedly, some 71 percent of Palestinians felt this way, as did majorities in Indonesia and Jordan and nearly half of those in Morocco and Pakistan.[60] What is more, the war in Iraq has sent support for the United States to record lows in the Muslim world.[61] It is important to keep in mind that al Qaeda targets not only the U.S. military in the Middle East but also U.S. public opinion, as did the Viet Cong during the Vietnam War.

Since the mid-1990s, the state system has become extremely vulnerable in many countries around the world. Several multinational states have imploded due to centrifugal ethnic rivalries. Large-scale immigration, the ascendance of multiculturalism, and the decreasing salience of the assimilationist paradigm could presage a similar situation in the United States. The American extreme right is one segment of the American society that is keenly aware of these trends. The September 11 attacks and their consequences could reinvigorate the American extreme right, as they increase the salience of the issues about which it feels strongly. It is conceivable that the extreme right could exploit the current crisis as a way to call attention to its critique of many of the government's policies. As history has on occasion demonstrated, long, protracted, and unpopular wars can have a radicalizing effect on a country's populace. For example, both Russia and Germany were beset with revolutionary upheaval in the aftermath of World War I. Likewise, the Vietnam War gave impetus to the counterculture, which would ultimately have a substantial impact on the social texture of the United States. If the war on terror should falter, then it could conceivably redound to the favor of the extreme right, as some segments of the public may be more easily swayed by unconventional political thinking that offers frank analysis on the pressing issues of the day.

It is difficult to predict how the unexpected and alarming convergence between militant Islam and the extreme right will unfold in the future. The cross-fertilization of rhetoric between the two parties reached new heights in December 2005, when Iranian President Mahmoud Ahmadinejad dismissed the Holocaust as a myth that has been used as a pretext for the creation of a Jewish state in the heart of the Islamic world. A few weeks before this pronouncement, Ahmadinejad called for the destruction of Israel—the country should be "wiped off the face of the map." Ahmadinejad's comments were condemned by officials in the West, but they drew praise in some quarters in the Muslim world. A spokesman for Hamas, Khaled Meshall, commended the Iranian president for his "courage" in speaking out on the Holocaust and called for a united front in support of Iran. Likewise, Mohammed Mehdi Akef, the leader of Egypt's Muslim Brotherhood, the largest opposition force in that country, echoed Ahmadinejad's comments that the Holocaust was a myth. For their part, representatives and organizations of the extreme right—including David Duke and the Institute for Historical Review—expressed satisfaction that a head of state had publicly impugned the accepted version of the Holocaust. This meeting of the minds among disparate groups and individuals could presage some strange alliances in the future.

Notes

CHAPTER 1. INTRODUCTION

1. See Horst Mahler, "Independence Day—Live," http://vanguardnewsnetwork.com/index 115htm, September 12, 2001, and "The Fall of the Judeo-American Empire," http://vanguard newsnetwork.com/h_mahler4htm. Downloaded November 5, 2001.

2. William Pierce, "Provocation and Response," *Free Speech* 7, 10 (October 2001), http://www .natall.com/free-speech/fs0110a.html.

3. Kurt M. Campbell and Michele A. Flournoy, *To Prevail: An American Strategy for the Campaign against Terrorism* (Washington, DC: CSIS Press, 2001), p. 6.

4. For more on this study, which was conducted by the Milken Institute, see "Study: Attacks Will Wipe Out 1.6m Jobs This Year," *USATODAY,* January 11, 2002, http://www.usatoday. com/news/attack/2002/01/11/jobs.htm.

5. J. Treastor, "For Insurers, Failures and Rate Jumps," *New York Times,* September 15, 2001, in Christopher Hewitt, *Understanding Terrorism in America: From the Klan to al Qaeda* (London: Routledge, 2003), p. 1.

6. The extreme right has frequently predicted an economic collapse that will supposedly usher in a revolutionary period and radicalize whites out of their complacency. In this sense, their analysis is Marxian, as they presage the demise of contemporary capitalism. Leonard Zeskind makes this observation in the essay "Redefining America" in the Southern Poverty Law Center's spring 1999 *Intelligence Report.* Likewise, in their survey of individuals in the white separatist movement, Betty A. Dobratz and Stephanie L. Shanks-Meile found that the respondents asserted that their movement grows in hard economic times. *White Power, White Pride! The White Separatist Movement in the United States* (New York: Twayne Publishers, 1997), p. 23.

7. Paul R. Pillar, *Terrorism and U.S. Foreign Policy* (Washington, DC: Brookings Institution Press, 2001), p. 1.

8. James F. Hoge Jr. and Gideon Rose, eds. *How Did This Happen? Terrorism and the New War* (New York: Public Affairs, 2001).

9. Samuel P. Huntington. *The Clash of Civilizations and the Remaking of World Order* (New York: Touchstone, 1996), p. 20.

10. Ibid., p. 84.

11. Ibid., pp. 117–119.

12. Jonathan D. Salant, "Census: U.S. Arab Population Is Surging," Associated Press, December 3, 2003. The article noted that the United States experienced a massive immigration of Arabs during the 1990s. Before the 1990s, Arabs were likely to come from countries with large Christian populations. However, current Arab immigrants increasingly trace their ancestry to heavily Muslim countries such as Iraq and Yemen.

13. As observed in David Frum and Richard Perle, *An End to Evil: How to Win the War on Terror* (New York: Random House, 2003), p. 41.

14. Huntington, *The Clash of Civilizations,* pp. 256–257.

15. Ibid., pp. 305–306.

16. James Kurth, "The American Way of Victory," *National Interest,* Summer 2000, p. 5, in Patrick J. Buchanan, *Death of the West: How Dying Populations and Immigrant Invasions Imperil Our Country and Civilization* (New York: Thomas Dunne Books, 2002), p. 243. Similarly, Hewitt points out that what the media describe as "American values" are in fact the dominant values of the powerful and far from reflective of national values. Hewitt, *Understanding Terrorism in America,* p. 21.

17. Pillar, *Terrorism and U.S. Foreign Policy,* p. 53.

18. Huntington, *The Clash of Civilizations,* p. 36.

19. Pillar, *Terrorism and U.S. Foreign Policy,* p. 65.

20. Benjamin R. Barber, *Jihad vs. McWorld: How Globalization and Tribalism Are Reshaping the World* (New York: Ballantine Books, 1996), p. 5.

21. Fareed Zakaria, "The Return of History," in James F. Hoge Jr. and Gideon Rose, eds., *How Did This Happen? Terrorism and the New War* (New York: Public Affairs, 2001), pp. 307–317.

22. Buchanan, *Death of the West,* p. 120.

23. Zakaria, "The Return of History," p. 315.

24. Weinberg and Eubank drew their data from ITERATE II and ITERATE III data sets for terrorist events between 1968 and 1990. They used the U.S. State Department's Patterns of Global Terrorism, the chronology of significant terrorist events for 1995 and 1996, and the RAND-St. Andrews Chronology for 1994 and 1996. Finally, they coded events for the years 1992 and 1995 from the ITERATE collection, Terrorism, 1992–1995. Leonard Weinberg and William Eubank, "Terrorism and the Shape of Things to Come" in Max Taylor and John Horgan, eds., *The Future of Terrorism* (London: Frank Cass, 1999), p. 97.

25. Weinberg and Eubank argue that the wave of street corner assaults by youth gangs in European cities in the 1990s constitute a form of between-civilization conflict. Weinberg and Eubank, "Terrorism," in Taylor and Horgan, *The Future of Terrorism,* pp. 99–104.

26. Niall Ferguson, "Clashing Civilizations or Mad Mullahs: The United States between Informal and Formal Empire," in Strobe Talbott and Nayan Chanda, eds., *The Age of Terror: America and the World after September 11* (New York: Basic Books, 2001), pp. 133–134.

27. Xavier Raufer, "New World Disorder, New Terrorisms: New Threats for Europe and the Western World," in Taylor and Horgan, *The Future of Terrorism,* p. 41.

28. Ibid., p. 42.

29. Abraham Foxman, *Never Again? The Threat of the New Anti-Semitism* (New York: HarperCollins, 2003), p. 8.

30. Ibid., p. 16.

31. Jeffrey Kaplan and Leonard Weinberg, *The Emergence of a Euro-American Radical Right* (New Brunswick, NJ: Rutgers University Press, 1998), pp. 109–110. Likewise, George and Wilcox asserted that extremist groups sometimes fulfill a "watchdog" function in society, insofar as they are especially sensitive to issues concerning their particular interests. John George and Laird Wilcox. *Nazis, Communists, Klansmen, and Others on the Fringe* (Buffalo, NY: Prometheus Books, 1992), p. 61.

32. William Pierce, "Who Is Guilty?" ADV Broadcast, September 22, 2001.

CHAPTER 2. THE CONTEMPORARY EXTREME RIGHT

1. Patricia Adler and Peter Adler, *Constructions of Deviance: Social Power, Context, and Interaction,* 4th ed. (Belmont, CA: Thompson Wadsworth, 2003), pp. 2–3.

2. Christopher Hewitt, *Understanding Terrorism in America: From the Klan to al Qaeda* (London: Routledge, 2003), pp. 19–20.

3. George Michael, *Confronting Right Wing Extremism and Terrorism in the USA* (London: Routledge, 2003), pp. 5–6.

4. Martin Durham, "The American Far Right and 9/11," *Terrorism and Political Violence* 15, no. 2 (2004): 96–111.

5. See "Reaping the Whirlwind," *Intelligence Report,* Winter 2001, http://www.splcenter.org.

6. According to this theory, in the eighth century, a Eurasian tribe known as the Khazars converted to Judaism, and their descendents comprise the vast majority of contemporary Jews. Anti-Semites and occasionally some anti-Zionists invoke this theory to reject contemporary Jewish ancestral claims to Palestine. Ironically, the esteemed Hungarian Jewish author Arthur Koestler unwittingly did much to popularize this theory in his book *The Thirteenth Tribe* (New York: Random House, 1976). Extremists have arrogated this book, which has become a staple in their literature. Many far-right book distributors sell the title.

7. For more on the National Alliance demonstrations at the Israeli embassy, see H. J. Brief, "White Supremacist Rally Draws Protestors." *Washington Times,* May 12, 2002; Allan Lengel, "Neo-Nazis, Foes, Clash at Israeli Embassy," *Washington Post,* May 12, 2002, A19; and Anti-Defamation League, "Neo-Nazis Rally in Nation's Capital." August 26, 2002, http://www.adl.org/Learn/news/Neo_Nazis_Rally.asp.

8. Nicholas Goodrick-Clarke, *The Black Sun: Aryan Cults, Esoteric Nazism and the Politics of Identity* (New York: New York University Press, 2002), p. 2.

9. Ibid., pp. 305–306.

10. Susan Miller, "Census Predicts Decline of Whites," *Washington Times,* March 18, 2004.

11. George Michael, *Confronting Right-Wing Extremism and Terrorism in the USA* (London: Routledge, 2003), passim.

12. Mark Potok, "The Year in Hate," *Intelligence Report,* Spring 2003, http://www.splcenter.org.

13. Jared Taylor, *Paved with Good Intentions: The Failure of Race Relations in Contemporary America* (Oakton, VA: New Century Books, 2004). The biographical information comes from Taylor, ed., *The Real American Dilemma: Race Immigration and the Future of America* (Oakton, VA: New Century Books, 1998), pp. 137–138.

14. Taylor, *The Real American Dilemma,* p. 135.

15. Quotes from Francis's speech were published in Dinesh D'Souza's treatise on race, *The End of Racism* (New York: Free Press, 1995), pp. 389–390. When his comments reached the general public, the management of the *Washington Times* decided to terminate his employment.

16. Kevin MacDonald, *Separation and Its Discontents: Toward an Evolutionary Theory of Anti-Semitism* (Westport, CT: Praeger, 1998), p. 28.

17. From the *Jewish Bulletin,* July 23, 1993, quoted in David Duke, *My Awakening* (Covington, LA: Free Speech Press, 1998), p. 447.

18. From the *Jewish Bulletin,* February 19, 1993, quoted in Duke, *My Awakening,* p. 448.

19. Interview with Mike Piper, April 2003.

20. Interview with Jürgen Graf, April 2003.

21. Anti-Defamation League, "Holocaust Denial in the Middle East: The Latest anti-Israel, Anti-Semitic Propaganda Theme," http://www.adl.org/holocaust/denial_ME/western/deniers.asp (downloaded January 16, 2002).

22. David McCalden, now deceased, an Ulsterman and one of the founders of the IHR, is reported to have arranged the organization's early funding from Arab sources. Gerry Gable, "The Far Right in Contemporary Britain," in Luciano Cheles, Ronnie Ferguson, and Michalina Vaughan, eds., *Neo-Fascism in Europe* (New York: Longman, 1991), p. 248. McCalden also once served as the "congressional district coordinator" for the National Association of Arab Americans. Anti-Defamation League, *Extremism on the Right: A Handbook* (New York: Anti-Defamation League, 1988), pp. 120–121.

23. Shortly after the release of his book in November 1977, Grimstad registered with the Department of Justice as an agent of the government of Saudi Arabia. In 1982, Grimstad is also believed to have distributed his Holocaust denial books to members of Congress through a Pakistani-based organization, the World Muslim Congress. A similar mailing was sent out to members of the British Parliament in 1981. Anti-Defamation League, *Extremism on the Right*, p. 99.

24. Martin Lee, *The Beast Reawakens* (Boston: Little, Brown, 1997), p. 225.

25. Interview with Jürgen Graf, April 2003.

26. This is consistent with Roger Griffin's notion of the palingenetic myth, which permeates fascist ideology (i.e., process of death and rebirth). See Roger Griffin, *The Nature of Fascism* (New York: Routledge, 1993).

27. J. Groebel, cited in Jonathan T. Drummond, "From the Northwest Imperative to Global Jihad: Social Psychological Aspects of the Construction of the Enemy, Political Violence, and Terror," in Chris E. Stout, ed., *The Psychology of Terrorism: A Public Understanding* (New York: Praeger, 2002), p. 59.

28. Drummond, "From the Northwest Imperative to Global Jihad"; H. H. A. Cooper, "What Is a Terrorist? A Psychological Perspective," in Jonathan R. White, *Terrorism: An Introduction* (Belmont, CA: Wadsworth, 2002), pp. 24–25. Originally published in *Chitty's Law Journal* 26: 8–18.

29. Drummond, "From the Northwest Imperative to Global Jihad," p. 60.

30. Ibid., p. 61.

31. Ibid., pp. 56–58.

32. Ibid., 67.

33. Ibid., pp. 73–75.

34. Paul Wilkinson, *Political Terrorism* (New York: Wiley, 1974), in White, *Terrorism: An Introduction,* p. 23.

35. Drummond, "From the Northwest Imperative to Global Jihad," pp. 76–79.

36. Ehud Sprinzak, "The Process of Delegitimation: Towards a Linkage Theory of Political Terrorism." *Terrorism and Political Violence* 3, no. 1 (Spring 1991): 50–68.

37. Ehud Sprinzak, "Right-Wing Terrorism in a Comparative Perspective: The Case of Split Delegitimation," in Tore Bjørgo, ed., *Terror from the Extreme Right* (London: Frank Cass, 1995), pp. 17–43.

38. Christopher Hewitt, "Patterns of American Terrorism 1955–1998: An Historical Perspective on Terrorism-Related Fatalities 1955–98," *Terrorism and Political Violence* 12, no. 1 (2000): 6.

39. A case in point is the murder of three civil rights workers (Michael Schwerner, Andrew Goodman, and James Chaney) in Philadelphia, Mississippi. Local law enforcement officers arrested the three on trumped-up traffic charges and then delivered them to the Klan.

40. Examples include the 1995 bombing of the Murrah Federal building in Oklahoma City; the Oklahoma Constitutional Militia's alleged plans to bomb federal facilities in 1995; the Virginia-based Mountaineer Militia's alleged plan to blow up the FBI's fingerprint facility in Clarksburg, West Virginia, in 1996; the Arizona-based Viper Militia's alleged plot to blow up federal buildings in Phoenix; the arrest of militia members for planning an attack on Fort Hood, Texas, in 1997; the Colorado First Light alleged plot to disrupt the federal government in 1997; and the Republic of Texas, which allegedly planned to infect selected government officials with deadly toxins.

41. Hewitt, *Understanding Terrorism in America*, p. 46.

42. George Eric Hawthorne, "The Brüders Schweigen: Men against Time," in David Lane, *Deceived, Damned, and Defiant: The Revolutionary Writings of David Lane* (St. Maries, ID: 14 Word Press, 1999), p. 157.

43. George Eric Hawthorne, "History in the Making," in Lane, *Deceived, Damned, and Defiant,* p. 229.

44. Ben Klassen, *On the Brink of a Bloody Racial War* (Niceville, FL: Church of the Creator, 1992), pp. 14–15. The number killed in Lebanon was actually 241.

45. Mattias Gardell, "Black and White Unite in Fight?" in Jeffrey Kaplan and Heléne Lööw, eds., *The Cultic Milieu: Oppositional Subcultures in an Age of Globalization* (New York: Alta Mira Press, 2002), p. 168.

46. Walter Laqueur, *No End to War: Terrorism in the Twenty-First Century* (New York: Continuum, 2003), p. 195.

47. Bruce Hoffman, "Responding to Terrorism across the Technological Spectrum," *Terrorism and Political Violence* 6, no. 3 (Autumn 1994): 365–389.

48. Benjamin Netanyahu, *Fighting Terrorism: How Democracies Can Defeat the International Terrorist Network* (New York: Farrar, Straus and Giroux, 2001), pp. 12–13, 19, 28.

49. A 1999 study by the New Century Foundation found that for the year 1994, of the approximately 1.7 million crimes of interracial violence involving blacks and whites, roughly 90 percent were committed by blacks against whites. Although the report received criticism because the New Century Foundation is a part of the racialist organization American Renaissance, the report used reliable data from the Federal Bureau of Investigation and the Bureau of Justice Statistics. See New Century Foundation, *The Color of Crime* (Oakton, VA: New Century Foundation, 1999).

50. Carol M. Swain, *The New White Nationalism in America: Its Challenge to Integration* (New York: Cambridge University Press, 2002), p. 2.

51. Kenneth Stern from the American Jewish Committee cites two studies on this issue. *The Ottawa Citizen* estimated approximately 600, whereas Gina Smith estimated 800. The Simon Wiesenthal Center (SWC) puts the number at 2,100. See Kenneth Stern, "Hate on the Internet" (New York: American Jewish Committee, 1999), http://www.ajc.org/pre/interneti.htm.

52. Swain, *The New White Nationalism in America,* p. 7.

53. Ibid., pp. 34–35.

54. Josef Meighy, *SS Freikorps Arabien* (self-published, 1995).

55. Richard Scutari, "Resistance Magazine Denigrates the Order: A Bruder Responds," posted on Alex Curtis' now defunct website, http://www.whiteracist.com (downloaded March 12, 2001).

56. Kevin Flynn, and Gary Gerhardt, *The Silent Brotherhood* (New York: Signet, 1990), p. 127.

CHAPTER 3. THE DEVELOPMENT OF MILITANT ISLAM AND ARAB NATIONALISM

1. See, for example, Samuel P. Huntington, *The Clash of Civilizations and the Remaking of World Order* (New York: Touchstone, 1996); and Kenneth R. Timmerman, *Preachers of Hate: Islam and the War on America* (New York: Crown Forum, 2003).

2. Bernard Lewis, "Islamic Terrorism?" in Benjamin Netanyahu, ed., *Terrorism: How the West Can Win* (New York: Farrar, Straus and Giroux, 1986), p. 66.

3. Jeffrey Record, *Bounding the Global War on Terrorism* (Carlisle, PA: U.S. Army War College, December 2003), p. 27.

4. Daniel Pipes, *Militant Islam Reaches America* (New York: W. W. Norton, 2002), pp. 38–44.

5. Yossef Bodansky, *Islamic Anti-Semitism as a Political Instrument* (Houston, TX: Ariel Center for Policy Research, 1999), p. 19.

6. Bernard Lewis, *What Went Wrong? The Clash between Islam and Modernity in the Middle East* (New York: Perennial, 2002), p. 47.

7. Amir Taheri, *Holy Terror: Inside the World of Islamic Terrorism* (Bethesda, MD: Adler and Adler, 1987), p. 199.

8. Ibid., p. 48.

9. Medea Institute and ummah.com, "The Muslim Brotherhood," in Adam Parfrey, ed., *Extreme Islam: Anti-American Propaganda of Muslim Fundamentalism* (Los Angeles, CA: Feral House, 2001), p. 76.

10. Ibid., pp. 76–79.

11. Al-Banna, "On the Doctrine of the Muslim Brothers," in Barry Rubin and Judith Colp Rubin, eds., *Anti-American Terrorism and the Middle East: A Documentary Reader* (Oxford: Oxford University Press, 2002), p. 28.

12. Taheri, *Holy Terror*, p. 54.

13. John Zimmerman argued that Qutb's animus toward the United States predated his stay there. Moreover, he believed that many of Qutb's anecdotes about the United States are probably apocryphal. Most notable is Qutb's allegation that while traveling on an ocean liner, a drunken American woman attempted to seduce him. He was particularly affronted by this experience. Zimmerman suspected that this experience was probably contrived. Qutb also expressed outrage over an alleged incident in which employees at the George Washington Hospital in Washington, D.C., upon hearing of the assassination of Hassan al-Banna, began a celebration. Subsequent research revealed no record of Qutb receiving treatment there. Moreover, very few Americans had even heard of al-Banna; even fewer had enough interest in him to celebrate his death. John C. Zimmerman, "Sayyid Qutb's Influence on the 11 September Attacks," *Terrorism and Political Violence* 16, no. 2 (Summer 2004): 222–252.

14. Ahmad S. Moussalli, *Radical Islamic Fundamentalism: The Ideological and Political Discourse of Sayyid Qutb* (Beirut, Lebanon: American University of Beirut, 1992), p. 26.

15. Sayid Qutb, *Milestones* (Cedar Rapids, IA: Mother Mosque Foundation, n.d.), pp. 7–8.

16. Moussalli, *Radical Islamic Fundamentalism*, p. 13.

17. To Islamists, democracy is often depicted as a slippery slope to degeneracy. The late Ayatollah Khomeini once remarked that democracy "leads to prostitution." Taheri, *Holy Terror*, p. 28.

18. Qutb, *Milestones*, p. 9.

19. Much of the far right could be characterized as "preservatist" in the sense that it often idealized some mythic golden age. However, there is quite a bit of variation in this theme among various far-right groups. For example, the patriot movement looks to the American Revolution for inspiration, whereas the neo-Confederates look to the Civil War. The Odinists idealize the Viking era, whereas the National Socialists and many of the historical revisionists admire Hitler's Third Reich. The World Church of the Creator idealizes not only the Third Reich but also the Roman Empire and the American Western frontier of the nineteenth century. And the Christian Identity followers identify with the lost tribes of Israel. George Michael, *Confronting Right-Wing Extremism and Terrorism in the USA* (London: Routledge, 2003), p. 91.

20. Bodansky, *Islamic Anti-Semitism as a Political Instrument*, p. 13.

21. Sayid Qutb, "Paving the Way," in Rubin and Rubin, *Anti-American Terrorism and the Middle East*, p. 30.

22. Qutb, *Milestones*, p. 118.

23. Ibid., p. 49.

24. Ibid., p. 160.

25. Yossef Bodansky, *Bin Laden: The Man Who Declared War on America* (Rocklin, CA: Forum, 1999), p. 34.

26. Gilles Kepel, *Muslim Extremism in Egypt: The Prophet and Pharaoh* (Berkeley: University of California Press, 1993), p. 16.

27. Jane Corbin, *Al Qaeda: In Search of the Terror Network That Threatens the World* (New York: Thunder's Mouth Press, 2002), pp. 10–11.

28. This is according to the statements of one of the Free Officers. See Moussalli, *Radical Islamic Fundamentalism*, p. 32.

29. "Do Not Call Jihad a Defense from Milestones, the Book That Killed Its Authors," in Parfrey, *Extreme Islam*, p. 63.

30. Timmerman, *Preachers of Hate*, p. 121.

31. Moussalli, *Radical Islamic Fundamentalism*, p. 42.

32. Marc Sageman, *Understanding Terror Networks* (Philadelphia: University of Pennsylvania Press, 2004), p. 2.

33. Ibid., p. 8.

34. Actually, Mawdudi had resurrected the *jahiliyya* discourse prior to Qutb. Mawdudi had used the term *jahiliyya* in an abstract way to describe the system of beliefs and ideas in India during the early twentieth century. However, Qutb took Mawdudi's ideas out of context and applied them to his own theories of jihad and *jahiliyya*. See Sageman, *Understanding Terror Networks,* pp. 6–9.

35. Taheri, *Holy Terror*, p. 57.

36. Qutb, *Milestones,* p. 70.

37. Moussalli, *Radical Islamic Fundamentalism*, p. 164–166.

38. Ladan Boroumand and Roya Boroumand, "Terror, Islam, and Democracy," *Journal of Democracy* 13, no. 2 (April 2002): 8.

39. M. A. Muqtedar Khan, "Radical Islam, Liberal Islam," *Current History,* December 2003, p. 420.

40. Ibid., p. 421.

41. Taheri, *Holy Terror,* p. 264.

42. Moussalli, *Radical Islamic Fundamentalism*, p. 37.

43. "Do Not Call Jihad a Defense from Milestones, the Book That Killed Its Authors," in Parfrey, *Extreme Islam,* p. 64.

44. Kepel, *Muslim Extremism in Egypt*, p. 34.

45. Timmerman, *Preachers of Hate,* p. 121.

46. Bodansky, *Islamic Anti-Semitism as a Political Instrument,* p. 58.

47. Qutb, *Milestones,* p. 125.

48. Bodansky, *Islamic Anti-Semitism as a Political Instrument,* p. 62.

49. Bernard Lewis, *Semites and Anti-Semites: An Inquiry into Conflict and Prejudice* (New York: W. W. Norton, 1986), p. 121.

50. See, for example, Martin Kramer, "The Salience of Islamic Antisemitism," lecture at the Institute of Jewish Affairs in London, October 1995, http://www.oct.org.articles/antisemit1.htm.

51. Timmerman, *Preachers of Hate,* p. 47.

52. Lewis, *What Went Wrong?* p. 154.

53. Roland Jacquard, *In the Name of Osama Bin Laden: Global Terrorism and the Bin Laden International* (Durham, NC: Duke University Press, 2002), p. 3.

54. Kepel, *Muslim Extremism in Egypt,* p. 111.

55. Ibid., p. 117.

56. Ibid., pp. 121–123.

57. Bodansky, *Islamic Anti-Semitism as a Political Instrument,* p. 23.

58. Ibid., p. 25.

59. Shaul Mishal and Avraham Sela, *The Palestinian Hamas: Vision, Violence, and Coexistence* (New York: Columbia University Press, 2000), p. 4.

60. Bodansky, *Islamic Anti-Semitism as a Political Instrument,* pp. 5–6.

61. Ibid., p. 157.

62. Daniel Pipes, *The Hidden Hand: Middle East Fears of Conspiracy* (New York: St. Martin's, 1998), pp. 142–151.

63. See, for example, George Michael, "The Revolutionary Model of Dr. William L. Pierce," *Terrorism and Political Violence* 15, no. 3 (Autumn 2003): 62–80; and Research Staff

of National Vanguard Books, "Who Rules America" (Hillsboro, WV: National Vanguard Books, 2000).

64. Benjamin Netanyahu, *Fighting Terrorism: How Democracies Can Defeat the International Terrorist Network* (New York: Farrar, Straus and Giroux, 2001), p. xvii, and Netanyahu, "Terrorism and the Islamic World," in Benjamin Netanyahu, ed., *Terrorism: How the West Can Win* (New York: Farrar Straus Giroux, 1986), pp. 62–63.

65. Pipes, *The Hidden Hand,* pp. 122–132.

66. Ibid., pp. 9–10.

67. Ibid., p. 104.

68. Julie Stahl, "Greater Danger in Islamic Anti-Semitism, Expert Says," CNS News, October 25, 2002, http://www.cnsnews.com/ViewForeignBureaus.asp?Page=\ForeignBureaus\archive\ 200210FOR.

69. *Washington Times,* November 4, 1992, cited in Pipes, *The Hidden Hand,* p. 154. The transcript of the recorded telephone conversation is reprinted in the chapter "Clinton Is the Best Guy for Us," in Jim Keith, ed., *Secret and Suppressed: Banned Ideas and Hidden History* (Portland, OR: Feral House, 1993), pp. 256–269.

70. This is according to a report by Israel Radio. Quoted in Mohamed Khodr, "Sharon to Peres: 'We Control America.'" Media Monitors Network, November 20, 2001, http://www.media monitors.net/ khodr49.html.

71. Statements from Osama bin Laden that appeared in the *Observer Worldview,* November 24, 2002.

72. Quoted in Jeffrey Belodoff and Elyce Milette, "The Franklin Prophecy: An Anti-Semitic Hoax Gets New Life on the Internet," *Jewish Post,* http://jewishpost.com/jp0809y.htm (downloaded June 9, 2004). For a rebuttal of the Franklin Prophecy, see Anti-Defamation League, "The Franklin 'Prophecy': Modern Anti-Semitic Myth Making," http://www.adl.org/special_ reports/franklin_prophecy/franklin_intro.asp (downloaded May 21, 2005).

73. Yosri Fouda and Nick Fielding. *Masterminds of Terror: The Truth behind the Most Devastating Terrorist Attack the World Has Ever Seen* (New York: Arcade Publishing, 2003), p. 193.

74. Abraham Foxman, *Never Again? The Threat of the New Anti-Semitism* (New York: HarperCollins, 2003), p. 198.

75. Ibid., p. 199.

76. Ibid., pp. 204–205.

77. Interview with Kevin MacDonald, March, 2003.

78. Bodansky, *Islamic Anti-Semitism as a Political Instrument,* p. 45.

79. This observation is made in Carol M. Swain, *The New White Nationalism in America: Its Challenge to Integration* (New York: Cambridge University Press, 2002), p. 68.

80. The creation of the state of Israel in 1948 is considered the first *Naqbah* among Arabs.

81. Robin Wright, *Sacred Rage: The Wrath of Militant Islam* (New York: Touchstone, 2001), p. 65.

82. John Esposito, "Political Islam: Beyond the Green Menace," *Current History* (January 1994): 19–24.

83. Walter Laqueur, *The New Terrorism: Fanaticism and the Arms of Mass Destruction* (New York: Oxford University Press, 1999).

84. Although Sterling was viewed as alarmist by some of her critics, the opening of Soviet archives has subsequently given credence to her original thesis. Claire Sterling, *The Terror Network* (New York: Berkley Books, 1984).

85. As Bruce Hoffmann observed, several elements of this incident made it unique. First, the terrorists made a bold political statement by hijacking prisoners for the express purpose of trading them for Palestinian prisoners held in Israel. Second, unlike in previous hijackings, in which the national origin of the aircraft that was seized did not matter, in this incident, the hijacked plane was an evident symbol of the Israeli state. Third, the hijackers created a potentially catastrophic

situation in which the plane could be destroyed and many passengers killed if demands were not met and, in doing so, forced the Israeli government to negotiate with the terrorists. Finally, through a combination of dramatic political statement and symbolic targeting, the terrorists demonstrated that they could engineer media events. Bruce Hoffman, *Inside Terrorism* (New York: Columbia University Press, 1998), pp. 67–68.

86. Hoffman, *Inside Terrorism,* p. 84. According to one estimate, the PLO established a sophisticated financial operation worth, according to one estimate in the mid-1980s, $5 billion. Return on investments was the group's largest source of income at that time, bringing in approximately $1 billion a year. James Adams, *The Financing of Terrorism* (New York: Simon and Schuster, 1986), p. 16.

87. Jillian Becker, "The Centrality of the PLO," in Netanyahu, *Terrorism,* p. 98; and Sterling, *The Terror Network,* pp. 269–280.

88. Samuel Katz, *Relentless Pursuit: The DSS and the Manhunt for the al-Qaeda Terrorists* (New York: Forge, 2002), p. 46.

89. Kepel, *Muslim Extremism in Egypt,* p. 192.

90. Walter Laqueur, *No End to War: Terrorism in the Twenty-First Century* (New York: Continuum, 2003), p. 37; and Sageman, *Understanding Terror Networks,* pp. 17–18.

91. Mark Juergensmeyer, *Terror in the Mind of God: The Global Rise of Religious Violence* (Berkeley: University of California Press, 2000), p. 81.

92. Katz, *Relentless Pursuit,* p. 49.

93. Boroumand and Boroumand, "Terror, Islam, and Democracy," p. 9.

94. Michael A. Ledeen, *The War against the Terror Masters* (New York: St. Martin's, 2003), p. 10.

95. Kepel, *Muslim Extremism in Egypt,* p. 16.

96. Ledeen, *The War against the Terror Masters,* p. 13.

97. Timmerman, *Preachers of Hate,* p. 132.

98. Shaul Shay, "Suicide Terrorism in Lebanon," in International Policy Institute for Counter-Terrorism, *Countering Suicide Terrorism* (New York: International Policy Institute for Counter-Terrorism and the Anti-Defamation League, 2002), p. 134.

99. Ledeen, *The War against the Terror Masters,* p. 20.

100. Bodansky, *Islamic Anti-Semitism as a Political Instrument,* p. 82.

101. Ibid., p. 86.

102. Ledeen, *The War Against the Terror Masters,* p. 23.

103. Ibid., p. 12.

104. Bodansky, *Bin Laden,* p. 22. Hekmatiyar would later make peace with his erstwhile rival Mullah Muhammad Omar. Reportedly in early 2003, Hekmatiyar met with Omar, bin Laden, and Ayman al-Zawahiri to form an alliance to resist the American occupation in Afghanistan. Paul L. Williams, *Osama's Revenge: The Next 9/11* (Amherst, NY: Prometheus Books, 2004), pp. 110–111.

105. Amal Saad-Ghorayeb, *Hizbu'llah: Politics and Religion* (Sterling, VA: Pluto Press, 2002), pp. 7–11.

106. Foxman, *Never Again?* pp. 232.

107. Martin Kramer, "The Moral Logic of Hezballah," in Walter Reich, ed., *Origins of Terrorism: Psychologies, Ideologies, Theologies, States of Mind* (Washington, DC: Woodrow Wilson Center Press, 1998), p. 134.

108. Wright, *Sacred Rage,* p. 82.

109. Saad-Ghorayeb, *Hizbu'llah,* p. 15.

110. Wright, *Sacred Rage,* p. 85.

111. Saad-Ghorayeb, *Hizbu'llah,* p. 104.

112. Ibid., pp. 16–17.

113. Ibid., p. 129.

114. Ibid., p. 20.

115. Ibid., pp. 20–21.

116. Michael Scott Doran, "Somebody Else's Civil War," in James F. Hoge, Jr., and Gideon Rose, eds., *How Did This Happen? Terrorism and the New War* (New York: Public Affairs, 2001), pp. 44–45.

117. Saad-Ghorayeb, *Hizbu'llah*, pp. 78–82.

118. Paul R. Pillar, *Terrorism and U.S. Foreign Policy* (Washington, DC: Brookings Institution Press, 2001), p. 134.

119. Kramer, "The Moral Logic of Hezballah," pp. 144–146.

120. Jessica Stern, "The Protean Enemy: What's Next from al-Qaeda?" *Foreign Affairs*, July–August 2003, pp. 32–33.

121. Mishal and Sela, *The Palestinian Hamas*.

122. "Charter," in Barry Rubin and Judith Colp Rubin, eds., *Anti-American Terrorism and the Middle East: A Documentary Reader* (Oxford: Oxford University Press, 2002), p. 55.

123. Mishal and Sela, *The Palestinian Hamas*, p. 71.

124. Quoted in ibid., p. 196.

125. Jean Rosenfeld observed that several Hamas suicide bombers did not fit the marginalized, lumpenproletariat profile. Some bombers had led well-adjusted, comfortable, and focused lives. As she noted, these organizations have succeeded in creating a "parallel world" in which seemingly normal people live normal lives, yet exemplary members sacrifice themselves for the good of their community by volunteering for suicide missions. Jean E. Rosenfeld, "The Religion of Usamah bin Ladin: Terror As the Hand of God," http://www.publiceye.org/frontpage/911/Islam/rosenfeld2001.htm.

126. A combined total of roughly 3,500 people, including both Palestinians and Israelis, had perished in the second intifada by February 2004. Roughly 900 Israelis had been killed—nearly half by suicide terrorism. Jim Winkates, "Suicide Terrorism: Precedents and Profiles" (Maxwell Air Force Base, AL: Air War College, March 17, 2004), p. 2.

127. Ledeen, *The War against the Terror Masters*, pp. 50–51.

128. Katz, *Relentless Pursuit*, p. 103.

129. Bodansky, *Islamic Anti-Semitism as a Political Instrument*, p. 99.

130. Pillar, *Terrorism and U.S. Foreign Policy*, p. 46.

131. Fouda and Fielding, *Masterminds of Terror*, p. 39.

132. Rubin and Rubin, *Anti-American Terrorism and the Middle East*, p. 43.

133. The most prominent of the identified apostates include Anwar Sadat, the assassinated Egyptian president who made peace with Israel; Hosni Mubarak, Sadat's successor and current Egyptian president, who has often allied his country with the United States; Hafez al-Assad, the late Syrian president whose brutal repression of the Muslim Brotherhood drew the ire of the Islamists; Ali Abdallah Saleh, the president of Yemen, who cooperated with American authorities in the wake of the attack on the U.S.S. *Cole;* Muammar Qaddafi, who had distanced himself from and spoken out against militant Islam; and King Fahd Bin Abdul al-Saud, the late Saudi king, who invited U.S. troops into his country, the custodian of the holiest sites in the Muslim world. See Paul L. Williams, *Al Qaeda: Brotherhood of Terror* (Upper Saddle River, NJ: Alpha, 2002), pp. 99–101.

134. Simon Reeve put the estimate at 14,000 to 17,000 in *The New Jackals: Ramzi Yousef, Osama bin Laden, and the Future of Terrorism* (Boston: Northeastern University Press, 1999), p. 3; Adam Robinson put the figure at 15,000 to 22,000 in *Bin Laden: Behind the Mask of the Terrorist* (New York: Arcade Publishing, 2001), p. 114.

135. Peter L. Bergen, *Holy War, Inc.: Inside the Secret World of Osama bin Laden* (New York: Free Press, 2001), p. 46.

136. Rohan Gunaratna, *Inside al Qaeda: Global Network of Terror* (New York: Columbia University Press, 2002), p. 19.

137. Taheri, *Holy Terror*, p. 169.

138. Ahmed Rashid, *Taliban* (New Haven, CT: Yale University Press, 2001), p. 85.

139. Steven Emerson, *American Jihad: The Terrorists Living among Us* (New York: Free Press, 2002), p. 41.

140. Wright, *Sacred Rage,* p. 264.

141. Ledeen, *The War against the Terror Masters,* p. 35.

142. Doran, "Somebody Else's Civil War," p. 44.

143. This is according to the testimony of one Sheikh Hisham Kabbani, the founder of the Islamic Supreme Council of America before the U.S. State Department. See Ledeen, *The War against the Terror Masters,* p. 76.

144. According to Pakistan's Ministry of Religious Affairs, 10–15 percent of the madrassas have links to sectarian militant groups or international terrorism. Fouda and Fielding, *Masterminds of Terror,* p. 42.

145. Rosenfeld, "The Religion of Usamah bin Ladin."

146. Ibid.

147. Reeve, *The New Jackals,* p. 4.

148. Bodansky, *Bin Laden,* p. 112.

149. Jacquard, *In the Name of Osama Bin Laden,* p. 54.

150. Rosenfeld, "The Religion of Usamah bin Ladin."

151. Kari Vick, "Muslim Rivals Unite in Baghdad Uprising," washingtonpost.com, http://www.msnbc.msn.com/id/4679155/ (downloaded April 7, 2004).

152. Robinson, *Bin Laden,* p. 97.

153. This is according to Hamza Muhamad, a Palestinian volunteer in Afghanistan. See Bodansky, *Bin Laden,* p. 19. See also Sageman, *Understanding Terror Networks,* p. 58.

154. Masoud was assassinated by the Taliban just two days prior to the September 11, 2001, attacks. Intelligence analysts believe that Masoud was assassinated in order to remove a potential leader in a U.S.-led campaign against the Taliban.

155. Sageman, *Understanding Terror Networks,* p. 3.

156. Ibid., p. 36.

157. Nearly a decade after the incident, a captured Pakistani al Qaeda member, Muhammad Saddiq Odeh, told his Pakistani and American interrogators that bin Laden had personally ordered the assassination of Azzam because he suspected that his former mentor had ties to the Central Intelligence Agency (CIA). Gunaratna, *Inside al Qaeda,* p. 24.

158. Bergen, *Holy War, Inc.,* p. 62.

159. Corbin, *Al Qaeda,* pp. 22–23.

160. Gunaratna, *Inside al Qaeda,* p. 23.

161. Bergen, *Holy War, Inc.,* p. 59.

162. Stern, "The Protean Enemy," p. 29.

163. Bodansky, *Bin Laden,* pp. 30–31.

164. See Hoffman, *Inside Terrorism,* p. 195.

165. For more on the history of the Iraqi national flag, see nationmaster.com, http://www.nationmaster.com/encyclopedia/Flag-of-Iraq (downloaded June 9, 2004).

166. Wright, *Sacred Rage,* p. 274.

167. Gunaratna, *Inside al Qaeda,* pp. 28–29.

168. Reeve, *The New Jackals,* p. 172.

169. Robinson, *Bin Laden,* p. 132.

170. Sageman, *Understanding Terror Networks,* p. 39.

171. Paul R. Rich, "Introduction,'" *Small Wars and Insurgencies* 14, no. 1 (Spring 2003): 10.

172. Paul R. Rich, "Al Qaeda and the Radical Islamic Challenge to Western Strategy," *Small Wars and Insurgencies* 14, no. 1 (Spring 2003): 43.

173. Jacquard, *In the Name of Osama Bin Laden,* p. 31.

174. Kurt M. Campbell and Michele A. Flournoy, *To Prevail: An American Strategy for the Campaign against Terrorism* (Washington, DC: CSIS Press, 2001), p. 42.

175. Gunaratna, *Inside al Qaeda,* pp. 7–9.

176. These observations are made in Campbell and Flournoy, *To Prevail,* pp. 47–48.

177. Essentially there are three general patterns of suicide terrorist campaigns. First, nearly all suicide terrorist campaigns occur as part of organized terrorist campaigns, not isolated incidents. Second, liberal democracies are uniquely vulnerable to terrorism (e.g., the United States, France, India, Israel, Turkey, Russia, and Sri Lanka). Third, suicide terrorist attacks are directed at a strategic objective. It is also worth mentioning that suicide terrorism is especially lethal; from 1980 to 2001 suicide attacks accounted for approximately 3 percent of terrorist incidents yet resulted in nearly half of the terrorist fatalities, even when the outlier of the 9/11 attacks was excluded. Robert A. Pape, "Dying to Kill Us," *New York Times,* September 22, 2003.

178. Martha Crenshaw, "Suicide Terrorism in Comparative Perspective," in International Policy Institute for Counter-Terrorism, *Countering Suicide Terrorism* (New York: International Policy Institute for Counter-Terrorism and the Anti-Defamation League, 2002), p. 26.

179. For more on this Islamist interpretation of suicide terrorism see Abdul Aziz, "Are Martyrdom Operations Lawful (According to Quran and Sunnah)?" http://myweb.tiscali.co.uk.al ghurabah/operations.htm (downloaded March 21, 2004).

180. Robinson, *Bin Laden,* p. 151; and Bodansky, *Bin Laden,* p. 70.

181. Corbin, *Al Qaeda,* pp. 41–42.

182. According to author Adam Robison, bin Laden did not think very highly of Aidid. He looked askance at his heavy drinking and use of profanity. However, they shared a common enemy in the United States and thus were able to work together. Robinson, *Bin Laden,* p. 149.

183. Salah Najm, "Transcript of Usamah Bin-Ladin, 'The Destruction of the Base: Interview with Usamah Bin-Ladin,'" June 10, 1999, http://www.terrorism.com/BinLadinTranscript .shtml.

184. John Miller, "Osama Bin Laden: The ABC Interview," May 18, 1998.

185. Robinson, *Bin Laden,* p. 147.

186. Emerson, *American Jihad,* p. 145.

187. Robinson, *Bin Laden,* p. 139.

188. Bruce Hoffman, "Terrorism Trends and Prospects," in Ian O. Lesser, Bruce Hoffman, John Arquilla, David Ronfeldt, and Michele Zanini, eds., *Countering the New Terrorism* (Santa Monica, CA: RAND, 1999), p. 9.

189. Michele Anini and Sean J. A. Edwards, "The Networking of Terror in the Information Age," in John Arquilla and David Ronfeldt, eds., *Networks and Netwars: The Future of Terror, Crime, and Militancy* (Santa Monica, CA: RAND, 2001), p. 34.

190. Bergen, *Holy War, Inc.,* pp. 34–38.

191. Bergen, *Holy War, Inc.,* p. 38.

192. Campbell and Flournoy, *To Prevail,* p. 40.

193. Phil Williams, "Transnational Criminal Networks," in Arquilla and Ronfeldt, *Networks and Netwars,* pp. 71–72.

194. Sageman, *Understanding Terror Networks,* pp. 99–135.

195. Francis Fukuyama, *The Great Disruption: Human Nature and the Reconstitution of Social Order* (New York: Free Press, 1999), p. 199.

196. Fouda and Fielding, *Masterminds of Terror,* p. 114.

197. Williams, *Al Qaeda,* pp. 2–9.

198. Gunaratna, *Inside al Qaeda,* p. 61.

199. Reeve, *The New Jackals,* pp. 184–185.

200. Corbin, *Al Qaeda,* p. 60.

201. Williams, *Osama's Revenge,* pp. 25–26.

202. Jacquard, *In the Name of Osama Bin Laden,* p. 39.

203. Bergen, *Holy War, Inc.,* pp. 92.

204. Williams asserts that al Qaeda and the Taliban established ties with transnational crime syndicates in Turkey to transport heroin to the West. Also, they allegedly recruited foreign chemists to process the opium into heroin. Williams, *Osama's Revenge*, pp. 23–35.

205. Bodansky, *Bin Laden*, pp. 102–104.

206. Michael Ledeen believed that "in all probability the working relationship between al Qaeda and Iran was forged in the Afghan war, and continued uninterrupted throughout the nineties." Ledeen, *The War against the Terror Masters*, p. 50.

207. Taheri, *Holy Terror*, pp. 99–111.

208. Robinson, *Bin Laden*, p. 188.

209. Ibid.

210. Ibid., p. 260.

211. Ibid., p. 261.

212. Ledeen, *The War against the Terror Masters*, p. 279.

213. David Frum and Richard Perle, *An End to Evil: How to Win the War on Terror* (New York: Random House, 2003), p. 44.

214. Ibid., p. 43.

215. Gunaratna, *Inside al Qaeda*, p. 150.

216. Bergen, *Holy War, Inc.*, p. 77.

217. Jacquard, *In the Name of Osama Bin Laden*, p. 112.

218. Reeve, *The New Jackals*, pp. 216–217.

219. Laurie Mylroie, *The War against America: Saddam Hussein and the World Trade Center Attacks* (New York: Regan Books, 2001), p. 252.

220. Frum and Perle, *An End to Evil*, p. 46.

221. Ledeen, *The War against the Terror Masters*, p. 179.

222. Alan M. Dershowitz, *Why Terrorism Works* (New Haven, CT: Yale University Press, 2002), p. 179.

223. The commission noted that bin Laden's organization supported anti-Hussein Islamists in the Kurdistan region of Iraq. By the early 1990s, however, bin Laden ceased that and by doing so, opened the way for a meeting with a high-ranking intelligence officer of the Iraqi government. At the meeting, bin Laden reportedly requested space in Iraq to establish training camps and assistance in procuring weapons, but the Iraqi government never responded. "9/11 panel sees no link between Iraq, al-Qaida," MSNBC, June 16, 2004. http://www.msnbc.msn.com/id/5223932/.

224. Bin Laden, "Declaration of War (August 1996)," in Rubin and Rubin, *Anti-American Terrorism and the Middle East*, p. 137.

225. Bin Laden, "Statement: Jihad against Jews and Crusaders (February 23, 1998)," in Rubin and Rubin, *Anti-American Terrorism and the Middle East*, pp. 149–151.

226. Ledeen, *The War against the Terror Masters*, pp. 87–89.

227. Ibid., p. 131.

228. Reportedly, in 1998 the Taliban struck a deal with Saudi officials to hand over bin Laden in exchange for Saudi support and U.S. recognition. However, following Operation Infinite Reach, the chief of Saudi intelligence, Prince Turki Faisal, met in Afghanistan with Omar, at which time he rebuffed Saudi requests to hand over bin Laden. Williams, *Osama's Revenge*, pp. 58–59.

229. Reeve, *The New Jackals*, p. 214.

230. Jessica Stern, *The Ultimate Terrorists* (Cambridge, MA: Harvard University Press, 1999), p. 60.

231. Williams, *Osama's Revenge*, p. 41.

232. "Bin Laden claims to have nuclear weapons," USATODAY, November 10, 2001. http:///www.usatoday.com/news/attack/2001/11/10/binladen.htm.

233. Quoted in Gunaratna, *Inside al Qaeda*, p. 48.

234. "Interview with Usama bin Ladin (December 1998)," in Rubin and Rubin, eds., *Anti-American Terrorism and the Middle East*, pp. 154–155.

235. Stern, *The Ultimate Terrorists*, p. 77.

236. Fouda and Fielding, *Masterminds of Terror*, p. 48. Researcher Paul Williams claims that as U.S. armed forces combed the tunnels of an al Qaeda base in Kandahar, they discovered low-grade uranium–238 in a canister. If this report is true, conceivably such material would suffice to create a dirty bomb and was presumably in the possession of al Qaeda before their withdrawal from the base. Williams, *Al Qaeda*, p. 75.

237. Burt Herman, "Experts Worry Terrorists Have Nuke Plans," Associated Press, February 4, 2003.

238. John Arquilla and David Ronfeldt, "Afterword (September 2001): The Sharpening Fight for the Future," in Arquilla and Ronfeldt, *Networks and Netwars*, p. 367.

239. Fouda and Fielding, *Masterminds of Terror*, p. 127.

240. Katz, *Relentless Pursuit*, p. 270.

241. Doran, "Somebody Else's Civil War," p. 47.

242. Gunaratna, *Inside al Qaeda*, p. 12.

243. Frum and Perle, *An End to Evil*, p. 48.

244. Huntington, *The Clash of Civilizations*, p. 111.

245. Frum and Perle, *An End to Evil*, p. 54.

246. Ibid., p. 176.

247. Paul R. Ehrlich and Jianguo Liu, "Some Roots of Terrorism," *Population and Environment* 24, no. 2 (November 2002): 183–192.

248. See Hoffman, *Inside Terrorism*; Michael Barkun, *Religion and the Racist Right: The Origins of the Christian Identity Movement* (Chapel Hill: University of North Carolina Press, 1994); and Thomas Flanagan, "The Politics of the Millennium," *Terrorism and Political Violence* 7, no. 3 (1995): 164–175.

249. Hoffman, *Inside Terrorism*, p. 94.

250. Bruce Hoffman cites numerous examples, including the 1995 Aum Shinrikyo cult's attack in the Tokyo subway; the 1995 assassination of Yitzhak Rabin; the 1993 bombing of the World Trade Center in New York by Islamic extremists; and the 1996 campaign of Hamas's suicide bombers. See Hoffman, *Inside Terrorism*, pp. 92–93.

251. Ibid., pp. 92–93.

252. Foxman, *Never Again?* p. 235.

253. For more on Lifton's analysis of apocalyptic groups, see Robert Jay Lifton, *Destroying the World to Save It: Aum Shinrikyo, Apocalyptic Violence, and the New Global Terrorism* (New York: Metropolitan Books, 1999). For an analysis of bin Laden and al Qaeda, see Perter Benesh, "Terrorism Expert Points to Bin Laden's Utopian Vision," *Investor's Business Daily*, September 26, 2001.

254. "Al-Qaeda 'Extinct within a Year,'" October 9, 2003, http://www.news.com.au/common/story_page/o,4057,7431422%5E1702,00.html.

255. Reuel Gerecht, "The Encyclopedia of Terror," in Ledeen, *The War against the Terror Masters*, p. 24. Originally published in *Middle East Quarterly* (Summer 2001).

256. Thomas R. Mockatis, "Winning Hearts and Minds in the 'War on Terrorism,'" *Small Wars and Insurgencies* 14, no. 1 (Spring 2003): 26.

257. Numerous "number three" al Qaeda leaders have been killed or captured since 9/11: Muhammad Atef, Abu Zubaydah, Khalid Sheikh Muhammad, and Saif al-Adel. Faye Bowers, "Al Qaeda's Profile: Slimmer but Menacing," *Christian Science Monitor*, September 9, 2003.

258. Paul R. Rich, "Al Qaeda and the Radical Islamic Challenge to Western Strategy," *Small Wars and Insurgencies* 14, no. 1 (Spring 2003): 47.

259. Campbell and Flournoy, *To Prevail*, pp. 42, 78.

1. The average income for Muslims appears to be higher than the average income in the United States; a 1996 survey found that their median household income was $40,000, versus $32,000 for the country as a whole. Daniel Pipes, *Militant Islam Reaches America* (New York: W. W. Norton, 2002), p. 157.

2. Pipes, *Militant Islam Reaches America*, p. 207.

3. Samuel Katz, *Relentless Pursuit: The DSS and the Manhunt for the al-Qaeda Terrorists* (New York: Forge, 2002), p. 46.

4. Laurie Mylroie, *The War against America: Saddam Hussein and the World Trade Center Attacks* (New York: Regan Books, 2001), p. 89.

5. Katz, *Relentless Pursuit*, p. 53.

6. Mark Juergensmeyer, *Terror in the Mind of God: The Global Rise of Religious Violence* (Berkeley: University of California Press, 2000), p. 66.

7. Peter L. Bergen, *Holy War, Inc.: Inside the Secret World of Osama bin Laden* (New York: Free Press, 2001), p. 66.

8. Juergensmeyer, *Terror in the Mind of God*, p. 67.

9. Steven Emerson, *American Jihad: The Terrorists Living among Us* (New York: Free Press, 2002), p. 33.

10. Katz, *Relentless Pursuit*, p. 57.

11. Yossef Bodansky, *Bin Laden: The Man Who Declared War on America* (Rocklin, CA: Forum, 1999), p. 11.

12. Bodansky, *Bin Laden*, p. 19.

13. Adam Robinson, *Bin Laden: Behind the Mask of the Terrorist* (New York: Arcade Publishing, 2001), p. 92.

14. Bergen, *Holy War, Inc.*, p. 133.

15. Emerson, *American Jihad*, p. 37.

16. Rohan Gunaratna, *Inside al Qaeda: Global Network of Terror* (New York: Columbia University Press, 2002), p. 6. One example of such an NGO is the Benevolence International Foundation (BIF). Based in Illinois, it is ostensibly a humanitarian organization dedicated to helping people suffering in wars in various Islamic territories. The BIF was founded in the 1980s by Saudi Sheik Adil Abdul Galil Batargy, a bin Laden associate. According to the FBI, the BIF's current leader, Enaam M. Arnaout, has a relationship with bin Laden that dates back to the late 1980s. The charity reportedly arranged a trip to Bosnia for Mamdouh Salim, who in 1994 traveled to Sudan in an attempt to acquire radioactive material for al Qaeda.

17. Yosri Fouda and Nick Fielding, *Masterminds of Terror: The Truth behind the Most Devastating Terrorist Attack the World Has Ever Seen* (New York: Arcade Publishing, 2003), p. 95.

18. John V. Parachini, "The World Trade Center Bombers (1993)," in Jonathan B. Tucker, *Toxic Terror: Assessing Terrorist Use of Chemical and Biological Weapons* (Cambridge, MA: MIT Press, 2001), pp. 190–191.

19. This is according to a statement that Ramzi Yousef made to FBI agent Brian Parr. Direct Examination of Brian Parr, *United States of America v. Ramzi Yousef and Eyad Ismoil*, S1293CR.180 (KTD), October 22, 1997, p. 4721, in John V. Parachini, "The World Trade Center Bombers (1993)," in Jonathan B. Tucker, ed., *Toxic Terror: Assessing Terrorist Use of Chemical and Biological Weapons* (Cambridge, MA: MIT Press, 2001), p. 202.

20. Quoted in Simon Reeve, *The New Jackals: Ramzi Yousef, Osama bin Laden, and the Future of Terrorism* (Boston: Northeastern University Press, 1999), p. 27.

21. Ibid., pp. 156–157.

22. Mylroie, *The War against America*, p. 106.

23. Reeve, *The New Jackals*, p. 20.

24. Laurie Mylroie, "Iraqi Complicity in the World Trade Center Bombing and Beyond," *Middle East Intelligence Bulletin* 3, no. 6 (June 2001); and Mylroie, *The War against America.*

25. Reeve, *The New Jackals,* p. 246.

26. Abu Sayyaf was founded in 1991 by Abdurazzak Abubakar Janjalani, a native Filipino from the island of Basilan. Janjalani fought with the mujahideen in Afghanistan and received terrorist training from Osama bin Laden, who urged him to extend al Qaeda's influence to the Philippines. Janjalani also befriended Ramzi Yousef. Janjalani was killed in a gun battle with Filipino police in 1998, but his organization remains active. For more on Abu Sayyaf, see Dirk J. Barreveld, *Terrorism in the Philippines: The Bloody Trail of Abu Sayyaf, Bin Laden's East Asian Connection* (Lincoln, NE: Writers Club Press, 2001).

27. Katz, *Relentless Pursuit,* p. 99.

28. Reeve, *The New Jackals,* p. 157.

29. Juergensmeyer, *Terror in the Mind of God,* p.129.

30. Mylroie, *The War against America,* p. 202.

31. Fouda and Fielding, *Masterminds of Terror,* p. 99.

32. Parachini, "The World Trade Center Bombers (1993)," pp. 205–206; and Reeve, *The New Jackals,* p. 24.

33. Mylroie, *The War against America,* pp. 24–26.

34. Ibid., pp. 28–32.

35. Laurie Mylroie pointed out that U.S. authorities intercepted a telephone call from Sudan's UN ambassador to Hassan al-Turabi, the leader of the National Islamic Front. The ambassador protested to Turabi that two agents from his own UN mission had been involved in the bombing plot, yet he had not been informed, whereupon al-Turabi responded, "Mind your own business." Ibid., p. 191.

36. Ibid., p. 183.

37. For more on the life of Muhammad, see Lance Williams and Erin McCormick, "Bin Laden's Man in Silicon Valley: 'Mohamed the American' Orchestrated Terrorist Acts While Living a Quiet Suburban Life in Santa Clara," *San Francisco Gate,* September 21, 2001, http://www.sfgate.com.

38. Emerson, *American Jihad,* p. 60.

39. Ibid., p. 80.

40. Ibid., pp. 84–85.

41. Ibid., pp. 93–98. In October 2003, Alamoudi was indicted on charges that he illegally accepted $340,000 from the Libyan government for his efforts to persuade the U.S. government to lift sanctions imposed on Libya for supporting terrorism. David Frum and Richard Perle, *An End to Evil: How to Win the War on Terror* (New York: Random House, 2003), p. 83.

42. Shaul Mishal and Avraham Sela, *The Palestinian Hamas: Vision, Violence, and Coexistence* (New York: Columbia University Press, 2000), p. 163.

43. Emerson, *American Jihad,* pp. 103–104.

44. Those charged were accused of planning to purchase night-vision goggles and cameras, stun guns, blasting equipment, binoculars, radars, laser range finders, mine-detection equipment, and advanced aircraft analysis and design software. Emerson, *American Jihad,* pp. 35–36.

45. Anti-Defamation League, "Dearborn Man Charged with Supporting Hezbollah," January 30, 2004. http://www.adl.org.

46. Anti-Defamation League, "Muslims of the Americas: In Their Own Words," http://www.adl.org (downloaded January 9, 2002).

47. Jerry Seeper and Steve Miller, "Militant Muslims Seek Virginia Base," *Washington Times,* July 1, 2002. http://www.washtimes.com/.

48. Emerson, *American Jihad,* pp. 111–116.

49. The Anti-Defamation League praised federal law enforcement for arresting Arian. ADL Press Release, "ADL Commends Law Enforcement for Arrests of Suspected Terrorist Supporters," February 20, 2003.

50. Anti-Defamation League, *Jihad Online: Islamic Terrorists and the Internet* (New York: ADL, 2002), p. 18.

51. See Mary Beth Sheridan, "More Serious Charges Possible in 'Va. Jihad Network' Case, *Washington Post,* August 2, 2003, p. B02; and Kevin Bohn, "'Virginia Jihad' Suspects Charged with Plotting to Fight U.S.," CNN.com, http://cnn.law.printhis.clickability.com/pt/cpt?action=cptandtitle=CNN.com+-+%27Virginia (downloaded February 10, 2004).

52. These figures are from the Middle East Policy Council, http://www.mepc.org/public_asp/workshops/musworld.asp

53. Pipes, *Militant Islam Reaches America,* pp. 38–127.

54. Mattias Gardell, *In the Name of Elijah Muhammad: Louis Farrakhan and the Nation of Islam* (Durham, NC: Duke University Press, 1996), pp. 31–37.

55. Ibid., p. 12.

56. For example, the Nation of Islam teaches that Wallace D. Fard was God and Elijah Muhammad was a prophet; traditional Islam teaches that Muhammad was the final prophet. Furthermore, the NOI subscribes to a racialist theology, which traditional Islam rejects (despite previous and current racism in the Islamic world).

57. Abraham Foxman, *Never Again? The Threat of the New Anti-Semitism* (New York: Harper Collins, 2003), pp. 185–186.

58. Gardell, *In the Name of Elijah Muhammad,* p. 265.

59. Foxman, *Never Again?* p. 161.

60. Foxman, *Never Again?* p. 173.

61. Mattias Gardell, "Black and White Unite in Fight?" in Jeffrey Kaplan and Heléne Lööw, *The Cultic Milieu: Oppositional Subcultures in an Age of Globalization* (New York: Alta Mira Press, 2002), p. 172.

62. Gardell, *In the Name of Elijah Muhammad,* p. 322.

63. Interview with Tom Metzger, October 15, 2005; and Gardell, "Black and White Unite in Fight?" p. 173.

64. Gardell, "Black and White Unite in Fight?" p. 174.

65. Ibid., p. 175.

66. Ibid., p. 176.

67. Foxman, *Never Again?* p. 179.

68. Gardell, "Black and White Unite in Fight?" p. 177.

69. Muammar al-Qaddafi, "The Green Book," in Adam Parfrey, ed., *Extreme Islam: Anti-American Propaganda of Muslim Fundamentalism* (Los Angeles: Feral House, 2001), p. 133.

70. Louis R. Mizell Jr., *Target U.S.A.: The Inside Story of the New Terrorist War* (New York: John Wiley and Sons, 1998), pp. 25–26.

71. Chuck Morse, *The Nazi Connection to Islamic Terrorism: Adolf Hitler and Haj Amin al-Husseini* (Lincoln, NE: iUniverse, 2003), p. 106.

72. Gardell, *In the Name of Elijah Muhammad,* p. 206.

73. Quoted in Gardell, *In the Name of Elijah Muhammad,* p. 207.

74. See Arthur G. Magida, *Prophet of Rage: A Life of Louis Farrakhan and His Nation* (New York: Basic Books, 1996), pp. 102–103.

75. Ibid., p. 190; Louis Farrakhan, "The Great Atonement," in Parfrey, *Extreme Islam,* pp. 238–246.

76. Magida, *Prophet of Rage,* p. 200.

77. Gardell, *In the Name of Elijah Muhammad,* p. 210.

78. "Islamic Terrorists and American Extremists," July 14, 2002, http://www.policeone.com/policeone/rontend/parser.fm?object.

79. For more on El Rukns and its ties to Libya, see Howard Abadinsky, *Organized Crime,* 7th ed. (Belmont, CA: Wadsworth/Thompson, 2003), pp. 136–137.

80. David Kaplan, "Made in the U.S.A.," *U.S. News and World Report,* June 10, 2002, http:// www.usnews. com/usnews/news/articles/10jihad.ht.

81. Aukai Collins, *My Jihad* (Guilford, CT: Lyons Press, 2002).

82. Sara Jess and Gabriel Beck, *John Walker Lindh: American Taliban* (San Jose: University Press of California, 2002), p. 167.

83. Lauri Kellman, "FBI: Lindh Assaulted at Federal Prison in California," Associated Press, March 6, 2003.

84. Tony Locy, "Authorities: Padilla Plot Included Plan to Blow Up Apartments," *USA TODAY,* June 1, 2004, http://www.usatoday.com/news/nation/2004–06–01-padilla_x.htm? POE=NEWISVA.

85. Ron Scherer and Alexandra Marks, "Gangs, Prison: Al Qaeda Breeding Grounds? With the Arrest of Jose Padilla, Roots of American Disaffection Get a Closer Look," *Christian Science Monitor,* June 14, 2002, p. 2.

86. For more on Gadahn, see the Associated Press, "Profile of Terror? American on List Turned to Islam, Vanished," May 27, 2004, http://www.msnbc.msn.com/id/5074719/; "Azzam the American Threatens U.S.," Fox News, October 29, 2004, http://www.foxnews.com/story/ 0,2933,136937,00.html; and Annette Stark, "Peace, Love, Death Metal," *Los Angeles City Beat* 66, September 9, 2004, http://lacitybeat.com/article.php?id=1212andIssueNum=66.

87. For more on Isa Abdullah Ali, see Mizell, *Target U.S.A.,* pp. 56–63.

88. "U.S. Soldier Charged in Grenade Attack on 101st in Kuwait," CNN.com.

89. The U.S. Department of Justice indicted al-Masri on May 27, 2004, for terrorism-related crimes, including attempting to establish a terror training camp in Oregon and assisting in the kidnapping of two other Americans in Yemen. "U.S. Indicts British Cleric on 11 Charges," May 27, 2004, http://www.msnbc.msn.com/id/5071534/.

90. Christopher Mansey, "Naval Reservist Investigated. He Could Have Ties to Radicals," *USATODAY,* July 27, 2002, p. 11A.

91. For more on Anderson, see "Soldier charged in al-Qaeda probe," *USA TODAY,* February 18, 2004, http://www.usatoday.com/news/nation/2004–02–18-soldier-charged_x.htm and Anti-Defamation League, "National Guardsman Suspected of Trying to Aid al Qaeda," February 13, 2004, http://www.adl.org.

92. For more on Chitigov, see "Warlord Killed in Chechnya Was Ex–U.S. Marine," March 24, 2005, http://www.globalsecurity.org/military/library/news/2005/03/mil–050324-rianovosti21. htm.

93. Paul R. Pillar, *Terrorism and U.S. Foreign Policy* (Washington, DC: Brookings Institution Press, 2001), p. 52.

94. Mizell, *Target U.S.A.,* pp. 54–55.

95. Ibid., p. 181.

96. Ibid., pp. 53–54.

97. Ibid., p. 181.

98. Ibid., p. 184.

99. Ibid., pp. 192–193. According to the journalists Yosri Fouda and Nick Fielding, both Mir Aimal Kansi and Ramzi Yousef spent time in the same guesthouse in Muridke, Pakistan, operated by Markaz ad Dawa wal Irshad—an organization formed under the influence of Abdullah Azzam and whose members attacked the Indian parliament on December 13, 2001. See Fouda and Fielding, *Masterminds of Terror,* p. 45.

100. Mizell, *Target U.S.A.,* pp. 194–195.

101. Ibid., p. 75.

102. Ibid., p. 75.

103. Ibid., p. 198.

104. Emerson, *American Jihad,* p. 30.

105. Bergen, *Holy War, Inc.,* pp. 139–140.

106. Bob Woodward, *Bush at War* (New York: Simon and Schuster, 2002), p. 295.

107. Frum and Perle, *An End to Evil,* p. 89.

108. Anti-Defamation League, "ADL Satisfied with Designation of the 2002 LAX Shooting as a Terrorist Act," April 14, 2003, http://www.adl.org.

109. Matthew Barakat, "Valedictorian Suspect in Plot on Bush's Life," *Detroit Free Press,* February 23, 2005, http://www.freep.com/news/nw/terror23e_20050223.htm.

110. Al Qaeda planners eventually ruled out the White House for "navigational reasons." The comparatively small building could not be easily spotted from the air. It is believed that hijacker pilot Ziad al-Jarrah intended to strike the Capitol. Fouda and Fielding, *Masterminds of Terror,* pp. 127–128. United Airlines Flight 93 was scheduled to depart from the Newark Airport at 8:00 A.M., but a forty-minute delay put the hijackers behind schedule. This delay allowed the passengers the time to hear of the initial attacks by way of their cell phones. Thus by mere accident, the hijackers may have been thwarted from carrying out their mission. Paul L. Williams, *Osama's Revenge: The Next 9/11* (Amherst, NY: Prometheus Books, 2004), p. 64.

111. Woodward, *Bush at War,* p. 40.

112. Kaplan, "Made in the U.S.A."

113. Such attacks are believed to have occurred in other countries. In Tunisia, for example, one Nizar Naouar is believed to have blown up a gas truck near the historic Ghriba synagogue in May 2002. "FBI Warns about Fuel Tank Attacks," *USATODAY,* June 21, 2002, http://www.usatoday.com.

114. Mohamad Bazzi, "Militant Combat Training Offered in U.S.," *Pipedream,* October 5, 2001, http://www.bupipedream.com/011005/news/n4.html.

115. Gunaratna, *Inside al Qaeda,* pp. 116–118.

116. Marc Sageman, *Understanding Terror Networks* (Philadelphia: University of Pennsylvania Press, 2004), p. 95.

117. Josie Appleton, "Fundamentalism Begins at Home," *Spiked,* December 14, 2004.

118. Claire Sterling, *The Terror Network* (New York: Berkley Books, 1984); and Pillar, *Terrorism and U.S. Foreign Policy,* pp.42–43.

119. Pillar, *Terrorism and U.S. Foreign Policy,* pp.50–51.

120. Walter Laqueur, *No End to War: Terrorism in the Twenty-First Century* (New York: Continuum, 2003), pp. 68–69.

CHAPTER 5. INTERACTION BETWEEN THE EXTREME RIGHT AND ISLAMIC/ARAB EXTREMISTS

1. "Report: Anthrax Could Be from Domestic Extremists," CNN, October 26, 2001, http://archives.cnn.com/2001/HEALTH/conditions/10/27/post.report.extremists/.

2. As quoted in Harold Brackman, *9/11 Digital Lies: A Survey of Online Apologists for Global Terrorism* (Los Angeles: Simon Wiesenthal Center, 2001), p. 16.

3. See Robert Pate, "The Anthrax Murders: The Israeli Connection," *National Vanguard,* pp. 3–5; 22–29.

4. Anti-Defamation League, *Beyond Anthrax: Extremism and the Bioterrorism Threat* (New York: Anti-Defamation League, 2003).

5. Amir Taheri, *Holy Terror: Inside the World of Islamic Terrorism* (Bethesda, MD: Adler and Adler, 1987), p. 50.

6. Chuck Morse, *The Nazi Connection to Islamic Terrorism: Adolf Hitler and Haj Amin al-Husseini* (Lincoln, NE: iUniverse, 2003), pp. 12–14.

7. Ibid., p. 20.

8. Kenneth R. Timmerman, *Preachers of Hate: Islam and the War on America* (New York: Crown Forum, 2003), pp. 102–103.

9. Ibid., pp. 104.

10. Quoted in ibid., pp. 105.

11. Ataullah Bogdan Kopanski, "Muslims and the Reich," *Barnes Review* (September–October 2003): 27.

12. Ibid., p. 29.

13. Ibid., p. 28.

14. Timmerman, *Preachers of Hate,* pp. 105–106.

15. Ibid., pp. 103–104.

16. Interview with Ahmed Huber, April 2003.

17. According to documented private conversations he had with his staff, Hitler lamented his alliance with Italy, insofar as it alienated some people in the Muslim world. Italian adventures were looked upon as imperialistic aggression by those countries in North Africa that Mussolini had invaded. Hitler expressed admiration for the solidarity of the Muslim people and believed that they could have been potentially useful allies against his enemies. See L. Craig Fraser, *The Hitler-Bormann Documents.* Date and publisher unknown.

18. Timmerman, *Preachers of Hate,* p. 107. See also Norman Cameron and R. H. Steven, trans., *Hitler's Table Talk, 1941–1944* (New York: Enigma Books, 2000), p. 547.

19. For more on the Handschar Division, see George Lepre, *Himmler's Bosnian Division: The Waffen-SS Handschar Division, 1943–1945* (Atglen, PA: Schiffer Military History, 1997).

20. Morse, *The Nazi Connection to Islamic Terrorism,* p. 74.

21. Yossef Bodansky, *Islamic Anti-Semitism as a Political Instrument* (Houston, TX: Ariel Center for Policy Research, 1999), p. 30.

22. Morse, *The Nazi Connection to Islamic Terrorism,* p. 80.

23. Kopanski, "Muslims and the Reich," p. 27.

24. Michael J. Martin, "Arab Nazism: Then and Now," FrontPage.com, February 24, 2003, http://www.frontpage.com/Articles/Printable.asp?ID=6291.

25. Kopanski, "Muslims and the Reich," pp. 30–31.

26. Ibid., p. 32.

27. Morse, *The Nazi Connection to Islamic Terrorism,* pp. 63–71.

28. Lenni Brenner, *Zionism in the Age of the Dictators: A Reappraisal* (Chicago: Lawrence Hill Books, 1983). Eichmann initially supported Jewish immigration into Palestine. After his trip to Jerusalem in 1937, however, he recommended that Jewish immigration be forbidden. He was apparently taken by the display of Nazi flags and portraits of Hitler that he saw during his stay there. Morse, *The Nazi Connection to Islamic Terrorism,* p. 45.

29. Martin A. Lee, *The Beast Reawakens* (Boston, MA: Little, Brown, 1997), p. 123.

30. Morse, *The Nazi Connection to Islamic Terrorism,* p. 142.

31. "Hitler's Promises to the Grand Mufti of Jerusalem," in Adam Parfrey, ed., *Extreme Islam: Anti-American Propaganda of Muslim Fundamentalism* (Los Angeles: Feral House, 2001), pp. 23–28.

32. Morse, *The Nazi Connection to Islamic Terrorism,* p. 57.

33. Ibid., p. 86.

34. Timmerman, *Preachers of Hate,* p. 111.

35. Kevin Coogan, *Dreamer of the Day: Francis Parker Yockey and the Postwar Fascist International* (New York: Autonomedia, 1999), p. 385.

36. Morse, *The Nazi Connection to Islamic Terrorism,* p. 94.

37. The Green Shirts went by different official names during its history, including *Misf al-Farât* in the 1930s, the Islamic National Party in 1940, and the Socialist Party in 1946. Its leader, Ahmed Hussein, also wrote a book in the style of Hitler's *Mein Kampf* titled *Imâni* and published a rabidly anti-Semitic journal called *al-Ichtirakya.* During a visit to New York in the late 1940s, Ahmed Hussein, the leader of the Green Shirt Party, addressed a meeting of the extreme right

National Renaissance Party (NRP). Kurt Mertig, the NRP's first chairman, hoped to get a post at Cairo University. Coogan, *Dreamer of the Day,* pp. 380, 387.

38. Morse, *The Nazi Connection to Islamic Terrorism,* p. 28.

39. Irving Sedar and Harold J. Greenberg, *Behind the Egyptian Sphinx* (Philadelphia: Chilton, 1960), p. 53.

40. Ibid., p. 59.

41. According to Anis Mansour, one of Sadat's closest friends and advisers, the peace treaty did not mean that Sadat had a change of heart toward Israel. Rather, the treaty was a diplomatic maneuver that allowed Egypt to sit down with Israel and settle its accounts. See Bodansky, *Islamic Anti-Semitism as a Political Instrument,* p. 78.

42. Sedar and Greenberg, *Behind the Egyptian Sphinx,* p. 45.

43. For more on this issue, see ibid.; and Lee, *The Beast Reawakens.*

44. Coogan, *Dreamer of the Day,* p. 382.

45. Lee, *The Beast Reawakens,* pp. 140–141.

46. Ibid., p. 146.

47. Ibid., pp. 126–130.

48. Glenn B. Infield, *Skorzeny: Hitler's Commando* (New York: Military Heritage Press, 1981), p. 209.

49. Sedar and Greenberg, *Behind the Egyptian Sphinx,* pp. 63–64.

50. Lee, *The Beast Reawakens,* p. 143.

51. Coogan, *Dreamer of the Day,* p. 382.

52. Sedar and Greenberg, *Behind the Egyptian Sphinx,* p. 69.

53. Coogan, *Dreamer of the Day,* p. 383.

54. Martin Lee, "The Swastika and Crescent," *Intelligence Report,* Spring 2002, http://www .splcenter/intelligenceproject/ip–4u3.html.

55. Sedar and Greenberg, *Behind the Egyptian Sphinx,* p. 76.

56. Coogan, *Dreamer of the Day,* p. 388.

57. Ibid., pp. 382–383.

58. Sedar and Greenberg, *Behind the Egyptian Sphinx,* p. 65.

59. Ibid., p. 67.

60. Infield, *Skorzeny,* p. 210.

61. Sedar and Greenberg, *Behind the Egyptian Sphinx,* p. 70.

62. Infield, *Skorzeny,* p. 217.

63. Yockey's *Imperium* was important to the development of postwar neofascism in that it modified the ideology to reflect the new conditions of that era. For more on Yockey see Francis Parker Yockey, *Imperium* 3rd ed. (Costa Mesa, CA: Noontide Press, 1991); Coogan, *Dreamer of the Day;* and Lee, *The Beast Reawakens.*

64. See, for example, Francis Parker Yockey, *The Enemy of Europe* (Reedy, WV: Liberty Bell Publications, 1981).

65. Coogan believed that Nazi scientists in Argentina may have been working on such a project. Just exactly what the "cobalt bomb" is, is unclear. Weiss described it as a "goose-egg bomb, capable of destroying four city blocks." It sounds as if it might have been a forerunner to the so-called suitcase nuclear bombs produced in the former Soviet Union. There is little information available to corroborate just how serious the cobalt bomb project was. See Coogan, *Dreamer of the Day,* pp. 380–381.

66. This is asserted by a representative of the Anti-Defamation League in an FBI Internal Memorandum, File Number 97–3835–33, July 13, 1959.

67. Nicholas Goodrick-Clarke, *The Black Sun: Aryan Cults, Esoteric Nazism and the Politics of Identity* (New York: New York University Press, 2002), p. 78.

68. Coogan, *Dreamer of the Day,* p. 389.

69. Lee, *The Beast Reawakens,* p. 181.

70. Claire Sterling, *The Terror Network* (New York: Berkley Books, 1984), p. 116.

71. Peter Wyden, *The Hitler Virus: The Insidious Legacy of Adolf Hitler* (New York: Arcade Publishing, 2001), p. 111.

72. Ibid., p. 111; and William Grim, "Neo-Nazi al Qaeda," Frontpagemag.com, March 4, 2004, http://frontpagemag.com/Articles/ReadArticle.asp?ID=12436.

73. Lee, "The Swastika and Crescent."

74. Wyden, *The Hitler Virus,* p. 112.

75. Sterling, *The Terror Network,* p. 113.

76. Ibid., p. 113.

77. Ibid., p. 114.

78. Lee, *The Beast Reawakens,* p. 180.

79. Ibid., pp. 180–181.

80. Ibid., pp. 158–159.

81. Bruce Hoffman, *Right-Wing Terrorism in Europe since 1980* (Santa Monica, CA: RAND Corporation, 1984), pp. 6–7.

82. Lee, "The Swastika and Crescent."

83. Benjamin Netanyahu, *Fighting Terrorism: How Democracies Can Defeat the International Terrorist Network* (New York: Farrar, Straus and Giroux, 2001), p. 61; and Lee, *The Beast Reawakens,* p. 205

84. Rand C. Lewis, *A Nazi Legacy: Right-Wing Extremism in Postwar Germany* (New York: Praeger, 1991), p. 157.

85. Ibid., p. 157.

86. Ibid., p. 161.

87. Lee, *The Beast Reawakens,* p. 202.

88. Morse, *The Nazi Connection to Islamic Terrorism,* p. 33.

89. According to a former Libyan minister of planning, Omar el-Meheishi, Qaddafi allocated approximately $580 million for terrorism and paramilitary activities for the year 1976 alone. Whitaker, *The Terrorism Reader,* p. 64. According to one estimate, between 1975 and 1985 Libya was responsible for approximately 200 terrorist operations, which resulted in the death of roughly 100 people and the wounding of 500 more. Warren Kinsella, *Unholy Alliances: Terrorists, Extremists, Front Companies, and the Libyan Connection in Canada* (Toronto, ON: Lester Publishing, 1992), p. 23.

90. Lee, "The Swastika and Crescent."

91. Cindy C. Combs, *Terrorism in the Twenty-First Century* (Upper Saddle River, NJ: Prentice-Hall, 1997), p. 101.

92. See, for example, Kinsella, *Unholy Alliances.*

93. Lee, *The Beast Reawakens,* pp. 182–183.

94. Kinsella, *Unholy Alliances,* p. 3.

95. Ibid., pp. 22–46.

96. Interview with Tom Metzger, March 2003.

97. Quoted in Kinsella, *Unholy Alliances,* p. 101.

98. Martin Walker, *The National Front* (Glasgow, Scotland: William Collins, 1977).

99. Nick Griffin's background is characteristic of the new, more professional racialist right: he received degrees in both history and law from Cambridge University. Nick Ryan, *Into a World of Hate: A Journey among the Extreme Right* (New York: Routledge, 2004), p. 62.

100. Gerry Gable, "The Far Right in Contemporary Britain," in Luciano Cheles, Ronnie Ferguson, and Michalina Vaughan, eds., *Neo-Fascism in Europe* (New York: Longman, 1991), pp. 250–261.

101. Ryan, *Into a World of Hate,* p. 55.

102. David J. Whitaker, ed., *The Terrorism Reader* (London: Routledge, 2001), p. 66.

103. "U.S.: Libya Takes Lockerbie Blame," CNN.com, February 10, 2004.

104. Michael Reynolds, "Virtual Reich," *Playboy,* February, 2002, http://www.vanguard newsnetwork.com/index181.htm.

105. Ibid.

106. See Stephen Jones, with Peter Israel, *Others Unknown: The Oklahoma City Bombing Case and Conspiracy* (New York: Public Affairs, 1998); and David Hoffman, *The Oklahoma City Bombing and the Politics of Terror* (Venice, CA: Feral House, 1998).

107. Dirk J. Barreveld, *Terrorism in the Philippines: The Bloody Trail of Abu Sayyaf, Bin Laden's East Asian Connection* (Lincoln, NE: Writers Club Press, 2001), p. 8.

108. Simon Reeve, *The New Jackals: Ramzi Yousef, Osama bin Laden, and the Future of Terrorism* (Boston: Northeastern University Press, 1999), p. 82.

109. Ibid., pp. 81–84.

110. Ibid., p. 83.

111. Ibid., p. 82.

112. Jim Crogan, "The Terrorist Motel: The I-40 connection between Zacarias Moussaoui and Mohamed Atta," http://www.apfn.org/apfn/OKC_motel.htm (downloaded March 14, 2003).

113. According to author Paul Williams, some FBI officials believe that there was an operational connection between Yousef and Nichols. However, I know of no public statement by the FBI that suggests this. Paul L. Williams, *Al Qaeda: Brotherhood of Terror* (Upper Saddle River, NJ: Alpha, 2002), pp. 145–146.

114. Yael Haran, "A Terrifying Alliance," http://www.enduring-freedom-operation.org/alliance.stm, January 14, 2002.

115. Laurie Mylroie, *The War against America: Saddam Hussein and the World Trade Center Attacks* (New York: Regan Books, 2001), p. 8.

116. "Oklahoma City Blast Linked to bin Laden," WorldNetDaily, March 21, 2001, http://worldnetdaily.com.

117. Jayna Davis, *The Third Terrorist: The Middle East Connection to the Oklahoma City Bombing* (Nashville, TN: WND Books, 2004), pp. 120–121.

118. Ibid., p. 299.

119. Ibid., p. 34.

120. Crogan, "The Terrorist Motel."

121. Eric Boehler, "Did Timothy McVeigh Have Iraqi Helpers?" Salon.com, December 2, 2002, http://www.salon.com.

122. Davis, *The Third Terrorist,* pp. 37–40.

123. Michael Piper, "Neo-Cons Hype New Book Pinning OKC Bombing on Saddam, Osama," *The American Free Press,* May 31, 2004, pp. 6–7.

124. Lou Michel and Dab Herbeck, *American Terrorist: Timothy McVeigh and the Oklahoma City Bombing* (New York: Regan Books, 2001), pp. 286–287.

125. Davis, *The Third Terrorist,* p. 60.

126. McVeigh fired a 25mm high-explosive round that struck an Iraqi soldier directly in the chest. As McVeigh recounted: "His head just disappeared. . . . I saw everything above the shoulders disappear, like in a red mist." After reflecting on his actions, McVeigh felt angry and uncomfortable. Michel and Herbeck, *American Terrorist,* pp. 72–75.

127. Davis, *The Third Terrorist,* p. 58.

128. Timothy McVeigh, "On Hypocrisy," http://www.vanguardnewsnetwork.com/vnn/showEssay.asp?essayID=1253 (downloaded April 24, 2003).

129. The story leaked by Defense Department officials of a possible link between McVeigh and Iraq was published in the "Washington Whispers" segment of the October 29, 2001, issue of *U.S. News and World Report.*

130. Wolfowitz confirmed to a *Vanity Fair* reporter that he seriously entertained the theory that "based on phone records and other evidence," Saddam Hussein was behind the 1995 attack in Oklahoma City. Davis, *The Third Terrorist,* p. 60.

131. Davis, *The Third Terrorist,* p. 138.

132. David Frum and Richard Perle, *An End to Evil: How to Win the War on Terror* (New York: Random House, 2003), p. 49.

133. These observations are made in Charles A. Morse, "The Nazi Background of Saddam Hussein," February 21, 2003, http://newsmax.com/archives/articles/2003/2/20/145726.shtml.

134. William Grim, "Neo-Nazi al Qaeda," www.TheJewishPress.com, March 4, 2004, http://frontpagemag.com/Articles/Printable.asp?ID=12436.

135. Center for Democratic Renewal, *International Connections of U.S. White Supremacists* (Atlanta, GA: CDR, n.d.), p. 71.

136. Michael O'Meara, *New Culture, New Right: Anti-Liberalism in Postmodern Europe* (Bloomington, IN: 1st Books, 2004), pp. 167, 172.

137. Harvey G. Simmons, *The French National Front: The Extremist Challenge to Democracy* (Boulder, CO: Westview Press, 1996), pp. 101–102.

138. Haran, "A Terrifying Alliance."

139. Vladimir Solovyov and Elena Klepikova, *Zhirinovsky: Russian Fascism and the Making of a Dictator* (Reading, MA: Addison-Wesley, 1995), pp. 122–123.

140. Ibid., p. 124.

141. Ibid., pp. 127–129.

142. Nabi Abdullaev, "Fundamentalism in Russia: An Interview with Islam Committee's Heidar Jamal," in Parfrey, *Extreme Islam,* pp. 281–284.

143. James Ridgeway, "White Power and al Qaeda Unite against America." *The Village Voice,* October 31–November 6, 2001.

144. Haran, "A Terrifying Alliance."

145. Abraham Foxman, *Never Again? The Threat of the New Anti-Semitism* (New York: HarperCollins, 2003), pp. 221.

146. Peter Finn, "Unlikely Allies Bound by a Common Hatred," *Washington Post,* April 29, 2002, page A13.

147. Ibid., p. A13.

148. Michelle Cottle, "White Hope," *New Republic,* November 21, 2001, http://www.tnr .com.

149. See Aryan Nations' Ministry of Islamic Liaison, http://www.aryan-nations.org/Islam/ index.htm.

150. Actually, the plight of Eastern European women trafficked into prostitution has caught the attention of human rights groups such as Amnesty International. The lack of attention this story had received in the major American media is cited by the far right as further proof of Jewish control of the media. For more on this issue, see U.S. Department of State, Bureau of Democracy, Human Rights, and Labor, "'White Slave' Prostitution in Israel: Non-Jewish Women Imported from Russia, Ukraine," March 31, 2003; and Matthew Gutman, "Pressured by U.S., Israel Battles a Burgeoning 'White Slave' Trade," *Forward,* June 28, 2002, http://www.forward. com/issues/2002/02.06.28/news10.html.

151. "A Turning Tide Is a Violent Tide," http://aryan-nations.org/Islam/index.htm.

152. According to Hoskins, throughout history righteous "Phineas Priests" have fulfilled a sacred role by assassinating those who have transgressed God's law. He cites some diverse historical examples, including Robin Hood, St. George, Beowulf, King Arthur, John Wilkes Booth, Jesse James, Gordon Kahl (the late radical tax protester and member of the Posse Comitatus), and Robert Jay Matthews (the late leader of the Order). Not long after the first publication of the book, several right-wing terrorists identified themselves as Phineas Priests and have engaged in criminal acts, including robbery and terrorism. For example, in 1996 a white separatist cell calling themselves Phineas Priests committed a string of bombings and bank robberies in Washington state. Other right-wing extremists have used the name as well; however, the name appears to denote more of a "state of mind" fellowship than a formal organization. According to Bruce

Hoffman, the name Phineas is taken from a character in the Old Testament (Numbers 25), who became an avenger priest by murdering a Midianite woman whom he discovered having sex with her Israelite lover. Bruce Hoffman, *Inside Terrorism* (New York: Columbia University Press, 1998), p. 119.

153. Amardeep Bassey, "Midland Nazi Turns to Islam," *Sunday Mercury,* February 16, 2003.

154. Ryan, *Into a World of Hate,* p. 55.

155. Some observers believe that Column 88 was a state-directed organization intended for various purposes, including discrediting the far right and serving as part of an anticommunist resistance movement in the event of war with the Soviet Union. Gerry Gable, "Britain's Nazi Underground," in Luciano Cheles, Ronnie Ferguson, and Michalina Vaughan, eds., *The Far Right in Western and Eastern Europe,* 2nd ed. (London: Longman, 1995), p. 258.

156. Ryan, *Into a World of Hate,* p. 17.

157. For more on the life of David Myatt, see "David Myatt Biographical Sketch: The Life and Times of David Myatt," http://www.geocities.com/davidmyatt/biog.html (downloaded February 1, 2003).

158. David Myatt, "Towards the Galactic Empire: Autobiographical Notes Part Two," http://www.geocities. com/davidmyatt/biog.html (downloaded January 30, 2003).

159. David Myatt, "Islam and National Socialism," http://www.geocities.com/david myatt88/islamandns.htm.

160. David Myatt, "National-Socialism and Muslims," http://www.geocities.com/david myatt88/ns_muslims.htm.

161. David Myatt, "My Conversion to Islam," http://www.davidmyatt.portland.co.uk/ texts/my_conversion_to_islam.htm (downloaded February 10, 2003).

162. David Myatt, "Why I Am a Muslim," http://www.davidmyatt.portland.co.uk/texts/ why_i_am_a_muslim.htm (downloaded February 10, 2003).

163. Myatt, "Towards the Galactic Empire."

164. David Myatt, "A Covert Life: The Fanatical Tale of David Myatt," http://www.geocities .com/davidmyatt/covertlife.html (downloaded January 30, 2003).

165. Myatt, "Towards the Galactic Empire."

166. Interview with David Myatt, April 2003.

167. Myatt, "A Covert Life: The Fanatical Tale of David Myatt."

168. "Islamic Sanctuary: The Real Cause of the War," http://www.aalhaqq.jeeran.com/ sanctuary.html (downloaded January 30, 2003).

169. "Why America Cannot Win Its Declared War against Islam," http://www.aalhaqq .jeeran.com/nowin.html (downloaded January 30, 2003).

170. Abdul Aziz [Myatt], "Why I Support Sheikh Usama bin Laden (hafidhahullah)," downloaded March 31, 2004. http://myweb.tiscali.co.uk/alghurabah/support/usama.html.

171. David Myatt, "Our Current Situation," *Situation Report: Reichsfolk,* emailed to me from David Myatt on January 21, 2002.

172. Ibid.

173. Interview with David Myatt, April 2003.

174. Lee, "The Swastika and Crescent."

175. Kevin Coogan, "Report on Islamists, the Far Right, and al-Taqwa," September 2002, http://coraclesyndicate.org/pub_e/k.coo_e/publ_09–02_1.htm.

176. Morse, *The Nazi Connection to Islamic Terrorism,* p. 101.

177. U.S. Department of the Treasury, "The United States and Italy Designate Twenty-Five Finances of Terror," August 29, 2002, http://www.ustreas.gov/press/releases/po3380.htm.

178. Jay Bushinsky, "Swiss Probe Anti-U.S. Neo-Nazi Suspected of Financial Ties to al Qaeda," SFGate.com, March 12, 2002, http://www.sfgate.com/cgi-bin/article.cgi?file=/c/a/ 2002/03MN192483.DTL.

179. Ibid.

180. In an interview with Huber, he mentioned meetings he had with American far rightists and Islamists, although he did not specify names. He reportedly had ties with the late Dr. William L. Pierce of the National Alliance. See Jim Oliphant, "The Hate Within," *Legal Times,* May 20, 2002.

181. Coogan, "Report on Islamists, the Far Right, and al-Taqwa."

182. "Swiss Holocaust Denier Admits Links to bin Laden's al Qaida," Jewish Telegraphic Agency (downloaded April 17, 2002). http://www.jewishsf.com/bk01113/i22.shtml.

183. Kevin Coogan, "The Mysterious Achmed Huber: Friend to Hitler, Allah and Ibn Laden?" http://coraclesyndicate.org/pub_e/k.coo_e/publ_05–02_1.htm, September 2002.

184. Interview with Ahmed Huber, April 2003.

185. Ibid.

186. Ibid.

187. Peter Finn, "Germany Bans Islamic Group," *Washington Post,* January 16, 2003, p. A14.

188. "Neo-Nazis Selling Weapons in Kosovo," Beta News Agency, January 6, 2004, http://news.suc.org/bydate/2004/January_10/2.html.

189. As reported in Paul Lungen, "Holocaust Denial Finds New Home," *Canadian Jewish News,* February 22, 2001, http://www.cjnews.com/main.asp.

190. "Strengthening Homeland Security Since 9/11," from the White House web page, http://whitehouse.gov/ homeland/six_month_update.html.

191. Stephen Schwarz, "Wahhabis in the Old Dominion: What the Federal Raids in Northern Virginia Uncovered," *Weekly Standard* 7, no. 29, April 8, 2002, http://www.weeklystandard. com.

192. Haran, "A Terrifying Alliance."

193. Rohan Gunaratna, *Inside al Qaeda: Global Network of Terror* (New York: Columbia University Press, 2002), p. 6. As a result of American retaliation after September 11, 2001, al Qaeda has become more dispersed and reportedly operates on much smaller sums than the estimated $30 million spent annually prior to the 9/11 attacks. "9/11 Panel Sees No Link between Iraq, al-Qaida," MSNBC, June 16, 2004, http://www.msnbc.msn.com/id/5223932/.

194. Howard Abadinsky, *Organized Crime,* 7th ed. (Belmont, CA: Wadsworth, 2003), p. 276.

195. Lee, "The Swastika and Crescent."

196. Interview with Ahmed Huber, April, 2003.

197. Bushinsky, "Swiss Probe Anti-U.S. Neo-Nazi Suspected of Financial Ties to al Qaeda."

198. Finn, "Unlikely Allies Bound by a Common Hatred," p. A13.

199. See the ADL website, www.adl.org, and the Simon Wiesenthal website, www.wiesenthal .com, for more on this issue.

200. ADL Press Release, "ADL Comments on Holocaust Denial Conference Held in Jordan," May 15, 2001.

201. Interview with Jürgen Graf, April 2003.

202. Foxman, *Never Again?* pp. 222–223.

203. *Jerusalem Post,* April 25, 2001, quoted in Foxman, *Never Again?* p. 220.

204. Foxman, *Never Again?* pp. 223–224.

205. Michael A. Ledeen, *The War against the Terror Masters* (New York: St. Martin's, 2003), p. 282.

206. "Revisionist Fredrick Töben Speaks at Iran's Intifada Conference," September 9, 2003, http://www.nationalvanguard.org/printer.hpp?id=114.

207. Reuven Paz, "Palestinian Holocaust Denial," *Washington Institute Peace Watch* no. 255, April 21, 2000. http://www.ict.org.il/articles/articledet.cfm?articleid+108.

208. ADL, "ADL Backgrounder: The Zayed Center," http://www.adl.org/Anti_semitism/zayed_center.asp (downloaded September 3, 2002).

209. ADL Press Release, "Arab League Think-Tank Labels Holocaust 'A Fable,'" August 28, 2002.

210. For more on Piper's lecture at the Zayed Center, see Abu Dhabi, "U.S. Scribe Urges Concern for Palestinians," *Gulf News,* March 12, 2003; and Syed Qama Hasan, "Israeli Lobby behind Iraq War Plan," *Khaaleej Times,* March 12, 2003.

211. In 1998 the *Sunday Times* of London reported that Israeli scientists were working on a form of biowarfare that would exploit medical advances and identify distinctive genes carried by Arabs. A genetically modified bacterium could then be created that would harm only ethnic Arabs. The disease could be spread by spraying the organisms in the air or putting them in water supplies. For more on this story, see Uzi Mahnaimi and Marie Colvin, "Israel Planning 'Ethnic' Bomb as Saddam Caves In," *Sunday Times,* November 8, 1998, http:www.the-times.co.uk.

212. Interview with Mike Piper, April 2003.

213. Richard V. London, "Malaysia Welcomes AFP," *American Free Press* 4, no. 37, September 13, 2004, pp. 1, 10.

214. Michael Collins Piper, *Final Judgment: The Missing Link in the JFK Assassination Conspiracy,* 5th ed. (Washington, DC: Center for Historical Review, 2000).

215. The fact that Jack Ruby was Jewish is cited often by Arabs and Iranians as compelling evidence that Jews were involved in the JFK assassination. See Daniel Pipes, *The Hidden Hand: Middle East Fears of Conspiracy* (New York: St. Martin's Griffin, 1998), p. 157. In an interview with Mike Piper at his office in the headquarters of the *American Free Press,* I noticed an advertising poster for his book *Final Judgment* in Arabic script. He told me that a Middle Eastern distributor had translated it and sold it in the region. He made no mention of the number of sales, claiming that it was not uncommon for books in the region to be pirated, thus making such figures hard to gauge.

216. Christopher Bollyn, "Vanunu Speaks: Israeli Whistleblower Risks Jail to Talk Exclusively to AFP," *American Free Press* 4, no. 32, August 9, 2004, p. 3.

217. Interview with Mike Piper, April 2003.

218. Foxman, *Never Again?* pp. 219–220.

219. ADL, "White Supremacist David Duke Invited to Give Anti-Semitic Lecture in Bahrain," November 14, 2002, http://www.adl.org.

220. Interview with David Duke, March 2003.

221. Ahmed Rashid, *Taliban* (New Haven, CT: Yale University Press, 2001), pp. 156–169.

222. Rashid, *Taliban,* pp. 176–177.

223. David Duke, "The Iraqi War: It's Not about Oil, Stupid!" *David Duke Online Report,* November 29, 2002, http:www.davidduke.com.

224. David Duke, "Evangelicals Who Serve the Anti-Christ!" January 25, 2003, http://www .davidduke.com/radio.

225. Duke, "Evangelicals Who Serve the Anti-Christ!"

226. See Daniel Pipes, "Canadian Islamists Host a Neo-Nazi," WorldNetDaily.com, January 7, 2004, http://www.danielpipes.org/pf.php?id=1431; and Gil Francisco White, "Islamist-Nazi Alliance Reborn on Campus?" *The Daily Pennsylvanian,* November 5, 2003, http://www.daily pennslyvania.com/vnews/display.v?ART/3fa8a3666637e.

227. Associated Press, "Ex-KKK Leader Duke Pleads Guilty to Charges," December 18, 2002.

228. For more on these demands, see "To: The Government of Israel," http://natall.com/ demands.index.html.

229. For more on the National Alliance demonstrations at the Israeli embassy see H. J. Brief, "White Supremacist Rally Draws Protestors." *Washington Times* (May 12, 2000); Lengel. "Neo-Nazis, Foes, Clash At Israeli Embassy." *Washington Post* (May 12, 2002), A19; and ADL. "Neo-Nazis Rally in Nation's Capital." August 26, 2002. http://www.adl.org/Learn/news/Neo_Nazis_Rally.asp. For a complete list of the demands see http://natall.com/demands/index.html. For more on the leafleting campaign see Anti-Defamation League. "Hate Literature Blitz Planned By Neo-Nazi Groups To Coincide With Jewish Holidays and 9/11." http://www.adl.org/PresRele?AUS_12/4148_12.asp, August 27, 2002.

230. ADL, "U.S. Anti-Semites Take Up Palestinian Cause," April 25, 2002, http://www.adl.org.

231. Pierce claimed that in September 2001 his website, natvan.com, received on average 19,000 hits a day—a 50 percent increase from a year earlier. William L. Pierce, "Provocation and Response," American Dissident Voices, September 15, 2001, http://natvan.com/pub/091501.txt.

232. As reported in Bill White, "Nazi Group Sees Explosive Growth in Wake of September 11 Attacks," November 15, 2001, http://overthrow.com.

233. Pierce, "Provocation and Response."

234. William Pierce, "Send Them All Back," American Dissident Voices, October 27, 2001.

235. William Pierce, "Terrorism and Hate," American Dissident Voices, November 10, 2001.

236. Eric Richardson, "Inside the 'Axis of Evil': A White Nationalist Visits Iran," National Vanguard 120 (May–June 2003): 3–7.

237. Kevin Alfred Strom, "Bring Our Troops Back Home," March 28, 2005, http://www.al-jazeera.com.

238. A transcript of the interview can be found in Kevin Alfred Strom, "Those Who Know Why," American Dissident Voices, May 29–June 4, 2005, http://nationalvanguard.org/story.php?id=5134.

239. William Pierce, "Bosch/Bin Laden," American Dissident Voices, August 14, 2002.

240. For example, the Jewish Defense League (JDL) has violently confronted both right-wing extremists and Muslims on previous occasions. In 1999, JDL members were involved in a fistfight with Klansmen on The Jerry Springer Show. Recently, the JDL has targeted Arabs and Muslims as well. In December 2001, JDL leader Irv Rubin and a fellow member were charged with plotting to bomb the King Fahd Mosque in Culver City and the San Clemente office of Darrell Issa, an Arab-American from California. "JDL Leader Charged in Bomb Plot Long Known for Extremism, Arrests," Baltimore Sun, December 14, 2001.

241. Jeffrey Fleishman, "Shared Hatred Draws Groups Closer," Los Angeles Times, January 19, 2003, http://www.boston.com/dailyglobe2/019/nation/Shared_hatred_draws_groups_closer?.shtml.

242. Bodansky, Islamic Anti-Semitism as a Political Instrument, p. 76.

243. Samuel Katz, Relentless Pursuit: The DSS and the Manhunt for the al-Qaeda Terrorists (New York: Forge, 2002), p. 235.

244. "Nazis Tied to Anthrax Attacks," Worldnetdaily, http://www.wnd.com/news/article.asp?ARTICLE_ID=25290 (downloaded November 16, 2001).

245. Paolo Pontoniere, "Al Qaeda Reaching Out to Non-Islamic Militant Groups," Pacific News Service, November 16, 2001. http://www.pacificnews.org.

246. For example, some Muslim scholars have attempted to show that Socrates, Lao-Tzu, Hammurabi, and Zoroaster were prophets of Allah and thus acceptable to Islam. Yahiya Emerick, The Complete Idiot's Guide to Understanding Islam (Indianapolis, IN: Alpha Books, 2002), p. 183. In this tradition, it might not be too much of a stretch to include Odin, Thor, and other members of the Norse pantheon into the framework of Islam.

247. Benjamin Netanyahu, "Defining Terrorism," in Benjamin Netanyahu, ed., Terrorism: How the West Can Win (New York: Farrar, Straus and Giroux, 1986), p. 13.

248. Martha Crenshaw, "Suicide Terrorism in Comparative Perspective," in International Policy Institute for Counter-Terrorism, Countering Suicide Terrorism (New York: International Policy Institute for Counter-Terrorism and the Anti-Defamation League, 2002), p. 22.

249. Alex Curtis praised the exploits of Benjamin Smith, a former member of the World Church of the Creator, who went on a shooting spree that killed two and injured several others. Just before he was about to be apprehended by the police, Smith committed suicide via a gunshot to the head. Curtis lauded Smith as an "Aryan kamikaze" in a subsequent newsletter. See "Aryan Kamikaze Terrorizes Midwest," Nationalist Observer, no. 15 (July 1999).

250. For groups that have sustained a protracted campaign of suicide terrorism, several layers of supporters are used. They include activists who initiate the attack by recruiting the terrorist

and providing him or her with training and intelligence on the target. Also, collaborators give logistical assistance to the suicide terrorist and his or her operational team. See "Benefits of the Suicide Attack," in *Countering Suicide Terrorism* (New York: International Policy Institute for Counter-Terrorism and the Anti-Defamation League, 2002), p. 149.

251. Specifically, numerous secular and religious benefits accrue to Islamic martyrs: (1) the family of the *shaheed* is showered with honor and praise, and their status is enhanced in the community; (2) the *shaheed* gains eternal life in paradise; (3) the *shaheed* gains permission to see the face of Allah; (4) the *shaheed* receives seventy-two young virgins, known as *houris*, who will serve him in paradise; (5) the *shaheed* is granted the privilege of promising life in heaven for seventy relatives; (6) the *shaheed* is revered in his community and mosque; and (7) Islamist groups and even some Arab governments will endow the family of the *shaheed* with material support. Jim Winkates. "Suicide Terrorism: Precedents and Profiles" (Maxwell Air Force Base, AL: Air War College, March 17, 2004), pp. 21–22.

252. Andrew Macdonald [William Pierce], *The Turner Diaries* (Hillsboro, WV: National Vanguard Books, 1993), p. 202.

253. Ibid., p. 202.

254. Ibid., p. 203. Italics in original.

255. The American Jewish Committee issued a press release announcing that members of a New York University student group, Arab Students United, distributed material written by David Duke. American Jewish Committee, "Arab Student Group Distributes David Duke Hate Material," October 8, 2001, http://www.ajc.org/InTheMedia/PressReleases. Also, the ADL issued a press release in which it disclosed several instances in which Muslims had used right-wing extremist propaganda to augment their anti-Zionist propaganda. See ADL, "ADL Says U.S.-Backed Anti-Semites Are Feeding Sept. 11 Rumor Mill," November 9, 2001, http://www.adl.org.

256. Abraham Foxman, "New Excuses, Old Hatred: Worldwide Anti-Semitism in Wake of 9/11," February 8, 2002, http://www.adl.org/main_Anti_Semitism_International/as_speech.htm.

257. "Speech by Prime Minister Muhammad Mahathir," October 16, 2003, http://www.adl.org/Anti_semitism/malaysian.asp.

258. See "Fallout from Mahathir" at the ADL website, www.adl.org.

259. Quoted in Simon Tisdall, "'Father' of Malaysia Savages Bush and Blair," *Guardian,* May 27, 2005.

260. Center for New Community. "CNC Uncovers Neo-Nazis Masquerading as Anti-Globalization Activists," June 21, 2002, http://newcom.org.

261. Reynolds, "Virtual Reich."

262. Rosebraugh's strategy is described in Michelle Malkin, "Eco-terrorists Declare War," *Washington Times,* March 24, 2003, http://www.washingtontimes.com

263. Kevin Coogan makes this observation in Reynolds, "Virtual Reich."

264. See, for example, Neil Clark, "Why the Left and Right Must Unite and Fight: The View from the Left," Anti-War.com, April 1, 2003.

265. Pipes, *The Hidden Hand,* p. 162.

266. Daniel Pipes, *Militant Islam Reaches America* (New York: W. W. Norton, 2002), pp. 212–213.

CHAPTER 6. THE U.S. GOVERNMENT'S RESPONSE TO POLITICAL EXTREMISM AND TERRORISM

1. Robert M. Blitzer, "FBI's Role in the Federal Response to the Use of Weapons of Mass Destruction: Statement of Robert M. Blitzer, Chief, Domestic Terrorism/Counter-terrorism Planning Section, FBI, before the U.S. House of Representatives Committee on National Security,"

November 4, 1997; and The White House, Office of the Press Secretary, "Fact Sheet: Combating Terrorism: Presidential Decision Directive 62," May 22, 1998.

2. The various new laws and initiatives nearly doubled the amount of money spent on counterterrorism, to $11 billion a year. Jim Redden, *Snitch Culture* (Venice, CA: Feral House, 2000), p. 71. Much of the money went to the FBI, whose antiterrorism budget jumped from $78 million to $609 million a year. Furthermore, between fiscal years 1993 and 2000 the number of FBI special agents assigned to counterterrorism programs increased from 550 to 1,669—approximately a 224 percent increase. Dale L. Watson, "The Terrorist Threat Confronting the United States: Statement for the Record of Dale L. Watson, Executive Assistant Director for Counterterrorism and Counterintelligence for the FBI before the Senate Select Committee on Intelligence," February 6, 2002, http://www.fbi.gov/congress/congress02/watson020602.htm; and Paul R. Pillar, *Terrorism and U.S. Foreign Policy* (Washington, DC: Brookings Institution, 2001), p. 80.

3. See Watson, "The Terrorist Threat Confronting the United States."

4. Bruce Hoffman, *Combating Terrorism: In Search of a National Strategy* (Washington, DC: RAND), March 27, 2001, p. 5; Federal Bureau of Investigation. *Terrorism in the United States 1999* (Washington, DC: FBI, 2001).

5. Much of this section is drawn from George Michael, "Right-Wing Extremism in the Land of the Free: Repression and Toleration in the USA," in Roger Eatwell and Cas Mudde, eds., *Western Democracies and the New Extreme Right Challenge* (London: Routledge, 2004), pp. 172–192.

6. James Kirkpatrick Davis, *Spying on America: The FBI's Domestic Counterintelligence Program* (Westport, CT: Praeger, 1992), p. 26.

7. Nathan Schachner, *The Price of Liberty: A History of the American Jewish Committee* (New York: American Jewish Committee, 1948), pp. 123, 159–162; Anti-Defamation League, *Not the Work of a Day: The Story of the Anti-Defamation League of B'nai B'rith* (New York: Anti-Defamation League, 1965), p 32; Morris Schonbach, "Native Fascism during the 1930s and 1940s: A Study of Its Roots, Its Growth, and Its Decline," Ph.D. diss., University of California at Los Angeles, 1958, pp. 436–437.

8. Arnold Forster, *Square One: The Memoirs of a True Freedom Fighter's Life-long Struggle against Anti-Semitism, Domestic and Foreign* (New York: Donald I. Fine, 1988), p. 55.

9. FBI Internal Memorandum, File Number 438611424445, September 8, 1964.

10. Phillip Finch, *God, Guts, and Guns* (New York: Seaview/Putnam, 1983), p. 158.

11. Davis, *Spying on America,* p. 93.

12. Ibid., p. 176.

13. Jessica Stern, *The Ultimate Terrorists* (Cambridge, MA: Harvard University Press, 1999), p. 149.

14. Michael A. Ledeen, *The War against the Terror Masters* (New York: St. Martin's, 2003), p. 71.

15. Oliver "Buck" Revell, *A G-Man's Journal* (New York: Pocket Star Books, 1998), pp. 254–255. Dr. James O'Connor, a former deputy assistant director of the FBI and currently a professor of criminology, communicated to me that the idea for the Hostage Rescue Team was conceived by the Training Division of the FBI. Telephone Conversation with Dr. James O'Connor, June 2002.

16. Danny O. Coulson and Elaine Shannon, *No Heroes: Inside the FBI's Secret Counter-Terror Force (*New York: Pocket Books, 1999), pp. 209–313.

17. Cheri Seymour, *Committee of the States: Inside the Radical Right* (Mariposa, CA: Camden Place Communications, 1991), p. 5.

18. Coulson and Shannon, *No Heroes,* p. 533.

19. David B. Kopel and Paul H. Blackman, *No More Wacos: What's Wrong with Federal Law Enforcement and How to Fix It* (Amherst, NY: Prometheus Books, 1997), p. 38.

20. Ibid., p. 61; Nancy T. Ammerman, "Waco, Law Enforcement, and Scholars of Religion," in Stuart A. Wright, *Armageddon in Waco: Critical Perspectives on the Branch Davidian Conflict* (Chicago: University of Chicago Press, 1995), p. 289; and Stuart A. Wright, *Armageddon in Waco: Critical Perspectives on the Branch Davidian Conflict* (Chicago: University of Chicago Press, 1995), pp. 88–89.

21. Michael Fortier and his wife Lori were accused of having foreknowledge of the planned bombing and not alerting authorities. Lori Fortier received "use immunity." Stephen Jones, with Peter Israel, *Others Unknown: The Oklahoma City Bombing Case and Conspiracy* (New York: Public Affairs, 1998), p. 96.

22. Redden, *Snitch Culture,* p. 71.

23. Daniel Klaidman and Michael Isikkoff, "The Feds' Quiet War: Inside the Secret Strategy to Combat the Militia Threat," *Newsweek,* April 22, 1996, p. 47.

24. David E. Kaplan and Mike Tharp, "Terrorism Threats at Home," *U.S. News and World Report,* December 29, 1997–January 5, 1998, pp. 22–27.

25. For example, the FBI spent two years investigating Alex Curtis as part of Operation Lone Wolf. Curtis's alleged offenses were amateurish and should probably have been handled by local authorities. For more on this investigation, see the FBI's report, "Operation Lone Wolf," 2000, http://www.fbi.gov/majcses/lonewolf1/htm.

26. Maria Glod and Jerry Markon, "Tracking Hate Groups Aids Terrorism Fight," *Washington Post,* May 19, 2003, p. B01.

27. For example, in 1998 the Anti-Defamation League released a report that warned of the growing influence of the National Alliance, calling it the "largest and most active neo-Nazi organization in the nation." The ADL attributed the National Alliance's strength to several factors: "its skillful embrace of technology, its willingness to cooperate with other extremists, its energetic recruitment and other promotional activities, and its vicious, but deceptively intellectualized propaganda." Anti-Defamation League, *Explosion of Hate: The Growing Danger of the National Alliance* (New York: ADL, 1998). In the last few years of his life, Pierce claimed that his organization had experienced substantial growth in members, financing, and influence. In an interview that I conducted with him in July 2000, he told me he had several full-time staff members at his national office and that the organization had even developed some "redundancy," whereby numerous personnel could perform multiple tasks such as Internet and computer operations.

28. For more on Cecchini, see Glod and Markon, "Tracking Hate Groups Aids Terrorism Fight," p. B01; and Heidi Beirich and Mark Potok, "40 to Watch," *Intelligence Report,* Summer 2003, n. 111, www.splcenter.org.

29. Bob Moser, "The Blotter," *Intelligence Report,* Spring 2003. http://www.splcenter.org/intelligenceproject.

30. Bill Torpy, "White Supremacist Held on Gun Charges Is a Victim of War on Terror, His Lawyers Say," *Atlanta Journal-Constitution,* July 22, 2003.

31. Anti-Defamation League, "ADL Welcomes Guilty Plea of White Supremacist Chester Doles," January 15, 2004, http://www.adl.org/learn/news/Chester_Doles2.asp.

32. Bill Torpy, "FBI Agent: Lawmen May Belong to Supremacist Group," *Atlanta Journal-Constitution,* March 12, 2003.

33. "Man Held for Months Reaches Plea Deal," October 29, 2003, http://www.theWBAL-Channel.com.

34. See Kevin Alfred Strom, "War against Whites, War against Freedom: An Interview with Elizabeth Wheeler," American Dissident Voices, July 26, 2003, www.natall.com; and Kevin Alfred Strom, "Lovell Wheeler Update: A New Interview with Elizabeth Wheeler," American Dissident Voices, August 23, 2003, www.natall.com.

35. "Don't Hate, Appreciate," *Baltimore City Paper,* November 15, 2003, http://www.citypaper.com.

36. See, for example, correspondence among readers on the Stormfront discussion forum at http://www.stormfront.org/forum/.

37. Over the 2004 Memorial Day weekend, various high-profile far-right leaders, including David Duke of the European American Unity and Rights Organization (EURO), Kevin Alfred Strom of the National Alliance, Willis Carto of *American Free Press,* Don Black of Stormfront, Dr. Ed Fields of *The Truth at Last,* John Tyndall of the British National Party, and Paul Fromm of the Canadian Association for Free Expression, endorsed the "New Orleans Protocol." Essentially the protocols contain three major tenets: (1) zero tolerance for violence; (2) honorable and ethical behavior in relations with other signatory groups; and (3) maintaining a high tone in arguments and public presentations. The protocols were formulated and announced during a conference, which welcomed David Duke from his release from prison.

38. See Mark Potok, "Against the Wall," *Intelligence Report,* Summer 2003, n. 111, http://www.splcenter.org. For an analysis of the problems from the perspective of the "movement," see Jerry's Aryan Battle Page, "The Decline of the National Alliance," December 2003, http://www.jabpage.org.

39. Kim Murphy, "Jury Verdict Could Bankrupt Aryans," *Los Angeles Times,* September 8, 2000.

40. Anti-Defamation League, "Police Arrest White Supremacists in Southern California," November 19, 2002, http://www.adl.org/learn/news/Arrest_Suprem_Cal.asp.

41. "Authorities Arrest Suspected White Supremacists," November 19, 2002, http://abclocal.go.com/kabc/news/111802_NW_SUPREMISTS.html.

42. Chelsea J. Carter, "Alleged White Supremacists Charged," Associated Press, November 18, 2002.

43. See "'White Supremacist' Leader Pleads to 120 Days on Weapons Charges," November 27, 2002, http://www.overthrow.com; and "Charges against Christine Greenwood Dropped," July 3, 2003, http://www.overthrow.com.

44. Seamus McGraw, "Aryan Alienation: Pa. Town Gives Racists Cold Shoulder," *Forward,* August 2, 2002.

45. Dennis B. Roddy, "Federal Investigators Infiltrate Extremist Groups," *Pittsburgh Post-Gazette,* February 23, 2003, http://www.post-gazette.com.

46. Anti-Defamation League, "Aryan Nations Member Arrested After Standoff with Police," May 25, 2004, http://www.adl.org.

47. Henry Schuster, "An Unholy Alliance," CNN, March 29, 2005, http://www.cnn.com/2005/US/03/29schuster.column/.

48. For more on the theology of the World Church of the Creator, see George Michael, *Confronting Right-Wing Extremism and Terrorism in the USA* (London: Routledge, 2003), pp. 78–81.

49. "Literature of Hate Hits South Hill," October 19, 2001, http://www.wiesenthal.com/social/press.

50. Matt Hale, *The Truth About 9–11: How Jewish Manipulation Killed Thousands* (East Peoria, IL: Creativity Publications, 2002).

51. According to prosecutors, the leader of the church's security detail, Anthony Evola, had been recruited by the FBI to work as an informant since 1999. Rudolph Bush, "Hale's Security Boss Was FBI Informer, E-mails, Tapes Led to Arrest, U.S. Says," *Chicago Tribune,* January 24, 2003, http://wwwchicagotribune.com/news/local/chi–0301240295jan24,0,7321287.story?coll=chi-news-hed.

52. John Beckham and P. J. Huffstutter, "Supremacist Guilty in Plot to Kill Judge," *Los Angeles Times,* April 27, 2004, latimes.com.

53. Ibid.

54. Karen McDonald and Andy Kravetz, "Some Feel the World Church Will Falter, and Hale Is Capable of Crime." *Peoria Journal Star Online,* January 9, 2003, http://www.pjstar.com/news/topnews/hold/g135498a.html.

55. ADL Press Release, "ADL Lauds Law Enforcement for Preventing Extremist Violence with Arrest of Matt Hale," January 8, 2003.

56. "Michael Chertoff, J.D., Assistant Attorney General in the Department of Justice, to Deliver Keynote Address at Seton Hall University School of Law Commencement," May 24, 2002, http://domapp01shu.edu/depts/special%20programs/pressrelease.nsf/f7b9c5bae1fc659852569d.

57. "Free Matt Hale Legal Defense Fund, http://www.matthale.org/ (accessed November 16, 2003).

58. Tony Willow, "'Creativity' Movement Leader, Jon Fox to Turn State's Evidence!" October 21, 2003, http://citizensagainsthate.com/home/modules.php?op=modload&name=News&file=article&sid=129&mode=thread.

59. Jeff Coen and David Heinzmann, "Police: DNA Matches," *Chicago Tribune,* March 11, 2005, http://www.chicagotribune.com/news/local/na/chi–0503110284mar11,1,4896586.story?coll=chi-news-hed.

60. Natasha Korecki and Frank Main, "Hale Sentenced to 40 Years," *Chicago-Sun Times,* April 6, 2005, http://www.suntimes.com/output/news/hale06.html.

61. Michael Hoffman explained that Zündel was unable to get advertising space for his Holocaust denial literature, so he came up with the idea of selling UFO literature, which advertisers would permit. His advertisements for his UFO books appeared in many comic books in the 1970s. Through this method, Zündel was able to entice those who inquired about his UFO book with neo-Nazi and Holocaust denial literature. See Michael A. Hoffman II, *The Great Holocaust Trial* (Torrance, CA: Institute for Historical Review, 1985), p. 18.

62. For more on the Zündel trial, see Stanley R. Barrett, *Is God a Racist? The Right Wing in Canada* (Toronto: University of Toronto Press, 1987); Hoffman, *The Great Holocaust Trial;* Warren Kinsella, *Web of Hate* (Toronto: Harper Perennial, 1995); and Manuel Prutschi, "The Zündel Affair," in Alan Davies, ed., *Anti-Semitism in Canada: History and Interpretation* (Waterloo, Ont.: Wilfrid Laurier University Press, 1992), pp. 249–277.

63. "Zündel Arraigned in German Court," ADL Law Enforcement Agency Resource Network, March 2, 2005, http://www.adl.org/learn/extremism_in_america_updates/individuals/ernst_zundel/zundel_update_2005–03–02.htm.

64. For more on Ernst Zündel's most recent legal battle, see Anti-Defamation League, "Ernst Zündel: Update," May 7, 2003. http://www.adl.org; and Associated Press, "Canada Prepares to Deport Publisher," May 3, 2004.

65. According to some sources, some of the top members of the administration of the university held strong anti-Zionist positions and even published a series of articles critical of Israel and Jews in the university-published magazine, *Personnel.*

66. John McQuaid, "Duke's Decline," *Times-Picayune,* April 13, 2004, p. 1.

67. Susan Schmidt, "Bush to Name Chertoff to Court," *Washington Post,* January 18, 2003, p. A14; "Michael Chertoff . . . to Deliver Keynote Address."

68. Shanna Sissom, "David Duke Leaves Big Spring Prison in Greyhound Bus," *Midland Reporter-Telegram,* April 9, 2004.

69. Cain Burdeau, "Duke Draws Support from Fractured Far-Right Groups," Associated Press, May 31, 2004.

70. For more on the Krar case, see "Feds: What Did Texas Couple Plan to Do with Cyanide?" *USA TODAY,* January 30, 2004, http://www.usatoday.com; "Prison Sentence for Possessing Chemical Weapons," *ATF News,* May 4, 2004. http://www.atf.org; and Camille Jackson, "Terror, American Style," *Intelligence Report,* Spring 2004, n. 113, http://www.splcenter.org.

71. Michael, *Confronting Right-Wing Extremism and Terrorism in the USA.*

72. Glod and Markon, "Tracking Hate Groups Aids Terrorism Fight," p. B1.

73. This is according to Ivan C. Smith, former head of the analysis, budget, and training section of the FBI's National Security Division. See Paul Sperry, "Why FBI Missed Islamic Threat,"

WorldNet Daily, July 25, 2002, http://www.worldnetdaily.com/news/printer-friendly.asp?
ARTICLE_ID=28400.

74. The report was released in 1999. David Holmes, who at that time was the head of security, is now a security official in the Transportation Security Agency. See Paul Sperry, "TSA Honcho Nixed Islamic Groups in Terror Report," WorldNet Daily, July 23, 2002, http://www.world netdaily.com/news/printer-friendly.asp?ARTICLE_ID=28374.

75. David Cole and James X. Dempsey, *Terrorism and the Constitution* (New York: New Press, 2002), p. 83.

76. The evidentiary criterion for a criminal predicate is slightly below the threshold of "probable cause," which is less than absolute certainty but greater than mere suspicion or "hunch."

77. Cole and Dempsey, *Terrorism and the Constitution,* p. 97.

78. Ibid., p. 119.

79. Ibid., p. 155.

80. Claire Sterling, *The Terror Network* (New York: Berkley Books, 1984).

81. Ledeen, *The War against the Terror Masters,* pp. 111–113.

82. For a synopsis of the Afghan political situation during this period, see Michael Parenti, *The Terrorism Trap: September 11 and Beyond* (San Francisco: City Lights Books, 2002), pp. 56–59.

83. Parenti, *The Terrorism Trap,* p. 40.

84. Samuel Katz, *Relentless Pursuit: The DSS and the Manhunt for the al-Qaeda Terrorists* (New York: Forge, 2002), p. 52.

85. Kenneth R. Timmerman, *Preachers of Hate: Islam and the War on America* (New York: Crown Forum, 2003), p. 138.

86. Milton Bearden, "Graveyard of Empires," in James F. Hoge Jr. and Gideon Rose, eds., *How Did This Happen? Terrorism and the New War* (New York: Public Affairs, 2001), p. 87; Simon Reeve asserted that according to one source, U.S. emissaries actually met directly with bin Laden, who reportedly first suggested that the mujahideen be provided with Stinger missiles. Simon Reeve, *The New Jackals: Ramzi Yousef, Osama bin Laden, and the Future of Terrorism* (Boston: Northeastern University Press, 1999), p. 167.

87. Salah Najm, "Transcript of Usamah Bin-Ladin, the Destruction of the Base: Interview with Usamah Bin-Ladin," June 10, 1999, http://wwww.terrorism.com/BinLadinTranscript. shtml.

88. Marc Sageman, *Understanding Terror Networks* (Philadelphia: University of Pennsylvania Press, 2004), pp. 56–59.

89. Ledeen, *The War against the Terror Masters,* p. 29.

90. Katz, *Relentless Pursuit,* p. 263.

91. Yosri Fouda and Nick Fielding, *Masterminds of Terror: The Truth behind the Most Devastating Terrorist Attack the World Has Ever Seen* (New York: Arcade Publishing, 2003), p. 166.

92. "Executive Order: Sanctions on the Afghan Taliban (July 6, 1999)," in Barry Rubin and Judith Colp Rubin, eds., *Anti-American Terrorism and the Middle East: A Documentary Reader* (Oxford: Oxford University Press, 2002), p. 218.

93. "Resolution 1267 (October 15, 1999)," in Rubin and Rubin, *Anti-American Terrorism and the Middle East,* p. 219.

94. For example, in the Senate by a vote of 98–0 and in the House of Representatives by a vote of 420–1, Congress passed a joint resolution authorizing President Bush to use "all necessary and appropriate force" for those responsible for the September 11 terrorist attacks.

95. Rubin and Rubin, *Anti-American Terrorism and the Middle East,* pp. 339–343.

96. GAO (General Accounting Office), *Homeland Security: A Risk Management Approach Can Guide Preparedness Efforts* (Washington, DC: General Accounting Office, October 31, 2001).

97. Dan Eggen and Jim McGee, "FBI Rushes to Remake Its Mission," *Washington Post,* November 12, 2001, p. A01.

98. Ibid., p. A01.

99. Ibid., p. A01.

100. Council on Foreign Relations, "Balancing Security and Civil Liberties," http://cfrterrorism.org/security/liberties_print.html.

101. U.S. Department of Justice, Civil Rights Division, "Civil Rights Division National Origin Working Group Initiative to Combat the Post-9/11 Discriminatory Backlash," January 16, 2002, http://www.usdoj.gov/crt/legalinfo/nordwg_mission.html.

102. Community Relations Service, "CRS Sponsors Briefing on the USA PATRIOT Act for Arab Americans and Muslim Leaders," December 19, 2001, http://www.usdoj.gov/crs/pr12192001.htm.

103. See, for example, "ADL Responds to Violence and Harassment against Arab Americans and Muslim Americans," 2001, http://www.adl.org/terrorism_america/adl_responds.asp.

104. Fouda and Fielding, *Masterminds of Terror*, p. 135.

105. Kurt M. Campbell and Michele A. Flournoy, *To Prevail: An American Strategy for the Campaign against Terrorism* (Washington, DC: CSIS Press, 2001), p. 83.

106. Ledeen, *The War against the Terror Masters*, p. 64.

107. "It Should Have Been a Wake-up Call," *USA TODAY,* February 26, 2003, http://www.usatoday.com.

108. Josh Meyer, "Ashcroft Rethinks Domestic Spying," *Los Angeles Times,* December 1, 2001.

109. Susan Schmidt and Dan Eggen, "FBI Given More Latitude: New Surveillance Rules Remove Evidence Hurdle," *Washington Post,* May 30, 2002, p. A01.

110. See, for example, Abraham Foxman, "Just Counter-terrorism," June 7, 2002, http://www.adl.org/Terror/ahf_counter_terrorism.asp; and Foxman, "Give Security Agencies More Room to Fight Terrorism," downloaded October 2, 2001, http://adl.org/terrorism_america/ op_ed_1001.asp.

111. Susan Herman, "The USA PATRIOT Act and the U.S. Department of Justice: Losing Our Balances?" *Jurist,* http://law.pitt.edu/forum/formnew40htm.

112. George Michael, "Homeland Defense Initiative and U.S. Counterterrorism Policy," in *Encyclopedia of World Terrorism 1996–2002* (Armonk, NY: M. E. Sharpe, 2003), p. 59.

113. Eric V. Larson and John E. Peters, *Preparing the U.S. Army for Homeland Security: Concepts, Issues, and Options* (Santa Monica, CA: RAND Corporation), 2001, pp. xv–xvi.

114. Michael, "Homeland Defense Initiative and U.S. Counterterrorism Policy," pp. 57–58.

115. See the U.S. Department of Homeland Security website, http://www.dhs.gov/.

116. Bob Woodward, *Bush at War* (New York: Simon and Schuster, 2002), pp. 48–60.

117. Ibid., p. 83.

118. The original name for the campaign was "Operation Infinite Justice." The name was soon changed to "Enduring Freedom" in order to avoid offending the sensibilities of Muslims, who believe that only God can deliver infinite justice. Woodward, *Bush at War,* pp. 134–135.

119. Warren Chin, "Operation 'Enduring Freedom': A Victory for a Conventional Force Fighting an Unconventional War," *Small Wars and Insurgencies* 14, no. 1 (Spring 2003): 64.

120. Ibid., p. 66.

121. Ibid., p. 69.

122. Noor Khan, "Taliban Regrouping in Southern Afghanistan," *Washington Times,* February 19, 2004.

123. Fouda and Fielding, *Masterminds of Terror*, p. 140.

124. Khalid Sheik Muhammad, the uncle of Ramzi Yousef, had been indicted years earlier for his role in "Operation Bojinka," which planned to explode U.S. airliners in flight over the Pacific Ocean. See Ibid., p. 88.

125. As Andrew and Patrick Cockburn pointed out at the start of the war in 1980, the Iraqi army began the war with ten divisions but ended with fifty-five divisions. The army ended the

war with a tank force of 4,000 and rockets that could reach both Tehran and Tel Aviv. Andrew Cockburn and Patrick Cockburn, *Out of the Ashes: The Resurrection of Saddam Hussein* (New York: HarperCollins, 1999), p. 82.

126. David Frum and Richard Perle, *An End to Evil: How to Win the War on Terror* (New York: Random House, 2003), p. 17.

127. According to an investigation by the UN Food and Agriculture Organization, it was estimated that by the end of 1995 alone, as many as 576,000 children had died as a result of the sanctions. Cockburn and Cockburn, *Out of the Ashes,* pp. 137–138.

128. Woodward, *Bush at War,* p. 330.

129. Ibid., p. 332.

130. Ibid., p. 346.

131. Ibid., p. 349.

132. "US Public Thinks Saddam Had Role in 9/11," *Observer,* September 7, 2003.

133. See, for example, Jack Kelly, "There's a War On: Better to Fight the Hard-Core Killers in Iraq," *Pittsburgh Post-Gazette,* August 24, 2003.

134. Neil MacFarquhar, "Rising Tide of Islamic Militants See Iraq as Ultimate Battlefield," *New York Times,* August 13, 2003.

135. Patrick Quinn and Katherine Shrader, "Foreigners Responsible for Most Suicide Attacks in Iraq," *Kingsport Times,* July 1, 2005, p. 5A.

136. Susan Page, "Poll: Muslim Countries, Europe Question U.S. Motives," *USA TODAY,* March 16, 2004.

137. Richard Benedetto, "Poll Shows Most Americans Feel More Vulnerable," *USA TODAY,* August 8, 2005.

138. Fouda and Fielding, *Masterminds of Terror,* p. 39.

139. Abraham Foxman, *Never Again? The Threat of the New Anti-Semitism* (New York: HarperCollins, 2003), pp. 29.

140. Ledeen, *The War against the Terror Masters,* p. 151.

141. Thomas Carothers, "Democracy: Terrorism's Uncertain Antidote," *Current History,* December 2003, p. 405.

142. Alan Sorensen, "The Reluctant Nation Builders," *Current History,* December 2003, p. 409.

143. Quoted in Michael Gove, "Why I Fear Today's Brave New World," http://www.timesonline.co.uk/article/o,7–681369,00.html (downloaded May 21, 2003). For Fukuyama, three cautions to this approach are in order. First, the scope of the current idealist project requires a consistent and long-term commitment to building legitimate and stable institutions in that region of the world. History has demonstrated that the United States is not good at either implementing or sticking to such a project over the long run. Second, inasmuch as building instructions will require that the United States occupy the region for considerable time, the idealist project may come to resemble an empire, at least in the short run. Finally, with regard to U.S. domestic politics, the public may be loath to support the idealist project over the long haul.

CHAPTER 7. THE ROLE OF NONGOVERNMENTAL ORGANIZATIONS IN THE AFTERMATH OF 9/11

1. This University of Florida study is cited in Maria T. Padilla, "Race Violence Leads to Rise in Anti-Racism Groups," *Salt Lake Tribune,* August 22, 1999, http://www.sltrib.com/1999/aug/08221999/ nation_w/17231.htm.

2. For a more in-depth analysis of NGOs in this area of policy, see George Michael, *Confronting Right-Wing Extremism and Terrorism in the USA* (London: Routledge, 2003), pp. 10–38.

3. These efforts include sharing information; arranging meetings with ICT terrorism analysts and representatives from the law enforcement, government, the media, and community

groups in the United States; bringing U.S. law enforcement to Israel for meetings on counter-terrorism; and distribution of joint publications. ADL Press Release, "ADL and Renowned Counterterrorism Institute Partner in Fight against Terrorism," November 1, 2001, http://adl.org/PresRele/TerrorismIntl_93/3947_92.htm.

4. Kenneth S. Stern, *A Force upon the Plain: The American Militia Movement and the Politics of Hate* (New York: Simon and Schuster, 1996). Stern also wrote a book on Holocaust revisionism, *Holocaust Denial* (New York: American Jewish Committee, 1993). Finally, he wrote a lengthy report under AJC auspices called "Hate and the Internet," 2000, and a report on the violence from "lone wolves" such as Benjamin Smith and Buford Furrow during the summer of 1999. See his "Understanding the Summer of Hate," 2000. The latter two reports are available on the AJC website at http://www.ajc.org.

5. J. J. Goldberg, *Jewish Power: Inside the American Jewish Establishment* (New York: Addison-Wesley, 1996), p. 6.

6. Interview with Chip Berlet, August 31, 2000.

7. For more on the political backgrounds of the staffs of the CDR and PRA, see Laird Wilcox, *The Watchdogs: A Close Look at Anti-Racist "Watchdog" Groups* (Olathe, KS: Laird Wilcox Editorial Research Center, 1999).

8. Steven Emerson, "Testimony before the United States Senate Committee on the Judiciary, DOJ Oversight: Preserving Our Freedoms While Defending against Terrorism," December 4, 2001, http://judiciary.senate.gov/print_testimony.cfm?id=128&wite_id=81; and Steven Emerson, *American Jihad: The Terrorists Living among Us* (New York: Free Press, 2002), p. 14.

9. Interview with Steven Emerson, June 12, 2005.

10. One exception is the 1980 bombing of the train station in Bologna, Italy, which killed 85 persons and wounded over 200 others. An underground, neofascist organization, Ordine Nuovo, was believed to be responsible for the attack as part of its "strategy of tension" to destabilize Italy and usher in authoritarian rule.

11. Emerson, *American Jihad*, p. 14.

12. John F. Sugg, "Steven Emerson's Crusade," *Extra!* January–February 1999, http://www.fair.org/extra/0091/emerson.html.

13. ADL, *The ADL Anti–Paramilitary Training Statute: A Response to Domestic Terrorism* (New York: ADL, 1995).

14. ADL Press Release, "ADL Commends President for Domestic Anti-Terrorism Initiative: Calls on 26 States to Enact Anti-Paramilitary Training Statutes," April 24, 1998.

15. As of 1998, those states were Arkansas, Georgia, Indiana, Kansas, Kentucky, New Mexico, New York, South Carolina, and Wyoming. Anti-Defamation League, *1999 Hate Crime Laws* (New York: Anti-Defamation League, 1998).

16. Morris Dees and Ellen Bowden, n.d., "Taking Hate Groups to Court," http://www.splcenter.org/legalaction/la–3.html.

17. ADL memorandum to FBI director William H. Webster, FBI File Number 100–530–526, December 10, 1980.

18. ADL Press Release, "ADL Says Pro-Palestinian Rallies Turn into Forums for Anti-Semitism," May 14, 2002, http://www.adl.org/PresRele/ASUS_12/4097_12.asp.

19. Independent researcher Laird Wilcox has thoroughly examined various FBI and ADL memoranda, which indicate a close working relationship between the two entities. See Wilcox, *The Watchdogs*, pp. 45–46. My review of Wilcox's archives on this subject confirms his assertion.

20. Morris Dees, *Hate on Trial* (New York: Villard Books, 1993), p. 19.

21. See, for example, Wilcox, *The Watchdogs;* and Michael, *Confronting Right-Wing Extremism and Terrorism in the USA,* pp. 192–193.

22. A good example is the case of the Liberty Lobby, which began airing a program called *This Is Liberty Lobby* over scattered radio stations in 1973. The program expressed views that

were highly critical of Israel and Zionism. Consequently, the ADL took an interest and sought to dissuade radio stations from carrying the program. To meet this challenge, the ADL chief fact-finder at the time, Irwin Suall, sent a directive to ADL regional offices with recommendations for action against the Liberty Lobby radio program. Regional directors were instructed to communicate directly with station managers and discourage them from airing the program. The ADL eventually prevailed in this battle as it dissuaded Mutual Broadcasting System to cancel its contract with the Liberty Lobby to air the program. For more on this affair see Liberty Lobby, *Conspiracy against Freedom* (Washington, DC: Liberty Lobby, 1986), passim.

23. As Pipes pointed out, Christian fundamentalists have been among the most stalwart supporters of Israel and would therefore not seem to warrant a significant level of concern from Jewish defense organizations. Daniel Pipes, *Militant Islam Reaches America* (New York: W. W. Norton, 2002), p. 157. Still, Jewish defense organizations are often uncomfortable with Christian fundamentalists with respect to the issue of separation of church and state.

24. Abraham Foxman, "New Excuses, Old Hatred: Worldwide Anti-Semitism in Wake of 9/11," February 8, 2002, http://www.adl.org/main_Anti_Semitism_International/as_speech.htm.

25. Melissa Radler, "NY Jews Start Counterterror Group," *Jerusalem Post,* September 28, 2001, http://cgis.jpost.com.

26. Abraham H. Foxman, "Blame the Terrorists, Not Israel," http://www.adl.org/ ADL_Opinions/Terrorism/blame_op_09212001.htm (downloaded September 24, 2001).

27. ADL Press Release, "Conspiracy Theories and Criticism of Israel in the Aftermath of Sept. 11 Attacks," November 1, 2001, http://www.adl.org/PresRele/Islme_62/3946_62.asp.

28. ADL, "New ADL Poll Shows No Anti-Semitic and Blame Israel Fallout from Sept. 11 Attack," November 2, 2001, http://www.adl.org/PresRele/asus_12/3948_12.asp.

29. American Jewish Committee, "Talking Points: The Agenda of Islamic Extremism, the War on Terrorism and the U.S.-Israel Alliance," October 8, 2001, http://www.ajc-chicago.org/ Terrorism/BriefingsDetail.asp?did=221&pid=735.

30. Simon Wiesenthal Center, "Trans-National Hate: Technology Unites Anti-Semites and Haters around the Globe." February 27, 2001, http://www.wiesenthal.com/site/apps/nl/ content2.asp?c=fwLYKnN8LzH&b=312451&ct=285352.

31. Growitz Institute, *Unraveling Anti-Semitic 9/11 Conspiracy Theories* (New York: Anti-Defamation League, 2003).

32. Harold Brackman, *9/11 Digital Lies: A Survey of Online Apologists for Global Terrorism* (Los Angeles: Simon Wiesenthal Center, 2001).

33. For more on the ADL's analysis of these rumors, see ADL, "Conspiracy Theories and Criticism of Israel in the Aftermath of Sept. 11 Attacks," November 1, 2001, http://www.adl.org/ PresRele/Islme_62/3946_62.asp; "4,000 Jews Absent during World Trade Center Attack," downloaded November 15, 2001, http://www.adl.org/Internet_Rumors/jews_rumors.htm; and ADL Press Release, "ADL Urges Western Leaders to Denounce 'The Big Lie' about 9/11 and to Help Educate against Anti-Semitism," September 10, 2002, http://www.adl.org/PresRele/ ASInt_13/4157_13.asp. All are available on the ADL's website at http://www.adl.org. For more on David Duke's allegations, see "How Israeli Terrorism and American Treason Caused the September 11 Attack," *David Duke Report,* no. 52 (November 2001).

34. ADL Press Release, "ADL Expresses 'Shock and Disappointment' with Saudi Claim That Israel was Behind 9/11 Terrorist Attack," December 5, 2002, http://www.adl.org/PresRele/ ASInt_13/4204_13.asp.

35. This figure is given in Abraham Foxman, "When Conspiracy Theories Are Taken Seriously," *Yale Daily News,* March 4, 2003, http://www.yaledailynews.com/article.asp?AID=22090.

36. Rachel Donadio, "Radical Islam, Neo-Nazis Are Seen Sharing Hate Rhetoric," *Forward,* November 23, 2001, http://www.forward.com/issues/2001/01.11.23/news3.html.

37. ADL Press Release, "ADL Says Pro-Palestinian Rallies Turn Into Forums For Anti-Semitism," May 14, 2002. http://www.adl.org/PresRele/ASUS_12/4097_12.asp.

38. Abraham Foxman, *Never Again? The Threat of the New Anti-Semitism* (New York: HarperCollins, 2003), pp. 10–11.

39. Ibid., p. 15.

40. Ibid., p. 27.

41. Ibid., p. 28.

42. Michelle Cottle, "White Hope," *New Republic,* November 21, 2001, http://www.tnr.com.

43. Donadio, "Radical Islam, Neo-Nazis Are Seen Sharing Hate Rhetoric."

44. Chip Berlet, "Third Position Fascism," Political Research Associates, http://www.public eye.org (downloaded April 17, 2002).

45. "Rep. Traficant Crosses the Wrong Line at the Wrong Time by Scapegoating Israel," National Jewish Democratic Council, September 14, 2001.

46. Philip Carmel, "French Jewish Leader Stirs Anger with Talk of Anti-Semitic Alliance," JTA, January 30, 2003, http://www.jta.org/page_view_story.asp?intarticleid=12371&intcategory id=2.

47. Adrian Humphreys, "Anti-Semitism Now Sprouts from the Left: Professor," *National Post,* February 11, 2003, http://www.nationalpost.ca.

48. Joseph Farah, "Islam's Unholy Alliance with Neo-Nazis, Leftists: Western-Made Terrorists Plot Joining al Qaida in 'Red Jihad,'" December 29, 2003, http://www.worldnetdaily.com/news/printer-friendly.asp?ARTICLE_ID=36350.

49. John Solomon, "U.S. Extremists' Links with Terror Groups Watched," Salon.com, February 28, 2002. http://www.salon.com/news/wire/2002/02/28/extremis.

50. For example, in the Senate by a vote of 98–0, and in the House of Representatives by a vote of 420–1, Congress passed a joint resolution authorizing President Bush to use "all necessary and appropriate force" to apprehend those responsible for the September 11 terrorist attacks.

51. See, for example, Anti-Defamation League, "ADL Applauds President Bush for Signing into Law Landmark Anti-Terrorism Bill," October 26, 2001, http://www.adl.org/presrele/teror_92/3944_92.asp.

52. Laurie Goodstein, "Jewish Groups Endorse Tough Security Laws," *New York Times,* January 3, 2002.

53. John Ashcroft, "Prepared Remarks of Attorney General Ashcroft," November 7, 2003, http://www.usdoj.gov/ag/speeches/2003/antidefamation.htm.

54. The Central Intelligence Agency (CIA) was criticized for its efforts to stymie the antiwar movement during the Vietnam era. An integral part of the antiwar movement was the underground press. In 1967 the CIA launched its MHCHAOS program, which sought to infiltrate and disrupt the antiwar underground press. "MH" stood for worldwide area of operations, while CHAOS stood for just that. Angus MacKenzie, *Secrets: The CIA's War at Home* (Berkeley: University of California Press, 1997), pp. 26–27.

55. ADL, "ADL Calls Bush Administration Military Commission Guidelines 'A Significant Step Forward,'" March 25, 2002, http://www.adl.org/PresRele/Teror_92/4062_32.htm.

56. ADL Press Release, "ADL Lists Top Issues Affecting Jews in 2002," December 22, 2002, http://www.adl.org/PresRele/Mise_00/4213_00.htm.

CHAPTER 8. HOW THE EXTREME RIGHT VIEWS THE CURRENT CRISIS

1. D. A. Snow, E. B. Rochford, Jr., S. K. Worden, and R. D. Beford, "Frame Alignment Processes, Micromobilization, and Movement Participation," *American Sociological Review* 51 (1986): 464–481.

2. Jonathan T. Drummond, "From the Northwest Imperative to Global Jihad: Social Psychological Aspects of the Construction of the Enemy, Political Violence, and Terror" in Chris E. Stout, *The Psychology of Terrorism: A Public Understanding* (New York: Praeger, 2002), pp. 56–58.

3. Peter Finn, "Unlikely Allies Bound by a Common Hatred," *Washington Post*, April 29, 2002, p. A13.

4. See Horst Mahler, "Independence Day—Live," http://vanguardnewsnetwork.com/index 115htm, September 12, 2001; and Mahler, "The Fall of the Judeo-American Empire," http://vanguardnewsnetwork.com/h_mahler4htm (downloaded November 5, 2001). The Balfour Declaration is named after Lord Arthur James Balfour, who promised Zionist leaders British cooperation with the establishment of a Jewish homeland if they would work to persuade American government leaders and pundits to declare war on Germany during World War I.

5. See Horst Mahler, "11 September 2001—'Cui Bono?'" http://vanguardnewsnetwork.com/h_mahler3.htm, September 21, 2001.

6. Quoted in Jim Nesbitt, "Many American Right-Wing Extremists Applaud Sept. 11 Attacks," Newhouse News Service, http://www.newhousenews.com (downloaded January 31, 2002).

7. Ibid.

8. ADL, "What They are Saying," December 11, 2001, http://www.adl.org.

9. ADL, "What They are Saying." September 14, 2001, http://www.adl.org.

10. Ibid.

11. ADL, "What They are Saying." September 24, 2001, http://www.adl.org.

12. David Duke, "The Big Lie: The True Reason behind the Attack of September 11," October 8, 2001, http://www.duke.org.

13. Sam Francis, "Mass Immigration + Feckless Feds = Anarcho-Tyranny," VDARE.COM, April 21, 2003, http://www.vdare.com/francis/patriot_act.htm.

14. William Pierce, "Terrorism and Hate," *American Dissident Voices,* November 10, 2001.

15. For a good analysis of the effect that 9/11 had on the Christian patriot movement, see Martin Durham, "The American Far Right and 9/11," *Terrorism and Political Violence* 15, no. 2 (2004): 96–111.

16. Interview with John Tyndall, June 3, 2003.

17. Interview with Mike Piper, April 2003.

18. Interview with Kevin MacDonald, March 2003.

19. Jared Taylor, "Will America Learn Its Lessons? Paying the Price for Foolish Policies." *American Renaissance* 12, no. 11 (November 2001): 1–8.

20. Interview with Sam Francis, April 8, 2003.

21. President George W. Bush, "Address to the Nation (September 11, 2001)," in Barry Rubin and Judith Colp Rubin, eds., *Anti-American Terrorism and the Middle East: A Documentary Reader* (Oxford: Oxford University Press, 2002), p. 319.

22. George W. Bush, "Address to Joint Session of Congress (September 20, 2001)," in Rubin and Rubin, *Anti-American Terrorism and the Middle East,* p. 323.

23. Michael A. Ledeen, *The War against the Terror Masters* (New York: St. Martin's, 2003), p. 213.

24. Interview with John Tyndall, June 3, 2003.

25. Interview with Nick Griffin, May 2003.

26. Interview with David Myatt, April 2003.

27. Interview with Jürgen Graf, April 2003.

28. Jared Taylor, "Teaching More Millions to Hate Us," *Battleflag,* October 2001, p. 4.

29. The Special Forces Underground (SFU) was a sub-rosa organization composed of members of the U.S. Special Forces that was active around the mid-to-late 1990s. Its leader, Sergeant Steven Barry, recounted that the impetus for the creation of the SFU was the Ruby Ridge and Waco incidents. According to some reports, during the army's deployment in Haiti to help reinstall the deposed Jean-Bertrand Aristide as president, Barry and some members of his SFU

helped certain anti-Aristide Haitian military and paramilitary forces hide weapons in direct defiance of official U.S. and UN efforts to disarm them. The SFU publishes a newsletter called *The Resister,* which humbly started out as a short mimeographed newsletter. For more on the SFU see George Michael, *Confronting Right-Wing Extremism and Terrorism in the USA* (London: Routledge, 2003), pp. 161–162.

30. Interview with Steven Barry, December 11, 2003.

31. Kevin MacDonald, "Hatred of the West?" http://www.csulb.edu/~kmacd/9–11.htm.

32. Interview with Rohan Gunaratna, January 17, 2004.

33. I am indebted to Jonathan Drummond for this observation. See Drummond, "From the Northwest Imperative to Global Jihad," p. 90.

34. Interview with Mike Piper, April 2003.

35. George W. Bush, "Address to Joint Session of Congress (September 20, 2001)," p. 321.

36. As *Haaretz* reported, those five are Alona Avraham, thirty, from Ashdod, who was onboard United Flight 175 from Boston, Massachusetts, to Los Angeles, California, that crashed into the south tower of the World Trade Center; Leon Lebor, fifty-one, who was born in London but later moved to Jerusalem and then New York and worked as a janitor in the WTC; Shay Levinhar, twenty-nine, who worked for the eSpeed subsidiary of the brokerage firm Cantor Fitzgerald in the north tower; Daniel Lewin, thirty-one, who was aboard American Airlines Flight 11 from Boston to Los Angeles, which crashed into the north tower; and Haggai Sheffi, thirty-four, who was on the 106th floor of the north tower when American Airlines Flight 11 struck. Haaretz.com, June 21, 2004, http://www.haaretzdaily.com/hasen/pages/ShArt.jhtml?itemNo=206453&contrassID=3&subContrassID=0&sbSubContrassID=0.

37. David Duke, "UPDATE: One Year Later 9–11 2002." The story of the Odigo employees receiving advanced warning appeared in Yuval Dror, "Israel's Odigo Says Workers Warned 2 Hours Before 911," *Haaretz Daily,* September 21, 2001, http://www.haaretzdaily.com/hasen/pages/ShArt.jhtml?itemNo=77744&contrassID=/has%5C.

38. Kenneth R. Timmerman, *Preachers of Hate: Islam and the War on America* (New York: Crown Forum, 2003), p. 18.

39. The USS *Liberty* was a U.S. Navy vessel that was attacked on June 8, 1967, during the Six-Day War between Israel and its Arab neighbors. The USS *Liberty,* an intelligence ship, was sailing in the eastern Mediterranean Sea when it came under attack by Israeli aircraft and Israeli motorboats for 75 minutes. Thirty-four U.S. sailors were killed, and 173 others were wounded. The Israeli government insists that the Israeli armed forces had mistaken the ship for an Egyptian vessel. Survivors of the attack maintained that American flags were prominently displayed on the vessel, rendering the Israeli explanation untenable. Far-right literature often cites the case of the USS *Liberty* as an example of Israeli malfeasance and mendacity. For more on the USS *Liberty,* see the USS *Liberty* memorial website, http://www.ussliberty.org/.

40. Interview with David Duke, March 2003.

41. For more on this theory, see the Growitz Institute, *Unraveling Anti-Semitic 9/11 Conspiracy Theories* (New York: Anti-Defamation League, 2003), p. 19.

42. Fox News, "Carl Cameron Investigates," December 17, 2001, http://www.whatreallyhappened.com/Israeli-Spying-Part–2.htm.

43. Fox News, "Carl Cameron Investigates," December 17, 2001, http://www.whatreallyhappened.com/Israeli-Spying-Part–3.htm.

44. Drummond, "From the Northwest Imperative to Global Jihad," p. 93.

45. Ledeen, *The War against the Terror Masters,* p. 41.

46. "SEC Secret Probe of Stock Dealing Before 9/11," http://www.tbrnes.org/Archives/a048.htm. Downloaded April 14, 2003.

47. Neil Mackay, "Five Israelis Were Seen Filming as Jet Liners Ploughed into the Twin Towers on September 11, 2001," *Sunday Herald,* November 2, 2003.

48. As quoted in "Special Report with Brit Hume," December 17, 2001. For more on the Mossad's putative new policy that allows assassination in the United States, see Richard Sale, "Israel to Kill in U.S., Allied Nations," United Press International, January 15, 2003.

49. Interview with Jürgen Graf, April 2003.

50. Interview with John Tyndall, June 3, 2003.

51. Interview with David Myatt, April 2003.

52. Interview with Ahmed Huber, April 2003.

53. Neil Mackay, "Five Israelis Were Seen Filming as Jet Liners Ploughed into the Twin Towers on September 11, 2001," *Sunday Herald,* November 2, 2003.

54. "No War for Israel," *The David Duke Report,* no. 60.

55. David Duke, "America on the Brink," *The David Duke Report,* no. 51, p. 3.

56. Interview with David Duke, March 2003.

57. Interview with Mike Piper, April 2003.

58. ADL, "What They Are Saying," October 11, 2001, http://www.adl.org.

59. Interview with Tom Metzger, March 2003.

60. Interview with Willis Carto, May 7, 2003.

61. Justin Raimondo, "Speech Delivered at Washington University, Missouri," October 9, 2002, http://wwwantiwar.com/justincol.html.

62. Ibid.

63. Ibid.

64. Justin Raimondo, *The Terror Enigma: 9/11 and the Israeli Connection* (Lincoln, NE: iUniverse, 2003).

65. Interview with Sam Francis, April 8, 2003.

66. Interview with Kevin MacDonald, March 2003.

67. Interview with Nick Griffin, May 2003.

68. Interview with Jürgen Graf, April 2003.

69. Interview with David Myatt, April 2003.

70. Benjamin Ginsberg, *The Fatal Embrace: Jews and the State* (Chicago: University of Chicago Press, 1993), p. 4.

71. Patrick Buchanan, "Whose War?" *American Conservative,* March 24, 2003, p. 14.

72. Quoted in "The Revolutionary," *Esquire,* p. 190.

73. Kathleen Christison and Bill Christison, "A Rose by Any Other Name: The Bush Administration's Dual Loyalties," *Washington Report on Middle East Affairs,* March 2003, p. 15.

74. Ibid., p. 15.

75. Ibid., p. 15.

76. Ibid., p. 15.

77. Richard Perle, Douglas Feith, and David Wurmser, "A Clean Break: A New Strategy for Securing the Realm," Institute for Advanced Strategic and Political Studies, Jerusalem, July 8, 1996.

78. Patrick Buchanan, "On to Damascus?" April 9, 2003, http://www.wnd.com/news/article.asp?ARTICLE_ID=31953.

79. As quoted in Buchanan, "Whose War?" p. 10.

80. Ledeen, *The War against the Terror Masters,* pp. 147–210.

81. David Frum and Richard Perle, *An End to Evil: How to Win the War on Terror* (New York: Random House, 2003), pp. 32–33.

82. Ibid., p. 233.

83. Ibid., pp. 97–145.

84. Ibid., p. 231.

85. Ibid., pp. 234–273.

86. Joshua Micah Marshall, "Practice to Deceive," *Washington Monthly* 35, no. 4 (April 2003): 29–34.

87. Buchanan, "Whose War?" p. 11.

88. Ibid., p. 12.

89. Buchanan reprints excerpts of his warnings in Patrick J. Buchanan, *Where the Right Went Wrong: How Neoconservatives Subverted the Reagan Revolution and Hijacked the Bush Presidency* (New York: Thomas Dunne Books, 2004), p. 15.

90. Buchanan, *Where the Right Went Wrong,* p. 34.

91. ABC *Nightline,* "The Plan," March 5, 2003.

92. Paul Findley, "Liberating America from Israel," 2002, http://www.countercurrents.org/pa-findley230704.htm.

93. J. J. Goldberg, *Jewish Power: Inside the American Jewish Establishment* (New York: Addison-Wesley, 1996), p. 13.

94. Moran is quoted in Spencer S. Hsu, "Jewish Groups Blast Moran for Comments," *Washington Post,* March 10, 2003, http://www.washingtonpost.com.

95. "Six Democrats Say Moran Should Not Run Again," Reuters, March 12, 2003. http://www.reuters.com.

96. Sam Francis, "James Moran: Questions Remain," vdare.com, March 17, 2003, http://www.vdare.com.

97. Hsu, "Jewish Groups Blast Moran for Comments."

98. Abraham Foxman, "Poisoners Are Back," March 23, 2003, http://www.adl.org/Iraq_war/op_ed_032403.asp.

99. Ernest Hollings, "Bush's Failed Mideast Policy Is Creating More Terrorism," *Charleston Post and Courier,* May 6, 2004, http://hollings.senate.gov/~hollings/opinion/2004506A17.htm.

100. "ADL Urges Senator Hollings to Disavow Statements on Jews and the Iraq War," May 14, 2004, http://www.adl.org.

101. "Allen Denounces Hollings Anti-Semitic Expression," May 20, 2004, http://allen.senate.gov/?c=story&t=press&story=2004052040084.403125.

102. "Sen. Hollings Floor Statement Setting the Record Straight on his Mideast Newspaper Column," May 20, 2004, http://hollings.senate.gov/~hollings/statements/2004521A35.html.

103. "Bush Sought 'Way' to Invade Iraq?" CBSNEWS.com, January 11, 2004, http://www.cbsnews.com.

104. Dan Eggen and Walter Pincus, "The Book on Richard Clarke," *Washington Post,* March 23, 2004, p. A01.

105. "Gen. Zinni: 'They Screwed Up,'" *60 Minutes,* May 21, 2004, http://www.cbsnews.com/stories/2004/05/21/60minutes/main618896.shtml.

106. Bob Woodward, *Plan of Attack* (New York: Simon and Schuster, 2004).

107. ADL Press Release, "ADL Commends President Bush's Message to International Community on Iraq, Calling It 'Clear and Forceful,'" September 12, 2002.

108. Colin L. Powell, "Remarks at the American Israel Public Affairs Committee's Annual Policy Conference," March 30, 2003, http://www.state.gov/secretary/former/powell/remarks/2003/19174.htm.

109. "President Speaks to the American Israeli Public Affairs Committee," Office of the Press Secretary, May 18, 2004, http://www.whitehouse.gov/news/releases/2004/05/20040518–1.html.

110. Paul Findley, *They Dare to Speak Out: People and Institutions Confront Israel's Lobby* (Chicago: Lawrence Hill Books, 1989).

111. Kevin MacDonald, *The Culture of Critique: An Evolutionary Analysis of Jewish Involvement in Twentieth-Century Intellectual and Political Movements* (Westport, CT: Praeger, 1998), p. 304.

112. Goldberg, *Jewish Power,* p. 18.

113. Thomas L. Friedman, *From Beirut to Jerusalem* (New York: Anchor Books, 1989).

114. Goldberg, *Jewish Power,* p. 17.

115. As cited in Abraham Foxman, *Never Again? The Threat of the New Anti-Semitism* (New York: HarperCollins, 2003), pp. 36.

116. "Holy War Ground Zero," in Adam Parfrey, ed., *Extreme Islam: Anti-American Propaganda of Muslim Fundamentalism* (Los Angeles: Feral House, 2001), p. 171.

117. Barry Rubin, "The Truth about U.S. Middle East Policy," in Rubin and Rubin, *Anti-American Terrorism and the Middle East*, p. 87.

118. Jared Taylor, "Blood, Soil, and Iraq," http://www.thornwalker.com/ditch/ (downloaded April 15, 2003).

119. "The al Basrah Interview," email from skinheadz list, received January 3, 2005.

120. Interview with John Tyndall, June 3, 2003.

121. Interview with Nick Griffin, May 2003.

122. Interview with Jürgen Graf, April 2003.

123. Interview with David Myatt, April 2003.

124. Interview with Jared Taylor, February 6, 2004.

125. William Pierce, "Regaining Control," American Dissident Voices, September 29, 2001, http://www.natvan.org.

CHAPTER 9. HOW MILITANT ISLAM VIEWS THE CURRENT CRISIS

1. See, for example, ADL, "What They Are Saying." September 13, 2001, http://www.adl.org; and ADL, "What They are Saying." October 11, 2001, http://www.adl.org.

2. "Broadcast by Iraqi President Saddam Hussein (September 12, 2001)," in Barry Rubin and Judith Colp Rubin, eds., *Anti-American Terrorism and the Middle East: A Documentary Reader* (Oxford: Oxford University Press, 2002), p. 283. This may have been an injudicious remark by Hussein, reflecting a degree of schadenfreude. In a subsequent announcement he and several members of his government, including his deputy prime minister Tariq Aziz and his permanent representative to the UN, Mohammed al-Douri, condemned the 9/11 attacks. See *Iraqi News Agency*, October 21, 2001, in Mustafa Al Sayyid, "Mixed Message: The Arab and Muslim Response to 'Terrorism,'" *Washington Quarterly* (Spring 2002): 181.

3. "Anthrax Should Be Put in US Water Supply, Says Hamas Columnist," in Adam Parfrey, ed., *Extreme Islam: Anti-American Propaganda of Muslim Fundamentalism* (Los Angeles: Feral House, 2001), p. 133.

4. Paul R. Ehrlich and Jianguo Liu, "Some Roots of Terrorism," unpublished paper.

5. Paul R. Pillar, *Terrorism and U.S. Foreign Policy* (Washington, DC: Brookings Institution Press, 2001), p. 64. In the winter of 1986, child soldiers of the Iranian Party of Allah organized a massive campaign of "purification" in northern Tehran against the fans of Michael Jackson. Hundreds of people were roughed up, and Jackson records and paraphernalia were destroyed in a bonfire. Amir Taheri, *Holy Terror: Inside the World of Islamic Terrorism* (Bethesda, MD: Adler and Adler, 1987), p. 94.

6. The Hubal was the stone idol that stood in the Kabba—the structure that resides in Mecca, which according to Islamic tradition was originally built by the prophet Abraham on orders from God as a sanctuary of Islam. Michael Scott Doran, "Somebody Else's Civil War," in James F. Hoge, Jr., and Gideon Rose, eds., *How Did This Happen? Terrorism and the New War* (New York: Public Affairs, 2001), p. 33.

7. Osama bin Laden, "Declaration of War (August 1996)," in Rubin and Rubin, *Anti-American Terrorism and the Middle East*, pp. 137–142; and Bin Laden, "Statement: Jihad against Jews and Crusaders (February 23, 1998)," in ibid.

8. Statements from Osama bin Laden that appeared in the *Observer Worldview*, November 24, 2002.

9. Kurt M. Campbell and Michele A. Flournoy, *To Prevail: An American Strategy for the Campaign against Terrorism* (Washington, DC: CSIS Press, 2001), pp. 43–44.

10. Salah Najm, "Transcript of Usamah Bin-Ladin, the Destruction of the Base: Interview with Usamah Bin-Ladin," June 10, 1999, http://wwww.terrorism.com/BinLadinTranscript.shtml.

11. "Bin Laden Rails against Crusaders and UN," BBC News, November 3, 2001, http://news.bbc.co.uk/hi/english/world/monitoring/media/_reports/newsid_1636000/1636782.stm.

12. In a recruitment video, bin Laden declared that the "American government is independent in name only" and that he believed that it "is controlled by Israel." "Al-Qa'ida Recruitment Video (2000)," in Rubin and Rubin, *Anti-American Terrorism and the Middle East,* p. 178.

13. John Miller, "Osama Bin Laden: The ABC Interview," May 18, 1998.

14. Yosri Fouda and Nick Fielding, *Masterminds of Terror: The Truth behind the Most Devastating Terrorist Attack the World Has Ever Seen* (New York: Arcade Publishing, 2003), p. 130.

15. Redacted versions of these documents can be found in Appendix I in Fouda and Fielding, *Masterminds of Terror,* pp. 187–196.

16. Najm, "Transcript of Usamah Bin-Ladin, the Destruction of the Base."

17. Harold Brackman, *9/11 Digital Lies: A Survey of Online Apologists for Global Terrorism* (Los Angeles: Simon Wiesenthal Center, 2001).

18. The FBI notified major movie studios in Los Angeles that they could be the targets of a terrorist attack in retaliation for U.S. intervention in Afghanistan. See Seth Schiesel, "FBI Warning: Movie Studios Possible Target of Terrorists," *New York Times,* September 21, 2001. For his part, Jon Drummond argues that there is evidence that there is a bias in the American media that favors Israelis over Palestinians. For example, in the first intifada (1987–1995) and the ongoing al-Aqsa intifada combined, more than 80 percent of those killed were Palestinians, and nearly as many Palestinian children have been killed (455) as have all Israelis combined (535). Yet as one observer noted, "There is a disturbing pattern in Western media in which Israelis are often presented as victims of 'terrorism' while Palestinian innocents targeted by the IDF are not similarly characterized." See Jonathan T. Drummond, "From the Northwest Imperative to Global Jihad: Social Psychological Aspects of the Construction of the Enemy, Political Violence, and Terror," in Chris E. Stout, ed., *The Psychology of Terrorism: A Public Understanding* (New York: Praeger, 2002), p. 59.

19. Jessica Stern, "The Protean Enemy: What's Next from al Qaeda," *Foreign Affairs* (July–August 2003), p. 30.

20. "Videotape of a Private Meeting (December 13, 2001)," in Rubin and Rubin, *Anti-American Terrorism and the Middle Eas,* p. 244.

21. Rohan Gunaratna, *Inside al Qaeda: Global Network of Terror* (New York: Columbia University Press, 2002), p. 238.

22. David Frum and Richard Perle. *An End to Evil: How to Win the War on Terror* (New York: Random House, 2003), p. 42.

23. Sheikh Muhammad Hussein Fadlullah of Hezbollah, quoted in Harold Brackman, *9/11 Digital Lies: A Survey of Online Apologists for Global Terrorism* (Los Angeles: Simon Wiesenthal Center, 2001), p. 8.

24. Sheikh Muhammed Al-Gamei'a, quoted in ibid., p. 9.

25. Kenneth R. Timmerman, *Preachers of Hate: Islam and the War on America* (New York: Crown Forum, 2003), p. 12.

26. Ibid., p. 16.

27. ADL, "American Muslim Clerics Join Malik Zulu Shabazz of Anti-Semitic New Black Panther Party for Press Conference on C-SPAN," http://www.adl.org/Anti_semitism/shabazz_backgrounder.asp (downloaded November 8, 2001).

28. Steven Emerson, *American Jihad: The Terrorists Living among Us* (New York: Free Press, 2002), p. 105–107.

29. See ADL, "American Muslim Clerics Join Malik Zulu Shabazz"; and ADL, "Media Watch: ADL Letter to C-SPAN," November 7, 2001, http://www.adl.org.

30. ADL. "What They Are Saying," November 28, 2001, http://www.adl.org.

31. Daniel Pipes, *The Hidden Hand: Middle East Fears of Conspiracy* (New York: St. Martin's Griffin, 1998), pp. 9–10.

32. Saleh Abdel-Jawwad, "Why Israel Wanted the War against Iraq," *Al-Ahram Weekly Online*, April 17–23, 2003, http://weekly.abram.org.

33. "Bin Laden Calls Americans 'Vulgar and without Sound Ethics,'" al-Jazeera, October 18, 2003, http://english.aljazeera.net/HomePage.

34. "Full text: 'Bin Laden Tape,'" BBC News, http://wwwnewsvote.bbc.co.uk/mpapps/page tools /print/news.bbc.uk/2/hi/middle_east/36280. downloaded April 27, 2004.

35. "Osama bin Laden Offers Peace to Europe: Terror Attacks for America, Allies, Zionists," *American Free Press* 4, nos. 17–18, April 26 and May 3, 2004, p. 16.

36. Louis Farrakhan, "America at the Crossroads: War Is Not the Answer," March 2, 2003, http://www.finalcall.com.

37. Nation of Islam, "Farrakhan: War Can End through Process of Atonement," October 17, 2001, http://www.noi.org.

38. Thanaa Imam, "Iraq Says Farrakhan Tells of U.S. Muslims' Support," *Washington Times,* July 9, 2002, http://www.washtimes.com.

39. "Iraq War Shows Up Divide between White and Black in US," April 7, 2003, http://www.smh.com.au/articles/2003/04/06/10495657570237.html.

40. Daniel Pipes, "The Snipers: Crazy or Jihadists?" *New York Post,* October 29, 2002, http://www.nypost.com/postopinion/opedcolumnists/60763.htm.

41. Excerpts from these speeches can be found in Anti-Defamation League, "Farrakhan in His Own Words," May 5, 2004, http://www.adl.org.

42. Interview with Ahmed Huber, April 2003.

43. See, for example, his audiotape released on November 16, 2003, "Alleged Saddam Tape Urges 'Road to Jihad,'" *USA TODAY,* November 16, 2003, http://www.usatoday.com/news/world/iraq/2003–11–16-saddam-tape_x.htm.

44. The CIA received a message from a European ally that the United States could face a chemical attack in a big-city subway. Iraq had admitted that it had produced tons of VX and two less sophisticated nerve agents, Sarin and Tabun. Furthermore, in its final report released in January 1999, the United Nations Special Commission (UNSCOM) stated that it could not account for 1.5 tons of VX known to have been manufactured in Iraq. Barton Gellman, "U.S. Suspects al Qaeda Got Nerve Gas from Iraqis," *Washington Post,* December 12, 2002, p. A01.

45. Al-Zarqawi has long been involved in the global jihadist movement. Reportedly, he was born in 1966 to a family of Jordanian Palestinians who resided in the village of Zarqo, not far from the city of Amman. He dropped out of high school to study the Koran, which he memorized by heart. He later married and started a family. In 1989, he left for Afghanistan to join the mujahideen against the Soviets, but the war had already ended by the time of his arrival. According to some accounts, this marked a significant change in Zarqawi's life, as he became deeply involved in Islamism. Upon returning to Jordan after the war, he was imprisoned by the government for seven years, presumably for his political and religious extremism. Upon his release, he became involved in terrorism and was suspected of masterminding a plot to strike U.S. and Jordanian targets in Jordan. He is believed to have established a network of contacts in several parts of the world, extending from London to the Iberian peninsula and the Pankisi Gorge region of Georgia. There is some speculation that he established ties with the regime of Saddam Hussein insofar as Zarqawi reportedly received medical treatment in Baghdad in 2002. For more biographical information on Zarqawi, see Michael Isikoff and Mark Hosenball, "The World's Most Dangerous Terrorist," *Newsweek,* June 23, 2004, http://www.msnbc.com/id/5280219/site/newsweek/?GT1=3584; and Nimrod Raphaeli, "'The Sheikh of the Slaughters': Abu Mus'ab Al-Zarqawi and the Al-Qa'ida Connection," July 1, 2005, http://memri.org/bin/articles.cgi?Page=archivesandArea=iaandID=IA23105.

46. For more on the meeting between Izzat Ibrahim al-Douri and al-Zarqawi, see "Izzat Ibrahim Pledges Allegiance to Abu Musab al Zarqawi," SITE Institute, June 9, 2004, http://www.site institute.org/exposing.asp?id=237.

47. Former regime loyalists have formed groups such as Al-Awdah (the Return), Jihaz al-i'Ilam al-Siyasi Lil Hizb al-Ba'ath (Political Media Organ of the Ba'ath Party), Saddam's Fedayeen, the General Command of the Armed Forces, Resistance and Liberation in Iraq, the Popular Resistance for the Liberation of Iraq, and the Patriotic Front. Several non-Ba'athist nationalist resistance groups have been created as well, including Thuwwar al'-Arak-Kata'ib al-Anbar al-Musallah (Iraq's Revolutionaries) and Munazzamat al-Alam al-Awsad (Black Banner Organization). Some of the more important Islamist groups include Ansar al-Islam, Mujahideen al-Ta'ifa al-Mansoura (Mujahideen of the Victorious Sect), Kata'ib al Mujahideen fi al-Jama'ah al-Salafiyah fi al-'Arak (Mujahideen Battalions of the Salafi Group of Iraq), and, of course, al Qaeda. For more on the various groups composing the Iraqi insurgency, see Ahmed S. Hashim, "The Insurgency in Iraq," *Small Wars and Insurgencies* 14, no. 3 (Autumn 2003): 1–22.

48. For an excellent exegesis on fourth-generation wars, see Thomas X. Hammes, *The Sling and the Stone: On War in the Twenty-First Century* (St. Paul, MN: Zenith Press, 2004). As Hammes explained, first-generation war arose with the nation-state and was characterized by the clash of large standing armies. This type of warfare reached its apogee in the Napoleonic Wars. The Industrial Revolution enabled second-generation war, which emphasized firepower. World War I was an exemplar of this type of conflict. The German blitzkrieg of France in 1940 was the first significant display of third-generation warfare, which emphasized maneuverability and mobility.

CHAPTER 10. PROSPECTS FOR COOPERATION BETWEEN MILITANT ISLAM AND THE EXTREME RIGHT

1. Jeffrey Kaplan and Leonard Weinberg, *The Emergence of a Euro-American Radical Right* (New Brunswick, NJ: Rutgers University Press, 1998).

2. Interview with David Duke, March 2003.

3. Ibid.

4. Interview with Ahmed Huber, April 2003.

5. Interview with Jürgen Graf, April 2003.

6. Interview with Steven Emerson, June 12, 2005.

7. Michelle Cottle, "White Hope," *New Republic,* November 21, 2001, http://www.tnr.com.

8. Interview with John Tyndall, June 3, 2003.

9. Interview with Nick Griffin, May 2003.

10. British National Party, "Islam, Bush and the BNP," http://www.bnp.org (downloaded April 6, 2002).

11. British National Party, "'Islam—a Threat to Us All!' BNP Launches Joint anti-Islam Campaign with Sikhs and Hindus," http://www.bnp.org.uk (downloaded April 6, 2002).

12. "Sleeping with the Enemy," *Searchlight,* February 2002, http://www.searchlightmagazine .com.

13. Interview with Nick Griffin, May 2003.

14. Nicholas Goodrick-Clarke, *The Black Sun: Aryan Cults, Esoteric Nazism and the Politics of Identity* (New York: New York University Press, 2002), p. 69.

15. Interview with Jared Taylor, February 6, 2004.

16. Interview with Steven Barry, December 11, 2003.

17. Susan Sevareid, "Italian Premier Puts Down Islam," *Washington Post,* September 27, 2001, http://www.washingtonpost.com.

18. Catherine Field, "Far Right's Drums Beat Hate Out against Islam," *New Zealand Herald*, October 5, 2001, http://www.nzherald.com.nz.

19. Walter Laqueur, *No End to War: Terrorism in the Twenty-First Century* (New York: Continuum, 2003), p. 59.

20. According to a 1988 study, countries with a large number of Muslims have a crude birthrate of 42 per 1,000 people; by contrast, developed countries have a crude birth rate of only 13 per 1,000 people. This comes out to a total fertility rate of 6 children per Muslim woman and 1.7 children per woman in the developed world. The annual average rate of natural increase is 2.8 percent in the Muslim world; in the developed world it is a mere 0.3 percent. John R. Weeks, *The Demography of Islamic Nations* (Washington, DC: Population Reference Bureau, 1988), p. 13, cited in Daniel Pipes, *Militant Islam Reaches America* (New York: W. W. Norton, 2002), p. 23.

21. Pipes, *Militant Islam Reaches America*, p. 24.

22. Francis Fukuyama, "Our Foreign Legion," *Wall Street Journal*, January 26, 2004, http://www.sais-jhu.edu/fukuyama/articles/WSJ%20Our%20Foreign%20Legions.htm.

23. Patrick J. Buchanan, *Death of the West: How Dying Populations and Immigrant Invasions Imperil Our Country and Civilization* (New York: Thomas Dunne Books, 2002), p. 109.

24. Ibid.

25. Ibid., pp. 115–116.

26. Samuel P. Huntington, *The Clash of Civilizations and the Remaking of World Order* (New York: Touchstone, 1996), p. 201.

27. "Haider: Curtail Immigrants to Fight Terrorism," *Washington Times*, September 27, 2001.

28. Martin Lee, "The Swastika and Crescent," *Intelligence Report*, Spring 2002, http://www.splcenter/intelligenceproject/ip-4u3.html.

29. Interview with David Myatt, April 2003.

30. Interview with Ahmed Huber, April 2003.

31. Interview with Jürgen Graf, April 2003.

32. Interview with Kevin MacDonald, April 2003.

33. Lothrop Stoddard was a very prominent nativist active during the 1920s. A respected academic (he received his Ph.D. from Harvard), Stoddard wrote several books warning of a demographic inundation of the Western world by nonwhites. In light of current demographic realities, his prognostications were indeed prophetic. See Lothrop Stoddard, *The Rising Tide of Color against White World-Supremacy* (Brighton, England: Historical Review Press, 1981).

34. Interview with Sam Francis, April 8, 2003.

35. Interview with Mike Piper, April 2003.

36. The far right gives many examples of how Jews allegedly work to effect miscegenation. Chief among them is through the mass media. It is argued that since Jews figure prominently in Hollywood, they as a group are responsible for the content of movies, which depict miscegenation in favorable ways. Another bête noire in this regard is MTV, which often features music videos from so-called gangsta rap artists in which white women are objectified. The most strident far-right critic in this regard was the late Dr. William L. Pierce of the National Alliance. For more of his analysis on this issue, see his various American Dissident Voices programs, which are archived at the National Alliance website at www.natvan.org.

37. Robert Weissberg, himself a Jew, presented a lecture at the American Renaissance conference in 2000 in which he echoed this sentiment, which is interesting, considering the fact that such a view is generally dismissed as an anti-Semitic canard. See Robert Weissberg, "Jews and Blacks: Everything the Goyim Want to Know But Are Afraid to Ask," unpublished transcript for the 2000 American Renaissance conference.

38. See, for example, Samuel R. Berger and Monna Sutphen, "Commandeering the Palestinian Cause: Bin Laden's Belated Concern," in James F. Hoge, Jr., and Gideon Rose, eds., *How Did This Happen? Terrorism and the New War* (New York: Public Affairs, 2001), pp. 123–128.

39. Interview with Ernst Zünel, October 5, 2000.

40. Ernst Zündel, "The West, War, and Islam," http://homein.tripod.com/3/id15.html.

41. Dr. William L. Pierce, "The Martyrdom of Wafa Idris," American Dissident Voices, February 9, 2002.

42. Kevin Alfred Strom, "Terror in Chicago," American Dissident Voices, January 18, 2003.

43. Duke covered these topics in greater detail in *My Awakening* (Covington, LA: Free Speech Press, 1998).

44. Interview with David Duke, March 2003.

45. Interview with Tom Metzger, March 2003.

46. In addition to David Duke, participants at the conference included Don Black of Stormfront, Sam Dickson, Dr. Ed Fields of *The Truth at Last* newspaper, Kevin Alfred Strom of the National Alliance, John Tyndall of the British National Party, Bob Whitaker, Gemar Rudolf, Paul Fromm, Edgar Steele, Roy Armstrong of European American Unity and Rights Organization, David Pringle of the National Alliance, and Willis Carto of the *American Free Press*.

47. For more on the conference, see the David Duke website, http://www.davidduke.com/.

48. Laqueur, *No End to War*, p. 161.

49. James Kurth, "Confronting the Unipolar Moment: The American Empire and Islamic Terrorism," *Current History* 101, no. 659 (December 2002): 403.

50. Ibid., p. 403.

51. See Robert Jay Lifton, "American Apocalypse," *Nation*, December 22, 2003, http://www.thenation.com/docprint.mhtml?i=20031222&s=lifton.

52. Christopher Hitchens, "Jewish Power, Jewish Peril," *Vanity Fair*, September 2002, pp. 194–202.

53. See, for example, Daniel Jennings, "Americans: The Jews of the World," *FrontPageMagazine.com*, April 23, 2003; Bernard Wasserstein, "Anti-Semitism and Anti-Americanism," *Chronicle of Higher Education* 1, no. 9 (2001): 28.

54. Laqueur, *No End to War*, p. 150.

55. Kevin Coogan, "The Mysterious Achmed Huber: Friend to Hitler, Allah and Ibn Laden?" http://coraclesyndicate.org/pub_e/k.coo_e/publ_05–02_1.htm, September 2002.

56. Interview with Ahmed Huber, April 2003.

57. "Bin Laden Calls Americans 'Vulgar and without Sound Ethics,'" al-Jazeera, October 18, 2003, http://english.aljazeera.net/HomePage.

58. Laqueur, *No End to War*, p. 175.

59. Kenneth R. Timmerman, *Preachers of Hate: Islam and the War on America* (New York: Crown Forum, 2003), pp. 2–3.

60. Ibid., p. 315.

CHAPTER 11. CONCLUSION

1. Walter Laqueur, *No End to War: Terrorism in the Twenty-First Century* (New York: Continuum, 2003), p. 125.

2. For a good discussion of the theoretical development of asymmetric warfare, see Bruce Berkowitz, *The New Face of War: How War Will Be Fought in the Twenty-First Century* (New York: Free Press, 2003).

3. Jonathan D. Salant, "Census: U.S. Arab Population Is Surging," Associated Press, December 3, 2003.

4. Daniel Pipes, *Militant Islam Reaches America* (New York: W. W. Norton, 2002), p. 23.

5. Jerry Seeper, "Islamic Extremists Invade U.S., Join Sleeper Cells," *Washington Times*, February 10, 2004.

6. Abraham Foxman, *Never Again? The Threat of the New Anti-Semitism* (New York: HarperCollins, 2003), p. 22.

7. Ibid., p. 28.

8. David Frum and Richard Perle, *An End to Evil: How to Win the War on Terror* (New York: Random House, 2003), p. 67.

9. Ibid., p. 71.

10. "Did 'Jihad' Arms Course Visit U.S.?" MSNBC, December 27, 2001, http://www. msnbc .com/news/668509.asp?cp1=1.

11. Frum and Perle, *An End to Evil*, p. 73.

12. Samuel Huntington, "The Hispanic Challenge," *Foreign Policy* (March–April 2004), p. 1, http://www.foreignpolicy.com/story/cms.php?story_id=2495etseq.

13. Samuel Huntington, *Who Are We? The Challenges to America's National Identity* (New York: Simon and Schuster, 2004), p. 143.

14. Huntington cited six factors that distinguish the current wave of Mexican immigration from previous waves of immigration. The first is contiguity: the United States shares a border with Mexico. The fact that the former is a First World country and the latter a poor Third World country makes the relationship all the more problematic. The second factor, scale, is unprecedented in that Mexican immigration composes a larger percentage of total immigration than any other ethnic group in previous immigration waves (with the English of the early years of the republic excepted). The third factor is illegality. A larger proportion of immigrants enter the country illegally than in previous immigrations. Fourth, Hispanic immigrants are regionally concentrated in the Southwest and California. This could conceivably transform this region into an area in which English-language proficiency would not be necessary for the majority of the population that resides there. Fifth, currently immigration differs from previous waves in persistence. The latter tended to fluctuate greatly and at times even slowed to a trickle, but the current wave of immigration shows no signs of abating, even during economic downturns. Finally, the historical presence of Mexico combined with huge immigration from that country could undercut American national unity, insofar as some Mexicans feel a sense of national grievance as a result of the Texas War of Independence and the Mexican-American War, which resulted in a huge loss of Mexican territory. Conceivably, this sentiment could heighten irredentist demands, as Mexicans come to comprise a larger share of the population in the American Southwest. Huntington, *Who Are We?* pp. 222–230.

15. Huntington, "The Hispanic Challenge," p. 9.

16. Huntington, *Who Are We?* pp. 310–313.

17. Jane Corbin, *Al Qaeda: In Search of the Terror Network That Threatens the World* (New York: Thunder's Mouth Press, 2002), p. xvii.

18. Paul Kennedy recognized a historical pattern in which empires expand beyond their capacity to maintain hegemony. At first, an imperial domain may buttress an empire, but eventually the costs outweigh the benefits and hence lead to decline and disintegration. Paul Kennedy, *The Rise and Fall of the Great Powers: Economic Change and Military Conflict from 1500 to 2000* (New York: Vintage Books, 1989).

19. Chief among those who hold this view is Rohan Gunaratna, arguably the most authoritative scholar on the subject of al Qaeda. He believes that al Qaeda never expected the United States to send ground troops to Afghanistan. Al Qaeda viewed the United States in light of previous attacks in Aden, Somalia, and Lebanon and therefore did not believe a ground response would be forthcoming after 9/11. Interview with Rohan Gunaratna, January 17, 2004. Marc Sageman suggested this position as well in *Understanding Terror Networks* (Philadelphia: University of Pennsylvania Press, 2004), p. 51. Thomas Hammes argued that al Qaeda committed a fundamental strategic error with the 9/11 attacks in that it sent the message that its organization was attacking the United States in its homeland rather than in some faraway land that the United States could be encouraged to leave. Thomas X. Hammes, *The Sling and the Stone: On War in the Twenty-First Century* (St. Paul, MN: Zenith Press, 2004), pp. 148–149.

20. Walter Laqueur, *The Age of Terrorism* (Boston: Little, Brown, 1987), p. 321.

21. Decision Support Systems, "Al-Qaida's Endgame? A Strategic Scenario Analysis," November 2, 2001, http://www.metatetempo.com.

22. Walter Laqueur, *Guerilla Warfare: A Historical and Critical Study* (New Brunswick, NJ: Transaction Publishers, 1998), p. 394.

23. Christopher Hewitt, *Understanding Terrorism in America: From the Klan to Al Qaeda* (London: Routledge, 2003), p. 120.

24. "Most of U.S. Forces Withdrawn from Saudi Arabia," *USA TODAY,* August 26, 2003, http://www.usatoday.com/news/washington/2003–0828-ustroops-saudiarabia_x.htm.

25. According to an April poll conducted by the *New York Times*/CBS News, 47 percent of those surveyed responded that the United States had done the right thing in taking military action against Iraq, whereas 46 percent replied that the United States should have stayed out of Iraq. Richard W. Stevenson and Janet Elder, "Support for War Is Down Sharply, Poll Concludes," *New York Times,* April 29, 2004, http://www.nytimes.com/2004/04/29/politics/29POLL.html?ex=1087099200&en=dd225f70d661f2a9&ei=5070&hp. Furthermore, a FOX News/Opinion Dynamics Poll conducted on June 8–9, 2004, indicated that only 39 percent of the respondents believed that the war on Iraq would make the United States safer. Forty-six percent of those surveyed believed that the war on Iraq would not make the United States safer. See PollingReport.com, http://www.pollingreport.com/iraq.htm. A CBS News/*New York Times* Poll conducted in April 2004 found that only 49 percent of those surveyed believed that the policies of the Bush administration have made the United States safer from terrorism. See PollingReport.com, http://www.pollingreport.com/terror.htm. More recently, a poll released in July 2005 that was conducted by *USA Today*/CNN/Gallup found that 58 percent of those Americans surveyed believed that the United States would not be able to establish a stable, democratic government in Iraq and 32 percent agreed that the United States could not win the war in Iraq. Susan Page, "Poll: USA Doubts Iraq Success, but Not Ready to Give Up," *USA Today,* July 26, 2005. See http://www.usatoday.com/news/nation/2005-07-26-poll-us-not-winning-iraq_x. htm. Finally, still another poll conducted by the same parties and released in August 2005 found that 57 percent of those Americans surveyed believed that the war in Iraq had made the United States more vulnerable to terrorism. Richard Benedetto, "Poll Shows Most Americans Feel More Vulnerable," *USA Today,* August 8, 2005. See http://www.usatoday.com/news/nation/2005-08-08-pollvulnerable_x.htm.

26. William E. Gibson, "U.S. Military Force Stretched to Limit by Global Missions," *South Florida Sun-Sentinel,* May 2, 2004, http://www.sunherald.com/mld/sunherald/news/politics/8575712.htm.

27. "Iraq Coalition Casualty Count," http://icasualties.org/oif/ (downloaded July 2, 2005).

28. See the U.S. Department of Homeland Security website at: http://www.dhs.gov/. It is worth noting that several pre-existing agencies have been reorganized under the Department of Homeland Security. Thus, much of the funding for these agencies preceded the creation of the new department. Suffice it to say, however, the new department will require a substantial amount of additional funding.

29. "What's Wrong with Social Security?" Social Security Network, http://www.socsec.org/facts/Basics/basics_wrong_1.htm (downloaded June 9, 2004). See also "Projections of Future Financial Status," Social Security Administration, downloaded June 9, 2004, http://www.ssa.gov?OACT/TR/TR03/II_project.html.

30. For example, the National Research Council estimated that the net fiscal cost of immigration ranges from $11 billion to $22 billion per year. Cited in Center for Immigration Studies, http://www.cis.org.topics/costs.html (downloaded May 23, 2004). A 1996 study by Rice University economic professor Donald Huddle estimated the annual cost to be roughly $24 billion. The Federation for American Immigration Reform, extrapolating from Huddle's estimates, estimated the annual cost to be roughly $61 billion in 2000. In his calculation, Huddle included the costs associated with various programs, including public education, food stamps, Social Security, housing, Medicaid, Medicare, Aid to Families with Dependent Children, Earned Income Tax

Credit, criminal justice and corrections, and local government services. See Donald Huddle, *The Net National Costs of Immigration: Fiscal Effects of Welfare Restorations to Legal Immigrants* (Houston, TX: Rice University, 1997). Also see the website of the Federation for American Immigration Reform, http://www.fairus.org/.

31. Robert Kaplan, "The Coming Anarchy," *Atlantic Monthly,* February 1994, http://www.theatlantic.com/politics.foreign/anarchy.htm.

32. Walter Laqueur, *The New Terrorism: Fanaticism and the Arms of Mass Destruction* (New York: Oxford University Press, 1999), p. 245.

33. See Lydia Saad, "Have Americans Changed? Effects of Sept. 11 Have Largely Faded," Gallup Organization, September 11, 2002, http://www.gallup.com/content/login.aspx?ci= 6790; and Karlyn H. Bowman, "Pride and Patriotism: Sept. 11 Affects American Feelings," American Enterprise Institute for Public Policy Research, June 27, 2002, http://www.aei.org/news/newsID.14041/news_detail.asp.

34. Joseph Scolnick identified several factors that enhance national unity and thus enable a country to face external threats more effectively: "(1) all groups within the state perceive the external challenge or dispute as a threat"; (2) "citizens of the threatened state cannot avoid the danger by moving away"; (3) "at least minimal social cohesion must obtain prior to the foreign threat"; (4) "the threat must not be linked to a domestic dispute where parties seek external assistance"; (5) "cooperation among the conflicting domestic groups will enable the state to succeed in repelling the threat"; (6) "the cost of the cooperative solution must be acceptable to the state's citizens, and it must be equitably shared"; and (7) "the citizens must believe that the government can prevail against the threat; accordingly, government policies must not be viewed as disastrous."

By inference, the corollary would be that the absence of these factors would diminish national unity and undermine effectiveness in reacting to external threats. Scolnick pointed out that a government facing an unpleasant domestic situation may manufacture a foreign crisis or exaggerate a seemingly minor threat as a major one. However, that tactic can be risky, when imaginary or exaggerated threats tend to fail because of their short duration. Joseph M. Scolnick, Jr., "How Governments Utilize Foreign Threats," *Conflict* 8, no. 1 (1988): 12–22.

35. Arthur A. Stein, *The Nation at War* (Baltimore, MD: Johns Hopkins University Press, 1980), in Huntington, *Who Are We?* p. 361.

36. Huntington, *Who Are We?* pp. 361–362.

37. Ibid., p. 38.

38. Ibid., p. 338.

39. Ibid., p. 340.

40. Yosri Fouda and Nick Fielding, *Masterminds of Terror: The Truth Behind the Most Devastating Terrorist Attack the World Has Ever Seen* (New York: Arcade Publishing, 2003), p. 196.

41. Interview with David Myatt, April 2003.

42. "Invasion USA: Could French-style Riots Happen Here?" November 8, 2005, http://www.worldnetdaily.com/news/article.asp?ARTICLE_ID=4728442.

43. This document was analyzed by the Norwegian Defense Research Establishment (FFI). See "FFI Explains al-Qaida Document," *Forsvarets forskningsinstitutt,* March 19, 2004, http://www.mil.no/felles/ffi/start/article.jhtml?articleID=71589.

44. John Solomon, "U.S. Extremists' Links with Terror Groups Watched," Salon.com, February 28, 2002.

45. Ibid.

46. For more on this development, see Jeffrey Kaplan and Leonard Weinberg, *The Emergence of a Euro-American Radical Right* (New Brunswick, NJ: Rutgers University Press, 1998).

47. Quoted in "US Says al-Qaeda Ready to Hit 'Hard,'" iafrica.com, May 27, 2004, http://iafrica.com/news/ worldnews/325459.htm.

48. John Diamond and Toni Lacy, "Non-Arab Recruits Scout for al-Qaeda," *USA TODAY,* August, 16, 2004.

49. Jessica Stern, "The Protean Enemy: What's Next from al Qaeda," *Foreign Affairs* (July–August 2003), p. 38.

50. In his suicide letter, Charles Bishop claimed an ideological affinity with al Qaeda, expressed anti-American and anti-Israeli sentiment, and justified his attack as a way to call attention to the oppression of the Palestinian and Iraqi peoples. Eric Lenkowitz, "Teen Suicide Plot: Super Bowl Was Next," NYPOST.COM, February 7, 2002, http://www.nypost.com/cgi-bin/printfriendly.pl.

51. Michelle Malkin, "Eco-terrorists Declare War," *Washington Times,* March 24, 2003, http://www.washingtontimes.com.

52. David Johnston and James Risen, "Agencies Warn of Lone Terrorists," *New York Times,* February 23, 2003, http://www.nytimes.com.

53. Alfred Schobert, a researcher at the Information Service against Right-Wing Extremism in Duisburg, Germany, made this observation with regard to the situation in Germany. He conceded, however, that some far-right leaders see potential in such an alliance. See Peter Finn, "Unlikely Allies Bound by a Common Hatred," *Washington Post,* April 29, 2002, p. A13.

54. Laqueur, *No End to War,* p. 160.

55. The ADL issued a press release in which it disclosed several instances in which Muslim extremists had used right-wing extremist propaganda to augment their anti-Zionist propaganda. See ADL, "ADL Says U.S.-Backed Anti-Semites Are Feeding Sept. 11 Rumor Mill," November 9, 2001.

56. Mark Juergensmeyer once referred to the networking of dispersed people tied culturally despite their diversity of places as "email ethnicities." Mark Juergensmeyer, *Terror in the Mind of God: The Global Rise of Religious Violence* (Berkeley: University of California Press, 2000), p. 194.

57. Joseph S. Nye, Jr., "The Changing Nature of World Power," *Political Science Quarterly* 105 (Summer 1990): 181–182, mentioned in Samuel P. Huntington, *The Clash of Civilizations: Remaking of World Order* (New York: Touchstone, 1996), p. 92.

58. John Arquilla, David Ronfeldt, and Michele Zanini, "Networks, Netwar, and Information-Age Terrorism," in Ian Lessler et al., eds., *Countering the New Terrorism* (Santa Monica, CA: RAND, 1999), pp. 53–54.

59. John Arquilla and David Ronfeldt, "What Next for Networks and Netwars?" in Arquilla and Ronfeldt, *Networks and Netwars: The Future of Terror, Crime, and Militancy* (Santa Monica, CA: RAND, 2001), p. 328.

60. Faye Bowers, "Al Qaeda's Profile: Slimmer but Menacing," *Christian Science Monitor,* September 9, 2003.

61. "Survey: World Support for U.S. at New Low," *USA TODAY,* June 3, 2003, http://www.usatoday.com/new/washington/2003–06–03-pew_x.htm.

Selected Bibliography

Abadinsky, Howard. *Organized Crime.* 7th ed. Belmont, CA: Thomson/Wadsworth, 2003.

Abdullaev, Nabi. "Fundamentalism in Russia: An Interview with Islam Committee's Heidar Jama," in Adam Parfrey, ed., *Extreme Islam: Anti-American Propaganda of Muslim Fundamentalism.* Los Angeles: Feral House, 2001, 281–284.

Adams, James. *The Financing of Terrorism.* New York: Simon and Schuster, 1986.

Adler, Patricia, and Peter Adler. *Constructions of Deviance: Social Power, Context, and Interaction.* 4th ed. Belmont, CA: Thomson/Wadsworth, 2003.

Al-Banna, Hassan. "On the Doctrine of the Muslim Brothers," in Barry Rubin and Judith Colp Rubin, eds., *Anti-American Terrorism and the Middle East: A Documentary Reader.* Oxford: Oxford University Press, 2002, 27–28.

Ammerman, Nancy T. "Waco, Law Enforcement, and Scholars of Religion," in Stuart A. Wright, ed., *Armageddon in Waco: Critical Perspectives on the Branch Davidian Conflict.* Chicago: University of Chicago Press, 1995, 282–296.

Anini, Michele, and Sean J. A. Edwards. "The Networking of Terror in the Information Age," in John Arquilla and David Ronfeldt, eds., *Networks and Netwars: The Future of Terror, Crime, and Militancy.* Santa Monica, CA: RAND, 2001, 29–60.

"Anthrax Should Be Put in US Water Supply, Says Hamas Columnist," in Adam Parfrey, ed., *Extreme Islam: Anti-American Propaganda of Muslim Fundamentalism.* Los Angeles: Feral House, 2001, 133.

Anti-Defamation League (ADL). *The ADL Anti–Paramilitary Training Statute: A Response to Domestic Terrorism.* New York: ADL, 1995.

———. *Beyond Anthrax: Extremism and the Bioterrorism Threat.* New York: ADL, 2003.

———. *Explosion of Hate: The Growing Danger of the National Alliance.* New York: ADL, 1998.

———. *Extremism on the Right: A Handbook.* New York: ADL, 1988.

———. *Jihad Online: Islamic Terrorists and the Internet.* New York: ADL, 2002.

———. *Not the Work of a Day: The Story of the Anti-Defamation League of B'nai B'rith.* New York: ADL, 1965.

Arquilla, John, and David Ronfeldt. "Afterword September 2001: The Sharpening Fight for the Future," in John Arquilla and David Ronfeldt, eds., *Networks and Netwars: The Future of Terror, Crime, and Militancy.* Santa Monica, CA: RAND, 2001, 363–369.

———. "What Next for Networks and Netwars?" in John Arquilla and David Ronfeldt, eds., *Networks and Netwars: The Future of Terror, Crime, and Militancy.* Santa Monica, CA: RAND, 2001, 311–361.

Arquilla, John, David Ronfeldt, and Michele Zanini. "Networks, Netwar, and Information-Age Terrorism," in Ian Lessler et al., eds., *Countering the New Terrorism.* Santa Monica, CA: RAND, 1999, 39–84.

Barber, Benjamin R. *Jihad vs. McWorld: How Globalization and Tribalism Are Reshaping the World.* New York: Ballantine Books, 1996.

Barkun, Michael. *Religion and the Racist Right: The Origins of the Christian Identity Movement.* Chapel Hill: University of North Carolina Press, 1994.

Barrett, Stanley R. *Is God a Racist? The Right Wing in Canada.* Toronto: University of Toronto Press, 1987.

Barreveld, Dirk J. *Terrorism in the Philippines: The Bloody Trail of Abu Sayyaf, Bin Laden's East Asian Connection.* Lincoln, NE: Writers Club Press, 2001.

Bearden, Milton. "Graveyard of Empires," in James F. Hoge, Jr., and Gideon Rose, eds., *How Did This Happen? Terrorism and the New War.* New York: Public Affairs, 2001, 83–95.

Becker, Jillian. "The Centrality of the PLO," in Benjamin Netanyahu, ed., *Terrorism: How the West Can Win.* New York: Farrar, Straus and Giroux, 1986, 98–102.

Bergen, Peter L. *Holy War, Inc.: Inside the Secret World of Osama bin Laden.* New York: Free Press, 2001.

Berger, Samuel R., and Monna Sutphen. "Commandeering the Palestinian Cause: Bin Laden's Belated Concern," in James F. Hoge, Jr., and Gideon Rose, eds., *How Did This Happen? Terrorism and the New War.* New York: Public Affairs, 2001, 123–128.

Berkowitz, Bruce. *The New Face of War: How War Will Be Fought in the Twenty-First Century.* New York: Free Press, 2003.

Berlet, Chip. "Third Position Fascism." Political Research Associates. http://www.publiceye.org (downloaded April 17, 2002).

Bin Laden, Osama. "Declaration of War August 1996," in Barry Rubin and Judith Colp Rubin, eds., *Anti-American Terrorism and the Middle East: A Documentary Reader.* Oxford: Oxford University Press, 2002, 137–142.

———. "Statement: Jihad against Jews and Crusaders, February 23, 1998," in Barry Rubin and Judith Colp Rubin, eds., *Anti-American Terrorism and the Middle East: A Documentary Reader.* Oxford: Oxford University Press, 2002, 149–151.

Bodansky, Yossef. *Bin Laden: The Man Who Declared War on America.* Rocklin, CA: Forum, 1999.

———. *Islamic Anti-Semitism as a Political Instrument.* Houston, TX: Ariel Center for Policy Research, 1999.

Boroumand, Ladan, and Roya Boroumand. "Terror, Islam, and Democracy." *Journal of Democracy* 13, no. 2 (April 2002): 5–20.

Brackman, Harold. *9/11 Digital Lies: A Survey of Online Apologists for Global Terrorism.* Los Angeles: Simon Wiesenthal Center, 2001.

Brenner, Lenni. *Zionism in the Age of the Dictators: A Reappraisal.* Chicago: Lawrence Hill Books, 1983.

"Broadcast by Iraqi President Saddam Hussein September 12, 2001," in Barry Rubin and Judith Colp Rubin, eds., *Anti-American Terrorism and the Middle East: A Documentary Reader.* Oxford: Oxford University Press, 2002, 283–284.

Buchanan, Patrick J. *Death of the West: How Dying Populations and Immigrant Invasions Imperil Our Country and Civilization.* New York: Thomas Dunne Books, 2002.

———. "Whose War?" *American Conservative,* March 24, 2003, 7–14.

Bush, George W. "Address to Joint Session of Congress (September 20, 2001)," in Barry Rubin and Judith Colp Rubin, eds., *Anti-American Terrorism and the Middle East: A Documentary Reader.* Oxford: Oxford University Press, 2002, 320–326.

———. "Address to the Nation September 11, 2001," in Barry Rubin and Judith Colp Rubin, eds., *Anti-American Terrorism and the Middle East: A Documentary Reader.* Oxford: Oxford University Press, 2002, 319–320.

Campbell, Kurt M., and Michele A. Flournoy. *To Prevail: An American Strategy for the Campaign against Terrorism.* Washington, DC: CSIS Press, 2001.

Carothers, Thomas. "Democracy: Terrorism's Uncertain Antidote." *Current History* (December 2003): 403–406.

Center for Democratic Renewal (CDR). *International Connections of U.S. White Supremacists.* Atlanta, GA: CDR, n.d.

"Charter," in Barry Rubin and Judith Colp Rubin, eds., *Anti-American Terrorism and the Middle East: A Documentary Reader.* Oxford: Oxford University Press, 2002, 54–60.

Chin, Warren. "Operation 'Enduring Freedom': A Victory for a Conventional Force Fighting an Unconventional War." *Small Wars and Insurgencies* 14, no. 1 (Spring 2003): 57–75.

Christison, Kathleen, and Bill Christison. "A Rose by Any Other Name: The Bush Administration's Dual Loyalties." *Washington Report on Middle East Affairs* (March 2003): 14–18.

"Clinton Is the Best Guy for Us," in Jim Keith, ed., *Secret and Suppressed: Banned Ideas and Hidden History.* Portland, OR: Feral House, 1993, 256–269.

Cockburn, Andrew, and Patrick Cockburn. *Out of the Ashes: The Resurrection of Saddam Hussein.* New York: HarperCollins, 1999.

Cole, David, and James X. Dempsey. *Terrorism and the Constitution.* New York: New Press, 2002.

Collins, Aukai. *My Jihad.* Guilford, CT: Lyons Press, 2002.

Combs, Cindy C. *Terrorism in the Twenty-First Century.* Upper Saddle River, NJ: Prentice-Hall, 1997.

Coogan, Kevin. *Dreamer of the Day: Francis Parker Yockey and the Postwar Fascist International.* New York: Autonomedia, 1999.

Cooper, H. H. A. "What Is a Terrorist? A Psychological Perspective." *Chitty's Law Journal* 26 (1977): 8–18.

Corbin, Jane. *Al Qaeda: In Search of the Terror Network That Threatens the World.* New York: Thunder's Mouth Press, 2002.

Coulson, Danny O., and Elaine Shannon. *No Heroes: Inside the FBI's Secret Counter-Terror Force.* New York: Pocket Books, 1999.

Crenshaw, Martha. "Suicide Terrorism in Comparative Perspective," in International Policy Institute for Counter-Terrorism, ed., *Countering Suicide Terrorism.* New York: International Policy Institute for Counter-Terrorism and the Anti-Defamation League, 2002, 21–29.

Davis, James Kirkpatrick. *Spying on America: The FBI's Domestic Counterintelligence Program.* Westport, CT: Praeger, 1992.

Davis, Jayna. *The Third Terrorist: The Middle East Connection to the Oklahoma City Bombing.* Nashville, TN: WND Books, 2004.

Decision Support Systems. "Al-Qaida's Endgame? A Strategic Scenario Analysis." November 2, 2001. http://www.metatetempo.com.

Dees, Morris. *Hate on Trial.* New York: Villard Books, 1993.

Dershowitz, Alan M. *Why Terrorism Works.* New Haven, CT: Yale University Press, 2002.

Dobratz, Betty A., and Stephanie L. Shanks-Meile. *White Power, White Pride! The White Separatist Movement in the United States.* New York: Twayne Publishers, 1997.

"Do Not Call Jihad a Defense from Milestones, the Book That Killed Its Authors," in Adam Parfrey, ed., *Extreme Islam: Anti-American Propaganda of Muslim Fundamentalism.* Los Angeles: Feral House, 2001, 61–67.

Doran, Michael Scott. "Somebody Else's Civil War," in James F. Hoge, Jr., and Gideon Rose, eds., *How Did This Happen? Terrorism and the New War.* New York: Public Affairs, 2001, 31–52.

Drummond, Jonathan T. "From the Northwest Imperative to Global Jihad: Social Psychological Aspects of the Construction of the Enemy, Political Violence, and Terror," in Chris E. Stout, ed., *The Psychology of Terrorism: A Public Understanding.* New York: Praeger, 2002, 49–95.

D'Souza', Dinesh. *The End of Racism.* New York: Free Press, 1995.

Duke, David. *My Awakening.* Covington, LA: Free Speech Press, 1998.

Durham, Martin. "The American Far Right and 9/11." *Terrorism and Political Violence* 15, no. 2 (2004): 96–111.

Ehrlich, Paul R., and Jianguo Liu. "Some Roots of Terrorism." *Population and Environment* 24, no. 2 (November 2002): 183–192.

Emerson, Steven. *American Jihad: The Terrorists Living among Us.* New York: Free Press, 2002.

Esposito, John. "Political Islam: Beyond the Green Menace." *Current History* (January 1994): 149–154.

"Executive Order: Sanctions on the Afghan Taliban July 6, 1999," in Barry Rubin and Judith Colp Rubin, eds., *Anti-American Terrorism and the Middle East: A Documentary Reader.* Oxford: Oxford University Press, 2002, 218.

Farrakhan, Louis. "The Great Atonement," in Adam Parfrey, ed., *Extreme Islam: Anti-American Propaganda of Muslim Fundamentalism.* Los Angeles: Feral House, 2001, 238–246.

Federal Bureau of Investigation (FBI). *Terrorism in the United States 1999.* Washington, DC: FBI, 2001.

Ferguson, Niall. "Clashing Civilizations or Mad Mullahs: The United States between Informal and Formal Empire," in Strobe Talbott and Nayan Chanda, eds., *The Age of Terror: America and the World After September 11.* New York: Basic Books, 2001, 113–141.

Finch, Phillip. *God, Guts, and Guns.* New York: Seaview/Putnam, 1983.

Findley, Paul. *They Dare to Speak Out: People and Institutions Confront Israel's Lobby.* Chicago: Lawrence Hill Books, 1989.

Flanagan, Thomas. "The Politics of the Millennium." *Terrorism and Political Violence* 7, no. 3 (1995): 164–175.

Flynn, Kevin, and Gary Gerhardt. *The Silent Brotherhood.* New York: Signet, 1990.

Forster, Arnold. *Square One: The Memoirs of a True Freedom Fighter's Life-long Struggle against Anti-Semitism, Domestic and Foreign.* New York: Donald I. Fine, 1988.

Fouda, Yosri, and Nick Fielding. *Masterminds of Terror: The Truth behind the Most Devastating Terrorist Attack the World Has Ever Seen.* New York: Arcade Publishing, 2003.

Foxman, Abraham. *Never Again? The Threat of the New Anti-Semitism.* New York: Harper-Collins, 2003.

Fraser, L. Craig. *The Hitler-Bormann Documents.* Date and publisher unknown.

Friedman, Thomas L. *From Beirut to Jerusalem.* New York: Anchor Books, 1989.

Frum, David, and Richard Perle. *An End to Evil: How to Win the War on Terror.* New York: Random House, 2003.

Fukuyama, Francis. *The Great Disruption: Human Nature and the Reconstitution of Social Order.* New York: Free Press, 1999.

Gable, Gerry. "Britain's Nazi Underground," in Luciano Cheles, Ronnie Ferguson, and Michalina Vaughan, eds., *The Far Right in Western and Eastern Europe.* 2nd ed. London and New York: Longman, 1995, 258–271.

———. "The Far Right in Contemporary Britain," in Luciano Cheles, Ronnie Ferguson, and Michalina Vaughan, eds., *Neo-Fascism in Europe.* New York: Longman, 1991, 245–263.

GAO (General Accounting Office). *Homeland Security: A Risk Management Approach Can Guide Preparedness Efforts.* Washington, DC: General Accounting Office, October 31, 2001.

Gardell, Mattias. "Black and White Unite in Fight?" in Jeffrey Kaplan and Hélène Lööw, eds., *The Cultic Milieu: Oppositional Subcultures in an Age of Globalization.* New York: Alta Mira Press, 2002, 152–192.

———. *In the Name of Elijah Muhammad: Louis Farrakhan and the Nation of Islam.* Durham, NC: Duke University Press, 1996.

George, John, and Laird Wilcox. *Nazis, Communists, Klansmen, and Others on the Fringe.* Buffalo, NY: Prometheus Books, 1992.

Gerecht, Reuel. "The Encyclopedia of Terror." *Middle East Quarterly* (Summer 2001). http://is-ci-ce-ct.com:85/article/showquestion.asp?faq=3&fldAuto=1543.

Ginsberg, Benjamin. *The Fatal Embrace: Jews and the State.* Chicago: University of Chicago Press, 1993.

Goldberg, J. J. *Jewish Power: Inside the American Jewish Establishment.* New York: Addison-Wesley, 1996.

Goodrick-Clarke, Nicholas. *The Black Sun: Aryan Cults, Esoteric Nazism, and the Politics of Identity.* New York: New York University Press, 2002.

Griffin, Roger. *The Nature of Fascism.* New York: Routledge, 1993.

Growitz Institute. *Unraveling Anti-Semitic 9/11 Conspiracy Theories.* New York: Anti-Defamation League, 2003.

Gunaratna, Rohan. *Inside al Qaeda: Global Network of Terror.* New York: Columbia University Press, 2002.

Hammes, Thomas X. *The Sling and the Stone: On War in the Twenty-First Century.* St. Paul, MN: Zenith Press, 2004.

Hashim, Ahmed S. "The Insurgency in Iraq." *Small Wars and Insurgencies* 14, no. 3 (Autumn 2003): 1–22.

Hawthorne, George Eric. "The Brüders Schweigen: Men against Time," in David Lane, *Deceived, Damned, and Defiant: The Revolutionary Writings of David Lane.* St. Maries, ID: 14 Word Press, 1999, 157–158.

———. "History in the Making," in David Lane, *Deceived, Damned, and Defiant: The Revolutionary Writings of David Lane.* St. Maries, ID: 14 Word Press, 1999, 228–231.

Hewitt, Christopher. "Patterns of American Terrorism 1955–1998: An Historical Perspective on Terrorism-Related Fatalities 1955–98." *Terrorism and Political Violence* 12, no. 1 (2000): 1–14.

———. *Understanding Terrorism in America: From the Klan to al Qaeda.* London: Routledge, 2003.

"Hitler's Promises to the Grand Mufti of Jerusalem," in Adam Parfrey, ed., *Extreme Islam: Anti-American Propaganda of Muslim Fundamentalism.* Los Angeles: Feral House, 2001, 23–28.

Hoffman, Bruce. *Combating Terrorism: In Search of a National Strategy.* Washington, DC: RAND, March 27, 2001.

———. *Inside Terrorism.* New York: Columbia University Press, 1998.

———. "Responding to Terrorism across the Technological Spectrum." *Terrorism and Political Violence* 6, no. 3 (Autumn 1994): 365–389.

———. *Right-Wing Terrorism in Europe since 1980.* Santa Monica, CA: RAND Corporation, 1984.

———. "Terrorism Trends and Prospects," in Ian Lessler, et al. *Countering the New Terrorism.* Santa Monica, CA: RAND, 1999, 7–38.

Hoffman, David. *The Oklahoma City Bombing and the Politics of Terror.* Venice, CA: Feral House, 1998.

Hoffman, Michael A., II. *The Great Holocaust Trial.* Torrance, CA: Institute for Historical Review, 1985.

Hoge, James F., Jr., and Gideon Rose, eds. *How Did This Happen? Terrorism and the New War.* New York: Public Affairs, 2001.

"Holy War Ground Zero," in Adam Parfrey, ed., *Extreme Islam: Anti-American Propaganda of Muslim Fundamentalism.* Los Angeles: Feral House, 2001, 171–188.

Huddle, Donald. *The Net National Costs of Immigration: Fiscal Effects of Welfare Restorations to Legal Immigrants.* Houston, TX: Rice University, 1997.

Huntington, Samuel P. *The Clash of Civilizations and the Remaking of World Order.* New York: Touchstone, 1996.

———. *Who Are We? The Challenges to America's National Identity.* New York: Simon and Schuster, 2004.

Infield, Glenn B. *Skorzeny: Hitler's Commando.* New York: Military Heritage Press, 1981.

"Interview with Usama bin Ladin, December 1998," in Barry Rubin and Judith Colp Rubin, eds., *Anti-American Terrorism and the Middle East: A Documentary Reader.* Oxford: Oxford University Press, 2002, 151–157.

Jacquard, Roland. *In the Name of Osama Bin Laden: Global Terrorism and the Bin Laden International.* Durham, NC: Duke University Press, 2002.

Jess, Sara, and Gabriel Beck. *John Walker Lindh: American Taliban.* San Jose: University of California Press, 2002.

Jones, Stephen, with Peter Israel. *Others Unknown: The Oklahoma City Bombing Case and Conspiracy.* New York: Public Affairs, 1998.

Juergensmeyer, Mark. *Terror in the Mind of God: The Global Rise of Religious Violence.* Berkeley: University of California Press, 2000.

Kaplan, Jeffrey, and Leonard Weinberg. *The Emergence of a Euro-American Radical Right.* New Brunswick, NJ: Rutgers University Press, 1998.

Kaplan, Robert. "The Coming Anarchy." *Atlantic Monthly,* February 1994. http://www.theatlantic.com/politics.foreign/anarchy.htm.

Katz, Samuel. *Relentless Pursuit: The DSS and the Manhunt for the al-Qaeda Terrorists.* New York: Forge, 2002.

Kennedy, Paul. *The Rise and Fall of the Great Powers: Economic Change and Military Conflict from 1500 to 2000.* New York: Vintage Books, 1989.

Kepel, Gilles. *Muslim Extremism in Egypt: The Prophet and Pharaoh.* Berkeley: University of California Press, 1993.

Khan, M. A. Muqtedar. "Radical Islam, Liberal Islam." *Current History* (December 2003): 417–421.

Kinsella, Warren. *Unholy Alliances: Terrorists, Extremists, Front Companies, and the Libyan Connection in Canada.* Toronto: Lester Publishing, 1992.

———. *Web of Hate.* Toronto: Harper Perennial, 1995.

Klassen, Ben. *On the Brink of a Bloody Racial War.* Niceville, FL: Church of the Creator, 1992.

Kopanski, Ataullah Bogdan. "Muslims and the Reich." *Barnes Review* (September–October 2003): 27–33.

Kopel, David B., and Paul H. Blackman. *No More Wacos: What's Wrong with Federal Law Enforcement and How to Fix It.* Amherst, NY: Prometheus Books, 1997.

Kramer, Martin. "The Moral Logic of Hezballah," in Walter Reich, ed., *Origins of Terrorism: Psychologies, Ideologies, Theologies, States of Mind.* Washington, DC: Woodrow Wilson Center Press, 1998, 131–157.

Kurth, James. "Confronting the Unipolar Moment: The American Empire and Islamic Terrorism." *Current History* 101, no. 659 (December 2002): 403–408.

Laqueur, Walter. *Guerilla Warfare: A Historical and Critical Study.* New Brunswick, NJ: Transaction Publishers, 1998.

———. *The New Terrorism: Fanaticism and the Arms of Mass Destruction.* New York: Oxford University Press, 1999.

———. *No End to War: Terrorism in the Twenty-First Century.* New York: Continuum, 2003.

Larson, Eric V., and John E. Peters. *Preparing the U.S. Army for Homeland Security: Concepts, Issues, and Options.* Santa Monica, CA: RAND Corporation, 2001.

Ledeen, Michael A. *The War against the Terror Masters.* New York: St. Martin's Press, 2003.

Lee, Martin. "The Swastika and Crescent," *Intelligence Report.* Spring, 2002. http://www.splcenter/intelligenceproject/ip–4u3.html.

Lee, Martin A. *The Beast Reawakens.* Boston: Little, Brown, 1997.

Lepre, George. *Himmler's Bosnian Division: The Waffen-SS Handschar Division, 1943–1945.* Atglen, PA: Schiffer Military History, 1997.

Lewis, Bernard. "Islamic Terrorism?" in Benjamin Netanyahu, ed., *Terrorism: How the West Can Win.* New York: Farrar, Straus and Giroux, 1986, 65–69.

———. *Semites and Anti-Semites: An Inquiry into Conflict and Prejudice.* New York: W. W. Norton, 1986.

————. *What Went Wrong? The Clash between Islam and Modernity in the Middle East.* New York: Perennial, 2002.

Lewis, Rand C. *A Nazi Legacy: Right-Wing Extremism in Postwar Germany.* New York: Praeger, 1991.

Liberty Lobby. *Conspiracy against Freedom.* Washington, DC: Liberty Lobby, 1986.

Lipset, Seymour Martin, and Earl Raab. *Jews and the New American Scene.* Cambridge, MA: Harvard University Press, 1995.

Macdonald, Andrew. *The Turner Diaries.* Hillsboro, WV: National Vanguard Books, 1993.

MacDonald, Kevin. *The Culture of Critique: An Evolutionary Analysis of Jewish Involvement in Twentieth-Century Intellectual and Political Movements.* Westport, CT: Praeger, 1998.

MacKenzie, Angus. *Secrets: The CIA's War at Home.* Berkeley: University of California Press, 1997.

Magida, Arthur G. *Prophet of Rage: A Life of Louis Farrakhan and His Nation.* New York: Basic Books, 1996.

Meighy, Josef. *SS Freikorps Arabien.* Self-published, 1995.

Michael, George. *Confronting Right-Wing Extremism and Terrorism in the USA.* London: Routledge, 2003.

————. "Homeland Defense Initiative and U.S. Counterterrorism Policy," in *Encyclopedia of World Terrorism, 1996–2002.* Armonk, NY: M. E. Sharpe, 2003, 55–61.

————. "The Revolutionary Model of Dr. William L. Pierce." *Terrorism and Political Violence* 15, no. 3 (Autumn 2003): 62–80.

Michel, Lou, and Dab Herbeck. *American Terrorist: Timothy McVeigh and the Oklahoma City Bombing.* New York: Regan Books, 2001.

Miller, John. "Osama Bin Laden: The ABC Interview." May 18, 1998.

Mishal, Shaul, and Avraham Sela. *The Palestinian Hamas: Vision, Violence, and Coexistence.* New York: Columbia University Press, 2000.

Mizell, Louis R., Jr. *Target U.S.A. The Inside Story of the New Terrorist War.* New York: John Wiley, 1998.

Mockatis, Thomas R. "Winning Hearts and Minds in the 'War on Terrorism.'" *Small Wars and Insurgencies* 14, no. 1 (Spring 2003): 21–38.

Morse, Chuck. *The Nazi Connection to Islamic Terrorism: Adolf Hitler and Haj Amin al-Husseini.* Lincoln, NE: iUniverse, 2003.

Moussalli, Ahmad S. *Radical Islamic Fundamentalism: The Ideological and Political Discourse of Sayyid Qutb.* Beirut, Lebanon: American University of Beirut, 1992.

"The Muslim Brotherhood," in Adam Parfrey, ed., *Extreme Islam: Anti-American Propaganda of Muslim Fundamentalism.* Los Angeles: Feral House, 2001, 74–79.

Mylroie, Laurie. "Iraqi Complicity in the World Trade Center Bombing and Beyond." *Middle East Intelligence Bulletin* 3, no. 6 (June 2001).

————. *The War against America: Saddam Hussein and the World Trade Center Attacks.* New York: Regan Books, 2001.

Najm, Salah. "Transcript of Usamah Bin-Ladin, the Destruction of the Base: Interview with Usamah Bin-Ladin." June 10, 1999. http://wwww.terrorism.com/BinLadinTranscript.shtml.

Netanyahu, Benjamin. "Defining Terrorism," in Benjamin Netanyahu, ed., *Terrorism: How the West Can Win.* New York: Farrar, Straus and Giroux, 1986, 7–15.

————. *Fighting Terrorism: How Democracies Can Defeat the International Terrorist Network.* New York: Farrar, Straus and Giroux, 2001.

————. "Terrorism and the Islamic World," in Benjamin Netanyahu, ed., *Terrorism: How the West Can Win.* New York: Farrar, Straus and Giroux, 1986, 61–63.

Nye, Joseph S., Jr. "The Changing Nature of World Power." *Political Science Quarterly* 105 (Summer 1990): 177–192.

Pape, Robert A. "Dying to Kill Us." *New York Times,* September 22, 2003, A17.

Parachini, John V. "The World Trade Center Bombers, 1993," in Jonathan B. Tucker, ed., *Toxic Terror: Assessing Terrorist Use of Chemical and Biological Weapons.* Cambridge, MA: MIT Press, 2001, 158–206.

Parenti, Michael. *The Terrorism Trap: September 11 and Beyond.* San Francisco: City Lights Books, 2002.

Perle, Richard, Douglas Feith, and David Wurmser. "A Clean Break: A New Strategy for Securing the Realm." Institute for Advanced Strategic and Political Studies, Jerusalem, July 8, 1996.

Pillar, Paul R. *Terrorism and U.S. Foreign Policy.* Washington, DC: Brookings Institution Press, 2001.

Piper, Michael Collins. *Final Judgment: The Missing Link in the JFK Assassination Conspiracy.* 5th ed. Washington, DC: Center for Historical Review, 2000.

Pipes, Daniel. *The Hidden Hand: Middle East Fears of Conspiracy.* New York: St. Martin's Griffin, 1998.

———. *Militant Islam Reaches America.* New York: W. W. Norton, 2002.

Prutschi, Manuel. "The Zundel Affair," in Alan Davies, ed., *Anti-Semitism in Canada: History and Interpretation.* Waterloo, ON: Wilfrid Laurier University Press, 1992, 249–277.

Al Qaddafi, Muammar. "The Green Book," in Adam Parfrey, ed., *Extreme Islam: Anti-American Propaganda of Muslim Fundamentalism.* Los Angeles: Feral House, 2001, 218–223.

"Al-Qa'ida Recruitment Video 2000," in Barry Rubin and Judith Colp Rubin, eds., *Anti-American Terrorism and the Middle East: A Documentary Reader.* Oxford: Oxford University Press, 2002, 174–183.

Qutb, Sayid. *Milestones.* Cedar Rapids, IA: Mother Mosque Foundation, n.d.

———. "Paving the Way," in Barry Rubin and Judith Colp Rubin, eds., *Anti-American Terrorism and the Middle East: A Documentary Reader.* Oxford: Oxford University Press, 2002, 29–32.

Raimondo, Justin. *The Terror Enigma: 9/11 and the Israeli Connection.* Lincoln, NE: iUniverse, 2003.

Rashid, Ahmed. *Taliban.* New Haven, CT: Yale University Press, 2001.

Raufer, Xavier. "New World Disorder, New Terrorisms: New Threats for Europe and the Western World," in Max Taylor and John Horgan, eds., *The Future of Terrorism.* London: Frank Cass, 2000, 30–51.

Record, Jeffrey. *Bounding the Global War on Terrorism.* Carlisle, PA: U.S. Army War College, December 2003.

Redden, Jim. *Snitch Culture.* Venice, CA: Feral House, 2000.

Reeve, Simon. *The New Jackals: Ramzi Yousef, Osama bin Laden, and the Future of Terrorism.* Boston: Northeastern University Press, 1999.

Research Staff of National Vanguard Books. "Who Rules America." Hillsboro, WV: National Vanguard Books, 2000.

"Resolution 1267 October 15, 1999," in Barry Rubin and Judith Colp Rubin, eds., *Anti-American Terrorism and the Middle East: A Documentary Reader.* Oxford: Oxford University Press, 2002, 219–220.

Revell, Oliver "Buck." *A G-Man's Journal.* New York: Pocket Star Books, 1998.

Rich, Paul R. "Introduction." *Small Wars and Insurgencies* 14, no. 1 (Spring 2003): 1–19.

———. "Al Qaeda and the Radical Islamic Challenge to Western Strategy.'" *Small Wars and Insurgencies* 14, no. 1 (Spring 2003): 39–56.

Richardson, Eric. "Inside the 'Axis of Evil': A White Nationalist Visits Iran." *National Vanguard* 120 (May–June 2003): 3–7.

Ridgeway, James. "Osama's New Recruits: White Power and al Qaeda Unite Against America." *Village Voice,* October 31–November 6, 2001. http://www.villagevoice.com/news/0144, ridgeway,29553,1.html.

Robinson, Adam. *Bin Laden: Behind the Mask of the Terrorist.* New York: Arcade Publishing, 2001.

Rosenfeld, Jean E. "The Religion of Usamah bin Ladin: Terror as the Hand of God." http://www.publiceye.org/frontpage/911/Islam/rosenfeld2001.htm.

Rubin, Barry. "The Truth about U.S. Middle East Policy," in Barry Rubin and Judith Colp Rubin, eds., *Anti-American Terrorism and the Middle East: A Documentary Reader.* Oxford: Oxford University Press, 2002, 81–106.

Rubin, Barry, and Judith Colp Rubin, eds. *Anti-American Terrorism and the Middle East: A Documentary Reader.* Oxford: Oxford University Press, 2002.

Ryan, Nick. *Into a World of Hate: A Journey among the Extreme Right.* New York: Routledge, 2004.

Saad-Ghorayeb, Amal. *Hizbu'llah: Politics and Religion.* Sterling, VA: Pluto Press, 2002.

Sageman, Marc. *Understanding Terror Networks.* Philadelphia: University of Pennsylvania Press, 2004.

Schachner, Nathan. *The Price of Liberty: A History of the American Jewish Committee.* New York: American Jewish Committee, 1948.

Scherer, Ron, and Alexandra Marks. "Gangs, Prison: Al Qaeda Breeding Grounds? With the Arrest of Jose Padilla, Roots of American Disaffection Get a Closer Look." *Christian Science Monitor,* June 14, 2002, 2.

Schonbach, Morris. *Native Fascism during the 1930s and 1940s: A Study of Its Roots, Its Growth, and Its Decline.* Ph.D. diss. University of California at Los Angeles, 1958.

Schwarz, Stephen. "Wahhabis in the Old Dominion: What the Federal Raids in Northern Virginia Uncovered." *Weekly Standard,* April 8, 2002. http://www.weeklystandard.com/content/public/articles/000/000/001/072kqska.asp.

Sedar, Irving, and Harold J. Greenberg. *Behind the Egyptian Sphinx.* Philadelphia: Chilton Company, 1960.

Seymour, Cheri. *Committee of the States: Inside the Radical Right.* Mariposa, CA: Camden Place Communications, 1991.

Shay, Shaul. "Suicide Terrorism in Lebanon," in International Policy Institute for Counter-Terrorism, ed., *Countering Suicide Terrorism.* New York: International Policy Institute for Counter-Terrorism and the Anti-Defamation League, 2002, 134–139.

Simmons, Harvey G. *The French National Front: The Extremist Challenge to Democracy.* Boulder, CO: Westview Press, 1996.

Snow, D. A., E. B. Rochford, Jr., S. K. Worden, and R. D. Beford. "Frame Alignment Processes, Micromobilization, and Movement Participation. *American Sociological Review* 51 (1986): 464–481.

Solovyov, Vladimir, and Elena Klepikova. *Zhirinovsky: Russian Fascism and the Making of a Dictator.* Reading, MA: Addison-Wesley Publishing, 1995.

Sorensen, Alan. "The Reluctant Nation Builders." *Current History* (December 2003): 407–410.

Sprinzak, Ehud. "The Process of Delegitimation: Towards a Linkage Theory of Political Terrorism." *Terrorism and Political Violence* 3, no. 1 (Spring 1991): 50–68.

———. "Right-Wing Terrorism in a Comparative Perspective: The Case of Split Deligitimation," in Tore Bjørgo, ed., *Terror from the Extreme Right.* London: Frank Cass, 1995, 17–43.

Stein, Arthur A. *The Nation at War.* Baltimore, MD: Johns Hopkins University Press, 1980.

Sterling, Claire. *The Terror Network.* New York: Berkley Books, 1984.

Stern, Jessica. "The Protean Enemy: What's Next from al Qaeda." *Foreign Affairs* (July–August 2003): 27–40.

———. *The Ultimate Terrorists.* Cambridge, MA: Harvard University Press, 1999.

Stern, Kenneth S. *A Force upon the Plain: The American Militia Movement and the Politics of Hate.* New York: Simon and Schuster, 1996.

———. *Holocaust Denial.* New York: American Jewish Committee, 1993.

Stickney, Brandon M. *All-American Monster: The Unauthorized Biography of Timothy McVeigh.* Amherst, NY: Prometheus Books, 1996.

Stoddard, Lothrop. *The Rising Tide of Color against White World-Supremacy.* Sussex, England: Historical Review Press, 1981.

Swain, Carol M. *The New White Nationalism in America: Its Challenge to Integration.* New York: Cambridge University Press, 2002.

Taheri, Amir. *Holy Terror: Inside the World of Islamic Terrorism.* Bethesda, MD: Adler and Adler, 1987.

Taylor, Jared, ed. *The Real American Dilemma: Race Immigration and the Future of America.* Oakton, VA: New Century Books, 1998.

Timmerman, Kenneth R. *Preachers of Hate: Islam and the War on America.* New York: Crown Forum, 2003.

"Videotape of a Private Meeting December 13, 2001," in Barry Rubin and Judith Colp Rubin, eds., *Anti-American Terrorism and the Middle East: A Documentary Reader.* Oxford: Oxford University Press, 2002, 243–247.

Walker, Martin. *The National Front.* Glasgow, Scotland: William Collins, 1977.

Wasserstein, Bernard. "Anti-Semitism and Anti-Americanism." *Chronicle of Higher Education* 1, no. 9 (2001): 28. http://chronicle.com/free/v48/i05/05b00502.htm.

Weeks, John R. *The Demography of Islamic Nations.* Washington, DC: Population Reference Bureau, 1988.

Weinberg, Leonard, and William Eubank. "Terrorism and the Shape of Things to Come," in Max Taylor, and John Horgan, eds., *The Future of Terrorism.* London: Frank Cass, 1999, 94–105.

Whitaker, David J., ed. *The Terrorism Reader.* London: Routledge, 2001.

Wilcox, Laird. *The Watchdogs: A Close Look at Anti-Racist "Watchdog" Groups.* Olathe, KS: Laird Wilcox Editorial Research Center, 1999.

Wilkinson, Paul. *Political Terrorism.* New York: Wiley, 1974.

Williams, Paul L. *Osama's Revenge: The Next 9/11.* Amherst, NY: Prometheus Books, 2004.

Williams, Phil. "Transnational Criminal Networks," in John Arquilla and David Ronfeldt, eds., *Networks and Netwars: The Future of Terror, Crime, and Militancy.* Santa Monica, CA: RAND, 2001, 61–97.

Woodward, Bob. *Bush at War.* New York: Simon and Schuster, 2002.

Wright, Robin. *Sacred Rage: The Wrath of Militant Islam.* New York: Touchstone, 2001.

Wright, Stuart A., ed. *Armageddon in Waco: Critical Perspectives on the Branch Davidian Conflict.* Chicago: University of Chicago Press, 1995.

Wyden, Peter. *The Hitler Virus: The Insidious Legacy of Adolf Hitler.* New York: Arcade Publishing, 2001.

Yockey, Francis Parker. *The Enemy of Europe.* Reedy, WV: Liberty Bell Publications, 1981.

Zakaria, Fareed. "The Return of History," in James F. Hoge, Jr., and Gideon Rose, eds., *How Did This Happen? Terrorism and the New War.* New York: Public Affairs, 2001, 307–317.

Zimmerman, John C. "Sayyid Qutb's Influence on the 11 September Attacks." *Terrorism and Political Violence* 16, no. 2 (Summer 2004): 222–252.

INTERVIEWS

Steven Barry, December 11, 2003.
Chip Berlet, August 31, 2000.
Willis Carto, May 7, 2003.
David Duke, March 2003.
Steven Emerson, June 12, 2005.
Sam Francis, April 8, 2003.
Jürgen Graf, April 2003.

Nick Griffin, May 2003.
Rohan Gunaratna, January 17, 2004.
Ahmed Huber, April 2003.
Kevin MacDonald, March 2003.
Tom Metzger, March 2003.
David Myatt, April 2003.
Mike Piper, April 2003.
Jared Taylor, February 6, 2004.
John Tyndall, June 3, 2003.
Ernst Zündel, October 5, 2000.

Index

Abdel-Jawwad, Saleh, 267
Abdu, Mohammed, 35
Abdul-Karim, Ali, 92
Abouhalima, Malmoud, 85, 86
Abrams, Elliott, 238, 246, 252
Abu Dhabi, United Arab Emirates, 159
Abu Nidal organization, 106
Abur-Raheem, Hammad, 93
Abu Sayyaf, 64, 89, 132, 306, 326n26
Achille Lauro hijacking, 193
Adel, Saif al-, 324n257
Aden, Yemen, 70, 79, 107, 121
ADL. *See* Anti-Defamation League
Advice and Reformation Committee (ARC; al
  Qaeda), 108
Afghan Arabs, 62, 71
Afghani, Jamal al-Din al-, 35
Afghanistan: British and, 113; extreme right
  and, 306; Germany and, 113; Iran and, 74; ji-
  hadists in, 87, 194; mujahideen in, 65–66,
  67, 68, 73–74, 86–87, 101, 102, 108, 113,
  194–95, 270–71, 326n26, 344n86; opium
  trade in, 74, 323n204; al Qaeda and bin
  Laden in, 73–74, 77, 91, 102, 147, 195–96,
  201, 319n104, 326n26, 344n86; Saudi Ara-
  bia and, 74, 195; Soviet war with, 57, 62, 68,
  101, 194–96, 254, 299; Taliban in, 73–74,
  147, 196; U.S. aid to, 194–95, 254; U.S.
  sanctions on, 196; U.S. war in, 78, 196,
  200–201, 261
Afghan Services Bureau (MAK), 65, 66, 86, 87
African Americans, Islam and, 94–101, 103, 107
Afrika Korps, 114, 119
Against All Enemies (Clarke), 252
Agca, Mehmet Ali, 128
Agiza, Ahmad Husayn, 85
Ahram, Al-, 265
Aidid, Muhammad Farrah, 70, 322n182
AIMA (Argentine Israeli Mutual Association),
  108, 168

AIPAC (American Israel Public Affairs Commit-
  tee), 48, 166, 186, 246, 251, 252, 253
AJC (American Jewish Committee), 175, 208,
  214, 218, 246, 339n255, 347n4
Akbar, Hasan K., 103
Akhdar, Elias Muhammad, 92
Alamoudi, Abdulrahman, 91, 326n41
Albrecht, Udo, 127
Albright, Madeline, 203
Alexander, Yonay, 91
Alfred P. Murrah Federal Building, 11, 133, 135,
  173, 178, 210, 314n40. *See also* Oklahoma
  City bombing
Algeria, 106, 121
Algerian National Liberation Front, 125
Ali, Abu, 107
Ali, Isa Abdullah, 103
Ali, Muhammad (boxer), 99
Ali, Muhammad (New York City cab driver),
  106
Ali, Noble Drew, 94
'Ali Zahran, Gamal, 265
al-Jazeera, 161–62, 166, 190, 263
Alkhifa Center, 87
Allen, George, 251
Alloush, Ibrahim, 22
"Al-Qaida's Endgame?" 300
Al Rashid hotel bombing, 88
Al-Risala, 259
Amaudruz, Gaston-Armand, 157
Amdocs, 233
America I Have Seen, The (Qutb), 38
American Airlines flight 11, 351n36
American Airlines flight 77, 1
American-Arab Anti-Discrimination Commit-
  tee, 259
American Conservative, 244, 251
American Dissident Voices radio program, 2, 15,
  16, 164, 165–66, 182, 227, 289
American Enterprise Institute, 246, 247

America First philosophy, 240
American Free Press, 20, 134, 159, 223, 228, 229, 239, 269
American House of Saud, The (Emerson), 209
American Israel Public Affairs Committee (AIPAC), 48, 166, 186, 246, 251, 252, 253
American Jewish Committee (AJC), 175, 208, 214, 218, 246, 339n255, 347n4
American Jihad (Emerson), 210
American Muslims for Jerusalem, 259
American Nazi Party, 124, 221
American Renaissance, 17, 222, 224, 254, 257, 278, 292
American Securities and Exchange Commission, 234
Americans to Counter Terrorism, 214
Amin, Hafizulla, 194
Amman, Jordan, 157
Amreekee, Jibreel al-, 103
Amriki, Abu Suhayb Al- , 103
Anderson, Ryan Gibson, 104
Andrews, Don, 129
Angeles, Edwin, 132
Ani, Ahmad Khali Ibrahim Samir al-, 76
Annan, Kofi, 262
Ansar al-Islam, 204
Anthrax attacks, 111, 259
anti-Americanism, 292–95
Anti-Defamation League (ADL), 19, 170, 211, 212, 266; on African American anti-Semitism, 94, 95–96, 98; Chertoff and, 187; description of, 208; on extreme right, 112, 142, 162, 165, 179, 181, 183, 184, 192, 213, 219, 341n27, 348n22; on Holocaust revisionism conference, 156–57; on international terrorism, 212, 214, 215, 219; on Iraq War, 252; U.S. government and, 175, 176, 179, 212, 218–19. *See also* Foxman, Abraham
Anti-Globalism Action Network (AGAN), 171
anti-Semitism: African American, 96, 98; American public and, 216; of bin Laden, 48, 75, 77; of David Duke, 162–63, 189–90; extreme right and, 14, 15–16, 17, 18–19, 20–23, 47, 52, 97–98, 161–63, 172, 187–88, 189–90, 208–9, 213, 215–19, 313n6; Farrakhan and, 95–96, 270; Islamic, 44–52, 93, 108, 136, 170–71, 217, 219; of Islamic militants in Europe, 8–9, 113, 127, 139; left-wing, 172; media and, 139; in Nazi Germany, 113; new, 216–17, 293; Western, 50–51. *See also* Holocaust revisionism
Anti-Terrorism and Effective Death Penalty Act (1996), 173, 193

Aqsa, al-, intifada, 8, 60, 61, 320n126, 355n18
Arab-American Institute, 259
Arab Commercial Bank (Geneva), 125
Arab Foreign Legion, 121
Arab League, 119, 121, 159, 280
Arab nationalism (pan-Arabism): anti-Semitism and, 46, 50; decline of, 52, 56, 61, 130; in Iraq, 68; militant Islam and, 36–37, 52–53, 56, 58–59, 60, 271; National Socialism and, 119–24; in Palestine, 60; rise of, 34–37
Arab News, 161, 230
Arab Students United, 339n255
Arafat, Yasser, 106, 119, 121, 124, 127, 128, 137
Arcand, Adrien, 187
Argentina, 59; bombings in, 167–68, 331n65
Argentine Israeli Mutual Association (AIMA), 108, 168
Arian, Sami al-, 93
Arkansas, 177
Armed Islamic Group, 75, 106
Armenia, 254
Armstrong, Roy, 359n46
Arnaout, Enaam M., 325n16
Arquilla, John, 308
Aryan Baby Drive program, 184
Aryan Barbarian, 15–16
Aryan Loyalist magazine, 221
Aryan Nations, 16, 17, 27, 173, 183–85, 212, 227; Ministry of Islamic Liaison, 140, 142, 163
Arya Samaj Movement, 277
Ashcroft, John, 197, 219, 223, 288, 306
Asi, Muhammad al-, 266
Assad, Hafez al-, 57, 58, 137, 320n133
Assimilation, 3, 298, 308
Atatürk, Mustafa Kemal, 35–36, 45
Atef, Muhammad, 324n257
ATF (Bureau of Alcohol, Tobacco, and Firearms), 25, 176, 177
Atlanta, Ga., 209
Atta, Muhammad, 76, 107, 133, 168, 231
Austria, 282
Austrian Freedom Party (FPÖ), 137, 282
Avraham, Alona, 351n36
Axis-Arab Manifesto of Liberation in Berlin, 114
Axis powers, Islamic world and, 114, 117, 118
Axman, Anton, 151
Ayyad, Nidal, 85
Azhar, al-, conference, 50
Azerbaijan, 254
Azzam, Abdullah, 62, 65–66, 86–87, 108, 298, 321n157, 328n99
Aziz, Abdul, 143, 146

Ba'ath (Renaissance) Party, 46, 67, 133, 136;
   Syrian, 58
Baghdad, Iraq, 76, 88, 115
Bahrain, 190
Baker, Bill, 163–64
Baker, James, 159
Bakr, Kadri Abu, 88
Balfour Declaration, 220–21, 350n4
Bali, 2002 bombing in, 83
Balkans, 4
Ball, Douglas B., 250
Ball, George W., 250
Baltimore, Md., extreme right in, 181
Banna, Hassan al-, 36, 37
Banu Nadir, 44, 45
Banu Qaynuqa, 44
Banu Quraiza, 44
Baraka, al, 154
Barber, Benjamin, 6–7, 109
Barbie, Klaus, 149
Barka, Ben, 139
Barnes Review, The, 20, 21
Barr, Bob, 181
Barry, Marion, 105
Barry, Steven, 227, 278–80, 350n29
Barzinji, Jamal, 154
Basayev, Shamil, 104–5
Bashir, Omar, 77
Basque Nation and Liberty, 168
Batargy, Adil Abdul Galil, 325n16
Baz, Rashid, 106
Beam, Louis, 29, 97, 171, 212
Beck, Zachary Loren, 185
Bedouins, 63
Begin, Menachem, 289
Beirut, Lebanon, 57, 156, 210
Belfield, David, 105
Benevolence International Foundation (BIF),
   325n16
Ben-Gurion, David, 160
Bennett, William, 345
Benoist, Alain de, 136, 137
Berclaz, Rene-Louis, 157
Berg, Alan, 27
Bergen, Peter L., 72
Berlet, Chip, 217
Berlusconi, Silvio, 280
Betar, 114
Bhutto, Benazir, 66
Bildeberger Group, 28, 47
Billig, Haupsturnführer, 117
bin Ali, Abdullah, 114
Binalshibh, Ramzi, 201

bin Laden, Muhammad, 62
bin Laden, Osama, 91, 108, 132; in Afghanistan, 65, 73–74, 77, 102, 147, 195–96,
   326n26, 344n86; Aidid and, 70, 322n182;
   attacks on U.S. interests by, 69, 70, 174;
   Azzam and, 62, 65–66, 86–87, 108, 298,
   321n157; background of, 62–64; Bosnian
   Muslims and, 64, 71, 262; extreme right and,
   154, 164, 166–67; Filipino terrorists and, 89;
   Saddam Hussein and, 76, 356n45; Iraq and,
   267, 323n223; on Iraq War, 267; on Israel,
   56, 78, 261, 262, 267, 268, 293, 355n12; on
   Jews, 49, 75, 77, 262, 294; as leader of al
   Qaeda, 62–67, 73, 74–75, 300; on martyrdom, 236; 9/11 attacks and, 1, 214, 264,
   300; Pakistan and, 66, 79; on Palestinian
   issue, 260–61, 262, 287; Qutb and, 38, 44;
   Saudi Arabia and, 24, 62–63, 66, 67–68, 73,
   154, 323n228, 325n16; Shi'ites and, 65; So-
   mali campaign and, 70–71, 196; Soviet-
   Afghan war and, 65–66, 86, 298, 299; in
   Sudan, 64, 68, 69, 71, 73, 77, 91; supporters
   of, 61, 64, 149, 220, 269, 308; on U.S., 24,
   56, 66, 76–77, 80, 195, 203, 228, 259–64,
   267–68, 293, 294, 304, 343n61, 355n12;
   WMDs and, 78–79; al-Zawahiri and, 54, 64,
   67, 73, 75, 76, 85, 298, 319n104
Bishop, Charles, 363n50
Black, Don, 292, 342n37, 359n46
Black International, 126–27
Black P. Stone Nation, 100
Black separatist movement, 95, 98, 99
Black September, 124–26
Black September war, 127
Blair, Tony, 235, 242, 244, 245, 277
Blais, Pierre, 189
Blood and Honor, 184
Bloomberg, Michael, 297
BNP (British National Party), 130, 190, 207,
   223, 226, 243, 255, 256, 276, 277, 282
Bodansky, Yossef, 35, 46, 133
Bolton, John, 246, 252
Bonaparte, Napoleon, 34, 35
Borghese, Prince Valerio, 126
Bormann, Martin, 125
Bornschain, Harald, 154
Bosch, Hieronymus, 167
Bosnia; bin Laden on, 64, 71, 262; Muslims in,
   64, 71, 117, 262; al Qaeda and, 306; U.S.
   and, 254
Bosnia-Herzegovina, 103, 154, 299
Bounding the Global War on Terrorism (Record),
   301

Brady bill, 13
Branch Davidian, 25, 177
Brandenburg Division, Aryan Nations, 183
Braun, Eva, 151
Brazil, 59
Brennenstuhl, Philippe, 157
British Intelligence Service (MI6), 66
British National Party (BNP), 130, 190, 207,
  223, 226, 243, 255, 256, 276, 277, 282
British Royal Commission, 113
Brokaw, Tom, 111
Bronfman, Edgar M., 294
Brooklyn, N.Y., 87, 91
Brotherhood Group, 71–72
Brown v. Board of Education of Topeka, 175
Bruey, Judith, 191–92
Brzezinski, Zbigniew, 194
Buchanan, Pat, 7, 244–45, 249–50, 251, 281,
  282
Buenos Aires, Argentina bombing, 167
Bulgaria, 118
Bureau of Alcohol, Tobacco, and Firearms
  (ATF), 25, 176, 177
Burns, William, 252
"Bush Doctrine," 203
Bush, George W.: on anti-Semitism, 170, 219,
  252–53; bin Laden on, 263, 267, 268; ex-
  treme right on, 2, 14, 225, 235, 239, 240,
  241, 242, 244, 277, 288; Farrakhan on, 269,
  269; on Saddam Hussein, 301; immigration
  and, 257; Iraq war and, 165, 200, 202,
  203–4, 205–6, 239, 242, 246, 252; on Israel,
  234–35, 252–53; 9/11 attacks and, 196, 197,
  198, 199–200, 201, 225, 229, 230, 344n94;
  war on terror and, 149, 196–97, 200, 202,
  203–4, 218, 222, 293, 303
Butler, Richard, 183, 185, 212
Butz, Arthur, 98

Cairo, Egypt, 121
California, 179, 183, 299
Cameron, Carl, 233
Camp David Peace Accords, 54
Canada, extreme right in, 129, 187–89
Canadian Association for Free Expression,
  342n37
Canadian Holocaust Remembrance Association,
  188
Canadian Immigration and Refugee Protection
  Act, 188
Canadian Jewish Congress, 188
Canadian Security Intelligence Service, 188
Cannistraro, Vince, 133–34

Cardin, Benjamin, 250
Carlos the Jackal, 149, 218
Carter, Jimmy, 159, 194
Carto, Willis, 20, 240, 342n37, 359n46
Castro, Fidel, 58
Cecchini, Byron Calvert, 180
Center for Democratic Renewal (CDR), 209
Center for Strategic and International Studies, 3
Central Intelligence Agency (CIA): 106,
  349n54; Afghanistan and, 195; on anthrax at-
  tacks, 111; antiterrorist measures of, 234; bin
  Laden and, 73, 321n157; on Egypt, 120; mil-
  itant Islam and, 85; 9/11 attacks and, 198,
  229, 335, 237; USA PATRIOT Act and, 219
Chapman, Seifullah, 93
Charles Martel Society, 17, 18
Charlotte, N.C., 92, 179
Chatila massacre, 289
Chechnya, 64, 78, 102, 104, 262, 306
Cheney, Dick, 203, 288
Chertoff, Michael, 187, 190–91
Chicago, Ill., 100–101
Chitigov, Rizvan, 104–5
Christian Identity, 14, 15, 64, 81, 142, 184,
  316n19
Christian patriot movement, 14, 222–23
Christians; fundamentalist, 2, 137, 159, 185,
  213, 256, 348n23; on Israel, 253, 348n23;
  Maronite, 57, 267; in Middle East, 35, 44,
  58, 57, 59, 60, 160, 297, 311; Muslims and,
  163–64, 273, 280, 286, 291, 292
Christians and Muslims for Peace (CAMP), 163
Christie, Doug, 188
Church of the Sons of Yahweh, 184
Churchill, Winston, 114
CIA. *See* Central Intelligence Agency
Cienfuegos, Ernesto, 305
Citron, Sabrina, 188
Clancy, Tom, 111
Clarke, Richard, 252
Clash of civilizations theory (Huntington), 5, 6,
  7, 8
"Clean Break, A," 246
Clinton, Bill, 47, 48, 77, 78, 89, 162, 173, 192,
  196, 261, 274, 298
CNN, 209, 210
Coast Guard, U.S., 200
Cohen, Eliot, 247
COINTELPRO (Counter Intelligence Pro-
  gram), 175, 198
Cold War terrorism, 193
Cole, USS, 79, 107, 320n133
Collins, Aukai, 101–2

Colonialism, in Middle East, 5, 35, 36, 115, 118, 128–29
Colorado First Light, 314n40
Column 88, 142, 335n155
"Coming Anarchy, The," (Kaplan), 302
Comintern, 109
Commentary magazine, 246
Committee of Three, 75
communism; extreme right and, 28, 131; Islam and, 45, 47, 109
Congressional Task Force on Terrorism and Unconventional Warfare, 133
Conseil représentatif des institutions juives de France (CRIF), 218
Consultation Council (al Qaeda), 73
Converse (Israeli firm), 233–34
Cook County Democratic organization, 101
Cooper, Abraham, 186
Cooper, H. H. A., 24
Corrie, Rachel, 171
Corriere della Serra, 154
Coulson, Danny O., 176
Council of American Islamic Relations (CAIR), 259
Council of Conservative Citizens, 17, 222, 292
Council on Foreign Relations, 4, 28, 47
Counter Intelligence Program (COINTELPRO), 175, 198
Counter-Terror Task Force, 180
Courdroy, Robert, 125
Covenant, Sword, and the Arm of the Lord (CSA), 176, 177
Creativity, 15. *See also* World Church of the Creator
Cukierman, Roger, 218
Culture of Critique, The (MacDonald), 18–19, 224
Curtis, Alex, 17, 179, 338n249, 341n25

Daley, Richard, 100
D'Amato, Alfonse M., 89
Dar el Ilm Lilmalayin, 159
Dar es Salaam, Tanzania, 78
Dar-us-salaan mosque, 104
Daschle, Tom, 111–12
Davis, Gray, 297
Davis, Jayna, 132, 133, 134, 135
"Day of Terror Plot, The," 89–90
Dean, Diana, 106
Debbaudt, Jean Roberts, 126
Decision Support Systems (DSS), 300
Dees, Morris, 183, 212
Defense Policy Board, 246

De Gaulle, Charles, 118
Deir Yassin massacres, 289
Deligitimization, 25
democracy: globalization of, 3–5, 6; Islam and, 34, 39, 41, 167, 205, 279, 316n17
Deutsche-Arabisches Infanterie Battalion 845, 114
Dhahran, Saudi Arabia, 73
Dickson, Sam, 292, 359n46
"Did Six Million Really Die?" (pamphlet, Zündel), 188
dirty bombs, 79, 102, 324n236
Discover Islam Center, 161
Doles, Chester James, 180–81
Doles, Teresa, 180
Doran, Michael Scott, 80
Douri, Izzat Ibrahim al-, 271
Droege, Wolfgang, 129
Drummond, Jonathan, 23–24
Duey, Randy, 32
Duke, David, 93; on alliance with militant Islam, 18, 161–64, 272–73, 291, 339n255, 359n46; on Iraq War, 238–39; on Israeli connection to 9/11 attacks, 222, 230–32, 237–38; on Jews, 215; on Palestinian issue, 289–90; racialist movement and, 17–18; U.S. government investigation of, 189–91
Dulles, John Foster, 120
Durham, Martin, 13

Earth Liberation Front, 171, 307
East, John P., 17
East Timor, 262
eco-extremists, 171
Egypt: anticolonial uprising in, 115; British occupation of, 120; intelligence of, 89; Islam and, 36, 53–54, 85; Islamic Jihad in, 67, 76; Israel and, 47, 54, 123–24, 266, 267; nationalism and, 37, 120; Nazis and, 119, 120, 121–23, 124; 1952 coup in, 37, 41, 120; Soviet Union and, 123–24; U.S. and, 120; Westernization of, 35, 36
Egyptian Islamic Group, 31
Egyptian Parachute Corps, 123
Ehrlich, Paul, 81
Eichmann, Adolf, 118, 125, 128, 149, 330n28
Eisenberg, Lewis, 233
Eizenstat, Stuart E., 294
El Al airline: hijacking, 53, 318–19n85; ticket-counter attack, 107
Elgabrowny, Ibrahim, 85
Ellison, James, 177
El Rukns, 100–101

Emerson, Steven, 91, 209–11, 212, 275
Encyclopedia of the Afghan Jihad, The, 82–83
Endelman, Todd, 218
"End of History, The?" (Fukuyama), 4
End to Evil, An (Perle and Frum), 248
Eretz Israel (Greater Israel) theory, 47, 239
Esquire magazine, 246
ETA (Euskadi Ta Askatasuna), 168
Eubank, William, 8
European American Unity and Rights Organization (EURO), 189
European New Order, 126
Europe, Tiers monde, même combat (Benoist), 137
Euskadi Ta Askatasuna (ETA), 168
Evola, Anthony, 186, 342n51
Executive Order 13228, 199
Executive Working Group on Domestic Terrorism, 178
extreme right: anti-American rhetoric of, 138, 288; anti-Semitism, 3, 14, 15–16, 17, 18–19, 20–23, 47–48, 52, 97–98, 161–63, 172, 187–88, 189–90, 208–9, 213, 215–19, 286–92, 293–95, 358n36; definition of, 12–13, 14–15, 20, 23–24, 25, 293; far left and, 171; globalization and, 7, 18, 30, 171, 221, 273; Holocaust/historical revisionism and, 20–23, 98, 139, 156–58, 160–61, 187–88, 256, 274–75, 287, 343n61; on immigration, 18, 30, 189, 224, 257, 272, 281–86; on Iraq War, 238–45, 243, 244, 247, 249–50, 254; Islam opponents in, 272, 277–80, 285–86, 290–91; Islam, supporters of ties to, 22, 31, 142–64, 166, 167, 170, 172, 184, 185, 273, 282–83, 284, 282, 288–89, 306; on Israel, 207, 228, 289–90, 348n22; leaderless resistance approach of, 27, 29–30, 97, 143, 179, 307; on neoconservatives, 241–44, 247, 248, 249; on 9/11 attacks, 1–2, 156, 215, 220–22, 224–27, 228–38, 250, 254–55, 256–57, 291, 308; Qaddafi and, 129–30; racism and, 13, 14–23, 26, 30, 31, 143, 144; similarities to militant Islam of, 2–3, 22–23, 29, 31, 52, 138, 140, 168–71, 217, 262, 267, 282, 283, 306; war on terror and, 9, 254–55, 256, 267, 309. See also extreme right, American; extreme right, European
extreme right, American: African Americans and, 97–98; anti-Semitism of, 3, 14, 15–16, 17, 18–19, 20–23, 28; civil rights era and, 26; Saddam Hussein and, 138; methods to counteract, 211–13; militia movement and,

13–14, 134, 177–78, 211; on 9/11 attacks, 1–2, 156, 215, 220–21, 224–25, 254–55, 256–57; 1990s resurgence of, 11; on Oklahoma City bombing, 134; opposition to U.S. government by, 25, 26; patriotism and, 23; in post–WWII Middle East, 124; racism and, 13, 14–23, 26, 30, 31, 143, 144; Third Reich and, 112–19; U.S. government response to, 173–92, 307; violence and, 13, 23–29
extreme right, European: Algerian war and, 121; on American culture, 293; British, 97, 129–30, 142–48, 223; Saddam Hussein and, 136–38; 1990s resurgence of, 8; Palestinian rejectionist group and, 124–28
extremism, definition of, 11–13

Faci, Michel, 136
Fadlullah, Muhammad Hussein, 57–58, 59
Faisal, King, 62
Faisal, Prince Turki bin, 195, 323n228
Falange, 137
Fall of Pan Am 103, The (Emerson), 209
Falwell, Jerry, 163
Faraj, Muhammad, 54
Fard, Wallace D., 94, 95, 327n56
Farhat, Hassan, 92
Faris, Mohammad Abu, 91
Farmbacher, Wilhelm, 123
Farouk, King, 37, 120
Farrakhan, Louis, 95–96, 97–98, 99, 100, 269–70
far right, definition of, 13
Fatah, 119, 125, 126
Fattouh, Zeinab Mansour, 148
Fatwas, 24, 42, 76–77
Faurisson, Robert, 156
Fawwaz, Khalid al-, 108
Federal Bureau of Investigation (FBI): on anthrax attacks, 111; counterterrorism section of, 197, 198–99, 306, 340n2; domestic terrorism and, 173, 174–79, 180, 181, 183, 184, 192, 307, 341n25; Hezbollah and, 92, 183; Joint Terrorism Task Force, 90, 92, 183; NGOs and, 175, 176, 178–79, 212; international terrorism and, 85, 86, 89, 102, 108, 192, 193, 218; 9/11 and, 197, 233; 1993 World Trade Center bombing and, 132; Ruby Ridge incident and, 177; USA PATRIOT Act and, 199; Waco incident and, 178
Federal Communications Commission (FCC), 213
Federal Emergency Management Agency (FEMA), 200

Graf, Jürgen: Holocaust revisionism and, 21–22, 157, 256, 274–75; on immigration, 284; on Iraq War, 243; on terrorist attacks on U.S., 226, 235, 256

Grand Mufti. *See* Husseini, Haj Amin al-

Gray Wolves, 128

Great Britain: Afghanistan and, 113; Egypt and, 123–24; extreme right in, 97, 129–30, 142–48, 223; imperialism of, 45; Iraq and, 114–15; Jewish state and, 113, 114; Muslims in, 108, 281; Race Relations Act, 207

Greater Israel (Eretz Israel) theory, 47, 239

Greece, 254

Green Book, The (Khaddafi), 99, 128, 129, 130

Green Shirts, 119, 330n37

Greenwood, Christine, 183–84

Griffin, Nick, 129, 130, 190, 226, 243, 256, 276–77, 332n99

Grimstad, William, 22, 314n23

Gritz, Bo, 227

Grobba, Fritz, 123

Groebel, J., 23

Guerilla Warfare (Laqueur), 301

Gulf War, 67, 68, 71, 100, 134, 137, 202–3, 245, 284

Gunaratna, Rohan, 67, 69, 75, 82, 228, 360n19

gun control laws, U.S., 13

Gurr, Ted Robert, 6

Gurwekht, 113

Haaretz, 230, 231, 351n36

Habash, George, 75, 127

Hadayet, Hesham Mohamed, 107

Haddad, Waddi, 126

Hadj, Louis al-, 122

Hage, Wadih el-, 85

Haider, Jörg, 137, 282

Hale, Matt, 17, 185–87

Halens, Christoph, 129

Halliburton, 268

Hamas, 60–61, 75, 154, 158, 193, 320n125; in U.S., 91–92, 133, 174

Hampton, Howard, 188

Hanafi Muslims, 105

Handschar Division, 121

Hariri, Rafik, 157

Harrington, Patrick, 97, 129

Harris, Kevin, 177

Harris, Larry Wayne, 111

Hashemites, 247

Hassan, Abdul Mawgoud, 124

Hassan, King, 139

Hassinger, Alex, 221

hate crime laws, 211

Hatfill, Steven, 111

Hausofer, Karl, 122

Hawthorne, George Eric, 27

Hayden Lake, Idaho, 183, 185

Hegel, G. W. F., 38

Hekmatiyar, Gulbadin, 56–57, 319n104

Hepp, Odfried, 127

Hersh, Seymour, 229

Hess, Rudolf, 187

Hewar Center, Al-, 259

Hewitt, Christopher, 11–12, 25, 26

Heydrich, Reinhard, 118

Hezbollah, 57–59, 65, 74, 75, 79, 139, 167–68, 210, 247, 306; in U.S., 92, 133

Hezbollah International, 74, 75

Hidmi, Nasser Issa Jalal, 92

Hikind, Dov, 89

Hilfskorps Arabien, 127

Hillard, Earl, 96

Himmat, Ali Ghaleb, 148–49

Himmler, Heinrich, 115

Hindus, 277

Hintersatz, William, 117

Historical revisionism. *See* Holocaust/historical revisionism

Hitchens, Christopher, 293

Hitler, Adolf, 139, 143; on Arab independence, 114, 118; extreme right and, 124, 125, 237, 316n19; al-Husseini (Grand Mufti) and, 115, 116, 118–19, 285; on Jews, 113, 118, 158; Middle Eastern admirers of, 115, 119, 120, 122, 128; Muslims and, 112, 113, 116, 123, 136, 151–52, 153, 285, 330n17

Hitler-Bormann Documents, 116

Hizb-i Islami, 57

Hizb ut-Tahir, 153

Hoax of the Twentieth Century, The (Butz), 98

Hoffman, Bruce, 29, 68, 81, 88

Hoffman, Karl Heinz, 127

Hoffman, Michael, 93

Hoge, James F., 4

Holland, Derek, 129, 277

Hollings, Ernest F., 251

Holmes, David, 344n74

Holocaust Denial (Stern), 347n4

Holocaust/historical revisionism, 20–23, 98, 139, 156–61, 187–88, 244, 256, 274–75, 287, 314n23, 316n19, 343n61, 347n4

Holy Land Foundation (HLF), 92

Holy War, Inc., 72

Homeland Security, Office of, 187, 196, 199–200, 223, 302, 361n28

Hoover, J. Edgar, 175
Horowitz, David, 238
Horrifying Fraud (Meyssan), 228–29
Hoskins, Richard Kelly, 142
Hostage Rescue Team (HRT), 176, 177, 340n15
"How We Can Coexist," 263
Hoy, Robert, 97
Huber, Ahmed, 115–16, 148–56, 168, 236, 270, 274, 283–84, 244, 256, 293–94, 336n180
Hull, David Wayne, 184
Hungary, 118
Hunter, 182
Huntington, Samuel, 81, 285, 298, 303, 304; clash of civilizations theory of, 5, 6, 7, 8
Hussaini, Hussain Hashem al-, 133
Husseini, Haj Amin al- (Grand Mufti): extreme right and, 124; in Iraq, 114; Hitler and, 115, 116, 118–19, 285; on Jews, 113, 117; Nazis and, 112, 115, 116–17, 118–19, 121, 122, 123, 125, 151, 285; PLO and, 119; Young Egypt and, 119
Hussein (seventh-century Shiite martyr), 56
Hussein, Ahmed, 330n37
Hussein, King, 124, 127
Hussein, Qusay, 75
Hussein, Saddam, 115; extreme right and, 136–38; fascism and, 136; Israel and, 247, 251; Kuwait invasion and, 61, 67, 202; militant Islam and, 67, 68, 88; 9/11 attacks and, 204, 259; on pan-Arabism/pan-Islam, 270; al Qaeda and, 76, 301, 356n45; Saudi Arabia and, 76; support for terrorists by, 76; Soviet Union and, 137; as U.S. target, 200, 203, 245, 302

Ibn Saud, King Abdul-Aziz, 63, 123
Ibn Taymiyya, 41
Ibn-ul-Khattab, 104
Ibrahim, Hassan, 119
Ichtirakya, al-, 330n37
Idaho, Aryan Nations in, 183
Idris, Wafa, 288
IHR (Institute for Historical Review), 20, 21, 22, 139, 156, 227, 313n22
Illuminati, 47
Ilyukhin, Victor, 138
immigration: in Canada, 188; extreme right on, 18, 30, 189, 224, 257, 272, 281–86; far left on, 172; in Great Britain, 129; Jewish, to Palestine, 112, 113, 118, 158, 313n6, 330n28; Mexican, to U.S., 257, 298,

360n14; multiculturalism and, 16, 19, 296–99; Muslim, in Europe, 5, 108–9, 280–85, 297; in U.S., 16, 19, 30, 84, 108–9, 224, 257, 272, 281, 283, 296–97, 302, 308, 311n12
Immigration Act of 1965, 303
Immigration and Naturalization Service (INS), 85, 187, 199, 200, 234
Imperium (Yockey), 124
India, 254
Indonesia, 80, 262, 308
InfoCom Corporation, 92
Information Services Against Right-Wing Extremism, 363n53
INS (Immigration and Naturalization Service), 85, 187, 199, 200, 234
Institute for Historical Review (IHR), 20, 21, 22, 139, 156, 227, 313n22
Internal Revenue Service (IRS), 190; Security Division, 176
International Association of Chiefs of Police, 179
International Conference on the Palestinian Intifada, 158
International Development Corp. (IDC America), 191
International Jew, The (Ford), 157
International Policy Institute for Counter-Terrorism (ICT), 208, 346–47n3
International Position, 130
International Third Position, 277
Internet, 130–31, 139, 170; ADL and, 215; extreme right and, 1, 11, 30, 111–12, 181, 182, 187; extreme right and Muslim communication on, 306, 307; FBI and, 198, 199, 272; 9/11 rumors on, 215
Inter-Services Intelligence (ISI; Pakistan), 74, 162, 195
intifadas, 158, 167; al-Aqsa (second), 8, 60, 61, 320n126, 355n18; first, 58, 60, 355n18
Investigative Project on Terrorism, 209–10, 275
Invisible Empire, 96
Iran, 247; Hamas and, 60, 75; Hezbollah and, 57, 59, 74, 75; Holocaust/historical revisionism and, 158–59; 1979 Islamic Revolution in, 34, 55, 202; nuclear weapons and, 79; al Qaeda and, 75, 323n206; shahs of, 55, 115, 194; as sponsor of terrorist groups, 74–75; Supreme Council for Intelligence Affairs, 74; Taliban and, 75; U.S. and, 56, 248
Iranian hostage situation, 53, 194
Iranian Party of Allah, 354n5
Iran-Iraq War (1980–1988), 202

Iraq: anti-Semitism in 136; army of, 345–46n125; bin Laden and, 267, 323n223; British and, 114–15, 123, 136; chemical weapons and, 356n4; extreme right and, 126, 136, 138; Israel and, 47, 267; National Socialism in, 119; 9/11 attacks and, 76; 1941 revolt in, 114, 123, 136; 1993 World Trade Center attack and, 88–89, 132; Oklahoma City bombing and, 132, 133, 134; al Qaeda and, 65, 75, 76, 271; Soviet Union/Russia and, 126–27, 137–38, 202, 204; U.S. and, 68, 90, 134–35, 202–4, 205; U.S. sanctions on, 76, 203, 226, 228, 260–61, 263, 281, 346n127

Iraq-Austrian Association, 137

Iraq War (2003): American Muslims on, 269; American public on, 207, 269, 301, 308, 361n25; Bush and, 200, 202, 203–4; extreme right on, 159, 162–63, 165, 166, 238–54, 270; Jews on, 165, 238–40, 241, 242, 244, 246, 250–53; left-wing radicals on, 171; militant Islam on, 267–71; oil theories and, 162–63, 243

Irish Republican Army, 168

Irving, David, 98

ISI (Inter-Services Intelligence, Pakistan), 74, 162, 195

Islam: African Americans and, 94–101, 103; anti-Semitism and, 44–52, 93, 108; clergy of, 42–43; communism and, 45, 47, 109; democracy and, 34, 39, 41, 167, 205, 279, 316n17; description of, 33, 35; in Europe, 117, 297; in Great Britain, 108, 281; growth of, 5, 107; Holocaust/historical revisionism and, 22–23, 156–61; ideology of, 33, 37–43; in Iran, 55–57; Nazi Germany and, 112–24; political authority and, 33, 39, 41, 53, 55; secularism and, 45, 46; universality of, 40; in U.S., 5, 63, 64, 84, 107, 259, 281, 311n12; violence and, 5–6, 45, 53. *See also* militant Islam

Islam and the Jews (al-Husseini), 117

Islambuli, Khalid al-, 54

Islamic Association of Palestine (IAP), 91

Islamic Center, 60

Islamic Committee for Palestine (ICO), 93

Islamic Committee, Russian Branch, 138

Islamic Concern Project, 93

Islamic Front for the Struggle against Jews and the Crusaders, 75

Islamic Group, the (al-Gamaa-i Islamiya), 65, 85

Islamic Guerrillas of American, 105

Islamic Jihad, 65, 75, 90, 91, 93; Egyptian, 67,

75, 76; Lebanese, 75; Palestinian, 75, 93; Yemeni, 70

Islamic National Party, 330n37

Islamic Republic of Iran Broadcasting (IRIB), 22

Islamic Study Committee (al Qaeda), 73

Islamic World League, 114

Islamists. *See* militant Islam

Israel: American criticism of, 250; attack on Palestinians in, 9; Christian right on, 253, 348n23; Egypt and, 47, 54, 123–24, 266; ethnic exclusivity in, 19; extreme right on, 207, 228, 289–90, 348n22; Hamas and, 60–61; Hezbollah and, 57–58, 59; Islamic opposition to, 45, 46, 50, 51, 214–15; Lebanon and, 57, 59, 267, 289; left-wing criticism of, 171; on Middle East secessionist movements, 267; Mossad in, 112, 122, 160, 215, 229, 230, 231, 232, 234, 235, 237, 265; National Alliance on, 164–65; 9/11 attacks and, 161, 185–86, 191, 215, 216, 218, 229, 230, 231, 233, 234, 235, 237, 242, 265; 1972 Olympic team murders, 124, 126; Palestinians in, 37, 121, 282; peace treaty with Egypt of, 54, 120, 331n41; policy toward Palestinians of, 171, 247, 289; Saudi opposition to, 263; U.S. and, 1, 46, 51–52, 57–58, 96, 159, 160, 185–86, 205, 214, 218, 227, 238, 241, 243, 245, 249–50, 253, 293, 297

Israeli embassy (Buenos Aires) bombing, 167

"Israeli Involvement in September 11" lecture (Duke), 161

Israeli-Palestinian conflict, 51, 245

Istanbul, Turkey, terrorist attacks in, 108

Italian-Libyan Friendship Society, 129

Italy; extreme right activists and, 129, 130; Middle East colonialism of, 118

Jabotinski, Vladimir, 114

Jackson, Jesse, 101

Jackson, Michael, 354n5

Jacquard, Roland, 65

Jahiliyya, 39–40, 42, 317n34

Jalabad, battle of, 65

Jama At al-Jihad, 54, 67, 85

Jamal, Heidar, 138

Janjalani, Abdurazzak Abubakar, 326n26

Jarrah, Ziad al-, 329n110

Jazeera, al-, 161–62, 166, 190, 263

Jebra, Abdul Moneim, 137

Jeddah agreement, 122

Jeddah, Saudi Arabia, 68

Jeffries, Leonard, 98

Jenkins, Woody, 190
Jersey City, N.J., 85
Jerusalem Post, 215, 231
Jewish Community Center (Buenos Aires) bombing, 167
Jewish Defense League (JDL), 86, 338n240
Jewish defense organizations, 208–9, 213, 218–19, 234. *See also individual organizations*
Jewish Supremacism (Duke), 189
Jewish tribes, 44–45
Jews: alleged control of U.S. by, 2, 3, 46–47, 48, 49, 140, 165, 217, 223, 237, 245, 255, 266, 293–95; in Argentina, 167–68; conspiracy theories about, 44, 46–47, 48, 215, 228–38; immigration of, to Palestine, 112, 113, 118, 158, 313n6, 330n28; intellectual movements of, 18–19; Iraq War and, 165, 238–40, 241, 242, 244, 246, 250–53; neoconservative, 165, 238, 239, 241, 242, 243, 246. *See also* Anti-Semitism; Zionism
Jihad, Abu, 127–28
"Jihadi Iraqi Hopes and Dangers" (documentary), 305
"Jihad in America" (documentary; Emerson), 209, 210
Jihadist movements, 69; in Afghanistan, 101, 194; Americans and, 101–5; global, 101; Hezbollah and, 58; Saddam Hussein on, 270–71; against Israel, 50, 60–61; justification for, 24, 42; in Pakistan, 101; Soviet-Afghan war and, 62; against U.S., 204. *See also* Islamic Jihad
Jilani, El Sheikh Sayyid Mubarik Ali, 93
John Birch Society, 13, 28
John Paul II, 89, 128
Johnson, Chalmers, 251
Johnson, Larry, 104
Joint Chiefs of Staff, 100
Joint Terrorism Task Force, 90, 92, 183
Jones, Stephen, 131, 135
Jordan: on bin Laden, 308; Black September war in, 127; historical revisionism conference in, 157; on Saddam Hussein, 61; Israel and, 247; PLO in, 124, 127
Jordanian Writers' Association, 157
Jordan, Montana, 178
Journal of Historical Review, 22
Junge, Gertrud, 151

Kabul, Afghanistan, 68
Kach movement, 86, 207
Kahane, Rabbi Meir, 85, 86, 207
Kaiser, Robert, 251

Kallstrom, James, 198
Kamal, Ali Hassan Abu, 106
Kame, Moustapha, 108
Kandahar, 324n236
Kansi, Mir Aimal, 106, 328n99
Kaplan, Jeffrey, 9, 272
Kaplan, Robert, 302
Karachi, Pakistan, 89
Karim, Abdul Basit, 88
Kashmir, 66, 93, 262
Katz, Harry, 48
Kengerle, Mehmet, 128
Kennedy, John F., assassination theory, 159, 160, 337n215
Kennedy, Paul, 299
Kennedy, Robert, 105
Kenya, 77, 121
Kepel, Gilles, 45
Kerkhoff, Frank, 154
Khaalis, Hamaas Abdul, 105
Khalifa, Muhammad Jamal, 88
Khamenei, Ayatollah Ali, 158, 266
Khan, Abdul Aadeer, 79
Khan, Masoud, 93
Khan, Mullah Mirza Ali, 113
Khartoum, Sudan, 68
Khatami, Hojjatoleslam Seyed Mohammad, 75
Khobar Towers bombing, 73
Khomeini, Ahmed, 138
Khomeini, Ayatollah Ruhollah, 37, 42, 55–57, 151, 202, 277
Khost, Afghanistan, 75
Kirkpatrick, Jeane, 245
Klassen, Ben, 27
Klinghoffer, Leon, 193
Knights of the Ku Klux Klan, 96, 189, 212
Koestler, Arthur, 313n6
Kommando Deutsch-Arabischer Truppen, 114
Kopul, Jan, 220
Koran, 39–40, 41; on Jews, 44–45, 50; on suicide, 59, 70
Kosovo, 254
Kourani, Haidar, 92
Kourani, Mahmoud Youssef, 92
Krar, William, 191–92
Krauthammer, Charles, 245, 251
Kreis, August, 183, 185
Kristol, William, 241, 245
Ku Klux Klan, 26, 96, 138, 175, 184, 189, 212, 314n39
Kühnen, Michael, 136
Kunstler, William, 86
Kurdish People's Party, 75

Kurds, 202, 267
Kurth, James, 6, 292
Kuwait, liberation of, 67
Kyna, Karl von, 127

Lantos, Tom, 250
Laqueur, Walter, 292, 293, 294, 300, 301, 307
Lashkar-i-Taiba (Righteous Army), 93, 103
Latif, Mahumd 'Abd al-, 37
Lavon affair, 266, 289
Lebanon, 156; bombing of French post in, 59; bombing of U.S. Marine barracks in, 59; Christians in, 57, 59; civil war in, 57, 137; extreme right and, 127–28; Hezbollah and, 57–59; Holocaust/historical revisionism and, 156–57; Islam terror network in, 53, 61; Israel and, 57, 59, 267, 289; Shi'ites in, 247; U.S. and, 59, 210
Lebed, Alexander, 78
Lebor, Leon, 351n36
Ledeen, Michael, 205, 225, 247–48
Lee, Martin, 121
Leers, Johan von (Omar Amin), 122
Leesburg, Va., 180
Lefkow, Joan Humphrey, 186, 187
left-wing extremists: ADL on, 225; anti-Semitism, 9, 172, 218, 248; decline of, 109, 177; extreme right and, 164, 171, 221, 288; FBI campaign against, 175; oil as motive for war theory of, 162–63, 259; Palestinian and, 60, 125; PLO and, 53, 124–25, 126, 127; terrorism of, 174, 194
Le Pen, Jean-Marie, 137, 190, 282, 284
Levi Guidelines, 175
Levinhar, Shay, 351n36
Levin, Sander, 250
Lewin, Daniel, 351n36
Lewinsky, Monica (scandal), 47
Lewis, Bernard, 33, 35, 44
Libby, Lewis "Scooter," 252
Liberal Democratic Party (Russian), 137
Liberation Tigers of Tamil, 168
Liberia, 97
Liberty, USS, 232, 289, 351n39
Liberty Lobby, 20, 97, 159, 347–48n22
Library of Congress, U.S., 212
Libya, 101, 103; Nation of Islam and, 99, 100; nuclear weapons and, 79; as sponsor of terrorism, 128; U.S. and, 130, 248, 326n41, 332n89
Liddawi, Mustafa Al, 74
Lifton, Robert Jay, 82
Likud Party, 242–43, 249

Lindh, John Walker, 102
Liu, Jianguo, 81
Locke, John, 43
Los Angeles, Calif., 107, 208; Aryan Nations and, 183
Los Angeles Times, 251
Louisiana, David Duke in, 189, 291
Lowey, Nita, 250
Lowy, Frank, 231, 233
Ludwig, Doug, 181
Lufthansa plane hijacking, 126

Macdonald, Ian Verner, 129
MacDonald, Kevin, 18–19, 50, 51, 223, 227, 242–43, 285
Macover, Michael, 230
Madole, James H., 124
Madrid train station attacks, 268, 305
Mahathir, Muhammad, 170–71
Mahdi, Fawsi Salim el-, 128
Mahfouz, Khalid bin, 154
Mahler, Horst, 220–21
Mahmood, Sultan Bashiruddin, 79
Mahon, Dennis, 138
Makashov, Albert, 190
Makhtab al-Khadimat (MAK), 65, 66, 86, 87
Makki, Hassan M., 92
Malcolm X, 95
Malik, Prince, 100
Malone, Mat, 97
Mandela, Nelson, 58
Manichaeism, 58
Mansour, Anis, 331n41
Mansour, Mohammed, 148
Mao Zedong, 29, 301
Marashov, Albert, 138
Markaz ad Dawa wal Irshad, 328n99
Maronite Christians, 57, 267
Marr, Wilhelm, 45
Martin, Anthony, 20, 98
martyrdom, 56, 58, 59, 69–70, 169, 236, 339n251
Marx, Karl, 38
Maryland, extreme right in, 181
Marzuq, Musa Abu, 91, 92
Masada, battle of, 65
Masoud, Ahmed Shah, 66, 321n154
Masri, Sheikh Abu Hamza al-, 104, 328n89
Masri, Aziz al-, 119
Matthews, Robert Jay, 27, 31–32
Mawdudi, Mawlana abu al-Ala, 42, 317n34
Mayer, Andreas, 117
May 15 Arab Organization, 105

McCabe, Patrick, 183, 184
McCalden, David, 313n22
McCloskey, Paul, 250
McKinney, Cynthia, 96, 217
McVeigh, Timothy, 25, 131–32, 133, 134–35, 177, 178
McWilliams, Brian, 230
Mecca, 44, 55, 67, 74, 354n6
media: alleged Jewish control of, 47, 49, 58, 95, 131, 134, 139, 172, 215, 264, 266, 273, 290, 334n150, 358n36; alleged U.S. favoritism of Israel in, 159, 233, 238, 242, 355n18; Iraqi, 269; on Iraq War, 239; militant Islam and, 263–64, 268, 278, 319n85; NGOs use of, 211, 213; al Qaeda and, 263–64; on reason for 9/11 attacks, 224, 226, 228; U.S. domination of, 260, 264
Media Committee for the Victory of Iraqi People, 305
Medina, 67, 74
Megret, Bruno, 280
Meheishi, Omar el-, 332n89
Mehlman, Kenneth, 252
Mehr News Agency, 166
Meighy, Josef, 31
Mein Kampf (Hitler), 119, 122, 152
Mercy International Relief Agency (MIRA), 168
Mertig, Kurt, 331n37
Metzger, John, 17
Metzger, Tom, 17, 96–97, 129, 212, 221, 240, 290
Mexico immigrants in U.S., 257
Meyssan, Thierry, 228–29
Mezer, Ghazi Ibrahim abu, 106
Michigan Militia Corps Wolverines, 14
Middle East peace agreement (1993), 4
Milestones (Qutb), 41, 43
militant Islam (Islamism): anti-American views of, 214, 228; anti-Semitism and, 9, 34, 44–52, 93, 108, 136, 170–71, 217, 219; anti-Western views of, 34, 53 60, 75; Arab nationalism and, 52–53, 56, 62, 271; bin Laden's reenergizing of, 69; definition of, 33–34, 80–81, 293; globalization and, 7, 109; Saddam Hussein and, 67, 68; in Iran, 55–57, 59, 60, 74, 75, 202; Iraq and, 205; on Iraq War, 267–71; new world order and, 7–8, 109, 146–67; on 9/11 attacks, 1, 264–66; Oklahoma City bombing and, 210; in Palestine, 60–61; Qutb, and, 37–44; resurgence of after 1967, 52–54; secularization and, 35–36, 60; similarities to extreme right of, 2–3, 22–23, 29, 31, 52, 138, 140,

168–71, 217, 262, 267, 282, 283, 306; terrorism and, 53–54; U.S. as target of, 259–60; U.S. threat to, 7–8; in U.S., 84–110. *See also individual organizations*
Military Committee (al Qaeda), 73
militia movement, 13–14, 134, 177–78, 211
millennialism, 58, 64
Million Man March, 98
Ministry of Islamic Liaison (Aryan Nations), 140, 142, 163
Minutemen organizations, 13
Mogadishu, Somalia, 70, 196
Mongols, 45
Montana Freemen, 178
Montgomery, Ala., 209
Moody, James, 187
Moore, Roger, 132
Moorer, Thomas, 232
Moorish Science Temple, 94
Moran, James, 250, 251
More in Common Than You Think (Baker), 163–64
Morocco, 308
Mossad, 112, 122, 160, 215; 9/11 attacks and, 229, 230, 231, 232, 234, 235, 237, 265
Moussaoui, Zacarias, 108, 133
Moynihan, Daniel Patrick, 5, 263
Mubarak, Hosni, 89–90, 320n133
Mueller, John, 197
Mughniya, Imad, 75, 167
Muhammad ali Amriki, Abu ("Muhammad the American"), 90–91
Muhammad, Alim, 97
Muhammad, Amin, 97
Muhammad, Amir, 266
Muhammad, Elijah, 95, 99, 100, 327n56
Muhammad, John, 269
Muhammad, Khalid Abdul, 96
Muhammad, Khalid Sheikh, 73, 89, 202, 324n257, 345n124
Muhammad, Omar Barki, 108
Muhammad, Prophet, 33, 41, 44, 74, 143, 151, 283–84, 327n56; Jews and, 44, 45, 50
Muhammad, Wallace, 95
Mujahedin-e Khalq Organization (MKO), 76
mujahideen: in Afghanistan, 65–66, 67, 68, 73–74, 86–87, 101, 102, 113, 194–95, 270–71, 326n26, 344n86; American, 101–5; in Bosnia-Herzegovina, 154; Saddam Hussein and, 270–71; Western experiences of, 108
multiculturalism, 3, 6, 13, 14, 16, 30, 296–99, 303–4, 308
Munich Olympic games (1972), 124–28

Munzel, Oskar, 123
Musawaar, Al-, 119
Muslim Brotherhood, 36, 37, 43, 53, 54, 55, 60, 63, 80, 112, 148
Muslim Council, 259
Muslims of America (MOA), 92–93
Mussolini, Benito, 112, 114, 330n17
Mutamar al-Alam al-Islami (Islamic World League), 114
Mutte, Claudio, 129
Muwafaq Foundation, 154
Myatt, David Wulstan (Abdul Aziz), 142–48, 168, 226, 235–36, 244, 256, 282–83, 304
My Awakening (Duke), 189
Mylroie, Laurie, 76, 88, 90, 132, 326n35

Nada Management, 148
Nada, Yousef, 148, 149
Naguib, Muhammad, 120
Nairobi, Kenya, 77
Nakleh, Issah, 22
Nasreddin, Ahmed Idris, 149
Nasser, Gamal Abdel: extreme right and, 124, 150; Germany and, 121, 122–23, 124; Islamists and, 37, 41, 43, 53; 1952 coup and, 37, 41, 120; Soviet Union and, 123–24
Nation, 251
National Alliance, 2, 15–16, 112, 164–67, 171, 173, 180–82, 221, 222, 289, 291, 341n27. *See also* Pierce, William L.
National Association for the Advancement of White People, 189
National Democratic Party (NPD; Germany), 167
National Front (NF), 97, 129, 130, 190, 207, 220, 277, 280
National Islamic Front, 69, 326n35
Nationalism in the Middle East. *See* Arab nationalism
Nationalist Movement, 254
Nationalist Observer website, 179
National Renaissance Party (NRP), 124, 315n49, 331n37
National Security Agency, 233
National Security Council, 246
National Socialism: Arab nationalism and, 119–24; extreme right and, 12, 15, 143–46, 151, 282–83, 305, 316n19. *See also* Nazis
National Vanguard (organization), 16
National Vanguard (publication), 9, 166
Natión Européene, La, 126
Nation of Islam (NOI), 94–100, 130, 327n56
Nayef Ibn Abd al-Aziz, Prince, 215

Nazis: Afghanistan and, 113; Egypt and, 121–23, 124; Iraq and, 136; Islam and, 112–24. *See also* Hitler, Adolf; National Socialism; Neo-Nazis
Nebi Musa, festival of, 112
Neglected Duty, The (Faraj), 54
neoconservatives, 134, 163, 165, 238–50, 252, 253, 256, 270
neo-Nazis, 2, 31, 97, 121, 125, 126, 127–28, 136, 167, 187, 218, 227, 275, 341n27, 343n61
Netanyahu, Benjamin, 29, 47, 237–38, 246
networks, 88, 308; extreme right and, 29–30, 169, 307; Internet and, 307; jihad, 195–96; jihad, in northern Virginia, 93–94, 154; militant Islamic, 61, 62, 72, 79, 109, 169, 192, 249, 271, 298, 356n45; al Qaeda, 64–65, 71, 72–73, 79, 82–83, 89, 90, 149, 154, 192, 196, 234, 300
Neurath, Konstantin von, 113
Never Again? The Threat of the New Anti-Semitism (Foxman), 216
Newark, N.J., 94
New Black Panther Party (NBPP), 265–66
New Century Foundation, 315n49
New National Front, 130
New Orleans Protocol, 291, 342n37
New Trends, 266
new world order, 3, 7–8, 109, 131, 146–47, 167, 244, 254, 305
NF (National Front), 97, 129, 130, 190, 207, 220, 277, 280
NGOs. *See* Nongovernmental organizations
Nichols, Lana, 131–32
Nichols, Marife, 131
Nichols, Terry, 131–32, 134, 178, 333n113
Nidal, Abu, 202
Nightline, 250
9/11 attacks: American academics on, 263; American Muslims on, 259, 265–66; Bush administration and, 196, 197, 198, 199–200, 201, 223, 229, 230, 344n94; conspiracy theories on, 228–38, 264–68; economic cost of, to U.S., 3–4; events of, 107; extreme right on, 1–2, 156, 215, 220–22, 224–25, 254–55, 256–57; Iraq and, 76; Israel and, 161, 185–86, 191, 215, 216, 218, 229, 230, 231, 232, 234, 235, 237, 242, 265, 351n36; Middle East reactions to, 264–66; al Qaeda and, 1, 80, 196, 201–2, 234, 299–300, 329n110, 336n193; reasons for, 1, 80, 214, 225–28, 299–300; U.S. government response to, 173, 196–201

9/11 Digital Lies (Simon Wiesenthal Center), 215

NOI (Nation of Islam), 94–100, 130, 327n56

nongovernmental organizations (NGOs): on extreme right, 174, 177, 178, 179, 211–12, 213, 307; Jewish defense organizations as, 208, 214–19; on militant Islam, 213–14; on Muslim American hate crimes, 198; al Qaeda infiltration of, 87; role of, 207–19. *See also individual organizations*

nonrevolutionary racialist right, 14, 17–19

Nordkaukasischer Waffengruppe (North Caucasus Armed Group), 117

North Atlantic Treaty Organization (NATO), 103, 244

Northern Alliance, 74, 102, 201

North Korea, 79, 248

Nosair, El Sayyid, 85, 86, 89

NPD (German National Democratic Party), 153–54

nuclear weapons, 78–79

Nuremberg Laws, 113

Nye, Joseph, 308

Ocalan, Abdullah, 75

Occupied Territories, 60, 61, 96

Odeh, Muhammad Saddiq, 321n157

Odigo, 230, 231

Odinism, 15, 185, 316n19

oil in Middle East, 162–63, 243, 244, 259, 260, 300

Oklahoma City bombing, 11, 13, 29, 131–36, 173, 174, 178, 192, 210

Oklahoma City, Islamist activities in, 133

Olson, Norm, 14, 277–78

Omar, Mullah Muhammad, 73–74, 78, 147, 319n104, 323n228

Onassis, Aristotle, 122

O'Neill, Paul, 252

Operation Anaconda, 201

Operation Bojinka, 89, 345n124

Operation Clean-Sweep, 176–77

Operation Defense Shield, 245

Operation Desert Fox, 203

Operation Desert Storm, 67, 203

Operation Enduring Freedom, 102, 200–202, 345n118

Operation Green Quest, 154

Operation Infinite Justice, 345n118

Operation Infinite Reach, 78, 196

Operation Iraqi Freedom, 202–4

Operation Lone Wolf, 179, 341n25

Operation Restore Hope, 70

Operation Smokescreen, 92

Orange County, Calif., 183

Order, the, 27, 28, 31, 32, 176, 183

Ordine Nuovo (New Order), 154, 347n10

O'Reilly, Bill, 93

O'Reilly Factor, The, 93

Organization of Petroleum Exporting Countries (OPEC), 54

Organization of the Islamic Conference, 170

Ortega, Daniel, 58

Oslo Accords, 60

Osman, Semi, 104

Ostturkisches Waffenverband, 117

Othman, Omar Mahmud, 108

Ottoman Empire, 35–36, 112

Our Struggle with the Jews (Qutb), 44

Padilla, Jose, 102

Pahlavi, Shah Mohammed Reza, 55

Pahlavi, Shah Reza, 115

Pakistan: Afghanistan and, 74; bin Laden and, 66, 78, 79, 308; Inter-Services Intelligence (ISI), 195; Islam in, 64, 204; nuclear weapons and, 78–79; Taliban and, 162; U.S. and, 162, 201, 254

paleo-conservatives, 7, 18, 222, 238, 241, 242, 281

Palestine Liberation Organization (PLO): financial operation of, 219n86; Germany and, 127–28; in Jordan, 124, 127; Khomeini and, 55; leadership of, 119; left-wing extremists and, 53, 124–25, 126, 127; nationalism and, 53; right-wing extremists and, 127, 130

Palestine: anticolonial uprising in, 115; anti-Zionism in, 112; Christians in, 60; Fatah and, 125, 126; financial supporters of, 92, 93; Israel and, 47, 96, 253, 261; Jewish immigration into, 112, 113, 118, 158, 313n6, 330n28; militant Islam and, 2, 47, 60–61, 66; Muslim Botherhood and, 37; Nazis and, 115; opposition to Jewish settlement in, 112, 118, 330n28; partition of, 113, 262; population of, 281–82

Palestinian Authority, 60, 61

Palestinian Information Center, 264

Palestinian issue, 261, 286–92

Palestinian rejectionists, 4, 31, 61, 125, 130, 193

Palestinians: attack on, in Israel, 9; attacks on Israel by, 121; bin Laden and, 260–61, 262, 287, 308; extreme right and, 2, 127–28, 280, 287–91; population growth of, 216, 282; support for, 51, 123–24, 214

Pamyat (Memory) organization, 138
Pan Am flight 103, 130
Pan Am flight to Japan, bombing, 105
pan-Arabism. *See* Arab nationalism
pan-Islam, 35, 46, 50, 66, 69
Panzerfaust Records, 180
Paraguay, 59
Parmenter, Denver, 32
Patriot Act, 165, 198, 199, 219, 223, 239
Paved with Good Intentions (Taylor), 17
Pearlman, Adam, 103
Pearlman, Phil, 103
Pelley, William Dudley, 49
Pelosi, Nancy, 250
Pentagon 9/11 attack, 107. *See also* 9/11 attacks
PENTBOM, 197
People's Democratic Party (PDP), 194
People That Shall Dwell Alone, A (MacDonald), 18
Peres, Shimon, 48
Perle, Richard, 238, 245, 246, 248, 249, 251, 252
Peshawar, 66, 86
Peters, Pete, 14
Philippines, 64, 66, 80, 89; Terry Nichols in, 131, 132
Phineas Priesthood, 142, 334–35n152
Phoenix memo, 198
Pierce, Bob, 105
Pierce, William L.: on antiterror measures, 222; on bin Laden, 164, 166–67; Doles and, 181; on Jews, 47, 58, 139, 166, 281, 358n36; on Muslims, 164–67, 276, 288; as National Alliance leader, 15–16, 164, 180, 341n27; on 9/11 attacks, 2, 9, 227, 239, 383n231; on suicide terrorism, 169; on U.S., 15, 188
Pillar, Paul, 6, 109
Piper, Mike, 159–61, 223, 229, 239, 286, 337n215
Pipes, Daniel, 33, 46, 47, 84, 172, 213, 266
Plan of Attack (Woodward), 252
Podhoretz, Norman, 238, 245, 246, 247
political correctness, 3, 30, 299
Political Research Associates (PRA), 209, 217
Pollard, Jonathan, 232, 289
Popular Front for the Liberation of Palestine (PFLP), 53, 75, 125, 127
Populist Party, 163
Posse Comitatus, 138, 227
Potok, Mark, 186, 217
Powell, Colin, 200, 203, 227, 235, 252
PFLP (Popular Front for the Liberation of Palestine), 53, 75, 125, 127
Prague, 76

Presidential Decision Directive (PDD) 39, 173
Pringle, David, 359n46
Privacy Act of 1974, 175
Project for a New American Century, 241
Project for the New Century, 250
Project Megiddo (FBI), 178–79, 192
Protocols of the Learned Elders of Zion, The, 46, 48, 61, 139, 253
Putnam, Robert, 263

Qaddafi, Muammar, 137, 277, 282, 320n133; as sponsor of terrorism, 99, 100, 101, 128–30, 332n89
Qadi, Yassin, al-154
Qaeda, al: Advice and Reformation Committee (ARC) office, 108; in Afghanistan, 91, 102, 196, 201, 344n86; Americans in, 102–5; bin Laden as leader of, 62–67, 69, 73, 74–75, 300; budget of, 73; dirty bombs and, 79, 102, 324n236; drug trafficking and, 74, 323n204; Saddam Hussein and 76, 301, 356n45; infiltration of U.S. armed forces by, 103–4; Iran and, 75, 323n206; Iraq and, 65, 75, 76, 271; Liberation Tigers of Tamil and, 168; 9/11 attacks and, 1, 80, 196, 201–2, 234, 299–300, 329n110, 336n193; 1993 World Trade Center bombing and, 88, 196; organizational structure of, 73, 82; religious orientation of, 81; in Sierra Leone, 168; in Spain, 168; in Sudan, 64, 69, 71, 91; tactics of, 69–70, 83; al-Taqwa and, 148–49, 154, 155, 156; terrorist network and, 64–65, 71, 72–73, 79, 82–83, 89, 90, 149, 154, 192, 196, 234, 300; Taliban and, 74, 201; USS *Cole* attack and, 79, 107, 192; in U.S., 88, 90, 174; U.S. on, 200; U.S. as target of, 228, 260, 263, 299–305, 360n19; WMDs and nerve gas and, 78–79, 271, 325n16, 356n44, 360n19. *See also* bin Laden, Osama
Qaradawi, Yusuf al-, 91
Qatar, 161
Qattan, Ahmed al-, 91
Qawka, Khalil al-, 91
Qutb, Muhammad, 62
Qutb, Sayid, 37–44, 62, 316n13

Raab, Earl, 19
racialist right, 12, 142, 185, 332n99; nonrevolutionary, 14, 17–19; revolutionary, 14–16, 17, 25, 29, 182, 183
racial separatism, 95–99
racism, extreme right and, 13, 14–23, 30, 31, 143, 144

radical right, definition of, 12–13
Radio Islam, 139–40
Rafsanjani, Ali Akbar Hashemi, 74, 158
Rahji, Suleiman Abdul al-Aziz al-, 154
Rahman, Sheikh Omar Abdel, 65–66, 84–86, 87, 90, 108
Raimondo, Justin, 241, 242
Rami, Ahmed, 139
Ramirez Sánchez, Ilich, 149, 218
Rand Corporation, 79
Rashid, Ahmed, 162
Rashid, Amir Abdul, 104
Rashid, Haruan al-, 117
Rashid Hotel bombing, 88
Raufer, Xavier, 8
Reagan, Ronald, 59, 100, 193, 194, 202, 238
Record, Jeffrey, 301, 302
Redfeairn, Ray, 183
Reeve, Simon, 76, 89, 131, 132
Reichsfolk organization, 143
Reid, Richard, 108
Reisz, Heinz, 136
Remer, Otto Ernst, 121, 125, 139
Resistance magazine, 166
Resistance Records, 182
Ressam, Ahmed, 106, 193
Revell, Oliver Buck, 176
"Reviving the Islamic Spirit" conference, 163
Revolutionary Guards (Iran), 57
revolutionary racialist right, 14, 16, 25, 29, 182, 183
Rexist Party, 126
Ribbentrop, Joachim von, 115
Rice, Condoleezza, 252
Richardson, Tex., 92
Ridge, Tom, 199, 218
right-wing extremists. *See* extreme right
Rimland, Ingrid, 187
Risala, Al-, 259
Riyadh, Saudi Arabia, 63, 73
Robertson, Pat, 163
Rockwell, George Lincoln, 124
Rodman, Peter, 246
Romania, 118
Rommel, Erwin, 114, 119
Ronfeldt, David, 308
Roosevelt, Franklin D., 175, 237
Roper, Billy, 164, 221
Rose, Gideon, 4
Rosebraugh, Craig, 171, 307
Rosenfeld, Jean, 64
Rosicrucians, 47

Ross, Bart A., 187
Roy, Olivier, 108
Rubin, Barry, 254
Rubin, Irv, 338n240
Ruby Ridge incident (1992), 13–14, 25, 177
Rumsfeld, Donald, 200, 252, 288
Rusk, Dean, 232
Russia: bin Laden on, 262; extreme right in, 138 U.S. and, 249; Iraq and, 126–27, 137–38, 202, 204, 309. *See also* Soviet Union
Russian-Chechen wars, 101
Rwanda, 4

Saar Foundation, 154
Sabra massacre, 289
Sadat, Anwar: assassination of, 31, 54, 67, 85; Islamists and, 41, 53, 54, 320n133; Nazis and, 119–20; peace treaty with Israel of, 54, 120, 331n41
Sadr, Moqtada, 65
Sageman, Marc, 72, 108, 195
Said, Homanned, 121
Said, Nur, 114, 115
Sakina Security Services, 297
Sala, Ahmed, 75
Saladin the Kurd, 40–41
Saladin, 64
Salafiyya movement, 63–64, 80
Salahuddin, Doud, 105
Salameh, Ali Hassan, 126
Salameh, Muhammad, 88
Saleh, Ali Abdallah, 320n133
Salem, Emad, 85, 89
Salim, Mamdouh, 325n16
Sampson Option, The (Hersh), 229
San Diego, Calif., 179
Sargent, Charlie, 142
Sarhad, 113
Saudi Arabia: Afghanistan and, 74, 195; bin Laden and, 62–63, 66, 67–68, 73, 154, 259; economics of, 81; formation of, 63; Germans and, 122; Holocaust/historical revisionism and, 22; on Israel, 263; National Guard building bombing in, 73; on 911/ attacks, 215, 263; on Saddam Hussein, 61; Taliban and, 63, 74, 323n228; U.S. and, 24, 67, 249, 259, 301
Saudi Bin Laden Group, 62, 65
Saud, King Fahd Bin Abdul al-, 320n133
Saud, Muhammad ibn, 63
Savehie, Mahdi Chamran, 74
Schacht, Hjalmar, 122, 123
Schily, Otto, 153

Schobert, Alfred, 363n53
Schroeder, Christa, 151
Schroeder, Gary, 138
Scutari, Richard, 31–32
Searchlight, 277
Secret Army Organization (OAS), 121
Secret Relationships between Blacks and Jews (NOI), 98
Secret Service, 180, 200
Secret Warriors (Emerson), 209
secularization of the Middle East, 35–36, 45, 46, 60
Separation and Its Discontents (MacDonald), 18
September 11, 2001 attacks. *See* 9/11 attacks
Shabazz, Malik Zulu, 265–66
Shah, Wali Khan Amin, 88, 131
Shalah, Ramadan Abdalah, 75, 93
Shaltut, Mahmud, 150
Shamir, Yitzhak, 289
Sharia, 39, 40, 43, 53, 58, 147, 204, 260
Sharon, Ariel, 23, 48, 60, 165, 243, 245, 249, 265
Shaukat, Nadif, 114
Shehi, Marwan al-, 133
Shelton, Robert, 212
Shere-e-Pubjab, 277
Shi'ites: Hezbollah and, 57, 247; in Iraq, 202–3, 247; in Lebanon, 247; militant Islam and, 34, 41, 55, 56, 59; nationalism and, 41; Sunni relations with, 42, 56, 65, 74, 80, 151
Shura (al Qaeda), 73
Sicherheitsdienst (Security Service), 118
Siddique, Kaukab, 266
Sierra, Bryan, 180
Sierra Leone, al Qaeda in, 168
Silver Shirts, 49
Silverstein, Larry, 232–33
Simon Wiesenthal Center (SWC), 156, 186, 208
Singh, Ammo, 277
Singh, Rhajinder, 277
Sirhan, Sirhan, 105
Six-Day War (1967), 52, 351n39
Six Million Reconsidered, The (Grimstad), 22
Skorzeny, Otto, 121, 122, 123–24
Skull and Bones Society, 47
Smith, Benjamin, 185, 187, 338n249
Social Democratic Party (Switzerland), 149
Socialist Party, 330n37
Social Justice in Islam (Qutb), 43
Somalia, 70–71, 90, 196
Somerville, Mass., 209
Soros, George, 170

Southern Poverty Law Center (SPLC), 176, 179, 181, 183, 186, 192, 209, 211–12, 213, 217
Soviet-Afghan war, 57, 62, 64, 68, 101, 194–96, 254, 299
Soviet Union: collapse of, 4, 28, 238, 299; Egypt and, 123–24; Gulf War and, 137; Iraq and, 126–27, 137–38, 202; Muslims in, 117; terrorism and, 53, 78, 109, 193–94
Spain, terrorists in, 168
Spann, Michael, 102
Special Forces Underground, 227, 350–51n29
SPLC. *See* Southern Poverty Law Center
Spotlight, 20, 97
Springfield, Va., 91, 92
Sprinzak, Ehud, 25, 26
Sri Lanka, 168
SS Freikorps Arabien (Meighy), 31
SS-Waffengruppe "Turkestan," 117
"Stay Out of Tall Buildings" (Pierce), 9
Steele, Edgar, 359n46
Steele, John Frederick, 183
Stein, Arthur, 303
Steiner, David, 48
Sterling, Claire, 109, 193, 194
Stern, Jessica, 78, 264
Stern, Kenneth, 208, 347n4
Stoddard, Lothrop, 285, 358n33
Stormfront, 292, 342n37
Story, Richard, 181
Strauss, Leo, 249
Strom, Kevin Alfred, 16, 166, 182, 289, 291, 342n37, 359n46
Suall, Irwin, 348n22
Subh, Atallah Abu al-, 259
Sudan, 90; bin Laden in, 64, 68, 69, 71, 73, 77; Iraq and, 57; Israel and, 267; U.S. bombing in, 78, 196
Suez Canal, 1956 seizure of, 123–24
Sufism, 63
suicide terrorism: extreme right on, 140–41, 165, 166, 169; Hamas and, 61, 320n125; al-Husseini and, 113; in Israel, 61, 76, 320n126; justification of, 59; in Kenya, 77; al Qaeda and, 69–70, 73, 74; strategy of, 322n177, 338–39n250
Sum of All Fears (Clancy), 111
Sunnis; militant Islam and, 34, 41, 55, 56, 58, 59, 174; Shi'ite relations with, 42, 56, 65, 74, 80, 151
Sunshine Project, 31–32
Sunstein, Cass, 30
Sutter, Joshua Caleb, 184
Swain, Carol M., 30

swarming, 79
SWC (Simon Wiesenthal Center), 156, 186, 208
Swiss National Front, 125
Switzerland, 156; extreme right in, 125, 149, 220, 294
Sykes-Picot agreement, 266
Syria, 115, 119; extreme right and, 164; Hamas, and 60; Hezbollah and, 57, 59; Saddam Hussein and, 61; Israel and, 47, 247; sponsorship of terrorism by, 248, 252
Syrian Ba'ath Party, 58
Syrian Public Relations Association, 164

Tabatabai, Ali Akbar, 105
Tafoya, Eugene, 105
Taft, Robert, 240
Taha Rifa'i, Ahmad, 75
Talaa' al-Fateh, 85
Taliban: in Afghanistan, 73–74, 102, 147, 201, 321n154; bin Laden and, 73, 323n228; drug trafficking and, 74, 323n204; extreme right on, 147; al Qaeda and, 74, 201; Saudi Arabia and, 63, 323n228; U.S. support for, 162; U.S. war with, 162, 201, 299
Tanzania, 78
"Tanzim 17," 128
Taqwa, al-, 148–49, 154, 155, 156
Taqwa mosque, 104
Taraki, Noor Mohammed, 194
Taylor, Jared, 17, 224, 226, 254, 257, 278, 286
Tehran, Iran, 75, 158
Tenet, George, 106–7, 196
Terror Enigma, The (Raimondo), 242
terrorism: religion and, 4, 81–82; state sponsorship of, 72, 88, 128–30, 168, 174, 248, 249, 252, 332n89; trends in, 7–8, 174, 175–76. *See also* suicide terrorism
Terror Network, The (Sterling), 109, 193
Testament of Adolf Hitler, 116
Te-Ta-Ma Truth Foundation, 186
Thatcher, Margaret, 129
Third Position, 96, 128–30, 217
Third Reich; extreme right and, 151–53, 316n19; Islam and, 112–24
Third World nationalism, 122, 218
Thiriart, Jean, 126
Thirteenth Tribe, The (Koestler), 313n6
Thirty Years' War, 8, 123
Thompson, H. Keith, 122, 124
Timmerman, Kenneth, 265, 294–95
Tito, Josip Broz, 301
Töben, Frederick, 158

Tobias, Glen A., 252
Traficant, James, 217–18
Transportation Security Administration, 200
Tribe of Shabazz from the Lost Nation of Asia, 94
Trilateral Commission, 28, 47
Truth about 9–11, The (Hale), 186
Tulfah, Khairallah, 115, 136
Tunisia, 329n113
Turabi, Hassan al-, 69, 71, 76, 326n35
Turan Shah the Mamluk, 41
Turkey, 35–36, 112, 204, 254
Turner Diaries, The (Pierce), 15, 169, 182, 191
"Turning Tide Is a Violent Tide, A," 140–42
Tyndall, John, 129, 130, 223, 225, 235, 255, 276, 342n37, 359n46

UFOs: Nazi Secret Weapons (Zündel), 188
Ul Haque, Anwar, 265
Umarov, Doku, 105
United Arab Emirates, 159
United Arab Republic, 124
United Association for Studies and Research (USAR), 91
United flight 175, 1, 351n36
United flight 93, 1, 107, 329n110
United Klans of America, 17, 212
United Nations (UN): on Afghanistan, 196; Iraq and, 203; Resolution 1267, 196; U.S. in, 246
United Nations Special Commission (UNSCOM), 203
United States: Afghanistan aid from, 194–95; Afghanistan sanctions of, 196; alleged Jewish control of, 2, 3, 46–47, 48, 49, 140, 165, 217, 223, 237, 245, 255, 266, 293–95; Arab population in, 296–97, 311n12; Egypt and, 120; fiscal cost of, 361n30; on extreme right, 173–92; foreign terrorist organizations in, 6; Hezbollah and, 59, 92, 133; immigration in, 16, 19, 30, 84, 224, 257, 281, 283, 296–97, 302, 308, 311n12; Iranian hostage situation and, 53, 194; Iraq and, 68, 90, 134–35, 202–4, 205; Iraq sanctions by, 76, 203, 226, 228, 260–61, 263, 281, 346n127; Islamic criticism of, 45, 57–58; Israel and, 1, 46, 51–52, 96, 159, 160, 185–86, 205, 214, 218, 227, 238, 241, 243, 245, 249–50, 253, 293, 297; Lebanon and, 59, 210; Libya and, 130, 248, 326n41; militant Islam in, 84–110; on militant Islam, 192–206; Muslims in, 5, 63, 64, 84–110, 259, 269, 281, 311n12; national identity in, 303–4; Pakistan and, 162, 201;

United States (continued)
  in Saudi Arabia, 24, 67, 249, 259, 301; in So-
    malia, 70–71; support of Muslim countries
    by, 254; Syria and, 57; on Taliban, 162; war
    on terror, 9, 200, 202, 218, 222–23, 299,
    302–3
Uniting and Strengthening America by Provid-
    ing Appropriate Tools Required to Intercept
    and Obstruct Terrorism. See USA PATRIOT
    Act
"Unknown Islam, The" (Huber), 293
Unocal, 162
Unraveling Anti-Semitic 9/11 Conspiracy Theories
    (ADL), 215
USA PATRIOT Act, 165, 198, 199, 219, 223,
    239
U.S. Army Special Forces School, Fort Bragg, 90
U.S. Army War College, 301
U.S. Customs Service, 199–200
U.S. Defense Department, 200
U.S. embassies: in Beirut, 210; in Israel, 263; in
    Kenya, 77, 196; in Tanzania, 78, 196
U.S. Justice Department, 100, 235; Civil Rights
    Division's National Origin Working Group,
    197; Community Relations Service, 197–98;
    FBI and, 132, 175; extreme right and, 176,
    180, 185, 187, 189, 190, 223; war on terror
    and, 197, 328n89
U.S. State Department, 6, 90, 157, 161, 190,
    246; Diplomatic Security Service, 196
U.S. Treasury Department, 154, 176–77

Vanunu, Mordechai, 160
Verité et Justice, 22, 156, 157
Vest, Jason, 251
Vichy France, 118
Vigilants of Christendom (Hoskins), 142
Virginia; extreme right in, 180; militant Islam
    in, 91, 93–94, 154
Voight, Udo, 167
Volcker, Paul, 294
Voss, Wilhelm, 123
Voz de Aztlan, La, 305

Waco, Texas incident, 13, 14, 25, 177
Wafd Party, 36
Waffen-SS Handschar Division, 117
Wahhabism, 36, 63–64, 65, 67, 80, 154
Wahhab, Muhammad bin Abdul al-, 63
Walker, Linda, 181
Walker, Shaun, 16
WAR (White Aryan Resistance), 17, 96–97,
    111, 129, 212, 221, 240, 290

War against the Terror Masters, The (Ledeen), 248
war on terror: American public on, 204; Euro-
    peans on, 204; funding of, 196–97, 302, 303;
    globalization and, 3, 4; Iraq and, 202–4, 205;
    treatment of Muslims and Arabs and,
    197–98; in U.S., 9, 200, 202, 218, 222–23;
    U.S. economy and, 3–4
Warsaw uprising, 117
Washington Institute for Near East Policy, 246
Washington Post, 204, 230, 231, 251
Watchdog groups. See Nongovernmental
    Organizations
Watson, Dale, 306
Waxman, Henry, 250
Waziri mujahideen, 113
weapons of mass destruction (WMD); Pakistan
    and, 79; al Qaeda and, 78–79
Weaver, Randy, 13–14, 177
Weaver, Sammy, 177
Weaver, Vicki, 177
Weber, Mark, 22
Webster, William, 176
Wehrsportgruppe-Hoffmann, 127
Weinberg, Leonard, 8, 9, 272
Weissberg, Robert, 358n37
Weiss, Fred, 124, 331n65
West Bank, 282
Westfield America, 233
Westphalia, Treaty of, 8
"West, War, and Islam, The" (pamphlet,
    Zündel), 188, 287
"What We're Fighting For: A Letter from Amer-
    ica," 263, 304
Wheeler, Artie, 181–82
Wheeler, Burton, 240
Wheeler, Elizabeth, 182
Where the Right Went Wrong (Buchanan), 250
Whitaker, Bob, 359n46
White Aryan Resistance (WAR), 17, 96–97,
    111, 129, 212, 221, 240, 290
White Knights of the Ku Klux Klan, 184
white nationalists, 16–17, 96, 129, 161, 224,
    273, 285, 292. See also individual organizations
"White power" movement, 15, 272
white separatists, 13–14, 27, 96, 97, 98, 311n6,
    334–35n152. See also individual organizations
Who Are We? The Challenges to America's Na-
    tional Identity (Huntington), 298
Wiedemer, Hansjuerg Mark, 156
Wilcox, Laird, 11
Wilkinson, Paul, 24
"Will America Learn Its Lessons?" (Taylor), 224
Williams, Ken, 198

Williams, Maurice, 105
Williams, Paul, 74, 78
wiretaps, 199, 233
"Without Borders" talk show, 161
WMD. *See* weapons of mass destruction
Wolfowitz, Paul, 135, 200, 241, 246, 251, 252, 333n130
Women for Aryan Unity, 183
Woodward, Bob, 203, 252
Woolsey, R. James, 133, 247
World and Islam Studies Enterprise (WISE), 93
World Assembly of Muslim Youth, 154
World Church of the Creator (WCOTC; Creativity), 15, 16, 27, 173, 185–87, 227, 316n19, 338n249
World Islamic Front for Jihad against Jews and the Crusaders, 75, 76
World Jewish Congress, 157, 294
World Muslim Congress, 22
"World's Most Dangerous Terrorist, The" (Duke), 161
World Trade Center bombing (1993), 84, 87–89, 132, 134, 196
World Trade Center bombing (2001), 80, 107, 215, 232, 351n36. *See also* 9/11 attacks
Wright, Robin, 52–53
Wurmser, David, 238, 246, 247
Wurmser, Meyrav, 246

Y2K terrorist threats, 192–93
Yassin, Ahmad, 60
Yeltsin, Boris, 137
Yemen, 62; hotel attacks in, 70; USS *Cole* attack in, 79, 107, 320n133

Yockey, Francis Parker, 124, 126, 331n63
Yom Kippur War, 54
Young Egypt, 119
Yousef, Ramzi, 88–90, 131–32, 134, 196, 326n26, 328n99, 333n113, 345n124
"Y2K Paranoia" (ADL), 179
Yugoslavia, 117, 254

Zachkeim, Dov, 246
Zagallai, Faisal, 105
Zakaria, Fareed, 7–8
Zarqawi, Abu Musab al-, 65, 271
Zawahiri, Ayman al-, 54, 64, 67, 73, 75, 76, 85, 298, 319n104
Zayed al-Nahayan, Sultan Bin, 159
Zayed Center for Coordination and Follow-up, 159
055 Brigade, 74
Zhirinovsky, Vladimir, 137–38, 190
Zinni, Anthony, 252
Zionism: extreme right on, 2–3, 15, 20, 125, 270, 221, 293; Islam on, 2–3, 20, 44–47, 58, 61, 93, 125, 138, 158, 286–87, 293; purpose of, 253; formation of Jewish state and, 112, 114, 118. *See also* anti-Semitism
Zionist Emergency Evacuation Rescue Operation (ZEERO), 86
Zionist occupation government (ZOG), 15, 24, 25, 28–29, 147, 217, 244, 245, 256, 293, 305
Zubaydah, Abu, 107, 201, 324n257
Zündel, Ernst, 187–89, 287, 343n61